DOCUMENTS OF PER
IN EARLY MODERN

As well as 'play-makers' and 'poets', playwrights of the early modern period were known as 'play-patchers' because their texts were made from separate documents. This book is the first to consider all the papers created by authors and theatres by the time of the opening performance, recovering types of script not previously known to have existed. With chapters on plot-scenarios, arguments, playbills, prologues and epilogues, songs, staged scrolls, backstage-plots and parts, it shows how textually distinct production was from any single unified book. And, as performance documents were easily lost, relegated or reused, the story of a play's patchy creation also becomes the story of its co-authorship, cuts, revisions and additions. Using a large body of fresh evidence, *Documents of Performance* brings a wholly new reading of printed and manuscript playbooks of the Shakespearean period, redefining what a play, and what a playwright, actually is.

TIFFANY STERN is Professor of Early Modern Drama at Oxford University, and the Beaverbrook and Bouverie Fellow and Tutor in English Literature at University College, Oxford. She specialises in Shakespeare, theatre history from the sixteenth to the eighteenth century, book history and editing. Her previous publications include *Shakespeare in Parts* (co-written with Simon Palfrey, 2007, and winner of the 2009 David Bevington Award for Best New Book in Early Drama Studies), *Making Shakespeare* (2004) and *Rehearsal from Shakespeare to Sheridan* (2000).

DOCUMENTS OF PERFORMANCE IN EARLY MODERN ENGLAND

TIFFANY STERN

CAMBRIDGE
UNIVERSITY PRESS

CAMBRIDGE UNIVERSITY PRESS
Cambridge, New York, Melbourne, Madrid, Cape Town,
Singapore, São Paulo, Delhi, Mexico City

Cambridge University Press
The Edinburgh Building, Cambridge CB2 8RU, UK

Published in the United States of America by Cambridge University Press, New York

www.cambridge.org
Information on this title: www.cambridge.org/9781107656208

First published 2009
3rd printing 2011
First paperback edition 2012

Printed in the United Kingdom at the University Press, Cambridge

A catalogue record for this publication is available from the British Library

Library of Congress Cataloging-in-Publication Data
Stern, Tiffany
Documents of performance in early modern England / Tiffany Stern.
p.   cm.
Includes bibliographical references and index.
ISBN 978-0-521-84237-2 (hardback)
1. English drama–Early modern and Elizabethan, 1500–1600–Criticism, Textual.
2. English drama–17th century–Criticism, Textual.
3. Theater–Production and direction–England–History–16th century.
4. Theater–Production and direction–England–History–17th century. I. Title.
PR658.T4S74 2009
822′.309–dc22

2009028996

ISBN 978-0-521-84237-2 Hardback
ISBN 978-1-107-65620-8 Paperback

To my uncle Patrick Tucker

Contents

Acknowledgements   *page* ix
Textual note   xiii

Introduction: Playwrights as play-patchers   1

1   Plot-scenarios   8
    Introduction   8
    Plot-scenarios: Content   11
    Plot-scenarios: Construction, appearance, use and preservation   16
    'Plotters': Scenarios as commodities   25
    Amateur plotters   30
    Conclusion   31

2   Playbills and title-pages   36
    Introduction   36
    Producing playbills   38
    Number and frequency of playbills   47
    'Posting' bills   50
    Bills, advertisements, title-pages   53
    Contents of bills and title-pages   56
    Conclusion   62

3   'Arguments' in playhouse and book   63
    Introduction   63
    Arguments as programmes; Arguments as paratext   65
    Conclusion   79

4   Prologues, epilogues, interim entertainments   81
    Introduction   81
    Prologues, first performance and revision   82
    Prologues and 'benefits'   93
    The circulation of prologues and epilogues on page and stage   97

Choruses and interim texts on page and stage   106
Authorship of prologues and epilogues   109
Players of prologues and epilogues   112
Conclusion   117

5   Songs and masques   120
    Introduction   120
    Explanations for songs lost and found   125
    Songs in the theatre: Real reasons for songs lost and found   135
    Songs, masques and revision   145
    Printers and 'separate' songs   153
    Traces of 'theatre' in printed plays   160
    Conclusion   168

6   Scrolls   174
    Introduction   174
    Theatre scrolls and their scribes   179
    Blank and cued scrolls   188
    Separate circulation of scrolls   190
    Conclusion   199

7   Backstage-plots   201
    Introduction   201
    The pre-plot   205
    Backstage-plots: Physical characteristics   207
    Backstage-plots: Contents   209
    Eighteenth-century prompters and their call-sheets   214
    Book-holders as prompters; backstage-plots as call-sheets   219
    Backstage-plots and playbooks   227
    Conclusion   231

8   The approved 'book' and actors' parts   232
    Introduction   232
    The approved book and performance   232
    Scribes and actors' parts   236
    Extemporisation by clowns and others   245
    Conclusion   251

Conclusion: Repatching the play   253

Notes   257
Bibliography   316
Index   346

Acknowledgements

It is impossible to come up with a list that will do justice to the many academics who have helped and encouraged me in my work. Several people have kindly read through drafts and answered specific queries; others have asked useful questions and given important direction and encouragement. People who have read substantial portions of this book include Alan Dessen, Gabriel Egan, Suzanne Gossett, Andrew Gurr, John Jowett, David Lindley, Leah Marcus, Gordon McMullan, Carol Rutter, Tracey Sowerby, Gary Taylor, Stanley Wells, Paul Werstine and an anonymous reader at Cambridge University Press, all of whose observations and advice immeasurably improved the text; its errors are, of course, my own. Other scholars were kind enough to supply me with their unpublished work and discoveries: thanks to Peter Blayney, Colin Burrow, Suzanne Gossett, Sonia Massai and Lucy Munro.

During the process of completion I have received so many incisive comments from colleagues all over the world that it has become impossible to list them all. Sustained time spent with the following people, however, has resulted in a productive mixture of intellectual discovery and food/drink: Sharon Achinstein, Pascale Aebischer, Alan Armstrong, John Astington, Tom Betteridge, Gordon Campbell, David Carnegie, Bill Carroll, Patrick Cheyney, Jean Chothia, Tony Dawson, Ross Duffin, Katherine Duncan-Jones, Richard Dutton, Charles Edelman, Paul Edmondson, Sarah Enloe, Lukas Erne, Alan Farmer, Ewan Fernie, Tim Fizpatrick, Brian Gibbons, Stuart Gillespie, John Golder, Margreta de Grazia, Andrew Hartley, Diana Henderson, Mary Hill-Cole, Peter Holbrook, Peter Holland, Jonathan Hope, Bill Ingram, Farah Karim-Cooper, Tom Keymer, M. J. Kidnie, Bernhard Klein, Ros Knutson, Zack Lesser, Todd Lidh, Joe Loewenstein, Jeremy Lopez, Ivan Lupic, Jack Lynch, Larry Manly, Jim Marino, Randall Martin, Russ McDonald, the late Scott McMillan, Gordon McMullan, Bob Miola, Michelle O'Callaghan, Stephen Orgel, Richard Preiss, Paul Prescott, Eric

Rasmussen, Paul Salzman, Jonathan Sawday, David Scott Kastan, Jim Shapiro, Bill Sherman, Emma Smith, Adam Smyth, Peter Stallybrass, Holger Syme.

The following universities invited me to give talks that arose from or became part of *Documents of Performance*, and listeners at those places made my chapters better with their suggestions and advice: Queensland, Australia; Sydney, Australia; Cambridge, UK; Exeter, UK; Glasgow, UK; King' College, London, UK; Oxford, UK; Shakespeare Institute, Stratford-upon-Avon, UK; Strathclyde, UK; Mary Baldwin, USA; North Carolina at Charlotte, USA; Pennsylvania, USA; Princeton, USA. I also wish to acknowledge the contribution of organisers, co-presenters and audience members at the following conferences: 'The Blackfriars Scholars Conference', Staunton, Virginia, USA; 'Redefining British Theatre History', Huntington Library, Los Angeles, USA; 'The Renaissance Society of America', Miami, USA; 'The Renaissance of Subjectivity Conference', Royal Holloway, London, UK; 'The Shakespeare Association of America' in Bermuda, USA, Minneapolis, USA, San Diego, USA, and Victoria, BC, Canada; 'The International Shakespeare Conference', Stratford-upon-Avon, UK.

Parts of this book have previously been published in other forms. A version of 'Chapter two: Playbills and title-pages' was published as '"On each Wall/And Corner Post": Playbills, Title-pages, and Advertising in Early Modern London', *English Literary Renaissance* (*ELR*), 36, 57–85; grateful thanks to *ELR* for permission to reprint this article. A considerably earlier version of 'Chapter four: 'Prologues, epilogues, interim entertainments' was published as '"A Small-Beer Health to his Second Day": Playwrights, Prologues, and First Performances in the Early Modern Theatre', *Studies in Philology*, 101, 172–99: thanks, too, to *Studies in Philology* for allowing me to reuse that piece.

It is a pleasure to have the opportunity to thank publicly the many others who supported me while completing this project. The Folger Shakespeare Library granted me a short-term fellowship as a result of which I was able to explore their extraordinary manuscript holdings in more depth. University College, Oxford, and the Faculty of English at Oxford kindly gave me a term's sabbatical; the AHRC provided me with invaluable help when it awarded me 'matching' research leave – without which this book would still be on my 'to do' list. The Museum voor Schone Kunsten, Gent © Lukas – Art in Flanders VZW graciously supplied the illustration for the cover of this book: Cornelis Geysbrechts' *Brivenbord met Dansmeesterviool en Pistool*, 1664.

My debts to libraries are great – and to librarians are greater still. I would like to thank the librarians of the following places: The Beinecke Library, The Bodleian Library, The British Library, The Cambridge University Library, Harvard Theater Library, The Houghton Library, The Huntington Library, The New York Public Library. In particular, the unstinting help and warm friendship of librarians at The Folger Shakespeare Library made researching this project truly pleasurable.

My research has also been honed and shaped by watching performances in reconstructed spaces. Ralph Cohen, whose American Shakespeare Center puts on plays from parts in the rebuilt Blackfriars Playhouse, Staunton, Virginia, has been an inspiration and delight, and his actors have enriched my understanding of the practicalities of early modern texts on stage: thank you Doreen Bechtol, John Harrell, James Keegan, J. P. Scheidler and Rene Thornton Jr. To the talented Paul Menzer and Thadd McQuade, who made Virginia my second home when they allowed me to stay, so often, in their first one, I owe more thanks and whisky than I can ever supply. I'd like also to give particular thanks to Jason Guy not just for his performances, his perspicacity, and his sofa, but also for his great and valued friendship, and the friendship of Vanessa Morosco.

At Univ my English colleagues – first John Mee and Catherine Clarke, latterly Tony Howe, Nick Halmi and Laura Varnam – have made working an intellectual and companionable pleasure. I'm also lucky enough to have an additional series of non-Eng-Lit friends who help me in good and difficult times with their friendship, humour, and intellectual – and frivolous – conversations: thanks to Frank Arntzenius (for boxes A and B); Michael Blome-Tillmann (for being my favourite Assistant Professor); Tim Brook (for Chinese violence – and, of course, the Zoon); Robin Butler (for tales of Mrs T.); Iwao Hirose (for chewing tobacco); Nadine Moeller (for sharing her own 'shepherd's pie' moment); Sandy Murray (for his tales of medieval suicide and despair); Mike Nicholson (for vodka); John Wilson (for trying to explain why 23 and 56); Alex Woell (for 'the sofa-couch' culture); and Oliver 'Monsieur Le Goeth' Zimmer. Friends elsewhere in Oxford who deserve special mention include Michael Burden, Sam/John (but always Sam to me) Eidinow, Sos Eltis, Bart Van Es, Laurie Maguire, Richard McCabe, John Morgenstern, David Norbrook, Simon Palfrey, Gonzalo Rodriguez-Pereyra and Ralph Wedgewood. Especial thanks to John Hawthorne for friendship, curry and rare books.

I would also like to make some personal acknowledgements to friends and family. Over the years that this book was being planned and written,

I have benefited enormously from the encouragement and friendship of James Canon, Becky Hewitt, Elspeth Jajdelska, Wojtek Jajdelski, Justyna Lesniewska, Bryan Magee, Gareth Mann, Zygmunt Mazur, Paige Newmark, Arkady Ostrovsky. My family, Jonty Stern, Elisabeth Stern, and Joy Moore, have as ever been a vital source of encouragement and affection. I do, however, owe a particular debt to uncles. My uncle Andrew Tucker suggested the image for the cover of this book; my uncle Patrick Tucker first made me enthralled by the staging of Shakespeare and continues to teach and challenge me with his ideas. It is to Uncle Patrick, inspiration and friend, that this book is affectionately dedicated.

Textual note

As typeface, pagination and layout are so often relevant to the argument
made here, all printed early modern texts are quoted from the original
early modern source where possible, though speech-prefixes have sometimes been expanded or regularised for the sake of clarity. As a result,
some plays are quoted under an authorship now disputed (for instance,
not all of the plays in the 1647 or 1679 Beaumont and Fletcher folio
include Beaumont's hand, whilst Massinger's major contribution to them
is not acknowledged); when this is the case, the identity of the people said
to be the 'real' authors will be added to the text in the footnote. As the
point being made, however, is how often certain passages even in plays of
seemingly undisputed authorship are in fact by other authors – or the
same author, but writing at another point in time – it need not be
assumed that any of the identified authors are in fact writers of the
fragment in question; similarly, dates of performance are not generally
supplied as it cannot be assumed that a 'fragment' shares a date with the
rest of its play (prologues, epilogues, songs often constitute later additions). All titles and character names are given in old spelling, with the
exception of Shakespeare's plays where, for ease of reference, the conventional modern spelling names of plays are used, though texts are quoted
from quartos (from the facsimiles prepared by Michael J. B. Allen and
Kenneth Muir: *Shakespeare's Plays in Quarto: A Facsimile Edition of Copies
Primarily from the Henry E. Huntington Library* (Berkeley: University
of California Press, 1981)) and the Folio (from the facsimile prepared
by Charlton Hinman, *Mr. William Shakespeares Comedies, Histories, &
Tragedies* (New York: Norton, 1968)), using the through-line-numbers
(TLN) of that edition. For plays in manuscript, an edition of that
manuscript preserving its features (a Malone Society edition or equivalent) is quoted when there is one; otherwise the manuscript itself is quoted

from source, as are all other unedited manuscript fragments. Manuscript compilations, variously catalogued as 'miscellanies', 'commonplace books', 'table-books', 'notebooks', are here called 'miscellanies': full shelf-mark numbers for them are supplied, and page or folio numbers when possible. For all manuscripts, spelling and punctuation are retained, but alphabetic conventions i/j and v/u are regularised and contractions are expanded.

Introduction: Playwrights as play-patchers

As well as being called 'play-makers' and 'poets', playwrights of the early modern period were frequently known as 'play-patchers' because of the common perception that a play was pieced together out of a collection of odds and ends: it was not a single whole entity. The term was unflattering and designed to wound, as was 'playwright', with its implication that constructing plays was a craft – equivalent to being a cartwright or a wheelwright – rather than an art. But, just as 'playwright' over time lost its pejorative implications, so 'play-patcher' too came to be seen as an unpalatable truth. Well may Randolph sneer at the poet who makes a 'Comedy' out of 'patches of his ragged wit, as if he meant to make Poverty a Coat of it', and Wither lament the men who can do little more than 'patch up a bald witlesse *Comedy*' out of 'rotten-old-worme-eaten stuffe'; there was something 'patchy' in the very substance of early modern plays.[1] Dekker articulates this when he describes a 'play-patcher' as 'a Cobler of Poetrie'.[2] Again, he is being uncomplimentary – to him plays are all too often 'cobbled together' – but 'cobbler' also simply implies that the writers of the texts are, like shoe-makers, constructing their artifacts of discrete and separate pieces; when the joins are ill-fitting or overly visible, that is a problem – but the patch remains a feature of the whole, that notwithstanding.

Other writers are specific about what constitutes a 'patch' of play. 'Constantia Munda', discussing poetasters who 'can but patch a hobbling verse together', finds patchiness inside the very verse form used by play-wrights; and a manuscript poem of the time is more pointed still: it refers to the men who out 'Of . . . other mens songs . . . patcht us up a play', where the 'patches' are the ditties and lyrics because they are authored by 'other men' and at other times from the rest of the dialogue.[3] George Whetstone takes this idea further, seeing 'patches' as the segments that, in a collabora-tive play, are contributed by separate authors; he writes of a selected group of 'Comedians' who conjointly are able to 'patch[] a Comedie together'.[4]

Whatever the nature of the 'patch' – and writers are more united in the idea that plays are patchwork than in their definitions of what a 'patch' is – the notion that a playbook is made up of 'patched rimes' was, at the time, self-evident.[5] But the segmentation of plays from their initial construction to their first performance and thereafter tends to be ignored by modern critics. It is usual now to concentrate on the poetic logic that unifies a text, as though a playbook is as coherent a piece of literature as an epic poem. A sense that the play is a complete and finely honed work of art leads to various linked assumptions: for instance, the idea that plays were written in the order performed, or plotted by the people responsible for the dialogue, or revised (when they were) in their entirety.

But in fact plays were from the start written patchily. They were composed to scenarios sometimes drawn up by professional 'plotters' (scenario-writers) rather than playwrights, and were parcelled out to be written in segments. Even the plays plotted and composed by a single playwright might be written out of order, so that comic and tragic sections, for instance, might come about at different times. Prologues and epilogues were frequently drawn up first on separate pieces of paper from the plays they flanked, and were not always by the author(s) of the rest of the text. Songs too were completed and sometimes written by composers, and disseminated to be learnt separately by singers; and they might then be brought textually onto the stage during performance; while scrolls (letters, poems, proclamations, challenges, epitaphs, etc. to be read on stage) were copied and occasionally even written by a scroll-scribe, and were regularly designed from the first on detached papers; in performance they too might be read on stage; outside performance they belonged together with other stage-props. Meanwhile, an abstract of a play's story, a passage that would never be spoken on stage, might be an important performance document though not part of the performed play. Known as an Argument, it was written to be handed to the audience – something akin to a primitive theatre programme – and would 'interpret' the play while it was being enacted; similarly another non-playable document, consisting of a briefer but more lurid summary, was printed and posted around London as a playbill; it too shaped understanding of the perform-ance in the theatre. Together with the playbooks, some or all of these papers would be submitted to the playhouse though not all of them would make it into or become the prompter's book (and, equally, any might).

The process of mounting a production then merely increased the patchiness that writing had already given a play. The dialogue – the one section that, though created patchily, had been given to the playhouse as something like a unified text – was resolved on receipt into a collection of fragments. As T. H. Howard-Hill writes:

the [prompter's] book was itself the origin of another set of theatrical documents: a casting table and list, the plot, and the actors' parts, not to mention such items as lists of properties and instructions to the musicians, which are virtually unknown to theatrical historians – all of which necessarily precede performance, and, for the most part, rehearsals. Once these documents were prepared, then the primacy of the book was diminished; it became one of a set of documents by which performances were governed.[6]

In fact, as *Documents of Performance* will also argue, the prompter's book is not necessarily the source for all these separate texts – but Howard-Hill's point remains key: the play in whatever form it reached the playhouse was either already a collection of scattered papers, or quickly became one. Even the playwrights who wrote their dialogue as a tightly unified document did so in the knowledge that it would be distributed as actors' parts, having been rewritten by a copyist; those parts would then be learnt by a player who may not have thought textual fidelity important. Entrance stage-directions, meanwhile, which define much of the action of the play, were likely to be extracted onto a backstage-plot – and even, sometimes, created there. So knowledge of parts and backstage-plots combined with other separable features of production will have shaped playwrights' thinking, their notion of the full play, and their relationship to each separate 'patch' of text.

Together, the fragments that the playhouse made, in conjunction with the fragments that play-writing had produced, and the additional fragments brought about for advertising and explaining the play, were the documents that amounted to 'the play' in its first performance.

Each patch, however, had a separate home, a separate circulation and, as often as not, a separate writer: the song lyrics going to composers or originating there; the parts going to actors' separate homes if not copied there; the scrolls being inscribed and perhaps written in the theatre by a scroll-scribe; the stage-directions being extracted by the prompter or his helper, again in the theatre, again in a process that involved authorship in addition to copying; the bill and Argument making their way to printers having been designed by author or playhouse. The first performance was a (re)uniting of separate texts: thereafter some would be relegated, some lost, some 'improved', while others would reside with the dialogue in the playhouse, perhaps written into the 'book', or perhaps placed in the loose folder made for playbooks and related material when the stiff backstage-plots were bent in two.

Thus each separate document that made up a play has its own story, its own attachment to the other documents, its own rate of loss and survival. And, as any fragment could be separately written aside from the play-script, so it could easily and at any subsequent time be updated or freshly composed or added to by someone else: the story of a play's patches is also the story of its cuts, revisions and additions.

This book will tell the story of the documents created for performance by playwrights and the playhouse. It will provide chapters that hover between bibliography and theatre history in that each section considers a different theatrical manuscript that contributed to the play's first (and sometimes subsequent) days, and each considers what this means for the fully written play in the form in which it survives. In addressing the manuscripts that actually made up a production, *Documents of Performance* will show that the early modern notion behind the term 'patchwork' for playtext – the early modern distrust of the unity and completion of the playscript – is just as visible now as it was then.

Much here relies on looking for and then thinking about the many play fragments that survive in manuscript and print and that, unlike full playbooks, are not generally addressed by scholars – although they collectively form a repository for lost plays, or rather, a series of 'found' sections for lost plays or lost moments in plays. Some of these fragments are hidden within surviving playtexts but have not been seen for what they are; others are in miscellanies or songbooks whose contents have not always been catalogued; others still, including rare printed ephemera, have been misidentified by libraries so that their true nature has been hidden. Many of the documents considered here are being discussed for the first time. Using a body of fresh evidence about early modern theatre and early modern texts, as well as taking a survey of printed and manuscript playbooks of the early modern period, this book explores the piecemeal nature of the playtext in the theatre, and so on the page, redefining in fundamental ways what a play actually is.

As entire chapters are given over to documents not extant (playbills), not hitherto known to have existed (Arguments), or not previously thought to survive in full (plot-scenarios), as rich a range of examples from as many sources as possible will be provided. For this reason, texts and fragments discussed here range widely: the book explores plays performed from the very beginning of the professional theatre, in the 1570s, to just before the interregnum, looking forward at some Restoration and eighteenth-century texts when they provide details for issues not exhaustively documented in the early modern period. This is because early modern information itself survives in patches; only by providing as wide a range of references as possible can patterns visible in later theatrical practice be shown to have their origins in the early modern period. The result, of course, is a book of tendencies, trends and likelihoods. In its nature *Documents of Performance* cannot absolutely determine which separate papers were created for one particular play in a particular play-house at a particular time; it can, however, say what documents were generally brought about when plays were readied for production, and how regularly plays of the period were discussed, thought of, and disseminated as a series of pieces.

The organisation of this book is determined by its two interests: the play in its first performance, and the way the play on the page manifests that. Its structure mirrors that bifold interest. It considers texts theatrically in the order in which their separate patches were created and/or encountered, with the proviso that several came into existence simultaneously. So it begins with the first document written towards the creation of a play, the plot-scenario, goes on to look at the documents an audience member might meet on the way to the playhouse (playbill), and in that house (Argument), and continues from there to discuss the documents that amounted to 'the play' in performance: first the prologue, and then the play itself, with its songs, scrolls, entrances from backstage-plots, dialogue from parts, and its guiding book that ran the performance but had not shaped all of its documents. But as *Documents of Performance* is equally interested in the effect of the separate dissemination of theatre documents on the printed playbook, its structure is simultaneously designed to mimic that of reading a play (for a playbook is set out in the order in which performance happened). So the playbill chapter is also the chapter on the title-page, the chapter on the performance Argument is also on a printed play's Argument, the prologue is what happens when the next page of the playbook is turned, as well as the way the play starts, and of course the songs, scrolls, entrances and dialogue make up the printed play as they do the performed play. The patchwork construction that defines early modern plays thus also defines the way this book has been designed and written.

In more detail: the first chapter will be about the plot-scenario, because the first time anyone confronted a playscript was as a fragment that promised a whole text: it could be judged, sold, stolen, and waved in front of a company as promise of a play to come. Physically and mentally the 'fragment' remained the unit in which a play was written and learnt. The second chapter is on the playbill, printed in large numbers and liberally scattered as flyers and posters over the London that had rejected playhouses. They advertised the play to be performed by using the same vocabulary and information as title-pages and hanging on the same posts as they did; that some title-pages may have inherited the playbill's content will naturally be considered. The next chapter turns to Arguments, also (usually) printed, which were an early form of theatre programme available only for some productions: they told the story of the play to come, and often contained a character-list; they were published at playwrights' expense and given out as souvenirs of what had been performed. These texts, like the Arguments to playbooks that they reflect or become, ensure that readers can follow what is happening in a complex narrative, but risk upstaging the very story they introduce by doing so; they were limited to special, court or first performances. Chapter 4 looks at prologues and epilogues, which were so often extracted from the play to be read out onstage that, like the scrolls they strongly resemble, they could frequently become 'lost' from the playbook, surviving elsewhere in books of poems or jests, as other forms of literature. A discussion of their relationship to benefit performances, and how often they and related interim texts were intended for single performances at court, or on first days, will lead to questions about the authorial nature of prologues and epilogues, the relationship they have to the real playwright(s), and whether they should be seen as temporary or permanent residents in the plays that contain them.

Documents of Performance then turns to the documents that made up the body of a performed play. It looks at the documents that descend from the full playbook or that were written in advance of its completion. Chapter 5 is on songs, which sometimes needed to be taken out from the playscript before it had even been completed in order to be sent to a composer: with their requirements for music from another source they represent collaborative moments even in single-authored plays. But if an old tune were to be used for a song, the text still continued to be regularly removed from the play and written out afresh, partly because it could, on its separate paper, be flanked by the musical notation to the words, partly because it also could sometimes be sung from onstage, and – when neither of those pertained – because it needed a particular variety of rehearsal from the actor, or actor and instrumentalist/singer combined. It too was frequently lost, removed, altered, added and written by someone other than the playwright. Then chapter 6 addresses the theatre 'scrolls', which were extracted and inscribed onto separate papers mimicking the documents they pretended to be – letters, bills, proclamations. They were often read out onstage, saving the actor from learning more than he had to, and so returning the enacted play at that moment to a paper medium (as songs sometimes did): plays performed were made up of a combination of the remembered word and the written one, part text, part action.

Chapter 7 is on the backstage-plots that hung in the tiring-house detailing entrances and 'personals' (the properties that actors were to take onstage with them). They were written to govern onstage performance from backstage, and were some of the theatre's most important manuscripts: they alone of all play fragments were mounted on special boards and penned with several quills for clarity and beauty. In this way they were more valued than the book they protected when not in use, the full 'approved' play. But that will be because backstage-plots really ran the performance, while, as chapter 8 shows, the full play only did in some respects: it had been divided, often before being approved, into 'parts' from which actors were to learn their characters; those parts, however, were not always faithful to the playbook from which they were copied, nor were they always faithfully followed by actors.

How does the printed book reflect these dislocated texts? If what was performed from the first was completed, disseminated, learnt or read on the stage in a series of large and small fragments, what documents did printers receive? Though published plays often have a 'finished' appearance, they will be shown regularly to be missing some of those sections written for manifestation in the theatre but also lost there, which might extend from prologues to epilogues to songs to choruses to interim entertainments to internal masques to Arguments to playbill lures as well as other paper witnesses of the text. So in telling the story of the theatre's separate documents, *Documents of Performance* also tells the story of printed playbooks, explaining where and why the patch is as visible in the printed whole as it is in the performance. Again, it will be shown that issues barely considered now were regularly in early modern discussion. Indeed, the same terms of opprobrium, 'patch' or 'patchy', were used for writers of print as for writers of performance: one poet is described by Rankins as having 'Thrust[] forth a patched Pamphlet into print', for instance. What is interesting, however, is the response of the readers to that patched pamphlet. They, according to Rankins, are conscious of the book's patchy nature, and delighted by it, gazing at it 'as on a pide coat'.[7] He calls them 'fooles' for so doing, but the patched text, with its various segments visible either in print or in performance, is well compared to a multi-coloured coat for the effect that it had: some, like Rankins, found it ugly because it lacked uniformity, and others, for exactly the same reason, found it stylish and beautiful.

CHAPTER I

Plot-scenarios

INTRODUCTION

Abraham Wright, the divine, had performed in plays when at Oxford in the 1630s; he had even written a play, *The Reformation*, now lost, that had been acted with some success. So when, in around 1640, he started taking notes about the plays he was studying, he did so as an afficionado. He realised, for instance, that lines might read poorly on the page but act well, saying of *Vittoria Corombona* (John Webster's *White Devil*) that it was 'indifferent' as a text, 'but for ye presentments I beeleeve good', and of Henry Shirley's *Martyrd Souldier* that its songs had been 'much taken' by the 'people', though it too had, to his mind, second-rate lines. Wright's method was to analyse plays for two features both of which he commented on separately. One was the writing style. The other was the 'plot'. Thus there were plays like James Shirley's *School of Complement* that Wright found to be 'a good play for ye plot rather then lines'; and there were plays like *The Lady of Pleasure*, also by Shirley, that Wright thought 'ye best play . . . for ye lines', whilst finding 'ye plot is as much as none'. Ideally the play should be strong in both, like Shakespeare's *Othello* which was 'A very good play, both for lines and plot, but especially ye plot'.[1]

Wright's notes are accompanied by excerpted passages from plays, often paraphrased, to be learnt and reused. Thus Wright's analyses of plot-versus-lines might seem to be, like his extracted texts, thoroughly rooted in the act of reading. But his reference to the response of the 'people' gives pause: he is also interested in how plays worked as performance texts for he is analysing them with an eye to the audience. Moreover, his subjects of concern match those of theatregoers. Picking their way through a production, spectators seem often to have considered deeply, and separately, the way plot contributed to the play's success. When Thomas Locke wrote a letter to Carleton on the reception of Fletcher and Massinger's *Sir John Van Olden Barnavelt*, his critique muddled political commentary (the play, depicting a real event, was causing ructions) with artistic choices about structure:

Our players have fownd the meanes to goe through with the play of Barnevelt, and it hath . . . receaved applause: yet some say that . . . Barnavelt should perswade Ledenberg to make away himself (when he came to see him after he was prisoner) . . . and [that] to tell him that when they were both dead (as though he meant to do the like) they might sift it out of their ashes, was thought to be a point strayned.[2]

Other audience criticisms similarly concern the way specific plot moments were liked or disliked. Hausted's Cambridge play, *The Rivall Friends*, was damned, grieves its author, principally because the four 'Gulls' in the third act were thought 'impertinent to the Plot'.[3] Even Charles I watched plays with strong views on plotting. 'Though the kinge commended the language' of Davenant's *The Wits*, writes Henry Herbert, he 'dislikt the plott and characters'.[4] Here Charles I simultaneously praises and criticises the same play because, like Wright, he is able to analyse 'plot' as a totally separate entity from dialogue.

Early modern playwrights presented their plays for criticism in exactly the same terms. Regularly dividing plot from language, it was they who, as Davenant had it, first 'taught you [the critical audience] how t'unweave a plot,/And tract the winding Scenes'.[5] Examples show him to be right. Playwrights continually regard the plot as something with merits or demerits separate from those of the dialogue. 'First for the Plot', writes Habington of *The Queene of Arragon* (1640), 'it's no way intricate', continuing, 'The Language too is easie'; Carlell insecurely fears the watchers of *The Deserving Favourite* who will say both that 'the Plot was dull,' and that 'The Language [was] rude'.[6] Shirley even appends a prologue to the start of his *The Brothers* that concludes, insecurely, 'two houres hence you may/(If not before) laugh at the plot, and play', as though simultaneously worried that the audience might laugh at the structure of the 'plot' (which would be a critical act), whilst hoping that they laugh at the substance of the 'play' (an appreciative act: this play is a comedy).[7] Indeed, R. D. compliments Tatham on his *Distracted State* by praising its masterful fusion of the two separate elements of the drama: 'if we may/Conclude Language and Plot do make a Play,/Here they are met'.[8]

Why do playwrights, and so audiences, have a sense that there is a separation amounting almost to a rivalry between a play's plot and its language? The answer lies in the fact that the two were created as, initially, separate documents: they were different texts. For 'plot' in this period did

not simply stand for 'story'. The prologue at the Blackfriars to Massinger's
The Emperour of the East, for example, can frankly confess that the 'story' of
the play is borrowed, whilst asking the audience to admire the 'proportion'
and 'drawing' – the structure – of its drama:

> Hee hath done his best, and though hee cannot glorie
>   In his invention, (this worke being a storie,
> Of reverend Antiquitie) hee doth hope
>   In the proportion of it, and the scope,
> You may observe some peeces drawne like one
>   Of a stedfast hand.[9]

'Structure', in this period, was created before the rest of the play was, and
was called in its initial formation 'the plot': these days it would be called
a 'scenario'.

Writing a letter to his friend William Walsh in 1693 Dryden casually
referred to the progress he was making with his play *Love Triumphant*:
'I have plotted it all,' he commented; '& written two Acts of it.'[10] He was
articulating the usual method for composing a play: first 'plotting' the full
outline, then 'writing' the play proper. His routine had long held in the
theatre, probably having its origins in the humanist educational process:
as students had been encouraged to resolve full texts into summaries and
to broaden summaries back into full texts, 'plotting' before 'writing' was
an obvious way to conceive of any literary document. Puttenham had,
years previously, recommended writing a play in layered form: 'our maker
or Poet is . . . first to devise his plat or subject, then to fashion his poeme,
thirdly to use his metricall proportions, and last of all to utter with
pleasure and delight'.[11] In this model the plot or 'plat' starts as everything,
what the play is, and is later encroached upon by different stages of play-
writing and perfecting. Using 'metricall proportions' – writing verse – is
presented as a decorative flourish on top of a written play on top of a plot,
while the plot's final end, an 'utterance' or performance, implies that the
document is still in some sense 'there' in the enacted play, blurring the
distinction between plot as a unit of construction and plot as a unit of
play.[12] Even playwrights excluded from practical theatrical concerns –
closet and female writers – knew that careful advanced plotting was the
secret to the success of any play, Margaret Cavendish drawing a distinction not between playwrights who plotted and playwrights who did not,
but, rather, between playwrights who devoted all their time to 'plotting',
and playwrights who also spared some effort for writing the text: 'some
take more pains a Plot to lay,/Than other some to plot, and write a Play'.[13]

Very little has been written on plot-scenarios, and it is sometimes said that only one, and sometimes that none, of them survive from the early modern period.[14] In fact several full and near-complete plots exist in manuscript; at least one can be found in print; and the contents of fragments of others are stranded in the middle of manuscript playbooks. This chapter will explore whole and partial plot-scenarios, paying attention to the variant titles given these pieces of paper – 'plots', 'arguments', 'devices', 'inventions' – which make them easily confusable with other varieties of plot. A familiarity with the existence of plot-scenarios and their uses raises a number of fundamental questions about the narrative order in which dialogue was written, for, with a plot mapping structural logic, a play itself could be composed out of sequence. Moreover, as plots were important objects in their own right that could be distributed between co-authors, stolen, or sold to companies or courtiers even before the play itself existed, the active and powerful life of the plot reveals the separate and separable importance of design and sequence to the success of a play. And, as traces of plots are there in the layout and sometimes in the stage-directions of completed plays, an argument will be made for considering the authorship of dialogue entirely separately from the authorship of structure (and linked stage-directions). Plots were crucial to a play's achievement, and 'plotters' emerge as the play-writing heroes behind many important texts, including texts to which they did not actually contribute a word.

PLOT-SCENARIOS: CONTENT

Several whole plots survive, one in print and some in manuscript. The first is most unusual, for plots are made obsolescent by the fact of the full play, and, though sometimes kept by the playhouse, as will be shown, did not tend to make it to the press. When, however, passages of an actual play were missing, for whatever reason, a plot summary was regularly used to represent what the full text might have been; on one occasion printing a plot served the same purpose.

The text that precedes the start of Ben Jonson's play *Mortimer* in the 1641 edition of his *Workes* consists of a list of the 'persons' to be in the story, nine in all plus a chorus, together with an act-by-act summary, here entitled 'arguments', for the play. So 'T*HE First Act comprehends* Mortimer's *Pride and Security*'; '*The Fourth Act*' is when Mortimer is discovered in the bedroom of Isabel the Queen Mother and is 'sent to execution'; the conclusion is summarised in full as '*The fifth Act, the Earle of* Lancasters *following the crie, and meeting the report. The Celebration of the Kings Justice*.[15] These two pages of preliminary matter at first glance look very similar to the person-list and 'argument' provided by Jonson for *Sejanus* (discussed in chapter 3), but the difference is that the actual play of *Mortimer* that then follows is, as the printer Moseley later described it, 'the very Beginning only (for it amounts not to one full Scene) of a Tragedy'.[16] On the first page of the play Mortimer speaks a soliloquy; on the second page Isabel enters, flirts with him, and recalls the haughty lords from whom Mortimer has rescued her. Mortimer assures her that she is now 'Queen of your self, and them'. There is no more. Instead, a terse note, provided presumably by the person charged with gathering Jonson's papers, Kenelm Digby, informs the reader: 'left unfinished' or, in variant states of the text, 'Hee dy'd, and left it unfinished.'[17] Whether Jonson died while writing the play, as the note indicates, or whether he gave up on the text, the demise of the author is the reason for the survival (and subsequent printing) of this particular plot: a summary from which to write a play never actually completed. Thus the 'arguments' to *Mortimer* preserve what is created by a playwright just before he embarks on the dialogue of a full text: a list of the people who will feature in the play, and a frank account of the bare story divided into distinct units – here acts.[18]

A plot in manuscript, but containing many of *Mortimer*'s features, is to be found inside a collection of notes kept by Milton in the 1640s. It has a telling name, *Paradise Lost*, and reveals that Milton's original notion, from which he preserved only the title, was to justify God's way to men in something like a mystery play. So the projection for the play of *Paradise Lost* starts, as *Mortimer* does, with a person-list: in fact this particular text has two different person-lists, both erased, for it is a crude working document, and these and its *currente calamo* corrections reveal that the structure was being actively created through the process of writing the plot. Looser grammatically than *Mortimer* (which may have been improved for the press), but divided into acts in the same way, *Paradise Lost* is lightly punctuated and gives every sign of being a working document, full of errors and rethinking:

Moses *prologizei* [speaks a prologue] recounting how he assumed a̶ his true bodie, that it corrupts not because of his [.] with god in the mount declares the like of Enoch and Eliah, besides the purity of ye pl[ace] that certaine pure winds, dues, and clouds praeserve it from corruption whence ~~Heavenly Love~~ [ex]horts to the sight of god, tells they cannot se Adam in the state of innocence by reason of ~~sin~~ thire sin.

After this initial outburst, it resolves into a bullet-point-like structure indicating what is to happen, more than how: in 'Act 4', for example, the opening instruction is

> Adam
>   fallen}[19]
> Eve

The very roughness of this document indicates how essential it was to perfect a plot before writing – moreover this particular document may have taught its author to give up on the dramatic form for his grand scheme: the play Milton started on this subject was quickly abandoned (as his friend Edward Phillips relates).[20] Sometimes the point of designing plots was precisely in order to see whether or not the resultant play would work. Dryden had kept a would-be play, *Sicilian Vespers*, 'Plotted by me above these seven years', but ultimately it warned him off composing the drama – for looking at it afresh he realised 'the Rape in my *Tragedy of Amboyna*, was so like it, that I forbore the Writing'.[21]

The most telling of the surviving plots was sold to the Folger Shakespeare Library as 'an original unpublished manuscript Scenario of an English tragedy, which was to bear the title *Philander King of Thrace*' (the title, and genre, are supplied from a Maggs Brothers Catalogue; both are open to question).[22] It contains, as ever, a list of the people to be in the play, followed additionally by useful information for writing the text – what the rivers in Thrace and Macedon are called, for instance. After that, there is a full and very detailed account of the story that is to unfold, but only until act 3, at which point the plot comes to an end: it may be that this is the plot for a collaborative play in which only acts 1–3 were of interest to this particular author; alternatively the plotter may have given up before completing the document.

When (rarely) discussed, the plot of *Philander*, for want of a better title, is said to be an anonymous but 'amateur' document, too unrelated to the public theatre to merit serious attention. Yet the authorship of this plot was identified by Laetitia Yeandle, the Folger's then Curator of Manuscripts, some years ago; she traced it to Sir Edward Dering in whose hand it is written: a regular, somewhat obsessive, London theatregoer who fraternised with actors and playwrights, kept a notably large collection of playbooks of his own, and had London plays copied and sometimes adapted to his taste. The earliest Shakespeare play to be found in manuscript – a conflation of Q5 (1613) of *1 Henry IV* and QB (1600) of *2 Henry IV* for private performance shortly before the First Folio was published – starts

in Dering's hand and was written up at his request.[23] The author/writer of
the plot of *Philander*, then, was a man thoroughly engaged with and by
the London professional theatre that he watched, read, imitated and
adapted on a regular basis. Though Dering may not be professional, he
was the most knowledgeable of amateur playwrights, who was in every
way keen to mimic and 'improve on' the practice of professional writers.

The scenario can be expected to be similar to those found in the
professional theatre of the time, though perhaps in an overblown version.
And this seems to be the case: *Philander* is divided not only act-by-act as
are the plots above, but also scene-by-scene. Act 1 is focussed and relatively
spare, elucidating what actions are to take place and which characters are
to be involved:

> ### Act. i.
> Scaen: i.
> Philander and his sister Suavina walke and conferre: she greives for ye warre.
> Sc. 2.
> Philander telleth Euphrastes ye cause why he will not marry Suavina to any but
> a present K.
> Scn: 3.
> Aristocles and Suavina discover theire passions and are discovered by Phonops.
> Sc: 4.
> Philander doth banish Aristocles.
> Sc: 5.
> Euphrastes doth counsel Aristocles to go to ye warres between ye Epirot and
> Achaian.[24]

By the third act, however, the plotter's literary and novelistic impulses
seem to be taking over. Details of each scene become fuller, and more
emotive, the verbs carrying such weight as to show an author confounding
plot summary with anecdote or tale. At the same time, Dering is simultaneously unsure which character will say what: he is still creating the story
even as it overtakes him, as 3.6 – fairly neatly written, but with erased text –
demonstrates:

> Sc. 6.
> Whilst he sitts bet[ween] ye two lady's ye two K[ing]s come in: each jea-lous
> and envious that Aristocles doth impede theire loves. they court theire severall
> mistresses. suavina breifely de-ferres him to ~~ye sibyll's~~ ye Phoebade *vertumna*:
> where ~~that~~ next night shee'l meete him: and so goes out.
>
> Salohcin ~~bidds~~ asketh Phonops if Ascania be deade: he sayth she shall that ~~dnight~~.
> Salo-hcin asketh Philander how he speedes, who sayth but coldly and condition-
> ally. Corintha leaves them Philander's vowe will not suffer him appeare

complaines to

in any sentence against Aristocles and therefore ~~winnes~~ Saolohcin to ~~banish him~~
who biddes him feare not he will but think on itt and take care. He biddeth
Phonops dispatch him att advantage. ~~Sc. 7~~
~~Aristocles complaynes of banishment unlook't for.~~

Is this plot, which ends abruptly at the conclusion of the third act, incomplete because the story became too complex for a single play? Or did it
successfully provide matter for a drama that has no longer survived – of
which, perhaps, Dering was only to write the first three acts? Either way,
combining the information from this and the two 'complete' plots discussed so far indicates both what plots provide towards plays structurally,
and where their traces can be found in extant playscripts. Evidently character-
lists are a key element, as is the division of the play, here into both acts
and scenes (in *Mortimer* and *Paradise Lost* into acts only).

As the individual unit, act or scene, is a constant concern of the plot, so
Dryden and subsequent authors even varied the word 'plot' with the term
'scenary' (with an 'a'), naming the document for the separate bits out of which
it was made, the scenes (*scena* in Latin), as much as for the whole that it
ultimately became. The plot insisted on the integrity of the scene or act in itself:

> To make a *Sketch,* or a more perfect *Model* of a *Picture*, is in the Language of
> *Poets,* to draw up the *Scenary* of a *Play*, and the reason is the same for both; to
> guide the Undertaking, and to preserve the Remembrance of such things, whose
> Natures are difficult to retain.[25]

Dryden's awkward phrasing here – his comparison with sketching
a picture, and his unfortunate use of the verb 'draw' for 'write' – has led
to the misapprehension that he is designing (wing) 'scenery' (with an 'e')
and has hidden what he is actually doing: coming up with an early form of
the word 'scenario' (*OED*, 1878). Thereafter 'scenary' remained in use for
many years, being described in Boyer's 1699 *Dictionary* as 'The ordering
of the Scenes of a Play'; and in Johnson's 1755–6 *Dictionary* as 'the
disposition and consecution of the scenes of a play'.[26] Here scenic order,
like act order, is said to be what the 'plot' is about; as Guillemard
maintained, 'he is . . . no good Poet . . . that doth not order al the acts
wel and discreetly unto the end'.[27]

The way the plot separated act from act, or scene from scene, naturally
dictated the methods available for writing a play. As a plot turns a play
into a series of separate units, the breaks and stops in the narrative are as
prominent as the action; scenic rather than narrative integrity is a source
of generative and creative power. Some playwrights therefore wrote

religiously to scene or act summaries, as seen in the few surviving printed plays in which plot-summaries are placed throughout at the start of acts or scenes. In these instances playwrights are shown first writing out the relevant passage from the plot and then composing underneath it, the result being a play written to the plot's summary moment rather than to the narrative of the whole. Each of the three acts of Jonson's *The Sad Shepherd* is topped with a summary, and, as the play is, like *Mortimer*, still in its unfinished state, '[wanting] two entire acts', these can hardly be, as is sometimes said, *inserted* into the text to highlight the play's Latinate and 'pastoral' construction.[28] And other 'non-classical' texts such as *The Misfortunes of Arthur* preserve similar 'internal' summaries; in this particular instance 'acts' are subdivided into 'scenes', giving them an appearance much like those of Dering's *Philander*.

The argument of the third Act.

1 IN the first Scene *Cador* and *Howell* incite and exhort *Arthur* unto warre: Who mooved with Fatherly affection towards his sonne, notwithstanding their perswasions resolveth upon peace.
2 In the second Scene, an Herault is sent from *Mordred* to commaund *Arthur* to discharge his armies under paine of death, or otherwise if he dare, to trie it by Battaile.
3 In the third Scene *Arthur* calleth his Assistants and Souldiers together, whom he exhorteth to pursue their foes.
4 In the fourth Scene *Arthur* between griefe and despaire resolveth to warre.[29]

Further examples of plays with inner summaries include Nabbes' *Hannibal and Scipio* (1637), and George Ruggle's *Ignoramus*, written in Latin for Cambridge University production in 1614 and printed in a translation by Robert Condrington in 1630. Though possibly these scene summaries are the scattered remains of 'Arguments' given to the audience for performance (see chapter 3), the division of their contents, and their dispersal over the playscript, suggests otherwise. Rather, it seems that the plot summary was sometimes so fundamental to the play that its presence, always felt there, remains written there, overtopping the grandiloquent dialogue with its stark account of actions to be taken and emotions to be felt.

PLOT-SCENARIOS: CONSTRUCTION, APPEARANCE, USE AND PRESERVATION

As plots are so elemental to the writing of a play, and as they so seldom survive, it becomes important to ask whether there is information detailing how closely they were written, and by whom. Exploring this reveals too what plots characteristically looked like, and why and where they were kept, all issues that help explain the tension between plot and 'play' covered in the introduction to this chapter.

There are not many stories about the occasion when a plot, as opposed to a play, was written – but there is one, and it survives in two very different forms: a manuscript poem hitherto unprinted, and a printed prose account. The first is hard to date; it is in a Restoration miscellany, but its story is from around 1610. It concerns both Beaumont and Fletcher who, it relates, walked into the countryside and picked a spot beside a road to begin 'Moulding ye Figure of an unborn play'; 'unborn' because at this juncture, to use Ben Jonson's description of plotting and then writing *Poetaster*, 'the Plot was but an *Embrion*'.[30] At a certain moment in the plotting process, the poem goes on, the two men reached a hiatus: they could not settle how 'The King' in their prospective play should be murdered.

> At winding up of ye well-labord scene,
> It was resolv'd, The King must die. But then
> About ye How, & Where Debates arose;
> One was for Stabbing; th'other poison chose.[31]

The play they are creating is fairly clearly *The Maid's Tragedy* (written *c.* 1608–11), in which Evadne kills the king by, as must have prevailed, stabbing; but what is interesting here is the fact that the 'winding up' of a specific scene is being so carefully 'laboured' before the writing of the text has started. That Beaumont and Fletcher should be working minutely on the internal structure of a specific scene conveys something of the logic behind plotting: plotting, particularly plotting for co-writers who might have to write apart from one another, had to determine not just which actions should occur, but which actions should take place in which point of the scene, as well as the other scenes that should come before and afterwards.

The well-known version of the same anecdote has a similar conversation taking place indoors in a tavern. In this account, only Fletcher is named, though he is obviously in discussion with someone over what is described as the 'rude draught' of a play. 'Rude draught' too, however, is the play's plot rather than its dialogue, for during this meeting Fletcher is, as above, still trying to determine what should happen to the king: 'Meeting once in a Tavern, to contrive the rude draught of a Tragedy,

Fletcher undertook to kill the King therein.' As both anecdotes go on to relate, Fletcher's king-killing plans are overheard:

> A Countrie-Fellow overhearing this
> (As every subject bound in Duty is)
> Had them secur'd; & up to Town he spurd,
> And swore ye same before ye Council-Board.

The conclusion of both anecdotes too depends upon Fletcher being at the plotting (rather than writing) stage of play-writing; the prose account even relies on a resonant verbal confusion between plotting *a play*, and plotting *an insurrection*: for when Fletcher was told to explain his treasonable actions 'the mistake soon [appeared], that the plot was onely against a Drammatick and Scenical King, [and] all wound off in a merriment'.[32] The plot of *The Maid's Tragedy*, whether co-contrived in the countryside or in a tavern, was determined in great detail before the play was written; nevertheless, as a document it is still called a 'rude draught' – 'draught', because it is a plot, not a whole play, and 'rude' because it is either 'primitive' (but both versions of the anecdote militate against that reading), or 'messy'.

Plots were, of course, both primitive *and* messy in the form in which they were first written: they were private documents made for the personal use of a small number of people. But it was their shambolic form that was a defining feature. So hectic were they in appearance that praising play-wrights for not blotting them was a truly extravagant way of extolling creative faculty, far more excessive than merely implying, as Shakespeare's friends did, an unblotted dialogue. West is in a frenzy of adulation when he claims that his brother-in-law, the playwright Randolph, could write plots on minute quantities of paper and with no blots, a masterpiece of spare precision that put him in an entirely different league from all other playwrights (whose multiply erased plots looked like the account-books of haberdashers): 'Hee was not like those costive Wits, who blot/A quire of paper to contrive a Plot./And e're they name it [the plot – and play], crosse it, till it look/Rased with wounds like an old Mercers Book.'[33] 'Blotted'/'crossed'/'rude' were within a 'normal' range of descriptive adjectives used to depict the appearance of a completed plot text, for a rough quality was fundamental to the document's nature.

As it happens, what appears to be a description both of the partial contents of a Fletcherian plot and of the messiness of the whole survives from the early modern period. It is to be found within the manuscript of the play *Bonduca*, which, though neat (it was probably written out for a private patron), is defective, missing the content of three-and-a-half scenes – 5.1, 5.2, 5.3 and part of 5.4. The scribe of this manuscript is the prompter of the King's Men, Edward Knight; the play from which he is copying must be damaged in some way, perhaps torn, or perhaps lacking pages that had not been properly secured. Whatever the reason for the deficiency in the underlying text, Knight needs to fill in for the missing scenes, and opts to do in miniature what Digby did for the whole of *Mortimer*: he provides plot summaries of the lost content, scene-by-scene:

Actus: Quinti: Scæna: pria:

~~Here should be A Scene of the Solemnitye of~~
~~penius his ffunerall: mourned by Caracticus:~~

Here should A Scæne. be betwene Junius. & petillius: (Junius mocking petillius for being in love with Bonducas Daughter that Killd her selfe: to them: Enterd Suetonius: (blameing petillius for the Death of pænius:

The next scæne. the solemnitye of pænius his ffunerall mournd by Caracticus:

---[34]

At this stage in the manuscript it is not yet apparent whether Knight is quoting from an actual plot-scenario that he has to hand, or writing summaries in his own words, though the language he uses is indicative. Description mingles with entrance stage-directions phrased in such a way as to sound like a backstage-plot – 'to them: Enterd Suetonius'; the origin of this text seems to be a 'treatment' for a play by a theatre afficionado, as is further indicated by the horizontal lines that divide one scene from another. This professional language could, of course, be traced to Knight himself, except that it is some years since the play has been performed by the company: the original play dates from *c.* 1613; Knight did not join the company until 1624; and the manuscript Knight is now writing dates to *c.* 1630. It would be unusual if Knight were to retain an action-by-action and scene-by-scene memory of what happened in performances of this particular text (if he had overseen a production at all – and he may not have done: any revival of *Bonduca* must have been long enough ago for the acting text to become damaged or lost). Moreover the erasure, which picks up the same words, '*the solemnitye of pænius his ffunerall mournd by Caractius*' and places them first at 5.1. and then at 5.3, though it may indicate confused recollection as Laurie Maguire suggests (if so, she adds, this would constitute the single unambiguous occasion of scenic 'reversal' offered by memorial texts), is much more likely to be traceable to eyeskip in transcription, or to an underlying scenario, here copied, that is divided as to when the 'funeral' should take place.[35] In other words, the writer shows signs of transcribing from a manuscript plot. In the later printed text of *Bonduca* found in the *Comedies and Tragedies* of 1647, which has a different source from the manuscript, the funeral is actually placed where the erased indication is that it should be, at 5.1, furthering the idea that the plot was toying with the position of this important theatrical moment.[36]

As it is, when Knight completes his scene summaries he explains to the reader the cause of them; his chatty account – almost always reproduced without the scene summaries that precede it – has, I suggest, been subsequently misunderstood, with profound ramifications:

The begining of this following Scæne betweene petillius & Junius is wanting. ---- the occasion. why these are wanting here. The booke where it by it was first Acted from is lost: and this hath beene transcrib'd from the fowle papers of the Authors wch were found:
---[37]

Lacking the scenes in question, explains Knight, he has transcribed 'this' from the 'foul papers'; it was losing sight of what 'this' might mean that perhaps led the great bibliographer W. W. Greg to make a singular error of interpretation.

Homing in on the fact that none of the manuscript was copied from the 'allowed' book ('the booke where by it was first Acted from', which 'is lost'), Greg decided that 'this' meant the entire text Knight was copying: thus he took it that there was an authorial draft in front of Knight that was called in its entirety 'the fowle papers of the Authors' and that consisted partly of text and partly of 'plot'. But the theory that he went on to develop – a 'scheme' for the construction of plays in which texts were written first in 'foul papers' and then in 'fair' text – came to exclude the bitty nature of the passage to which Knight's explanation was attached, as Werstine forcefully points out: the 'explicit sense in which Greg used *foul papers* appears at odds with the sense in which the terms *foul sheet* or *foul papers* were used in the Jacobean and Caroline documents from which Greg drew these words, where they seem to have referred to fragmentary or incomplete copies of plays'.[38] For Greg's later account of play-construction, though stemming from 'the "foul papers" we . . . find Edward Knight transcribing', was that 'foul papers' constituted 'the play more or less as the author intended it to stand, but not . . . clear or tidy enough to serve as a prompt-book'.[39] Yet what Knight appears to say is that he has been obliged to turn *away* from a defective text *to* 'foul papers' from which he has been able to copy 'this'. So 'this' is most likely to mean 'this section made up of scene summaries'; the explanation is, after all, written at the end of the section of scene summaries (rather than at the end or beginning of the 'book'). The 'foul papers', in Knight's rare early modern use of the term, seem, in this instance, to mean 'the plot', 'foul papers' being an equivalent description to 'rude draught'.[40] Scholars of the early modern period have not considered this, partly because they are not familiar with 'plots' of which a 'foul' or 'rude' nature was a primary feature, and partly because they are not familiar with the context of Knight's pronouncement.

Other early modern scribes confronted with deficient playbooks dealt with the problem in exactly the same way. The Latin university manuscript play *Senilis Amor* is missing a final section, for example, and a new scribe has written on the verso of what is now its last page (all other verso pages in the rest of the document are blank) a plot summary for the play's conclusion and, like Knight, a chatty explanation of what has happened:

> Titubis & Collosus having cheated the woman of her henns, make a feast & sing Io Bacche venus: & Cat: are sett in the stocks being drunke: there Call for drinke & fall a sleepe; this sceane full of sport was basely torne out of this place.[41]

Like Knight, the annotator of *Senilis Amor* makes plot summary stand in for lost dialogue: that he too is copying from an actual plot rather than simply remembering the scene can be suspected for similar linguistic reasons – he is writing largely in the present tense (rather than the past tense of recollection); he is varying the language he uses, from summary to specific song name to something like a stage-direction, 'call for drinke'. This passage, in combination with Knight's above, indicates that 'plots' may sometimes have been preserved for emergencies even when the full play had been completed.

This suggestion is furthered still by another moment of plot summary in another play that may also have Fletcher's hand in it: the anonymous *Faithful Friends* (*c.* 1614). Though it survives in a neat and carefully corrected manuscript text, the purpose of this copy of *Faithful Friends* is not entirely clear – it might be for a censor or a printer or for performance.[42] How its scribes relate to its playwrights is also uncertain: the text is largely written out by 'A', but whether he is the primary playwright or simply the copier is not evident; similarly it is not obvious whether 'B', who revises and corrects the whole shortly thereafter, is a theatre functionary, an interested reader – or a (or the) playwright. One fact about the play's construction, however, is obvious. At the moment when 'A' copies the play, the content for one scene, 4.5, is absent. This is not because, as in the earlier two cases, a defective text underlies this one, for 'A' confidently expects the arrival of the missing scene, and leaves a gap in the manuscript long enough to contain the entire section when it arrives. This means that at the point of writing out the play in neat, 'A' has text for 4.4 and 5.1 and knows enough about 4.5 to anticipate its length. The same is true of songs, also missing, for which 'A' also leaves gaps. 'A' is writing a neat manuscript placing 'in order' a play he is receiving in piecemeal fashion.

At some point 'A' gives up on acquiring the missing 4.5. To fill his gappy manuscript he does what the scribe does for missing text in *Bonduca* and *Senilis Amor*: he plugs the hole with the content of the plot for that scene, which, in this case, he has to write out in unnaturally large letters to fill the space. After a heading describing the nature of the insertion, the contents follow:

The Plott of a Scene of mirth to conclude this fourth Acte.

Enter Sr Pergamus the foolish knight like a Bridegroome leading Flavia his Bride, Bellario the singing souldier, Black Snout the Smith, Snipp Snapp the Tayler and Cauleskin the Shomaker.

An Altar to be sett forth with the Image of Mars. Dindinus the Dwarfe bearing Sr Per: launce and shield wch are hung up for trophees, and Sr Perg. Vowes for the love of Flavia never to beare Armes agen, the like dos Bla: Snout who hangs up his sword and takes his hammer vowing to God Vulcan never to Use other Weapon, The Taylor and the Shoomaker to vowe the like to God Mercury Then Bellario t̶ ̶s̶o̶ sings a songe how they will fall to there old Trades, a clapp of Thunder and run of /

finis 4 Act.[43]

Actually, at some point after this, another scribe, 'R', finally provides the dialogue for the missing scene; it is written on a loose sheet of quarto-sized paper (the rest of the play is in folio), and has been placed within the text rather than affixed onto it, being described in 1812 as a 'detached manuscript'; it is now correctly situated on fol. 37, having resided for many years, as damp marks indicate, pressed between two 'wrong' pages around fol. 4.[44]

Here the plot summary does not stand for a scene once written and now missing; it stands, rather, for a passage either parcelled out to a different author to complete (who was slow in the process), or not completed by the writer who has written the rest of the play. In either case, the play is being written 'out of order', as plots allow, and the comic and largely irrelevant scene (as well as all of the songs) are the last sections of the full text to be completed. As these are also the most 'disposable' bits of text, and are not necessary for the story, it seems that the play is being written in 'priority order', most important sections first, comic 'additions' or disposable text last (songs and their creation also have their own narrative, covered in chapter 5). Plots allowed plays to be written in non-linear fashion according to whatever set of priorities the author or authors held; they also allowed the simultaneous co-writing of plays by two different writers. Finally, plots gave whoever possessed copies of them (in the case of *Bonduca* and *Faithful Friends*, seemingly the playhouse) a substitute that could both describe a piece of text that was missing and prescribe how it was to be written up were another playwright to be found.

Many dramatists, including Chapman, Chettle, Daborne, Dekker, Drayton, Ford, Munday, Samuel Rowley, Tourneur, Wilson and Webster, signed contracts or left correspondence 'specifying that they had each produced an act, scene or some other closely delineated portion of a play': they had written out of narrative order to plot-units, signifying that co-writing required multiply distributed plots.[45] So Daborne writes to Henslowe on 5 June 1613 about two plays he is concurrently completing. Rushed for time, he has parcelled out a section of one of his plays to Tourneur in a private agreement, for which, presumably, he is either paying or collecting (or creating) a favour: 'I have not only labord my own play which shall be ready before they [Lady Elizabeth's Men] come over but given Cyrill Tourneur an act of ye Arreignment of London to write yt we may have yt likewise ready for them.'[46] Daborne has transferred to Tourneur enough information for the writing of a single act out of context from the rest of the play: he has, presumably, given him a plot.

Heywood was probably the recipient of multiple such plots, for he claims often to have written what appear to be single acts in others' plays. He records how he had had 'an entire hand or at least a maine finger' in 220 plays: a hand has five digits, so a main finger is likely to mean 'a crucial act' in a play.[47] Shakespeare, too, is thought to have co-written to plots, Gossett in her edition of *Pericles* suggesting that Shakespeare plotted the collaborative work but became sole author of one section; Melchiori arguing likewise that *Edward III* was outlined by Shakespeare who then also revised the play in its final stages.[48] Letters of the period do confirm that 'simultaneous' collaboration from plot summaries was an entirely normal method of putting a play together. John Day writes to Henslowe, 'about the plott of the Indyes I have occasion to be absent therfore pray delyver it to will hauton'.[49] He wants a copy of the plot for the play he is co-writing with Haughton and Smith to be given to him by Haughton, and is happy to receive it without attending a meeting on the subject; presumably all three co-writers were each supplied with a copy of the plot, regardless of its actual author (who is evidently not Day).[50] Dekker too co-wrote in a fashion that implies shared access to a careful plot. When he was taken to court to explain the part he had taken in writing the scandalous play, now lost, of *Keep the Widow Waking* (also called *The Late Murder in Whitechapel* and *The Late Murder of the Son upon the Mother*), he was obliged to explain which sections of the text had originated with him. The play was co-authored with Ford, Rowley and Webster, but Dekker's particular contribution had been, he stated, 'two sheetes of paper conteyning the first Act' of the play together with 'a speech in the last Scene of the last Act of the Boy who had killed his mother'.[51] His unit of writing is both an amount that will fit on to 'two sheets of paper' ('the usual practice seems to have been to write . . . plays on separately folded [folio] sheets, in units that is of four pages'), and an amount that makes 'part' sense (a speech) and plot sense (an act).[52]

Much the same is indicated by Nashe's account of writing *The Isle of Dogs*. He claims that he is responsible only for 'the induction and the first act of it', and that 'the other foure acts without my consent, or the least guesse of my drift or scope, by the players were supplied' – but this is disingenuous.[53] What got *The Isle of Dogs* into trouble was its parody of particular people, seemingly the Queen and/or Henry Brooke, 8th Lord Cobham: these are plot points, not writing points. Nashe's insistence that the players had no sense of his 'drift' is his way of implying the play was completed without access to his plot. But as the company had some of Nashe's already-written scenes this is likely to be untrue, not least because, as will be shown, they were probably supplied with a copy of the plot when they commissioned the play. Presumably Nashe is really the plot-writer but is hoping to hide that behind the fact that he only part-wrote the actual play.

As these illustrations indicate, there could be several plot summaries in circulation for any one play: if an author did not complete his section of a play, the plot could record what should be there, enabling someone else to write the requisite text; if the play had been completed but subsequently damaged, the 'plot' or scenario both supplied the content of the absent passage and, again, instructed another author what to write if the missing scene were to be recreated. A plot anticipated that the whole would come into being for the first time – and enabled it to come into being again – but only if the theatre itself retained a copy of the document.

'PLOTTERS': SCENARIOS AS COMMODITIES

As plots were often independently purchased by theatres long before the play itself existed, the retention of the plot as 'security' is highly likely. Daborne dangled a good scenario in front of an emissary from the impresario Henslowe, threatening to take it elsewhere if he did not receive forty shillings for it. As the actor Nathan Field summarises in a letter written at the end of June 1613:

Mr. Hinchlow ['Henslowe']

Mr. Dawborne and I, have spent a great deale of time in conference about this plott, wch will make as beneficiall a play as hath Come these seaven yeares, It is out of his love he detaines it for us, onely xl. is desir'd in hand, for wch, wee will be bound to bring you in the play finish'd upon the first day of August; wee would not loose it, wee have so assured a hope of it, and, on my knowledge Mr. Dauborne may have his request of another Companie.[54]

Here Field is particularly keen on buying the plot for forty shillings as he is sure the piece will be 'beneficiall' (by which he means, financially lucrative) though not a word of it yet exists. Thus a plot is not only a practical document for the author or authors, it is also a 'pitch' providing an essential foretaste of the final play. It is its own advertisement.

Two records document how, some years earlier, twenty shillings (half the amount Daborne asked for) was lent to Ben Jonson for a plot, with the promise of further money when the actual play was delivered:

Lent unto Bengemen Johnsone the [2] 3 of desembz 1597 upoon a Bocke wch he was to writte for us befor crysmas next after the date herof wch he showed the plotte unto the company I saye lente in Redy money unto hime the some of xxs.[55]

Obviously this plot, on which money was lent rather than given, was also something like a contract or promise of the play to come. But here the fact that Henslowe had secured his own copy of the plot as a result of the financial transaction was to redound onto Jonson. On 23 October 1598 Henslowe records in his diary giving money 'unto mr Chapmane' for 'ii ectes of a tragedie of bengemens plotté': Henslowe, it seems, has distributed the writing of two acts to assure the timely completion of Jonson's play.[56] This means, however, that Henslowe, not Jonson, is choosing co-writers for a Jonsonian plot: in raising money on his plot, Jonson had parted with his sole interest in the telling of his story. Later in life the same seems to have happened again – perhaps it regularly did. In a tight-lipped preface to his King's Men play *Sejanus*, Jonson tells the reader that the text was originally written with a collaborator. Again the Jonsonian plot appears to have been 'shared' against its author's will, for, as the preface goes on to say, Jonson has now painstakingly removed the second writer's work, replacing it with his own, never-acted, passages:

> this Booke, in all numbers, is not the same with that which was acted on the publikke Stage, wherein a 2nd pen had a good share; in place of which I had rather chosen, to put weaker (and no doubt less pleasing) of mine own, then to defraud so happy a Genius of his right, by my lothed usurpation.[57]

Jonson appears to be more reliable as a plotter than as a writer.

This fits in with other accounts of Jonson. Though widely tipped as a genius, he was also famously 'Sure and Slowe', as his friends put it; or, as his critics scoffed, his 'Witt/As long upon a Comoedie did sit/As Elephants bring forth'.[58] Jonson was not a fast writer. And given that Jonson's name is, in his younger days, associated with several collaborative texts, including the lost *Hot Anger Soon Cold* with Henry Porter and Henry Chettle, the lost *Page of Plymouth* with Dekker, and the lost *Robert II*, also known as *The Scot's Tragedy*, with Chettle, Dekker '& other jentellman', it is possible he was at that stage being hired specifically for his plots rather than, or as well as, for his leisurely writing.[59] After all, when early modern writers wanted to praise Jonson, they often turned to his plots first – 'Publius Naso' (a veiled reference to Jonson) in Parrot's *The Mastive* is said to have 'compoz'd a Play,/Of such a plot' that 'The best in London payes for his invention'.[60] Similarly, when writers of the period wanted to goad Jonson, they rounded on his plots, accusing him of a heavy-handedness befitting (his former profession) a bricklayer:

> . . . Ben, In this strickt Age
> A brickehills fitter for the then yt stage
> Thou better knowes A groundsell how to Laye
> Then lay the plott or grounde worke of A playe.[61]

Even after death, Jonson retained a good name for his plotting. Flecknoe mourned his loss with 'few know, now he's gone, to plot a Play', elaborating elsewhere, 'Now every one writes Playes, the Art is almost lost, and instead of neatly and closely plotting them, we have nothing but loose ends and Thrums.'[62] Perhaps even some of the surviving plays in which Jonson was co-contributor are written to his plots rather than written *by* him. *Eastward Hoe*, co-authored with Chapman and Marston, and *The Widow*, co-authored with Fletcher and Middleton, are both plays in which the absence of Jonson's 'voice' has been regularly commented upon.[63] Granted, other commentators on the plays have 'found' Jonson's voice, but, then again, they have looked for it with the assumption that it is there in the text. Actually, there is no reason to suppose a plot collaborator was also a dialogue-writer – though he may have been.

The tension regularly expressed between the plotters and the writers of plays, however, implies how often the two were different – and how, when they were different, it was a matter of dispute who had authored the text. In the busy workaday companies of the time, plays were regularly plotted by those best at plotting and written by those best at writing. Hence Middleton could slightingly refer to 'the best Common Play-Plotter in England': being a play-plotter was an entire job, and not, to his mind, very prestigious compared to being a play-writer (or '-maker' as the term more often had it, 'make' being perhaps in apposition to 'plot').[64] Nashe, too, in admitting that Greene outranked him in only one thing, 'plotting Plaies, wherein he was his crafts master', demonstrated how praising that particular aspect of the job could be a criticism in itself.[65] The criticism will be because the power of words, the use of lyricism or euphuism, the creation of apt analogies and startling metaphors, were nothing to do with the plot. Yet though words may have bespoken a verbal richness, without the plot they would have been nothing: a fact the detractors were probably conscious of too.

Talented plotters were actually cherished and revered not just by their companies but also by the more knowledgeable spectators. One religious tract even compared God to a play-plotter, enjoining the spectators of the world's 'Tragick-Comedy' (us) to remember that 'the whole plot [was] contrived by infinite Wisdome and Goodness'; elsewhere, in a poetic comparison, Phaon's clasping of Sappho's hand is a sign that 'Love' the playwright has 'laid the scean' and 'draw'd the tragick plot, whereon must lean/The ground of all his Acts', because Love has determined a structure that will produce the play he has in mind – both the scenes and, in a pun, the 'acts' that ensue from them.[66] Of playwrights writing in the early modern period, Massinger was held up as a writer 'that knows/The strength of Plot to write in verse and prose'; while, in a list of the best comedy-writers of his age, Francis Meres views playwrights and play-plotters as equally worthy of veneration. His heroes for writing comedy are '. . . eloquent and wittie *John Lilly, Lodge, Gascoyne, Greene, Shakespeare, Thomas Nash, Thomas Heywood*', after which he lists '*Anthony Mundye* our best plotter'.[67] He will also have been ironic: Munday was a spy and informer against Catholics and was undoubtedly known for 'plotting' in every sense of the word. As has been indicated, early modern sensibility relished the loaded nature of the verb 'to plot'.[68] Nevertheless, that superlative 'best' for plotting was genuine praise, taken literally enough to provoke jealousy from Jonson, who had been omitted from this particular list altogether (though he is down amongst the 'best' for tragedy). Perhaps because he thought plotting not worth praising as an art in its own right, but probably because he wished he had received that praise himself, Jonson has 'Antonio Balladino', a parody of Anthony Munday in *The Case is Altered*, depicted as someone so obsessed with 'plaine' plays that all he cares about is their plots, while he disdains the writers of their language: 'let me have a good ground, no matter for the pen, the plot shall carry it'. The retort, sourly made by 'Onion', is, 'Indeed that's right, you are in print already for the best plotter.'[69] The title of 'good plotter' was one to which Jonson at least aspired.

That will be because a good plot had a high market value: so much so that theatre people, who seldom record their fear of losing a play, sometimes record their fear of losing a slick plot. In Tailor's *The Hogge Hath Lost his Pearle*, Haddit the playwright worries that the actor Change-coate, to whom he has revealed his new jig, has 'powdred up my plot in your sconce', and will 'home . . . and instruct your Poet over a pot of ale, the whole methode on't'; in *The Spanish Gipsie*, Sancho, like a playwright, checks that Roderigo 'will not steale my Plot': ''tis not my fashion,' replies Roderigo; 'but', Sancho responds, 'now adayes,'tis all the fashion'.[70] The prolific Heywood is said regularly to acquire plots for his plays from elsewhere. In a poem of invective, it is held that 'Shakespear's a Mimicke, Massinger a Sot,/Heywood for Aganippe takes a plot': for his muse – Aganippe was the fountain of the Muses – Heywood 'takes' plots rather than makes them.[71]

With a plot by one writer and a playscript by another, however acquired, the danger was always that either the plotter's or the writer's work might not in the final instance be acknowledged; there was continuously a battle concerning who had really 'authored' the text. Shirley, it is implied, plotted (some of) Edward Howard's plays, a fact Howard did not recognise publicly. One poem imagines a moment when the two men meet in the afterlife. Asked to put forward their best artistic contributions for judgement by Apollo, Edward 'Ned' Howard 'rose and commended the Plot of his Play':

> Such Arrogance made Apollo stark mad,
> But Sherly endeavour'd to appease his Chollar,
> By owning the Play, and swearing the Lad
> In Poetry was a very pert Scholar.[72]

Later in time, 'Ned's' brother Robert Howard was to dispute with Dryden about the authorship of the *Indian Queen*. Here the problem was reversed: Dryden had written all the verse, but Howard, who had written the plot only, published the play as his own work.[73] But Dryden could give as good as he got. He himself, it was claimed, let it be thought the play *Oedipus* was 'his' and ignored Nathaniel Lee's sizable contribution to it. Defending himself from this accusation, he explains defensively, 'I writ the first and third Acts of *Œdipus*, and drew the *Scenary* of the *whole Play*: whenever I have own'd a farther Proportion, let my Accusers speak.'[74] Dryden, like Howard, is confounding plotting a whole play with writing it; as it seems, authoring a plot could lead its writer to think that he 'owned' more of the final text than he did – or perhaps the writers of plots really did have some cause to say the resultant play was theirs. In the publishing trade of the time, after all, the purchaser of a licence to print acquired a right not to a single book but to all books bearing that title and story: 'Shakespeare's *Taming of the Shrew* and *King John* could not have been included in the First Folio without the consent of the owners of the anonymous *Taming of a Shrew* and *Troublesome Reign of King John*';[75] perhaps similarly the owner of a story, particularly an owner who had shaped the very way that story is told, felt all the resultant literature to be his, whether or not he had written it.

'Collaborating' at the level of plot alone is a notion often not con-sidered when looking into early modern co-authorship. Yet it remained a prominent option for co-writing in the minds of early modern writers. Jasper Mayne in his poem 'To the Memory of the incomparable Paire of Authors, Beaumont and Fletcher' does not automatically assume the two both wrote dialogue, though he has it on his list of possibilities. He equally wonders: 'Whether one did contrive, the other write,/Or one fram'd the Plot, the other did indite'.[76] Later anecdotes, dating from the time when Jonson's name was on the wane, maintained that Ben Jonson 'availed himself of [Beaumont's] judgment at least in the correcting, if not even in the contriving all his plots', which, though doubtless untrue, does illustrate a continued tendency to identify a plotter and a plot as separate from a playwright and a play, as does the similar idea that 'after Beaumont's Death, Mr. James Shirly was consulted by Fletcher in the plotting several of his Plays'.[77] Given the necessity of a good plot to a good play it seems that on occasion someone who had only plotted the text was still thought of as an active co-author – and even sometimes as the 'main' or 'real' author, a fact that should be borne in mind when looking at collaborative plays. Given the nature of plotting and the esteem in which it was held, an 'author' named on a title-page might not be responsible for any of the sentences in the play at all. Modern critics, struggling to 'discover' which of a handful of collaborative authors wrote which passage of a play, are not always asking the right question.

AMATEUR PLOTTERS

Because the plot was such a separate document from a play, it was capable of circulating 'secretly' in ways that will never be obvious in the subsequent full text. For in a world full of skilled plotters and would-be playwrights, a private transaction to purchase a plot alone was always possible. In Middleton's *Puritaine*, Pyeboard, running away from debtors, takes refuge in a gentleman's house and claims that the householder is about to pay him five pounds for 'the Device of a Maske here, drawne in this paper'. Given the sum of money he names, he may be claiming that he has written an entire masque for the gentleman; nevertheless, the play strongly suggests that he is asking extravagant money for the plot of the piece only, for the puns between the 'wholsomly plotted' house and the paper plot seem to underline the comedy of the scene, as do puns on the nebulous word 'device' which often also meant 'plot'. 'I told them there was a Device for a Maske drawne int,' says Pyeboard, presenting his document to the Gentleman; 'May it please your good Worship then, but to uphold my Device.' The Gentleman, picking up on the audacious trick being played on the debt collectors, remarks that it is 'an excellent device', takes the paper and says he was never better pleased.[78] Plots were undoubtedly purchased in this fashion in, often, an underhand manner. An admirer of the playwright Thomas Randolph, who does not approve of acquiring a plot other than by writing it yourself, condemns both the 'sneaking tribe' who buy play-plots, and the 'panders' who sell them: 'The sneaking Tribe . . . That Pandars fee for Plots, and then belie/The paper with --- *An excellent Comedie,/Acted . . . With great applause*'.[79] How the 'sneaking Tribe' are belying the paper is by claiming that the excellent play is theirs when its plot is written by another. Again, contriving a plot is rated as a highly 'authorial' action.

Only occasionally was the entire issue reversed – and then the separation between plot and play emerged as more prevalent than ever. This was when an aristocrat or member of the royal family came up with a device to which a playing company had a dutiful text written and performed. Examples include some court masques, even though they consist largely *of* plot. *Britain's Burse*, a masque written up by Jonson, was seemingly made to order to a plot of Sir Robert Cecil's design ('The deseigne is to have three persones only actors according to yor lo[rdshi]ps conceit') – a plot to which, moreover, Cecil's secretary Wilson appears to have had access in advance of production, for he relates it in full in a letter.[80] *The Masque of the Inner Temple and Gray's Inn*, meanwhile, was first published as being 'By Francis Beamont, Gent.', but a cancel was then almost immediately issued to eliminate his name from the title-page. That seems to stem from a hesitancy about who 'authored' the play for, as Chamberlain wrote, Sir Francis Bacon was the 'cheife contriver' (presumably the plotter though perhaps the inventor) of the show.[81] Finally, one entire play was plotted by a royal hand though written by a regular playwright. *The Gamester* was, records Herbert, Master of the Revels, 'made by Sherley, out of a plot of the king's'; it was 'well likte' especially by the King who 'sayd it was the best play he had seen for seven years'.[82]

Plots, then, did not only have an independent existence on their own separate sheets of paper; they could be separately sold, separately distributed, separately 'stolen', or separately given as gifts, and they could, and regularly did, also have a separate authorship from the rest of the text. In fact, when plotter and writer *were* one, that was a special circumstance worthy of recording. Ford relates how he has not 'layne in wait/For any stolne Invention, from whose height/He might commend his owne'; while Nabbes justifies his own play *Covent Garden* with ''tis no borrow'd Straine,/From the invention of anothers braine./Nor did he steale the Fancie'.[83] Clavell, a thief in real life, boasts of *The So[l]ddered Citizen* that 'the Plott, & language, all/Hee his owne proper Coyne, may call,/H[']as robbd noe Authors'; finally Digges praises Shakespeare because 'all that he doth write,/Is pure his owne, plot, language exquisite'.[84]

CONCLUSION

Though most plots are now lost, some few have been shown still to survive, and more yet may be discovered, particularly as they can take a number of forms. While the *Philander* plot occupies the first six sides of a small booklet made up of sheets folded into a quire of twelve leaves, *Paradise Lost* is on one side only. Plots written for purchase or as tasters of a play to come might be mildly different from the plots for writing a play; with the longer plots raising the possibility that, on occasion, when companies write of receiving 'papers', 'sheets' or even 'books' towards a play ('book', as Ioppolo indicates, meant a complete text, irrespective of whether the format resembled one or more stitched quires or a printed book), they are referring to plots rather than playscripts.[85]

For, once written, plots often multiplied, being given to co-authors when there were any, and to the company at least when there were not. Even a playhouse that had not paid for a plot in the first instance usually ended up acquiring one, either handed over as an 'abstract' (what might these days be called the 'leave-behind'[86]) to advertise what the full play would be like, or handed over with the full play as an account of the contents. At the playhouse it could, further, aid in the analysis of cast numbers, indicate where revision or cutting should take place, and help in the construction of other (backstage- or Argument) plots. For whatever reason, the plot seems often to have been not simply acquired but retained by the playhouse as a unique document, where it doubled as 'protection' for the loss of any passages of the play.

Plotting was, as has been indicated, a separate skill from play-writing, because plots themselves were different documents from plays. Jonson has emerged as a writer with two skills, a plotting talent and a writing talent – at only one of which was he speedy. This continued separability of plot from dialogue, even in an author who wrote both, encouraged an audience to keep the firm sense that the two could be separately analysed, and that a play could simultaneously be good in the one and bad in the other.

Critics who try to pick out the voices of two or more co-authors without a sense of the varied ways collaboration could work should bear in mind the importance, respect, authority – and authoriality – accorded to plots in the early modern period. All too often scholars confine their questions about collaborating to who wrote which scene or act (a form of co-writing that the plot brought about), but do not ask who wrote plot and who wrote dialogue (another form of co-writing that the plot brought about). Scholars looking to stylometrics or other forms of analysis to separate the voice of one co-author from another need to realise that a major co-writer, someone even prepared to think himself the main or sole 'author' of the play, may not be the writer of any of its words.

Similarly, though modern critics assume a linear sense of play-construction, the plot often allows non-linear writing that may explain certain muddled time-schemes and confused naming-habits. For play-wrights had a relationship to a play that was not dissimilar, according to Parkes, to the relationship between a tailor, his cloth, and his final piece of completed clothing:

The Poet first casts his plot, then divides his Sceane: so the Taylor first his stuffe, then his fashion, then divides it into severall skirts and quarters, in the end knits it all together in an equall proportion, so makes his garment. So likewise the Poet.[87]

Plays here are described as though they are, like a garment, made from units discrete and 'finished' in themselves; the result of writing from plots in this way allowed authors to complete the 'best' bit first, or follow through one particular strand or plotline before turning to another, or write the tragic section before the comic (or vice versa): the full sense of the play in its entirety sometimes belonged only to the plotter, who may or may not have been the playwright, while the play's units of construction may have been what shaped the dialogue-writers' lines.

For all these reasons the 'shadow' of the plot and the things that it has brought about is present in all plays, visible when structure is markedly crisp but the execution of the story is flabby, or when one section of a play is more polished than another. On other occasions an extract from the plot has made it into the playscript, not just when an entire passage has been written out, but perhaps when, far more usually, a 'person-list' (or 'table' or 'character-list' or 'dramatis personae') is supplied for the play that is to follow.[88] That this moment of paratext frequently has its origin in the person-list of the plot would explain why it is so often oddly 'out of date' against the play it introduces, giving one name to a character who actually has another name in the text, or a generic title to a character who is named in the playbook – errors revealing that the person-list has not necessarily been written *from* the play. The manuscript of Mountfort's *Launching of the Mary*, for instance, gives the Captain's name as FitzJoseph in the person-list, though in the play he is called Fitz-John; while in Shakespeare's Folio the list for *Measure for Measure* provides only 'Clowne' for the character who, in the play, is 'Pompey', omits Justice and Varrius, calls Lucio a 'Fantastique', and gives the Duke a name, Vincentio, that is never used in the text itself.[89] 'Person-lists', like various prologues, epilogues and songs, may have been amongst the set of documents that related to, and sometimes accompanied, a manuscript play; for playhouses sometimes had them or acquired them even after an author's death, as their use by Knight and the scribe of *Senilis Amor* and *Faithful Friends* indicates.[90] At least those occasions where 'person-lists' and the characters in the plays differ may preserve leftovers from the play at the plot stage of its writing.

Other passages that may have made it straight out of plots into plays are those sections where action is summarised – for instance, dumb-shows – which are 'uninflected' by dialogue. They can simply be lifted straight from plots, and probably often were. But in other less obvious ways the plot may be manifested even in fully written playbooks. Some writers, it has been suggested, seem to have written with slavish observance of the plot-scenario, while others may have preserved odd moments of plot in stage-directions, such as '*Enter two serjants to arrest the Scholar George Pyeboord*' in Middleton's *Puritan*.[91] Shakespeare provides several potential examples. In *All's Well* 'Parolles and Lafew stay behind, commenting of this wedding' (TLN 1089–90), which seems to tell the writer what to dramatise rather than telling the actors what to do.[92] *Timon of Athens*, often said to be a play that is not in its final form, is full of such occasions: '*Enter Lord Timon, addressing himselfe curteously to every Sutor*' (TLN 118–19); '*Enter Lord Timon, the States, the Athenian Lords, Ventigius which Timon redeem'd from prison. Then comes dropping after all Apemantus discontentedly like himselfe*' (TLN 338–41); '*Flamineus waiting to speake with a Lord from his Master, enters a servant to him*' (TLN 916–17). So what Richard Hosley denominated '"fictional" stage-directions', defined by Dessen and Thomson as directions that 'usually refer not to theatrical structure or equipment but rather to dramatic fiction', may have their source not so much in a dramatist carried away by the power of his narrative as in a dramatist working so closely to a plot that it has 'bled through' into his stage-directions.[93] Were this so, then some of the features of Shakespeare's and others' plays traditionally thought to be markers that the text was prepared for a 'literary' readership – long or overly 'telling' stage-directions – may be the reverse: signs that they are in a primitive stage of development particularly close to the plot. This too should give pause for critics using stylometrics to analyse plays: if some stage-directions might be lifted from plots, then they need not be by the author of the passages surrounding them.

On occasion, more full-scale devotion to plots may manifest itself. Sometimes traces of plot-reuse, perhaps even plot-theft, can be found in extant plays, when scenic structure (rather than story or words) closely resembles scenic structure in another text. Examples include Shakespeare's *King John* and the anonymous *Troublesome Reign of King John*, where, famously, 'In all that can be put under the heading of vocabulary or versification or atmosphere the plays are worlds apart; in their construction and unity of impression they are as close together as two very different pieces can be.'[94] Even the oddity of the one or two similar stage-directions in these two different texts may relate to the fact that phrases from a shared plot have been lifted into each play.[95]

On the other hand, plots or plot elements could also have been wrested from these or other plays, for, unlike other 'lost' playhouse documents, plots can be 'back-created' from full playscripts. So desirable was a good plot, so likely to lead to a good play, that plots not stolen before a performance might be stolen during one. Explaining how his *Queen Elizabeth* had been taken by audience members using 'stenography' or shorthand, Heywood complains that:

> the cradle age,
> Did throng the Seates, the Boxes, and the Stage
> So much; that some by Stenography drew
> The plot: put it in print: (scarce one word trew:).[96]

If he is right, then the creation of plots out of performed plays might supply one explanation for how memorial texts came about. Often long stage-directions are features of plays thought to be inadequate reports of performance ('suspect' or 'bad') texts. This may be because they contain large fragments of 'plot', having, as Heywood opined, been 'reconstructed' from plot summaries created by spectators in the playhouse. Even if this is not the case, the idea that a play's plot might specifically be targeted by thieves speaks for itself. Plots were the backbone of a good play; they preceded plays, but were also visible within them, setting up the notion that a play in its final performance form could still be stripped down to the root document that made it up. In this construction, where the words of the dialogue merely flesh out what the play is, language emerges as equal to or less important than structure: a gloss, sometimes, to a carefully crafted plot.

CHAPTER 2

Playbills and title-pages

INTRODUCTION

On any single day a Londoner of the early modern period would be confronted with a widely different selection of plays to see: he or she could never simply know what was in performance the way we can now. That is because there was no fixed repertory. Tiny London of the early modern period could not sustain a long run of the same play as it would be unable to produce the audience for it. Hence the extraordinary fuss made when Middleton's politically provocative *Game at Chesse* was actually performed for an unbeatable nine days in a row. As Henslowe's 'diary' implies, it was normal to perform a different play every day, repeating it for as long as it brought in an audience, dropping it when it lost its appeal. Even a new play might not be performed above once, as chapter 4 illustrates. How, then, would a Londoner keen to go to the playhouse learn what plays were on offer at each theatre on a particular day?

There were actually a number of ways to obtain information about what was being staged. One was to attend a theatre and find out, or even determine, the play for the next day. At the end of each performance an announcement would be made asking the audience to sanction a particular choice of play for the following afternoon; Antimo Galli writes from London on 22 August 1613 telling how this task had fallen to his servant, who went to the Curtain and 'at the end of the performance . . . invited the public to the play for the next day, and named one. But the people, who wanted a different one, began to call out . . . because they wanted one that they called "Friars".'[1] Generally, as will be shown, information about the next day's play was already in the public domain, and the question was a courtesy. But even if it were not, attending a playhouse would only give information about one particular theatre, and then only for the afternoon immediately following. So another option for the interested Londoner was to wait for the actors to parade through the city 'crying the play', which is to say broadcasting the title of the play to be performed accompanied by drums and trumpets, a habit that they may have reserved for country performances after about 1600.[2] What, though, if you had missed the actors, or, at any rate, missed one of the companies? You can always, of course, hope that a friend knows what is on, as Pontus does, whose tedious daily greeting is 'How doe you Sir? Come, what's the Play?'[3] But how do his friends know what to reply? The answer is the same for all literate people: through reading the advertisements hanging on the posts of London.

Why do we not study these playbills? The answer is simple: because they no longer exist. Posters were and are ephemeral, and no playbills are known to have survived to the present day; the earliest bill for a professional indoor production found so far dates from 1687.[4] Modern critics have inevitably shied clear of the entire subject, and nothing significant has been written about players' advertisements since W. J. Lawrence's thought-provoking but incomplete account of 1913, unhelpfully called 'the Origin of the Theatre Programme', and a short and useful article on billposting in the time of Elizabeth written by Holzknecht in 1923.[5] Yet if a batch of playbills were to turn up, many questions at the very intersection of theatre history and bibliography would be answered. We would see what forms of advertisement playbills resembled and where they fitted in generically with other publications in early modern London. In particular, we would know whether playbills and playbooks resembled one another in advertisement, which would affect our approach to the presentation of 'the text' as performance and as literature. We would learn practical details too: whether playbills for different theatres were made to appear alike or unalike (helping us see whether competing playhouses marketed themselves as separate or similar). We would know which aspects of the play the bill deemed worthy of advertisement and which it rejected: were companies or theatres cited, were parts of the play's story selected as important, were playwrights named?

Despite the absence of playbills, single examples of other kinds of poster have survived. There is a manuscript bear-baiting bill from the 1590s, a 'plot' for the hoax entertainment *England's Joy* of 1602 (see chapter 3), a printed rope-dancing advertisement from *c.* 1630, a challenge from 1629, and a Bartholomew Fair puppet playbill said to date from around 1655. In addition to this meagre handful there are the odd foreign bills to swell the numbers: a manuscript Spanish playbill of 1619, a printed French playbill of 1629, and a printed German playbill of *c.* 1628.[6] Using these in conjunction with a range of contemporary references, most of which have not been culled before, it is possible to reconstruct in detail the look and content of playbills of the period, in ways that are also revealing about play title-pages. This chapter sets out to do that, concentrating on five major playbill questions. (1) How were bills produced? (2) In what numbers? (3) Where were they found? (4) What were they hung with? (5) What specific information did they provide, and what does that say about printed plays? The answers will give a visual and bibliographical context for the bill; determine how visible playbills were in a London that had rejected the theatre itself; suggest whether bills 'belonged to' specific places and how those places themselves can be 'read'; give bills a *milieu* and show the first context – preceding the theatrical one – in which plays were to be found; explore how theatres and playwrights were dealt with in the bill; reflect on questions of bill-authorship; and hint at the story behind playbooks with lavish titles.

PRODUCING PLAYBILLS

A joke told in *Mery Tales* (1567) illustrates how, from early on in the life of the theatre in London, playbills were an important and very visible preliminary part of the entertainment. The story concerns a swindler called Qualitees who managed to entice a large audience into Northumberland House in London by advertising the performance of an 'antycke plaie'. Having collected a half-penny to a penny from each of the incomers at the gate, Qualitees absconds, leaving a full theatre behind him wondering when the performance will begin, until they realise they have been duped. The play never existed beyond its description on the bill. This is an early example of an advertising scandal: the spectators came to the performance specifically because they had been, as the anonymous writer of the story puts it, 'moved' by the bills Qualitees had set up 'upon postes aboute London'.[7] But advertising scandals can only work in a world informed by advertisements. Often the claim is made that planned and careful advertising did not come into being until the Restoration: 'it can scarcely be said', writes Marjory Plant, 'that there was much deliberate advertising before the middle of the seventeenth century'; Paul J. Voss opens a section of his extremely good article 'Books for Sale' with a scoffing 'scholars have not uncovered roadside billboards or a sixteenth-century Yellow Pages'.[8] But Qualitees' joke, which tellingly dates from the establishment of the first permanent professional theatre in London, is just one of many stories about widespread intrusive advertisements of the early modern period. Londoners by the time of this early jest are already trained to find their would-be pleasures staked out on posts all over the city.[9] Versions of Qualitees' trick are, predictably, a refrain throughout this chapter.

Most playhouses were situated across the river outside London. As a consequence, they relied on heavy advertising throughout the city for their audience: a potential viewer could hardly be expected to commute over the Thames to the theatre without knowing in advance what was on. Accounts frequently record the importance of advertisements, showing that posters were put up as soon as actors were ready to perform: 'Upon a little Abatement of the Plague, even in the first Week of Lent, the Players set up their Bills, and began to play in the Black-Fryars and other Houses.'[10]

It is hardly surprising to discover from the Stationers' Register that playbills were printed from at least 1587 onwards, for printing makes easier the production of bills in substantial numbers. And, as only one printer at a time was allowed to produce playbills, the name of the bill-printer at any time during the early modern period can be definitely stated. Between 1587 and 1642 (when the theatres closed) four printers/printing families held that desirable post: John Charlewood, James Roberts, William and Isaac Jaggard, and Thomas and Richard Cotes. These printers were of vital importance to each and every playhouse, all of which relied on advertising for revenue; the playhouses needed the printers more than the printers (who were all, also, publishers) needed the playhouses.

The post of printer for 'all manner of Bill*es* for players' was first accorded to John Charlewood on 30 October 1587 (on the same day, Thomas Purfoot was given similarly exclusive rights to the printing of bills for fencing prizes).[11] Charlewood also printed plays – hardly surprisingly, given that his job greatly increased the likelihood of a playscript coming his way. He even prefixed his text to Lyly's *Endimion* (1591) with the following note to the reader: 'Since the Plaies in Paules were dissolved, there are certaine Commedies come to my handes by chaunce . . . This is the first . . . if this may passe with thy good lyking, I will then goe forwarde to publish the rest.'[12] In 1593 Charlewood died; immediately William Jaggard, later to print so many Shakespeare plays, started making strenuous attempts to acquire 'the printinge of the billes for players as John Charlwood had'.[13] He was granted the position provided Charle-wood's wife, Alice, consented, died, or married a non-stationer. In fact she did none of those: she married James Roberts, also a printer; and in so doing gave him not just herself but also her dead husband's types, ornaments, and rights over 'The billes for plaiirs' (that last passed

officially to Roberts on 31 May 1594).[14] Jaggard, therefore, did not become
playbill-printer, a fact that led to tension between him and Roberts some
years later. Meanwhile, Roberts, as well as printing playbills, also printed
Shakespeare quartos including *The Merchant of Venice* (1598, 1600), *Titus
Andronicus* (1600), *Hamlet* (1604–5), and other well-known plays, including *Arden of Feversham* (1599) and *A Larum for London* (1600).

As Roberts' health declined, he started sharing printing tasks and
premises with Jaggard. In about 1606 Jaggard succeeded entirely to
Roberts' business, and at some point between then and 1615 inherited
his types, his ornaments, and the rights to print playbills he had so long
sued for. While also printing the bills he, and later his son Isaac, printed
various plays including *The Miseries of Inforst Mariage* (1607), *West-ward
Hoe* (1607), *A Woman Killde with Kindnesse* (1607), *Edward the Second*
(1612), *A Woman is a Weather-cocke* (1612). They also published a number
of Shakespeare plays, some 'legitimately', others (the 'Pavier' Quartos)
with false dates, made to look as though they had been printed by Roberts
(easy given that Jaggard had inherited Roberts' types). So in 1619 the
Jaggards produced *Sir John Old-castle* ('1600'); *A Midsummer Night's
Dream*; *The Merchant of Venice*; *Sir John Falstaff* (*Merry Wives*); *King Lear*
('1608'); *A Yorkshire Tragedie* by 'W Shakespeare'; *The First Part of the
Contention* (*1 Henry VI*); *The True Tragedy of Richard Duke of York*
(*2 Henry VI*) and *Pericles*. In 1623 they printed the First Folio of Shakespeare.

In 1620, however, crisis threatened the playbill-printing monopoly. The
King took it upon himself to grant Roger Wood and Thomas Symcocke
rights 'for the sole printing of paper and parchment on the one side' no
matter what the content, extending to, and including

All Indentures for Apprentices, . . . All Bondes and Recognizances for Vicualers,
Alehouse = keepers and others, and all Licences whatsoever. All Billes for Playes,
pastimes, showes, Challenges, prizes, or sportes whatsoever. All Licences and
passports, All Epitaphes, or other Coppies, either in prose or in verse . . . And all
other Mandates, briefes, coppies, publications, Chartes and Tabels whatsoever.[15]

The list, which continues in this vein, usefully indicates just how filled
London would have been with printed documents: the city was reliant
on massive amounts of paper advertising and paper discourse of all kinds.
It is instructive, though, that out of the general furore what worried
John Chamberlain most, as he wrote to Dudley Carleton, was 'how far
yt may concerne ballades and play-bills': he seems to feel that threatening
these papers might detrimentally affect life in London altogether.[16] In fact,
the problem was soon resolved. Thirty-one named stationers including

William Jaggard took their complaints to parliament and, pointedly, posted their petition in a bill; they argued that if they were to lose the right to print paper on one side 'it will not onely be a great hinderance unto them who have beene brought up in this Art . . . But also to all other his Majesties loving subjects that have occasion to use any of the things mentioned in the said Letters patents'.[17] The new patent was reversed by parliament and, as a consequence, bill-printing returned to the Jaggard family.

On the death of Isaac Jaggard the printing house was acquired by the brothers Thomas and Richard Cotes (4 June 1627); in that month or the next the two men were granted rights to print 'Bills for players', an entitlement they kept to the interregnum when the playhouses closed.[18] During that time they also had other Jaggard rights transferred to them; Thomas Cotes reprinted Shakespeare's Folio in 1632; he was also responsible for printing many other plays including *The Faithful Shepheardesse* (1629), *The Two Noble Kinsmen* (1634), *Pericles* (1635), *The Ball* (1639); he ceased printing in 1641. Richard, meanwhile, separately printed *Titus Andronicus, The First Part of the Contention* (*2 Henry VI*), *The True Tragedy of Richard Duke of York* (*3 Henry VI*), *Henry V, 1 Sir John Oldcastle, A Yorkshire Tragedy* (all 1630); he continued to print plays until 1651. The interregnum, of course, put a stop to legitimate playbill-printing.

One other piece of historical information about the bill-printers should be brought in here. It concerns a time in 1602 when Roberts was playbill-printer but Jaggard made a private and illicit arrangement to print bills for one company, Worcester's Men. Roberts discovered what Jaggard was doing and mounted a complaint, but finally, on 13 December 1602, agreed that

the said William Jagger shall have the onely and sole imprinting of the said billes for the said company of players nowe apperteyninge or hereafter to appertyne to the said Erle of Worcester . . . The said William yielding and payinge therefore to the said James [Roberts] and his said wife or one of them monethely foure shillings . . . And the said William Jagger to meddle with the printing of no other billes for players, but these only.[19]

What this arrangement does is to confirm that generally *all* bills for *all* companies were printed by one printer. This means that all bills must have looked similar up to a point, no matter which company, play or theatre they were printed for. Between 1602 and the time when the full reversion of all bills came his way, Jaggard is the only printer who acquired a specific right for the bills of one company (and he was probably only able to do so because of his friendship with Roberts). Jaggard's arrangement with Worcester's Men provides practical information too. If the printer is prepared to pay four shillings a month to produce bills for a single company, then he anticipates making a profit of well over four shillings per month from bill-printing: the printer of the playbills must have made about six shillings or more, per month, per company, for his simple job.[20] As there were usually six acting companies at London at any one time, the playbill-printer would have made a clear profit of at least £3 a year. The right to print players' bills, then, was always profitable: it would provide a small, steady, regular income that had the additional advantage of not being linked to sales.

So from at least 1587 onwards four printing houses had a particularly strong connection with the playhouse. But they also had an unusually close connection to one another: as a result of the marriages and take-overs listed above, presses, types and ornaments were also all inherited through the four printing establishments. In playbill terms this almost certainly means that all bills would have looked similar not just to each other but also over time. Advertising explains why: it is useful for a playbill to be instantly recognisable as such irrespective of theatre, play or period. That said, there must have been a way for one playhouse to differentiate itself from another on the bill – perhaps each advertisement included the 'sign' (generally hung on the flag) of the theatre in question, a rose for the Rose, a swan for the Swan, Hercules carrying the globe for the Globe.[21] But the implication is that each 'detached' theatrical company advertised in a similar way: each sent out similar visual signals. Though the separate playhouses were at odds with one another, printing-house contingencies may have brought them together; representatives of each playhouse, moreover, must have met as they converged in the one place they mutually relied on for publicity: the bill-printer's establishment.

Various left-overs suggest how intimate were connections between the four printing houses and playhouses in general. A surviving Jaggard bill for a shooting contest is among the papers belonging to the actor Edward Alleyn; perhaps Alleyn acquired it as a consequence of knowing Jaggard. The fact that so many plays, in particular so many Shakespeare plays, fell into the hands of these four printer/publishers is particularly interesting. The printers would have known from bills which plays were doing well and which were doing badly: would they have sued for specific texts? Or is it that the players, who met these printers on a regular basis, had a habit of handing over playbooks for publication, some legitimately, some illegitimately? One other possibility is an advertising one. As has been seen, playhouses relied on publicity and marketing – might they have selectively sold (or given) plays to the printers of the playbills as other, alternative, means of advertising? Critics who stress the tension that there was between playhouse and printing house underestimate the extent to which they shared interests. Performances were 'published' or publicised by having their title and other details hung over London in printed texts; every play ever put on was first met in printed form whether or not a passer-by could read it. Plays readied for performance already belonged to the world of the printing house – indeed every play was a little bit printed.

So it is important to try to reconstruct what the printed advertisements might have looked like. Were they, for instance, ever flanked with a picture as some playbook title-pages were? Vague accounts indicate that entertainment bills may sometimes have been illustrated. A manuscript poem relates how a widow's death is indicated by 'A scutcheon, Drawn by Painter's skill, . . . plaiced up, like a Play-house Bill', though whether the 'drawing' or 'placing' makes the shield bill-like is open to question.[22] As other one-day advertisements might be topped with woodcuts, however, the occasional illustration of playbills seems likely: when fencers 'set up bills in publique places' advertising challenges, they would sometimes 'to content and provoke the multitude . . . [expose] to publique view those tragicall sports in painted tables'.[23]

Bill content and layout can be more definitely established as cognate advertisements from the period do survive. One of the surviving bills, for a rope-dancing entertainment, is, for instance, printed by the last of the four playbill printers, the Cotes brothers, so it indicates not just the content but the look of professional bills.[24] It has decorated edges, ornamental first letters, and black-letter text given elegance and variety by bursts of English double pica: it is visually striking and carefully organised on the page. The most telling aspect of the bill, however, is its small gap or blank for performance venue, as that explains how bills for popular plays could be bulk-produced for use on different occasions.

[ms: At 9 a Clok]

At the [*ms: Rose in in winestreet*]

this present day shall bee
showne rare dancing on the
Ropes, Acted by his Majesties
servants, wherein an Irish Boy of eight
yeares old doth vault on the high rope,

the like was never seene: And one Mayd
of fifteene yeares of age, and another
Girle of foure yeares of age, doe dance on
the lowe Rope; And the said Girle of foure
yeares of age doth turne on the Stage,
and put in fourescore threds into the eye
of an Needle. And other rare Activityes
of body, as vaulting and tumbling on
the Stage, and Egges dancing upon a
Staffe, with other rare varietyes of
Dancing, the like hath not beene seene in
the realme of England. And the merry
conceites of Jacke Pudding.
If God permit.
Vivat Rex.

This advertisement specifies an entertainment to be performed 'today', but neither identifies the day nor the place of performance. It is a 'stock bill' for travelling rope-dancers, and at every new town the name of the site for the enactment can be slotted into the gap provided.[25] As the one surviving printed French playbill also has a gap for the place of entertainment to be inserted, a pattern for the bills of stock plays can be conjectured: such bills could be printed in large numbers with empty space left for unfixed information.[26] As for the text of the rope-dancing bill, it appears to have been written by someone who knows the dancers' routine very well, and who is keen to use what can be called 'advertising language' to promote the performance ('the like was never seene . . . the like hath not beene seene in the realme of England'). The writer is likely to have been a performer or manager for the rope-dancers, and unlikely to have been one of the printers, who had no financial stake in the success of the production. The point seems obvious, and yet issues of rope-bill authorship redound on playbill authorship.

For new plays, plays that had been altered, and plays that were irregularly performed, fresh bills would have had to be written. Hints at what a 'specific' playbill might have been like can be gathered from the German bill provided for English players on a visit. In translation it reads:

Know all men, that a new company of Comedians have arrived here, who have never been seen before in this country, with a right merry Clown, who will act every day fine Comedies, Tragedies, Pastorals, and Histories, intermixed with lovely and merry Interludes, and to-day Wednesday the 21 April they will present a right merry Comedy called Love's Sweetness turned into

Deaths Bitterness. After the Comedy will be presented a fine Ballet and laughable Droll. The Lovers of such plays must make their appearance at the Fencing-house in the afternoon at 2 o'clock, where the play will begin at the appointed hour precisely.[27]

Here is a 'one-day' bill, also printed, showing how print simply was the normal medium in which bills were produced even in small quantities. Narratively the bill introduces the players, and provides date, genre of play, title of play, two added lures (clown and droll), time and place.[28] It is a full bill but, unlike the rope-dancing one, gives no details of the 'story' the audience is to see: it is less descriptive and more generalised in its promotional matter, as befits a performance where it is unclear which aspect of the play will win favour. It could have been written by anyone.

Another surviving printed bill, also for one day, is a 'Challenge', printed in 1629. It is telling because the single day's entertainment it promotes is to be provided in a theatre, the Red Bull: printed bills even for single theatrical occasions were entirely normal. This one, as above, contains date and place, provides enough professional bravado to act as a lure, and is written in the voice and first person of its protagonists, not its printers. Its close of 'Vivat Rex' will be covered below:

> ## A Challenge,
> From *Richard Gravener*, Gentleman and
> Souldier . . .
> against *Thomas Blunne*, Shoo-maker . . .
> this to be perfor-
> med at the Red Bull in St. Johnstreet, on Tuesday next, being the
> 20 of October, 1629, if God permit.
>
> J udicious Gentlemen and others. I being
> a Souldier, from me expect not comple=
> mentall phrases, for in my opinion that
> more stuffes the eare, then please the eye;
> . . . I in plaine termes challenge
> the said Thomas Blunne at these eight severall wea=
> pons hereunder named . . . desiring from the
> spectators stage-roome, and from him his uttermost
> of his mallice . . .
>
> ### The names of the Weapons.
>
> {Long Picke,   }   {Halfe Picke,   }
> {Blacke Sword,   }   {Sword and Buckler }
> {Single Rapier,   }   {Rapier and Dagger, }
> {Sword and Dagger. }   {Holberd.   }

And I the said Thomas Blunne will be ready at the
time and place appointed, to answer this Challen=
ger,   If God permit.   Vivat Rex.

A final kind of 'one-day' bill, different again, is the single surviving
bear-baiting bill, which can be found in Dulwich College. It is a different
kind of 'challenge' levelled by some men of Essex who have brought their
bear to London for a one-day match:

aie
Tomorrowe beinge Thursd
in
shalbe seen at the Beargard
on the banckside a greate ~ ~ ~
Mach plaid by the gamstirs
of Essex who hath chalenged
all comers what soever to
plaie v dogges at the single
beare for v pounds and also
to wearie a bull dead at the
stake and for your better ~ ~
t
content shall have plasant spor
with the horse and ape and
whiping of the blind beare
Vivat Rex [29]

'Tomorrowe being Thursdaie' makes the advertisement relevant only for
'today', Wednesday (Thursday itself will require a new bill): theatrical
events, this bill indicates, could be advertised anew on successive days. As
for the writing of the bill, the adjectives 'great' match, 'pleasant' sport and
the assured 'for your better content' show once again measured use of
'advertising language'; the suggestion is that this bill was authored either
by one of the Essex men or, if they had one, by their manager. Narratively
the place of entertainment is stated, and what will happen there; the whole
ends, as the rope-dancing bill and challenge had ended, with 'Vivat Rex'.
In fact 'vivat rex' which, as will become clear later, also concluded
playbills, is a feature that ties English bills for all varieties of entertainment
with one another as one species of event. Why 'vivat rex'? Lawrence
suggests that the tag is an attempt to give players' advertisements the
legitimacy of a proclamation, but actually the reverse is the case, for
proclamations did not end with 'vivat rex' but with a number of other
formulae, typically 'God Save the King/Queen'.[30] 'Vivat rex' was probably

actually used to prove that the entertainment in question has royal sanction; the implication would be that the entertainment was in no way seditious. A final point: this bill is a 'challenge' and challenges, as will be shown, were advertised at the challenger's expense. Hence, perhaps, the reason why the bill is in manuscript: maybe the Essex men, coming to London to make money, did not want to run to the expense of print. On the other hand, maybe this surviving paper is the rough for the printer (the day, the place and some of the words are mis-spaced on the page and have to be concluded on the line above).

NUMBER AND FREQUENCY OF PLAYBILLS

Firstly it is evident from the bear-baiting bill that entertainments could be advertised not just on the day of performance itself but in advance. 'Great Captaine Sharke' indicates that the same was true of plays when he already knows that 'the day that next ensues' will not provide him with playhouse pleasures as 'There's no Play to be playd, but he hath seene.'[31] It is intriguing to investigate how much advance notice was given before performance. Often 'days' rather than 'a day' are mentioned. Writing to Henslowe between 5 and 8 August 1613, Daborne suggests advertising the performance of his new play for Wednesday (rather than, as a lost letter must have suggested, Monday), and performing a stock play on Monday instead: 'let ye boy giv order this night to the stage keeper to set up bills agst munday [9 August] for Eastward hoe & one wedsday the New play', giving something under a week's warning for a new performance, and a few days' warning for a ready-prepared one.[32] This matches Vennar's advertising of his hoax play *England's Joy*, for which he gave a week's warning.[33] Northbrooke attests to the fact that players tend 'to set up their billes upon postes certain dayes before, to admonish the people to make resort unto their Theatres'.[34] As it would seem, planning began a week or so before performance for an original entertainment, with slightly less warning for a stock production, which could be mounted at any time by the company.

If bills for every production in every theatre for each day of the coming week were all to be found in London at the same time, then playbills must have been a significant feature of the city. Many references suggest as much when they depict bills 'sett upp', as a writer as early as 1587 put it, 'in sondry places of the cittie'.[35] Playbills are a staple of the jest-book world up to the interregnum: their look and, more specifically, their number are two of the visually striking aspects of early modern London in general. In his *Wit and Mirth* (1629), John Taylor, the Waterpoet, tells how Nathan Field, star actor of the early modern period (he died in 1619 or 1620), was riding up Fleet Street at a great pace, when a gentleman called to him and asked what play was on that day. Field, angry at having been stopped for such a frivolous reason, answered 'that he might see what Play was to be playd upon every Poste. I cry you mercy (said the Gentleman) I tooke you for a poste, you road so fast.'[36] Anyone literate could be assumed, suggests the gag, to have read the playbills.[37] Weak as Taylor's merry tale is, it was popular and, over ten years later in 1640, still had a home in jest-books. By this time, though, some of its specific details had given way. Field, the hero of Taylor's story, is now long dead; in the revised joke the interlocutor simply names the particular theatre he wants to know about to a passing horseman: 'One seeing a fellow ride along London street extreamly fast, called after him [and] asked him what play was that day to be playd at the red Bull?' The answer is the same: 'he was an asse to aske him such a question, being it was a question every post could tell him'.[38] What is evident is that, though the details of the story have to be altered over time to make contemporary sense, the fact that play information is so visible that any pedestrian – or horseman – capable of reading can be expected to have assimilated not just title but also playhouse and day of performance is as valid in the 1640s as in the 1610s (and, as Qualitees' tale above attests, the 1560s). Playbills, then, were more than just a common sight over London. They were so present and so numerous that it was hard for the casual observer not to read them.

One of the main objections to playbills, indeed, was that they were visible enough and widespread enough to get themselves noticed and read, whether or not that had been the passer-by's intention. In other words, they 'worked' as advertisements. One epigram depicts an 'inconstant' man who leaves his house in order to go to a sermon. But

> by the way a Bill he doth espie,
> Which showes there's acted some new *Comedie*;
> Then thither he is full and wholly bent,
> There's nothing that shall hinder his intent.[39]

As the poem spells it out, the bill for the 'new Comedy' gets at the man and literally 'diverts' him, though it is situated far away from any actual playhouse. Hence another objection to playbills: like plays, they sidetrack the readers/watchers away from moral pursuits. The bill has functioned like a play, but it is more insidious, for while you can choose not to see a play, you can hardly avoid reading a playbill. The theatre has, through the medium of bills, corrupted the pedestrians in the streets of London.

The only early modern accounts that give any actual sense of numbers of bills printed refer to very specific events – to 'challenges'. In 1599 Toby and George Silver challenged the Italian fencers Vincentio Saviolo and Jeronimo to a contest on the Bel Savage stage, famous for its high and dangerous scaffold. 'We caused . . . five or sixe score Bills of challenge to be printed,' relates George.[40] The nervous Italians failed to attend the enforced contest, leaving the audience disappointed but the Silvers victorious. Similarly John Taylor, the Waterpoet, reports an unhappy arrangement he made with William Fennor. Both men agreed to perform in a trial of wit together on the Hope stage, 7 October 1614: another event that took place in a theatre for which records remain, for Taylor 'caused 1000 bills to be Printed' publicising the fact.[41] What then happened is a variation of the Qualitees story. On the day of performance, the audience, who had paid a particularly large sum for this one-off production, crowded into the playhouse. Everyone waited expectantly, but Fennor, 'this Companion for an Asse', had run away, leaving Taylor 'for a Foole, amongst thousands of criticall Censurers'.[42] The audience then tore Taylor, metaphorically, and the theatre, literally, apart.[43] Particularly bitter over the bills, Taylor refers repeatedly to the printing and distributing he undertook for the challenge: both had happened at his own expense, and it rankled. He had, he points out, needed

> . . . to print a thousand Bils and more,
> And daily on the Posts to clap up store,
> For thousand Readers as they passe the way,
> To see my name engag'd to play a Play
> 'Gainst William Fennor . . .[44]

As Taylor implies, in wit battles the challenger took it upon himself to have bills made up, printed and distributed round London (by contrast, it was the prompter or 'stage-keeper' who posted bills for professional players, as Daborne's letter, already quoted, reveals). Even if exaggerated, Taylor's story provides an upper limit for the number of bills that might be produced for a special, single occasion, parallel perhaps to the first performance for a new play, which caused similar interest and, like Taylor's wit challenge, inflated its entrance charges.[45] It is worth balancing Taylor's 'thousand' with the Silvers' more modest hundred-odd and with records for bills of other kinds printed for distribution around London, bearing in mind that large numbers are a function of print: what takes time is setting type; that done, many bills might as well be printed, paper providing. The city printer, who, as the name suggests, published for

London only, was asked on 16 March 1692–3 to deliver 'Two Thousand Copies of the late orders of this Court against the Prophanation of the Lords day and other Impieties' in addition to a number he had already had printed.[46] Those bills, too, have not survived: just because bills are ephemeral does not mean that there were few of them.

Taylor's story also reveals that, as was illustrated by the bear-baiting bill and the challenge, it was normal to post bills 'daily' for the same event. Thus the daily bill-posting routine of the players is a reliably predictable fact about living in London: when Breton, in 1626, writes a record of the events that happen hour by hour in an average London morning, he remarks that at nine o'clock in the morning 'The Players Billes are almost all set up.'[47] Daily rebilling implies the daily removal of bills from their posts. But what were 'posts' and why were bills taken from them? Why was daily billing necessary?

'POSTING' BILLS

In order to 'view what is plaid to day', as references repeatedly maintain, you simply had to 'Goe read each post'; over time bills are, with increasing insistence, described as being on 'each post' and 'every post' of London.[48] But though the modern noun 'poster' has derived from the verb 'to post', which seems to have its roots in the habit of sticking bills *on* posts, no one has given posts much attention. What posts were gives context to the parts of London where bills were appropriate.

A variety of struts impaled the city. There were regular tethering posts for horses outside taverns, alehouses, playhouses, shopping streets, inns of court and the Old and (after 1609) New Exchanges. Those same public places often also provided 'pissing posts' to encourage urinating in designated areas; their use as advertising spaces (though negative ones) is evident from Taylor's threat to name the subscribers who will not pay him for his journey from Scotland 'On every pissing post'.[49] Roads for horses, which were filthy with ordure, were separated from pedestrian areas by wooden posts, and it is probably these that General Columbo in Shirley's *Cardinal* talks of when he mentions 'a Post that's carv'd/I'th' common street, . . . holding out [its] forehead/To every scurrill wit to pin disgrace/And libells on't'; these posts were often highly attractive and visible, as was necessary in badly lit streets, making them ideal hosts for advertisements: 'Look upon a painted poast . . . whose colour is laid in oyle, how the rain beats upon it in stormy weather . . . and leaves it rather more beautiful then before.'[50] There were also whipping posts, and posts on which depended signs illustrating trades or establishments. The general use of posts as advertising spaces everywhere in London undoubtedly took in some or all of these.

Those aside, there were particular sections of the city where entertainment bills could reliably be found: the obvious 'publick places' where Phylander will set his challenge 'by the Play-Bills'.[51] One site was the place of performance itself: Flecknoe's commonwealth woes are stimulated by passing the Blackfriars playhouse and finding it shut up with 'never a *Play-bil* on the Gate'.[52] Other areas were those famous for providing general information: the internal columns of St Paul's Cathedral where social and business needs were advertised, outside St Paul's where the booksellers were, and major shopping buildings and streets, particularly the Old and New Exchanges and Cheapside.[53] Some of the areas noted for bill-posting are suggested by a text referring to 'all famous places of the City' for setting up information: 'Queen-Hithe, Newgate, the Stocks, Pillory, Pissing Conduit, and . . . Bridewell'; the fencers Toby and George Silver posted their bills 'from Southwarke to the Tower, and from thence through London unto Westminster'.[54] To those can be added 'London Stone', which is where the bill in Nashe's *Returne of the Renowned Cavaliero Pasquill* is set up; and the Inns of Court: Pepys, on Christmas Day 1666, goes 'to Temple . . . thinking to have seen a play . . . but there missing of any Bills, concluded there was none'.[55]

The main place for hanging playbills, however, was the heart of the city: the houses themselves. For the most popular places for attaching playbills, as references indicate, were the walls, doors and doorposts of London homes. 'Post' seems, in its general sense, to have referred to a doorpost rather than anything else. A 1581 precept of the Lord Mayor of London set out particularly to stop, ward by ward, people from fixing 'anye papers or breifes upon anye postes, houses, or other places . . . for the shewe . . . of anye playes'.[56] Interestingly this also indicates that each ward – each separate administrative section of London – was in danger of playbilling: bills were widespread indeed. The Mayor was singularly unsuccessful, and years later Heath referred to the normality of seeing Blackfriars' playbills throughout London on 'each wall/And corner poast'.[57] Doorposts not only had the advantage of being spread throughout the city (and towns and cities in general), they were also protected from the weather: playbills on doorposts were unlikely to be destroyed by the elements before doing their jobs. The result was, though, that plays, through the medium of bills, were present street by street in the city that had so pointedly rejected them: 'Players,' as Rankins put it, 'by sticking of their bils in London, defile the streetes with their infectious filthiness.'[58] Though playhouses themselves were banished to Southwark or the outskirts of the city, their names and plays were written across its breadth and in its most localised and domestic space; London at its most intimate was filled with printed mementos of what it hated. Hence the fact that plays were a constant source of tension; hence, too, the fact that playbills, their contents and their presentation of their contents, were a matter of considerable concern to the people of London.

Starting from the outside of houses, bills moved easily to the inside. Keen theatregoers would have bills collected from around town to be pondered over at home; one of the jobs given to society servants was to acquire playbills for each different playhouse, present them to the lady of the house, and then attend her on her trip to the theatre. A 'panarete' ('an all-virtuous woman' – here used ironically) thinks 'time's lost/Till a Playbill be sever'd from the Post/. . . [to] informe [her] what's to play'.[59] As for the type of woman only interested in pleasure, 'the *Playbills* [must be] brought her by her *Pentioner*, her eye views and reviewes, and out of her feminine judgement culls out one from among them which shee will see'.[60] But as well as taking bills from posts, servants might, too, have gathered bills from sites where they were provided for distribution. At any rate a 'free-floating' playbill, perhaps something like a modern-day 'flyer', features in Jonson's *Divell is an Asse*, for when Ingine sells Fizdottrell an overpriced cloak to wear to the theatre, he induces him to see the play with 'O here's the bill, s[i]r. I, had forgot to gi't you'; a stage-direction confirms '*He gives him the* Play-*bill*'.[61] Similarly, when the Italian fighters tried to ignore the challenge of the Silvers 'many gentlemen of good accompt, carried manie of the bills of challenge unto them, telling them that now the Silvers were at the place appointed, with all their weapons, looking for them'.[62] So the bill gets easily into the domicile; Brathwait repeatedly returns to the image of the lady of the house picking over playbills with a servant hovering at her shoulder, the two unhealthily close. Of a gentleman usher Brathwait writes:

It is . . . his Element to be versed in the perusal of *Play-bils*, which he presents to his Lady with great *devotion*; and recommends some especiall one to her view, graced by his owne judicious approbation. His choice she admits: to the Play-house she resorts.[63]

Here bill, again like playhouse, is disturbingly levelling: it is available to all irrespective of class, and brings about the over-familiar relationship of servant to mistress in anticipation of the theatrical event to come; the bill has corrupted its readers well away from the theatre itself. Likely as it was that a bill would end up in a house or a pocket, the theatre thus became present not just in every street of London but also inside many of its homes and about its people.

Entertainment bills were not, however, the only kinds of advertisements to be found on the posts of London. Cotgrave makes this clear in his dictionary of 1611 when he describes a 'plaquard' as 'a Bill, siquis, or Libell stucke upon a post, &c.'.[64] Each variety of posted advertisement, as Cotgrave maintains, was differentiated by name; each also, as will be shown, differed in look and verbal formula. The siquis, also sometimes called a 'bill', nearly always began either with 'si quis' or with a version of its English equivalent, 'if anyone': hence its name. It was an advertisement that might be for a broad range of goods or skills. It could offer amateur legal help ('thou hadst bills/Set up on every post, to give thee notice,/ Where any difference was, and who were parties'), or health-care ('On many a post I see *Quacke-salvers* Bills/Like *Fencers* Challenges, to shew their skills'); lessons were advertised 'on every post, for Arithmetique and writing Schooles'; while amateur stenographic teachers were accused of having 'with their Bills . . . be-sprinkled the posts and walls of this Citie'.[65] A siquis features in Barten Holyday's *Technogamia* (1618), 1:7, and provides the tenor of advertisements of the time, revealing how they differed from entertainment bills:

If there be any Gentleman, that, for the accomplishing of his natural indowments, intertaynes a desire of learning the languages; especially, the nimble French, majestike Spanish, courtly Italian, masculine Dutch, happily-compounding Greeke, mysticall Hebrew, and physicall Arabicke; or that is otherwise transported with the admirable knowledge of forraine policies, complementall behaviour, naturall dispositions, or whatsoever else belongs to any people or country under heaven; he shall, to his abundant satisfaction, be made happy in his expectation and successe, if he please to repaire to the signe of the Globe.[66]

The siquis advertisement begins diffidently, conditionally, 'if'. Playbills, against siquises, would have looked bold and forthright: they inform rather than wonder. Moreover, a playbill would have been visually different from a siquis, being nearly always printed and, as has been discussed, ending, as all entertainment bills ended, 'vivat rex'.

Libels, too were posted and in the same space as siquises and playbills. Adam Fox in *Oral and Literate Culture in England 1500–1700* presents many accounts about libels being attached to doorposts in small towns, and reproduces a fascinating picture of libellers in Holland sticking texts to the door and corner wall of a man's house.[67] He also explains how the space in which libels were hung was understood to be different from the 'legal' space, providing a story that tells of how, in 1611, a libel was pasted to one arm of the market cross in Highworth, Wiltshire. The libellers then decided that their paper 'was not sett up publiquely enough' on the lateral they had chosen; they 'enquired of some there present uppon which poste of the crosse [the king's] proclamacons used to be sett and there caused . . . Hewes to past[e] the said libell on that parte of the same crosse'.[68] This shows that space on the cross itself had a meaning, a hierarchy – the libellers made a point of intruding onto the very place that had been identified as 'royal' and 'legal'. Space itself was 'read'; playbills not only hung with siquises and libels, but in doing so were situated in apposition to the formal, sanctioned, authorised space of the printed legal bill.

So legal space was separate from advertising space. Other spaces too were specifically designated for particular bills: ship-owners, in advance of making a journey, had to print the full particulars 'and affix the same unto some Post or other open space in Lombarde street, there to remayne by the space of vii daies'.[69] More generally, there were proclamations that were not hung on posts but placed in 'tables', seemingly a protective frame hung in a public place, usually in markets and churches, 'where they might best be seen and redd of all men'; Strafford writes of 'an Order of the Lords of the Council hung up in a Table near *Paul's* and the *Black-Fryars*, to command all that Resort to the Play-House there to send away their Coaches', while the proclamation to establish standard weights and measures, issued first on 16 December 1587, should be read aloud in every market town before 12 of January and then

> hanged up and fastened in a table in the marketplace by an officer, where it may hang dry, to continue and be seen and read by any that will; and further that it . . . be also hanged up and fastened and preserved in every church in a table to be seen and read at all times.[70]

In London, which was divided into a variety of administrative districts, 'official' places for legal billing would, according to subject, have been parish churches (where, for instance, plague bills were posted), ward courts (for legal matters) and city guilds (for anything concerning that guild); presumably official city notices were also affixed to the city gates. Different kinds of text were expected to occupy their appropriate spheres; information was ranked, and the site reveals the nature of the content.

But if libels, advertisements and playbills belong to the same space, and if that space is differentiated from legal space, then the status of the three is equated and each becomes a comment on the other. The post is an intellectual context that defines the *milieu* in which bills were presented to the people of London. Which gives the world of the play quite a different appearance. A play, first met in its advertisement form, will not have been viewed in the context of theatre or author primarily, but in the context of the aggressive non-moral world of the pushy post with its promoting and invading strategies, and its equality of dubious subjects.

There is one further kind of advertisement, however, that has not yet been covered. It is the kind that most closely resembles the playbill: the printed advertisement for a printed book.

Advertisements for books consisted of title-pages separately printed and hung up on the posts of the city.[71] Title-page advertisements were widely visible and widely despised. Ben Jonson does not want the bookseller responsible for his poems to put 'my title-leafe on posts, or walls, . . . For termers, or some clerk-like serving-man,/Who scarce can spell th'hard names': he, snobbishly, does not want his book in the realm of the serving-men (and the assumptions about the class of person who reads posts is illuminating).[72] Jonson illustrates that post-advertising was thought of as 'low', whilst also implying that his works, popular poetry and plays, are likely to be so advertised. Parrot makes just the same request as Jonson, right down to the reasoning; he askes that his book of epigrams 'on Posts, by th'eares . . . stand not fixt,/For every dull Mechanicke to beholde'.[73] That said, there were authors who made specific vindictive door-post use of their title-page advertisements. When Doctors Fludd and Foster had an intellectual quarrel, they posted their accusatory title-pages on places bound to be irritating to the other: Foster went to Fludd's house at night and there set up 'two of the frontispieces or Titles of his booke . . . one on each post of my doore'.[74] Here, then, is testimony that if books of poetry often were 'posted', so too were medical books.[75] To this can be added pamphlets whose titles 'sue to be sold' on posts; and religious works – 'When I first saw the Title-page of M. Cary's Book posted up, professing a clear demonstration, that the Resurrection of the Witnesses, spoken of in Revel. 11 was accomplisht; I was glad . . .'[76] A. H. in *A Continued Inquisition against Paper-Persecutors* indicates that in general 'Titles each Terme on the Posts are rear'd,/In . . . abundance'.[77]

As McKerrow argues, the information on any book title-page of the period, informing the reader where the book in question is to be bought, is hardly of relevance to the owner of a book: it is only of relevance to someone who might wish to purchase that book; relevant, that is to say, as an advertisement.[78] Nashe writes of casual readers who 'torment Title Pages on everie poast, never reading farther of anie Booke, than Imprinted by *Simeon* such a signe', showing, actually, how likely such essential information was to register.[79] And having written of the importance of space and look, it is fascinating to find an actual reference to printed title-pages rubbing their edges up against printed playbills. Robert Heath, the author of a book of poems called *Clarastella*, instructs his bookseller not to 'prostitute' his work: do not, he begs,

> show it barefac'd on the open stall
> To tempt the buyer: nor poast it on each wall
> And corner poast close underneath the Play
> That must be acted at Black-Friers that day.[80]

Though he is writing much later, it is worth recording here that in 1673 Marvell jokes about an illiterate servant who completely confuses bill and title-page because they look the same and are found in the same place: 'I have seen a Lacquey that could not read, having been sent to take down the Play for the afternoon, has by mistake brought away the Title of a new book of Theology.'[81] Title-page and playbill, book and play, so often treated as being at opposite ends of the spectrum, even as being at odds, here are visually similar and perform the same function. As the book of T.B.'s play *Rebellion of Naples* notes, conflating booktitle and playbill, '*though* Naples *be the Scene, yet he plasters his bills upon the walls and gates of* London'.[82] Both, after all, are products of the printing house. Both hang on posts all over London. Both consistently work their way into the domestic space, title-pages continuing to 'advertise' even as they are part of a printed book. Both are advertisements – indeed, both often promote the same work, one in performance form, one in written form. Moreover, it was as printed playbill and printed title-page that most people met a theatrical production: for more people would read the bills than see the play *or* read the book. For many, the bills were the nearest they would get to play or book, and the grounds on which they would build all their theories about what was going on inside the theatre or inside the text. The specific information bills and title-pages provided, and the language in which they did so, had to be carefully chosen.

CONTENTS OF BILLS AND TITLE-PAGES

As suggested above, bills could be brief or complex: probably brief if for a new entertainment; complex if for a stock play. Always the title was a given, 'for Playes' records Peacham, if a covetous person 'read but their titles upon a post, he hath enough'.[83] In this way titles of popular plays became known and could themselves be used for political reasons. In a sinister parody-playbill, objectors to Charles I set up 'a Paper . . . near the Gates of *Whitehall,* importing that on the Morrow next there was to be Acted in the House of Peers a famous Tragie-Comedie, called, [*A King and no King*]'.[84] A minimal bill might feature little more than the title, raising, too, the possibility that some plays were advertised concurrently in two forms – a brief flyer, and a fuller poster. As the newssheet *Perfect Occurrences* relates, 'Tickets [small handbills] were thrown into Gentlemens Coaches, thus. At the Bull this day you may have Wit without Money, meaning a Play.'[85]

Fashion determined whether playbills named the theatre in which the actors would perform, or the title of the acting companies themselves. At first there was a habit for naming playing companies: in 1587 'the players billes are sett upp in sondry places of the cittie, some in the name of her Majesties menne, some the Earle of Leic', some the E. of Oxford, the Lo. Admyralles, and dyvers others'.[86] Later records seem to favour theatres over companies. Quotations already given about playbills of the 1620s onwards name the Red Bull (above, and in the 1640 'post' joke); and Blackfriars (see Heath's 'corner poast' reference). Hesitant as these references are, Alan B. Farmer and Zachary Lesser's 'Vile Arts' shows that a fashion for naming companies on book title-pages is bolstered by one for naming theatres between the 1580s and 1600s. Are playbill and title-page doing similar things?[87]

The naming of the genre of play to be performed went in and out of fashion. At one stage it seems to have been usual for playbills to tell the audience what type of play was on offer – tragedy, comedy, history. Wither, for instance, refers to being tempted by a bill advertising 'some new Comedy'.[88] But, as Tragedy complains in *A Warning for Faire Women,* 'history' and 'comedy' were starting to overtake tragedy in popularity in the 1590s, and it was becoming better simply not to address what form a play was going to take. 'You', says Tragedy accusingly to History and Comedy, in the induction to his play, 'have kept the theatre . . ./painted in play-bils upon every poast,/That I am scorned of the multitude' (performed 1596–1600).[89] The title-page for that same play, which dates from 1599, roughly the same time as its performance, does not name genre.[90] The prologue to Shirley's *The Cardinal,* performed in 1641, is as cagey as the bill seems to have been about what variety of play the audience is going to see.

> Think what you please; we call it [*The Cardinal*] but a Play:
> Whether the comic Muse, or Ladies love,
> Romance, or direfull Tragedy it prove,
> The Bill determines not.[91]

Its title-page for the play in book form, on the other hand, reads *The Cardinal, A Tragedie*; but the prologue dates, presumably, from performance, while the book of the play dates from 1653. For what it is worth, genre went through fashions on title-pages too; in 1641, when Shirley's play was performed, genre tended not to feature on title-pages either.[92]

Playbills also promoted novelty – as has been suggested, new plays had a particular *cachet* and cost more to see. The Prologue to *Arviragus and Philicia* provides 'a new Play' as 'promis'd . . . by our bill'; the sons of the rich, says Peacham, have as their study to 'stare at every post to see where the newest play is that afternoone'.[93] Newly revised plays and plays with new additions were also popular: an altered text might encourage a theatregoer to return to a play that he or she was already familiar with. This too worked its way into the advertising, as is evident from Campion who refers casually to 'the Players Bill that is stiled, *Newly revived, with Additions*'.[94] But exactly the same qualities can be found extolled on title-pages for printed plays. The book of Dekker's *If It be not Good, The Divel is in it* (1612) is 'A New Play, As it hath Bin lately Acted, with great applause . . .', while the 1619 title-page of *Dr Faustus* is 'With new Additions'.[95]

It is usually said that the playwright was never named in a playbill. This is because of Dryden's astonishment when, in 1668/9, he saw Congreve's name in the bill for *The Double Dealer*. He called it 'a new manner of proceeding, at least in England', and his judgement has seldom been questioned on the subject since.[96] But the earliest surviving French playbill of 1629 names its author, Scudéry; what in reality happened in England? In Marston[?]'s *Histriomastix* (1610), the actor Belch relates of the playwright Post-hast that 'it is as dangerous to read his name at a playe-dore, as a printed bil on a plague dore': playwrights, suggests the reference, might be named; here Belch, perceiving that Post-haste's name will demote the play, is arguing specifically for suppressing the writer's identity.[97] Advertising considerations seem in fact to have determined whether or not to name the playwright. Habington's prologue to *The Queen of Aragon* (Blackfriars', 1640) describes how the play's plot is not so outrageous 'That we might have given out in our Playbill/This day's the Prince writ by Nick Machivill'.[98] Again, the suggestion is that the author *could* be named, but would not necessarily be. The name of an unknown author might, after all, do a play no good service: Glapthorne writes of the audience who martyr a play 'yet have t'excite that flame,/Only distrust in the new Authors name'; such incidents (suggesting that in this case the name of the author had been advertised in some way) forced a careful attention to the use only of known authors' names. Moody writes a poem to Philip Massinger referring to 'The thronged audience' that came to the theatre 'Invited by your fame'; presumably in this instance the playbills positively touted authorship.[99] What does this recall? A habit of selective naming is, of course, exactly what is found in title-pages. If an author's name will sell a book, it starts to feature: 'Shakespeare', not named on any title-page before 1598, is, by 1605, featuring even on plays he had not written like *The London Prodigall*, and from then on Shakespeare appears regularly on a variety of plays by and not by the writer.[100] Perhaps, much like title-pages to books, the fashion for naming authors, which grew on title-pages after the 1590s, grew, too, on playbills.[101]

A look at the few full bills whose content survives confirms the similarity between bills and title-pages. So a 'short bill' for strolling players is recorded as part of a legal case. It was hand-written (Francis Wambus, one of the actors in the Lady Elizabeth's provincial company, confessed to its being in his 'hand writinge'), and read:

Here w^th^in this place at one of the clocke shalbe acted an excelent new Comedy called the Spanishe Contract By the Princesse servants vivat Rex.[102]

Compare this to a 'short title-page' like, for instance, that to Marmion Shackerley's 1632

HOLLANDS LEAGUER. AN EXCELLENT COMEDY AS IT HATH BIN LATELY and often Acted with great applause, by the high and mighty Prince CHARLES his Servants; at the private house in Salisbury Court.

Here shared advertising language is visible even on short bills and title-pages. Both the bill and the title-page name the play, both say which men, which 'servants', will perform or have performed the text, both name a place where performance will happen/happened. Both, significantly, use the same promotional 'excellent'; the word came to be so over-used at the time that one satirist described a second-rate play as 'a collusive flourish onely fronted with the name of excellent'.[103]

As for 'full bills', the narrative content of one is suggested by a Fizgeffrey epigram that depicts a couple discussing the details of a play they have drawn from the bill. 'Pre'thee whats ye Play?' asks one. The other replies:

> . . . A new Invented Toy of *Purle*
> That jeoparded his Necke, to steale a Girle
> Of 12: And (lying fast impounded for't)
> Hath hither sent his Beard, to Act his part.
> Against all those in open Malice bent,
> That would not freely to the Theft consent.
> Faines all to's wish, and in the Epilogue,
> Goes out applauded for a famous ------ [104]

This kind of 'long bill' is confirmed by the one surviving Bartholomew Fair bill, dating, it has been said, from the 1650s. It is for a puppet-show made from drolls and reads:

> John Harris's BOOTH,
> in Bartholomew-Fair *between the* Hospital-
> gate *and* Duck-lane-end, *next the Rope-dancers,*
> *is to be seen,*
> THe Court of King *Henry the Second*; And the Death
> of Fair *Rosamond*: With the merry Humours of
> *Punchinello,* and the *Lancashire*-Witches. As also the fa-
> mous History of *Bungy* and Frier *Bacon*. With the merry
> Conceits of their Man *Miles*. And the brazen speak-
> ing Head; wherein is represented the manner how
> this kingdom was to have been walled in with *Brass*.
> *Acted by Figures as large as Children two years old.*[105]

Here, even though so many different drolls are described, details of the most compelling aspect of *Friar Bungay and Friar Bacon* are specifically provided: 'wherein is represented the manner how this kingdom was to have been walled with Brass'. Compare this to, for instance, the longer but no less simplistic summary of Shakespeare's *Richard III* from its 1597 title-page:

The TRAGEDY OF King Richard the third. Containing, His treacherous Plots against his brother Clarence: the pittiefull murther of his innocent nephews: his tyrannicall usurpation: with the whole course of his detested life, and most deserved death.

Title-page and bill seem not only to have looked alike, but also to have read alike. Both can be brief, both can be narrative. When narrative they use the same advertising vocabulary – 'excellent', 'famous', 'merry'; both draw the reader in with short summaries of the most sensational scenes. What can be concluded from this? One is that books and plays, marketed using the same lurid language, were almost certainly intended for the same people. Another is that surviving play title-pages might just preserve the content of some of the lost playbills.

When printers had to produce title-pages for plays that had been advertised once already (probably to the same people), would they really have written their advertisements anew? Why do so, when the old advertisement, the playbill, was partly responsible for the success of the play in question? Though printers were renowned for making up titles to the books they published, play-printers would not have *needed* to do so: all the material they required to promote a play would as likely as not have been already available to them.[106] At least in the case of Shakespeare's plays – in general, but specifically when issued by the four playbill printers – it must be worth reconsidering the heritage of some of the more extravagant title-pages for plays. For, to enter the world of conjecture for a moment, why should the playbill/title-page for, say, *The Merchant of Venice*, not actually be composed as a playbill by the performing company? And if by the company, then why not by its resident wordsmith/ businessman/playwright? Why should the promotion of the play not be as 'authentic' as the rest of its text? That is, why should the playbill/title-page not be by Shakespeare?

The most excellent
Historie of the *Merchant*
of Venice.
With the extreame crueltie of *Shylocke* the Jewe
towards the sayd Merchant, in cutting a just pound
of his flesh: and the obtayning of *Portia*
by the choyse of three
chests.
As it hath beene divers times acted by the Lord
Chamberlaine his Servants.
Written by William Shakespeare.

This text, published as a title-page in 1600, has been planned. It is centred and draws the eye to key features by careful use of line-ending: in the title 'merchant' and 'Venice' both end lines, and before them is the lure 'excellent'; in the narrative, key elements of the story end lines: 'Jewe' is balanced with 'pound', 'Portia' with 'chests', and the two are set in apposition to one another. That Shylock does not succeed in cutting the pound of flesh is hidden – indeed this vivid account might suggest the thrilling reverse to a reader who does not already know the play. Here is a version of the full story of *The Merchant of Venice* that identifies Antonio and Shylock's bond, together with Portia's choice of chests, as the main elements of the tale. The fact that this is a love-story does not feature, nor is there any question as to Shylock's nature. Of course, the play itself complicates this description: but did this kind of lure 'work' to bring the punters into the playhouse? As has been argued, in the early modern period, as now, there was a language for writing advertisements that was promotional, sensational and different from the language in which plays were written. Just because this summary of *Merchant* is grossly reductive does not mean that it was not effective, and does not mean that it was not authorial.

CONCLUSION

These days title-pages are typically treated as the most 'disposable' bits of a playbook. While every other aspect of a play is treated with the intense concern for textual accuracy that typifies modern editorial practice, early modern title-pages, such as the one above, are an embarrassment. Offering a trivial summary of the play so introduced, this particular page, for instance, is squirrelled away without commentary, even by the most meticulous editors; it is usually to be found separated from the play proper in some corner of a modern text, either flanking the textual notes or in the introduction.[107] Title-pages, that is to say, are not considered to be part of the 'real' play. But this chapter has argued for the importance of title-pages both as particular varieties of advertising and as, perhaps, preservers of the lost playbills. Moreover, by linking the two it has indicated how performed plays and read books were linked, both notionally in the mind of the reader, and in fact; playhouse and printing house were not at odds but had, often, a mutual dependency.

From this has emerged, too, the fact that plays were heavily advertised all over London and that early modern streets were inscribed with a huge variety of texts, playbills being some of the most notable; title-pages being some of the others. Such references show an aspect of London frequently ignored: the city was textual, not in a new historical sense so much as in a literal one: it was covered in texts. Festooned with advertisements, plague bills and proclamations, London's pleasures, their consequences and their prevention were inscribed on almost every street, and playbills and play-book title-pages were a major way in which the playhouse intruded into the city.

CHAPTER 3

'Arguments' in playhouse and book

INTRODUCTION

There is one variety of front matter or 'paratext' for a printed play that seems entirely 'literary'. It is the Argument ('plot', 'device', 'subject', 'model') or play summary that is sometimes supplied in playbooks just before the dialogue begins. Critics seldom address it, because the very fact of an Argument is puzzling. Arguments give away a story's ending, and so remove dramatic suspense from the reading of a text, as these closing lines from plot summaries illustrate: 'Antonio marries Margaretta, . . . and . . . fals in love with Dionysia, . . . but the women come to tragicall ends, and Antonio for upbraiding Julianus with selling his King and Country to the Moore, is by Julianus slaine'; 'Whereupon, hir brother Cæsar . . . maketh warre upon *Antony*, and overcometh him, first at *Actium*, and then at *Pelusium*, to the utter ruine and destruction, both of *Antony* and *Cleopatra*.'[1]

The few scholars who consider Arguments at all see them in relation to the plays of Terence, Seneca and Plautus, which are regularly preceded by an *argumentum* (themselves copying the Greek plays of Euripides and Aristophanes that were fronted with a 'hypothesis'). Arguments before English plays are said to be self-conscious references to classical plays – and to classical plays in a particularly non-performative form, for classical *argumenta* and hypotheses had, themselves, been added to the texts some decades after performance as aids to readers.[2] Some press the point further, calling attention to the fact that other classical texts that were not plays at all had *argumenta* added to them, Virgil's *Aeneid* providing one example. Are Arguments supplied to untheatricalise plays entirely, aligning them not just with classical literature, but with classical literature's more serious form, the epic poem?

Jonson's use of Arguments is traced, as are so many of his textual affectations, to a mixture of classical pretension and antitheatricality that lets its author down: of his Argument before *Sejanus*, Lowenstein writes: 'It pre-empts, and thus partly disables the power of specifically theatrical suspense'; of the Argument to *The New Inne*, Kidnie adds a warning for any new reader of the play: 'There are some unexpected twists in the fifth act . . . readers unfamiliar with the plot . . . are advised not to read the argument and character list before reading the play.'[3] This wish to protect the reader from the Argument highlights the problem with the form: it seems positively to threaten enjoyment of the subsequent text. Classical scholars too confront this problem, but their explanations do not work for early modern texts. Thus Euripides' 'hypotheses' are said to be 'for readers who wished to be familiar with Euripidean plots without reading the plays themselves'; while Seneca's are explained as appendages 'meant to remind the reader of a content he or she is already supposed to know'.[4] But plot summaries to early modern plays often tell fresh stories (or fresh versions of old stories), and are supplied together with published texts, seemingly in the anticipation that they will be read, if at all, as part of the process of reading the play.

Granted, a selection of the writers who use Arguments attach them to closet dramas, often on classical themes, like Samuel Daniel's *Cleopatra* (1611), Mary Herbert, Countess of Pembroke's *Antonius* (1592), William Alexander, Earl of Stirling's *The Alexandraean Tragedie* (1637). It might be thought that such books do indeed use Arguments to show themselves as 'reading' texts as well as to highlight their 'classical' status. Nevertheless, Heywood's cold preface to *The Fair Maid of the West* complicates the issue, for his play, though published specifically for 'thy private reading', is vigorously anti-Argument: '*I hold it no necessity to trouble thee with the Argument of the story, the matter it selfe lying so plainly before thee in Acts and Scenes, without any deviations, or winding indents.*'[5] Arguments, implies Heywood, are not so much features of 'reading' plays as features of plays that are over-complicated. He is probably pointing a finger here directly at Jonson whose *New Inne* had been published with its Argument earlier that same year.

A further look at playbooks containing Arguments will reveal that, like Jonson, plenty of other writers published Arguments before theatrical texts – often texts that do not seem to be trying to be 'literary'. William Rowley's *All's Lost by Lust*, the Argument to which is quoted above, boasts on its title-page that it has been 'Divers times acted' and that it was lately played 'by her Majesties Servants, with great applause, at the Phoenix'; Chapman's *Pompey and Caesar* (1653), prefixed with an 'Argument' (A4b), was 'Acted at the Black-Fryers'; while Thomas Goffe's *Careles Shepherdess*

(1656), which has one of the few Arguments in verse (A1b), was 'acted before the King & Queen, and at *Salisbury-Court*, with great Applause'. Of course, these were texts published during the interregnum, and it could be argued that the addition of an Argument was a way of refashioning staged plays for the page. Nevertheless, in printed texts of masques, often written by consummate men of the theatre, an Argument is viewed as standard, though the event summarised by such texts was a visual and aural spectacular: George Chapman provides an 'aplicable argument' for *The Memorable Maske of the Two . . . Inns of Court* (1613?); William Davenant has an 'Argument' to *The Temple of Love* (1634 for 1635); Inigo Jones gives a 'Subject' to *Britannia Triumphans* (1637); *Maske of Flowers* begins with 'the Device of the Maske' (1614). It seems as though the kind of person who might opt to read a masque, a closet drama, or, sometimes, a public theatre play, might be expected to hope for, or be pleased to receive, an Argument for it along with its text.

This chapter will consider the purpose and use of the Argument; it will question and counter the idea that the Argument revealed writers of fiction 'engaged in construction, imagining and positioning their reader-ship', and will maintain instead that the Argument was a frank piece of theatre available to a particular tier of audience and reproduced in some playbooks.[6] To do this, it will consider specific occasions when the audience at a theatrical entertainment was supplied with a text, generally printed, that was analogous to the book's printed Argument. These sheets, also called Arguments (or 'plots', 'devices', 'subjects', 'models'), tie together, through the printed word, playbooks and performances, con-founding book history with theatre history – or, in Genette's terms, questioning what is part of the frame of the book, 'peritext', and what is part of the world outside the book, the 'epitext' – particularly when both are in print, both share a title and contents, and both precede the play proper.[7]

ARGUMENTS AS PROGRAMMES; ARGUMENTS AS PARATEXT

The grander the audience, the more it was paying or the more power it had, the more it seems to have wanted – or, at any rate, been given – things to read. For particularly important and *visual* productions, additional play-specific texts might be supplied for audience members. These documents, sometimes called 'plots', sometimes Arguments, were summaries of the entertainment, and they accompanied productions thought to need extra elucidation: court entertainments, academic entertainments, masques, puppet-shows, and, occasionally, public theatre performances.

Much has been written about the interplay between pageants and the written texts that describe them.[8] But nothing has been written about the Arguments, often printed, for masques and plays, and the way they mediated theatrical performance, as well as, of course, the way they linked plays to processions and other semi-theatrical occasions. This is because Arguments have not been specifically recognized or identified for what they are. Despite the fact that the rest of Europe has collected and discussed its Arguments – the Spanish their *relación*, the French their *ballets*, the Italians their *argomenti*, the Austrians their *perioche* – the English equivalent has been ignored.[9] The problem is partly to do with the name: historians of British theatre have been side-tracked by the title 'plot', confusing Arguments or 'plots' for audiences with backstage-plots for actors (see chapter 7) or plot-scenarios for playwrights (see chapter 1).[10] In fact, the audience's Argument was a separate text: unlike the 'plot-scenario' which it closely resembles, but which *precedes* the written play, the audience-plot is the narrative abstracted from a play *after* it has been written (though sometimes the 'scenario' may have fed into or become the Argument – see chapter 1). In having an existence after the play itself had been completed, the audience-plot somewhat resembles the 'back-stage-plot', a scene-by-scene list of entrances and props for actors, also written *from* the completed text, which again occasionally fed into that text (see chapter 7). The difference was that, while there was one back-stage-plot exclusively for theatre personnel, and one or two playhouse scenarios for the use of authors and companies, there might be several hundred 'plots' or Arguments for the audience, for these little texts tended to be printed.

Why? Partly to feed the literate audience's desire to have productions footnoted, edited and explained to them through the medium of the written word. And partly because the high cost of entrance to 'spectacular' shows (Arguments were often for masques or masque-like productions, and were invariably for first or court performances only) might in some way be offset by the present of a printed 'souvenir'. Meanwhile, from the performers' point of view, Arguments positively 'advertised' productions during performance and after it: they wooed the spectators' acceptance by forming a permanent link between them and the production, much as theatre programmes do today.

Characters in plays who receive Arguments illustrate how the texts were designed to be disseminated before production and read *during* it, 'making', as Jonson put it in one of his masques, 'the spectators understanders'.[11] So the Prince in Ford's King's Men's play *The Lover's Melancholy* is given what is called in the stage-direction a '*Paper-plot*' of *The Masque of Melancholy* by its author Corax. As Corax instructs the Prince, he is to 'Hold and observe the plot,' because ''tis there exprest/In kind, what shall be now exprest in action'.[12] Here the Prince is asked to read in advance the story of the masque; he can then retain the plot for further reference during performance as necessary. Whilst the action goes ahead, its written plot gives logic to what is happening: eschewing the actual words of the drama, the plot will provide narrative focus that might be said to complete, or to upstage, the masque, making the performance partly a reading one. Nor was the competition between playscript and its summary always subtle. When Mr Beveril in *No Wit/Help like a Woman* enters to introduce his masque, it is with a large 'Pastboord' – quite possibly designed to be visible to the real audience – which he presents to the Widow, explaining 'Here is an abstract, Madam, of what's shown.'[13] Similarly, for the masque in Shirley's play for Dublin performance by Ogilsby's Men, *The Constant Maid*, '1 Lady' gives 'papers' to both the King and Sir Giles; these she describes as 'the subject of the Masque', as ever distinguishing the plot from the action and the words: 'the subject' is something designedly extractable from the performance.[14] Fabritio in Middleton's King's Men play *Women Beware Women*, meanwhile, gives the Duke what he calls 'the model/Of what's presented'; it contains 'the Argument', which is then read out loud to the Duchess before the performance:

> *There is a Nymph that haunts the Woods and Springs,*
> *In love with two at once, and they with her;*
> *Equal it runs; but to decide these things,*
> *The cause to mighty Juno they refer,*
> *She being the Marriage-Goddess; the two Lovers*
> *They offer sighs, the Nymph a Sacrifice,*
> *All to please Juno, who by signs discovers,*
> *How the event shall be, so that strife dies:*
> *Then springs a second; for the man refus'd*
> *Grows discontent, and out of love abus'd,*
> *He raises Slander up, like a black Fiend,*
> *To disgrace th'other, which pays him i'th' end.*[15]

As this text, recited by the Duke, makes clear, the Argument tells the entire story of the production. There can now be no suspense in the masque itself, for the plot (both 'plot' and 'Argument' are used in the play for this document) has told all in advance: in a sense, it has upstaged the performance. Like the Argument to a playbook, then, this text dictates how moments in the play are to be understood; negative words like 'strife', 'discontent', 'abus'd' and 'disgrace' tell the Duke what to find, and how to react to it, in the performance itself. When the masque begins, the Duke interprets from the Argument so avidly that he resents diversions from it, and as the play he watches becomes more and more bizarre and murderous clings to it for solace: 'but soft! here's no such persons in the Argument,/As these three . . .'; 'This swerves a little from the Argument'; 'Why, sure, this plot's drawn false, here's no such thing.'[16] He believes the text he has been given has, or should have, an authority above that of the performance itself; the written narrative is supposed to trump as well as complete the actual production.

One group of plot summaries that survive from the early modern period are for occasions such as the ones described above: spectacular, often masque performances, on special or royal occasions. These include manuscript Arguments such as that for *Cupids Banishment. A Maske Presented To Her Majesty by Younge Gentlewomen of the Ladies Hall in Deptford at Greenwich the 4th of May 1617*; that for *Vertumnus*, 'as it was acted and plaide at oxeford before the Kings and Queenes Majesties, the Prince and Nobilitie'; and what seems to have been an Argument, now lost, for Jonson's *Pleasure Reconciled to Virtue*, which was sent round by friends to people who had missed the court occasion itself: a letter from Edward Sherburn to Carleton written on 10 January 1618 discusses 'the Maske wch wee had on Twelveth night' and goes on, 'yr L: will perceive the conceipt by perusing this little book'.[17]

These documents were also often printed, and at the playwright's expense, even though they were to be used for one occasion only. In such instances they may, as Heywood said of printed Arguments, indicate an insecurity on the part of the author: a fear that his deeper meaning cannot emerge merely through performance. For when employed for a production the Argument also jeopardizes the play it supposedly enhances; the audience risk missing some of the action by reading about it. Nevertheless, as the fashion for Arguments had its root in court performance, so, perversely, the grander the performance – which usually meant the more sumptuous it was on the eye and ear – the more likely it was to be preceded by the dissemination of a printed explanation. So a fragment headed 'The Ante-Masques' and including an Argument ('the Subject of the Masque') was published to be distributed on the single performance in which Aurelian Townshend's masque was performed inside Montagu's play *Shepheards Paradise*.[18] For at least one masque, *Neptunes Triumph*, Jonson even intended to stage a 'poet', probably played by himself, who was to enter the fiction specifically to distribute the Argument: '*The POET entring on the STAGE, to disperse the Argument, is call'd to by the Master-Cooke.*'[19] It is to be expected that Jonson would hand out booklets to accompany his masques, for such publications could subtly upstage Inigo Jones' fantastic designs or, rather, render them back into words.

As the above are references to Arguments for masques, it might be thought that only those entertainments were provided with additional printed texts. But Arguments are casually referred to as elements of other kinds of entertainment in ways that indicate a wider-spread, if occasional – and perhaps first-performance – use. So Lodowick in John Day's Red Bull play *The Knave in Graine, New Vampt* is responsible for bringing events to a conclusion and compares what he is about to 'perform' to a puppet-show. As with any 'motion', he explains, given the complexity that will ensue, 'you'le never understand without an interpreter, or a short plot, which I have drawn': the explication of a puppet-show might too be determined on paper.[20] Lodowick's account, as this suggests, will 'interpret' the action as it happens. More than that, as Lodowick, the 'author' of subsequent events, has composed the plot in advance of performance, so the Duke will see what occurs through the medium of a pre-determined explanation. In the scene that follows, the Duke receives this text, like his counterpart Duke in *Women Beware Women*, and watches the action whilst reading the prescribed interpretation of it: he is, for instance, in a position to correct the Doctor who describes himself as a 'fool' – 'more knave than foole, the plot's false drawne else'.[21] Again, the Argument is viewed as having more authority than the performance: a written text received in advance is shaping as well as sanctioning the enacted one.

There is also at least one depiction of the provision of an Argument for a straightforward play, here in court performance. Hieronymo in Kyd's *Spanish Tragedy* provides the King with two souvenirs before his performance of *Solyman and Perseda*, 'a Copie of the Play' and 'the Argument of that they show'.[22] Seemingly it is to this Argument that the King refers when he observes the entrance of Lorenzo and asks his brother to 'looke upon the plot,/And tel me . . . what part plaies he?', though it is also possible that his brother, who has been made book-keeper, is in a position to look at the backstage-plot.[23] Either way, though, it should be observed that the King asks for, and receives, 'footnotes' from a written text about the production while he is watching it. The King, that is to say, expects and hopes that his watching experience can be enhanced by text, as it is in the above examples. When Arguments were provided, they rendered the performance a conflation of staged action and written, textual, information, just as a modern opera programme does, which still often contains a summary of the story to be enacted.

As far as this book is concerned, however, the most important question is whether Arguments were ever distributed for plays in the public theatre. Are playbook Arguments potentially linked to a performance moment; and may they, on occasion, even simply have been lifted straight out of performance? At least one manuscript plot from an indoor private theatre, and one printed plot from an outdoor public theatre, survive, so the answer to both questions is potentially 'yes'. This also means that other plays for which there is no record of an Argument may, in principle, have had them (if the playwright or playhouse thought it worth the expense). Though not every production will have had an Argument, at least some did.

The manuscript private theatre plot at the Houghton Library is inscribed inside *A Register of all the noble men of England*, a document containing a selection of pieces on different subjects and in different hands. That makes the plot hard to date – it may be from any time between 1572 and 1590 – though its title explains who performed it and what they performed: 'Children of Paules pla[y]: *Publii Ovidii Nasonis Meleager*'. This plot is more than just neat; like the masque Arguments for royalty, it is elegantly inscribed, with names picked out in italics and the title carefully and elaborately presented in gothic hand. Comprising three sides of writing, it goes through the play act by act and scene by scene, interpreting what is happening theatrically to the watching/reading audience; its present-tense narrative, like the present-tense narrative of masque Arguments, highlights that it is to be read concurrently with watching.

Actus. I.
Melpomene the Tragicall muse, is presented wth a dumbe showe of the ffatall Sisters . . . who by consuming a bronde wth ffier, showe therby the fate and desteney of *Meleager* . . . The Lordes standing in doubte of the infortunate sequell, of so unhappie a beginning, are appoynted by *Melpomene* to sitt as *Chorus* over the stage to vewe the ende of everie accident, & explaine the some of everie Acte . . .[24]

At the same time, there is a question as to how many such elegant plots could have been written out and circulated. Each text like this would have taken time to prepare, and it is hard to imagine that such papers were distributed to many people.

The other surviving theatre Argument, for a public performance, and in print, was for wider dissemination, though still undoubtedly for one day only. It is *The Plot of the Play, called Englands Joy. To be Playd at the Swan this 6 of November. 1602*, and has not been considered very carefully having been, for some years, wrongly identified as a playbill.[25] In order to look more closely at what it is, and why it is not a playbill, the story of the preparing and mounting of the performance it accompanied, Vennar's *England's Joy,* must be told.

Richard Vennar widely advertised his intention to mount a one-day production of his play *England's Joy* at The Swan. But when the hour of performance arrived, he spoke only a few words of the prologue before running away from the theatre, taking the proceeds with him. This caused an outcry that was not mollified by Vennar's later and rather unlikely apology: he had never intended to dupe anyone, he claimed, he really had prepared a performance of an entire play, but he had been arrested by bailiffs just as the production was beginning.[26] The people who attended the Swan playhouse felt that they had been cheated out of what they had been promised in the playbills (and had paid twice the normal entrance fee to see): a performance played by members of the gentry in which women – gentlewomen no less – would play parts. Both Chamberlain in a letter and Manningham in his diary wrote about *England's Joy* in the month in which Vennar's fiasco took place. Chamberlain records 'a cousening prancke of one Vennar . . . that gave out bills of a famous play . . . to be acted only by certain gentlemen and gentlewomen of account'; Manningham confirms that 'Vennar . . . gulled many under couller of a play to be of gent. and reverens'; Vennar himself in his defence says, 'The report of Gentlemen and Gentlewomens actions . . . was not merely falcification, for I had divers Chorus to bee spoken by men of good birth.'[27] Twenty years later, the women who were to have performed stood out in popular memory: Slug, in Jonson's *Masque of Augurs* (1622), makes reference to 'three of those Gentlewomen, that should have acted in that famous matter of *Englands Joy*'.[28] But *The Plot of the Play, called Englands Joy* contains no reference either to the gentility or the sex of the players; moreover, it is printed by John Windet, though the single official printer of playbills at the time was James Roberts. The surviving plot is, evidently, not the playbill.

Instead the plot is, like other plots or Arguments, a printed document explaining the performance. Its description, which includes 'Musicke' and 'strange fireworkes', suggests that the 'play' was to have those spectacular qualities for which plots are so often provided; the entertainment may even have been (in intention) a public theatre masque. The document obviously relates to Arguments given out at court and perhaps indicates

that Vennar is equating his gentlemen and women players to a courtly
or royal entertainment. It takes the reader scene-by-scene through the
action that will ensue – the story of the rise of Queen Elizabeth – lightly
interpreting it:

4 Fourthly is exprest under the person of a Tyrant, the envy of Spayne, who to
shew his cruelty causeth his Souldiers dragge in a beautifull Lady, whome they
mangle and wound, tearing her garments and Jewels from off her: And so leave
her bloudy, with her hayre about her shoulders, lying upon the ground. To her
come certaine Gentlemen, who seeing her piteous dispoylment, turne to the
Throne of England, from whence one descendeth, taketh up the Lady, wipeth
her eyes, bindeth up her woundes, giveth her treasure, and bringeth forth a band
of Souldiers, who attend her forth: This Lady presenteth Belgia.[29]

As a scene-description, this combines explanation (the man and the
woman are identified as Spain and Belgia) with prescription. The tyrant
is 'cruel', the woman 'beautifull', and the depiction of what seems a
stylised rape – a woman stripped, wounded and despoiled – serves to
titillate the reader of the page, supplying a relish that actual performance
might not, and did not, give. If there is also a literary trickiness in the
writing, the obsessive use of words suggestive of four in this, the fourth
scene ('bringeth *forth* a band of Souldiers, who attend her *forth*'), then it
should be remembered that this is the designing work of a trickster.
Perhaps Vennar enjoyed the idea that his money-making plot should have
a 'plot' to go with it; perhaps he used the plot for 'proof' that a play really
existed; and perhaps he merely had it created as a bluff to entertain the
audience while its author ran away. Nevertheless, this counterfeit plot had
to be enough like other such plots not to arouse immediate suspicion in
the observers.

With *England's Joy* the plot is, absolutely, the play, in that the play may
never have existed. So this sheet does more than mediate the performance
to the observer, though that is what it offers to do: it creates, and then
edits, the non-existent event. True, while in the compter in 1614, Vennar
gave the poet confusingly named William Fennor £2 to mount *England's
Joy*, proof that by then at any rate a playscript had come into being.[30] This
may, however, be a fascinating example of how what purports to be an
audience-plot in reality becomes a plot-scenario, in that Vennar (or
perhaps Fennor) then wrote a play *from* the plot.[31]

Here are two Arguments that raise exciting possibilities. Arguments, as
indicated, seem to have been usual at court, especially for masques; might
be provided for puppet-shows; and would, on rare occasions, accompany
private theatre plays and 'spectaculars' in the public theatre. Certain kinds

of classy performances, that is to say, exploited the textual, seemingly with the theatre's approval. And as, throughout the tale of Arguments, authors have been responsible for printing or producing the texts (and presumably writing their narrative), so it remains possible that other productions were, if the author felt like it and his pocket ran to it, enhanced with paper explanations: the writer could intervene to control one version of the event, a special or first performance, in the fashion he knew best: in writing.

Various poems comparing man's life to a performed stage-play (rather than a play for reading) assume that an Argument precedes performance in the theatre. These are texts with an academic flavour, and may be referring to university performances in particular. Nevertheless they further highlight the connection between Arguments and performances of *plays* (as well as masques). One comparison sees Sir Francis Drake's life as being like a play, demanding:

> BE Drakes heroique deedes the argument,
> His name the prologue of your tragedie,
> The acts and scenes, his acts all excellent,
> Himselfe chiefe actor of Spaines misery . . .[32]

Another, originating in a Latin epigram by John Owen, was published in translation under the title 'Man is a Stage-Player' in 1619:

> Mans Life's a Tragike Comedie,
> Hope is his Argument;
> The Prologue Faith; the Acts are Love,
> The Stage Earths Continent.[33]

And an interregnum source just may imply more general use of Arguments before plays in the public theatre. *The Lively Character of the Malignant Partie*, written in 1642, is designed to recall a theatre plot, presumably because of the consonance between play 'plot' and political 'plot'. It is a systematic denunciation of most groups of people politicking in the early 1640s, from Papists to Cavaliers, and it begins by naming 'the chiefe of them, who have been (and are still designed) maine Actors in the fearefull Tragedie of this lamentable Age' (A1b). It goes on, like audience-plots, to take the reader scene by scene through the dreadful play being performed in the country: 'In the first Sceane, ye may behold . . . Papists [who] have ever plotted the promoting of horrid warre'; 'In the next scean, enters upon the Stage, to be presented to your view, the Prelaticall Partie, who have acted a great part in this Tragicall Story of the malignant Partie' (A2a). For 'the sixt Scene ye may behold . . . the Hotspurres of the Times, who are call'd the Cavaliers' (A4a). With its sudden reference to an actual playscript, Shakespeare's *1 Henry IV*, the 'plot' may imply that theatre plays, perhaps even Shakespeare's plays, could have been performed with plots of their own.

By the Restoration, Arguments were regularly used in the public theatre, though the subject has not been written about by scholars. In George Villiers, Duke of Buckingham's 1672 *The Rehearsal*, the parody playwright, Bayes, disseminates published material to help the audience understand his laughably complicated play; he explains, 'I have printed above a hundred sheets of papyr, to insinuate the Plot into the Boxes.'[34] Scholars from Johnson onwards have assumed this 'paper plot' passage is a parody of Dryden, who gave the audience what is now prefixed to the printed play of *The Indian Emperour*: the 'Connexion of the Indian Emperour, to the Indian Queen'. So Bayes' action is presented by critics as being one-off, recalling an equally unique and ridiculed event.[35] Actually, however, Bayes is, while still obviously parodying Dryden (again, with the implication that the play is over-complicated, and so inexplicable without extra 'helps'), reflecting a sometimes-chosen theatre habit. For the use of plots continues to be referred to right into the eighteenth century. In *The Play is the Plot* (1718) Sir Barnaby, keen to know who is going to enter next in the extraordinary tragedy he is watching, turns to a piece of paper he has been given: 'I have the Plot down here in Writing—[*puts on his Spectacles.*] *reads.*—Perseus resolving to pick a Quarrel with Phineus his Rival before he leaves Ethiopia, finds him walking in the King's Garden . . .'[36]

Several Restoration Arguments also survive. From 1662/3 is a pamphlet for a production of Εγχυχλοχορεια to be dispersed as the production began: the pamphlet includes itself in its story, much as Jonson had done all those years ago, describing its own dissemination when the 'Clownish Carrier' enters bearing 'a Packet of Books to be distributed by the Master of the Ceremonies, wherein is described the whole designe': the imperatives of narrative are here taking over from the imperatives of the enacted performance.[37] For the 1697 play *The Novelty*, the author, Peter Motteaux, provided 'a Preface to that Masque' (the play's third act *Masque of Hercules*) which was 'printed for the use of the Audience, the first day of the Novelty's being Acted'.[38] Interestingly, each of these Restoration Arguments is dated and reaffirms that, in the public theatre, only the first performance was graced with this additional, and apparently free, literature; like prologues and epilogues, Arguments were 'presents' for the first-performance audience.

As a result of such instances, the question that confuses editors about Arguments in printed books extends from a reading problem to a performance problem: why did players ever sanction the distribution of texts that, seemingly, threatened or displaced the performed or read play in this way? A look at one variety of surviving Arguments for one variety of audience makes some of the general reasons clearer.

Two small printed pamphlets flank not a masque but an unpublished manuscript Latin play in the Folger Shakespeare Library. One of them is in Latin, *Wernerus Martyr, Hoc Est, Comico-Tragoedia*, and one in German, *Wernerus Martyr, Das ist ein Lust unnd Trawriges Schawspil.*[39] They are both for the same German production performed in two parts on 15 and 16 October 1630, as their title-pages state, and they both have the same content: a title-page, the 'short' version of the plot ('Argumentum' and 'Argument unnd Innhalt' respectively), and a longer, scene-by-scene, summary of the tale being enacted. Each Argument also contains a 'person-list' providing the characters who will be in the story, without revealing which actors will perform them. In this way the Arguments closely resemble plot-scenarios (see chapter 1) and perhaps, partly, reproduce them.

As these Arguments for *Wernerus Martyr* explain (and as the manuscript play depicts), Werner was murdered by Jews as he returned from holy communion in Oberwesel in 1286. The play itself intersperses scenes from Werner's childhood with pastoral shepherds, evil Jews, students, the Virtues and the Rivers of Germany. In English, the plots for act 1 scenes 1 and 2 read:

Act 1, Scene 1
Urban, the stepfather of Werner, treats his stepson harshly on account of some minor grievance. In this matter, Werner displays a sample of his forbearing and endurance.

Scene 2
Since Werner's endurance towards the love of suffering increases, Christ (appearing in the form of a young man) offers him the gifts of heaven and the crosses of the various Virtues . . .[40]

The survival of the same Argument in two different languages highlights a practical purpose that could be served by such pamphlets: translation. The German-language Argument for a production that was itself in Latin allowed non-Latin speakers to 'understand' the story. It was, in the most literal sense, the play's 'interpretation'. But it also analyses the play in other ways, for in this account Werner's actions are 'interpreted' too: Werner illustrates forbearance, endurance and love of suffering; each description gives a title to what the actors are doing and limits what they achieve in performance even as it defines it. By doing this, however, the Argument promotes the play to the watching spectators who will imagine they see what they are told they see (or read what they are told they read): an Argument points basic emotions that may not in reality be picked up in the play itself; an Argument therefore makes sloppiness in a playscript less likely to be noticed.

By isolating the play's structure, the Argument also ensures that during performance (or reading) concentration can be given to the literary style of the piece – for, with Argument in hand, none of the audience will lose the thread of a complicated play (*Wernerus* took two days to perform); on the contrary, they can now enjoy additional anticipation in that 'the rest of the play is a process of expectation fulfilled, of progression toward a known end'.[41] Other literary aspects too can be abstracted, highlighted and extolled by the Argument. For *Wernerus*, the 'historical' sources of the tale are listed, contextualising the play both as literature and as 'truth': 'Diss schreibt *Surius* den *19 Aprilis, tom 7* und mit ihm *Abrahamus Bzoruius*'.[42] Playbook Arguments sometimes do much the same, providing a literary context ('*Plutus* . . . being by *Aristophanes, Lucian. &c.* presented naturally blind, . . . is here by his love of Honor, made see') or vouching for the truth of the story ('after his Grandfather *Abbas* his decease . . . in the year 1629. the young Prince took upon him the Empire; aged sixteen years . . . so fresh in memory is this sad story').[43] And given that Arguments were often explicitly trusted, so an upbeat, dictatorial, Argument might bully a reader/watcher into approving a play. They are also more about the narrative of the play than about the performance of it, showing an authorial concern to broadcast the play's structure and its literary qualities. Indeed, the Arguments of *Wernerus* will not only outlive performance but redefine what it was: *Wernerus* in production may have been ragged, unclear or amateur, but a permanent reminder of what should or may have been seen remains in Argument form in print. Over time, the Argument can become what the audience saw: again, modern theatre programmes can have a similar effect.

Plots, then, on every level 'interpret' a play, and are regularly found with plays that need explanation, in one or both senses of the word. They can be linked to the widespread popularity of short Latin Arguments to what were at the time inaccessible Greek plays; most 'foreign-language' plays, as well as most masques, can be assumed to have had 'plots'.[44] Though almost no critics are conscious of translation-plots, Suzanne Gossett, in a fascinating article, records how Latin drama performed in the English College in Rome was accompanied by Arguments in English. Though the English Arguments themselves are lost, surviving accounts written in Italian describe their production and dissemination: they were, in the early days, written by a scribe (payments are made to a scribe in 1632 for 'tanti copie di argomenti della comedia'), later they were printed – in 1646, for example, payments are made for '300. argomenti in un foglio'.[45]

An English Argument that included 'translation' amongst its features also survives for a masque that was performed in French, *Florimène*, in Whitehall for King Charles I in 1635. Again, the play has never been printed, though *The Argument of the Pastorall of Florimene with the Discription of the Scoenes and Intermedii* was; moreover, in this instance a little is known about the circumstances of the Argument's publication, for it was allowed for the press by Henry Herbert, Master of the Revels, a week in advance of performance.[46] As before, the plot is a scene-by-scene account of the action that mingles interpretation with something more. It provides, like *Wernerus*, first a brief Argument, then a fuller one, and also a list of the characters who will appear in the production (again, it does not name the actors who will perform those characters). The full content of the narrative is told, but the actual words in which the tale happens are not translated: the plot keeps the play's text 'secret' whilst making its structure public:

Above all, ranne a large Freese . . . in the midst was placed a rich compartment, in which was written FLORIMENE . . . Florimene appears; Florelle goes to her, and tells her the sentence of Diana, concerning her marriage, with which Florimene was much joyed, she presently perceiveth Filene with all the other shepheards and shepheardesses standing before the Temple . . . *Here the Heavens open, and there appeare many deities, who in their songs express their agreements to these marriages.*[47]

As is manifest from this and other Arguments, the text provided in no way competes with or replaces a playbook. Indeed, a text such as this seems bare and unsatisfactory without a production to enhance it: it needs to be 'completed' by performance. Yet such documents continued to be distributed. From 30 August 1661 there is a 'translation-plot' from a French troupe's one-day Drury Lane production of Chapoton's *La Descente d'Orphée aux Enfers*; it is called *The description of the Great Machines of the Descent of Orpheus into Hell, Presented by the French Comedians at the Cock-pit in Drury-Lane: The Argument.*[48]

So Arguments can be seen to have a recognisable form and structure. As it seems, some entertainments were flanked with texts that foregrounded the importance to them of writing and print, making the printed word seminal to the creation and dissemination of a fully intelligible spectacle.[49] For such productions, the playwright might have collaborated with a printer as much as, and perhaps more than, with actors.

The publication of Arguments after performances (seemingly a reproduction of the actual performance-plot, but rephrased in the past tense) is strange, but analogous to the publication of accounts of pageants, often put out a few days after the pageant itself. An Argument, read after the theatrical event, cannot remake the occasion, though it can make what the occasion should have been: it can shape, or falsely create, memory, or simply allow readers to have 'been' at an event where they were absent. Such, presumably, was the reason for printing a post-masque Argument for *Masque of Blackness*, which was described by Dudley Carleton in a letter written the day after the performance: 'The maske at night requires much labor to be well described; but there is a pamflet in press wch will save me that paynes.'[50] It likewise explains another 'translation'-plot, this one for a school play, *Princeps Rhetoricus or πιλομαχια the Combat of Caps* (1648). Though printed shortly after performance, it seems to be a copy of a text actually provided for the women in the audience:

> As for the scene that lies in Grecian-Rome,
> A piece new weaved ith Greek and Latian lome;
> Yet for your sakes (sweet Ladies) all along,
> The work's imbroder'd in our Mother Tongue.[51]

This pamphlet, like others, also 'interprets' the design of the play ('The whole draught of the Invention moves upon two principall Hinges ...'), and the meaning of the clothes and objects used ('The 3 Golden Keys lay open this Conceipt; that logick, Rhetorick, and Grammar, are ... taught fundamentall in Schools; but the work is left to be crowned and matured in the Academies'). It thus does ham-fistedly what other plots do more subtly: teaches the reader how to understand what he (or presumably, in this instance, she) is seeing. It contains the usual character-list, and a scene-by-scene summary. So for act 1 scene 1:

A Curtain is displaied . . . the prime School monitor appears in a studying posture: is interrupted by the entrance of the 2 Text-bearers, inducing . . . the wandring scholar Lose-Cap to the sight and speech of the Monitor, with a Petition tendered . . . for the recovery of his Cap, defunct; the Petition is accepted . . . [52]

Here, where Arguments survive or come into being after the event, and dialogue does not, the fundamental feature of a text is seen to be its abstracted story, not its words, as though story alone embodied what the performance was: a notion that the use of and regard given to the plot-scenario has also suggested.

CONCLUSION

It is hardly surprising that playwrights during the Renaissance and Restoration periods found methods to 'explain' their narrative and structure for, from the medieval period onwards, authors had sought ways to do this. The staging of a particular character, a 'presenter' (sometimes called an 'interpreter' or 'tronchman'), to tell the story and introduce its conceits had been variously utilised. Looking back from the vantage of the civil war, Edmund Gayton becomes theatre historian, explicating the various 'incongruities and absurdities of our owne stage':

> it being a long time us'd to historicall arguments, which would not be dispatched but by Chorus, or the descending of some god, or a Magitian: As in the playes of Bungy, Bacon and Vandarmast, the three great Negromancers, Dr Faustus, Chinon of England, and the like. Every act being supported by some long narrative, which was the Apology for the soloecisticall appearances of children, become men in an instant, within the space of two musicks.[53]

Dumb-shows provided alternative ways to give advanced warning for what was going to happen: the dumb-show in *Hamlet* gives the whole story to follow, and, though this is said to be unusual (based on other surviving dumb-shows), the play also seems to recall an earlier occasion on which the Argument was read out, at least to Hamlet: 'Have you heard the Argument,' asks the King, 'is there no Offence in't?' (TLN 2100).[54] Allowing some royal authority to read through an Argument and choose on that basis whether or not to have the play itself performed may have been commonplace. Spanish and Flemish Ambassadors, when staying at Trinity College, Cambridge, were invited to a play but were also told its argument beforehand: learning that 'yt consisted chiefly of a Jesuite and a puritan, they wold not adventure, but wisht they had not had notice, for they semed to like all their intertainment so well that they desired to have all the orations . . . that they might be printed'.[55] And a rather illiterate Argument for Ben Jonson's *Masque of Queens* is sometimes thought to be not a plot for performance, but a plot for selection purposes (though pre-play Arguments and audience Arguments are somewhat hard to distinguish from one another).[56]

Another even earlier theatrical habit, predating the establishment of the permanent London theatre, had been to supply full Arguments inside the prologue or before the play began, as one prologue from 1560 recalls:

> Knowe that among the Poets comicall,
> In breef sentence it was usuall.
> To showe the whole contents of the Comedye:
> In the argument which did wel verily.[57]

Later time grew wary of this. H. M. describes as a feature of a 'course Prologue' that it will 'betray . . . The Authors Subject', and Suckling maintains a 'Woman enjoy'd' is like knowing a play-plot: 'Fruition's dull, and spoils the Play much more/Than if one read or knew the plot before.'[58] Nevertheless, the variety of methods playwrights sought over time to explicate the narrative structure of their plays in the theatre explains why the audience was primed to receive written plots when these were handed out: an Argument suited well with their way of thinking (and alleviated problems they might otherwise have with the play's actual plot); Arguments seem to be a continuation of a theatrical habit of giving away the story. Those authors who put themselves to the expense of supplying Arguments were choosing through the medium of the printed page to become their own presenters and maintain a highly personal interpretative presence throughout performance.

The existence of the Argument at all provides yet another indication of the to-and-fro between the paratexts of enacted and printed play. The point is not only that printed Arguments interpreted plays during performance, but that some printed playbooks assumed the same habit: early modern playbooks that open with Arguments and character-lists not only hint towards, but might even actually preserve, audience-plots. These Arguments perform the same function as theatrical Arguments, clarifying the structure and themes of the text, providing a useful guide to characters, and supplying 'courtly' or 'first-performance' associations: they will, from their title 'Argument' onwards, have suggested those theatre texts to the early modern reader.

So Arguments in playbooks, far from being 'untheatrical', reflect one of the elements that linked play in performance to audience – and, equally, linked audience to printed book. The division between play as printed text and play as enacted performance is not as stark as it is often said to be, and Arguments provide one of the thrilling moments at which the two intersect, belonging to a strange textual hinterland where performance is most bookish and, conversely, where the playbook is most performative.

CHAPTER 4

Prologues, epilogues, interim entertainments

INTRODUCTION

'Let fancy', shrugs the Prologue to George Powell's *Alphonso* (1691), 'save my Play,/And then I'll laugh at Wits on my *Third Day*.'[1] What he is saying is that he hopes the audience will accept his play by applauding it. Provided they do so, *Alphonso* will be put on at least another two times; if the reverse happens and it is 'damned', it will never be staged again. Powell is particularly anxious that the play survive to 'my *Third Day*' because the third day was, in his time, the 'benefit' performance: the performance for which the author would be given a portion of the revenue as part-payment for his text. Because benefit performances were the major (and sometimes only) payment that playwrights received for their writing, cruel 'wits', whose taunting might result in a play's 'damnation' (in which case it would never be performed again – meaning there would be no third night), were a constant threat. As is clear from the prologue's concerns and frame of reference, this particular discourse is written specifically for the play to which it is attached, but is nevertheless not a permanent feature of that script. It belongs to the play at one crucial moment of its performance life, and is therefore angled, not towards all audiences, but towards the audiences who will determine the play's survival to the benefit – which is to say, the audiences who will attend days one and two of the production. Nor is this prologue unique. Every prologue of the Restoration was written to be similarly temporary, as were all epilogues, so that what was surprising was never the disappearance from the stage of a stage-oration but the random circumstance that might make it outlive the benefit night. This is expressed in the puzzled admiration accorded the extraordinarily popular epilogue for Ambrose Philips' *Distressed Mother*, which, 'Contrary to all other Epilogues, which are dropp'd after the third Representation of the Play . . . has already been repeated nine times'.[2] It is entirely usual for bibliographers and theatre historians of the Restoration to draw attention to the three-day nature of late seventeenth- and eighteenth-century prologues.[3]

But despite the fact that Caroline, Jacobean and some Elizabethan prologues and epilogues address exactly the same issues as their Restoration counterparts – the role the audience will have in assuring the play's survival or damnation, and the playwright's fears and desires for his 'benefit' performance – no critics of the early modern theatre have drawn attention to this, or dealt with its corollary: that most surviving prologues and epilogues in the early modern period were also temporary and also the preserve of early performances only. This chapter will argue that 'public theatre' prologues and epilogues from after around 1600 (and perhaps from before) are generally for first performances, not all performances, and will show how they were regularly changed, lost, found, and printed elsewhere, as befits manuscripts written outside the playbook and not necessarily intended to survive with it. Plays in performance, this chapter will suggest, were differently packaged depending on the stage of production they had reached; a prologue or epilogue heralded a play in its freshest and so most fluid state – and a prologue or epilogue in a printed play therefore did likewise. And as first-performance *revision* (as opposed to simple first-performance condemnation-or-approval, which has an older heritage) was instituted around the establishment of benefit performances, so prologues and epilogues may even have come to advertise a play ripe for reformation and change, while a play lacking them appeared to have been audience-tested and approved. The result is not only that some printed playbooks have prologues and/or epilogues and some do not; but that those lacking prologues/epilogues are making statements as strong as those containing them.

PROLOGUES, FIRST PERFORMANCE AND REVISION

There is a variety of prologues and epilogues seldom found in playbooks but published instead in miscellanies, poetry books and books of jests, or discovered in manuscript in commonplace books. These are the prologues or epilogues that are not so much play-specific as occasion-specific, acting as the theatre's notice-board, and explaining exceptional circumstances that relate to company, theatre or audience. They might celebrate the first time a boy-player performs a man rather than a girl ('For Ezekiel Fen at his first Acting a Mans Part'), or the day when a young boy is allowed to play an adult role ('A young witty Lad playing the part of Richard the third: at the Red bull: the Author . . . to incourage him, wrot him this

Prologue and Epilogue').[4] Alternatively, they are apologies or defences for the occasions when a play written for one theatre has to be performed in another ('Prologue at the Globe to . . . The doubtfull Heire, which should have been presented at the Black-Friers') or when a whole company has had to relocate ('Prologue spoken upon removing of the late Fortune Players to the Bull'; 'A Prologue spoken at the *Cock-pit*, at the coming of the *Red Bull* Players thither').[5] All these stage-orations could scarcely be repeated above once without becoming irrelevant: after he has performed once, Ezekiel Fen will no longer be new to men's parts; the role of Richard III will be returned to its 'real' adult performer (as is anticipated at the end of this special prologue); the *Doubtful Heir* will either shift to the Blackfriars or be reshaped so as not to irritate the audience at the Globe; the Fortune and Red Bull players will return to their old homes or adapt to their new ones. Occasion-specific stage-orations seem to be for single performances.

Of other stage-orations, those specifically addressed to the monarch, or any other named person or event, were obviously also written for single performances: 'The Prologue at Court' is for when the play is at court; 'The Prologue to the King and Queene' is for the occasion when those two illustrious people are at the performance; 'The prologe to a Presentmt of a Playe before bpp Thornburie & his Chauncelor, in his vissitacion at Corchester' speaks for itself.[6]

So 'occasional' and 'court' prologues and epilogues were all temporary. But, by extension, might the stage-oration itself be a temporary form? Heywood's prologue for *Loves Mistresse* entitled 'The *Prologue* to this Play, the first time it was Presented on the Stage' ('the stage' means The Phoenix playhouse rather than court), suggests as much, showing that particular prologue to be, like the others, tied to a single day – though in this instance the single day is that of the opening performance in the public theatre.[7] The connection between prologue and first performance gives pause for, when looked at more closely, the vocabulary of other prologues and epilogues of the period implies that they also are about the play in its 'first-time' form.

To turn to prologues first: it is standard to find day-specific words and references within prologues that signify their concern with a single occasion. They might stress that their play is new 'today' ('*THe* DIVILL *is an* ASSE,*' declares a Jonson prologue, '*That is, to day,/The name of what you are met for, a new Play*'); or they might refer to that day's special playbill (the prologue to *Arviragus and Philicia* fronts 'a new Play' as 'promis'd . . . by our bill').[8] The induction to Jonson's *Bartholmew Fayre*, which functions, as a selection of them do, like an elongated prologue, states the specific day on which it is to be (and presumably was) spoken, 'the one and thirtieth day of *Octob.* 1614', while the 'Introduction' to Cavendish's (perhaps unperformed) *Loves Adventures* describes the play it heralds as 'a new Play . . . writ by a Lady' and relays a conversation between two gentlemen who 'know not' what the play will be like.[9] It is normal for a prologue to stress the novelty of the play it introduces – though novelty is itself a time-limited state; the more successful a play is, the more tried and true, the further away it will be from its 'new' form. Yet *The Platonick Lovers* has appended to it a prologue that expresses the hopeful desire that because the play '[is] new/'Twill take'; ditto the prologue to *The Humorous Lieutenant* which is for 'a new Play . . . such a Play/You were wont to like'.[10] Similar points are made in prologues for plays by Beaumont and Fletcher ('New/. . . it is'); Philip Massinger ('Our Author with much willingnes would omit/This Preface to his new worke'); Nathaniel Richards ('the Play . . . is new'); Thomas Nabbes ('Some. . . Because this *new Play* hath a *new foundation*/We feare will cry it downe'); and James Shirley ('The worst that can befall at this new Play,/Is, we shall suffer, if we loose the day').[11] Moreover, so associated were prologues with plays that were 'new' that when Christopher Brooke sought to define the normality of writing an epistle in front of a book, he came up with 'an *Epistle* to the Reader is as ordinary before a new Book, as a *Prologue* to a new Play'.[12] A prologue *was* ordinary – but, as all these instances suggest, it was ordinary when a play was at a particular and early moment of its performance life. Shirley directly articulated this. Asked to provide a prologue for a revival, he claims to have shuddered, confused by the idea that an 'old' play should have a feature belonging so specifically to a play in its minority; he then writes a humorous prologue about his internal struggle: 'A Prologue you expect, we ask'd for one,/Our Poet said twas old, and should have none.'[13] He is being disingenuous, of course, for prologues were usual for revived plays too; but he does at least articulate the way prologues shied away from the 'old': they were the preserve of new – or, grudgingly, newly revived – plays.

Other prologues have lewder ways of drawing out a connection between themselves and the young and vulnerable state of the play they flank. Some, particularly those attached to plays about marriageable women, compare their texts to 'maids' at the very point of losing their virginity. They include Nabbe's *The Bride* which is 'a Mayden yet' – the 'yet' implying how soon a change will be undergone – and Fletcher's *A Wife for a Moneth*, which is similarly, at the moment described, 'a Virgin'.[14] As the salacious prologue to Shakespeare and Fletcher's *The Two Noble Kinsmen* explains, '*NEw* Playes, and Maydenheads, are neare a kin/Much follow'd both, for both much mony g'yn': money was hurled at both for the pleasure of participating in the transition from youth to experience; novelty was fleeting – and that was a main part of the attraction.[15]

Epilogues, similarly, often link themselves to first performances in vocabulary and theme. They are spoken by players who do not know, but are about to know, how the play has gone down. When the Epilogue to Shakespeare's *Henry VIII* gloomily prognosticates that, 'ten to one' (TLN 3450), the play will not please all the assembled spectators, he means that he is still uncertain whether or not the play will 'take'. He is matched by contemporary and later Epilogues, all wondering the same thing: 'we attend/To know if your acceptance crowne the end'; 'what your censures are,/If with, or against Arts industrie . . . We know not yet, 'till judgement give us ease'; 'whether you/conceave wee have wth care dischargd what*es* due/rest*es* yet in supposition'; 'I [Epilogue] am sent forth to enquire what you decree/Of us and our Poets.'[16] This is true whether it be for a child's production or for an adult one: one epilogue asks, 'for the children ere I goe,/Your censure I would willing know'.[17] As these epilogues also have specific 'new play' concerns, they, like prologues, can bluntly state the fact – 'his old new play,/Was never (in English) acted, till this day'; 'Our Play is new. . . 'tis in your powers,/To make it last; or weare out, in two houres.'[18]

So far, every prologue and epilogue discussed has linked itself with the play when 'new' – and 'new' has appeared to mean 'first performance'. 'What thinkst thou of this great day, *Baltazar*?' asks the King in Rowley's *Noble Souldier* (1634) – 'Of this day?' replies Balthazar, 'why as of a new play, if it ends well, all's well.'[19] But why write entire texts for one single performance? And why not then repeat them once they have been written – or, rather, why write such day-specific vocabulary into stage-orations as to make their repetition scarcely possible? The answer to both lies in the nature and purpose of the first performance.

It should, for a start, be pointed out that first days were, like those of the Restoration, for an audience different from that at subsequent performances. Entrance charges were highly inflated for a play's opening, yet the struggle to get into the theatre and hold a place there was still so intense that only people with wealth and time could attend the playhouse for an opening day. From as early as 1585, when the German Samuel Kiechel observed of London players that they 'take from fifty to sixty dollars, at a time, particularly if they act any thing new, when people have to pay double', to as late as 1661 when Pepys said of the new opera that 'it being the first time, the pay was doubled', first performances seem to have cost twice the amount of any other performance; they continued to do so well into the eighteenth century.[20] Yet despite the high cost, as word of the upcoming new production spread, so did the desire to get to it. Hearing of a new tragedy '(before/Not Acted), men prease round about the dore/Crowding for Entrance'; coaches hurtle to 'a new play' at Black-friars, and then wait in such a crush together that 'like (Mutton-pies in a Cookes-oven) . . . hardly you can thrust a pole betweene'.[21] Dekker thought the crowding of the dead on the banks of Elysium/Hell would be of an equivalent magnitude 'as if it had beene at a new Play'.[22] This is why ten performances of Jonson's popular *Volpone* are described admiringly in comparison to its first performance: each subsequent performance, it is claimed, was as crowded and urgent as the first – though, naturally, the remuneration garnered from them was less: 'when thy Fox had ten times acted been,/Each day was first, but that 'twas cheaper seen'.[23]

This desperate audience loved new plays partly *for* the price they had paid to see them: for 'at publique Stage-playes' it was a given that 'whosoever censures' felt 'entitled to it . . . for his money'.[24] This was because, in a highly ritualised theatrical moment, the spectators' 'judgement', solicited at the end of the first performance, would shape what was to be altered or cut from the play – and, more than that, would determine whether or not the play would 'survive' to be performed again. So immediately after the epilogue preceding the benefit performance, of which more below, the audience would be asked to give their final response to the play: should it be allowed further performance, yes ('ay') or 'no':

> Yf then this please (kinde gentlemen) saye so
> Yf yt displease affirem yt wth your No.
> your, I, shall make yt live to glad the sire
> your, No, shall make yt burne in quenchles fire.[25]

Theatrical habit being what it is, the same process continued to haunt first (or, depending when the 'benefit' was, first and second) performances for the next few centuries. When it was time to announce the third-day 'benefit' performance of Dryden's execrable (now lost) play *Ladies à la Mode* 'both he that said it, Beeston, and the pit fell a-laughing': the play was never performed again; Cibber ponderously assured the audience as they damned his play *Love in a Riddle* on its first performance 'that after this Night, it should never be acted agen . . . [and] I . . . [gave] out another

Play, for the next Day, though I knew the Boxes were all lett, for the same again'.[26] As late as 1827, Dibdin describes how at the end of a first performance audiences were still ritualistically asked whether 'under the sanction of your kind approbation' they would allow the new play to be performed again. 'The Ayes or the Noes', he goes on, 'generally interrupt the remainder': theatrical habit was long-lasting indeed.[27]

The early modern audience did sometimes opt, like its later counter-part, for a play's immediate 'death'. Jonson's *Sejanus* was a drama that the multitude 'Like hissing snakes' decided should 'die'; *New Inne* (1631) was censured by the 'hundred fastidious *impertinents . . .* present the first day', for whom Jonson wrote a special epilogue 'in the poets defence, but the play liv'd not, in opinion, to have it spoken'.[28] Other damned plays include Peter Hausted's *The Rivall Friends* (1632) which was, snaps its title-page, 'Cryed downe by Boyes, Faction, Envie, and confident Ignor-ance'; and two plays which in revised form became popular: *The Knight of the Burning Pestle*, which 'The wide world . . . for want of judgement . . . utterly rejected'; and Massinger's *Emperour of the East*, which was ori-ginally 'cri'd downe/By . . . malice'.[29] *Love's Kingdom*, meanwhile, was 'condemn'd . . . on the Stage, for want of being rightly represented unto [the people]'; while *The Marriage of Arts* was killed, writes its outraged author, King, simply because it did not use the cheap crowd-pleasers gauchely employed by Shakespeare in *Twelfth Night*:

> Had there appear'd some sharp cross-garter'd man
> Whom their loud laugh might nick-name Puritan,
> Cas'd up in factious breeches and small ruffe . . .
> Then sure they would have given applause to crown
> That which their ignorance did now cry down.[30]

Naturally one of the reasons so many prologues are insecure is that they do not know whether they are fronting a play that will be loved or hated; they are spoken in an ecstasy of question and anxiety: 'Our Author hopes . . . that in this Play/He . . . may/Gain liking from you all, unlesse those few/Who wil dislike, be't ne're so good, so new'; 'I . . . know not till/Y'approove of't whether w'have done well or ill.'[31] One of the themes of petrified epilogues, meanwhile, is the fearful sound of disapproval – the snake's or goose's hiss – and the wonderful sound of applause.[32] Creating the latter was the particular task of the epilogue: applause for the epilogue could easily be conflated with the final verdict reached on the playscript, so a smartly written tail piece could 'save' a questionable play. That is why puns on 'clapping' abound at the end of epilogues: so that the witticism,

and so the epilogue, and so the play will then be 'clapped' – 'I love
Thunder, when you make the clap'; 'Bells are the dead mans musicke: ere
I goe,/Your Clappers sound will tell me I, or no'; 'All the best men are
ours; for 'tis ill hap,/If they hold, when their Ladies bid 'em clap' (*Henry
VIII*, TLN 3462–3).[33] That 'clapping' pun was itself punned on by Shakespeare in his bleakest years: he made Pandarus in the epilogue of *Troilus
and Cressida* not ask for *a* clap *from* the audience but bestow *the*
clap (*OED* 1587) *onto* them.[34] Other epilogue devices included positing
fictional events that could only be brought about by applause, a metathea-
trical resource used years later in Barrie's *Peter Pan*, where Tinkerbell's life
or death is reliant on the strength of the clapping offered by the children.
So Prospero in Shakespeare's *Tempest* will have to remain suspended for
ever within his fictional world unless the audience will, by entering that
world, praise and simultaneously destroy it; a trick that worked powerfully enough to be reused in much the same words in other plays: in
Neale's *The Warde* Thomauzo asks the audience, 'if you will not give,/
from your full store, to make Thomazo live;/yet to Release him from his
taedious bands,/you'l freely offer to set too your hands'.[35]

No wonder, given the judgemental process undergone at a new performance, that the vocabulary of the law courts came so regularly to be
applied to it. The spectators who damned Fletcher's *Faithful Shepheardesse*
during its first performance, and before they had seen all of it, are
described ironically as 'The wise, and many-headed *Bench*, that sits/Upon
the Life, and Death of *Playes*'; while it is the 'judiciall spirits' of the
audience who will either banish Heywood's *Golden Age* or allow it to
appear upon the stage again.[36] Dekker 'knows what Judges sit to Doome
each Play'; while playwrights and players too stand at the 'bar' waiting to
hear the censure of the spectators.[37] Over time, the first day of the
performance came itself to be called 'the trial'.[38] So Nabbes writes, 'That
you should authorize [the play] after the Stages tryall was not my intention'; and Ford that, 'The Court's on rising; tis too late/To wish the Lady
in her fate/Of tryall now more fortunate.'[39] Shakespeare's 1623 Folio plays,
on the other hand, come pre-approved by the audience – they 'have had
their triall alreadie', boast Heminges and Condell, 'and stood out all
Appeales' (A3a). In some ways this further illustrates the link between
playhouse and Inns of Court; it is likely that members of the Inns of
Court took active part in the play-judging process. But another issue is
being underlined by the vocabulary of the trial. What is being tested in
the first performance and through the medium of stage-orations is not,
needless to say, the players, for they can put on another play if this one

is damned; their livelihood is not affected by one play specifically. The trial is, as prologues and epilogues so repeatedly illustrate, of the playscript itself.

Yet the trial was not merely for the life and death of a play. There were gradations of criticism, and a play that 'passed' might well do so only with provisos. When in Middleton's *Ant, and the Nightingale* a young gallant is advised go to the Bankside to see what is described as 'the first cut of a Tragedie', that implies that a second cut, or a reshaping of the play, will happen as a direct result.[40] Similarly, when the prologue to Marston's *Antonio and Mellida* asks his audience to 'polish these rude Sceanes', that, again, implies that audience criticism will dictate how the play is to be improved.[41] And particular texts even discuss how it was the first performance that brought about their alterations. Jonson's *Every Man Out of his Humour* had originally concluded with the appearance of Queen Elizabeth, whose presence drove out Macilente's vitriolic humour; but, as Jonson explains when providing a new ending to his 1600 quarto: the '*Catastrophe* or Conclusion' that the play had had 'at the first Playing: . . . many seem'd not to rellish . . . and therefore 'twas since alter'd'.[42] It seems that, from a time in theatrical history hard to date precisely, some plays on their opening performances were offered as mutable texts ready for audience revision, with the presence of the stage-orations broadcasting that fact.

The likelihood of post-first-performance revision is strongly indicated too by later theatrical practice. In the seventeenth and eighteenth centuries, adaptation in the light of first-night censure was normal. Audience criticism might result in subsequent alteration to entire plots of plays – 'after the first Representation of this Play, the Conclusion was alter'd: *Agamemnon* is left to continue in a Swoon, and the Scene is clos'd with these few lines . . .'; to their humorous content – Dennis removed a satire from *Liberty Asserted* 'after the first Night'; or to their characterisation – Count Bellair was excised from *The Beaux Stratagem* after the initial performance. Alternatively, material might be added in the light of the first performance: Mary Manley was highly distressed when one of her lead actresses, Mrs Bracegirdle, left the theatre before *Almyna* was to have its second night, because by that time 'the Alterations' had been 'annex'd' onto the play.[43] Most often, however, plays were shortened after first performances, the bits audiences most disliked being cut away: Dodsley in *Sir John Cockle at Court* apologises for 'some Things which the Audience very justly found Fault with' on the first performance 'and which, the second Time, were left out or alter'd as much as possible: And the Author takes this Opportunity of thanking the Town for so judiciously and favourably correcting him'.[44] D'Urfey likewise explains how his *The Old Mode and the New* had, by its second performance, been 'shorten'd at least an hour in the action'; of *The Banditti* he had hoped, wrongly, 'that tho' my Play might be too long, which is a general fault . . . not to be remedy'd' till the first day is over, and tho' some Scenes might seem Tedious 'till it was shorten'd, which is allways the Second Days work' the play might be accepted anyway.[45] The play's second or third night (depending on the date of the benefit) would usually then be delayed until improvements had been completed – easy to do when there was no fixed repertory, and many different plays were performed in a season. So, of *The Livery Rake*, which was 'not approved by the Audience', a promise was given: 'the Company of the Revels will not perform it again till proper alterations are made by the Author'.[46]

Though unequivocal instances of first-performance revision or shortening are not so clearly articulated in the early modern period, the effects of it are. 'Into how many pieces a poore Play/Is taken still before the second day,' exclaims the Epilogue to Suckling's *Goblins*.[47] Harding makes a point of publishing his play as performed in order specifically to show 'for what a nothing I esteeme their censures; whatsoever syllable there be, that they ever cavill'd at, is therefore not omitted'; it seems that pressure had been put on him to alter his play in the light of criticism – and that he had chosen not to yield.[48] In 1635 the fate of Killigrew's new play *Pallantus and Eudora* is portrayed as hanging in the balance while a member of the audience vociferously objects to a particular piece of characterisation. The point of contention is that 'Cleander', who in the story is supposed to be seventeen years old, has a dialogue that makes him speak more like a man of thirty. The rest of the audience at the Black-friars' first performance are dragged into discussion of the matter, all during the production itself:

The Answer that was given to One, that cried out upon the *Monsterousnesse* and *Impossiblitie* of this thing, the first day of the Presentation of the Play at the *Black-Friers*, by the Lord Viscount *Faulkland*, may satisfie All Others . . . The Noble Person, having for some time suffered the unquiet, and impertinent Dislikes of this Auditor, when he made this last Exception, forbore him no longer, but . . . told him, Sir, *'tis not altogether so Monsterous and Impossible, for One of Seventeen yeares to speak at such a Rate, when He that . . . writ the whole Play, was Himself no Older.*[49]

One audience member almost has the play damned; another saves it: this is minutely focussed criticism wholly determined by the people present.

And prologues and prefaces of the time indicate just how local and detailed the critiques could be: audiences might pass remarks on the plot (''tis too thinne'), make specific analyses of the scenes ('This was flat'), or have something to say about the language used at particular moments ('Here the Sceane/Fell from its height').[50] Of the critics in these first performances, some of the most dangerous seem to have been other playwrights (who often had free entrance into playhouses).[51] They sat clutching their 'blacke condemning Cole[s]' ready to write down their objections; the most cruel amongst them were those who had tried play-writing once and been 'hist from Stage'.[52] At least some theatrical cuts, thought to have been the result of careful deliberation, are potentially traceable to first-performance demands, the presence of the stage-oration signifying that alteration as well as damnation is allowable on this occasion, and the audience emerging as the 'cutters' of the play at least if not more.

This is obviously contrary to the idea that the premiere marked the time when textual 'collaboration' stopped and textual 'corruption' began.[53] For it is to suggest that well before the interregnum the first performance was one occasion on which the audience's 'collaboration' set the final touches to the text: the audience's contributions may have been an accepted (if resented) part of the process of textual revision. Were this the case, it would mean too that from some point in history (perhaps the institution of the benefit performance onwards) playscripts were potentially fluid between first and second performance; some texts that survive in more than one version may be showing the result of speedy first to second performance 'revision'. That at least is what the eighteenth-century playwright Colman imagined as true in the time of Beaumont and Fletcher, basing his ideas, obviously, on theatrical practice in his day:

A writer in his closet often silently acquiesces in the excellence of a continued declamation; but if at any time the audience, like Polonius, cry out, 'This is too long,' such passages are afterwards naturally curtailed or omitted in the representation.[54]

Possibly this revision question ties in with an issue raised by Andrew Gurr in another context. He gathers evidence indicating that plays may well habitually have existed in more than one form: a longer, ideal, 'maximal' text that was passed by the Master of the Revels, and a shorter 'minimal' text that the company performed. While not looking at the moment at which revision takes place, he tentatively wonders whether the playhouse manuscript was routinely cut in performance and questions how it was that speeches were selected for trimming.[55] Evidence supplied above suggests that plays were written in long form first and potentially shortened in the light of performance; one reason for long versions of published plays is that they may be in first-performance state; shorter texts may show that cutting has been made in the light of audience criticism.

With the first performance so crucial to the success of the play, a number of special one-off events came to be linked to it. The playwright might, for instance, try to buy his approval by arranging a '*faction* in a partiall way,/Prepard'd to *cry it up*, and boast the *Play*', as a prologue to a Nabbes play put it; or bring 'friends to magnifie his play', as a Brome prologue called it disdainfully.[56] In the prologue/induction to John Day's *Isle of Gulls* (1606), a prologue-speaker holds a conversation with three gentlemen. Here the whole point is that the playwright, though nervous of the 'trial' or first-performance audience, is above using underhand means:

2:      where sit [the Poet's] friends? Hath he not a prepared company of gallants, to applaud his jests, and grace out his play?
PROL: None I protest. Do Poets use to bespeake their Auditory? . . . Our Author . . . is unfurnisht of . . . a friendly audience . . .
1:      Then he must lay his triall upon God and good wits.[57]

A bolder approach was to send thugs out into the first-performance crowd to coerce them into acceptance. Gayton recalls a production in which bullyboys were sent by the author (or perhaps the actors) to terrorise the audience, making obscene hand gestures and even setting fire to the clothes of any woman seemingly about to disapprove of the play. In his description, the play was

most ridiculously penn'd and acted, [but] the Auditors . . . durst dislike nothing, but gave great Plaudites to most things that were to be hiss'd off the Stage with the Speakers; [because] the exhibitors of that shew politiquely had plac'd Whiflers arm'd and link'd [i.e., carrying weapons and burning torches] through the Hall, that it was the spoyl of a Beaver hat, the firing a Gown, beside many a shrew'd Bastinado, to looke with a condemning face upon any solaecisme, either in action or language.[58]

The expensive first performance and its concomitant judgemental audience explains why 'new play' prologues and epilogues were so often written in the first place. They were focussed, purposeful, and occasion-specific: the first and the last in a series of playhouse 'gifts' designed to make the critical audience more likely to accept a play. When supplied, they were additional sweeteners that celebrated the singularity of the first performance and the audience that had come to it, whilst working to put that audience in a forgiving frame of mind. When not supplied, that could be because their authors would not play the game; Jonson creates an induction in which his actors explain that he has given up on the prologue. 'The Author', it says:

will not be intreated by us, to give it a *Prologue*. He has lost too much that way already, hee sayes. Hee will not woo the gentile ignorance so much. But carelesse of all vulgar censure, as not depending on common approbation, hee is confident it shall super-please judicious Spectators, and to them he leaves it to worke.[59]

PROLOGUES AND 'BENEFITS'

From the practice of giving benefit performances onwards – special performances for which a share of the revenue would be received by the playwright – prologues and epilogues were written to encourage the audience not simply to 'save' the play *per se*, but to let it reach its benefit day (and perhaps then to attend that benefit). As a 1632 epilogue explains, '[the poet's] promis'd Pay/May chance to faile, if you dislike the Play'; and, as another confirms, 'the next night when we your money share/ Hee'll shrewdly guesse what your opinions are'.[60] Hence it becomes important to determine when 'benefits' started, for, after the institution of benefits, almost all stage-orations seem to have been generally for first performances only, while, before benefits, prologues and epilogues could have been spoken more than once easily. The trouble is that benefits were eased into the theatrical process, existing for some authors on some days in some theatres before 1600 or so, and existing for most authors in most theatres (and largely on the second day) only from the late 1620s. So in *Playhouse to Be Let* Davenant maintains that playwrights 'us'd to have the second day' – meaning some of the revenue from the second day as benefits – back in the days 'of mighty *Tamberlane,*/Of conjuring *Faustus,* and the *Beauchamps* bold' (in other words, the time of Marlowe and Heywood), yet Henslowe's accounts suggest that he is only partly right. Though Henslowe documents some playwrights being given 'the overplus of the second day' (the benefit Daborne received), these references are neither regular nor consistent.[61] Munday '& the Reste of the poets' are given money 'at the playnge of Sr John oldcastell the ferste tyme', Day is paid extra 'after the playnge of the 2 part of strowde', and Dekker was allowed additional cash 'over & a bove the price of his boocke called A medysen for A curste wiffe': a series of first-performance benefits for which prologues and epilogues could only plead.[62] Henslowe's records are also not consistent as to playwright: of the many playwrights mentioned in Henslowe's 'diary', the others do not seem to have been allowed benefit performances – or, at least, if they were, it is not clearly recorded.

Benefit performances are, however, already established enough in a generalised way by around 1611 for Dekker to criticise, in a play first performed that year, the kind of playwright who cares only that 'he *Gaines,/*A Cramd *Third-Day*' (here a third-day benefit is predicted), and for the Bardh who speaks the epilogue to a play by 'R. A.', *The Valiant Welshman*, for performance *c.* 1610 to hope that, rather than be sent to his tomb, he will be permitted to give 'second birth' (a second day) to the play.[63] By 1617 *The Law of Drinking* tells of giving a pipe of tobacco to a thread-bare poet in the expectation that he will pay back for it 'at the next new play he makes, if the Doore-keepers will bee true to him': another reference to performance-based revenue for a new play but, again, one not necessarily secure as to day.[64] In other words, the 'day' of benefits in the sixteen-teens still seems to be moveable, though the fact of them seems, from that time onwards, quite normal. Looking at Henry Herbert's now lost office book, Malone, the eighteenth-century theatre historian, summarised what he found there: 'that between the year 1625 and 1641, [authors'] benefits were on the second day of representation'.[65] This is evident anyway from the prologues and epilogues of the late 1620s onwards, for they insistently refer exclusively to second-day benefits – and so equally insistently indicate that they themselves precede that second performance: 'Every labour dyes,/Save such whose second springs comes from your eyes,' maintains *The Costlie Whore* in 1633; 'a Play/ Though ne'r so new, will starve the second day', observes the Prologue to Shirley's *Sisters*; Jasper Mayne's play is 'One, whose unbought Muse did never feare/An Empty second day, or a thinne share'; Sir John Denham suggests, 'if yee dislike the Play . . . Pray make no words on't till the second day . . . be past'; and Henry Harington, 'On Mr. John Fletcher's . . . Dramaticall Works', writes of the audience 'who the Poet and the Actors fright,/Lest that your Censure thin the second night'.[66] Playwrights penning these stage-orations were not necessarily looking for lasting fame from their work but, as Cartwright disgustedly observed, wrote 'not to time, but to the Poets day'.[67]

For revived plays, too, second-day benefits were offered, and these were (if the author were dead or no longer involved in the company) distributed around the people 'deserving' of additional payment. Herbert, the Master of the Revels, was given by the King's Men from 1628 onwards 'the benefit of too dayes in the yeare, the one in summer thither in winter, to bee taken out of the second daye of a revived playe, att [his] owne choyse'.[68] From this fact, and from a few of his surviving records, it is even possible to guess at the sums of money a playwright might hope for through a successful benefit: Herbert's 'winter' benefit for 22 November 1629, the second day of Shakespeare's *Othello*, earned him £9 16s; his summer benefit for 12 June 1631, the second day of Shakespeare's *Richard II*, earned him £5 6s 6d; while a winter benefit for Fletcher and Massinger's *The Custom of the Country* earned him £17 10s.[69] As the sum of money actually paid to a playwright to purchase a play might be around £5, though it seems to have risen to £8 and finally to around £20 (depending on author), a benefit could potentially double, treble, or perhaps quadruple a playwright's payment.[70] Naturally, he often chose to write special stage-orations to help bring that about.

As the second performance had an importance of its own, it may sometimes have been given its own prologue and epilogue, though the only occasions that specifically record them are royal or special in other ways. Cartwright's *The Royall Slave* had a second-performance epilogue written for the production of his play when repeated in front of the University, 'Thus cited to a second Night, wee've here/Venturd our Errours to your weighing Eare'; Heywood had a second-performance epilogue written for court, 'Spoken to the King and Queene, at the second time of the Author's Play cald Cupids Mistresse or Cupid and Psiche, presented before them. Cupid, the Prologue'; and a manuscript for an Oxford play records a series of complicated rules relating to the use of its prologue and epilogue: 'The second night being ye last Publique night had ye same speeches onely a new epilogue'; 'The third night being private ffor Gentlewomen, had onely a new Prologue ye Epilogue was ye same wth the ffirst Publique night.'[71] On all these occasions, of course, a 'first-performance' prologue and epilogue is superseded by a second-performance one: though the implication is still that prologues and epilogues are for single performance.

Benefits undoubtedly had a huge effect on the purpose and nature of the prologue and epilogue, though, even before the institution of the benefit, damnation could still take place at the end of a performance with all the shame and humiliation that implied. Nevertheless, it may be that pre-1600 (or so) some stage-orations, not automatically negated by benefits as happened later, had a longer life. Certain prologues and epilogues from before 1600, like the prologue to *Faustus* which is found in two different forms in two different texts, may even have been permanent or semi-permanent attachments to their plays: there is no demand that a 'relevant' stage-oration not be spoken more than once, though, as will be argued, the speed at which the texts were lost, in combination with the need to flatter the first-performance audience specifically, often indicates otherwise. A problem is that considerably fewer plays survive from before 1600 than from after 1600; of the 159 plays extant from between 1560 and 1600, as calculated by Bruster and Weimann, only 68 have prologues; conversely, of the 512 plays extant from between 1600 and 1639, 200 have prologues (others from before and after 1600 have epilogues, but their numbers have not been calculated).[72] Given that prologues and epilogues dropped away from plays easily, that is no surprise, but the result is that less material collectively survives from before the turn of the century than from after, making conclusions therefore much harder to draw, both about benefits and about their connection to stage-orations. The only article to address the issue dates from the beginning of the last century, and contends that the accession of King James in 1603 brought about the rise of the poet's benefit – if so, James' accession brought about the greater impermanence of the prologue or epilogue too.[73]

As the above quotations have indicated, prologues and epilogues became, if they were not always, generally impermanent residents in their plays. That does not mean that they *had* to be impermanent, any more than did prologues and epilogues from before 1600. There was no law against the repeated use of a stage-oration, and those that do not contain specific first-performance markers may, perhaps, have been used on other occasions. There are, however, clear tendencies not to do so. At least one manuscript play, *Self-Interest*, a translation and adaptation by Reymes, indicates that its epilogue is simply expected to leave the text after the first performance. The final words of the play are: 'He is content . . . that ffflaminio, (for to end all strife)/Do wed Virginia wch conclude's the play)/But where's the Epilogue Quoth you? Pray stay.' The epilogue prepared for by this speech is not however provided, and is 'lost' as a result. These last lines are, however, also marginally annotated 'leave out these two lynes after ye first acting of ye play'; two alternative lines are provided for subsequent performances that contain no reference to an epilogue.[74] This play thus anticipates having two performance forms: one with an epilogue on the first performance; one without an epilogue on subsequent performances. That, I would suggest, is relatively normal, and explains the many discarded and lost prologues and epilogues that will be addressed below.

The exception is with strolling players, who are likely to have spoken prologues and epilogues at every performance: each performance by travelling players was a 'first' for that particular audience, and each performance thus had to solicit the same audience to approve (and so return to see) another play by the same company the next day. Whether some of the surviving stage-orations in front of plays are 'strolling' ones remains open to question, though the few references that survive to such texts imply that special and different prologues and epilogues were written for travelling (amounting potentially to another series of largely lost stage-orations). On record are only a few hesitant accounts. There is a prologue insulting a country audience by the actor and playwright William Barkstead, 'Bee blith Fopdoudells for our Authour knows/How to delight your eyes, your Eares, your nose'; an anecdote about a 'Sarcasticall' prologue issued by Tarlton – instead of the real prologue he was supposed to give – to a set of townspeople who would not stop hissing; and the story of an epilogue delivered to the substantial hostess of an Oxford Inn that started 'great Caesar': it gave such offence that the hostess delivered the play's 'Plaudit' soundly 'about the Eares' of the epilogue-speaker.[75]

THE CIRCULATION OF PROLOGUES AND EPILOGUES ON PAGE AND STAGE

A throwaway reference in the 'bad' quarto of *Romeo and Juliet* (1597, c1a) to a prologue that had to be 'faintly spoke/After the Prompter', combined with an allusion to a player's nightmare – that the prologue itself 'hist at him, because he spake it so scurvily' – indicates that orations had a particular reputation for being ill-learnt by performers.[76] This may stem from their temporary status: perhaps players were not always committed to learning a text for a single repetition, though by fluffing the prologue they risked the damnation of the entire play. The situation was not helped by the fact that prompters' books did not always contain prologues: 'help' with a forgotten text was not necessarily available. In *The Returne from Pernassus*, a university play, the 'boy', who has not learnt his prologue properly, peters out after 'Spectators we will act a Comedy'; the prompter cannot, however, come to his aid for 'A pox on't', he swears, 'this booke hath it not in it.'[77] *Careles Shepherdess*, another university play, mean-while, has a man who enters '*to speak the Prologue*' and '*being out, looks in his hat, at which an Actor plac't in the Pit, laughs*' – here the fiction is that the actor has secreted his text in his head-gear, already sure that the prompter will be unable to assist him.[78] In the induction to *Thorny-Abbey*, on the other hand, the Fool has his own expedient. Expecting to need assistance with his lines, he enters '*with a Paper in his hand for a* Prologue', which he then hands to the prompter for surety: he knows his text is likely to need prompting; he also knows it is not in the 'book' of the play.[79]

As is to be anticipated, the temptation simply to take the paper text of the prologue onto the stage and read it sometimes proved too strong for resistance. Amongst the holdings for a fifteenth-century German production of a carnival play is a separate prologue showing signs of use that indicate it was taken on stage and read there. It is made from a folio sheet cut in half lengthways; verses are written on the front, with some more inscribed upside down and on the back, allowing the prologue-speaker to read the first side, flip the paper over, and read the second side; grease and dirt spots on the top and bottom of the sheet indicate where it was held during performance.[80] Presumably something similar could happen in English productions too, for the Prologue's separate piece of paper became explicitly associated with his character. The one woodcut that purports to depict a prologue-speaker, for instance, shows a man with a cloak on his arm and, prominently, a single written sheet in his hand. As the figure himself has been extracted from a larger engraving – he was originally a messenger bringing a paper to a concerned bishop, the words 'rede and considar' scrolling out of his mouth – it is the clutched paper that seems to have suggested his reuse as a prologue-speaker: in all other respects he is interchangeable with woodcut men who do not need to be doctored to fit the bill.[81] Accompanying what is significant in itself, a 1642 separately printed prologue and epilogue to Cowley's university play *The Guardian* – the play itself was not to be printed until 1650 – the prologue-speaker's held text can now double as the paper his character will 'read' on the stage, and, simultaneously, the paper the reader will purchase and read now.[82] Prologues, always 'liminal' and 'non-organic' in relationship to a play, as Bruster and Weimann illustrate, could also be 'whole' without it.[83]

Part of the joy of the prologue and epilogue resided not just in their existence away from the playscript but in their resultant separate circulation. Perhaps because they were 'rarer' than the play, being heard less often, perhaps because they were self-sufficient enough to make sense without the attendant playbook, they were independently copied, and sometimes independently purchased. Strolling players might pay for their food or 'Ordinary' with 'the Copie of a *Prologue*'; and one such free-floating prologue, for Massinger's *The Maid of Honour* in revival, made its way to a reader who had never seen the play: 'Sr:', he wrote to Carew, 'I have mett wth a coppie of the Prologue of the mayde of honour wherein it is apparent the poet points at you, yet I was tould you wanted not Confidence to heare it one ye stage whilst I forfeited my patience but to reade it in my Chamber.'[84] Even when desired, stage-orations' popularity was separate from that of their plays, resulting in the odd story of the internal prologue to *Hengist*'s play-within-the-play, 'A Prologue to the Mayor of Quinborough'. It was printed as a freestanding poem in Sir John Mennes' 1658 *Wit Restor'd* many years after Middleton's play had been performed, but some years prior to its printing in 1661.[85]

Other plays whose stage-orations found print were never published at all, and only their stranded head and tail pieces survive: the single passage now known of John Tatham's lost play *The Whisperer* is 'A Prologue spoken at the Red-Bull to a Play called the Whisperer, or what you please', which is preserved in a printed book of poetry; the single fragments known of Richard Lovelace's *The Scholars* are 'A Prologue to the Scholars. A Comaedy presented at the White-Fryers' and 'The Epilogue' printed in his *Lucasta*; and all that is published of William Gager's Latin Oxford play *Rivales* is the 'Prologus in Rivales Comoediam' for its revival, which is printed at the end of Gager's *Ulysses Redux*.[86] Manuscript prologues and epilogues similarly survive from lost playbooks. An epilogue for the lost Latin Oxford tragedy by Richard Eedes, *Caesar Interfectus* of 1581, is preserved in a miscellany, 'Egit triumphus Caesar de repub. Brutus de Caesare'; and a prologue for a court performance thought to be by Shakespeare, 'As the diall hand tells ore', is found in a single miscellany: with no further information supplied with it, it is impossible to be sure what play – by Shakespeare or someone else, extant or lost – this text once flanked.[87]

Comfortably inside books of poetry and miscellanies, 'severed' prologues find a new non-play life as 'poems' amongst other poems, or as jests amongst other jests: one 'nonsense prologue' in the *Booke of Bulls* keeps its theatrical affiliation but does not even reveal the play, lost or surviving, to which it was once connected:

> A Bull Prologu, to a foolish Audience.
> You who sitting here,
> doe stand to see our Play;
> Which must this night,
> be acted here to day.
> Be silent, 'pray,
> Though you alowd doe talke,
> Stirre not a jot,
> Though up & down ye walk . . .[88]

So prologues and epilogues, having been separately studied, and separately supplied to the stage, could then be separately memorialised in manuscript and print, for readers who perhaps had never encountered the play of which these were once a part. It is the habit of prologues and epilogues to circulate outside their plays, which resulted both in their 'recovery', as above, and, naturally, in their regular loss: one reason why printed plays often lack prologues or epilogues is that the papers containing them had wandered, not that they never existed.

When two copies of a single playbook survive, one of the most common lines of difference between them is that one will contain prologue and/or epilogue and the other will lack them. An incomplete list of manuscript plays with stage-orations that their printed counterparts have lost (or, if they are revival texts, not yet acquired), include: the manuscript of Carlell's *Arviragus* which contains a prologue to part two, 'Twas promis'd rather hop't the second part/would please more then ye first', that is absent from the printed text; Goffe's *Courageous Turk* which has an epilogue, 'Horror on the stage is ceast but wee within/To feele a second tremblinge do begin', not in the printed play; William Berkeley's *Lost Lady* of *c.* 1637 which has a prologue to the King, 'Most royall Sr could I yet lower bend', also in manuscript only (there may have been an epilogue too: the manuscript is missing a final page); and two manuscripts of Walter Montagu's *The Shepheards Paradise* which contain the prologue, 'What newes Apollo, from the Highest spheares', that three do not – and, again, nor does the printed text.[89] But this is not a one-way difference, manuscript versus print: for it is the printed text of *The Womans Prize* (*Tamer Tamed*) that, conversely, has a prologue ('Ladies to you, in whose defence and right') and epilogue ('The Tamer's tam'd . . .') both of which are absent from the manuscript of the play.[90] Brome's *The English Moore*, meanwhile, has one prologue, 'I come to welcome yee; and not to boast/o[u]r Authors skill . . . or any Cost/in o[u]r new play', and one short epilogue, 'I yield to Fortune wth an humble knee', in manuscript that are simply different from the prologue and epilogue in the printed text ('Most noble, fair, and curteous, to ye all' and 'Now let me be a modest undertaker').[91]

When there is no manuscript version of a play, but there are printed texts in multiple editions, they too may well still differ with respect to prologues and epilogues in particular. Examples include Chapman's *Bussy D'Ambois* which has a prologue added to its 1641 edition that is absent from the version of the play printed in 1607–8: that prologue is obviously for the play in revival, as it mentions as now dead the actor Nathan Field

'Whose Action first did give it name'; and May's *The Heire*, which was published with one epilogue in 1622, 'Our Authors heire if it be legitimate', and republished in 1633 with a revival prologue, 'Judicious friends, if what shall here be seene . . .', and a new epilogue, 'Our Heire is fall'n from her inheritance'.[92] Marston's *Malcontent* was published three times in 1604 by V. S. for William Aspley, firstly with neither prologue nor epilogue; then with an epilogue; and then, finally, in the same year and with the same publisher, minus the epilogue but plus Webster's new induction at the start of the playscript and, at the end, a prologue to the play.[93] Two versions of the play are involved here: Marston's version, in two forms, and Webster's revised version, but the prologues and epilogues float around aside even from that.

Only one book explains and articulates a specific (and author-related) reason for its difference in published stage-orations. Aston Cokain's *The Obstinate Lady* was acquired by his one-time friend William Godbid who procured an 'acquaintance' to supply its final missing page 'wherein my conclusion to the play with the Epilogue were'; he reduced the epilogue to two lines, '*thus have you seen by patience great/You may o'recome a Lady Obstinate*', and then printed the whole under Cokain's name. Cokain however prints anew the entire play, returning (or, at least, writing himself) the ending and his own epilogue, '*Ladies and Gentlemen, you that now may/Approve (or if you please) condemn our Play . . .*'.[94] But it is a rare author who cares so much about the oration's relationship to the play. As will be seen, many other writers were content not to compose stage-orations, or not to save them, or not to mind if they were lost and/or replaced.

Sometimes, of course, the presence or absence of stage-orations relates to the age of the play. The examples above include instances where prologues and epilogues had been added for revival. But there are equally a number of instances when stage-orations are present in an earlier text only and are later removed. Mason's *The Turke* had, in 1610, a prologue and epilogue that have gone by the 1632 edition, in which, instead, an 'Argument' for the play fills the space.[95] *Wily Beguiled* had an epilogue in its 1606 printing, but not in its 1614 edition (looking for a 'reason' for this, it is sometimes thought that the 1614 edition must have been printed from a defective copy of the 1606 edition); Shakespeare's *Romeo and Juliet* was published in 1597 and 1599 with a prologue, and in 1623 without (this, too, is sometimes attributed to printers' error: it is said that, working from a copy of the 1599 quarto, compositors neglected to turn the 'prologue' page).[96] But arguments 'excusing' the lack of stage-orations in later texts neglect the fact that 'losing' stage-orations was normal in performance when a play aged, and that there were logical arguments for omitting stage-orations in print. Publishing a play with its prologues and epilogues implied that the text was young – fresh, but also not yet approved; publishing it without them had the potentially useful psychological effect of making the text seem established, reliable and popular: a text that had 'passed' the 'trial' some years before. The 'loss' might even be designed to make the play look as though it had already won its audience approval.

Many early modern playbooks suspected once to have had prologues and/or epilogues are published without them. Though individually the fashion for prologues versus epilogues varied – *The Birth of Hercules* explains how, at the time of writing 'thepilogue is in fashion', while Phillips records how at one time prologues were so in fashion that 'without them the Audience could not be pleased' – most plays probably had at least one and, from the late 1620s onwards, both.[97] Yet some of the plays published without either utterly assume the existence of them: Falstaff sees kissing as 'the prologue of our Comedy', but the comedy in which he makes the comparison, *Merry Wives*, has no prologue in either of its two forms (TLN 1744–5); in *2 Henry VI*, also lacking a prologue, Gloucester says his death will be 'the Prologue to their Play' (TLN 1451); 'We are cast,' observes Antonio in *The Tempest*, another play without a prologue, 'to performe an act/Whereof, what's past is Prologue' (TLN 947). *Hamlet* and *Othello* too contain jibes about the regularity with which a prologue precedes a tragedy; both plays are, themselves, published with none. So Shakespeare expresses the idea that a prologue is normal to a production in plays that now lack them. Does this indicate that he wrote prologues that no longer survive for these plays? Probably. The unlikely rescue of what may be a Shakespeare prologue from the period illustrates just how easily others of his (and other people's) prologues could have been lost.

The prologue to *Troilus and Cressida* ('In Troy there lies the Scene'), when read, seems to be crucial to the play, situating the story to come in the middle of the Trojan war; 'in its desecration of epic language', writes Lombardo, 'and its use of images of chance and uncertainty, it encapsulates the actual nature of the play which follows'.[98] Nevertheless, that prologue was not printed in either of the variant first (1609) quartos of the text, and was absent, too, from the first setting of the play in Folio. When the compositors in Jaggard's printing house originally started to set type for *Troilus and Cressida*, they printed its first page (without prologue) following on from the last page of *Romeo and Juliet*, as a variant state of the page makes clear. Then, however, news reached Jaggard's printing house that legal rights for *Troilus and Cressida* still belonged to someone else. The compositors therefore stopped printing the pages, and reset their type, placing *Timon of Athens* after *Romeo and Juliet*, with, again, its first page on the verso after the last page of *Romeo*. Much later, when the rest of the Folio had been set, the rights to *Troilus* were finally acquired, at which stage type was set up all over again; the play was placed after *Henry VIII*, where it is now to be found. Hoping to use the old, preserved sheets already printed that included the start of *Troilus and Cressida* on the back of *Romeo*, however, the compositors had a problem. True, they could (and did) simply 'cancel' with a cross of erasure the *Romeo* page on the sheets that had it, but for the new sheets to be compatible in space-terms with the old the recto sheet that was the equivalent to the last *Romeo* page would have to be filled with some other text. It was at this stage, it seems, that the printing house acquired the prologue to the play, which they placed in type so extravagantly large as to fill the entire page. A prologue was rustled up from somewhere very late in the publication process to fill what had, for quite other reasons, become a spare space before the start of the play: a seemingly essential text was preserved through a printing fluke.[99]

In other printed playbooks, the look and placement of prologues and epilogues shows that the compositors were handed these texts 'separately': and, of course, at any stage from writing to printing such separate texts might be lost. It is entirely usual to find the epilogue printed immediately after the prologue, linking the two texts with one another more than with the play, and indicating how they had been supplied 'together' to the printer who then published them in the order received. They huddle like joint pre-thoughts or after-thoughts on the preliminary pages before the numbering starts, or at the back of the book after the numbering has ended. Prologues and epilogues even when present in printed editions, that is to say, are not always treated as though they are one with their plays, a unity, sharing the same rights. Indeed, they are regularly printed with their own generic headings, 'The Prologue', 'The Epilogue', identifying them, like 'The Song' and 'The Letter' considered in chapters 5 and 6, as generic forms of writing in themselves (rather than as subsets of playtexts at all). Also like songs and scrolls, they are regularly printed in italic rather than roman type, indicating either that they have come from a different source, or that they are intended to be made into one. So in look and placement they exist in the textual periphery, kept with the play, but not seen as entirely part of it.

Occasionally a printer, anxious to produce a text more orderly and perfect than the papers he has received, resituates a prologue or epilogue so that it is in the 'correct' place. In the playbook of Brome's 1640 *The Sparagus Garden*, some issues contain the epilogue directly below the prologue before the play starts, but others have it accurately placed at the conclusion of the playbook: seemingly the printer picked up the block of 'epilogue' type when he realised that he actually had room for it where it should be, producing a playbook with a logic and order that (first) performance would have given it, but that the manuscripts he received did not.[100] The printer of Mason's *The Turke*, meanwhile, leaves an apology for the reader (or, perhaps, author) together with the epilogue at the front of the play: 'This *Epilogue* should have bene printed at the end of the booke, but there was no spare place for it.'[101] Yet even the very lack of space tells something about the relationship between printer and epilogue: when counting his way through the text deciding how much to put on which page ('counting copy'), the compositor(s) either did not yet have access to, or had neglected to think about, the epilogue, presumably because it was not in the 'correct' place in the playbook (or not in the playbook). In 'cleaner' examples of the same thing, an entire play may be printed in two issues, one with and one without stage-orations, seemingly dependent on when the printers received the little texts (or realised they had been given them): William Cavendish's *Country Captaine* was printed in 1649 without a prologue and epilogue, then printed again that same year with an additional leaf containing them (it is thus the opposite of the playtexts that 'lose' prologues and epilogues over time).[102]

All the above instances reflect a printer who received a 'bundle' of prologues and epilogues and, separately, a playscript, and had to sort them out, a happening hard enough to deal with when working on a single play, and impossibly complicated when working on a group of plays. Collected works particularly suffered with respect to the correct placement of prologues and epilogues as a result. The stage-orations in Beaumont and Fletcher's *Comedies and Tragedies* of 1647, for instance, reveal a number of confusions in the printing house. Fletcher's hefty tragedy of *Valentinian* is flanked by a perky epilogue that says the story is 'so light . . . That ye may new digest it everyday'.[103] That same epilogue is, in a collection of poems by Beaumont, more convincingly ascribed to *The Fair Maid of the Inn*: an epilogue for a comedy seems to have become latched to a tragedy by mistake.[104] Meanwhile, the epilogue appended in the same collected works to Beaumont/Fletcher/Massinger's *Loves Cure*, 'Our Author feares there are some Rebell hearts', had been published eighteen years earlier at the end of Carlell's *Deserving Favourite* of 1629: either the playhouse had chosen to apply the same epilogue to both plays (a possibility), or a free-floating epilogue from elsewhere had simply made its way into the bundle handed the printers of *Comedies and Tragedies* by mistake.[105] What is clear is that the printers of the 1647 works received a collection of stage-orations varying in date and source, and then situated them as best they could in the complete works. While some stage-orations emerge as (potentially) 'originals', others are definitely for the plays on the first day of their revival – meaning that they are of neither the same date nor, probably, the same authorship, as the dialogue they introduce: 'It were injustice to decry this now/. . . being like'd before,' says one, and 'The worke . . . when it first came forth,/In the opinion of men of worth,/Was well receiv'd, and favour'd,' says another.[106] In a note tucked away at the end of the preliminary matter and before the plays begin, the printers themselves recognise that some of the 'rogue' prologues and epilogues originate from a different source from the plays: 'We forgot to tell the Reader,' they remark, 'that some Prologues and Epilogues (here inserted) were not written by the Authours of this Volume; but made by others on the Revivall of severall Playes.'[107]

The same issue dogged the next 'Bookseller' to put together a (fuller) complete works for a Beaumont and Fletcher complete edition in 1679, for he received yet more prologues and epilogues for the plays, also from a separate source. As a result, he boasts, his *Works* contain 'several Prologues and Epilogues, with the Songs appertaining to each Play, which were not in the former Edition': these prologues, epilogues and songs too seem often to date to revivals of the plays, and their context, as their acquisition makes plain, has long been one another, not the plays themselves.[108]

No wonder, given the freedom with which prologues and epilogues circulated, the errors in playbooks that indicate printers acquired, or were given, the 'wrong' stage-orations entirely for plays, or, alternatively, chose to use stage-orations from other plays to fill gaps. Quite aside from the muddled history behind Beaumont and Fletcher's 1647 *Comedies and Tragedies*, that text, once printed, became the source for a number of later plays' prologues and epilogues. When *Beggars' Bush* was separately printed in 1661 it was copied from the text supplied by the 1647 *Comedies and Tragedies*, but given the prologue and epilogue that had been attached there to *The Captaine*. This may be due to a simple misunderstanding on the printers' part: the leaf containing the stage-orations in the 1647 text is after *Beggars' Bush* and before *The Captaine*, and the printer may have lifted the wrong passages in error.[109] Not so the stage-orations to the 1647

The Noble Gentleman that were frankly plundered: the prologue to that play was published as the prologue to Fletcher's *The Tragedy of Thierry* when it was separately printed in 1649; the epilogue was published as the epilogue to Beaumont's *Woman Hater* in 1649 (it had not been attached to the earlier 1607 or 1648 editions).[110] It is as though any old Beaumont and Fletcher prologue or epilogue would do for any of their texts.

With Heywood it is the same. The 1639 edition of Heywood's *If You Know Not Me, You Know No Body* was published – not by the author – with a prologue and epilogue seemingly lifted out of the collection of stage-orations to be found in Heywood's *Pleasant Dialogues and Dramas* of 1637; the epilogue's statement that the play has shown Elizabeth 'in the Regall Throne/a potent Queene' is blatantly untrue, for *If You Know Not Me* had ended with Elizabeth's coronation; it is the second part of that play to which this epilogue rightly belongs.[111] A similar error, though this one perhaps traceable to a binder or a misguided collector, is found in the single copy of Middleton's 1607 *The Phoenix* to which the prologue and epilogue to Mason's 1610 *The Turke* have been appended.[112] Printers, but perhaps binders too, might 'mend' or 'improve' one play with the stage-orations from another. That said, though, so 'separate' were these texts that even a playwright himself might simply forget which play required which oration. Shirley included in a book of poems he published a 'prologue to his Tragedy call'd The Cardinall', which begins 'Does this look like a Term?'[113] Yet that text is later printed, also by Shirley (who dedicates the play to William Paulet) before *The Sisters* – to which it seems rightly to belong; *The Cardinal*, when published in full also under Shirley's auspices (he dedicates that play to 'R. B.'), has its own prologue specifically linked to the text, 'The Cardinal, 'cause we express no scene/ We doe believe most of you Gentleman/Are at this hour in *France* . . .'[114] In other words, Shirley, in his poems, appears to misremember the play to which one of his own prologues belonged. Prologues had a separate life from playscripts, and sometimes the connection between the two was forgotten over their years of separation.

CHORUSES AND INTERIM TEXTS ON PAGE AND STAGE

The dislocation between prologues, epilogues and plays extended to related 'interim' texts too. *Romeo and Juliet*, not always published with its full quota of stage-orations, also has a disjointed history with respect to its choruses: the chorus that in Q2 and Folio divides the first from the second act is missing from the 'bad' Q1; again, practical and printerly reasons are regularly given for this – and yet, looked at more widely, choruses like (and sometimes with) prologues and epilogues seem also to have been separate documents on separate papers; in their nature they too were impermanent. *The Winter's Tale*, for example, joins *Romeo and Juliet* as a text that retains one chorus whilst, it appears, losing at least one other. There, when 'Time' enters to explain the passing of sixteen years, he chattily assumes that he is half-way through a conversation with the audience/readers: 'Remember well', he enjoins, 'I mentioned a sonne o'th'Kings, which Florizell/I now name to you . . .' (TLN 1600–2). As the play stands, this is Time's first entrance, and the first opportunity he has had to mention Florizell, but presumably he once intervened on at least another occasion, of which this single chorus is the last vestige. Both plays join another Shakespearean text likely to have had more orations than it now bears. *The Taming of the Shrew* contains an induction that introduces the 'Christopher Sly' story, and some interact dialogue that continues it mid-play; the framing, however, is abandoned without con-clusion. Presumably, like the closely related play *The Taming of a Shrew*, Shakespeare's *Taming* once concluded with an epilogue-playlet that saw through its secondary plot.[115] In this way it will have echoed the relation-ship between the two manuscripts of Thomas Middleton's *Hengist, King of Kent*, both of which have a prominent 'presenter', 'Raynulph', who, Gower-like, speaks the prologue and the epilogue and intervenes at other crucial moments as chorus.[116] By the time of the printed text, however, the final epilogue is missing and the end of the last act has been rewritten, so that Raynulph never sees through the tale he has begun.

These three Shakespearean plays, with only some of their interim material surviving, can be compared to Daniel's *Hymen's Triumph* which, though only performed once, survives in two forms: a printed text containing a 58-line prologue and seven songs, five of which are choral, and a manuscript with no prologue and only three of the songs.[117] This in turn resembles the complicated story of the choruses in the various texts of Fulke Greville's closet play *Mustapha*. That play seems on both of its two printing occasions to have reached the printers with dialogue in one document and (incomplete?) choruses in another. As a result it was, like the texts above, published in a state of flux in 1609 with its choruses partially present and partially absent. So, though five choruses are antici-pated by the playbook, only three are provided at the end of acts 1, 3 and 4; at the end of act 2 a heading 'chorus' is given without a text to accompany it; for scene 5.2, an entrance is given for a chorus-speaker but, again, no text is supplied.[118] And, lest it be thought that the later reprinted text of the same play, published inside Fulke Greville's *Workes* with five choruses intact, represents *Mustapha* in a more settled form, a marginal note handwritten into one copy should be taken into account. The famous 'Chorus Sacerdotum', 'O wearisome condition of humanity', is annotated in the copy owned by Sir Kenelm Digby, who saw the *Works* through the press for Sir John Cokes: 'This chorus is misplaced; but rather than loose it, I caused it to be inserted here to fill up this page.'[119] As the Chorus Sacerdotum is entirely absent from the Warwick manuscript of the play, and is placed at the end of act 1 in the printed 1609 text, it was obviously having trouble finding a home; perhaps it was in the process of being removed from the play when Greville died.[120] Other plays' 'interim' entertainments are also misplaced because separately acquired. In the quarto text of Middleton's *Your Five Gallants*, two comic interludes are printed out of play sequence: they are situated together in the 'wrong' act interval (after act 4 instead of between acts 2 and 3), though the business they contain implies where they should be placed. They too had an existence independent from the play – and, in this instance, as John Jowett argues, seem to have been late additions to the play that the printer has tried to integrate.[121] Likewise, in the 'A' text of *Faustus* a comic scene and a chorus for the fourth act are misplaced after 3.1; again, this seems to be because the passages were written out on loose sheets of paper, perhaps by a collaborator, and misplaced in the play as a consequence, as Bevington and Rasmussen conjecture.[122] Like stage-orations, interim texts were as likely as not from a different date to that of the playtext they enlivened; and, for as long as they occupied separate papers from the main play, were always more subject to removal (or addition).

That prologues, epilogues and choruses sometimes constituted a collection of linked scrolls, so that they were created as a group or lost as a group, is indicated by the habit of writing plays first and epilogues and choruses, as a group, second: Samuel Daniel's manuscript for the wedding entertainment of Lord and Lady Roxborough, *Hymen's Triumph*, indicates he wrote the prologue and three choruses last and added them just before performance.[123] It is also visible when plays are extant in more than one form, containing the whole lot, or lacking the whole lot. Shakespeare's *Henry V* is an obvious example. It is often pointed out that *Henry V* was first published in corrupt form in 1600 (the year of its performance) without prologue, epilogue or chorus; that group of texts only reached print in the 'good' version of the play which came out in 1623. Those 1623 stage-orations, however, are less likely to be additions to *Henry V* than sections removed from it: James Bednarz produces parallels between

Henry V's prologue and chorus and Ben Jonson's *Every Man Out of his Humour* (1600) that date the stage-orations and chorus to 1599, overturning recent ideas that the passages entered the play late.[124] That would mean, though, that these texts had dropped away from *Henry V* by the time it was published in the year of its performance; the prologue and chorus, seemingly so crucial to an understanding of the play – because, like other such counter-narratives, they provide a different angle on the story to that of the dialogue – seem to have left the text almost immediately. In fact this is obvious, for time-specific references in one chorus, seemingly to the Earl of Essex, mean that these interim texts are relevant only during a very narrow period, usually isolated as between March and June 1599.[125] Perhaps the complex text was for the first-performance audience especially; perhaps it was for court – but whoever it was aimed at, the pattern is the same as that visible also in the story of the stage-orations and choruses to Richard Farrant's *The Warres of Cyrus King of Persia*. In the single print-run of that play there is, stranded in the middle of act 2, a seriously misplaced prologue. Headed 'To the audience', the prologue links itself to a no-longer-extant singing 'chorus' as co-commentators prepared to express a different opinion from the play's and speak out 'against' the hero: 'In stead of mournefull plaints our Chorus sings,/Although it be against the upstart guise.'[126] Here, too, prologue and chorus will have enriched the text, presenting another viewpoint to the narrative; here too, these additional texts, designed to be spoken together, were to have left the play together – and logically had to do so, as the one refers to the other; this surviving prologue-trace was, it seems, blindly copied by the printers where it had slipped in to the manuscript (a further illustration, obviously, of the fact that the prologue was on a different document from the play).

There are, in other words, particular types of text that stand separate from the main story and that can be added and removed aside from issues of wholesale revision. These might alter performance by performance: as prologues are generally linked to first days, choruses on occasion may, too, belong only to first or special days, not to all performances – or, rather, any 'removable' text might sometimes, perhaps often, have been removed (for any removable text can also be returned at any time).

AUTHORSHIP OF PROLOGUES AND EPILOGUES

Because of the separation of stage-orations from play, it can never be assumed that the author of a prologue or epilogue (or chorus) is the author (or are the authors) of the play. Stage-orations could, after all, be created entirely independently from the playscript, and at a different time, for unlike the dialogue they do not seem to have required official approval before performance. From the time of Queen Anne comes the complaint that 'Prologues, Epilogues, & Songs wch are often indecent, are brought upon ye Stage wth out his [ye Master of ye Revels'] License,' but it is notable that none of Herbert's records of the 1620s–40s are for new prologues or epilogues (and see chapter 8 for the Master of the Revels' generally light touch); one of the few manuscripts that retains Revels' imprimatur, *Believe as You List*, did not include its prologue or epilogue when sent for approval: those texts are written in later and placed *after* Herbert's hand-written licence; they are in a different handwriting from the rest of the play.[127] This meant that the prologue-writer was not even bound to have his text ready by the time the play was.

This will have been a product of the fact that prologues and epilogues were regularly written by someone other than the playwright. For the creating of these all-important passages was sometimes, from the first, given to a skilled prologue-writer; not all playwrights were good at the kind of obsequious pleading that was elemental to the stage-oration form. Fletcher was not a sharp prologue-writer, for instance, and anecdote records that he shied away from writing them, calling them 'needless and lame excuses'; one story relates how, demanded by the actors to provide a special prologue for a court performance, he in 'his indigna-tion rendred them . . . the onely bad Lines his modest Thalia was ever humbled with'; another relates how Fletcher 'scorn'd this crowching veine':

> We stabb'd him with keene daggers when we pray'd
> Him write a Preface to a Play well made.
> He could not write these toyes; 'twas easier farre,
> To bring a Felon to appeare at th'Barre.[128]

From Henslowe's 'diary' onwards examples of playwrights commissioned for their stage-orations alone abound. Middleton, in 1602, was paid by Henslowe to write a prologue and epilogue 'for the corte' performance of Greene's *Friar Bacon*; Dekker was paid for a prologue and epilogue to a play – seemingly some kind of revival – called *Pontius Pilate*.[129] Later Heywood's 'Prologues and Epilogues [are] here inserted' into his version of Marlowe's *Jew of Malta*; 'a Dialogue . . . by way of Prologue' is 'newly added' to Fletcher's *Faithful Shepheardesse* for 1632 performance before the King and Queen at Whitehall; while three manuscripts survive detailing

'The Prologue and Epilogue to [Middleton's] ye Game att Chesse by Pooley [Cowley?]', different from those printed or in the various manuscript texts to the play.[130] Later still, during the interregnum, William Cavendish was criticised for the fact that 'in the ruines of his Country' he found the leisure time 'to make Prologues and Epilogues' for plays by a runaway English company performing in Paris.[131]

When there was a resident or regular company dramatist, of course, he was likely to be a main prologue- and epilogue-writer: writing stage-orations may have been (perhaps like writing the text of the playbills) an aspect of his job as company wordsmith. Richard Brome, defending the accusation that he had breached his contract with Salisbury Court, insisted that he had worked hard for the company even if he had not come up with his full quota of plays, detailing that he had made 'many prologues and epilogues . . . songs, and one induction' for their productions.[132] Shakespeare, too, may have shared this responsibility for his company. 'W. S.' 'set foorth' and revised the old Queen's Men play of *Locrine*, according to its printed title-page; that reviser was undoubtedly responsible for its epilogue which, with its reference to the 'eight and thirty years' of Queen Elizabeth's reign, has a considerably later date than the rest of the play: as Sonia Massai maintains, there is every reason to think that Shakespeare as a company man was reviser/epilogue-writer of this text.[133] The most obvious place to look for fresh Shakespeare passages is amongst the prologues and epilogues of other Chamberlain's Men/ King's Men plays.

On other occasions playhouses, or perhaps playwrights (or, just possibly, printers), were content, rather than trying to write new prologues or epilogues, simply to reuse old ones that had worked before. The prose prologue printed at the start of the 1635 edition of Beaumont's *Knight of the Burning Pestle*, 'Where the Bee can sucke no Honey', is an appropriation, with one sentence removed, of the prologue published with Lyly's *Sapho and Phao* in 1584; while Dekker's *Wonder of a Kingdom* and Rowley's *All's Lost by Lust* are also published with exactly the same prologue even though it refers specifically to instructions from 'the poet' – 'Thus from the Poet, I am bid to say . . .'.[134] Beaumont and Fletcher's *The Tragedy of Thierry*, published in 1649, contains not only a prologue taken from their *Noble Gentleman*, but an epilogue taken from Shirley's *The Changes*, published in 1632.[135] If the playhouse did reuse stage-orations on occasion, that was because it was less concerned with the connection between play and stage-oration than with the ability of a single, good oration to get a play approved.

Once a play was in revival, its prologue and epilogue were almost universally written by someone who was not the author. The prologues James Shirley wrote to be spoken in Ireland in the 1630s (he was there between 1636 and 1640) are for plays by, amongst others, Jonson ('A Prologue to the Alchimist Acted there'), Middleton ('A Prologue to a Play there; Call'd, No wit to a Womans'), and Fletcher ('A Prologue to Mr Fletchers Play in Ireland' and 'A Prologue to another of Master Fletcher's Playes there') – prologues he kept and published even when he could not entirely remember the specific plays' names, as with 'To another Play there'.[136] Davenant in a 1638 book of poems prints his own 'Prologue to a reviv'd Play of Mr Fletchers call'd The Woman-hater', beginning 'Ladies! take't as a secret in your Eare' – it is a carefully written rhymed text which became linked enough to the play to be printed before that drama in its 1649 publication, yet it differs entirely from the prose prologue printed with the 1607 edition of the same play, which had been specifically against the rhyme form: 'A Prologue in Verse is . . . stale.'[137] As prologues were revised, revived, changed and added, as well as lost, at a pace of their own, there is no reason to be sure that plays published with stage-orations some years after performance are being printed with the 'original' prologues and epilogues by their authors.

PLAYERS OF PROLOGUES AND EPILOGUES

Some of the fluctuation around head and tail pieces related to the fact that the little texts performed a series of such specific theatrical duties that they barely 'translated' to the printed page at all. The visual effect of the Prologue and the rousing nature of the Epilogue are of the stage, and perhaps some authors were content to leave them there.

Understanding the Prologue and Epilogue in the theatre, however, elucidates their relationship to the staged play, which in turn explains the tension between oration and play that affects survival into print. Whether by the author of the play or not, the prologue and epilogue were in a sense anti-author, for they were spoken not just by ritualised characters but by ritualised and phoney versions of 'the playwright'.

In Heywood's *Foure Prentises of London*, the Prologue describes himself as wearing a 'long blacke velvet cloke'; this remained regulation wear well into the 1630s: the Prologue to Davenant's *Love and Honour* (1649) sports a 'grave long old cloak'; and the woman prologue-speaker to Shirley's *Coronation* (1640) declares she has the same rights as 'he/that with . . . a long black cloak,/With a starch'd face, and supple leg hath spoke/Before the Plays the twelvemonth'.[138] So far so good: the cloak reminds the audience that the stage-oration is something between a beggar and a scholar. His other features were also standardised. His stiff, colourful beard and fixed, whitened face are regularly spoken of – he is called 'the man in the long cloak with the coloured beard'; the man with 'a starch'd formall Beard and Cloake'; the man with the 'bearde so starched, and . . . countenance so set, that [he is] meet for a prologue before a Comedy'; and even the man 'with a smoothe Anus countenance, [like] a prologue to a play'.[139] It is the final item of dress, also entirely standard, however, that indicated 'who' the stage-oration notionally was: the wreath of laurels – 'bays', as it was sometimes known – worn around the temples. This too makes its way into the analogies of the time, so that '*Some*', writes Rowlands, '(as bold *Prologues* do to *Playes*),/With *Garlonds* have their *Fore-heads* bound'; Chapman describes how 'One Prologue here, puts on her wreath with ease'; Randolph advises, 'Burne that withered Bayes,/And with fresh Laurell crowne thy sacred Temples.'[140] 'Bays' symbolised poetic creativity; they were descended from the garland given to reward a conqueror or poet (*OED*, 'bay' n 1.3). So the Prologue crowned in bays represented more than just a triumphant person – he represented the triumphant 'author' of the text.[141]

Yet prologues were of course enacted by performers, whose most notable feature was their depersonalised and ritualised appearance: they were playable by anyone, and were self-consciously unlike any individual real person. This was because 'the poet' the Prologue stood in for was not – and was seldom intended to be – the actual playwright. He was, rather, a theatrical fiction, acting occasionally as though he wrote the plays (the Prologue to Harding's (unperformed) *Sicily and Naples* says, 'thus your Poet stands,/Expecting his owne destiny from your hands'), but more usually as though he did not – but knows who did: 'Thus from the Poet am I bid to say . . .'; 'hee [the playwright] doth now,/In mee present his service'.[142] The Prologue is, however, *visually* the 'author' of the play and takes on himself *theatrical* ownership of the text. He offers the play in the most positive way possible, standing wreathed in laurels won for the success of other plays (by other playwrights), and remembered fondly by the audience for the last new play 'he' introduced – and the one before. He it is who begs acceptance for the text in its youthful form, and he it is who takes responsibility for its faults; he also represents the range of special first-performance events that can happen to the play.

As there was a Prologue uniform that united most Prologues together and to each other as a single across-play character, even those eschewing traditional Prologue garb simply adopted another kind of standard wear that, in a different way, symbolised their function. This was the more combative 'armed Prologue' costume, worn by a speaker who visibly expected the worst from a critical audience; it was particularly popular during turbulent times. Such is the Prologue to Jonson's *Poetaster* (1602), who wears a 'forc't defense' against his potentially inimical audience; and the Prologue to Glapthorne's *Wit in a Constable*, whose speaker (the actor who is to play the part of the constable) appears already in office and armed for the same reason.[143] Even then, though, Prologues did and said similar things: they were seldom supposed to be unique, and combative Prologues in one playhouse were matched by combative Prologues in another. As the world-weary Prologue to Fletcher's *Humorous Lieutenant* (1647) put it, ultimately the 'Prologue, usuall to a play,/Is tied to . . . an old forme of Petition/. . . The cloakes we weare, the leggs we make, the place/We stand in, must be one.'[144] Prologues were instantly identifiable as such, linked in appearance to a long line of Prologues, rather than to the particular play they were introducing; the 'same' pretend author introduced all new plays.

The reason why the actual playwright, though a feature of the Prologue's address, remains so often unnamed in the oration is part of the theatrical reauthoring process: the 'author' represented by the Prologue is more important than the actual author. So the real writer, when referred to at all, is 'poet', 'writer', or 'play-maker', a function of his job rather than a named individual. Only when a writer is dead is a stage-oration likely to state who the true playwright of the play was. But the Prologue himself, on the other hand, sometimes does have a name, and a writer's name at that – though, if so, his title relates to the fiction of the play, not the fact, like 'Bardh' in *The Valiant Welshman*. As Eggers indicates, it was Gower in *Pericles*, not Shakespeare or Wilkins, who carried bays and dressed in the Prologue's cloak (see the drawing of Gower on the title-page of George Wilkins' 1608 *Painfull Adventures of Pericles*), heralding the authorship and success of *Pericles*.[145] In a number of ways prologues (also epilogues) were thus the least playwright-related bits of the text, irrespective of who wrote them, illustrated by the fact that a collaborative play, by Beaumont and Fletcher for instance, would still be introduced by a single Prologue-author.[146]

The Epilogue in look, movement and frame of reference also shared his approach and devices not with the plays to which he was attached, but with other Epilogues and with Prologues. This is why the famous Epilogue to *2 Henry IV* links himself not just with Shakespeare's play but also with another that he recently concluded and that the audience damned: he, the Epilogue, is the same character; the plays, however, are different – 'I was lately here in the end of a displeasing Play, to pray your Patience for it, and to promise you a Better.' Fascinatingly, that Epilogue then goes on to express the hope that this play will be accepted as payment for the last, once again speaking as though he has authored all the plays his theatre has offered ('I meant . . . to pay you with this'), a hope that sits oddly with his later distinction between 'our humble author' and himself (l.1b). Like Prologues, Epilogues too might come dressed as beggars or rigged up in defensive armour. The Epilogue deals slightly differently with the fact/fiction of his situation, however, sometimes simply standing up from his position on stage and directly addressing the audience whilst still within the story being performed, as 'Rosalind' in Shakespeare's *As You Like It*, 'Prospero' in *The Tempest*, or 'Ulysses', left alone on the stage at the end of Heywood's 1612–13 *Iron Age Part II* (1632): 'since I am the man soly reserv'd/Accept me for the Authors Epilogue'.[147] Like Prologues, though, this simply indicates that the fictional story is more important than the fact of authorship. The phrase 'Author's Epilogue', and the 'humble Author' of *2 Henry IV*, reveal Epilogues might equally represent an all-purpose 'author'.

Bearing this in mind, the first showing of a new public theatre play emerges as a site of division between the real author and a 'theatrical' one, and not just because of their rival ownership of the play. For Prologues and Epilogues also allowed textual criticism, textual change and textual revision that actual playwrights could find difficult to take.

The subject becomes the very matter out of which prologues and epilogues are made, the phoney authors apologizing for, or goading, the real one 'listning behind the arras, to heare what will become on's Play'; or 'pensive in the Tyring-house to heare Your Censures of his Play'; or waiting 'like a subtle Spie' in order 'to heare his destinie:/Just i'th pav'd-Entry as you passe; the place/Where first you mention your dislike, or grace'.[148] The playwright's state of first-performance nerves as he awaited the result of the trial was relished and pitied. He was described 'stand[ing] within biting his nayls' as 'Sometimes his hope, sometimes his fear prevails'; and it was a standard theatre joke that a nervous playwright could not distinguish between the opening of bottled ale and a hiss.[149] So a poet's 'shakings and quakinges, towardes the latter end of [his] new play' are described in the dialogue of *The Woman Hater*, where 'he standes peeping betwixt the curtaines, so fearefully, that a bottle of Ale cannot be opened, but he thinkes some body hisses'.[150] From the prologue onwards, the genuine author saw the play as a series of carefully defined hurdles to be got over. 'You'd smile', says one Prologue of his playwright, 'to see, how he do's vex and shake,/Speakes naught but if the Prologue does but take,/Or the first Act were past the Pikes once, then –/Then hopes and Joys, then frowns and fears agen,' though Brooke adds a cautionary note: that plays can still be, as he feelingly puts it, 'exploded, though the Prologue be never so good, and promising'.[151] Speech by speech, the prologue depicts a playwright conscious of, and terrified by, the opinion of the audience; one prologue describes the author standing with his cloak and hat muffling his head 'to hinder from his eare,/The scorns and censures he may shortly heare'.[152] And yet this prologue broadcasts the author's fear whilst at the same time reminding the audience of the right they have paid extra for – the right to scorn, censure, mew, hiss and throw apples. The Prologue is a contradiction, allowing the very things that he begs should not happen.

The division between Epilogue and actual author is depicted feelingly in the close of Shirley's *The Cardinal.* The idea here is that the real writer, standing in the tiring-room to hear how his play is doing, has thrust the actor playing the Epilogue onto the stage with too much force. One 'author' pushes another. So the Epilogue decides to be revenged on 'Mr Poet' with the audience's help:

> I have a teeming mind to be reveng'd.
> You may assist, and not be seen in't now.
> If you please Gentlemen, for I do know
> He listens to the issue of his cause,
> But blister not your hands in his applause,
> Your private smile, your nod, or hum, to tell
> My fellows, that you like the business well;
> And when without a clap you go away,
> I'l drink a small-be[e]r health to his second day;
> And break his heart, or make him swear, and rage
> He'l write no more for the unhappy Stage.

At the last minute, he relents:

> But that's too much, so we should lose; faith shew it;
> And if you like his play, 't[i]s as well, he knew it.[153]

The epilogue is startling in its brusqueness given that Shirley, a well-known prologue- and epilogue-writer as has been seen, almost certainly wrote it. But as a professional writer he would have known that the audience's opinion could be shaped by the prologue and epilogue (and that siding with the audience against the playwright might be just the kind of joke it liked); and he would have known also that prologues and epilogues, spoken as they were by players, had a player's stake in the play's success, not a writer's.

The epilogue's final repentance, as quoted above, is barbed: it ultimately decides against losing the author his 'second day', only because the actors too would lose out if that were the case. Careful actors might even tactically distance themselves from the play in its early days; describing a 'common player' Stephens writes disdainfully of someone so ready to take on the audience's opinion that he will not risk praising the play he is in 'till he hath either spoken, or heard the *Epilogue*: neither dares he entitle good things *Good*, unless hee be heartned on by the multitude' – until, that is to say, he knows that the play has taken with the audience.[154] In many ways prologues and epilogues were about the concerns of the playhouse on the first day, as much as the concerns of the author for his benefit. Well might the play need stage-orations, and need them to succeed in performance; the actors only needed a stage-oration to succeed in its own right, so that if the play *were* 'displeasing' the reputation of the acting company would not suffer as a result: a poet's failure must not pull down the players. Hence the division: playwrights and players did not have the same stake in the play's success and prologues and epilogues were conflicted features of that.

CONCLUSION

As has been argued, in performance (at least after *c.* 1600) stage-orations broadcasted a play's virginity and its author's fear, and were therefore a site of tension between author and play. Plays in performance were in some ways more comfortable without prologues and epilogues, though that had implications for the play's self-presentation. A play in performance with a prologue/epilogue looked like another play performed with them and unlike a play without: new plays resembled other new plays; and old successful plays resembled other old successful plays. Obvious as that may sound, it is telling to realise that a play in its first performance resembled other, different plays in first performance, rather than itself in subsequent performance. This is bound to have its ramifications, too, for a play on the page.

The presence or absence of stage-orations in a printed book made a statement in itself situating the reader on or not on a specific performance day with all the ramifications that came with it. It can be broadly suggested that a printed text *with* one or other (or both) prologue and epilogue promotes itself consciously or unconsciously as an exciting, fresh 'new' play, with all the implications for danger that that suggests; or as a freshly designed version of an old play (a revival), with all that that suggests. And plays with courtly prologues or epilogues are, obviously, not just presenting themselves as exclusive: they are asking the readers to imagine an event at which they were not actually able to be present. So prologues and epilogues are always 'event'-related in a way the rest of the text may not actually be. Though prologues and epilogues were enjoyed, having no stage-orations will inevitably have made a comment too: it will have been a healthy sign indicative of a lasting text. Stage-orations on the page not only imply that a play is in a particular form, but contribute to – and in part create – that form, irrespective of the real 'reason' for the preservation/loss of those documents.

The main problem with extending this argument to the nature of the play so flanked (is a play with a prologue actually in its 'new' form? is a play without a prologue in its 'approved' form?) is that, as illustrated, stage-orations so often have a different heritage from the play to which they are attached that they may reveal nothing about the underlying nature of the text they adjoin: they are only undoubtedly revelatory about themselves. More often than not a play's dialogue text is manifestly in a form in which it was written for prompter or by author, but its prologue is for a different, courtly or revised version of the play. It becomes clear, indeed, that anyone who tries to date a play from prologue, epilogue and, by extension, some choruses or interim entertainments is on dangerous ground: dating a prologue, epilogue, interim entertainment or chorus may well date just that text, not the play it flanks, for any text written and circulated separately could drop out and be replaced by others, or with none, at a different rate from the rest of the play. For a similar reason, including such texts, when they are present, in stylometric analyses is problematic: prologues and epilogues may well have been written by company authors, or at least different authors from the rest of the play, and, if written for revival by the play's author, may have been penned some years later.

What can be said is that critics writing about Shakespeare, and assuming prologues and epilogues were permanently part of the text, might profitably reconsider their position.[155] Shakespeare too straddles that vague 1600 divide, but his surviving prologues and epilogues manifest most of the concerns covered in this chapter, so offering some telling comments on their attachment to the plays to which they are latched.

They are full of nervous anxiety about what the judgemental audience will think of the play, and whether it will be 'approved' or condemned – typical first-performance concerns. The prologue to *Henry V* asks the audience 'Gently to heare, kindly to judge our Play' (TLN 35); the epilogue to *2 Henry IV* says that Falstaff will be seen again only if he has not already been 'kill'd' by the audience's 'hard Opinions' (TLN 3347); the prologue to *Henry VIII* hopes that 'the play may passe' (TLN 12); *As You Like It*'s epilogue hopes that the play 'may please' (TLN 2791). And perhaps they do more than that. At the end of *A Midsummer Night's Dream*, Puck asks the spectators not to 'reprehend' him; he also offers the promise, 'If you pardon, we will mend' (TLN 2218, 2214). This seems to go somewhat further than a simple request to 'save' the play. It suggests the possibility for first-performance revision too. Shakespeare's stage-orations seem to have been as mutable, and as threatening to their texts, as anyone else's.

CHAPTER 5

Songs and masques

INTRODUCTION

Characters in Marston plays keep on calling for songs. 'Wee must have the descant you made upon our names, ere you depart,' says Catzo to Flavia in Marston's *Antonio and Mellida*, and it is obvious why: 'Catzo' signified 'a man's privy member', and 'Dildo', his fellow page's name, speaks for itself.[1] The exchange leads up to a moment of song that will titillate the audience whilst simultaneously introducing the bleak sexuality of the play. Other characters in *Antonio and Mellida* also exhibit their natures as well as their emotions through the medium of song. The grief-stricken Andrugio proposes, 'Let's have a song,' though the song he hears will, in the event, be incapable of mimicking his sorrows: 'and thou felt'st my griefe . . . Thou would'st have strook division to the height;/And made the life of musicke breath'.[2] Throughout the play, songs extend beyond their tunes and words: they are important dramatic devices, depicting and creating mood, enhancing characterisation and defining emotional states; Sabol writes of the 'highly dramatic – at times even melodramatic' use Marston makes of songs; O'Neill calls him 'a writer-musician'.[3]

What is extraordinary in the circumstances is that hardly any of the actual words to Marston songs survive. The two songs discussed above, which are so carefully prepared for in their text, are lost: all that stands to mark the place where they should be is the single capitalised word 'CANTANT'. This is particularly surprising as Marston was one of the writers who carefully prepared his plays for publication – *Antonio and Mellida* itself has an irritated dedication written to the 'Lord protector of oppressed innocence', 'No-body', flirting with the worth (and lack of worth) of a printed playbook.[4] Under the circumstances, the words to the songs might be expected to be preserved as a part of Marston's 'defence' of his play in print, or as an exemplar of the writing skill he boasts, yet 'cantant', 'cantat', 'song', or 'the song', with no lyrics supplied, are substituted for over thirty songs in the Marston canon.[5] Marston's reliance on songs that are now lost has had a lasting negative affect on his standing amongst critics, for his plays, as he presented them to posterity, lead with disappointing frequency to charged emotional moments the cores of which no longer exist.

Immediately this raises questions about the way early modern play-books were prepared by their author-playwrights for a readership. A current critical obsession with the 'literary' nature of playbooks has carried a number of assumptions with it, not least the idea that an authorially prepared text is more 'complete' than a text that is not; indeed, it is the over-long nature of some of Shakespeare's plays that is used as 'proof' that they were prepared for the page.[6] Yet Marston is not the only playwright who provided his scripts for the printing house and neglected to include his songs in them. Seventeen of the songs called for in Shirley's dramatic works, often fronted with dedicatory material by their author, are not supplied. Chapman's songs, mainly lost, are absent from plays in which the author took especial care. There are no songs preserved at all in *All Fooles*, though a manuscript poem by Chapman written on the flyleaf to one of the issues of the playbook gives the piece 'my passport'.[7] And even if, as is sometimes suspected, this particular handwritten sonnet is a forgery by John Payne Collier, Chapman's concern with the publication of his plays is independently verified through the printed dedications that, like those of Marston and Shirley, are used to bolster his editions: in the front of *The Revenge of Bussy D'Ambois*, to give just one example, he boasts that his play represents an 'autentical Tragedie'.[8] Absent songs cannot therefore be taken as a sign of an uncaring author; rather, they demand a rethinking of what constituted textual completion or lack of completion as far as an author was concerned.

A careful look at printed and manuscript plays of the period more generally reveals that, irrespective of whether their plays were prepared for the press by the author, or acquired by some other means, most play-wrights of the period have 'lost' songs. The 1647 folio of Beaumont and Fletcher's *Comedies and Tragedies* requires thirty songs it does not supply – a number that is reduced to twenty by the 1679 publication of a new folio, *Fifty Comedies and Tragedies*, bolstered with prologues, epilogues and songs 'not in the former Edition' (and not necessarily authorial), donated by an anonymous gentleman.[9] Of the eight plays undoubtedly by Lyly and printed in his lifetime, seemingly with his consent, only *The Woman in the Moone* provides song lyrics. The other plays feature no songs, though when a small collected works of Lyly's *Six Court Comedies* was published years later by Blount, twenty-one songs were added to what was otherwise a reissue in a single volume of the earlier quartos.[10] It is still a matter of dispute as to whether these songs are recovered 'lost songs'; new or different songs written for the plays in revivals; or even songs specially composed to 'complete' the plays for publication, by, it has been suggested, Dekker.[11] Whose songs these are, and from when they date, will be discussed later; here it is simply important to note that Lyly is another writer whose texts made their way to the printing house during his lifetime, and potentially under a judgemental authorial eye, yet lacking the songs they had contained in performance.

Shakespeare's texts as a whole preserve more songs than most, though they indicate at least six lost songs, and perhaps more: the Welsh song in *1 Henry IV* is encapsulated in the stage-direction 'Heere the Lady sings a Welsh Song' (TLN 1790); there are two witches' songs in *Macbeth* that stop at the first line, '*Come away, come away, &c.*' (TLN 1467) and '*Blacke Spirits, &c.*' (TLN 1572) – the complete songs are only known because they exist in an independent source, Middleton's play *The Witch* (from which they have been borrowed).[12] *Love's Labour's Lost* is missing a song of which the title may or may not be preserved. Don Adriano asks his page Moth to 'Warble childe' and 'make passionate my sense of hearing'; Moth's response is a single incomprehensible word, 'Concolinel', to which Don Adriano responds 'Sweete Ayer' (1598, c3b). Whether 'Concolinel' is the title of a lost song (perhaps from the Irish 'Can cailin gheal', 'sing maiden fair', or the French 'Quand Colinelle', 'when Colinel'), or whether it represents some other corruption, a song has been sung by the time Don Adriano comes up with his 'Sweete Ayer' response, but is, as ever, missing from the playbook.

A Midsummer Night's Dream, meanwhile, contains no missing songs, or one, or perhaps two, depending on how they are counted: Oberon demands that the fairies sing 'this Ditty after me' (TLN 2179); Titania then requests them to 'rehearse this song by roate' (TLN 2180). There follows a heading, '*The Song*'. In the Folio of the play, the lines after '*The Song*', 'Now untill the breake of day' (TLN 2185), are indented, in italics and without a speech-prefix, as though they *are* the song Titania has asked for. But in the earlier quarto (1600), the same passage is set in roman letters and given to Oberon to speak (H4a). As 'Now' implies a resumption of speech after a song, Oberon probably does speak these words rather than sing them: 'The Song' is, then, simply the familiar title given to a missing lyric, though the Folio compositor, assuming or hoping that the subsequent lines constituted the words, set them as such. Samuel Johnson proposed that a second ditty had also been lost:

The truth is that two songs are lost. The series of the scene is this: . . . Oberon enters, and calls his fairies to a song, which song is apparently wanting in all the copies. Next Titania leads another song, which is indeed lost like the former, though the editors have endeavoured to find it.

His reading is that the text proposes a song battle between the two fairies, and that both their contributions have dropped away.[13]

Finally, there are two songs lost from Shakespeare plays that, like the lost Marston songs, would have given important emotional weight to their scenes. In *Pericles*, Marina is asked to come up with a song that will rouse the melancholy King. Later in the scene she will discover she is his daughter; at this stage, however, she knows only her own sufferings, and it is on that level that she identifies with Pericles and tries to draw him out:

MAR. Sir I will use my utmost skill in his recoverie, provided that none but
           I and my companion maid be suffered to come neere him.
LYS. Come, let us leave her, and the Gods make her prosperous.
           The Song.
LYS. Marke[d] he your Musicke? (1609, H3b)

Like other 'art' songs, Marina's lyrics will doubtless have reflected on the themes of the play – perhaps family, or love, or loss – which to the audience will have commented poignantly on both singer and listener. Much the same can be said of the lost 'sleepy Tune' that cannot lull Brutus' guilty conscience in *Julius Caesar*, and that instead sends its singer to sleep: it is heralded simply as '*Musicke, and a Song*' (TLN 2277–8), but is so carefully framed as to suggest that its words too will have contributed 'to the mood and character' of the scene and conditioned the understanding 'not primarily of their singer, but of the persons to and for whom [it was] performed'.[14]

One other Shakespeare song suffered a near miss. The 'willow song' in *Othello* is evidently prepared for and yet absent from the 1622 Quarto of that play, in which Desdemona explains how her maid Barbary died singing 'a song of willow . . . that . . . to night,/Will not goe from my mind' (L2b) without ever providing the words (rendering this reference extraneous). In the 1623 Folio, however, the passage is expanded and Desdemona sings a significant portion of the song which reflects on her emotions and bleakly foretells what is to happen: 'The poore Soule sat singing, by a Sicamour tree./Sing all a greene Willough . . . I call'd my Love false Love: but what said he then?/Sing Willough, &c./If I court mo women, you'le couch with mo men' (TLN 3011–26). It is obvious that both texts 'intend' this important song to be sung, but only one supplies it: the 'willow song' owes its preservation to the fact that a different source text from the Quarto, containing the song's content, was used for the Folio *Othello*.

Were songs lost because they were not authorial, so that playwrights did not care to retain them? That is provably not the case. In James Shirley's 1638 play *The Dukes Mistris*, Horatio raves about a song that he has written 'to shew I hate all hansome women', finally reciting it in full – though all the playbook supplies at this moment are the words '*He reads*'.[15] Shirley's 1646 *Poems*, however, contain a verse called 'One that loved none but deformed Women', which also survives in two musical settings of the period; these are self-evidently the words to the play's missing song:

> What should my Mistris do with hair?
> Her frizling, curling I can spare;
> But let her forehead be well plough'd,
> And Hempe within the furrowes sow'd . . .[16]

Similarly Heywood, who remembered to include songs written by the actor who played Valerius in his 1608 *Rape of Lucrece*, appears to have forgotten at least one (and quite possibly more) of his own lyrics. He starts his playbook with a stern preface: he is printing the text 'in his native habit' because he is annoyed by the numerous corruptions published under his name that he has not overseen.[17] Yet the native habit – the manuscript he was working from – must have lacked the songs, for it contains an exchange between Brutus and Horatius in which the former asks to hear a song 'whilst we may, for I divine thy musique and my madness are both short liv'd'; no song is provided.[18] In the 1630 *fourth* edition of the play, however, also published by Heywood, words are finally supplied. Beginning '*Packe clowdes away, and welcome day*', they are definitely by the author, for he publishes them elsewhere as one of his Epithalamiums in *Pleasant Dialogues and Dramma's* of 1637.[19] A further ditty, also not provided until the 1630 edition, is '*The* Spaniard *loves his antient slop*'; again, it is authorial, for it also occurs in another Heywood play, *A Challenge for Beautie* (1636), though in this case the song may have been added at a later date.[20]

That songs often circulated in a different way from – and so 'outside' – playbooks, meaning that they were easily lost, is the irresistible conclusion to be drawn from these instances. But the observation begs as many questions as it asks; questions that this chapter will address. How did so many songs anticipated in playbooks come to be lost? Given that so many were lost, how were so many others *not* lost but published along with their texts? How can songs be lost for one edition and found for another? If songs circulated away from their plays, what does this say about the moment when their lyrics are written, the moment when their tune is written, and the moment when the play's dialogue is written? Behind these questions are others. Did the same people who 'owned' plays 'own' the words of their songs? Is it even the case that the people who wrote plays wrote their songs? When plays were revised or updated, how often was that specifically along song lines? Finally, what can be concluded about printed playbooks that so regularly lose, misplace or forget author-ial passages, and what is to be thought of the 'literary' qualities of texts that so regularly lack their emotional heart?

EXPLANATIONS FOR SONGS LOST AND FOUND

Few critics have considered the phenomenon of lost songs as a group – they are, after all, lost – and those who have addressed them at all curiously call them 'blank' songs, though 'blank' signifies two varieties of paper both very much present: the 'blank' in theatrical use was a real piece of paper that lacked genuine writing (see 'Scrolls', chapter 6); the 'blank' in non-theatrical use was a piece of printed paper with gaps to be filled in manuscript – an indulgence, an indenture, etc. This chapter, using the term 'lost songs', will consider lost and found songs that are specifically written for the play performed. It will not look at the more general use of song in act breaks at the private theatres, assuming that any of a handful of theatre songs might have been adopted for such occasions, and that 'the play' was not shaped around them; when the specific words to act-break songs make their way into playbooks, however, they will be borne in mind along with all other play-specific lyrics. Similarly, it will not and cannot consider the moment given over to 'random song' indicated in the text by such stage-directions as 'He plays and sings any odde toy, and Orlando wakes'; '*After a solemne service, . . . musical songs of marriages, or a maske, or what prettie triumph you list*'; 'A songe Iff you will'; 'after some short song, enter'.[21] On such occasions, what the song is to be, and who will sing it, has obviously been left to the playhouse itself to decide. This is interesting in its own right, showing that playwrights were, on occasion, ready to submit a play 'incomplete' in terms of song, and quite happy to let the theatre use its own judgement on the matter; it also illustrates how the theatre must have had not simply singers but songs that could be drawn on for 'random' occasions. But it is the poignancy of a play-specific lost song that will be the focus here, for such songs are part of the meaning of that play – but part of the meaning that has been allowed to slip away. Unless it is thought that songs 'mattered' less than words, and plays do not suggest that, what must be confronted is that songs important to the play in which they had featured were simply vulnerable to different vicissitudes from the rest of the text.

Puzzled commentators, searching to explain how crucial songs are missing, usually ask their questions on a play-by-play basis; as a result, a number of misguided explanations that do not make sense of 'lost songs' generally still have currency. One such explanation is that the musical composer may have technically owned an entire song – not just the music he wrote for it, but also the words he inherited. The playwright, the argument then goes, could not publish his songs as they were not his to print.[22] But the reverse is in fact the case. So little control did composers have over their music, or, when they wrote them, their lyrics, that words by composer-lyricists – who, of all people, might be expected to want to guard their creations – are regularly printed without ascription in other people's plays: playwrights did not consider 'ownership' of a song any bar to publication. 'Have you never a song of maister *Dowlands* making?' asks a Page in *The Returne from Pernassus*, soliciting from within a play the singing of a musician-lyricist's song; and snippets of that popular composer's music are to be found throughout texts of the period: William Percy in his manuscript play *Necromantes* cannot even decide whether or not to adopt a Dowland tune – he has written some fresh words, but on second thoughts realises Dowland's music to a different set of lyrics might be better; he requests three 'maids' to dance using the 'song underwritten, or . . . some ditty to the tune of dowlands cock [probably 'Lachrimae Coactae'], which may do well, and best in this Place, els . . . some other note to this our ditty, if so it may be'.[23] Dowland's words, meanwhile, as with words by other composers, regularly find themselves, unacknowledged, in plays. 'Now O Now I Needs Must Part' is correctly printed in *Everie Woman in her Humor* and misquoted in *Eastward Hoe*; lines from 'sleepe wayward thoughts' too are printed in *Everie Woman* and *Eastward Hoe*; part of 'Wilt Thou Unkind Thus Reave Me' and part of 'Sorrow Stay' are in *The Knight of the Burning Pestle*; and 'Say Love if ever Thou Didst Find' is parodied in Chapman's *Widdowes Teares*.[24]

Robert Jones, the composer, was used in just the same way. Marston, though he produced lamentably few of his own songs, provides in a comic 'Dutch' accent a chunk of 'My Mistris sings no other song' ('mine Mettre sing non oder song') in *Dutch Courtezan*, though its tune and words were both by Jones – the song is also twice quoted in *Everie Woman in Her Humor*; Dekker and Webster's *North-ward Hoe* picks up on a different Jones song, 'My Thought this other night' and parodies it; *The Knight of the Burning Pestle* and *Twelfth Night* (TLN 806–9) both quote Jones' 'Farewell, dear love'.[25] Morley, too, provided a resource for playwrights. A snatch of his 'Sing Wee and Chaunt It' is printed in *The Knight of the Burning Pestle*; and *As You Like It*'s 'It was a Lover, and his lasse' (TLN 2546) is likely to be a Morley song too – he set its music and printed it in his *First Booke of Ayres*, 1600, but there is every reason to think he is printing his own lyrics as well as his tune; Lindley asks 'how far one might assume that Shakespeare wrote any of the lyrics for songs here and elsewhere'.[26]

Even when songs had not (as the last few quoted had) been printed first under the composer-lyricist's name, they were still treated as fair game by playwrights. The song printed in Middleton's 1608 *A Trick to Catch the Old-One*, '*Let the Usurer cram him, in interest that excell*', was only later published by its composer Thomas Ravenscroft; he appears to have been its lyricist too, for he prints the text with an opening couplet which adds logic to the whole:

> My master is so wise, so wise, that hee's proceeded wittall,
> my Mistres is a foole, a foole, and yet tis the most get-all.
> Let the Usurer cram him in interest that excell . . .[27]

As it seems, the opening couplet had simply been sloughed away by Middleton who, for play reasons, wants the word 'usurer' to be sung in the first line. Other Ravenscroft songs printed in plays before being published by their composer may comprise 'Give us once a drinke', to be found in Marston's *Jacke Drums Entertainment*, though on this occasion perhaps Marston himself wrote the words; and 'Love for such a cherrie lip', which reached print first in Dekker's play *Blurt Master Constable*, but was set by Ravenscroft to words written by his childhood tutor 'Edward Piers [Pearce]', as the composer is careful to record when he prints the piece, twelve years later, under its title 'The Mistris of her Servant'.[28]

So there was no sense that a playwright gave up a song for its composer. On the contrary, the songs that *are* printed in plays often have lyrics written by composers rather than playwrights (how often is hard to gauge: it may be that the words to many more of the songs thought to be by playwrights are actually by composers). Nor is it even that snippets only were fair game, for the composer-writer Campion has the whole of his

'What if a day, or a month, or a yeare' taken and printed without ascription not just in one play but two: Brome's *The Queen and Concubine*, and the anonymous *Philotus* (first quarto only); another set of lyrics to be found in Brome's *Joviall Crew* is thought actually to be by Campion; and the burden to Campion's 'Mistris since you so much desire' ('But a little higher, but a little higher') is sung (and printed) in *Eastward Hoe*; while two lines and a refrain of his 'My love hath vowd' ('If such danger be in playing') are in *The Knight of the Burning Pestle*.[29] As Philip Rosseter's 1601 *Booke of Ayres* – whose contents are divided between Rosseter and Thomas Campion – shows, songbooks provided theatrical source material, and words and music by composers were regularly adopted and adapted for the stage; thirteen pieces subsequently sung in plays for children originate from this book.[30] Songbooks, both printed and in manuscript, *supply* lyrics and tunes (rather than taking them out of circulation) for playwrights and, subsequently, for printed playbooks.

A second explanation offered for the lost songs is, again, to do with ownership. Given that, in the world preceding copyright, 'ownership' did not necessarily reside with the artistic 'creator' – the playwright or the composer – but to whomever had paid for a named piece of text, it is sometimes thought that songs were purposely excised from plays before printing because their content did not legally belong to the publishers. This explanation has been used to justify the loss of the 'willow song' from the Quarto of Shakespeare's *Othello*: the 1622 publisher, it is contended, did not own the willow song's words.[31] This begs the question what happened between 1622, when the Quarto was published, and 1623, when the song was printed in the Folio, to 'release' it: did Blount, publisher of the Folio, enter into financial negotiations to purchase rights for that particular passage of text (but not for the other lost Shakespearean songs)? That could just about be argued: as Blount 'recovered' so many lost Lyly songs, it could be said that he had a particular interest in plays' lyrics. But in neither Shakespeare's Folio nor Lyly's *Sixe Court Comedies* does Blount broadcast his success in reacquiring (or having specifically written for him) the words to the ditties, even though he writes a dedication to Lyly's works strongly associating the playwright with music in an extended analogy. Rather than attributing the absence of the willow song in the Quarto to the publisher's not owning the text, it is more pertinent to consider the blasé way in which it *is* published in the Folio although it is non-authorial: surviving versions of the song, sung from the point of view of a man rather than a woman, are found in more than one broadside from the early seventeenth century.

As a matter of fact, it will be seen that when two versions of a play exist, like *Othello*, and like Lyly's comedies, often one of the books contains songs and the other does not, irrespective of publisher. And, when one of the texts is in print, and one in manuscript, it is as likely to be the manuscript text as the print text that is wary of the songs. It is, for instance, the manuscript of Fletcher's *Humorous Lieutenant* (called *Demetrius and Enanthe* and written by the King's Men scribe Ralph Crane for Sir Kenelm Digby's private reading) that provides merely 'Musiq is heard, and an Antick of litle Fayeries enter, & dance about ye Bowle', while the printed text gives the words, '*Rise from the shades below*'.[32] It is, likewise, the manuscript of William Cavendish's *The Country Captain* that contains only a direction, 'A Song i'th taverne', while, again, the printed text supplies words to that song – '*Come let us throw the dice who shall drinke*' – despite the fact that the song is not by Cavendish but Shirley, and is, furthermore, a text of which its actual author was particularly fond: he published it in his 1646 *Poems* as an intensely visual poem, not a song at all, but a rebus embellished with pictorial illustrations of the dice it describes.[33] Of the two manuscripts of Phineas Fletcher's *Sicelides*, the songs missing from one manuscript, 'Olinda if thou yeeld not now' and 'Hymen, Hymen come', are provided in the other and in the printed text.[34] Conversely, the two manuscripts of Thomas Middleton's *Hengist, King of Kent* contain two songs, 'Boast not of high birth or blood' and 'If in musique were a powre', absent from the printed text; Richard Brome's manuscript for *The English Moore* has a song, '*Love, where is now thy Deitie*', that is simply indicated by 'Song' in the printed text, though the words occasion an entire dramatic argument – 'Call you this mournful. Tis a wanton air./Go y'are a naughty child indeed, Ile whip you/If you give voice unto such notes'; and the manuscript of *Beggars Bush* has the song, 'He ran at me first in the shape of a Ram', which is prepared for, but then missing from, the 1647 text of that play, leading Fredson Bowers to speculate whether 'the play's songs were . . . written on separate sheets, the sheet for the devil-gelding song having been lost after transcription into the prompt-book'.[35]

Finally, the manuscript of *Calisto* (or *The Escapes of Jupiter*), Heywood's conflation of his own plays *The Golden Age* and *The Silver Age*, is likewise the only text to provide words for the song that is nevertheless responsible for a crucial moment in his *Golden Age*. Thus *Golden Age* has a command, 'Let musick through this brazen fortresse sound/Till all our hearts in depth of sleepe be drown'd'; and a song is then sung which is so soporific it lulls the protective Beldams to sleep, leaving Calisto to the mercy of

Jupiter. The equivalent moment in the manuscript of *Calisto* supplies what the missing words are:

> A songe
> whether they bee awake or sleepe.
> wth what greate Care ought virgins keepe.
>   wth what art and Indever,
> The' Jewell wch they ought to pryse.
> Above. the ritchest marchandise.
>   And once Lost, lost for ever
> virginity is a rare gemme.
> Rated above a diadem.
>   And was despised never
> Tis' that att wch the most men ayme.
> wch beeinnge gott they Count theire game
>   And once lost, lost forever.[36]

The 'jewel' of *The Golden Age* is not a gem, says the song, but virginity itself – thus giving a new logic to financial metaphors in the play. At the same time, this 'warning' to the heroine to protect her virginity ironically induces the sleep that allows the rape to occur; in this way it is a foreshadowing directed outside the text and to the audience, now alerted to, and so primed for, the sexual encounter that is about to take place. Heywood's performed *Golden Age* would have relied on this song; his printed *Golden Age* suffers for its absence.

Collectively, as there is not a logic that determines whether a printed or a manuscript text will contain the song, the loss or recovery of a song must be an issue aside from publisher's ownership. For even when plays survive in variant texts in manuscript – so having nothing to do with publishers – they still differ as to the presence or absence of song: of the five manuscripts of Walter Montagu's *The Shepheards Paradise*, two contain the specially written songs between the acts and the prologue and three do not (there are neither songs nor prologue in the printed text);[37] similarly, of the three manuscript copies of William Percy's collected plays, two have the songs, but one lacks them, 'instead often indicating their place simply with a title or a first line'.[38]

Moreover, that publishers did not go out of their way to determine who had the right to songs in the playbooks they were printing is illustrated by the regularity with which lyrics by one playwright or poet are casually enwrapped in the plays of another and, like those lyrics written by composers, published there without acknowledgement. Shirley's poem 'Fye on Love' found itself in a play probably by Thomas Goffe (or perhaps by John Gough), *The Careles Shepherdess*, though Shirley is not thought to have befriended either author.[39] Then again, Shirley may have done just the same to another writer: his *Wittie Faire One* contains a verse, 'In Loves name you are charg'd hereby', which shortly afterwards saw print amongst Carew's *Poems* (though there may be some ambiguity about the authorship of this poem: Carew was dead by the time his works were gathered).[40] The pattern, however, is clear. The anonymous *Wisdome of Doctor Dodypoll* has a lyric, 'What thing is love?', that seems to have come from George Peele's *The Hunting of Cupid*; two Suckling lyrics, 'Some drinke' and 'A health to the Nut browne Lasse' from *The Goblins*, are found within Simon Sheppard's play *The Committee-man Curried*.[41] The existence of '*Hence all you vaine Delights*' in *Nice Valour* has resulted in those words being attributed to Beaumont and Fletcher, though miscellanies circulating from some years before reveal that they predate the play, and their authorship is questionable: they were written perhaps by the Oxford poet and preacher William Strode, as miscellanies often claim, and more probably by Middleton.[42] Manuscript plays too show authors ready enough to turn to other writers' texts when necessary. The outrageous William Percy sticks an entire lyric by Sir Philip Sidney, 'The Tyme hath beene that a Taudry lace . . .', inside his *Faery Pastorall*, adding in a casual stage-direction that it is to be sung 'to the tune of Green sleeves, being but a by-song to this Pastorall'.[43] This raises a linked issue. The words to songs obviously did not come with the requirement for novelty that hung about the rest of a play; borrowing a tried and tested 'good' song might be as astute in a playwright as coming up with a new one of his own.

Even the three occasions on which the real authorship of song lyrics is acknowledged have nothing to do with publishers. Instead, it is the playwrights who separate themselves from the songs in their plays, and for particular stated reasons. So, for example, the publisher appears to have been content with printing the words to 'Armes, and Honors, decke thy story' inside Webster's *Dutchesse of Malfy*; it was the playwright who intervened during the printing process. The page containing the words of the song is, in some issues of the play, unannotated, and in other issues embellished with a marginal note: 'The Author disclaimes this Ditty to be his.'[44] Webster, this suggests, entered the printing house while the sheet was being printed, and made the compositors insert his additional note before pulling any more pages. Yet his urgency to abjure the song does not relate to the actual song-writer, for that person is not named; it seems that Webster is more concerned that the song should not be linked to himself, than with attributing it to its actual author. So the words remain flanked with Webster's dismissal, while another song in the same play, 'O let us howle', that just may be by Campion, goes unannotated.[45] On another occasion, the publishers – or, at least, the printers – are ready in principle to integrate songs by different authors into one text, advertising on the title-page to Heywood's *Rape of Lucrece* that '*the severall Songes . . . by* Valerius, the merrie Lord' will be situated '*in their apt places*', where it will be difficult to see what is by Heywood and what is not. But someone aside from the printing house, probably Heywood himself, had the additional songs instead collected together at the back of the playbook: 'Because we would not that any mans expectation should be deceived . . . we have inserted these few songs, which were added by the stranger that lately acted *Valerius* his part in forme following.'[46] Here again, though the comment remembers, or asks the audience to recall, the fictional character the song-writer performed, Valerius, it also neglects to come up with a real name for the songs' author. Both Webster and Heywood, the playwrights, not the publishers, distance the songs from the text; on each occasion, who the real author was remains undisclosed; and on each occasion the songs are still published anyway.

Only one play is proud to acknowledge the source of its borrowed song, and this too is an authorial decision, not a publisher's one. '*From whence was first this Fury hurl'd*', placed in Killigrew's *The Second Part of Cicilia and Clorinda*, is flanked by a long note; but as that note is equally present in the play's handsome undated manuscript text, it appears to represent a story the playwright yearns to tell:

This Chorus was written by M. *Thomas Carew*, Cup-bearer to *Charles the First*; and sung in a *Masque* at *White-hall, Anno* 1633. And I presume to make use of it here, because in the first design,'twas writ at my request upon a dispute held betwixt Mistress *Cicilia Crofts* and my self, where he was present; she being then Maid of Honour: this I have set down, lest any man should believe me so foolish as to steal such a Poem from so famous an Author; or so vain as to pretend to the making of it my self; and those that are not satisfied with this Apology, and this Song in this place; I am always ready to give them a worse of mine own.
Written by THOMAS KILLIGREW.[47]

Here Killigrew's use of the song is vigorously justified by his friendship with its author and his part in its creation. Actually, the song would have been desirable for Killigrew in a number of ways – it had fine music penned for it by the King's composer, Henry Lawes (Carew prints the same song in 1651 in a book that boasts on its title-page 'the *Songs* were set in *Musick* by Mr. Henry Lawes'), and its original masque source would have brought with it pleasingly courtly associations.[48] Killigrew's profit in 'taking' the song is evident; there is no indication, however, that the 'Apology' has involved asking permission from Carew for the use of his lyrics. Indeed, the self-righteous language of the acknowledgement suggests that a more normal policy would be to 'steal a Poem' and 'pretend to the making of it'. The fact is that unless a playwright 'confessed' – to the publisher, as well as to the reader – that he was not the author of one of his songs, no one would guess. They still cannot.

In other ways, too, publishers are evidently not *au fait* with the heritage of the songs they print, whilst playwrights are. It is often difficult to know who the primary author of a song is: a careful exploration amongst the plays of the period reveals that one set of song lyrics can regularly find itself in more than one play, by more than one author, at least one of whom, and perhaps both of whom, are therefore not its writer. Of two of the 'recovered' songs printed in Lyly's *Campaspe* (first performed by Oxford's Boys, 1584, printed for Edward Blount, 1632), one, 'O For a Bowle of fatt Canary', is also, in a slightly variant form, in the second quarto of Middleton's *A Mad World my Masters* (Paul's Boys, 1606, printed for Walter Burre, 1608), while 'what Bird so sings, yet so does wayle?' is also in the belated 1656 quarto of Dekker and Ford's *The Sun's-Darling*, a masque licensed for the Cockpit on 3 March 1623–4 (printed for Andrew Penneycuicke).[49] Here there is not a consonance of acting company or publisher, though the passage of time, and the unclear story behind the reacquisition of Lyly's songs, may partly account for that.

Just the same issue haunts some songs that may – or may not – be by Shakespeare: 'And wil a not come againe' (L1b) is in Shakespeare's *Hamlet* (Chamberlain's/King's Men, 1601, printed for Nicholas Ling, 1604) and, in altered form, in Jonson/Chapman/Marston's *Eastward Hoe*, where what may be a parody of it begins '*His head as white as mylke*' (Queen's Revels, 1605, printed for William Aspley, 1605); '*Take, oh take those lips away*' is printed in the single surviving Folio text for Shakespeare's *Measure for Measure* (TLN 1771) (King's Men, 1604, printed for Edward Blount, 1623), and, with an extra stanza, in Fletcher, Jonson, Chapman and Massinger's *The Bloody Brother* (also known as *Rollo, Duke of Normandy*, King's Men, 1617, printed for Thomas Allott, 1639).[50] Here the problem of dating the songs (as opposed to dating the plays) raises its head: *Measure for Measure* was first performed by the King's Men in 1604, but its song is thought to have been added later and placed into the play to create an act break when the text was revised, perhaps by Middleton. That means it is not even certain whether *Bloody Brother* took its song from

Measure, or is the source for it; yet the two plays handle the music in a way that would have been startling for an audience hearing one version with a consciousness of the other: *Bloody Brother*'s additional stanza concentrating on the foresworn lover's beautiful breasts, her 'hills of Snow', demands that the subject of the song be a woman, while in *Measure* the subject appears to be a man, Angelo.[51] Or is it? Depending on when the song was taken, the song's story of the abandoned lover could be being deliberately misread by Mariana: her grief is leading her to 'reinterpret' everything.

Other playwrights offer equally confusing questions about song-authorship and all have ramifications for the reading of the text. '*How blest are they that wast their weary howers*' is in Quarles' *The Virgin Widow* (privately acted, 1641, printed for R. Royston, 1649), and Brome's *The Queen and Concubine* (King's Revels, 1635, printed for A. Crook and H. Brome, 1659), and either playwright – or neither – may have written it: but who is it who originally wastes those hours?[52] On other occasions, playwrights borrow songs from their earlier selves, a policy that in some ways complicates yet further the meaning of the text. 'CUPID is VENUS onely Joy' is in Middleton's *Chast Mayd in Cheape-Side* (Lady Elizabeth's, 1613; printed for Francis Constable, 1630) and *More Dissemblers Besides Women* (King's Men, 1615; printed for Humphrey Moseley, 1657); and Beaumont and Fletcher include '*Tell me (deerest) what is Love?*' in two of 'their' plays, Beaumont's *The Knight of the Burning Pestle* (Queen's Revels?, 1607, printed for Walter Burre, 1613) and *The Captaine* (1647) (King's Men, 1612, printed for Humphrey Robinson and Humphrey Moseley).[53] This habit of repeating someone else's songs, or one's own (or one's collaborator's) and giving the whole lot to the publisher is evidently not a printing-house issue. It relates instead to theatrical practicalities. Playwrights putting texts together at speed sometimes took whatever song was to hand, playing with its earlier meanings on some occasions, hoping to subsume them with new meanings on others. The result is that songs did not always belong as powerfully to a single play as did other aspects of the text: their potential to wander was inherent within their relationship to plays.

It is not, then, disputed 'ownership' by composer or publisher or playwright that prevents the publication of certain songs; such songs as are published indicate a cavalier attitude to authorship indicative of the reverse: 'ownership' of a song was difficult to isolate or retain, for songs had a way of circulating outside the play manuscript and between theatres.

SONGS IN THE THEATRE: REAL REASONS
FOR SONGS LOST AND FOUND

There are a number of reasons for lost and found songs and all have the theatre at their root. For the way songs were written, rehearsed and learnt for performance affected their circulation and final presence in (or absence from) the printed text; it was plays as performance texts, not plays as 'literature', that affected which documents were to hand for performance, and which documents were available when playwrights readied plays for printers.

One actual reason for the missing songs, when those songs are author- ial, relates to the moment of their creation. Songs in plays were, of course, always ultimately collaborative, because music had to be supplied or acquired for them from an external source. But when a playwright came up with lyrics to be set to a brand new tune, two people, the playwright and the music-writer, needed to be concurrently creative in order to finish the play. Whilst the rest of the dialogue was still being written by the playwright, lyrics could simultaneously be set by a musician; so there was every reason to extract the words to songs from their play context as early as possible. It was actually wise for a playwright to inscribe 'songs' onto a separate piece of paper in the first place. And, from a later time, one such separate 'authorial' song survives. A document in the Folger Shakespeare Library is headed 'Song.' and contains four verses beginning 'That Money will multiply care', which is sung in Richard Cumberland's *Jew of Mogodore* (1808). But here it is well outside the playbook and annotated with two additional pieces of information: 'Composed by, and in the Handwriting of, Richard Cumberland', and 'given to me [Wm Upcott] by Michael Kelly the Musical Composer': Cumberland seems to have done exactly what has been projected above – written out his words and conveyed them to the composer on a separate paper aside from the playtext.[54]

Though no songs written out for composers in this fashion have been found from the early modern period, their presence can be guessed at. Amongst the composer George Jeffreys' musical settings for Peter Hausted's *The Rivall Friends* is one song called 'Cruell but once againe'. To it is attached an explanation, 'This song was made for the Comodie but I thinke not sunge,' and clearly this is so, for the printed text of *The Rivall Friends* lacks 'Cruell but once againe' altogether. In this instance a set of words have made their way from the playwright to the composer, where they have been set, but they have not been captured by the extant playbook, having been revised away earlier in the play's life.[55]

The two-way transaction has become a one-way transaction, but it shows how the words to songs circulated well away from their play context and before, in some cases, a need to use them had been determined. Alternatively Leonard Willan's indecisive *Astraea* contains one 'SONG' beginning 'When Days bright Star' followed by, on the next page, 'Or thus in Dialogue by a Treble and a Base', which begins 'What Star is that shoots through the Skie?'[56] On this occasion, the play's dialogue is fixed, but which song would be best for the play is dependent on, originally, the composer's (or, in the printed form in which it is presented, the reader's) choice.

On other occasions aspects of the 'way' playwrights handed their songs over can be guessed at. At least in the cases of companies or playwrights with strong links to musicians (see below) playwrights seem not just to have sent composers their lyrics, but also to have given them careful guidance, if not access to the passage of text in which the song was to feature – hence the subtlety and 'fit' of so many early modern musical compositions. To cite a few examples: in Jonson's *Cynthias Revels* Hedon sings a song, '*O* That Joy so soone should wast!' and then asks Amorphus his impression of it. The latter answers with a criticism aimed, as it seems, not at the words but the tune: 'A pretty *Ayre*; in generall, I like it well. But . . . your long *die-Note* did arride me most . . . it was somwhat too long.'[57] Music survives for this song, perhaps by Nathaniel Giles, in which the collaborative joke becomes evident: there is such a long note given to 'die' that the word's sense of sexual ecstasy, as opposed to death, is luxuriously brought out. Here is a textual moment that relies on an aural moment, signifying careful instruction of the composer by the writer.[58] Much the same seems to have happened between Beaumont and Fletcher and Robert Johnson the composer: surviving Johnsonian music for 'away delights' from *The Captaine* coyly lingers on all potentially sexual words, bringing out innuendos and consciously inflaming the very lust that, notionally, the song sets out (unsuccessfully) to cure; collaboration, again, was necessary to ensure the song was appropriately inappropriate.[59]

Sometimes not certain words so much as certain feelings, a 'foreshadowing' of events to come, needed to be issued through the tune of a song, which was to convey something opposite to the tenor of the words. In such cases, in particular, the composer must have had careful instruction. 'Care charming sleep', sung to the dying emperor in Fletcher's *Valentinian*, is, in terms of words alone, a lullaby; the music that accompanies this song, by Robert Johnson, is however composed of a series of jarring notes in disjunctive sections. In the play, at the time when the song is sung, Valentinian is burning with the poison that will later kill him in torment, but only close understanding of the song's irony in its context will have enabled Johnson to write music so seemingly against the meaning of the lyrics (but actually so appropriate).[60] This suggests that playwrights with access to specific songwrights discussed the kind of music they wanted; they may even have done this 'first' before coming up with their words, in which case the composition of the song was, from the start, a joint venture, aside from the (perhaps) singular composition of the rest of the play. On occasion the generation of a song may even have come from the composer rather than the playwright. In February 1615 Robert Lane writes to Owen Gwyn, master of St John's Cambridge, about preparations for entertaining King James on a visit; he has secured the composer Robert Johnson to write music for the occasion and appears to have implored Ben Jonson to write words for it – in that order: 'we have bene with Mr Johnson our Musition & entreated Ben: Johnson to penne a dyttye, which we expect upon Satturday'.[61]

The second reason for the separation of songs from texts connects to the first. However and in whatever form the composer received a songtext, the next process, the composition of a tune to the music, will automatically have necessitated the creation of a fresh document, dislocated from the text. For the composed text would contain both words and music, and it was that document (or those documents) which was returned to the playhouse, and which resulted in the song sung on the stage. Any differences the composer made in the text, including cuts or embellishments for the sake of musical clarity, will also have been recorded in this finalised paper, though these reformations will not automatically have made their way back into the playbook: the 'book' may well have had in it a pre-composer version of the song, or no version of the song, while the performance contained the final, composed song. The composed paper, containing song and conjoined music, could be furthest from what (if anything) the prompter had to hand.

A third reason explains a different instance: the playwright who is not collaborating with a composer in the search for a fresh tune, but is collaborating instead with a tried and tested 'old' tune, for which no discourse is necessary. His method of composition here will be shaped by what kind of music he is using. If he is borrowing a tune from a theatrical company's library, he will have had to travel to the playhouse to see the music or speak to someone familiar with it (perhaps its singer) and will have had to shape his lyrics in homage or apposition to the 'known' lyrics supplied for the text. In this case, too, he is likely to have composed 'apart' from his playscript, as a series of musical themes would have dictated his options.

Take, for example, the choice made by William Percy in his manuscript play *Arabia Sitiens* (dated 1601). His intense desire to have his texts performed by Paul's Boys is boldly stated at the start of the manuscript book in which the play is contained; he then pointedly writes a set of lyrics shaped metrically to what must be a Paul's Boy tune. So one of his songs reads:

> Sing, to Mahomet, mourning layes,
> To ease us of these partching dayes,
> Nor Man, nor Heifer, no nor wether
> May endure this soultery weather.
> They in grief, pining in this drough
> Loe ligge in grasse, with Toungs lolled furth.
> Eheu, Eheu let us sing
> To Mahomet our good king.

As M. Hope Dodds points out, this text obviously glances at Lyly's song in *Mydas* and almost certainly adopts its music:

> Sing to *Apollo*, God of Day,
> Whose golden beames with morning play,
> And make her eyes so brightly shine,
> Aurora's face is call'd Divine;
> Sing to *Phoebus* and that Throne
> Of Diamonds which he sits upon;
>   Io, Paens let us sing,
>   To Physickes, and to Poesies King.[62]

In other words, Percy's writing was part of his marketing strategy; he was consciously taking on what these days would be called the 'brand' of Paul's Boys.

It is the same with another Paul's Boy play, the *Antimasque of Mountebanks* (1618) attributed to Marston/Campion; the second Mountebank's song seems to require the same tune as the song of the nymphs to Cupid from *Gallathea*, again, for reasons between homage and parody. The Mountebank sings:

> Is any deaf? Is any blinde?
> Is any bound or loose behinde?
> Is any foule that would be fayer?
> Would any lady change her haire?
> Does any dreame? Does any wa<l>ke?
> Or in their sleep affrighted talke?
>   I come to cure what ere you feele
>   Within, without, from head to heele.

As Bond points out, this is a 'coarse parody' of a *Gallathea* song; it probably, again, demands the same music:

> Lar.　Is anyone undone by fire,
> 　　　And Turn'd to ashes through disire?
> 　　　Did ever any Lady weepe,
> 　　　Being cheated of her golden sleepe?
> All. 3.　Stolne by sicke thoughts! The pirates sound,
> 　　　And in her teares, hee shalbe drownd.
> 　　　　　Reade his Inditement, let him heare,
> 　　　　　What hees to trust to: Boy give eare.[63]

Both occurrences, incidentally, indicate that Lyly's songs – the songs that were not published until 1632 – are original: indeed, Blount, their publisher, with his collection of 'recovered' songs seems actually to have had access to Paul's Boys' music library.[64] When writing to a 'company tune' like this, a playwright was particularly likely to design his lyrics aside from his play and on their own paper, or even to come up with them before he came up with the rest of his text, as part of his sales-pitch.[65]

Other companies too seem to have had 'libraries', and playwrights for them also would have felt a need to utilise these already-extant resources.[66] A King's Men's 'library' is evidenced by the fact that several collections of their theatrical music circulated independently of the plays. Matthew Locke, musician of the King's Men, copied a pool of 'masques and other tunes' composed by Robert Johnson; John Wilson, who took over from Robert Johnson as theatre composer for the King's Men, published in his *Cheerfull Ayres* (Oxford, 1660) Robert Johnson's *Tempest* songs, and later adapted theatrical music by William Lawes; he too seems to be reworking a set of 'company' songs made available to him *en masse*.[67] Nineteen of the King's Men dance tunes even made it to Germany in a context that did not involve the plays, where they were published in William Brade's *Newe Ausserlesene Liebliche Branden* (Hamberg, 1617); as Brade had left England for Germany in the 1590s, some intermediary must have sent or given him a bundle of King's Men's theatre music.[68] And such a pooled collection may even have survived to the Restoration, for William Davenant's *Macbeth*, performed in 1666 (published in 1673), was based textually on the Folio – though elaborately updated – but contained the full words to the Middleton songs (from *The Witch*) that, in the Folio, are indicated only by first lines. As Middleton's *The Witch* had not been published in Davenant's time, and as its single surviving manuscript was then unknown, Davenant seems to have had access to a specific source containing the words to the songs: a musical collection.[69]

Shakespeare, as befits a resident playwright, may frequently have employed his company's music manuscripts, reusing tunes over several plays. Sometimes it is very clear when he does so, for instance when he provides a new verse to his epilogue song to *Twelfth Night*, '*When that I was and a little tin[i]e boy*' (TLN 2560), with its chorus of '*the raine it raineth every day*', in his *King Lear* (TLN 1729–33). But Ross Duffin, the musicologist, illustrates in *Shakespeare's Songbook* how often lost tunes for Shakespeare's plays may in reality be extant: he maintains that Iago's '*And let me the Cannakin clinke, clinke*' (*Othello*, TLN 1182), for which no music survives, could easily have been sung to the same tune as Ophelia's 'To morrow is S. Valentines day' (*Hamlet*, TLN 2790) which does survive; both have a closely matching metre.[70] Shakespeare's lyrics too may be being written on pages containing 'old' music or 'old' words on which he can work his variations: he too may let the writing of a new song be shaped not to a play, but to a collection of theatrical tunes.

Even when a well-known, popular or ballad tune was to be used, for which no careful negotiation was needed, 'collaboration' between lyric and tune still had to take place which may have occasioned the song's separate construction. Examples include the Harper in George Peele's *Edward the First* who enters singing a song 'to the tune of Who list to lead a Souldiers life'; or Cagurcus in *Misogonus* who sings 'A songe to the tune of hartes ease', or Haltersycke in Pickering's *Horestes* who 'Entrithe & syngeth this song to ye tune of have over ye water to floride or selengers round'.[71] Having a known tune in mind, the playwright fitted his words to a pre-designed structure, and the shape and emphases of the music dictated where he placed his words for maximum effect. Though a song of this kind did not require a journey away to a composer or a theatre music library, and might, at the moment of writing, be placed directly inside the playscript where it belonged, that does not mean that it always was, for it was normal for a playwright to construct a song's words on a separate document. Why? The reason is simple and relates again to theatrical necessity: rehearsal.

For the fourth reason for the loss of songs is that player-singers, irrespective of the origin of their songtexts, would need to learn and practise songs differently from the way they learnt and practised lines (which would be different again from the reading of a 'letter' on stage, a text that might not be practised at all). Hence a linked reason for the separation of song from play: even an old or known song would need rehearsal, if only to decide whether the singer was up to singing it (voice-breaking was a constant problem in the theatre of the day) and, if so, the pitch at which it was to be sung. References of the time reveal that songs were generally rehearsed away from the dialogue, and under the instruction of different people. The boys in Chapman's *Gentleman Usher*, for instance, are heard 'practising' the song for their play, though none of the other performers are rehearsing with them:

> LASS.   And will these waggish pages, hit their songs?
> 2 PAG.   *Re mi fa sol la?*
> LASS.   O they are practising; good boyes, well done.[72]

This is because songs needed to be practised in front of a musical instructor, perhaps the composer, or the theatre's most musically knowledgeable member. And for this rehearsal the singer needed at least a text containing the words and, depending on musical knowledge (usually significant in a performing company), the music, for 'songs usually were, and are, rehearsed from a sheet of music containing text and tune, and such sheets are generally kept separate from the body of the play'; the song, perhaps never in every version of the playtext, could be lost and found accordingly.[73]

In fact, those separate theatre songtexts, consisting of words, or words and music combined, were so crucial to the accurate performance of the song onstage that they often came to be used in performance itself. Here again, there was a discrepancy between the song in the playbook, less likely to feature there than ever now that its words could be read out onstage, and the song on its staged paper, which, like a scroll (it was, indeed, a version of a scroll), was a confusion between a written text and a prop. Plenty of plays elaborately stage a moment when, with a flourish, a paper containing words and music for a song is physically produced to be sung from during a performance. In Shirley's *Changes* the love-sick Gerald has written his own lyric and sent it away to be set to music by a professional; the resultant songscript is brought back by the Page who is asked by Gerald first to 'read it' and then to sing it ('Tis yet no Song, infuse a soule into it'), a cumbersome piece of dialogue to explain the presence of the composed song in paper form on stage.[74] Likewise Horatio in Brome's *Novella* has written a poem, and now 'the words are set'; it is this set song that he hands to Victoria as a love token, reading out its words and then giving it to the maid at the suggestion 'my mayd shall sing 'hem for you'; again, the dialogue is manufactured to bring both words and music to the performers.[75] Both these examples are Caroline, but earlier illustrations can also be found, for example, when Amorphus in Jonson's *Cynthias Revels*, asked for a song, explains that he happens to have 'both the *Note*, and *Ditty* about me'; he is thus able first to 'reade the *Ditty* to your Beauties here' and, later, when requested 'let's heare it sung', to sing it from the paper.[76]

Other plays in which songs are on a piece of paper that is separately 'read' and 'sung from' presumably also refer to staged paper texts, which may be texts of words only or which may additionally contain the musical notation. Imperia, handing '*Hipolitoes* Sonnet' to her maids in *Blurt Master Constable*, is quick to advise that they 'first read it and then sing it'; when Subtle enters in Field's *Amends for Ladies*, 'with a paper, and his BOY', he reads out the words on the paper, a set of lyrics beginning '*Rise Ladie Mistresse, rise*', and then hands them over to his boy to sing.[77] It is typical of Jonson that he should regularly have his texts brought onstage so that they cannot be misremembered, and equally regularly have them both sung and read – so that the lyric as poetry would not be subsumed by the lyric as song. In his *New Inne* Lovel reads out 'It was a beauty that I saw' as a 'meditation'; later it appears to be the same piece that is performed as a song – the epithalamium – at the end of the play; in his *Sad Shepherd*, the direction preceding one of the songs, 'The Song. Which while *Karolin* sings, *Aeglamour* reads', may mean that Aeglamour simply looks over Karolin's shoulder while the singing takes place, but offers the strange possibility that recitation happened concurrently with the singing.[78]

Presumably other plays, too, brought their songs physically onto the stage. Moments like that in *As You Like It*, where, though there is no explicit direction for a piece of paper, Jaques in some way gives Amiens 'a verse . . . That I made yesterday' (TLN 933–4), may suggest the more widespread use of paper texts for songs onstage; and even the 'part' for Orlando in *Orlando Furioso*, which contains a fragmentary direction '<he> singes', and an indication of what might be the start of the song, 'I am orl<a>nd<o>', seems to anticipate that the text be provided externally: the tune 'Orlando' preserved in a Welsh manuscript may independently record the song's music.[79]

The habit of bringing a paper song onto the stage rid the prompter's book of any need to contain the words to the song. So the manuscript of *Believe as You List*, written by Knight the prompter, pools the business of the music on one side of paper (deleting a song-related speech at the top of one page and writing it at the bottom of the page before) for prompting clarity; nevertheless, the song itself is not supplied.[80] At other times the song is simply 'cued' into the text by its first few words, resulting in partly lost songs which, much like 'lost' scrolls, resolve into an 'etc.'

after a phrase or so. In Middleton's *The Widdow* Latrocinio is asked to sing 'Kuck before, and Kuck behind, &c'; in *Everie Woman* Phylautus is pardoned having been arrested, after which he sings 'My love can sing no other song, but still complaines I did her, &c. I beseech your Majestie to let me goe'; in Heywood's *Edward the Fourth*, the 'threemans Song', which begins 'Agencourt, Agencourt, know ye not Agencourt', peters out at 'O the French were beaten downe,/Morrys pikes and bowmen, &c.'[81] As with other lost songs, these may well be authorial and important to the play, as was 'From the honor'd dead I bring' in Fletcher's *The Wild-Goose Chase*, of which only four and a half lines are given in the printed playbook:

> Song.
> From the honor'd dead I bring}   {Take it nobly, 'tis your due
> Thus his love and last offring:}   {From a friendship ever true
> From a faith &c.[82]

A music manuscript containing words to the whole song reveals what the 'etc.' actually stands for – five and a half further lines:

> from a faith yt had no end,
> towards Heaven & to his freind,
> from a gratitude as true,
> as these are rich I bring to you
> This little Moddell hould it deere,
> and for yor Dead freind shedd a teare.[83]

These words, lost from the play, introduce what the supposed gift brought from the 'honor'd dead' is – not only jewels but a 'little Moddell' of himself (his sister); it is the human part of the gift that affects the rest of the play's story, for Mirabell subsequently offers to marry the sister as homage to his dead friend.[84] Seemingly on all these occasions the printer has received, as his base text, some kind of prompter's book, which knows the song to be sung (and so is written at a time when its lyrics already exist) but does not need the words.

A fifth reason for the loss of songs from playbooks concerns the way music circulated post-performance amongst the theatre audience: the people the music was, after all, designed to entertain. 'I have often gone to plaies more for the musicke sake, then for action,' says Ratsey in *Ratseis Ghost*; and some music-loving spectators wanted not just to hear but to have the play songs for themselves.[85] Just as fragments of text circulated in the table-books of the time, new songs had a *cachet* that made them desirable amongst the people with the talent to read music, play an instrument, or sing. As this was a somewhat elite market, smaller than that for printed playbooks, its concerns were met (when they were) in manuscript, a form that survives less well over time than print, but that also necessitates the circulation of separate song documents. A song, 'Press me no more kind love', from Montagu's *Shepheards Paradise*, for example, seems to have circulated away from its play, making its way in parody form into a Cambridge commonplace book of the interregnum; at least 49 copies of songs from Jonson's *Gypsies Metamorphosed* were in separate circulation dating from before, during and after the printing of the text of the masque.[86] But there was some pressure to make sure that these documents were not handed around too freely: keeping a song back from a yearning audience obliged them to revisit the theatre to hear the tune, and some writers were therefore possessive over their songtexts. Glapthorne's *Lady Mother* depicts a spectator's desire to have a copy of a new song, and the writer's desire not to hand it over:

CRA: Now on my life this boy does sing as like the boy at the whitefryers as ever
        I heard . . .
SU: I and the Musicks like theires, come Sirra whoes yor Poett
CRA: Some mad wag I warrant him, is this a new song
MU: Tis the first edition sir, none else but we had ever coppie of it
SU: But you wilbe intreated, to let a gent' have it
MU: By no meanes the Author has sworn's to the contrary least it should grow
        soe wonderous old & turne a Ballad.[87]

As Bowden indicates, this passage explains how pride in having authored a fascinating new lyric might induce a playwright specifically to withhold his songs and preserve their mystery: hence perhaps the plays like *Bonduca* that are published containing the words to catches and balladic snatches, but without the words for songs of import – here, a love song and a hymn.[88] That also meant that playwrights had a conflicted and divided impetus with respect to their own songs: a consciousness that the song is good might equally drive them to publish, or not to publish it with a play, and might make them release it or hold it back during the play's performance life.

The song, though a different variety of text from other scrolls (which are complete from the moment of writing, and do not need to be shaped to a known metrical structure or to the ability of a particular player), tends to be indicated in the same way: its words are often in italics though the dialogue is not; there is often a 'song' heading, indicating that the text is to be written on a separate piece of paper headed 'song'; and song-layout is often preserved. However, numerous people shaped the creation and circulation of the song, so that a song in a playbook usually had a different life from the rest of the playtext *and* a different life from the rest of the scrolls: it might be written from the start as a paper containing lyrics only, or be extracted as one to be sent to a composer; it might return from a composer as a paper or series of papers containing a combination of words and music; it might be learnt by a singer as a paper containing either words and music or just words – this text might also then make its way physically into performance as a prop; it might reside, with its music, amongst a collection of other theatre-related songs in the playhouse or with a musician; and it might, if it were a song of great theatrical popularity, be held back from a printed text as a separate paper consisting of music and text. From the moment of writing to the moment of performance and beyond, the song had often at least two paper lives separate from the play, one that consisted of words only, one that consisted of words with music, neither of which was necessarily ever fully integrated into the play that housed it.

SONGS, MASQUES AND REVISION

One attendant reason for all of this might be to do with revision. It has already been shown that, when two versions of the same play exist, one often contains songs that the other does not. Though the easy loss of songs is one explanation for this, the separation of song from play leads to another linked theatrical habit: songs are some of the first texts to be revised from an overlong drama (they can easily be removed to shorten a text without disturbing dialogue), and songs are also some of the first texts to be added to plays (as they do not give extra work to any players other than the singers themselves). Songs always present a major line of textual uncertainty.

To turn to cutting first: when a play had a long running time, the obvious passages to cut – passages that would not alter the narrative of the play or put out actors performing from parts – were the songs. This is directly confronted by William Percy, who writes a note to the Master of Paul's Boys to whom he intends to send (and perhaps did send) a copy of his collection of plays. He advises:

that if any of the fine and foremost of these Pasturalls and Comoedyes conteynd in this volume shall but overreach in length (The children not to begin before

Foure after Prayers And the gates of Powles shutting at six) the Tyme of supper,
that then in tyme and place convenient, you do let passe some of the songs and
make the consort the shorter, For I suppose these Plaies be somewhat too long for
that Place.[89]

The songs, though largely written for the plays in which they feature, are
seen as in their nature semi-permanent, an attitude that may explain how
other lyrics too were removed very early on in their plays' lives: the
manuscripts of *The Faithful Friends*, and *The Honest Mans Fortune* have
lyrics erased by the manuscript's 'corrector'.[90] Printed plays calling for
songs or masques that are not provided indicate that later theatrical cuts
have homed in on just those sections. Beaumont/Fletcher/Massinger's *The
Coxcombe*, in the single text in which it survives, lacks the masque
anticipated in Uberto's question, 'come, wher's this masque'; given that
the prologue insists that those who 'condemn'd' the play 'for the length'
will find 'that fault's reform'd', a masque was probably removed to
shorten the play's running time.[91] Perhaps songs and masques in plays
always had to be somewhat optional. With the necessity of additional
practice, additional singing, and additional instrumental skill that they
require, they may only ever have been performed when the right singer
was to hand or the right theatrical space was on offer. Some 'lost' songs
and masques may actually have been consciously removed.

The weakness of performers' voices meant that cutting a song entirely,
or turning it into a spoken poem, could be imposed by circumstance.
If the words were valued enough, but the singer incapable, the text might
be said or read. Shakespeare's *Cymbeline*, for instance, contains what looks
like a series of hasty revisions that turn a song to be sung by two people
into a song to be sung by one person and spoken by the other, and finally
into a song that is to be spoken by both. So in what seems to be a passage
of layered revisions, Arviragus feels that though his voice and Guiderius'
'Have got the mannish cracke' the two should nevertheless 'sing . . . to' th'
ground' the 'dead' Fidele; Guiderius, however, answers, 'I cannot sing: Ile
weepe, and word it with thee'; Arviragus then agrees 'Wee'l speake it then'
(TLN 2549–56), Shakespeare hounded by adolescence as he writes and
writes again. Linked to this are the songs for which contemporary music
survives but which are seemingly read rather than sung in the plays in
which they feature. Examples include 'Deare, do not your fair beauty
wrong' in Thomas May's *The Old Couple*, which Dotterel asks for 'leave
to read' – Johnson's music survives for this lyric, and Barnet, in the play,
claims to 'know the *song*' (italics mine); similarly '*Goe happy heart for thou
shalt ly/Intomb'd in her for whom I dy*' is in Fletcher's *Mad Lover* a 'read'

paper, though it was obviously once handed from one character to another (probably to a singer; but with the singer lost, the owner of the paper reads it himself); theatre music survives in several versions for this song too:

> Pol.　Next read this,
> 　　　But since I see your spirit somewhat troubled
> 　　　Ile doe it for ye.[92]

On other occasions it was simpler just to cut the song altogether; hence the real reason why the willow song was removed from the Quarto of *Othello* may be that the voice of 'Desdemona' had broken: it has been pointed out that Shakespeare's company seems to have had regular use of a singing and lute-playing boy between 1601 and 1604, accounting for Ophelia, and one form of Desdemona, and that the subsequent tragedies no longer expect a singing heroine.[93] 'Bad voices', after all, account for cuts in other plays, as a plaintive stage-direction printed after a song for two spirits in Nathaniel Richards' *Tragedy of Messallina* elucidates: '*After this song (which was left out of the Play in regard there was none could sing in Parts) Enter the Ghosts*'.[94]

Cut or reduced songs are countered by the reverse: songs added either for a court production, or because of the acquisition of a marvellous new singer. Here follows the story of 'added songs' with this caveat: that various of the songs mentioned as though they were written concurrently with the playtext may be added songs; and some of the songs seemingly cut from a play may, on the contrary, only have been added to a later version: without a play surviving in various forms (and music manuscripts surviving in various other forms), it is not always possible to date songs independently from the text.

To turn first to 'updating', in which one song in a play is replaced by another, refreshing the text specifically along song lines: when a stage-direction in Middleton's *Chast Mayd* asks for 'Musicke and Welch Song', and the song that follows, 'CUPID is VENUS onely Joy', is not only not in Welsh, but also borrowed from another play, *More Dissemblers Besides Women*, there is a strong likelihood that the song has been changed, an English song being substituted for an original Welsh one for ease of performance (and ease of understanding).[95] Similarly in *Twelfth Night*, as is often pointed out, a singing Viola seems to have been replaced by a singing Feste and the songs to be sung changed accordingly. Though only one text of the play is extant, in it Viola offers to go to the house of Count Orsino dressed as a eunuch 'for I can sing,/And speake to him in many sorts of Musicke' (TLN 109–10), though she never then sings anything. She is on one occasion, however, asked to sing by Orsino who begs her for 'That old and Anticke song we heard last night' (TLN 886), a song relished, he explains, by country women, knitters and spinsters. Curio then 'reminds' Orsino that the singer of the song was actually Feste who, as luck would have it, is in Orsino's house; the clown enters and sings '*Come away, come away death*' (TLN 941). This entire exchange is a surprise and for three reasons: it is a surprise that Feste, Olivia's jester, should be in Orsino's house at all; it is a surprise that Orsino misremembers who sang the song the night before; and it is a surprise that the song finally produced in no way accords with Orsino's description of it. Feste's artful verses, a lover's lament for a broken heart, imply that the lyrics have been changed; this play, too, has been updated along song lines, perhaps to showcase the company's new singing clown, Armin; and perhaps, as elsewhere, to rescue the boy-player of Viola from a vocal challenge he could no longer meet.[96]

A look at the layout of printed texts sometimes reveals which are the added songs. For example, when songs are absent from earlier play editions, but present in later ones, they are likely to be 'new' songs (though they could, of course, be 'found' songs); illustrations include 'O For a Bowle', attached to Middleton's *Mad World* in its 1640 edition, but absent from its 1608 quarto; '*Filena's* song' and 'Another Song', added to Flecknoe's *Love's Kingdom* in 1664 (a revised version of *Love's Dominion* of 1654 in which the songs did not feature); 'Lay a garland', 'I could never' and an additional song for the masque, '*To bed, to bed, come Hymen lead the Bride*', all absent from the 1619 edition of Beaumont and Fletcher's *The Maids Tragedie* and present in the 1622 edition; and 'Run to Love's lottery' and ''tis in good truth', added to Davenant's *Unfortunate Lovers* as late as the 1673 folio text of the play (having been absent from the 1643 and 1649 editions of the text).[97] In the latter two instances, additional characters are also written in to sing the songs, so the fresh nature of these texts is particularly visible. Heywood's *Rape of Lucrece*, meanwhile, swells by the addition of songs almost every time it is printed: the 1608 and 1609 editions contained twelve songs (some of which, added by the actor who played Valerius, postdate the first performance); the 1638 edition added four more songs to make a text of sixteen songs; the 1640 edition added a further five songs to make an edition of twenty-one songs.

In other plays, the fact that the songs are newer than the rest of the text is immediately obvious. There is the title-page of the second issue of *A Faire Quarrell* (both editions of that play are printed in 1617) that boasts of '*new Additions of Mr. Chaughs and Trimtrams Roaring, and the Bauds Song*'. In the printed text, those new additions make up a gathering flown into the already-printed play; it is headed: 'Place this at the latter end of the fourth Act', an instruction that has itself been printed.[98] Something similar may have happened with Dekker's *Shomakers Holiday*, in which, again, the songs seem to date from a revision of the play, but the text of the play appears to come from an earlier, pre-song, stage in its existence; Peter Smith points out that the play contains no cues for the songs (and that their placement is open to question as a result).[99] The result, in all these instances, is that the dialogue text is one age, but its songs are newer and younger. Plays should not, without due care, be dated from their songs.

It was frequently the theatre's needs (rather than the playwright's) that brought about the addition of a new song or masque into an old play. With the advent, first, of James I who liked music a great deal, and then of Charles I, who loved it, adult companies – whether students or professionals – closest to the king, or keenest to impress him, started to need regular music in their performances to please their most important patron. Over time, a pattern seems to have developed involving an interchange between court composers and specific theatrical companies, so that, when a play was to be put on before royalty, either the court lent, or the companies purchased, court composers to set music to the text. When playwrights were living, active and involved in the company, they were often part of this process – when they were not, the process went on regardless.

So, from about 1608 onwards, music for the King's Men is written by three court composers successively, though it is not apparent whether the King's Men *employed* the composers, or whether the composers were borrowed – or issued – from court (King's Men and King's composers had the shared aim of pleasing the King, after all). Robert Johnson's surviving theatre music is for King's Men plays, for instance, and dates from 1608 onwards. Amongst the texts for which he is known (or heavily suspected) to be composer are tunes to songs in 'Fletcher''s *Captaine, The Chances, The Lovers Progress, The Mad Lover* and *Valentinian*; Jonson's *Divell is an Asse* and *The Gypsies Metamorphosed*; perhaps Massinger's *The Fatall Dowry*; May's *The Old Couple*; Middleton's *The Witch* (including the songs that were subsequently used in *Macbeth*); Shakespeare's *Cymbeline, Tempest, Winter's Tale* and, perhaps, *Cardenio*; Tourneur's lost *The Nobleman*; and Webster's *Dutchesse of Malfy*.

John Wilson, who co-wrote with Johnson for a time, seems to have taken over from him as a theatre composer in about 1617; included in his repertoire are compositions for Brome's *The Northern Lasse*; Fletcher and company's *The Beggars Bush*, *The Bloody Brother*, *The Faithfull Shepheardesse*, *The False One*, *Loves Cure*, *The Loyal Subject*, *The Mad Lover*, *The Pilgrim*, *The Queene of Corinth*, *Valentinian*, *The Wild-Goose Chase* and *Women Pleas'd*; Ford's *The Lovers Melancholy*; and Middleton's *The Witch*.

Then, from about 1634 onwards, William Lawes seems to have set most surviving King's Men play songs, including tunes for Berkeley's *The Lost Lady*; Cavendish's *The Country Captaine*; Davenant's *Love and Honour* and *The Unfortunate Lovers*; Denham's *The Sophy*; Fletcher's *Faithful Shepheardesse*, *The Mad Lover* and *The Spanish Curat*; Jonson's *Epicoene*; Mayne's *The Citye Match*; Middleton's *The Widdow*; Shirley's *The Cardinal*; and Suckling's *Aglaura*, *Brennoralt*, *The Goblins* and *The Sad One* (unacted).[100] He additionally wrote for two other companies with royal connections: amongst his surviving music are settings for a song in Shirley's *The Dukes Mistris*, a play belonging to Queen Henrietta's Men, and for verses in Brome's *Joviall Crew*; Fletcher's *Cupid's Revenge*; Ford's *The Ladies Triall*; and Glapthorne's *Argalus and Parthenia*, which were put on by Beeston's Boys. As is obvious from these lists, composers inherited and reworked the tunes of their predecessors for the same play (so that sometimes it is hard to say which composer originally wrote a tune, and which embellished it). What can be seen is that popular plays were revived and revised musically by court composers, and that they often accommodated new songs over time.

The same can be said of masques in plays; from about 1608 onwards, when King's composers started writing for the King's Men, aspects of court masques started to be cut down and put into plays, despite the fact that their authorship, both in lyric and musical terms, was usually by someone other than the playwright(s). Masque elements in plays are often additions, often authorially complex, and often part of a negotiation between play and court.

A section of Jonson's *Masque of Oberon* (performed on 1 January 1611), for example, seems to work its way into a Shakespeare play. That masque began with an antimasque of 'Satyres' for which music, written by Robert Johnson, survives. As Shakespeare's *Winter's Tale* requires '*a Dance of twelve Satyres*', and as that dance is introduced by the servant's pointed comment, 'three of [the dancers], by their owne report (Sir,) hath danc'd before the King' (TLN 2158–64), and as the same troupe was performing the masque and the play in quick succession, it seems probable that the satyrs' dance in *Winter's Tale* is a reuse, with light rewriting, of the satyrs' dance in the *Masque of Oberon*. Did Shakespeare add this masque into the play? Did someone else ease it in? Was its purpose a public one: to give a moment of court glamour to a theatre audience who could '[bask] in reflected glory, feeling that they were in touch with spectacular, aristocratic entertainment'?[101] Or was the masque added specifically, and perhaps only, for a *court* performance of the play (like the one that took place on 5 November 1611) as a reprise of a loved event? In other words, is *Masque of Oberon*'s antimasque successfully and permanently melded into Shakespeare's play, or is it only a temporary visitor there?

The same question dogs other masques in plays also seemingly borrowed from court entertainments. Paired dancers perform a 'Country pastime' morris round a maypole in Shakespeare and Fletcher's *Two Noble Kinsmen*, a dance that appears to be, in reduced and simplified form, taken from the second antimasque in Francis Beaumont's *Masque of the Inner Temple and Gray's Inn* (performed on 20 February 1613 in the Banqueting House, Whitehall Palace), described in its argument as 'a May daunce or Rurall daunce, consisting . . . of all such persons as are naturall and proper for Countrey sports'.[102] By the same token, John Webster's 'Daunce' in his *Dutchesse of Malfy*, 'consisting of 8. Mad-men, with the musicke answerable thereunto' (and perhaps their song 'o let us howle', for which music survives by Robert Johnson), is thought to have been transferred from the court antimasque of 'Frantics' who 'fell into a madde measure, fitted to a loud phantasticke tune' in Campion's *The Lords Maske*, performed on 14 February 1613.[103] Other surviving Robert Johnson masques seem to have been similarly reused. His music from *The Masque of Amazons*, preserved in the British Library and intended for use at Lord Hay's residence on Twelfth Night 1618, was never performed because 'neither the Quene nor King did like or allow of yt'; but, rather than get rid of it, the company, probably under Middleton's direction, seem to have placed it in *Timon of Athens* where 'a masque of ladies as Amazons, with lutes in their hands, dancing and playing' is crowbarred into the play.[104] An earlier, more successful masque, for the same aristocrat, Campion's *A Maske . . . in Honour of the Lord Hayes* (performed in Whitehall on Twelfth Night 1607), may survive in *Pericles*, where the dance of the knights 'in your Armours' oddly recalls a courtiers' dance of knights with helmets.[105] The most intriguing example of the transferred masque, however, is the dance from Jonson's *Masque of Queenes* that seems to have made its way into Shakespeare's *Macbeth* via Middleton's *The Witch*. In 1609 Jonson wrote his *Masque of Queenes*, which started with an 'antimasque' in which twelve figures were to dance 'in the habit

of *hags*, or *witches*'.[106] This was played by the King's Men at Whitehall on
2 February 1609, with, as usual, the professional players performing
the antimasque, and the courtiers joining in the masque itself. But
Middleton's *Witch* (written between 1609 and 1616) contains an offhand
request, '*here they Daunce ye witches Dance & Ex*[i]*t*', which implies
reuse of the masque dance, for it refers to a witches' dance already
known to the company.[107] When Middleton's *Witch* was itself unsuccessful, its songs were stripped to bolster *Macbeth*, and its dance was, it
seems, taken too: in *Macbeth* the 'bloody baby' scene starts with three
witches already onstage, but then Hecate enters with, say the stage-
directions, 'the other three Witches' (TLN 1566), though the play, up to
this point, has required only three witches in total. When, slightly later
in the scene, '*The Witches Dance, and vanish*' (TLN 1680), the reason for
the swelled witches' entrance seems to emerge; the additional witches are
needed for the dance – which can now take place in pairs: the companies' 'witches dance' would appear to have found its third and final
home.

Whether masques 'stayed' in plays is always open to question. At least
two added masques in plays are noticeably occasion-specific. The masque
inserted into Shakespeare's *Tempest* seems to be substituted for another,
more suitable masque or dance, and does not sit comfortably in the text
that contains it. So Prospero sends Ariel off to return in 'a twinckle' (TLN
1698) with dancers; but Ariel comes back twelve lines later with a single
goddess. Prospero then asks Ariel to come again and 'bring a Corolary/
Rather then want a Spirit' (TLN 1713–14); this time Ariel goes off, but does
not come on again, and Iris enters instead. The dissimilarity between what
Prospero asks to happen, and what does then happen, implies that the
performance prepared for by the play is different from the one now found
in it: a thoughtful article on this subject by Irwin Smith proposes that the
masque as found in the play is written for the *Tempest*'s second court
performance as part of the wedding festivities of Princess Elizabeth and
the Elector Palatine.[108] Similarly, while the masque in the 'bad' quarto of
Shakespeare's *Merry Wives* is, it seems, for a public theatre audience, the
grander masque in the Folio *Merry Wives* appears to be for a specific
court occasion, perhaps the investiture of the Knights of the Garter.[109]
Undoubtedly one-day masques are sometimes found in plays: a document
headed 'The Ante-Masques' and providing 'the Subject of the Masque',
attributed to Aurelian Townshend, seems to have been distributed
on the single performance when his masque was performed inside
Montagu's play *Shepheards' Paradise*.[110] In fact, the more court-like the

play-masque is, the more likely it is to be an impermanent, court-only, resident of its play.

The question can even be raised as to whether all masques in plays were actually the preserve of the court alone. When Middleton and Rowley explain the masque adopted in the *World Tost at Tennis* with the line 'You shall perceive by what comes first in sight,/it was intended for a Royall Night', or when Dekker's *Old Fortunatus* emerges as a version of the play specifically rewritten and elongated with music for court performance, the court associations of masques in plays – or masques in some plays – are strongly suggested.[III]

Here the nature of the playbooks that survive is brought into question. If masques have a different and more select audience from the rest of their texts, then printed plays with masques may reproduce scripts in their 'special' or 'select' form rather than in their daily form. Some overlong texts may actually preserve court productions (rather than literary productions). This would make some sense: a court manuscript is more likely to circulate and so survive to be printed. If so, however, some published playbooks will then contain a confusion of occasions, mingling court-only moments with dialogue from another source, just as court-only prologues and epilogues regularly flank printed plays. It is, though, also possible that songs and masques added specifically for court performances may then – once they existed – have been brought into the public theatre for ordinary performance.

So songs and also masques were regularly removed to tighten a text; they were equally regularly added to enliven it literally or elevate it symbolically – in that some varieties of song, like the 'art song', came with courtly associations. Other songs, and particularly masques, could be temporary not permanent residents in the play in which they featured, resulting in 'composite' playbooks where the dialogue represents one form of text, and a song/masque represents another form, another authorship and another moment in time.

PRINTERS AND 'SEPARATE' SONGS

As has been seen, the simple fact that lyrics were so hesitantly linked to plays results equally in their regular loss and their unexpected insertion. Because each song or masque has its own story, there are often cases when one song is missing and another, in the same play, is not, raising questions about the nature of the playbooks that printers received. The first point to make is that, though the loss of songs might be related to the theatrical events dealt with above (as might the addition of songs), the presence of songs may or may not relate to texts in theatrical form. The story of a song and the story of a playbook containing that song need not be linked, particularly when, as so often happens, the printer was clearly given lyrics still on separate papers which he then integrated.

Take the ditties in the third play of Brome's *Five New Playes, The Weeding of the Covent-Garden*, performed in 1632, and published after the death of its author in 1659. Most of the songs for that play have their own story and, perhaps, their own separate origins. One is frankly lost, and its title 'song' is left stranded amidst the banter about its no longer extant lyrics:

> NIC. Pox on ye peace.
> *Song.*
> NIC. O most melodious.
> CLOT. Most odious, did you say? It is methinks most odoriferous.[112]

Another song is printed in full precisely where it should appear in the text; it consists of the title 'song' that the lost song above had had, succeeded by its lyrics – this is a song either correctly inserted by the printer, or already present in the play's manuscript (in which case 'song' is a 'scribe direction' indicating that the text should be written on a separate paper – see chapter 6):

> CLOT. Take you no care for that. Set your eyes and begin.
> SONG.
> To prove the Battoon the most noble to be.
> Of all other weapons observe his degree . . .[113]

Lastly there is a 'song of Sack' that Nick and Captain Driblow demand and the stage-direction asks for, but the play does not supply; it appears to be another lost song, indicated only by a complex stage-direction on how to divide the absent lyrics between various singers:

> NICK. I say, a song of Sack.
> CAPT. I, let it be of Sack.
> NICK. Now you pump, do you?
> COCK. No, sir, but think of a tune.
> CLOT. If he can pump us up a spring of Sack, we'll keep him, and break half
> the Vintners in Town.
> (*Song.* Now *B.* and *Clot.* askes *Gabriel,* Are you a brother. They fall in the burthen.)
> NICK. I vow, well-said.[114]

But the words to the song are not lost. After the title-page to *The Weeding of the Covent-Garden* but before the start of the dialogue, where one might expect to find a prologue, is a small collection of poetic pieces, only some of which relate to the playtext. First is a poem, 'Upon AGLAURA printed in Folio', which is an attack by Brome on Suckling's 1638 play *Aglaura*: it has nothing to do with *Weeding*. Second comes 'A SONG'; it begins 'Away with all grief and give us more sack': it is the 'song of Sack' required by the dialogue above. Third is 'A PROLOGUE' which, though vague in its terms, seems to be for the original first performance of *Weeding* and is likely to have been written by Brome; fourth is 'Another Prologue' which is obviously for *Weeding*, though equally obviously for that play in revival: it asks the audience to 'take the same surveigh . . . as our Poet took,/Of Covent-Garden . . . Some ten years since . . .'; fifth and finally is a poem 'To my LORD of Newcastle, on his PLAY called THE VARIETY', an obsequious piece by Brome about a play published in 1649 (and performed in 1641) which, again, has nothing to do with *Weeding*.[115] After these five different lyrics, the play proper begins. Thus the 'song of Sack' and the two prologues to *Weeding* are 'topped and tailed' by poems irrelevant to their play, indicating that the printers were given a playbook accompanied by a separate manuscript, or manuscripts, containing randomly relevant additional texts, including one of the songs (in the company of prologues), which they rendered into type in the order received.

Here follows the song of Sack in full as printed at the front of the playbook:

> A SONG.
> Away with all grief and give us more sack.
> 'Tis that which we love, let love have no lack.
> Nor sorrow, nor care can crosse our delights,
> Nor witches, nor goblins, nor Buttery sprights,
> Tho' the candles burne dimme while we can do thus,
> We'll scorn to flie them: but we'll make them flie us.
> Old Sack, and old Songs, and a merry old crew
> Will fright away Sprights, when the ground looks blew.[116]

As can be seen, though this is the song asked for by the dialogue, it is not in the form the dialogue requested: '(*Song.* Now *B.* and *Clot.* askes *Gabriel*, Are you a brother. They fall in the burthen.)'. This text does not separate its 'burden' (meaning its refrain carrying 'the gist or theme of the whole poem') or indicate where the conversation mooted in the dialogue is to be interspersed.[117] Then again, the request for the song in the dialogue is itself some kind of revision, for neither 'Gabriel' nor Betty, the only 'B' in the play, is in this scene as written. So the play, largely a good text, is provided in incomplete revised form at this moment, while the correct song dates from a different moment in the life of the stage-play, or, at least, from a different source. It is undoubtedly authorial, for what must actually be its burden, the last two lines, are reprised twice in another Brome play, *Joviall Crew*: '*Old* Sack, *and old* Songs, *and a Merry old* Crew, /*Can charm* ['fright' at the second singing] *away* Cares *when the Ground looks* blew.'[118] The 'Song of sack' then is authorial, for a revision, and kept in a bundle that includes prologues and unrelated poetry (so probably not in its musical form). What emerges from this is an indication of what is repeatedly evident in this chapter: songs often have separate sources from the plays they are in, with the result that the lyrics are not of an age and stage with the rest of the printed playbook.

Regularly songs circulated in the company of prologues, epilogues and other scrolls as a bundle, for they are often lost and found as a group. Song lyrics with prologues and epilogues for Cartwright's *Royal Slave* are bound together in a manuscript miscellany, and songs, prologues and epilogues for other plays too are grouped together in books of poetry, including Shirley's *Poems* (1646), and Beaumont's *Poems* (1653, republished in 1660 as *The Golden Remains of those So Much Admired Dramatick Poets, Francis Beaumont & John Fletcher . . . Together with the Prologues, Epilogues, and Songs, Many of Which were Never Before Inserted in his Printed Playes*).[119] Brome's songs regularly arrived at the printing house in a group with their stage-orations; they are printed in a cluster together before his playbooks as a result. So two songs are situated one after the other following on from the 'Drammatis Personae' in his *The Queen and Concubine* (published in the same edition of *Five New Playes* as *Weeding*). In this instance, they contain precise instructions as to where in the printed text they *ought* to belong, indicating that they were acquired after the rest of the text had been printed, or 'forgotten' until that point; they are entitled '*The first Song, for pag. 88.*' and '*The second Song, for pag. 111*'.[120] And before it is thought that both these circumstances relate principally to the state in which the dead Brome's playtexts were preserved, it should be pointed out that another Brome play, published during its author's lifetime, has a song separated in just the same fashion. Brome and Heywood's *The Late Lancashire Witches*, a play thrown relatively hurriedly together to capitalize on a current public affair, and printed the same year it was performed, has a single song printed at its end entitled 'Song. II. Act'; it follows next after the dialogue-play's final word 'Finis' which it thus renders erroneous, again implying a 'free-floating' song handed over to the printers with the playbook, and tacked on by them rather than inserted.[121] But then Brome had signed an agreement with Queen Henrietta's Men in July 1635 to come up with prologues, epilogues, revised scenes and songs for revivals, so will naturally have thought of all such sections as discrete entities anyway.[122] He is not, however, alone in this.

When songs precede or follow plays, and occupy the 'liminal' space of the prologue and epilogue, often joining those documents, their 'separate' origin is evident. And songs by – or at least, attached to plays by – many other writers are so placed. At the beginning of Massinger and Field's *Fatall Dowry* of 1632, four songs ('*First Song*', '*Second Song*', '*Cittizens Song of the Courtier*', '*Courtiers Song of the Citizen*') are published; there are two blackletter songs, '*The first Three-mans* Song' and '*The second Three-mans* Song (subtitled '*This is to be sung at the latter end*'), next to one another and preceding Dekker's 1600 *Shomakers Holiday*; as well as a 'SONG', 'Oares, Oares, Oares, Oares', after Dekker and Webster's *West-ward Hoe*.[123] 'The drinking Song, to the Second Act', meanwhile, is printed before Fletcher *et al.*'s *The Bloody Brother* (also known as *Rollo, Duke of Normandy*); there is a single song called 'The Song' printed at the end of Belchier's 1618 *Hans Beer-Pot* (also called *See Me and See Me Not*) and followed by another afterthought, '*An Addition to the Moores last speech*', with no indication as to which of the six songs required by the play (of which the other five are lost) it actually is.[124] The words to 'I. SONG' and 'II. SONG' are printed following on from one another and preceding the epilogue at the end of Massinger's 1655 *The Guardian*; the words to 'The Song in the second Act' and The Song in the fourth Act' similarly follow one another at the back of Habington's *Queene of Arragon*; and a single copy of Henry Glapthorne's *Wit in a Constable* (1640) contains 'Song the first' ('Youth, and beauty; strength, and grace') and 'Song the second' ('Beautie, vertue, wealth, and wit') on an additional leaf at the end that the others do not have.[125] *Philotus* has Campion's 'What if a day' appended to its 1603 printing (the song is absent from the play when it is reprinted in 1612); other songs, that are undoubtedly later additions to their plays, are placed after Heywood's *Rape of Lucrece* and Middleton's *Mad World* (1640 edition only).[126]

So when a playbook made its way to a printing house, it did not simply do so with or without its songs. It might have some songs written in place and others handed over in a bundle of scrolls or separate and alone – depending, perhaps, on whether the lyrics were in set 'musical' form (in which case their circulation was often with other musical manuscripts) or simple written form (in which their circulation was often with other scrolls). A careful look at where songs are situated in printed plays, as well as what is and is not printed as part of them, illustrates that even some printed playbooks with songs in the correct place have been constructed in the printing house out of separate documents: correctly placed songs may still have an entirely different origin in date, authorship and time from the book they are in. The odd printed play even boasts of this: Heywood's 1608 *Rape of Lucrece*, as has been discussed, claims on its title-page that 'the severall Songes' are positioned 'in their apt places' (at least some of these actually follow on from the end of the playtext, so the claim is not entirely true); while the 1679 Beaumont and Fletcher folio is proud not only to have acquired copies of hitherto lost songs, prologues and epilogues but, additionally, to have 'inserted [them] in their proper places' – which, in this case, it has for the most part successfully managed to do.[127]

Other printers did their best to place songs accurately without discussing the separate papers they received; only when they err are traces of this visible. Out of eight songs that should fall before the direction 'Exeunt' in Blount's edition of Lyly's plays, seven are misplaced after it.[128] That these particular songs were separately acquired has already been discussed, but the same mild misplacement can be seen in other plays too, and presumably for the same reason. Several songs in the Beaumont and Fletcher 1647 folio were, it seems, printed from a 'separate' source (meaning that, as in the Beaumont and Fletcher 1679 folio, some of the songs were independently supplied). In *Loves Cure* the 1647 text contains a passage in which Piorato wants to see Malroda, and the exchange is printed thus:

ALG.   Ile call her to you for that.
PIO.   No, I wil charme her.   *Enter Malroda.*
ALG.   She's come.
PIO.   My Spirit.
MAL.   Oh my Sweet,
        Leape hearts to lips, and in our kisses meet.
PIO.   *Turn, turn thy beauteous face away,*   Song.
        How pale and sickly mak't the day,
            In emulation of thy brighter beams! . . .
ALG.   Wel, I wil leave you to your fortitude.[129]

Actually, as Dyce first pointed out, the song is supposed to be the 'charme' that lures Malroda forth, and should therefore be placed in the text directly after 'I wil charme her' and before Malroda's entrance. The misplacement is the result of a printer's not knowing where exactly to put a freestanding songtext.[130] Similarly, confusion around a stage-direction for 'Musicke, Song, wreath' in *Valentinian* seems to have 'arisen from the provision of the lyric in a separate manuscript':

> the evidence is fragile, but I think what there is points towards the printer's copy as being a scribal transcript of Fletcher's working papers made before the lyrics of the songs were available . . . the printer's copy was, of course, provided with the song lyrics, these perhaps having been added to the manuscript on separate leaves during the course of revision.[131]

Traces on a Fletcher manuscript may even give a sense of the kind of confused play that the printer on these occasions received. In the manuscript for *Womans Prize* (*Tamer Tamed*), there is no song supplied for act 2 (as there is in the printed text of that play); there is, however, on the relevant page, a clump of sealing wax in which fibres are visible. It appears that a song – perhaps a theatre scroll, or perhaps an authorial addition – was once plugged onto the relevant area, but has subsequently dropped away.[132] A roughly attached, or wholly unattached, songtext would result in just the kind of light misplacement as is visible on *Loves Cure* and *Valentinian*.

Occasionally even correctly placed songs bear indications of their independent origins. Again, the Beaumont and Fletcher 1647 folio provides an example: there, when songs are labelled by number, the numbers do not match the numbers of songs in the actual play (so the numbering does not appear to be 'lifted' from the theatre). *Maid in the Mill* contains songs numbered '1 Song.', '2. Song.', '3. Song.', '4. Song', '5. Song.' though '1 Song' is actually the third song: the numbering, which may be by acts, seems to be a labelling policy helpful for a printer who has received a play and five separate song documents to be set in the correct order.[133]

Related to the placement of lyrics is the fact that songs that are to be read or sung twice in plays are often reproduced only once in the printed book, and not always at the first time of singing/speaking. Again, in such instances, the compositors may have had only one theatre document for a song that features twice; alternatively, the playtext itself only contained once what the author relied on a scribe to copy and circulate correctly – both options are also discussed in chapter 6 with respect to letters spoken twice but provided only once. It is interesting that two Jonson plays – despite, again, the author's care to have the text presented well on paper – reproduce the song the second, rather than the first, time it features.

In *Epicoene* the boy is asked to sing a song about Lady Haughtie that 'will get . . . me a perfect deale of ill will at the mansion . . . whose lady is the argument of it'.[134] When finally prevailed upon to voice the insulting text, he, as the playbook has it, then 'sings' what looks superficially like a normal 'lost' song:

> Cle.   . . . sir, you shall goe there no more, lest I bee faine to seeke your voyce in
>   my ladies rushes, a fortnight hence. Sing, sir. Boy sings.[135]

Later in the play, however, Clerimont boasts that it was he who 'made a song' to acknowledge Haughtie's 'autumnall face' and 'peec'd beauty'. At this stage he recites his words and they *are* printed: 'Still to be neat, still to be drest,/As, you were going to a feast.'[136] These are obviously a repetition of the words for the song the boy has sung. In *The Divell is an Asse*, similarly, '*Doe but looke, on her eies!*', the song that Manley sings and Wittipol says, is also supplied only for the second of the two occasions on which it features.[137]

In other words, faced with a playbook and some loose songs, a printer might place the songs accurately where they belonged in the narrative, fit the songs into the text somewhere else – the beginning or end of the playbook, for instance – or neglect to print them at all. Whatever the printer did, each of the 'inserted' songs might have its own form: might be 'theatrical' when the play was 'literary', might be 'literary' when the play was theatrical. Songs should always be regarded as potentially cohabitants of the play they are in, rather than as elements of that play.

TRACES OF 'THEATRE' IN PRINTED PLAYS

But if a song can come from a different paper and have a different source, then it can reveal interesting details about itself and its origins (and can muddle the reader looking for information about the playtext from the songtext). As discussed, not all 'free-floating' songs have a shared origin; some seem to have been acquired in the form in which they originated with the playwright – as, essentially, a poem; some seem to be in the form in which they were used in the theatre – as, essentially, a copied stage paper, perhaps cued, and perhaps containing music.

To look at what appear to be preserved theatre texts first: very occasionally, in printed books, 'cues' are provided with song lyrics. When this happens, the printed playbook seems to contain what otherwise is lost: the song in the form in which it was to be learnt or read by actors, perhaps the rehearsal text, perhaps the text to be sung from onstage. So in the printed playbook for John Suckling's *Brennoralt*, one song ends with the non-rhyming line '*Wine,---Wine.---*:

GRA.   *Wine, Wine, oh 'tis divine*
       Come fill it unto our brother:
       What's at the tongues end,
       It forth does send,
       And will not a syllable smother
       Then,
       It unlocks the brest
       And throwes out the rest,
       And learnes us to know each other.
       Wine,---Wine.---
DOR.   Mad lads, have you been here ever since?[138]

As it happens, a musical setting for the song from this text survives; a setting that appears to reflect what was sung in the theatre. It is essentially the same as far as words go, except that it lacks the '*Wine,---Wine.---*' line, ending on the more likely 'each other'. And, as the '*Wine,---Wine.---*' line would make better sense outside the song – the song praising wine is followed by a cry for some – it looks as though the compositor has simply printed on from the song into what should be a dialogue line. How? The implication is that he received a separate 'cued' songtext where the song and the words to be spoken after it were supplied, and he failed to note the difference between song and speech.

This is all the more likely because, despite the fact that very few theatre songs with their music survive from the period – so there are not many occasions on which a song as sung and as printed can be compared – on another occasion a printed playbook, again, takes the song a line too far. The song in the printed text of William Berkeley's *The Lost Lady* is, again, presented with a last line that does not rhyme with the other lines and sits uncomfortably amongst them:

SONG.
Where did you borrow that last sigh,
    And that relenting groane:
For those that sigh and not for love,
    Usurpe what's not their owne.
Loves arrowes sooner Armor pierce,
    Then your soft snowy skinne,
Your eies can onely teach us love,
    But cannot take it in.
Another sigh, then I may hope.
    The Song being ended, Enter PHILLIDA.[139]

This time there are two manuscripts for the song, both of which are in collections of music that seem to have a theatrical origin, and both of which lack the ambivalent last line. The printed play too may reveal cue-confusion resulting from a song provided in theatre form.[140]

That theatrical texts were cued in just this fashion can be guessed at not only backwards through printed texts such as these, but also forwards through looking at later theatrical habit. Documents for Garrick's 1766 production of *A Midsummer Night's Dream* include a paper with the words to a song on it, written in neat and flanked with cues: it starts with a cue 'Will we sing, and bless this place', goes on to present 'SONG, by a Fairy of Oberon's Train' and, having provided the lyrics, then gives the next cue, 'Obe. Now, until the break of day'.[141] Similarly, the eighteenth-century interludes for *The Musick in Mackbeth* by Purcell survive in theatre form in a manuscript where a spoken cue, 'ha! What can this be', is followed by a musical interlude leading on to the line 'speak sister speak': texts taking the same broad form, perhaps with music, perhaps without, appear to have been what the printers were given in the plays above.[142]

The second kind of cued texts are found in some of Shakespeare's plays. These are songs that are interspersed with instructions containing advice about who should join in the chorus, refrain or 'burthen'. So *As You Like It* contains a song that, as set in print, looks like this:

> Musicke, Song.
>
> *What shall he have that kild the Deare?*
> *His Leather skin, and hornes to weare:*
> *Then sing him home the rest shall beare this burthen;*
> *Take thou no scorne to weare the horne,*
> *It was a crest ere thou wast borne . . .* (TLN 2136–41)

The third line '*Then sing him home the rest shall beare this burthen*' regularly concerns editors, some of whom leave it in the song, some of whom have just '*Then sing him home*' in the song with '*the rest shall beare this burthen*' in a stage-direction, some of whom turn the whole line into dialogue. Whatever the case, the line was not part of the original song: it is absent from such early musical versions as the Folger manuscript copied around 1625, and such later settings as John Hilton's *Catch That Catch Can* (1652).[143] And '*the rest shall beare this burthen*' matches most closely the tone of stage-directions: 'Brain: Sings & his crue Keepes the Burthen'; 'Enter the wassaile . . . singinge the songe, & all of them bearing the burden'; 'Widgine . . . sings this Song. They all beare the burden'.[144] That said, if this line were, alternatively, a spoken instruction rather than a stage-direction – in Juliet Dusinberre's edition of *As You Like It* the line is given to Jacques, so he can articulate the fact that the burden of 'the lusty horn' is really to be borne by everyone – it remains a cue, but a spoken one.[145] A similar point can also be made of *The Tempest* where 'Come unto these yellow sands' (TLN 521) seems to muddle instructions for the chorus with lines of the song: '*Foote it featly heere, and there, and sweete Sprights beare the burthen*' (a stage-direction adds 'Burthen dispersedly' (TLN 525–6)); as a music score has not been found for this song, however, it is impossible to sort out exactly how to separate song from instruction. It seems that printers were sometimes given songs containing staging instructions, quite possibly because they originated in theatre papers.

Sometimes, even without any cues, there are suggestions that the printed songs are in post-composer, rather than authorial, pre-composer, form. As will be shown, composers could cut or rephrase lyrics in the process of setting them; if a printed text reflects those cuts then it represents the song as it left the composer, not as it was sent to him. Again, there is not usually enough information surviving to judge when that happens – two separate sets of lyrics are required – but on the odd occasion it is possible to get a sense of which text has made it to the printing house.

'Hence all you vaine Delights' is a set of lyrics often said to have been written by William Strode, though they are probably by Middleton. They were, either way, published in the Beaumont and Fletcher 1647 folio (in a play thought to be substantially by Middleton), *The Nice Valour*.[146] In that play, the song is an unusual nineteen lines long; it is usually, these days, printed in the form in which that text presents it:

> *Ther's nought in this life sweet,*
> *If man were wise to see't,*
> *But onely Melancholy,*
> *O sweetest melancholy.*
> *Welcome folded Armes, and fixed eyes,*
> *A sigh that piercing mortifies . . .*[147]

Yet a jokey contemporary parody of this song, 'Come all my deare delights', lacks the 'echo' line to 'O sweetest melancholy':

> Ther's nought in this world sweete,
> If Men had Eyes to see't;
> Save only Wine, & Wenches.
> Welcome circling Armes, & rowling Eyes,
> A Laugh that peirceth through ye skies . . .[148]

In fact the lyrics as reproduced in many a commonplace book of the period – including several that, together with a printed version, precede the play – are generally presented as eighteen lines long, and are often divided into three verses of six lines each accordingly.[149] 'O sweetest melancholy' enters the poem for the first time at the 1647 printing; it is, as surviving music for it suggests, inserted into the lyrics to facilitate a musical flourish.[150] Here is a printer seemingly given a theatre text for the song, with the composer's changes included on it.

Very occasionally, and usually only for masques, the musical notation will be printed together with the words for some of the songs. Such notated songs are pooled together and situated at the back of the play-book; these may be the closest to completed composer's texts to survive in print. Examples include the appendix of five musical settings attached to *A Maske . . . in Honour of the Lord Hayes*, produced on 6 January, 1607; and the appendix of five musical settings attached to *A Maske: presented . . . on Saint Stephens Night Last at the Mariage of the Right Honourable the Earle of Somerset* of 1614. In the latter, an even closer glimpse is provided of the way in which the musical texts were given to the printer. The final song has a printed heading: 'A Song, made by *Th. Campion*, and sung in the Lords Maske at the *Count Palatines* Marriage, we have here added, to fill up these emptie Pages.'[151] A song from a different masque, that is to say, has been supplied in the '*Somerset*' masque to fill a gap. Obviously the 'spare' song with its music was such a detached and separate document from its own masque physically, but also intellectually, that it was thought able to retain its integrity tacked to the back of another masque altogether.

All these have been examples of the printer receiving, irrespective of the origin of the playscript, a theatre or composer's version of the song (or a document that doubled as both). But the printer could also receive the reverse: a song document in a form further from the moment of performance than the rest of the text.

Sometimes the printer seems to have been given a 'short' version of a song that, when discovered in a miscellany or musical manuscript, is found to have extra lyrics. Of course there is a variety of reasons to explain this: the printer may have been given a 'theatre' song that was 'cut down' for performance; or may have received a song in its original 'authorial' version that was only subsequently elongated. But sometimes the 'long' song is so closely linked to the play, or so pertinent to the rest of the story, as to indicate that it must once have featured in performance, and that the printer has received a doctored text (or has, perhaps, forgotten to turn a freestanding song-page over).

For example, all the printer has of '*Courtier, if thou needs wilt wive*', the third song added to the beginning of Massinger and Field's *Fatall Dowry* of 1632, is the following set of verses – which, were there not a separate source for them, might seem to be complete in themselves:

> *Cittizens Song of the Courtier.*
>
> *Courtier, if thou needs wilt wive,*
> *From this lesson learne to thrive.*
> *If thou match a Lady, that passes thee in birth and state,*
> *Let her curious garments be*
> *Twice above thine owne degree;*
> *This will draw great eyes upon her,*
> *Get her servants and thee honour.*

In context in the play, this will be the 'new Song . . . cal'd The happy husband' that Aymer sings to 'please/Two companies'; it prevents Charalois from hearing that his wife Beaumelle is committing adultery, while simultaneously adding fuel to the sexual act.[152] The song's concentration on what constitutes an ideal wife is ironic, but it is the second verse, preserved in a miscellany, that accounts for the tenor of the song – and that, with its last-line reference to (happy) 'husbandes', also explicates the title Aymer gives it. With a wife who is given free rein, explains the second verse, 'thou at night shalt nothing miss', moreover most other courtiers constitute such 'husbands':

> let hir talke & court & kiss,
> thou at night shalt nothing miss,
> paint she must, perfume, & ride.
> have hir ffoote = man by hir side.
> horse hir well. & let hir will
> be thy law in good or Ill.
> search the court, & doe not lye
> Yf not such husbandes thou espy.[153]

Without the second verse, the song does not see itself through from the wife to the husband, and so does not entirely make sense in context. With the second verse, on the other hand, a moment of heightened theatre is created when the words all but reveal the adultery to the enraptured Charalois.

Another example is 'From the Temple to the Boord', the third song of Daniel's *Hymen's Triumph*. The printed text and manuscript to that play discreetly stop at 'wt or joyfull bridal Song', but another manuscript text of the song reveals its coarser continuation: a description of exactly what the joys of the marriage bed consist of; it too was undoubtedly written by Daniel.[154]

Shakespeare, also, provides an instance. 'Get you hence' from his *Winter's Tale* is, in the Robert Johnson music manuscript for it, a whole verse longer. The first verse, described as 'passing merry' (TLN 2110), is about a man loved of two women; its theme of a rake and his two heartbroken paramours is a dangerous reversal of events in the story of the play, reminding the audience of the chaste Hermione who 'dies' for being loved by two men. In the music manuscript's additional verse, however, the rake changes: he leaves dances and fairs for ever, while the women who love him, Phill ('fill') and Frize ('frize'), will either sit sadly, walk madly or weep in dark corners. A renouncement of the sheep shearing, and a consideration of the reality of love and its potential to cause great suffering, become the 'new' message of the longer song. Perhaps the second verse was cut because it was too bleak, beyond the remit of the story, except that it brings out an undercurrent running throughout the scene and the play. And, as Autolycus the clown offers to 'have this song out anon by our selves' (TLN 2134) later, there is every possibility that the entire text was sung, or that at least the second verse was added, like *Twelfth Night*'s 'The rain it raineth every day', as a reflective commentary at the end of the play. Reads the extra verse:

> nevermore fore lasses sake
> will I dance at fare or wake
> Ah mee A Ah me Ah mee
> who shall then were a raced ['raised'?] shooe
> or what shall ye bagpipe doe
> recant or elce you slay mee
> recant or elce you slay me
> if thou leave our Andorne greene
> where shall fill or frize be seene
> sleeping what sleeping sleeping
> no Ile warrant the sitting sadly
> or Idely walking madly
> in some darke
> in some darke darke Corner weeping
> in some darke darke Corner weeping.[155]

One more example is a song from Thomas May's *The Old Couple*, which, in the music manuscript, contains some more, utterly relevant, lines; moreover, the full words, including the phrases absent from the printed text, also circulate as a freestanding poem.[156] The printer may here have received a theatrical songtext containing the lyrics cut down for speaking; or may, again, have acquired the text in an earlier authorial state, or simply in a defective state. For whatever reason, the words of the song as the music manuscript presents them have a richness stripped from the words as they are in the play: the italic sections represent the words in manuscript only:

> Deare doe not your faire bewty wronge,
> in thinkinge still you are to younge:
> the rose & lilly in your cheeke,
> flourish, & no more ripeninge seeke:
> *inflaming beames shott from your eye,*
> *doe shew loves Midsummer is nighe:*
> your cherry lippe, redd soft & sweete
> proclaymes such fruite for taste is meete
> *Love is still young a buxumme boy,*
> *and younglings are alowde to toy,*
> then loose no time for love hath winges
> & flyes away, *and flyes away, and flyes away* from aged things.[157]

Other printers have received manuscripts more scrappy or damaged than the rest of the playscript; this can be seen when they are unable to read all the text in a song, and so print a 'gap' for the illegible words; examples include two of the songs in Jonson's masque *Pleasure Reconciled to Virtue*: '*O More, and more, this was so well*', which includes a line '*Just to the -------- you move your limbs*' (in the Crane transcript of this masque, the line is 'just to ye tune you move your limbes'); and '*It followes now you are to prove*', which includes a line '*It should be such should envie draw, / but ----------- overcome it*' (in the Crane transcript, the line is 'It should be such shold envy draw, but ever overcome-it').[158]

Songs in plays, then, may not be correctly placed; may represent composer's rather than author's texts; may be sourced from theatre documents or, alternatively, from authorial documents (either of which may have a different nature from the playtext); and may not provide the song as it was actually manifested in performance. Occasions on which a song is longer in musical manuscript than it is in printed text only add to the implication that lyrics as written and as set to music were altered, and that the lyrics gathered back by printers and placed in plays may be in one form or the other, and may or may not represent the form in which they were staged and/or the form in which they were authorially written.

CONCLUSION

Just as playwrights often neglected to provide the words to their songs, so
theatre composers, anxious to preserve their other music, were remarkably
unwilling to publish their theatrical compositions: Robert Johnson and
William Lawes, songwriters for the King's Men, published none of their
many theatrical compositions; John Wilson, also a composer for the
King's Men, only published some of his, muddled in with new settings
of songs by Johnson, when down on his luck during the penny-pinching
interregnum. Was this because theatre music was thought only to make
sense in the context of the rest of the play? That would be intriguing,
with its suggestion that a theatre song was so different from another
kind of song that it could not have an independent life outside its
drama. Yet everything in this chapter has militated against that idea,
from the fact that audience members might demand theatre songs,
to the survival of the music for theatre songs in non-theatre contexts –
two Jonson songs, 'Come my Celia' and 'have you seen but a bright
lily grow' from *The Divell is an Asse* are in a songbook that has no
theatrical origins, for instance.[159] The question then is whether songs-
with-music were not valued highly, which equally does not work with
the information in this chapter, in which songscripts circulated as far
as Holland and Germany as desired texts. As composers do not seem to
have been ashamed of their theatrical writing, the reason is probably
much more humdrum: the post-performance demand for play *words*
was not matched by a post-performance demand for play *music*,
probably because music could only make sense to people who could read
and perform it, a self-selecting group much smaller than the group of
people who could read (and enact) plays. This does, however, have a
major effect on the circulation of songs. As musical texts they, in their
entirety, circulated almost wholly in manuscript, while the rest of a play
had a real possibility of circulating in print. Songs thus travelled with all
the kudos and all the real possibilities for loss or extinction that other
manuscripts had, and were, like manuscript poems, a different entity from
their print neighbours.

   This explains how, against all the stories of songs lost from plays, there
is a counter story of 'found' songs in music manuscripts, the plays of
which are 'lost'. For it was never that songs were more suppressed than
plays; simply that their methods of survival depended on different people
and texts. One playless song, for which a home can perhaps be identified,
is set by John Wilson; it survives in two music manuscripts. In it

the singer commands a storm – as it is manifested in sea, roaring winds, mountainous waves – to treat tenderly a boat that has been left to its mercy:

> downe downe be still you seas
> waters your dread mistris pleas
> downe downe I say
> all beegenth as the day
> you that sing and roar aloft
> whissling winds bee still and soft
> not an angrey breath let fly
> you proud mountaines fall and die
> tumble noe more
> nor kicke nor rore
> nor troble hir keel
> to make hir reell
> but safe from surges rokes and sand
> kiss hir and stroke hir and sett hir a land.[160]

In Fletcher's *The Pilgrim* a mad Scholar has a song in which he first imprecates the storm in Lear-like fashion, then, taking himself to be Neptune, commands the waters, then the winds, then the waves to be at peace; finally he asks that the fish and seamonsters not terrorise the sailors whose bark, he entreats, should be kept unbruised. The scholar's outburst is also followed by a request for '*Musick, Song*' that calms him from his fit. And, as Wilson, the setter of the song above, was a theatre composer, and as the words take up the terrified scholar's frames of reference and soften them to end on a lullaby, this song probably belongs to the play, either constituting its '*Musick, Song*' or replacing the scholar's '*Down ye angry waters*'.[161] Here is the text that seems to negotiate with the song in some way, whilst not containing it:

> SCHO. Be not shaken,
>   Nor let the singing of the storm shoot through ye,
>   Let it blow on, blow on: let the clouds wrastle,
>   And let the vapours of the earth turn mutinous,
>   The Sea in hideous mountaines rise and tumble
>   Upon a Dolphins back, Ile make all tremble,
>   For I am *Neptune*.
> MAST.   Now what think ye of him?
> 2 GENT. Alas poore man.
> SCHO.   Your Barke shall plough through all,
>   And not a Surge so saucy to disturbe her.
>   Ile see her safe, my power shall saile before her.

> *Down ye angry waters all,*
> *Ye loud whistling whirlwinds fall;*
> *Down ye proud Waves, ye stormes cease;*
> *I command ye, be at peace.*
> *Fright not with your churlish Notes,*
> *Nor bruise the Keele of Bark, that flotes:*
> *No devouring Fish come nigh,*
> *Nor Monster in my Empery,*
> *Once shew his head, or terror bring;*
> *But let the weary Saylor sing:*
> *Amphitrite with white armes*
> *Strike my Lute, Ile sing Charmes.*

MAST.   He must have Musicke now: I must observe him.
         His fit will grow to full else. *Musick, Song.*
2 GENT. I must pitty him.
MAST.   Now he will in himselfe most quietly,
         And clean forget all, as he had done nothing.[162]

A more extreme example is when a song or music remains for which the entire play is lost: just because a play is no longer extant does not mean that its music is gone, in the same way that just because a play *is* extant does not mean that its lyrics and/or its music have survived. Music, though not words, entitled 'The Nobleman' may be the last surviving morsel of Cyril Tourneur's lost play *The Nobleman*; it appears to offer the tune of the masque element of the play.[163] And John Jowett argues that 'CUPID is VENUS onely Joy', which has been described already as a song Middleton used for two of his other plays, *A Chast Mayd in Cheape-Side* and *More Dissemblers Besides Women*, is the sole survivor from Middleton's now lost *Masque of Cupids*.[164] Even the well-known Robert Johnson song 'Woods rocks & Mountaines, and you desert places/Where nought but bitter cold and hunger dwells . . .' might constitute the single unadulterated surviving moment from Shakespeare and Fletcher's lost play *Cardenio*.[165] That song, which is found in two separate manuscripts – containing a single verse in one, and two verses in the second – has terminology that closely resembles what is thought to be the source text for *Cardenio*, Shelton's 1612 translation of *Don Quixote*. In that book, Dorotea asks 'the solitarinesse of these rockes . . . these craggs and thickets . . . [to afford] me leisure to communicate my mishaps to heaven' and laments that having 'found neyther rocke nor downefall' she is obliged to 'hide my selfe againe among these desarts'.[166] Intriguingly, similar phrasing (though a different song) is to be found, too, in Theobald's *Double Falshood*, which claims to contain the bones of a 'Shakespeare' play on the Don Quixote theme, and is often thought to be based on *Cardenio*. There Violante exclaims:

> How much more grateful are these craggy Mountains,
> And these wild Trees, than things of nobler Natures,
> For These receive my Plaints, and mourn again
> In many Echoes to Me.[167]

Like these two extracts, 'Woods rocks & Mountaines' depicts a moment where the singer asks rocks, trees, downfalls ('fountaines') and the desert to listen to and then echo her grief. Written by the main theatre musician for the King's Men, and contained in manuscripts full of musical settings for plays, the song probably belongs to a lost play; *Cardenio* offers one – and the most exciting – of its potential homes. If so, the words for that song, too, might be (though need not be) by Shakespeare or Fletcher:

> Woods rocks & Mountaines & you desert places
> where nought but bitter cold & hunger dwells
> heare a poore maids last words killd with disgraces
> slide softly while I sing you silver fountaines
> & lett your hollow waters like sad bells
> Ring ring to my woes while miserable I
> Cursing my fortunes dropp dropp dropp a teare & dye.
>
> Griefs, woes, and groanings, hopes and all such lyes
> I give to broaken harts yt dayly weepe
> To all poore Maids in love, my lost desiringe.
> Sleepe sweetly while I sing my bitter Moaninge
> And last my hollow lovers that nere keepe
> Truth [truth] in their harts, while Miserable I
> Cursinge my fortunes, drop [drop drop] a teare and dye.[168]

It is possible other surviving music manuscripts contain songs belonging to plays that, shorn of indications of what they are, are 'lost' while still extant.

Alternatively, as has been argued, even when songs circulated without their music, as their verbal content alone, they were likely not to be written into the playtext from the start, and to circulate in a bundle containing prologues and epilogues; in that case, their survival or lack of survival depended on the popularity and availability of paratext to the printer.

Immediately this raises questions for modern editors: the situation of a song in an early modern play should not be blindly accepted, for it may have been inserted into its place by a printer, and that printer may not have had instructions as to where the lyrics should go. Linked to this is a series of other problems not always fully considered when dating plays: the channels by which songs were written, added, rewritten and changed have an entirely different trajectory from the story of the creation of a play's dialogue, so that dating a play *from* its songs – dating *As You Like It*, for instance, from its Morley song – is always a questionable idea: dating a songtext only actually dates the lyrics themselves, not the play that surrounds them. Similarly, using stylometrics on a play and including its songs in that equation is dangerous: a song may well come from a different period as well as having a different author from the rest of the play.

Finally, songs have such an odd relationship to the playwright that they query notions of the play as 'literature', at least in the modern sense of 'literature'. In the early modern period, context-defining lyrics, as has been shown, were often not printed by their authors, even though the literal and emotional meaning of the play suffered as a direct result. The author concerned enough to prepare his plays for the press is often not faithful either to all the words he wrote or to the performance: Shirley, publishing his own *Bird in the Cage* in the very year of its performance, 1633 (having taken the time to produce for it an ironic dedication to Prynne), has already lost a song that will have encapsulated and eroticised the themes of a scene it was in.

CAT.   Shall we try our Lutes Madam?
DUG.   And voices if you please.
DON.   Yes you may try, they say Musicke built the wals of Thebes, it were
       a greater myracle if you could charme these to fall . . . Now would I give
       all my jewels for the sight of a paire of breeches, though there were nothing
       in em.
                                Song.
       This but feedes our dulnesse.[169]

This absence is not, it has been argued, because Shirley lacked rights to his songs, but because playhouse contingencies led songs to circulate in dislocated form: Shirley did not have his ditties to hand. What is more striking, though, is that Shirley did not mind the absence – but of course he did not. If the song was missing because it was popular and the theatre was holding it back, then the very lack of the song bespoke its reputation on stage. If the song was lost because it was in a pile of music manuscripts in the theatre or in the home of the singer, that was fine too: its absence manifested the successful performance of Shirley's play, suggesting that it and/or its tunes were still in current use, and tempting the reader back to the playhouse. While if a keen reader-musician hunted London for the music, spending time on the acquisition of the morsels that made up the full play, that was flattering to the author – and, again, all to the good of the theatre as an advertisement. In other words, an absent song, though it would affect a play's literary progress, could boost its theatrical reputation, and some authors were capable of trading the one for the other at the musical moments. Of course, this raises further questions about the playwright's relationship to songs in the first place. If a playwright was always conscious that a song would be extracted from his play, and if he even, himself, was part of the extraction process, what does that say about the way he conceived of the lyrics: was the song, at the moment of writing, part of the drama, or was it always aside from the text?

Much the same can be asked too of the reader of the play, then and now, for whom even extant songs are, in their nature, not entirely integrated into the text in the way they would have been in performance. Watching a theatrical entertainment, an audience member can be as interested in the music as in the words of a song, and sometimes more interested: but, lacking the music, a paper playbook always shows the reader how far from the genuine experience of performance he or she is. Existing songs in a play are always moments of loss, for songs are so performative as to be already semi-'lost' when without their music: their widespread actual loss may be linked to this. Every lost song, however, indicates that a theatrical need has overtaken a literary need; this chapter has offered some of the practical, theatrical and printing-house reasons to suggest why that might be.

CHAPTER 6

Scrolls

Before a word of an early modern playbook has even been read, certain sections of its contents already stand out as distinctive. While 'dialogue' is generally printed in roman text, and stage-directions and, often, speech-prefixes are generally in italics, there is a separate variety of text printed within the 'dialogue' section that may be in large type, in italics, or simply spaced in such a way as to separate it from the words that flank it. This variety of text is – or, rather, these varieties of text are – 'scrolls': the papers that are to be delivered onstage, such as letters, proclamations, bills, verses, challenges, schedules, epitaphs, itemised lists, prologues and epilogues (discussed in chapter 4) and songs (discussed in chapter 5).

A typical example can be found in Massinger's *Great Duke of Florence* in which Lidia '*Opens the Letter*', then speaks, then reads what she holds in her hand. Here the scroll is in italic type, differentiating it from the dialogue that surrounds it, whilst associating it with the stage-directions, as though its contents, too, will 'direct' the actor:

                        I

With Eagles eyes will curiously peruse it.   *Reads the Letter.*
Chast Lidia: the favours are so great
   On me by you conferr'd, that to intreat
The least addition to 'em, in true sense
   May argue me of blushlesse impudence.
. . .
How to prevent it, if your goodnesse finde
   You save two lives, and me you ever binde,
          The honourer of your vertues, Giovanni.[1]

Layout additionally isolates the letter here: the salutation, 'The honourer of your vertues, Giovanni', whilst abandoning the italic form, is instead set to the far right, creating an internal distinction between the part of the letter that conveys content, and the part of the letter that names the sender; a distinction created by layout in actual letters. Thus the letter made, and makes, visual sense to a reader of the playscript, whilst providing no obvious additional information to the actor of Lidia whose dialogue, 'I . . . will peruse it', and stage-direction, '*Reads the Letter*' (if reproduced on his actor's part), would have told him everything he needed to know about the text he was to recite.

Another equally typical example of the 'separated' scroll in the printed playbook can be found in the layout and typeface of the proclamation that is read out in Beaumont and Fletcher's *Love's Cure*. It, too, is in italics when the rest of the text is not; it additionally starts with an initial capital letter so large in size as to take up over two lines of 'normal' text; again the close, consisting of a centred ''Save the King', abandons the italic form, but is set so as to demarcate the conclusion of the proclamation, conforming to the habit of closing real proclamations with a set phrase in a different typeface. As with the letter, these are details that make their point visually but will be hard for a player to indicate in performance. They make the proclamation look like a real proclamation, but that fact hardly needs underlining given that the dialogue leading up to it contains the words 'Read the Proclamation . . . read aloud' before 'Herald reads':

> *Assis.* Read the Proclamation,
> That all the people here assembled may
> Have satisfaction, what the Kings deere love,
> In care of the Republique, hath ordained;
> Attend with silence: read aloud.
>
> Herald reads.
> *Forasmuch as our high and mighty Master,*
> *Philip, the potent and most Catholique King*
> *of Spaine, hath not onely in his own Royall person,*
> *been long, and often sollicited, . . . This to be read*
> *aloud for the publique satisfaction of his Maje-*
> *sties welbeloved Subjects.*
> 'Save the King.²

A third example is to be found in the itemised reckonings reproduced in Quarles' *Virgin Widow*. In that play, 'Quack' the doctor is to enter reading out two bills, one after the other: the first is Penelope Trippet's; the second is Master Lustyblood's. Yet though in performance Quack will speak the contents of the bills 'continuously' in a stream of prose that resembles the parody list in *Twelfth Night* ('Item two lippes indifferent redde, Item two grey eyes, with lids to them: Item, one necke, one chin, & so forth', TLN 538–9), each of these bills in the printed text is presented in 'bill form'. Both scrolls have their own headings in extra-large type; the contents of each are written out as a 'list' with items set to the left and separate costs to the right; the collective cost of both lists, '*summ. tot.*', is placed in the bottom right-hand corner below the individual prices. None of these features can be easily manifested in speech; nor can the retention of italic lettering for '*Item*' (a feature that recognises the Latinity of the term), nor the long dividing line extending the length of the printed page that separates one bill from the other:

Quack, reading a Bill.

Mistresse *Penelope Trippits* Bill, *April* 20.
    For 2 ounces of syrrop of Savin, and keeping her councell 0---13s–4d.
    Item for one ounce and a half of surfling Water   0---7---6.
    Item for a glasse of the best Mercury-}
        water, and a box of *Pomatum*   0---6---8.
    Item for 2 ounces of Talk   0---2---2.

Master *Lustybloods* Bill, *June* 9.

    For a Sweating Chaire   0---10---0.
    For a Purge   0---3---4.
    Item for the same again   0---5---4.
    Item for Turpentine Pills   0---3---2.
    Item for a Diet drinke   0---10---0.
    Item for a Serynge   0---2---6.
    Item for fluxing his body   0---12---0.
    Item for 2 penny-worth of *Diascordium*   0---1---1.
                          summ. tot.

A pretty Reck'ning!³

Although the features of these three types of scrolls are scarcely, and sometimes not at all, 'actable', they all provide information to the reader of the page: as each resembles the 'real' document it represents, each is an internally unique document in the play, for letter does not resemble proclamation, nor proclamation bill.

    'Headings' or marginal annotations referring to scrolls likewise insist on their otherness from one another and the text that contains them. It is very usual, for instance, to find a scroll topped with its own title: ['A'/ 'the'] 'letter'/'writing'/'challenge'/'paper'/'bill'/'schedule'. In the following examples, 'letter' and 'challenge' simply confirm what context and layout has already made plain, while 'The Writing' and 'A paper' provide information seemingly too nebulous to be worth recording:

Enter Artemia *with a Letter in each hand.*
Ar. I will againe peruse them ere I yeeld beleefe
to either. My fathers letter first.   *Letter.*
So may a hungry Lion crouch and bow,
Till by that crost, he get within his power
That pray which he intends for to devoure: . . .[4]

AMO. So. Keepe up your ruffe: the tincture of your necke is not all
so pure, but it will aske it. Maintayne your sprig upright; your cloke on
your halfe-shoulder falling; So: I will reade your bill, advance it, and
present you.   Silence.
Be it knowne to all that professe courtship, by these presents (from the white sattin   The challenge
reveller, *to the cloth of tissue, and bodkin) that we,* ULYSSES-POLYTROPUS-
AMORPHUS, *Master of the noble, and subtile science of courtship, doe give leave
and licence to our* Provost, ACOLASTUS-POLYPRAGMON-ASOTUS, *to play
his Masters prize . . .*[5]

Assist me breath a little to unfold, what they include.
I that have writ these lines, am one, whose sinne   *The Wri-*
Is more then grievous; for know, that I have beene   *ting*
A breaker of my faith, with one whose brest
Was all compos'd of truth: but I digrest . . .[6]

'Tis but a Sonnet, Gentlemen, that I fitted
To my fair Mistris here. *Euph.* Let us be happy
To heare it Sir. *Dot.* Take it as it is: *A paper.*
Deare, do not your fair beauty wrong,   *He reades.*
In thinking still you are too yong . . .[7]

Confronted with such heading 'statements', modern editors usually remove them entirely or turn them into actions: '[she reads] The Letter', though, perversely, the equally generic headings 'The Prologue' and 'The Epilogue' are generally allowed to stand as they are. 'External' paratext is thus accepted as generically different from the play – the liminality of prologues and epilogues means they are allowed to remain aloof from the playbook – while paratexts 'internal' in the play are made to conform to the rest of the book.

None of these devices separating scroll from text is the preserve of print only. Manuscript playbooks bearing the hallmarks of acting texts also often (and also not always) separate scrolls from dialogue using a selection of similar visual signals: the 'l[ett]re' in the manuscript of *Tom a Lincoln* (prepared by a series of copyists, possibly students and possibly professionals, for performance at Gray's Inn) is placed in quotation marks;

the letter in Jaques' manuscript play *Queen of Corsica* (written up by a scribe, perhaps for private performance, perhaps for reading) is in 'letter layout'; the oath in at least one copy of Montagu's *Shepheards' Paradise* (there are five copies in all of this play, which was performed at court by Queen Henrietta and her ladies; all are in scribal hand) is in large italic script when the rest of the text is in 'typical Caroline secretary hand'.[8] Generic headings too are found equally often in manuscript, again irrespective of provenance. After Andrucho's question, 'Where is the Epitaph?' in Wilson's manuscript play *The Swisser* (written for the King's Men) is the unnecessary heading 'Epitaph' before the words of the text follow; while the anonymous *Edmond Ironside* contains not simply an obvious heading of 'The Letter' for the letter, but also a second equally obvious direction 'finis Letter', both of which winch the content of the letter out of its textual enclosure whilst providing entirely self-evident information:

> Edm:
> What winde doth Cause yor Mr writte to us
> all is not well I doute give mee the Letter
> The Letter
> Prepaire Perillus Bull to punish mee
>   or some new never-hard of torteringe paine
>   to scourge me for my foule ingratitude
>   . . .
>   I come againe like to a strayed sheepe
>   tainted god watt wth naught but ignorance
>   oh take mee to yor mercye, or yf not soe
>   kill mee yor self death is the eand of woe
>   finis Letter.[9]

At first the temptation is to put all this information together – the special layout of certain scrolls, the angled headings of others – to conclude that the 'separation' of the scroll is an aspect of the famous 'literising' of texts for the page so often currently written about. According to this argument, the distinction made between scroll and text would be a design feature traceable to scribes or to the printing house, intended to clarify the reading experience whilst, simultaneously, ridding the play of its performance features (given that the layout and headings cannot be performed). So, not conscious of the strange rules governing all scrolls in plays, modern critics concerned with 'letters' (other scrolls do not excite the same interest) in Shakespeare's plays (other playwrights do not excite the same interest) conclude that the scrolls' 'differences' constitute extra-textual information for the insightful reader. In particular, the italic type that so often distinguishes scroll from dialogue is seen as a commentary on the letter itself and its contents. The 'bibliographical distinctness' of the typeface for letters in *The Merchant of Venice*, for instance, has been said 'to embody or to locate characters [who] are themselves radically disembodied and dislocated from the surface of the play-text'; while the italic typeface of the letters in *Hamlet* prompts Goldberg to ask:

> Do italics . . . mark the letter as *not* part of the play, or not part of the script produced by the hand that wrote the rest of the text? But in that case, to whom does the letter belong when the signature is not in the same hand as the letter, but instead marked the same way as the hand that produces the rest of the text?[10]

These are questions that the playbooks prompt, for the *Merchant* and *Hamlet* letters really do look different, but the reason for this is practical and links them not just to each other but to scrolls throughout manuscript and printed plays of the period. Far from representing carefully contrived literary or reader-focussed moments, scrolls are the reverse: sometimes a would-be stage-property and sometimes a preserved one.

THEATRE SCROLLS AND THEIR SCRIBES

Years after any of the plays considered in this chapter were written, the actor Cape Everard wrote a memoir in which he recorded working for Garrick in the 1770s. One anecdote he relates concerns a near crisis that he averted through his careful preparation for performance. As he tells it, Everard went onstage to perform 'Dick' ('Richard') in Robert Dodsley's *The Miller of Mansfield*. In the second scene of that play, Dick is to receive a long letter that he then reads out loud to the audience. Accordingly, Everard was handed a letter during the scene, but when he opened it he found it, to his horror, 'a mere blank!'. As Everard goes on to record, with some boastfulness, 'I had always made it a rule to study my Letters, as well as my character; it was well I did.'[11] Everard had expected genuinely to read his letter onstage, but on being handed a dummy 'blank' letter instead was able to save the day because, he is delighted to relate, he had learnt his letter as well as his lines. Everard had reason to brag: he would have had to put himself out even to acquire the letter's text, for sizable scrolls were so often given to actors onstage that they were not always additionally supplied inside the 'length' (as actors' 'parts' were then called).[12]

As the one professional actor's part remaining from the early modern period, for Orlando in Robert Greene's *Orlando Furioso*, does *not* contain the words of the roundelays the actor is to find on the trees and read (the content of which is known from the play Quarto in which they are printed in full), scrolls in the early modern period were, it can be guessed, 'staged' in the same way.[13] The reason in either case would have been the same: in the days before long theatrical 'runs', actors had to perform in many different plays each season, and anything that reduced learning was a God-send; reading a scroll on stage saved the overworked actor from memorising more text than was absolutely necessary. Here is the moment from the actor's part in which Orlando finds love poems to Angelica hanging on trees; though the 'dittyes' are not supplied, they need to be read out loud at this point, for it is their content that alerts Orlando to the name of his love-rival, 'Medor':

> yet more are muses maskine in these trees
> forrming ther dittyes in conceited lynes
> making a goddese in despight of me
> that have no goddess but Angelica
> ——————————————————— sorowes dwell.
> what ~~Italiano per dio~~
> dare Medor court my venus . . .[14]

The '~~Italiano per dio~~' is an oddity that may suggest the poems found were originally in Italian; perhaps it was crossed out when a decision was made to supply them in English, for scrolls, provided they are not written into the part, can change nature and content at any time.[15] Here is the equivalent moment from the Quarto of *Orlando Furioso*, a text of a later date and provenance, but only minutely different in dialogue-content for this passage. The scrolls and their rhyming contents are shown here to be central to the concerns of the scene (as well as the inspiration for the bad rhymes hanging in trees in Shakespeare's *As You Like It*). Oddly, but for a reason that will later be explained, when Orlando speaks, reads a scroll, and speaks again, his speech-prefix is 'unnecessarily' repeated:

> ORL: Yet more are Muses masking in these trees,
> Framing their ditties in conceited lines,
> Making a Goddesse in despite of me,
> That have no other but Angelica.
> SHEP: Poore haples man, these thoughts containe the hell,
> Orlando reades this roundelay.
> Angelica is Ladie of his hart,
> Angelica is substance of his joy,

> Angelica is medcine of his smart,
> Angelica hath healed his annoy.
> ORL: Ah false Angelica. What have we more?
> Another.
> Let groves, let rockes, let woods, let watrie springs,
> The Cedar, Cypresse, Laurell, and the Pine,
> Joy in the notes of love that Medor sings,
> Of those sweet lookes Angelica of thine.
> Then Medor in Angelica take delight,
> Early, at morne, at noone, at even and night.
> ORL: What dares Medor court my Venus?[16]

Some directions around scrolls even highlight when texts are to be *really* written out for their actor. *The Passionate Lover* asks that Selina enter '*with a Letter seal'd and writ out*'; *The Lovers' Progress* has Clarange '*Enter . . . (with a Letter writ out) and Frier*'; *The Spanish Curate* tells Leandro to '*Enter . . . (with a letter writ out) Milanes & Asermo*'; and *James the Fourth* commands, '*Enter* Slipper, Nano, *and* Andrew, *with their billes readie written in their hands.*'[17] Directions for specifically 'written' scrolls, too, continue to be found in promptbook markings of later texts: theatrical habits die hard. The 1790 promptbook for *Try Again* (*The Suspicious Brother*), made from an annotated printed text, brackets the scrolls to be read onstage in manuscript adding the note 'wt' by them, indicating that the papers given to the actors are to be 'w[ri]t[en]'; while Samuel Foote's *The Devil Upon Two Sticks* (1778), also printed and also annotated with manuscript notes, has a commanding 'all wrote' scrawled by the side of one whole letter and 'wrote' by the side of another two.[18]

Why a 'genuine' layout is so often provided for scrolls in early modern printed and manuscript texts can now be guessed: the italic lettering, the extravagant first capitals, the carefully spaced endings and salutations, are all ways in which the playbook itself indicates what the scroll, when extracted, should look like (or, depending on source, shows what the scroll, when extracted, did look like, a point that will be returned to). Similarly, generic headings such as 'the letter', 'a song', or 'epitaph' indicate that this is a scroll, not part of the dialogue, and thus, again, highlight it as a text for recopying (or preserve the fact that it was).

But who are these written and visual instructions for? Not the prompter: he will hold the entire book in performance, by which time the scroll must already have been extracted and written out. Not the actors either, who performed from actors' parts in combination with backstage-plots or their equivalent, and who were reliant on scrolls ready-written to be handed to them onstage. And not, when it comes to it, the reader, who hardly needs to be told or shown that a letter is a letter, a challenge a challenge, a bill a bill. Instructions in the playbook like this belong to a pre-performative moment when the play is yet to be divided into parts and scrolls. They are forms of direction to the person who will write out the scroll in the first place: the scroll-scribe.

Directions around scrolls are often obviously aimed at scribes. They include the explanatory 'finis Letter' already discussed at the end of *Edmond Ironside*, which condescendingly informs the scroll-writer when to stop; or, similarly, the equally patronising 'The Contents of the Letter' that tells the scroll-writer when to start in *The Hector of Germany*:

> *King.* Weele read them instantly.
>   *The Contents of the Letter.*
> Alls lost, our elected friend Savoy taken prisoner . . .
> Your Friend in Armes, ROBERT the Palsgrave.[19]

Even the direction 'read', so often found before scrolls, is at least as much scribe-direction as stage-direction, for whilst it tells an actor what he is to do, it also tells the scribe what to create to enable that actor to do so. Hence the number of directions that hover between scribe and actor. The printed text of *Solyman and Perseda* has '*Then he takes up a paper, and reedes in it as followeth*' preceding the scroll, instructing that the contents be taken out of the play and put on paper, as well as telling the actor then to read them; the manuscript play *Charlemagne* has a stage-direction '*Enter Richard readinge a letter*' but then brackets the entire contents of the letter together, labelling it sideways across its length 'read' – the 'reading' that possesses the entire contents of all the letter also indicates, of course, what to write:

Enter Richard readinge a letter

Rich {Myne Enemyes have labord muche, but my worst afflyctyon is thy lamente<
read {absence, wch may indaunger us alike, thee by wantinge my dyrectyons, me
    {by dispayringe of thy welfare . . . thy best on earthe: *Ganelon.*[20]

On other occasions the start of a scroll is 'cued' for the prompter and scroll-writer when it begins in italics, but continues in regular roman script (if in print), or italic hand and secretary or related hand (if in manuscript): the start of the scroll is presented as textually different. One such example is offered by the manuscript of the *Welsh Embassador* (hardly surprisingly, given the title, both the speech and scroll by Penda are transcribed in a 'Welsh' accent):

```
ARM:   you promist mee my lord that I should heare
       some of yor poetrie, a sonnet you would write . . .
PEN:   will you awle heare her welse muses pallad or madrigals
OMN:   rather then anie other
PEN:   tawsone then          Reads
       Wud you kanaw her mris face
       See the moone wth starrs in shace . . .²¹
```

Directions for the scribe did not merely indicate which text to write out. They could extend to which ink to use, which medium to write on, and what decorations to append to the documents. So in *The Spanish Tragedy* 'A Letter written to Hieronimo' is thrown down that is, in the fiction of the play, a letter written in blood; it begins 'For want of incke receive this bloudie writ'. In the margin are the words 'Red incke', addressed not to the actor, reader, prompter or person in charge of props (for the ink itself is not to feature onstage), but to the writer of the stage-letter, who must use the ink to create the letter's bloody appearance.²² Red ink would have to be especially purchased or made up for the occasion, and here the scribe is warned or reminded of the fact. Similarly the direction to use not paper but parchment and, further, to decorate it with a large seal ('zeale'), in *Promos and Cassandra* is, again, not for the actor or reader, but for the writer of the following proclamation:

```
[PROMOS]   Phallax, reade out my Soveraines chardge.
PHAL.      As you commaunde, I wyll: give heedefull eare.
           Phallax readeth the Kinges Letters Patents, which must be fayre written
           in parchment, with some great counterfeat zeale.²³
```

In Jonson's *Bartholmew Fayre* an even more complicated scribe-direction – or perhaps a direction to the writer of large text-letter notices – demands the creation of a labelled, pictorial sign: 'Little-wit *is gazing at the signe; which is the Pigs-head with a large writing under it.*'²⁴

Occasionally scribe-directions asked even more of the copier: sometimes the scribe seems to have been expected to create the content of a minor scroll himself; in the example above, for instance, the contents of the letters patents to be read are not supplied by the playbook. Likewise, in the second part of *Promos and Cassandra*, the scribe is specifically told to provide a list of names without, again, being given any suggestion as to what they might be:

```
Ul[rico].
. . .
I showe no more, then witnesse prov'd by oth,
Whose names and handes, defends it heare as troth.
           Ulrico delivers the King a writing with names at it.²⁵
```

Though this is hardly a major authorship question, it is also not an isolated instance. In Marlowe's *Edward the Second* Spencer, like Ulrico, appears to need a list of names to recite; that list too is nowhere supplied in the surviving playbook, either because the printed text derives from a prompter's book in which the contents of the list were not given (because the author wrote them directly onto a scroll?), or because the printed playbook reflects an authorial text in which the writing of the list is left to the scroll-scribe. (Of recent editors, Rowland maintains that the play is in authorial form, and Forker that the play is marked up with a view to theatrical production, but is not itself a promptbook. Earlier editors had thought that the play was set from a promptbook):[26]

> EDW. Why man, they say there is great execution
> Done through the realme, my lord of *Arundell*
> You have the note, have you not?
> MATR. From the lieutenant of the tower my lord.
> EDW. I pray let us see it, what have we there?
> Read it *Spencer.*   *Spencer reads their names.*
> Why so, they barkt a pace a month a goe,
> Now on my life, theile neither barke nor bite.[27]

Here too the scribe-direction is in a form reminiscent of a stage-direction ('reads their names'), but names can only be read when they have been written out. This use of the scroll-scribe as potential creator of 'unimportant' texts raises authorship questions about other internal scrolls. Might the scribe ever have composed, or added or embellished, in his own right other scrolls? With so little evidence surviving it is hard to say, though it remains possible that scrolls read onstage were not entirely replicas of the scrolls written (when they are written) in playbooks.

A whole bank of 'stage-directions' that have long puzzled editors can be explained when they are understood to be scribe-directions. It is only use of the eighteenth-century term 'stage-direction' (first recorded *OED* usage, Malone in 1790, though seemingly in fact coined by Theobald in the 1730s[28]), in combination with too performance-focussed an understanding of playbooks, that has pooled together with one description instructions intended for more than one person.

Other information for the scroll-scribe occasions what is often misunderstood as textual error: wayward speech-prefixes on and around scrolls. It is very usual, for instance, to find speech-prefixes for a single character 'unnecessarily' repeated after the scroll, as in the quarto of *Orlando Furioso* and the manuscript of *Edmond Ironside* both quoted above, or in the following instance from the 1604 Quarto of *Hamlet* for Polonius:

POL. Good Maddam stay awhile, I will be faithful.
      Doubt thou the starres are fire.   *Letter*
      Doubt thou the Sunne doth move . . .
POL. This in obedience hath my daughter showne me . . .[29]

The Fayre Mayde of the Exchange of 1607 provides a similar example:

ANTH.   Ile reade it or'e againe:
          A Letter.
          Sir, I did never like you, I doe not nowe thinke well of you,
          and I will never love you . . . Not yours, but her owne.
ANTHO. Blancke, I am strucke blancke, and blind, and mad withal[30]

But who is the repeated speech-prefix for? The answer is, again, the scroll-scribe, or, rather, the scroll-scribe and part-scribe (who are probably the same person). The scroll-scribe needs to know which bit of text to write on which separate paper, and when it ends; the part-writer needs to know which speeches to write on which actors' parts. To exemplify, using Shakespeare's *Merchant of Venice*: when Morocco is to approach the casket, open it, read its contents and then reflect on what he has found, he has, in the full Quarto, the following, including an 'unnecessary' speech-heading:

MOR. O hell! What have wee heare . . . Ile reade the writing.
      All that glisters is not gold . . .
      Fareyouwell, your sute is cold.
MOR. Cold indeede . . . (D3b)

To prepare this for performance, Morocco's first speech must be written onto the part for the actor playing Morocco; the scroll must be written onto a separate piece of paper, furled up, and put into the eye of a skull enclosed within the golden casket; and Morocco's next speech must, again, be written on the actor's part. So the repeated speech-prefix simultaneously heralds the end of the scroll and indicates on which part – here, the same part as before – the subsequent speech is to be written. This pattern, with its repeated speech-headings, is used throughout *Merchant of Venice*.[31]

Other speech-prefix problems that attend on scrolls are harder to explain. Scrolls that are not straddled in the middle of speech–scroll–speech, all by one person, as detailed above, can be hard to 'attribute' to anyone, for they are regularly not, as normal dialogue is, preceded by a conventional speech-prefix detailing the name of the speaker/reader. 'The omission of a speech prefix . . . before some quoted document to be read or proclaimed is not unusual,' writes Bevington; 'it is not always clear by whom matter is read', notes Chambers.[32] But a look at a surviving stage-scroll may explain how this happened.

Though theatrical scrolls are for the most part, like other ephemera, no longer extant, the early modern period does contain one preserved property letter for a 'staged' occasion. The document is a pretend letter that formed part of the Gray's Inn and Inner Temple revels held between Christmas 1594–5 and Shrove Tuesday and known as *Gesta Grayorum*: an extended feast of misrule. On 20 December, Henry Helmes, gentleman and student of Gray's Inn, was elected 'Henry, Prince of Purpoole, Knight of the Most Heroical Order of the Helmet, Archduke of Stapulia and Bernardia, and Duke of High and Nether Holborn'. At the same time, an 'Emperor', 'Frederick Templarius', was elected to the Inner Temple; for the next few weeks homages and tributes were sent from 'ambassadors' of one inn to the other. Associated revels held over the same period included ceremonies of investiture into the Knighthood of the Helmet; 'foreign wars'; daytime events such as sea-fights, processions and jousts; and evening events such as masques and plays: famously, Shakespeare's *Comedy of Errors* was chaotically performed for the 'Prince' and assembled (real) dignitaries on what came to be called the 'night of errors'. The text of *Gesta Grayorum* – or, rather, a series of texts making up moments of it – was published in 1688, and includes exchanges between Henry of Purpoole and Emperor Frederick as well as a number of their 'ambassadors' from 'overseas'. There is, for instance, a letter from 'Theodore Evanwhich, the great and mighty Emperor of all Russia' delivered by an ambassador who came 'in Attire of Russia' to the Prince.[33] But the surviving 'letter' from the *Gesta Grayorum*, not printed in the 1688 collection, is the remnant of another 'ambassadorial' visit that was obviously intended not to be so courteous. In it – its answer is not preserved – the Prince exchanges angry words with a 'Turke' over use of the Islamic crescent. The letter actually seems to prepare for a sea-battle, in which the waiting 'Acmirall' ('Admiral') will trounce the Turkish warlord: it is one side of an exchange leading up to a performed moment. It is, nevertheless, in form and content, an elegant and seemingly 'real' letter:

Henricus P Ps
Turke

Thy proud and insolent demand came into our Princly hands but not a *Nuncio* was seene that durste avowe the bearing of it. The respeclesse manner of thy Embassee and thy hauty arrogance we take notice of with as high disdaine as may spring from the inborne magnanimity of a Prince, And as much we slight it: Knowe our resolucion is to maintaine our right in bearing of the Crescent.   ffor thy threatened hostility we entertaine it thankfully, and accept of it as of thy triumphes to congratulate our late installment. We have given command to our Acmirall to waite thy coming and give the entertainment on the Sea, thy better receiving at thy landing shalbe our neerer Care. ffarewell and weare thy three Moones till we make them make upp the fower quarter = Changes of our Crescent. *From our Pallace of Portpoole.* 27. Dec. 1594.[34]

This letter is not only neatly written; it contains individual features that match those to be found in printed texts that contain scrolls in 'realistic' form. Specifically, the change of manuscript style for its salutation – here, from secretary hand into italic – directly reflects the different typeface so often used in the salutation in printed texts. Most importantly, however, having been carefully folded, the letter contains a direction written on its outside detailing to whom it is to be delivered ('To the Greate Turke'), and a direction on the inside detailing from whom it emanates, 'Henricus P P'. That the addressee is named on the front of the property letter may explain why that detail did not always make it into plays, for, with any 'real' document, it is the outside only that needs to name the person to whom the text is to be given (a crucial piece of information for players). As that piece of information, however, belongs to the scroll as much as, or more than, to the playbook, it is information that the playwright does not necessarily have to provide or even decide. In *2 Henry VI*, a direction leaves the choice of reader to be made by actor or scribe: '*Bullingbrooke or Southwell reades, Conjuro te*' (TLN 644–5). Even when a scroll-speaker is identified, his or her name is often written into the scribe-direction rather than the speech-prefix, so that the reader of the letter becomes one of the details for the scribe as much as or more than for the 'literary' reader or prompter:

> Qu. Elinor.   . . . Reede *Ned* thy Queenes request lapt up in rime,
> And saie thy *Nell* had skil to choose her time.
> *Read the paper Rice.*
> The pride of Englishmens long haire,
> Is more then Englands Queene can beare . . .[35]

On other occasions, however, even the scribe may not have been told the fictional name of the character for whom the scroll was intended. In the documentary property-list supplied by the prompter at the back of the manuscript for Massinger's *Believe as You List*, for instance, scrolls are titled by the name of the actor who is to receive them. Mr Swanston will get a 'writing' taken 'out of the booke' (i.e., copied from the prompter's book); and the other papers, 'notes', 'writings' and 'letters', are to go to Pollard, Taylor, Robinson, Lowen and Benfield – actors listed by real rather than fictional name, perhaps because the prompter is deciding who will receive each scroll.

> writing out of the booke wth a small peece of Silver
>> for Mr Swanston:

>   .3. notes for Mr pollard:

Act: 2:   A writing for Mr Taylor:
Act: 3: A letter. for Mr Robinson
     .2. letters for Mr Lowin:
Act: 5: A letter for Mr Benfeild/[36]

It is the prompter, too, who then goes through the playscript adding the scrolls to the entrances of characters (so this time by fictional name). To the authorial 'Syrus' is added 'wth a writing' (the writing for Mr Swanston); to the authorial 'Berecinthius a flamen' is added 'Ent: Berecinthius: (with.3. papers:)' (these will be for Mr Pollard); to 'Enter Flaminius' is added 'wth. 2. letters' (the '.2. letters for Mr Lowin'); to 'Enter Lentutulus' is added 'Ent: Lentulus: mr Rob: wth a letter' (the 'letter. for Mr Robinson'); while at the beginning of 5.1 the author's 'Ent: Marcellus (proconsul of Scicilie)' is, again, glossed 'wth a letter' (the one for Mr Benfield).[37]

The nearer a scroll is to a performance document, particularly in the case of a letter, the more it may not have required a speech-prefix in a playscript, because the prompter works out who is to read the document, though surrounding speech-headings for the scroll-scribe sometimes name its intended speaker.

BLANK AND CUED SCROLLS

There were, however, varieties of scroll that were less 'genuine' than any covered so far. Of the list attached to Massinger's *Believe as You List* above, not all the letters, though distinguished from 'notes' and 'writings' (so they must have looked 'different' from other scrolls) were actually to be read onstage. They were, in the terminology of that time and later, 'blanks': documents that were not genuine, lacking real content, but that resembled written scrolls in appearance. The manuscript of the anonymous play *The First Part of the Reign of King Richard the Second* singles out the special non-written letters that the play demands, using a marginal direction for 'blankes' on one occasion, and, later, an abbreviated request for '3:B' – a demand for another three blanks.[38] Again, subsequent theatrical practice retains the same designations, the 1832 call-book for Rowe's *Jane Shore* containing an act 3 box 1 call for Alicia to enter with 'W Paper No 1', and Jane Shore to enter with 'B Paper No 2': the first actress is to have a 'Written' paper, the second to have a 'Blank' one.[39] A play might often require a combination of written and blank documents, all to be kept together, but each to have a different use – which explains how Everard was given the 'wrong' letter for his crucial scene. That implies that, in the tiring-house, documents, whether simply props or written pieces of the actual play, resided together.

But there may also have been a third kind of document in theatrical use: not quite a blank, but not a conventional scroll either. For even if only a blank scroll were required by staging, it could still be put to another use. A manuscript annotation on a 1761 printed playbook of Shakespeare's *Othello*, marked up for performance at the King's Theatre on 8 August 1766, asks for '4 B[lank] Letters 1 with Cues'.[40] Four of the letters to be used in this production will be straightforward blanks, not actual documents; the fifth letter will, depending on how one reads this note, either be a blank letter that is marked up with cues, or a full letter that is marked up with cues: it will be a theatrical document that resembles an extract of an actor's part, whatever it is, allowing the actor receiving it to 'situate' its contents with cues. And, as the only instance in this particular edition of *Othello* when a letter is read out involves the interruption of that letter, so the nature of this particular cued document can up to a point be determined. The moment for receiving and reading the missive occurs in 4.1, when Othello is handed the scroll that commands him to return home to Venice:

> DES.   My lord!---------
> OTH.   *This fail you not to do, as you will* ------ [Reads.
> LOD.   He did not call; he's busy in the paper.
>   Is there division 'twixt my lord and Cassio?
> DES.   A most unhappy one; I would do much
>   T'attone them, for the love I bear to Cassio.
> OTH.   Fire and brimstone![41]

The content of the letter itself, '*This fail you not to do, as you will*', is so brief as hardly to need transcribing. So the possibility is that the actor of Othello is given in writing his disjointed response to the letter including cues – after all, the words are to be spoken whilst Othello closely observes the paper in his hand. This would reduce yet further the amount the busy actor had to learn, and would aid the player in the simultaneously crazed and focussed reaction he is to have:

> Sir, she can turn and turn, and yet go on!
> And turn again. And she can weep, sir weep!
> And she's obedient: as you say, obedient:
> Very obedient ------ proceed you in your tears ------
> concerning this, sir, ------ oh well painted passion! ------
> I am commanded home ---------- get you away,
> I'll send for you anon. ------ Sir, I obey the mandate,
> And will return to Venice ------ Hence, avaunt! ------[42]

Here it is worth recording that modern actors at the Blackfriars' Play-house in Staunton, Virginia, putting on plays from actors' parts in their yearly 'Renaissance Season', came independently upon the idea of adding cues to letters, and, further, of writing difficult passages of dialogue into their blanks. James Keegan noted that Barabas in Marlowe's *Jew of Malta* receives many letters to be opened and waved around but not read aloud onstage; when he played the part, he enclosed fragments of his dialogue inside them; John Harrell always made sure his letters to be read onstage were written in full with cues on either side so that he could place them. It is possible that in the early modern theatre too, at tiny moments, the per-formance switched from the actor's memory to a written paper cued like other actors' texts (traces of cued song-scrolls are discussed in chapter 5): the fact of a stage-scroll brought 'text' into the forefront of performance.

SEPARATE CIRCULATION OF SCROLLS

As scrolls were designed to be written out by other people and at other times from the writing of the full play, they were capable of circulating well outside the playhouse. Sometimes they might then function as though they really were the documents they pretended to be. A number of later theatre anecdotes rely on the fact that stage letters were superficially interchangeable with real letters, for instance. So the nineteenth-century actor and prankster Edward Sothern, going through his pockets in a hotel breakfast-room, discovered he had with him the 'property letter' he was to read onstage in Bulwer-Lytton's *The Lady of Lyons* when playing Claude Melnotte:

A property letter, you know, means a letter used on the stage, and this one read as follows:—
'*Young man, I know thy secret—thou lovest above thy station: if thou hast wit, courage, and discretion, I can secure to thee the realization of thy most sanguine hopes, etc etc.*'

Sothern amused himself over breakfast by having the missive delivered to an irascible old man sitting near him; he then sat and watched the outcome:

'D-n the breakfast!' he exclaimed, almost kicking over the table. 'I want to see the lunatic who calls me a "young man," and says he knows my secret, and can secure the realization of my fondest hopes. I haven't got any secret, and my fondest hope is to kick the idiot who sent me this insane note!'[43]

Despite its heavily stilted language, the letter is 'genuine' enough to deceive the old man. Other stage letters even became prized objects, and survive today, much as the *Gesta Grayorum* letter to the 'Turke' does, as mementos of entire versions of a play otherwise not recorded. The actor Lawrence Barrett, playing Bassanio in the *Merchant of Venice* in 1888, took it upon himself to divide the letter sent by Antonio, 'sweet Bassanio, my ships have all miscarried' into two parts: his way of coping with the tension between who of Portia and Bassanio reads the letter. This 'division' had been suggested to him by the editor Furness, and, as a thank-you, Barrett sent Furness his property letter at the end of the run. That paper memento of the 1888 touring production of *Merchant of Venice* still remains, a sole surviving textual remnant of the 1888 tour; it is amongst Furness's effects in the Furness Memorial Library, University of Pennsylvania, Philadelphia.[44]

Are there any examples of early modern stage-scrolls existing outside their text? Just possibly. Some scrolls that are to be read in plays also find their way into other books. The 'sonnets' read onstage by the King and his men, Dumaine, Longaville and Berowne, in *Love's Labour's Lost* (published in Quarto in 1598), 'Did not the heavenly Rethorique of thine eye' (E3a), 'If Love make me forsworne, how shall I sweare to love?' (E1b), and 'On a day, alacke the day' (E3b) are, for instance, reproduced as poems in *The Passionate Pilgrim* (published in 1599); Burrow calls them 'portable property' for this reason.[45] Nevertheless, in *Passionate Pilgrim* they differ from the form they took in the printed play. Generally the explanation given for the alterations is traced to the publisher of *The Passionate Pilgrim*, William Jaggard; Jaggard is said to have taken the texts from the printed Quarto of *Love's Labour's Lost*, but lightly updated them so that they could work out of context.[46] That may, of course, be so: Burrow writes that only poems highlighted by layout in the Quarto are extracted (and that the poem by the king, printed to look like dialogue, is not selected for *Passionate Pilgrim*).[47] At the same time, it is worth considering some of the differences between poems that are in *Passionate Pilgrim* and

those same poems in the play; are the original scrolls wedded to context –
and do the alterations serve to undo that? Take 'If Love make me
forsworn', as it is represented in *Passionate Pilgrim*; variant words from
Love's Labour's Lost are noted in brackets at the end of the line:

If Love make me forsworn, how shal I swere to love?
O, never faith could hold, if not to beauty vowed: [Ah]
Though to my selfe forsworn, to thee Ile **constant** prove, [faythfull]
those thoghts to me **like** Okes, to thee like Osiers bowed. [were]
Studdy his byas leaves, and makes his booke thine eies,
where all those pleasures live, that Art **can** comprehend: [would]
If knowledge be the marke, to know thee shall suffice:
Wel learned is that toung that well can thee commend,
All ignorant that soule, that sees thee without wonder,
Which is to me some praise, that I thy parts admyre:
Thine **eyes** Joves lightning **seems**, thy voice his dreadfull thunder [eie, beares]
which (not to anger bent) is musick & sweet fire
Celestiall as thou art, O, **do not** love that wrong: [pardon]
To sing heavens praise, with such an earthly toung. [That singes][48]

Alterations here do not really seem to be connected to either the lyric's
presence in or its absence from the play. These are, rather, the kinds of
changes found when a manuscript is twice copied (see chapter 8). Yet
these are not the kinds of changes that printers usually make: printers,
though they may add punctuation, tend to be faithful to words themselves, and chary of substituting synonyms like 'constant' for 'faythfull'.
Changes of this kind are actually much more like the kinds of alterations
made by scribes (see chapter 8). So perhaps Jaggard had alternative sources
for the *Passionate Pilgrim* sonnets: free-floating stage documents that had
been altered through the process of copying.

Whether or not this is the case, the circulation of scrolls aside from
playscripts had a practical manifestation. Again, as with songs and
prologues, stage-scrolls, precisely because they had their own, separate
circulation, are sometimes not written out in playbooks where they are to
be spoken: in this instance they had their complete manifestation *only*
outside the surviving playscript. The most simple example of this is when
a scroll is to be read twice onstage, but is supplied just once in the
playbook. In performance this will not be noticeable, for the paper scroll
will be handed over whenever, and as many times as, it is needed. Yet
take *The Thracian Wonder*, where the full content of the 'paper' the priest
reads is supplied first time round, but cued second time round:

PRIEST READS. Content shall keep in Town and Field,
When *Neptune* from his Waves shall yield
A *Thracian Wonder* . . .
. . .

PHE. READS. *Content shall keep in town and field,*
When Neptune *from his waves, &c.*[49]

Similarly, in the manuscript fragment of an unknown play, sometimes said to be by Webster, sometimes by Shirley, a character is to read a letter, which is supplied, and then to 'read againe'; on the second occasion it is not supplied, meaning that the letter sounds twice in the performance, but only exists once in the read text.[50] Willan's play *Orgula*, though a closet text, still opts to give a direction that requests '*Let*[*ter*]. *read by* Fi. *according to the contents of the former only signed* Ambigamor': the directions forcing the reader to hunt for the original letter in order to create the moment – because the author is projecting a staging in which a scribe can copy out the contents of the letter twice with different names.[51]

As these instances illustrate the incomplete nature of the printed text against the performed one, it can be asked whether Helena, at the end of *All's Well*, 'reads' Bertram's original letter – and, if so, how much of that letter she then speaks out loud. Earlier in *All's Well* the whole letter has been supplied – '*When thou canst get the Ring upon my finger, which never shall come off, and shew mee a childe begotten of thy bodie, that I am father too, then call me husband: but in such a (then) I write a Never*' (TLN 1460–3) – but for the second reading the text provides merely the opening of an inaccurate summary of the missive:

When from my finger you can get this Ring,
And is by me with childe, &c. This is done,
Will you be mine now you are doubly wonne? (TLN 3050–2)

The reiteration of the actual letter may be signalled by the word 'etc.', which as it stands creates a line that does not scan, in a summary of the missive that does not entirely work; Stanley Wells and Gary Taylor wonder whether 'the &c suggests that Shakespeare perhaps meant to check the original wording'.[52] If Helena is given the actual scroll to read, Bertram's original '*but in such a (then) I write a Never*' adds a new focus to Helena's boast of having 'doubly won' him.

Certainly other occasions where documents are end-stopped in an 'etc.' means 'read the stage scroll', for which reason those 'etc.' documents not supplied elsewhere in the manuscript are lost. So, in the printed playbook of Yarington's *Two Lamentable Tragedies*, the content of the Will is not supplied, though the surrounding dialogue indicates that it must have been read out on the stage:

> SCRIVE. Then give attention, I will read the Will.
> *Reade the Will.*
> *In the name of God, Amen. I, &c.*
> PAN. Thus if my sonne miscarry, my deare brother,
> You and your sonne shall then enjoy the land.[53]

Similarly, in the manuscript play of *Ghismonda*, a Latin scroll resolves into a simple 'etc.' after a few words, though, again, the whole would be needed were the play ever staged (the provenance of the play is unclear):

> GAB. Come, 'tis well now.
> PASQ. Read it.
> GAB. Noverint universi per etc.
> PASQ. The condicion?
> GAB. The condicion is, that if you pay to
> Gabriello foure shillinges upon the day apoynted,
> That then this bond of eight shillinges is voyd.[54]

In Cooke's *Greenes Tu Quoque* Rash likewise reads out a document of which all that is supplied is: 'How now! what have we heere, a Sonet and a Satire coupled together like my Ladies Dogge and her Munkie; *As little children &c.*'[55] Even a rude rhyme in *The Dutch Courtezan* seems to have been read onstage, but leads to an '&c.' after its start in the printed playbook, though here the text might have been really cut short or censored for publication. Nurse Putifer demands to hear again Freevil's poem about a kiss and is answered with:

> BEATR. Sha'te good Nurse,
> Purest lips soft banks of blisses,
> Selfe alone, deserving kisses:
> O give me leave to, &c.
> CRISP. Pish sister *Beatrice*, pree thee reade no more, my
> stomacke alate stands against kissing extreamly.[56]

One Shakespearean 'etc.' has regularly confused editors. It is in Shakespeare's *3 Henry VI* where an important proclamation seems to peter out:

> HAST. Sound Trumpet, *Edward* shal be here proclaim'd:
> Come, fellow Souldior, make thou proclamation.
> *Flourish. Sound.*
> SOUL. *Edward the Fourth, by the Grace of God, King of*
> *England and France, and Lord of Ireland, &c.*

MOUNT.   And whosoe're gainsayes King *Edwards* right,
By this I challenge him to single fight.
                        Throwes downe his Gauntlet (TLN 2578–85).

Cox and Rasmussen in their edition of the play wonder whether the 'etc.' indicates that the actor should supply the content of the scroll himself according to a known formula, equating this with the 'etc.' that signifies extemporisation (but that is not used for paper documents; see chapter 8); Marten and Hattaway maintain the &c. indicates a speech that is interrupted and – as in the Quarto there is no '&c.' – that may be so, though the 'stranded' heading hardly makes sense in its own right.[57] This document gives every sign of gesturing to a scroll that is not recorded in the book, and shares company with another lost scroll in *2 Henry VI*: '*Bullingbrooke or Southwell reades, Conjuro te, &c.*' (TLN 644–5). 'Conjuro te', 'I conjure you', is the beginning of a Latin invocation that needs, at the very least, completion.

Because of these separate documents, playscript and scroll, it might also be possible that on occasion what was given to the printing house was not an 'entire' play, but a play and, separately, one or more of its scrolls, as happened sometimes with songs and prologues (see chapters 5 and 4). And, like songs and prologues, there are some printed texts in which the scroll, even when present, contains indications that it may have been separately received. For example, every now and then, when several scrolls are called for in close succession, the texts will be not only 'titled' but embellished with a number. These numbers are, of course, entirely unnecessary for a reader, who will automatically read the scrolls in the 'correct' order (the order in which the playbook presents them); they are similarly useless for the actor whose dialogue dictates which text is spoken first and which second – information that will, probably, also be provided by the cues on his part. What seems to have made their way into the playbook, then, are either separate papers numbered for the property-man, separate papers numbered for the printer, or internal scrolls with numbering supplied for the scroll-writer who is to write them up as properties. Jonson's *Every Man Out*, for instance, distinguishes the 'first' and 'second' bills from one another in ways that provide nothing further for player or reader but speak instead of some other guiding principle:

PUNT. 'Fore god, CARLO, this is good; let's reade 'hem againe.

The first bill. *If there be any lady, or gentlewoman of good carriage, that is desirous to entertaine (to her private uses) a yong, straight, and upright gentleman, . . . who*

> *can serve in the nature of a gentleman usher, . . . Let her sub-*
> *scribe her name and place, and diligent respect shall be given.*

PUNT. This is, above measure, excellent! ha?

CARL.   No, this, this! here's a fine slave.

The second bill.   *If this city, or the suburbs of the same, doe affoord any young*
> *gentleman, . . . affected to entertaine the most gentleman-*
> *like use of tabacco: . . . most*
> *sweet attendance, with tabacco, and pipes of the best sort, shall be*
> *ministred*: STET QVÆSO CANDIDE LECTOR.[58]

Similarly, in the printed playbook of Goffe's *Raging Turke*, the bracketed
mottoes are numbered with '1' and '2' – numbers that will not themselves
be spoken out; the '3' for the third motto is not supplied but was probably
present on the manuscript behind this text:

> *Selym.* Those good *Trinm uri* what is't they speake?
>   *Opens the Letters.*
> 1 (To feede on hopes is but a slender dyet)
> 'Tis short, but full of weight: to feede on hope
> Is but a slender diet. Let it be.   *Descants.*
> I'le mend my table though no feast with me.
>   2 (Faire oportunity is bald behind)   *Reades second.*
> 'Tis true indeede *Mesithes.* Never feare
> I'le twist my fingers in her golden haire.
> What speakes the third? This writes more at large,
> And comments on the prefixt principalls.
> (Your Father did proclaime who should succeede   *Reads.*
> Publique denialls nullified his deede,
> Your hast will be convenient; things concurre
> To blesse your hopes, Fate bids you not demurre)
> Yours *Isaack* Bassa.[59]

In each instance it is always possible, of course, that the numbers
were supplied earlier by a thoughtful playwright preparing texts for
property-men, but Jonson and Goffe were playwrights concerned with
publication and were likely, if anything, to have removed performance
traces from their texts. Besides, the separation of scroll from playtexts
bolsters a point regularly noticed, but often left unexplained: the way
spelling and punctuation within scrolls is regularly different from the
spelling and punctuation adopted in the surrounding dialogue. In *Measure
for Measure*, for instance, 'The Letter', which, as so often, is already
separated by italics and a heading, contains a spelling of the name
'Barnadine', 'Bernardine', not found anywhere else in the surviving Folio
text. The dialogue itself is thought to have been printed from a text copied

out by Ralph Crane the scribe. But might, as Dover Wilson wondered, but no one has explored further, a 'stage-letter' have been given as copy for the compositors, to fill what was a gap in the 'book'?:[60]

Duk. Pray you let's heare.
The Letter.
Whatsoever you may heare to the contrary, let Claudio be executed by foure of the clocke, and in the afternoone Bernardine: For my better satisfaction, let mee have Claudios head sent me by five. Let this be duely performed with a thought that more depends on it, then we must yet deliver. Thus faile not to doe your Office, as you will answere it at your perill.
What say you to this Sir? (TLN 1984–93)

Indeed, the scene surrounding this letter seems to be from a wholly different version of the play than that preserved in the scroll: again, as with other scrolls, the text might have one date and the scroll another. At the start of the scene the Provost tells Abhorson to prepare for the execution of Claudio and Barnadine at four the next day (as the letter above confirms), but when he talks separately to Claudio later that same scene he tells him that the execution will occur at eight. It is as though a reviser, perhaps the compositor, perhaps Middleton or some other theatre aficionado, took the letter's 'four' and inserted it back into one passage of the text, without noticing the later 'eight'.

Other texts too show scrolls that are in a different state from the surrounding dialogue. Stephen Longstaffe in his edition of *Jack Straw* (1594) considers why the Proclamation is not only in black letter when the rest of the play is not, but is written with more care than the play surrounding it:

Given the complexity and length of the speech, it is likely that the actor playing Morton read from a transcript of the pardon onstage, so a . . . possibility is that the printer had access to this 'prop' pardon, and from that decided to accentuate its documentary status by using black letter, the lettering conventionally used for proclamations.[61]

Another Shakespearean example of, perhaps, a separately supplied scroll occurs in *Twelfth Night*. In that play, which survives in Folio only, Malvolio has a long speech in which he speaks, reads a letter, and speaks. But as the printed text presents it the whole lot are run together in a confusing fashion, though the start of the letter is cued by italics; as layout is relevant here, the speech and letter are set exactly as they are in the printed text:

Mal.
M,O,A,I. This simulation is not as the former:
and yet to crush this a little, it would bow to mee, for e-

very one of these Letters are in my name. Soft, here followes prose: *If this fall into thy hand, revolve.* In my stars
I am above thee, but be not affraid of greatnesse: Some
are become great, some atcheeves greatnesse, and some
have greatnesse thrust uppon em. Thy fates open theyr
hands, let thy blood and spirit embrace them, and to in-
ure thy selfe to what thou art like to be: cast thy humble
slough, and appeare fresh. Be opposite with a kinsman,
surly with servants: Let thy tongue tang arguments of
state; put thy selfe into the tricke of singularitie. Shee
thus advises thee, that sighes for thee. Remember who
commended thy yellow stockings, and wish'd to see thee
ever crosse garter'd: I say remember, goe too, thou art
made if thou desir'st to be so: If not, let me see thee a ste-
ward still, the fellow of servants, and not woorthie to
touch Fortunes fingers Farewell, Shee that would alter
services with thee, the fortunate unhappy   daylight and
champian discovers not more: This is open, I will bee
proud, I will reade politicke Authours, I will baffle Sir
Toby . . . (TLN 1145–66)

It is necessary to try to imagine what variety of text the compositor has
been given. He may have an entire manuscript playbook on which the
words '*If this fall into thy hand, revolve*', are in italics and the rest of the
letter is not, as with *The Welsh Embassador*. But as Mahood, when editing
the play, pointed out, the letter contains an important but odd transcription error. Malvolio here reads out the phrase 'Some are become great',
though the sentence, repeated twice later on in the play, reveals that the
word intended is 'born' (or 'borne' as it was often spelled). 'Borne' and
'become' are, of course, confusable in a scrawling secretary hand, and it is
likely that the compositor is misled by the handwriting he is reading at
this moment. Given that, in addition, 'the punctuation of the letter is . . .
uncertain, by comparison with the careful punctuation of the rest of the
play', the implication is that the compositor is working with a difficult
or unfamiliar hand, perhaps on a particularly worn or untidy document:
the letter may originate in a different source text from the text of the play,
perhaps again, a property letter.[62] Other features of this text too may
suggest that the scroll is 'inserted'. The end of the letter 'the fortunate
unhappy' occurs mid-sentence and is followed by a couple of spaces
before the start of what is actually the next sentence: 'the fortunate
unhappy   daylight and champian'. This implies there is some kind
of gap at the end of the letter, but also that the next words follow closely
upon it. Given that the first few lines of the letter are in italic, suggesting

a cue line, it could be that the compositor is working from a cued property letter; if that was the case, and if the last line of the letter was followed by the next few words of Malvolio's speech, that would explain the 'gap'; it is a manifestation of something like a cue line.

CONCLUSION

Collectively all this information makes it abundantly clear why the typographical examples discussed at the start of this chapter exist (why letters in playbooks often look like letters and proclamations like proclamations, etc.), and why this cannot be traced to any philosophical sense of the separate meaning of scroll from text, though the separation might, of course, be said to produce that effect. The typographical distinction serves the same purpose as all the other examples looked at: it provides in visual form the same information that the headings provide in narrative form, alerting the scroll-scribe to the presence of a scroll, and depicting exactly how the document is to look on its own piece of paper.

That said, no scroll *had* to be written on a separate paper: there was, indeed, never any necessity to realise the scrolls onstage save that the policy relieved the actor of some of his work, and if he were to receive a property anyway, it might as well have the 'correct' writing on it. So it is not always possible to say which scrolls actually were extracted and which were not; just which scrolls have features that indicate they probably were, or that they could be. This explains why two alternative texts for the same play often differ as to the presentation of scrolls: sometimes one 'intends' or allows scrolls to be taken out; and one, which may be closer to the authorial text, or closer to a readers' text, does not care about the separation of the scroll in the same way. In Middleton's *Game at Chesse*, as Orgel highlights, presentation of one of the letters differs in both print manifestations of it, and in manuscript.[63] In *King Lear*, however, both Quarto and Folio care about the separation, but in different ways: in Q1 Edmund's feigned letter beginning 'Let your reciprocall vowes bee remembred' is not in italics, but is headed '*A Letter.*' (κ1a) (that heading, absent in the same page in its uncorrected form, is purposely added in); in the Folio the heading is 'reads the letter', but the entire letter is in italics (TLN 383–9).

Regularly extracted from the play and given an additional, separate life on a piece of paper, scrolls for the stage were designed to have potentially two lives: one inside the text, as written (generally) by the author; one outside as retranscribed (but occasionally as written) by the scribe. That means that some playbook scrolls take us nearer to the play in perfor-mance than any other section of text, for they provide a description about what the concomitant stage-property was to have looked like or perhaps transcribe what it did look like. They are, that is to say, 'internalised' props, retained fossilised inside the playbook itself. Outside, they occu-pied a space together with other stage-props including 'blank' scrolls, which they closely resembled, yet as pieces of writing they were different from other stage-props, having also to work in the way all written text for reading onstage worked. For when read out they became, with songs and prologues, both the most textual passages of the play, and potentially the least authorial: simultaneously most vulnerable, because separate from the book, and most fixed, because not victims to lapsed memory. For the spectator of a performance these different pieces of paper are visibly separate from the rest of the play; for the reader of the playbook, they are inside the text, and published in reading order (for the most part), but still isolated by treatment. Both on stage and page they are a strange confusion of text and paratext: they are permanent yet continuously unstable texts, and plays are unstable around them to contain their oddities.

CHAPTER 7

Backstage-plots

INTRODUCTION

When, in Thomas Jordan's masque *Fancy's Festivals*, the character Fancy drops 'a bundle of Masking toyes' she also loses 'two Papers'. A poet, finding the fallen objects, details what he picks up: first the props, 'Ribons, Bells, bawbles, Masks, and dancing shooes'; then 'two papers' of which 'this is the Plot,/And this the language'.[1] Here 'plot' is kept together with 'language', but does not occupy the same papers, so that 'plot' denotes not a generalised or vague account of a story, but a variety of text in its own right. Given that the masque appears to have been recently completed, what, in this instance, is 'the plot'?

The 'plot' in *Fancy's Festivals* might be the Argument or summary of the masque sometimes given out to an audience and described in chapter 3, except that such plots, designed to be distributed in multiple quantities, are unlikely to have been carried around singly with the playscript. It might be the 'author-plot' or scenario from which the writer constructed his play or masque in the first place, except that the masque in *Fancy's Festivals* has already been hastily completed and is now about to be performed, as the gathering of props related to it indicates. Either use of 'plot' would be interesting because either would highlight the way separate written papers that did not constitute the actual playtext still flanked the playbook without ever being integrated into it. But as the plot to *Fancy's Festivals* is kept with its text in the lead-up to perform-ance, this particular piece of paper seems most likely to have been yet another form of text called, confusingly, 'plot' (or, sometimes, a variant of the word, 'plat'): the mounted paper consisting largely of a series of entrances for actors, to be used by theatre personnel either before performance or during it. It is the plot most closely identified with the playbook in that the two were not only, as above, kept together, but kept inside one another.

The document entitled *The Platt of The Secound Parte of the Seven Deadlie Sinns*, now to be found carefully mounted in a nineteenth-century cover, has a label preserved with it. It reads 'The Booke and Platt of the second part of The. 7 deadly sinns', indicating that this plot was once to be found in the same place as its playbook.[2] Yet by the time the document was discovered in the eighteenth century, it was wrapped around an entirely different playscript, making up 'a cover for an anonymous manuscript play entitled *The Tell-tale*'.[3] Even now, the manuscript of *The Telltale*, long separated from this plot, bears a leftover coversheet in an early modern hand that repeats the information of the plot's label, 'The Booke and platt of the second part of the 7 deadly sinns'.[4] So the plot of *Seven Deadly Sins* seems once to have flanked and probably clasped its own play, the two wrapped together with a coversheet naming their union, for the document appears to have spent many years bent in two, and has decayed significantly along its central fold. And, as two other plots, *The plott of the deade mans fortune*, and *The plott of Frederick & Basilea*, are similarly cracked down the middle (the others still extant are too decayed to tell), it seems likely that they all once doubled as folders for their theatrical playbooks. The connection between book and this variety of plot is a close one: the plot, though a separate document, occupies the same place as the book, implying that when the one is necessary, so is the other.

In the circumstances it could be seen as odd that a complete playbook-and-plot coupling does not survive, and that all plots have lost their books (and, presumably, all books their plots). Is it that plots only belonged to a particular period of theatre history, or to a particular company, or even to a particular moment in time? The uncertainty is not helped by the fact that the seven plots known about have an unclear provenance that makes them hard to date. Divided, now, between the British Library, which purchased five of them in the nineteenth century (*The plott of the deade mans fortune, The plott of Frederick & Basilea, The P<lott of the Seco>nd Par<t of> Fortu<ns Tenn>is, <The plot of Troilus and Cressida>, The Plott of the Battell of Alcazar*), Dulwich College, which purchased one of them, also in the nineteenth century (*The Platt of the Secound Parte of the Seven Deadlie Sinns*), and an unknown location (*The plott of The first part of Tamar Cam*, transcribed by George Steevens and published in 1803 but now lost), it is not evident whether the texts were ever kept together in one place, or whether they came from a variety of sources.[5] Five of the plots were sold by the estate of James Boswell the younger, an early nineteenth-century editor of Shakespeare; as his materials were largely inherited from the library of George Steevens, the eighteenth-century editor, the plots are likely to have come with Steevens' effects. And, as Steevens, after recording his discovery of the plot of the *Seven Deadly Sins* in Dulwich College, then 'acquired' that plot for himself, it is often thought that the other plots, too, originated in Dulwich and were later bought or taken by Steevens. Three of the plots, *Dead Man's Fortune*, *Tamar Cam* and *Frederick and Basilea*, are recorded by Steevens as being 'in my possession' in 1793, though as he also speculates about their connection to Dulwich he must have obtained them through an intermediary.[6]

Yet even if it could be demonstrated that *all* the plots came from Steevens, and even if it could thence be shown that Steevens' source was Dulwich College, that still would not conclusively prove that the plots themselves had a shared theatrical origin. Though Dulwich College was founded by the great early modern actor Edward Alleyn – so many of the theatre documents there are his – another performer, the Restoration actor and bookseller William Cartwright, also left his effects to Dulwich. Cartwright's holdings included documents and properties inherited from his father, also called William Cartwright, who was a player and Alleyn's direct contemporary. With no early catalogue to indicate what comes from Alleyn and what comes from Cartwright, it is impossible to know whether some or all of the plots belonged to Alleyn (who is named in three of them), whether some or all belonged to Cartwright's father (who is also named in three of them), or whether some or all belonged to another person or other people entirely (as a bookseller and bookbuyer, Cartwright the younger could have acquired theatrical documents like these at any time and from any source). This means that the companies and theatres that used the plots, and the periods of time from which the plots date, are all open to debate: do plots amount to a wide-ranging sample of ephemera created for every play in performance, or a narrow range of the material issued by a limited group of people over a brief period of time? Though the plots are traditionally dated between 1592 and 1602, all of those dates are somewhat open to question, as promoters and detractors of redating the *Seven Deadly Sins* plot from 1592 to 1594 to 1598 to 1602 know only too well.[7]

Not knowing how 'usual' plots were makes their purpose hard to construe. Backstage-plots are simultaneously the most well-known (for the most part, the only known) and the least comprehended form of 'plot' from the early modern theatre. And, because so little is understood about them, the various 'readings' offered over time to determine what they might be, when in the production process they were used, and by and for whom they were written have all been markedly different. Collier thought these plots were rough outlines of plays from which actors might extemporise, taking his pattern from the scenarios used by actors of the Commedia dell'Arte during the same period; his model would have it that the plot was 'the play' (there was no other text), and that it was written by an author for actors.[8] Greg, however, thought plots were written to hang backstage during performance; in his model, the plot was written by a scribe, or a prompter, from a playbook, for tiring-house use by either theatre functionaries or the actors themselves.[9] Tribble thinks a variant of this, maintaining that plots were so obviously intended for actors that those who think otherwise 'reflect a desire for these artefacts to tell us not what the players needed to know but what *we* want to know'.[10] King and Ioppolo, on the other hand, have it that backstage-plots are the same documents as plot-scenarios, arguing that what acting companies purchased when they bought 'plots' were lists of actor-entrances: for them, the plot is written by authors for prompters before (King) or after (Ioppolo) the play exists.[11] David Bradley, however, thinks plots were written from the book by prompters to sort out the casting and doubling of a play; he believes plots were later used for directing what he takes to be several rehearsals while the 'book' was away with the Master of the Revels: information 'stored' on plots during rehearsal might then, he argues, migrate back to the returned playtext – in his model, the plot both descended from and fed into the playbook, though its practical and theatrical use was over by the time performance started.[12]

Each suggestion posits not only an entirely different use and author for the plot, but an entirely different relationship between plot and playbook: in the first (Collier), there is no playbook; in the second (Greg and Tribble), the plot is written partially from the stage-directions in the playbook; in the third (King and Ioppolo), the plot provides the entrance-directions from which the playbook will be written; and in the fourth (Bradley), the plot's stage-directions partially come from the book but partially go into it.

This chapter will analyse afresh the seven known plots and the one act of what seems to be a 'pre-plot' document, attempting to sort out what plots are, when they were created, by whom, and hence, finally, how they relate to playbooks and other textual materials of the playhouse. It will do this by comparing plots with the information supplied by eighteenth- and nineteenth-century documents that appear to be their descendants. In the light of its discoveries, it will examine a handful of early modern references to plots, for it is not the case that, as Greg believed, 'no contemporary allusion to these Plots has been discovered'.[13] As a result, it will explain why none of the twelve books identified by Greg as prompters' books survives with a plot; and will argue that more theatrical playbooks may survive than has previously been thought.[14] Finally it will attempt to define the complex relationship between stage-directions in plays and stage-directions in plots. Which text is influencing which, and how does this affect the manuscript circulation of play fragments?

THE PRE-PLOT

The easiest way to start thinking about plots is to consider what elements were crucial to them in their most elemental and primitive state. Fortunately, notes towards a plot – a 'pre-plot' – survive on the underside of a letter, its play unnamed. The letter itself, from the actor Robert Shaa to Philip Henslowe, concerns Robert Wilson's 2 *Henry Richmond*: the pre-plot on the back of the letter is in Robert Wilson's (italic) hand and seems to concern that play.[15] It is a strange document, stopping at the end of one act, and showing who is to enter by fictional name only; who is then to enter to them (also by fictional name); and when the stage empties (signified by a line). No properties are supplied in the text and there is no marginal annotation:

~~Enter Richard~~

~~i se~~

1. Sce: *Wm Wor: & Ansell &* to them ye plowghmen
 ---- *Q. & Eliza*:
2. Sce: *Richard ˆ Catesbie, Lovell, Rich ap Tho: Blunt, Banester ˆ*
 ----
3. Sce: *Ansell Davye Denys Hen: Oxf: Courtney Bou'chier & Grace*
 to them *Riche ap Tho.* & his *Soldiors*
 ----
4. Sce: *Mitton Ban:* his *wyfe & children*
~~6. Sce~~: ----------------------
5. Sce: *K Rich: Catesb: Lovell. Norf. Northumb: Percye*

This pre-plot, written by the play's author, appears to constitute part of the way his text is marketed to the company. Perhaps Wilson is illustrating how stageable his completed play is (Shaa explains in the letter overleaf, 'we have heard their booke and lyke yt'); perhaps he is providing a document that establishes the number of players needed for the first act in order to help with casting issues.[16] He may additionally be indicating which characters are to be found in consecutive scenes (so indicating which roles can and cannot easily double); which incidents follow after which other incidents (so indicating which scenes could, if necessary, be cut); and which characters enter into which scene (so indicating which parts the part-scribe should collect as he embarked on copying a section into its constituent documents). Certainly this pre-plot shows the playwright himself contributing material to what eventually became the theatre's plot, and by extension illustrating that, from the very first, the kind of direction that belonged on a plot might never be written onto a playbook.

The qualities that the pre-plot lacks also reveal issues about the construction of full plots. Plots must have been made by combining documents that the theatre had separately created onto one piece of paper: a 'pre-plot' being just one of those documents. To be 'completed' as a plot along the model of the others, for instance, this pre-plot would have to be combined with a cast-list, a list of 'personals' (properties to be held or worn by entering actors), perhaps a general properties-list, and perhaps a music-list. But it is always possible that some productions did not combine their lists on a single plot document. It is worth considering here the 'scrowle of every mans name . . . thought fit . . . to play in our Enterlude' (TLN 272–4) that Quince holds in his hands for the rehearsal of the Mechanicals in *A Midsummer Night's Dream* and his promise to 'draw a bil of properties' (TLN 365–6): this cast-list and property-list seem to be the only documents produced towards rehearsing and performing *Pyramus and Thisbe*. Different productions might construct documents in the form that worked best for them: plots may not always have been that form.

The large number of papers that survive for the staging of the main masque of Shirley's spectacular *The Triumph of Peace*, put on by the Inns of Court in Whitehall for a royal performance on 3 February 1634, illustrate how a production can be run from a series of documents rather than a plot. These papers include a list that gives a processional order (information that, alternatively, a plot could offer – a numbered processional order is given in the last scene of *Tamar Cam*); a cast-list (again, full plots sometimes provide this information); and a cue-list for songs (plots with marginal annotation provide song-warnings – but a cue-list for them would still have been needed, as plots are not accurate as to 'moment'). Further documents for the masque include detailed diagrams of where performers are to stand for the dances, and costume-lists of the colours to be worn: information that plots do not supply, but that the playhouses may have come up with somewhere else.[17] Though Shirley's masque cannot be compared directly to a public theatre performance, what can be observed is that different performances create different documents to design their staging needs. Those documents can be written up into one single solid plot, but can also be used collectively to run the production in their own right. The performative advantage of having a plot is that it combines several flimsy documents onto one permanent theatrical board; its disadvantage is the same: the more theatre personnel who are to rely on this single document, the harder it will be for an individual to get a purchase on the text during a busy performance. In other words, all productions needed organisational documents; not all productions therefore needed plots.

With that caveat, the seven surviving plots can now be addressed. What does their physical structure reveal about their use? What do their contents show? To turn to the first question: plots were, as everything about them broadcasts, made with heavy and repeated use in mind. All surviving plots are made of substantial pulp boards onto which fresh sheets of good folio-sized paper (roughly 12 by 16 inches) are affixed. The pulp remains perfectly preserved for the plots of *The Dead Man's Fortune* and *Frederick and Basilea*, but traces of it can still be seen on the fragmentary remains of other plots. In the case of the *Seven Deadly Sins*, rebound and remounted in the nineteenth century, a testament to what the document was originally like survives from the eighteenth century: George Steevens, in his description of the plot published in the 1790s, portrays it as 'fairly [i.e., neatly] written out on paste-board in a large hand'.[18] Plots were, from the start, written as placards, a form that demanded their preservation, as well as aiding their probable second use as stiff covers to the playbook they helped to stage.

Written at the top of the folio sheet stuck onto the board is the nature of the document (the word 'plat' or 'plot'), and the title of the play for which it is the map. With the exception of *Dead Man's Fortune*, which does not magnify its heading, plots all have extremely large titles written in embellished gothic script: a script, a size and a form so magnificent that it will have required a special quill – Cocker recommends for gothic or, as he calls it, 'German Text' to adopt 'a great Pen having two slits'; but anyway the outsize and calligraphic nature of the plot-headings makes use of the average feather impossible.[19] Such headings may have been written by the same people who wrote the contents of the plots, but also may not: embellished large text-letters were often required on the stage, and the headings may have been penned by the playhouse scribe responsible for painting title- and scene-boards.[20] What these headings do share is, again, a close link with theatrical playbooks: the heading-writer to the plot of *Seven Deadly Sins* also pens the large and elaborate gothic titles to the manuscripts of *Thomas More* and *John a Kent and John a Cumber*. With their tremendous titles, the plot and plays' names alike are readable from a distance; in both instances some pride in the very creation of the documents is advertised too.

Under the title, and using most of the rest of the sheet in every plot (and seemingly spilling onto the back of the document in *Battle of Alcazar* and *Troilus and Cressida*), are two vertical columns ruled in ink in a thin nib. The boxes into which these are subdivided are filled with writing that fits exactly into its space, meaning that the columns were inked in first, and that the scribe then wrote in the text, sealing each box with a line as it was completed. As a result, no space is wasted; also as a result, the boxes are not of uniform dimensions, and one boxed stage moment is visually differentiated from another. The effect, as Tribble argues, is that the documents are made with 'a shape easily graspable by all members of the company': varying box-size aids users of the plot, whoever they are, to remember or find their 'place' quickly in the text.[21]

As for the appearance of the writing in the boxes themselves, all of the plots are inscribed with the utmost concern for clarity. Their contents are written in what George Steevens called a 'large' hand, meaning that the letters formed are universally bigger in size than conventional handwriting; one, *Seven Deadly Sins*, is, further, penned in unjoined letters, unusual at the time, but helpful if the text is to be read quickly or by unsophisticated or semi-literate readers.[22] Even the plot that appears to have been a little more speedily written, *Troilus and Cressida*, still breaks difficult words and names into print letters. It seems that plots set out to be intelligible to people not entirely familiar with their contents or even with reading – which is to say, people other than their scribes. It also appears that plots were written in 'neat' – so copied in some way, meaning that the scribes of the plots were not necessarily the same people as the composers of the plots.

Lastly, after some of the documents have been marginally annotated by another hand, they are pierced through by an oblong hole inserted about a third of the way down the central margin; this is visible on any plot for which the top half of the text survives, and was present, too, on the lost plot, being 'drawn' in Steevens' replication of the document. The relationship of this hole to the contents is telling: it was obviously added only after the entire text had been fully written *and*, when necessary, acquired its first set of annotations. The plot of *Dead Man's Fortune*, for example, has a hole placed high in the board to avoid cutting into marginal text. Thus hanging the documents on a square peg was the last in the act of making them, and the first in the act of publicly using them.

In sum, plots are carefully written and ornately headed documents, mounted onto placards to be hung on a peg, and, when not in use, wrapped around their playbooks. These are, as structure reveals, texts to be observed repeatedly by several people on the same occasion on which the book is to be used. Only undervaluing the plots' palaeographical dimension and absolutely ignoring their physical features could suggest that these were other than public documents designed for performance-use – a point made by Martin Wiggins some years ago.[23]

BACKSTAGE-PLOTS: CONTENTS

The single consistent concern of all plots is, as in the pre-plot, the initial entrance of characters, though in full plots this is explicitly spelled out. Boxes starting with 'enter' (never, though sometimes several people enter, the plural 'entrant') constitute: every single box in *Dead Man's Fortune*; every single box in *Battle of Alcazar*; every single box in *Tamar Cam*; every surviving visible box in the decayed manuscript plots of *Troilus and Cressida* and *Fortune's Tennis*; and all but one box in *Frederick and Basilea*. In the *Seven Deadly Sins,* where seventeen of the twenty-five boxes start with 'enter', there are a few exceptions. The first box of the plot relates to a character who is to be already onstage when the play begins, and therefore cannot be seen to enter onto it; the direction in this case reads 'A tent being plast one the stage for Henry the sixt. He in it' (1). The other six 'non-enter' boxes seem specifically to relate to one single character, Lydgate: 'A Larum wth Excursions After Lidgate speaks'; 'Henry and Lidgat speaks'; 'Lidgat speake'; 'A larum'; 'a Dumb show. Lidgate speakes'; and 'Lidgate speaks to the audiens and so Exitts' (within V, IX, within XIII, within XV, within XXII, XXIV). This character-focussed anomaly is hard to explain without the playbook, but as Lydgate's 'boxes' are generally smaller than the others (and are sometimes situated inside the others) staging obviously differs around that single character. Lydgate seems to have had a role somewhat 'outside' that of the main play; perhaps continually onstage as its chorus or narrator (in reality, Lydgate had been a chronicler of the fall of princes). That character aside, all boxes in all plots are designed to determine a flow of people in one direction, from backstage onto the stage: plots belong to the tiring-house.

The second concern of each box in each plot is a variant of the first concern: also entrances, but this time entrances mid-scene. For this, the formula used is 'to him/her/them', depending on who is already onstage, the word 'enter' being understood. Yet as none of these mid-scene entrances are cued, they must all be 'warnings' of some kind: more specific information will be required to isolate the specific stage moments to which they refer. A typical example of the first and second kind of entrances can be seen in boxes iv, v and vi of *Frederick and Basilea*:[24]

Enter Myron=hamec, lords. Tho: Towne. Tho Hunt ledbeter To them Heraclius, Thamar, Sam Charles
Enter Governor Mr Dunstann, To hym Messenger Th: Hunt To them Heraclius Sam, To them Myranhamec, Soliors.
Enter ffrederick, Basilea, R Allen. Dick, To them Kinge Mr Jubie To them Messenger Black Dick, To them Sebastian, Heraclius, Theodore, Pedro, Philippo Andreo Thamar. Mr Allen, Sam: Mr Martyn. leadb: Dutton Pigg. To them Leonora, will,

In this second concern too, plots emerge as documents to control entrances onto the stage in one direction – and so, again, as 'backstage' in their nature.[25]

Mid-scene exits are considerably less important than entrances in all the plots; the word 'exit' does not even occur in *Dead Man's Fortune, Frederick and Basilea* and what remains of *Fortune's Tennis*. In the other plots, 'exit' and 'exeunt' are sporadically supplied, but just as often inferred from circumstance; on several occasions a character enters and then enters again without an exit ever having been given, as happens with the 'keeper' in the *Seven Deadly Sins*, 11 – 'Henry Awaking Enter A Keeper J sincler. to him a servaunt T Belt. to him Lidgate and the Keeper'. So another document or documents must have been primarily responsible for mid-scene exits, an idea that will be returned to. The plots that do use the terms 'exit' and 'exeunt', *Tamar Cam, Battle of Alcazar* and *Troilus and Cressida*, also use the term 'manet', 'remain', for moments when an actor or actors are to stay onstage; this may not, however, be so much a way of indicating which actors are to remain as an alternative way of indicating the term 'exit', as Greg claims, for 'manet' allows the scribe to list the single characters who stay onstage, rather than the group who go off it.[26] Either way, 'manet' cannot convey information to anyone already onstage, for they cannot get backstage to read that they stay onstage: it is useful only to a backstage person. But, while plots take from little to no interest in 'internal' exits, those exits that empty the stage are of concern to all of them: the line ruled across the bottom of each box represents a moment when the stage empties, meaning that final exits are tacitly present on all the documents, whether explicitly written in or not. As a result of plots' concern for movement out onto the stage and exits at the end of scenes from the stage, plot 'boxes' sometimes do not map onto 'scenes', for the line along the bottom of a box may represent a dumb-show-end or an induction-end – any moment, scenic or not, at which everyone leaves the stage. Hence the use, here, of 'box' rather than 'scene' to describe the content of plots: for a box is not so much a dramatic unit as a unit of stage occupancy. These are documents about the structure of the play's movement, more than the play's narrative.

The third interest of plot boxes closely relates to entrances: it is with the properties that will be brought on by the entering actor. 'Enter Tesephon … disguisd wth meate' (*Dead Man's Fortune*, III.iii); 'to them … pescode wth spectakles' (*Dead Man's Fortune*, III.iv); 'Enter Sarda wth as many Jewels robes and Gold as he ca<n> carry' (*Seven Deadly Sins*, xv) are entrances that include the props collectively known, in the modern theatrical world, as 'personals', meaning the props that are to be carried or worn by the person of the entering actor. 'Personals' are the responsibility of the actor (unlike larger pieces of property that are the responsibility of backstage functionaries).

The fourth concern of boxes is, as with the pre-plot, fictional characters. Every plot names every fictional character who is in the play; and every entrance is to a character by fictional name. Some fictional names are then additionally glossed with the names of the 'real' actors who will play the parts, but this does not happen consistently. Of all the plots, only *Tamar Cam* assigns actors' names to every single fictional character; at the other extreme, in *The Dead Man's Fortune*, only four actors (but all fictional characters) are ever named. Even those 'real' names that are

present on the documents, however, are often placed oddly distanced
from the character name. When one character who is to be played by one
actor enters, that is well and good, and the entry is easy to read, following
the pattern of 'Enter Muly Mahamett mr Ed: Allen, his sonne Antho:
Jeffes' from *Battle of Alcazar* (1, chorus).[27] But when there is a 'massed
entry' in which several characters are to enter at the same time, the plot
often becomes confused. It will list, first, fictional characters, then (when
it does so) real actors' names, but the order of the real names will not
necessarily match the order of fictional characters. So one entry asks for
'Lucius and Damasus mr Bry T Good' (*Seven Deadly Sins,* VI), as though
Lucius is played by 'Mr Bry[an]' and Damasus is played by 'T[homas]
Good[ale]'; yet a later entry shows that 'Mr Bryan' must actually have
played Damasus, for in VIII he is already onstage when 'Lucius' enters:
'Lords R Cowly mr Brian. To them Lucius Running'. Plots have some
interest in casting, that is to say, but are not documents that sort it out
(where matching name with character would be the specific point of the
document). Nor is it the case that minor characters, who may have been
played by apprentices and hirelings, are consistently given 'real' as well as
fictional names, while major characters, who may have been played by
sharers, are given fictional names only, though this is often put forward to
explain the lack of casting information on plots.[28] Names of minor 'real'
actors are not supplied for some of the very moments when 'casting'
concerns might have made them most important. There are, amongst
the plots, five requests for 'attendants' (of which only one, from *Dead
Man's Fortune,* is later glossed in the margin with three names), two for
'soldiers', and one each for 'lords', 'satyrs', 'children', and 'spirritts', all
without further annotation.[29] In other words, when collective groups
of characters are required, they are not generally glossed with real actors'
names.

So plots seem, in a somewhat lackadasical fashion, to reflect some of
the casting choices made elsewhere, a fact underlined by layout too: names
of real actors, when provided, are not squeezed in after names of fictional
characters, but are instead written in with perfect spacing; the scribe is
already cognisant of casting choices by the time of writing. Thus this
document reflects some aspects of a casting process or series of processes,
without being that process in its own right. This would hardly need
articulating, were it not for the fact that an influential book by David
Bradley concluded that plots, despite their sturdy structure and neat
handwriting, were private ephemeral papers the main purpose of which
was as casting documents. He took the *Battle of Alcazar* – the only plot for

which a playscript, published in a considerably earlier version, survives – and importantly showed how casting decisions were part of the artistic creation of its performance. So interested was he in his revolutionary conclusions, however, that he came to believe the plots were drawn up *for* casting, rather than documents that erratically recorded that process. Scholarship about the plots has been misled ever since.

But if plots are mainly interested in fictional characters, they are strangely uninterested in fictional place. The court or city where the play is staged, be it Alcazar or Rome, is never mentioned, nor is the imaginary stage building – courthouse, gaol, senate. There are merely occasional references to the more general fictional locations in which the characters perform, 'upon the walls' (*Frederick and Basilea*, XI), 'a tent' (*Seven Deadly Sins*, 1). These smaller locales seem, however, as with equivalent stage-directions, to be used when the fiction maps very obviously onto the stage-construction: 'upon the walls' is 'above', in 'a tent' is in 'a stage construction resembling a tent'; on plenty of other occasions the simple stage-words themselves are employed, like 'above' (*Battle of Alcazar*, 11, chorus) and 'at one dore' (*Seven Deadly Sins*, VII).[30] Thus the plots flirt a little with the local edges of the fiction, but not enough to use its main situational terminology. No attention at all is paid to the locale backstage (so no real or fictional words for the tiring-house are used – there is no 'within' and 'without' in plots and the word is never applied). As ever, content shows plots to belong backstage whilst concerning issues onstage in largely practical configurations.

On some plots, however, further information is supplied outside the boxes. This information is not about entrances, fictional players, or 'personals'. It is about larger stage concerns: the gathering of major props, the sound effects. When present, this new marginal information is written by scribes other than the plot-writers, like the second hand that has marked extra properties in the plot for *Battle of Alcazar* including '<box>es for pre<s>ents' (II.i), '3. Violls of blood & a sheeps gather' (III, chorus), and 'Dead mens heads & bon<es>' (IV, chorus). Second scribal hands in the margin have likewise placed additional information about sounds in *Dead Man's Fortune*, *Fortune's Tennis*, *Battle of Alcazar* and *Tamar Cam*: against the box containing a command for '<He>au>lds' to enter and then 'Menalaus and Dimoded' and then 'Hector' and '<Dei>phobus, and then Cassandra' is a marginal note '3 severa<ll> <T>ucketts (*Troilus and Cressida*, a); the word 'Sound' is regularly found outside boxes in *Tamar Cam*; 'Alarum' is to be seen by boxes in *Troilus and Cressida*, *Battle of Alcazar* and *Tamar Cam*. *Dead*

Man's Fortune even enhances its four marginal demands for 'Musique' by a line of crosses marked along the bottom of the relevant box, creating four musical interludes that cut across the drama and impose a five-act structure onto the play. None of this information in the margins is, however, cued; it is, like the contents of the boxes, general rather than specific.

Plots, then, define box-by-box when the stage is empty and when it is full, but they are interested only in what is happening onstage, not off it; in particular, they carefully list who is to enter first and who is then to enter to them, but are only sporadically taken with mid-scene exits, and are really only concerned when exits empty the stage. Though they have a major investment in characters by their fictional names, they do not always provide the names of the actors who will play those characters, and, even then on crucial occasions neglect to name them. Property interests within plot boxes are confined to the 'personals' belonging to entering actors, but sometimes marginal notation in a different hand adds more general sound and property warnings. No cues are ever given on plots, however, so all the information they supply demands that more specific documents also be produced. Who will have written such placards and who will have used them? To answer this, it becomes helpful to examine other documents in the later history of theatre that resemble backstage-plots.

EIGHTEENTH-CENTURY PROMPTERS AND THEIR CALL-SHEETS

In the Folger Shakespeare Library, amongst a collection of documents relating to Garrick's 1763 production of *A Midsummer Night's Dream*, is a piece of paper folded in two and then folded into two again, creating a document made of columns.[31] In spite of its flimsiness, it has an immediate similarity in appearance to the plots, for each of its pages is treated as two columns, and each column is subdivided into numbered boxes. Column two is headed 'Act 2d', so clearly relating to the business that takes place in the second act; it consists, however, of a series of boxes numbered 1–9 (evidently not representative of scenes, therefore, as act 2 of *A Midsummer Night's Dream* contains only two scenes); similarly 'Act 3d' is made up of boxes numbered 1–10 (though, again, there are convention-ally said to be just two scenes in act 3 of the play). As with plots, the boxes are concerned only with entrances and players: they contain an actor's name and a reference to a door or wing of entrance – either 'PS' for 'Prompt Side', or 'OP' for 'Opposite Prompt' (both conventional theatrical acronyms at the time). They have no interest in internal exits or in what is happening backstage, though the end of a box also seems to indicate stage-clearance.

An example of the right-hand column of the first page of the document provides a sense of the look and contents of the boxes:

Act 2d

[1	Miss Mathews Mrs: Atkins	meet
[2	Y: Cauthery all ye. Boys Miss Sinisen all ye. Girls	PS OP
[3	Mr: Holland Macklin Miss ~~Macklin~~ Pritchard	OP
[4	Y: Atkins a flower	PS
[5	Miss Simson all ye. Girls Miss Young	x
[6	Y: Cautherly a flower	

This is stark compared to early modern plots, and yet the format is similar to them in other ways too. As with plots, there is a surprising laxness when the document asks for a group of people: no individual names are given, and the group is simply referred to by collective title – 'all ye. Boys' and 'all ye. Girls' are asked for in the example above. The document also reduces its property interests to those 'personals' that entering characters must have with them, like 'a flower' in the example above or, later, 'a paper w[rit]t[en]'.

In another way, too, this document seems to be a descendant of the plot. It contains a few additional 'warnings' for objects or groups which take the form 'dance ready' and 'ass's head ready OP', rather like the additional and more general property notes added to the margins of the plots. It is, finally, also like plots in not providing cues, so never giving the precise moment at which its actors or props are needed. Both documents, then, are loosely structured in the same way, having a sense of chronology, in terms of which actor comes on first, and who comes on later to join them, but lacking a sense of absolute moment.

It therefore becomes incumbent to ask who it was in the eighteenth-century theatre who was greatly interested in entrances and personals, moderately interested in the preparation of some properties, and moderately unconcerned about exits. Obviously this is some backstage person. And on one level it must be the prompter, for he is in charge of managing stage traffic. Nevertheless, he is not the automatic user of the document, for during productions he has to sit in one of the wings (as 'PS' and 'OP' suggest) holding, as one eighteenth-century account put it, 'a book before him, from which he . . . suppl[ies] those that are *out* in their parts with hints and directions proper to set them right'.[32] He does, however, have help; that same account describes the 'scouts and messengers' attending on the prompter: through dispatching them 'he can, at a minute's warning, bring the greatest characters of antiquity, or the pleasantest of the present times, upon the stage'.[33] But how does the prompter direct those scouts as to which actor is about to enter? As the theatre historian Kalman A. Burnim realised, the prompter created documents for his helpers such as the one quoted above: writes Burnim excitedly on a note he leaves with this particular document in the Folger, 'This is the earliest call-book I've encountered.'[34]

Call-books (also called 'call-lists' or 'call-sheets') were papers created by the prompter or under his auspices, but not for his own use. They were given to menial members of the backstage staff named, in the early eighteenth century, 'prompters' boys' and later, for obvious reasons, 'call-boys'. Call-boys allowed actors who were not performing to wait unworried in the 'scene' or 'green-room', and then be summoned to their door of entrance with a few minutes to spare, so that they would not have to hover in the wings indefinitely listening out for their cues of entrance: 'The want of . . . a Call-boy', wrote Brownsmith, the prompter of Salisbury theatre, at about the same period as the Garrick document was put together, is 'an inconceivable detriment to the conduct of a Play' as 'the mind of a performer [will be] always embarrassed and unsettled . . . who is obliged every minute to attend to the scene in action'.[35]

Colman the Younger goes into somewhat more detail about the job of the call-boy, detailing in particular the relationship between call-boy and prompter, and, concomitantly, the relationship between call-sheet and prompter's book:

> The Prompter's boy, Messieurs! Must stand
> Near the Stage-Door, close at the Prompter's hand;
> Holding a Nomanclature that's numberical,
> Which tallies with the Book prompterical:
>
> And as the Prompter calls, 'One, Two, Three, Four,'
> Mark'd, accurately, in the Prompt-Book page,
> These numbers mean the Boy must leave the Door,
> To call the folks refer'd to, for the Stage.[36]

Vandenhoff enlarges:

> the prompter . . . about 5 minutes, or three lengths (120 lines) before a character has to enter on the stage, finds marked in his prompt-book of the play a number thus [3]. He then says to his attendant imp, who has a list in his hand, (a call-list – very different from a New Year's call-list,) 'Call three;' – the boy looks at his list, walks to the Green-Room door, and calls the character marked [3] in that act; or the prompter orders him to call 4. 5, 6, 7: he consults his list for the act, finds these numbers, and at the Green-Room door calls the characters they represent, thus: –
>   Hamlet,
>   Horatio,
>   Marcellus,
>   Ghost.
> The gentlemen who represent these characters, on being thus called, rise, leave the Green-Room, and go and stand at the wing – the side-scene – at which they are presently to enter.[37]

As Vandenhoff indicates, once positioned by the appropriate door, actors were then on their own, awaiting the specific 'cue of entrance' as set out by their parts ('lengths' as they were then called): call-books, that is to say, gave generalised information designed to work in tandem with the specific information on actors' parts and in the book.

So far, plots seem like call-sheets in appearance. But in one way the Garrick call-sheet differs from the plot. While the plot had named all actors by fictional name and only some by real name, this document does the reverse. It names all actors by real name and only on particular occasions, when something akin to doubling is to occur – like the entrance for the Mechanicals in *A Midsummer Night's Dream* in their internal-play characters and costumes – does it supply fictional characters:

> Mr. Vaughan
> Mr. Yates
>   as Pyramus
> Mr. Philips
>   as Thisbe
> [4 Mr Ackman
>   as wall
> Mr. Perry
>   as moonshine
> Mr. Clough
>   as Lyon.

Yet the choice of whether to call actors by fictional names, or real names (or, on occasion, both), is explained by the nature of the call-book: provided a complete set of names is given, either will do. In the 1842 call-book for a production of Nicholas Rowe's *Jane Shore* (played at Drury Lane) all actors are called by their fictional names: Gloster, Ratcliff, Catesby, Lord Hastings are required for Act 1, box 1.[38] Vandenhoff explains, at any rate for the nineteenth century, that the choice of whether to call an actor primarily by name or primarily by fictional character simply differed from theatre to theatre (and country to country):

In many theatres, the calls are made by the name of the actor or actress representing the character called. It was so, if I recollect, at Covent Garden; at the Haymarket it is otherwise; and generally throughout the theatres of the United States, the calls are made by the names of the characters; and it is the safer plan, and less liable to mistakes on the part of the call-boys.[39]

Plot and call-sheet, then, remain similar, the 'plots' simply electing fictional characters, the Garrick call-sheet electing real actors.

The other difference between the Garrick call-sheet and the plot is physical. The Garrick document is flimsy; 'plots' are not, as discussed. Yet, there again, much depends on particular documents and their theatrical longevity. The look of eighteenth- and nineteenth-century call-books actually varied considerably, a fact that is probably responsible for their varied names: 'call-sheets' best describes the simple papers making up the Garrick example above, 'call-book' better describes the smart and carefully written book that was created for the 1842 production of Nicholas Rowe's *Jane Shore*.[40] The elegant or scrappy form the document takes may depend on the number of such texts distributed, and the length of time they were intended to last. A special one-off production for a particular occasion might require its own one-day call-sheet; while a 'stock' production might require one or several smarter call-books, always remembering that a significant change in company personnel would entail a rewriting of any call-sheet tied to real names. So it may have been with plots, where one sturdy document or several flimsy ones (like the ones produced for Shirley's *The Triumph of Peace*) could be used according to occasion.

Are plots a variety of call-sheet in an earlier form? For this to be the case, further correspondences would be needed between the early modern and the eighteenth-century theatre. Early modern theatre would require a prompter who spent his performance staring at his 'book', and a call-boy who aided him during production.

BOOK-HOLDERS AS PROMPTERS; BACKSTAGE-PLOTS AS CALL-SHEETS

Theatre changes slowly and it is a good bet that, if something happened in the eighteenth century, something like it happened in the sixteenth and seventeenth centuries: only recently has a close and repetitive attachment to our theatrical heritage been lost. It is to be expected that there was, in the early modern period, as later, a prompter whose main duty in performance was to 'prompt' the actors, for which reason he was constantly occupied, during performance, with the book he held in his hand. That there was just such a character was self-evident for centuries, but a strange idea that 'prompting' is not an early modern concept has confused recent scholarship. Belying that is the fact that 'prompter' is by far the most regularly used word for the functionary during the early modern period: it was the only term that Shakespeare ever used for him, referring to the actor so badly prepared that his prologue must be 'faintly spoke After the Prompter' (*Romeo and Juliet* [1597], C1a) and, alternatively, to the actor so sure of his stage actions that 'Were it [his] Qu. to fight, [he] should have knowne it,/Without a prompter' (*Othello*, TLN 301).

As with eighteenth-century actors, early modern players did not perform in 'long runs' and had such heavy learning and performance schedules that they often found themselves 'out' or 'at a non plus' on stage. When they were so, they turned to the prompter, blaming him if he did not instantly set them back on track: the Prologue to *The Careles Shepherdess* who '*being out, is laught at*' rounds on the prompter at once – 'Pox take the Prompter'; in the same way, Gingle, having had to prompt himself in *Apollo Shroving*, turns on the functionary: 'I am to say your

Monkey will recover. Master Prompter doe your part'; while, when Fairefield is 'out ons part', Caroll asks whether he does not have a 'prompter to insinuate/The first word of your studied Oration'.[41] Prompters had to spend so much of their performance actually prompting that they were a constant heard presence onstage, meaning that an actor had to modulate his tone accordingly – a good player was one whose 'voice tis not lower then the prompter, nor lowder then the Foile and Target'.[42]

As the prompter needed full access to the entire text to be spoken onstage, he would, as in later time, hold a complete copy of the play in his hands, known often as the 'book'; hence his main other title, 'book-holder'. Dictionaries over time, however, came to gloss the one term with the other, prompting being so essential to the job that Higgens in his 1585 *Nomenclator* described 'he that telleth the players their part when they are out and have forgotten' as 'the prompter or booke-holder'.[43] Pamphlets likewise varied the two randomly, Hugh Peters being described pejoratively as 'a *Prompter* at a Play-house' by one pamphlet, and 'a Book-holder at the Bull-play-house' by another.[44] But as what the book-holder mainly did from his book was to prompt, so the very verb 'to hold the book' came to mean 'to prompt'. Francis Bacon maintains that the 'Dowager Queen' (Henry VII's mother-in-law Elizabeth Woodville) thought her daughter was being suppressed when in fact 'none could hold the *Booke* so well to prompt and instruct this *Stage-Play,* as she could'; Timon, the playwright in Lodge's *Lady Alimony,* warns Siparius the prompter to 'Besure, that you hold not your Book at too much distance' because 'the Actors, . . . once out, [are] out for ever'; and Will Summers in Nashe's *Summers Last Will* asks the prompter to 'holde the booke well' in order that 'we be not *non plus* in the latter end of the play'.[45]

As prompting was such a regular activity, it naturally made its way directly into plays of the time. Davenport in *The City-night-cap* depicts one Lodovico who is saddled with the task of prompting the clown, only to find that he has to speak almost as much as the clown does:

Enter Lodovico, Clown and Masquers; a Stag, a Ram, a Bull and a Goat.

CLOWN. Look to me, Master.
LOD.   Do not shake, they'll think th'art out.---A Mask.
CLOWN. A Mask, or no Mask; no Mask but a By-clap;
       And yet a Mask yclep'd a City-Night-Cap.
LOD.   And conve---
CLOWN. And conveniently for to keep off scorns,
       Considerately the cap is hedg'd with hornes.

LOD.   We insinuate.
CLOWN.   Speak a little louder.
LOD.   We insinuate.
CLOWN.   We insinuate by this Stag and Ram so pritty,
         With Goat and Bull, Court, Country, Camp and City.
LOD.   Cuckold
CLOWN.   Cuckold my Lord.
LOD.   'Tis the first word of your next line.[46]

Similarly, in the 'Prelude' to *Thorny Abbey*, the prompter is handed the text of the prologue so that he can prompt the fool who tries to speak it:

FOOL.   . . . I have a part to say to you, if the *Prompter* would come to tell
             me, when I am out.
Enter Prompter, and takes the Fool's Paper, and stands behind him.
FOOL.   *We're to present you* ---(Ha! ha! he thinks I have pigs in my belly.)
PROMPTER.   Sirrah! go on. *We're to present you* ---
FOOL.   I won't have't non-sence *We're* to present you ---but I'le hav't
             I am to present you ---
PROMPTER.   And what are you to present them, I pray?
FOOL.   A P---a P---a P---a Pick-pocket.
PROMPTER.   A fools' head: are not you? a *Pick-pocket*, quoth he; a *Prologue*
             you mean.[47]

As all of these indicate, the prompter's task during performance was, as it remained over time, to hold text in hand and to prompt from it.

Yet there were other aspects of performance on which somehow the prompter also had to keep an eye. He was responsible for entrances, for instance. 'When/My cue's to enter', says Caesar in *The Roman Actor*, placing the responsibility for his entrance squarely on the act of prompting, 'prompt me.'[48] As a result, when actors missed their entrances, it was the prompter who took the blame, and the prompter who was, therefore, furious. Philantus, with his swearing and stamping, is described as being almost as angry as 'a play-house book-keeper, when the actors misse their entrance.'[49] The prompter was involved, too, with the beginnings of scenes more generally: his 'Begin, begin' is 'heard' and related by Will Summers in *Summers Last Will*; his 'Mend your lights, Gentlemen. *Master Prologue*, beginne' is scripted into Jonson's *Staple of Newes*; while Bassiolo, playing the prompter in Chapman's *Gentleman Usher*, orders 'Bring lights, make place.'[50] Similarly, he was concerned with exits that empty the stage – the prompter in Brome's *Antipodes* is heard commanding 'Dismisse the Court', leaving the actor Letoy to enlarge,

'Dismisse the Court, cannot you heare the prompter.'[51] These starts of scenes, preliminary entrances and final exits had to be managed whilst the prompter also paid close attention to the words of the book: a hefty task. To achieve this, the prompter, as in later times, would see to it that actors were 'called' or 'warned' some time in advance of the actual entrance; placed by the doors, the performers could listen for their actual moment of entrance as identified on their parts. So the prompter in Chapman's *Gentleman Usher*, Bassiolo, is heard shouting 'Sound Consort; warne the Pedant to be readie.'[52] And, as ever, it is analogies that go into some detail about the warning or 'calling' process. The royal heir awaiting his time to ascend to the throne is compared to a good actor primed and ready for entrance; as soon as the previous scene ends and providence 'calls' the heir/actor, he will go out onstage: 'a Royall Heire apparent . . . is he . . . who standeth at all howres, at all times and seasons, ready and prepared to enter (when providence shall call him) upon the Royall Stage, to act a Kingly part, assoone as the Sceane is . . . after a divine order cleared.'[53] Similarly, the minister, 'O. E.', who has attacked Robert Parsons is compared to an actor who 'is cauled up to the stage. Now his cu cometh in . . .'[54]

So 'calling' took place and was an early modern prompter's concern – but how did he do it? Eighteenth-century writers believed that the prompter in Shakespeare's time had had the same backstage help as they did. More than that: a story recorded in 1756 had it that Shakespeare first made his way into the theatre 'in quality of prompter's boy'; this tale is later recorded as 'traditional' by Malone, though it is impossible to know how far back that tradition goes; 'There is a stage tradition, that [Shakspeare's] first office in the theatre was that of Call-boy, or prompter's attendant; whose employment it is to give the performers notice to be ready to enter, as often as the business of the play requires their appearance on the stage.'[55] The tale is interesting as much for its expectation that call-boys were a fixture in the early modern theatre, as for its probably spurious claim. Practical theatrical lore, seemingly uncon-nected to the 'call-boy' story, certainly had it that Shakespeare's use of playhouse terminology related to the job of 'calling' actors. Glossing a line in *King John*, 'a fellow by the hand of Nature mark'd,/Quoted, and sign'd to do a deede of shame' (TLN 1946–7), Thomas Davies enlarges, 'The word *quoted*, occurs several times in Shakspeare, and it is a playhouse word. The characters who are to be called by the prompter's boy to be ready for the scene, are quoted by him in the margin of the play' (the distinction between marginal calls and call-book calls will be considered shortly).[56]

There were certainly general helpers in the tiring-house. John Gee compares a Jesuit trick, in which a visitation from a Catholic 'ghost' is used to draw people to the 'Romish church', with an actor onstage: 'though there be but one Actor appearing here upon the Stage, yet . . . there are diverse others within the tiring-house, that take a great deale of paines to project the plot, to instruct the Actor, and to furnish him with habit and ornament'.[57] Backstage functionaries, in his language, 'project the plot', a telling phrase in the circumstances. What is difficult is to find who the backstage people were. As well as those whose job was in their title (like 'tire-' men and women, responsible for clothing actors) there were general backstage boy-helpers whose specific tasks are never fully articulated. They are known as 'players' boys' (a term confusingly interchanged with 'boy-players', though maybe these boy-helpers were apprentice boy-players). Players' boys attended on the front of house before performances started, being paid to fetch stools, cushions and water for audience members, but seem then to have become stage-hands: a jest about a clown called to the stage has 'his Boy that then served him' later ordered onstage from the tiring-house to place onto his head a forgotten cap.[58] These 'boys' do not feature amongst Henslowe's payments, but then nor do property-men or other stage-hands, perhaps because they were hired and paid for by sharers, or perhaps because accounts relevant to them were kept in a different book. Nevertheless, as shown, there were calls and there were boys in the early modern theatre: that there might have been call-boys, though the title did not yet exist, is suggested again by analogy. In Marston's *Antonios Revenge* 'observation', personified, is asked to hurry over to 'cote' the plot in order to see what is to happen next: 'Now workes the sceane; quick observation scud/To coate the plot, or els the path is lost'; later in that same play a second request to 'observation' is made: 'Be gratious, Observation, to our sceane:/For now the plot unites his scattred limbes.'[59] 'Observation' emerges as some kind of overseer responsible for conveying information from the plot to the actors; as Baldwin put it, 'observation' is here either 'a deputy of the prompter', or 'one of the actors, [the plot] being a self-help device'.[60]

The very existence of a plot hints at a helper additional to the prompter: only when other people are to take over the calling will the prompter have needed a plot (otherwise he could simply call from the playbook). And, besides, the prompter sometimes himself wrote the plot, self-consciously doubling information he already had in the playbook – again suggesting that plots are not for his own use. The one early modern poem that refers to the person who 'scenes out' a play and allots roles to players (so a backstage-plot-writer, not plot-scenario-writer) gives the task to 'natures arte'; given the combination of plot-writing and casting, a prompter seems to be gestured at:

> An Epitaph one Mr Burbige
> This lifes a play sceaned out by natures arte
> Where every man hath his allotted part
> This man hath nowe, as many men can tell
> Ended his part, and he hath acted wel
> His play now ended, thinke his grave to be
> The retiringe howse of this his tragedye . . .[61]

Moreover, two of the surviving plots, *Fortune's Tennis* and the *Seven Deadly Sins*, are in a shared hand (though their headings seem to have been written by other people); tellingly, this hand is that of the writer who theatrically revised the manuscript 'books' of *Thomas More* and Anthony Munday's *John a Kent and John a Cumber*, known as 'hand C'.[62] 'Hand C' on the plays is always said to be that of the prompter. So a prompter seems to have written two of the plots and revised two playhouse 'books'; once again, the performance concerns of plot and book are linked: the same writers who are interested in preparing plays for the stage are interested in writing plots.

On other occasions, however, the prompter appears to have asked someone else, perhaps even the call-boy, to compile or copy the plot in neat from information supplied. Two plots, *Troilus and Cressida* and *Battle of Alcazar*, are in a shared hand that has not been found elsewhere; the other two are in uniquely different hands (the lost *Tamer Cam* only survives in print form, so the handwriting cannot be known). The writers of these plots, however, do not seem to have been the contrivers of them. A 'false start' preserved on the back of the *Dead Man's Fortune* plot indicates this is a copied document: the scribe of that particular text seems to be 'writing up' information rather than creating it:

False start:

The plotte of the deade mans fortune
Enter the prolouge /
Enter laertes Eschines and urganda
Enter *Tesephon* allgerius laertes wt\<h\> atendantes: Darlowe lee & b samme to them alleyane and statyra

Real start:

The plotte of the deade mans fortune
Enter the prolouge /
Enter laertes Eschines and urganda
Enter pesscodde to him his father
Enter *Tesephon* allgeryus laertes wth atendantes: Darlowe: lee: b samme: to them alleyane and statyra[63]

Both texts are similar enough to suggest a shared root text or source of information: the same words are provided in the same order in each, minus only an '&'. Moreover, the few errors to be found on that plot appear to be 'aural', as Wiggins illustrates, implying that this writer is copying from dictation rather than (or as much as from) a document: the mistaken letter 'x' written and deleted before the word 'executioner'; the mistaken 'is' written and deleted before 'his' are the kinds of mistakes that happen when copying by ear: 'Enter kinge Egereon allgeryus tesephon wth lordes the ~~x~~ executioner ~~wthis~~ his sworde and blocke' (*Dead Man's Fortune*, v.ii).[64] Aural copying, combined with errors suggestive of a writer not familiar with the text already, is a sign that the plot is being dictated; aural copying is observable on other plots too, and would explain why, when two boxes mistakenly both read 'Enter Hector & Antenor exeunt' (B and I of *Troilus and Cressida*), they are then both 'corrected' (Antenor deleted and 'Priam: Mr Jones' inserted), as though the copyist is being told which box to change by content only; it might, further, account for chattier moments on the plot ('then after that the musicke plaies & ther Enters . . .' v.i), which may record a person speaking through a documentary list. It is worth recalling that in later times stage-related plots were written or copied by call-boys, their jobs including doing 'odd jobs for the manager, and copying work for the prompter, form[ing] "plots" of the scenes marking the arrangement of the "wings", &c; also "property" plots'.[65]

Once it emerges that a plot is likely to be a call-list/book/sheet, various of its confusing features are automatically explained. The 'inversion' found in massed entries in plots is, if the placards are call-lists, no problem, for if 'Lucius and Damasus mr Bry T Good' (*Seven Deadly Sins*, vi) are called, this will not be confusing: 'mr Bry[an]' knows that he is

Damasus; similarly 'T Good[ale]' knows he is Lucius, and the use of both fictional and real names is simply a double security both for caller and called. In the same way the absence of actors' real names at certain points is explained: it does not matter whether the caller knows which players make up a group – he simply needs to call them, and it is up to the members of the group to recognise who they are; hence 'Soldiers', 'lords' and 'spirritts' (or 'all ye girls') can be called without an itemised list of players supplied. Other problems are solved too if the plots are call-sheets. What was on the plot was enough for the user of the plot, and was designed to work in tandem with the part: when Bradley asks how an actor was to know what 'excursions' on the plot means, or how Ajax is to know about his exit unmarked on the sheet, the answer is that he will know because it is on his main text, his actor's part.[66] Bradley's other question, why does the plotter not refer to all players by name, using instead terms like 'gils his boy' (*Tamar Cam*, v.iii), again is fine if that description works for the caller (or if 'Gils' might have used one of two boys on any particular performance).[67] Faced with the fact that various of the plots did not fit his 'casting' model, even Bradley had to concede that the plot of *Dead Man's Fortune*, which names hardly any of its actors, 'does in a manner serve as a call-sheet for bringing the cast on stage scene by scene'.[68]

As the plots are constructed as 'public' documents, however, they must have been available to more than one person: such plots as have marginal annotations for property and music calls anticipate use by at least three sets of caller. This recalls the definition of a plot given by Adams over sixty years ago, who saw it as 'a skeleton outline' serving 'as a very necessary and practical guide to actors, stage-hands, and other employees of the theatre in the smooth performance of the play'.[69] While these plots seem to be primarily for call-boys, who may have been several in number (particularly if some actors, like the 'clown' in the joke told earlier, had their own personal boy), public placards open for consultation by anyone could serve a use rather like that of a notice-board. Actors could look at plots if that would be helpful, using them as a 'safety net' capable of giving, in the words of Beckerman, a 'guide to memory' for a nervous player should he wish to take it.[70] In this plots resemble their most recent descendants, call-sheets for films, which are placed where anyone who needs their assurance can look at them: 'a copy of the Call Sheet is . . . posted in the production office so that every member of the cast and crew will know exactly what is planned for each shooting day'.[71] As a whole, plots, with their concerns to sort out practical backstage matters in order to make better the performance onstage, are not *for* actors, who are primarily concerned with *being* onstage, but they seem to have been available to them.[72]

BACKSTAGE-PLOTS AND PLAYBOOKS

Plays so near to staging that their backstage-plots have been drawn up, that are yet frustrated of actual performance, are a resonant poetic image of the period. The flamboyant Essex's failed rebellion was described as a 'Trageide' that 'was plotted but not acted'; and Henry Cuffe, sent to execution for his part in Essex's unsuccessful plotting, punned dismally: 'I am here adjudged to dye, for plotting a plot never acted.'[73] Behind both references is a sense that once a plot for action (so not a scenario, which is for writing) has been drawn up, performance should follow: the plot itself is the last creation before performance – meaning that it arises *from* the book. This is obvious anyway from the contents of the plot: entrances can only be determined when a text exists, whether or not those entrances are written into that text. This was 'self-evident' to Greg and everyone writing after him: only with the advent of Bradley's ideas did it become possible to dispute that notion, and even then a moment's thought should dismiss the question: an author is hardly likely to compose a scene to fit around a predetermined and unchangeable series of actor and property entrances.[74] And Beckerman's idea of plots arising from process, being produced *during* a long rehearsal period, demands a long rehearsal period, and, moreover, a rehearsal period given over to 'discovering' staging or, rather, entrances; that there were not many rehearsals, and that the rehearsals that were held were perfunctory and practical, has been explored elsewhere.[75] Plots imply in a variety of ways the fact that they link and relate to the stage-directions of a book. All of them make repeated use of the Latinate words of stage-directions and the inverted syntax that attends on them: 'enter', 'exit' and 'manet' are in plot and stage-directions alike still treated as Latin enough verbs for a character's name to follow rather than precede them. As the Latinity of stage-directions in books is largely found in 'directions to enter, exit or remain upon the stage', entrance-related directions always stand out as 'other', and this may (even partially) be because potential plot-matter is designed to isolate itself immediately from the other stage-directions in the text; it should be remembered that stage-directions are, more than any other part of a playbook, written by theatre practitioners, or at least with them in mind.[76]

Greg argued that 'literary terms' like 'upon the walls' found their way into the plot because of the close book–plot relationship; Calore demurred, maintaining that, as a plot's vocabulary must have worked for it as a document in its own right, some of its fictional and descriptive terms may have 'originated' with the plotter. Her first point is stronger than her second: evidently 'literary' terms were practical enough to work in a thoroughly theatrical document (though, a phrase like 'Enter Porrex sad' (*Seven Deadly Sins*, viii) might have either a practical or a literary manifestation depending on how it is read), but her argument that they may therefore not be sourced from the book implies a plotter who thinks within the fiction even when the playbook he is looking at does not.[77] That is unlikely: plots in many respects are simple poolings of entrances and, with no reason to deviate from source, probably do not do so. Yet, as not all entrances and certainly not all personals are determined in books (perhaps because they will be sorted out on plots instead) there are moments when plots may have come up with their own terminology – and to do so had 'factual' or 'fictional' options. One further potential source for their language is in other varieties of theatrical plot. The plot-scenario (see chapter 1), which presents the story of the play before it is muddled with words, would obviously be a useful document to have to hand when writing the backstage-plot, providing, as it does, the characters to be in each scene: possibly some fictional terms came into the plot from this source.

Might the plot ever have fed back into the playscript? That is not so clear. Plot-directions do not need to be manifested in the 'allowed' book: and the playtext sought by editors – a theatrical document relatively complete in terms of staging – will not automatically have existed in one place, being spread on occasion over at least book and plot, if not additionally over other plot-like documents. This may explain the many printed playbooks that survive lacking crucial directions for entrances (though it should also be remembered that printers setting a manuscript play might only include those stage-directions in the 'body' of the script, and exclude marginal notes).

Revision, however, does allow for the possibility of plot observations working their way into a rewritten passage of a playbook: particularly if the rewriting were undertaken because of a plot-discovery. Scott McMillin explains that the additional notes for a scene written into the margin of the plot of *Dead Man's Fortune* just prior to the conclusion of the play (in the hand of the music-call-annotator, not the plot-writer) constitute a late insertion added to give time for doubling actors to change their clothes.

His belief is that the necessity for the additional scene was highlighted by the fact of the plot.[78] Moreover, later full-play revision could always take place plot in hand, for the backstage-plot would reveal logics of scene-order and actor-use that would make obvious which characters were and were not available for additions or restructuring. So plots arose from playscripts, glossed them, and were used in tandem with them; but occasionally might shape later revisions.

It should however be borne in mind that a plot might well have a shorter life than a playbook. Any plot that names a series of minor actors is going to date quickly, and, when enough hirelings have changed, a new plot will be needed. So plots, though designed for repeated use, were likely to be less rather than more permanent than playbooks: every new acting season may well have required a new plot, even for an old play. A revision or revival too will have required a new plot; the discrepancies between the plot of *Battle of Alcazar* and its printed playbook illustrate how quickly a plot became outdated: the play as printed will have required an entirely different plot from the one that survives. So though plot-into-playbook is a remote possibility; playbook-into-plot remains far more likely.

All of the foregoing chapter, however, has acted as though every play-book had its plot: and clearly some did not. It is evident from the way some playbooks are marginally annotated that warning 'calls' such as those found on plots are sometimes found on 'books' either additionally or instead. Those calls are, in fact, what have traditionally been used to catalogue a playbook as a prompter's text. So 'bee redy Penda' is found in *The Welsh Embassador* 20 lines before Penda enters 'like a common soldier'; 'bee redy Edmond & Edlred' follows a little later; while 'Fellowes ready palestra: . . . Sarly' in *The Captives* is about 30 lines before the actual entrance.[79] Equally, 'books' might contain warning notes for properties: the revelation behind the curtains in *Thomas of Woodstock* is preceded by 'A bed/for woodstock' written 54 lines in advance; a table and banquet for *The Waspe* are readied 25 lines in advance; 'sett out a table' occurs in *The Welsh Embassador* 28 lines in advance of its disclosure; 'gascoine & Hubert below: ready to open the trap doore for mr taylor' precedes King Antiochus' prison entrance in *Believe as You List*, and there are regular warning notes for magical effects in *John of Bordeaux*.[80] The twenty surviving Restoration playbooks from 1660–1700 with prompt markings, and the further ten said to have 'prompt traces', similarly are marked up with advanced calls.[81] Thus 'Jamy Leander & ascanio be ready' and many other such notes are to be found in the manuscript markings of

Fletcher and Massinger's *Spanish Curate* made in 1660; 'Call Lovel,/Careless' and many other such notes are to be seen in the manuscript markings of Ravenscroft's *The Careless Lovers* made in 1673; and, more confusingly, simply the name of the actor and/or character, with no accompanying note, are written into the margin a page or so before entrance in the promptbook of Shirley's *The Ball* made in the 1660s or 1670s (as in 'Ambrose' and other such notes in the manuscript markings).[82]

As there is no cause for thinking that the theatre doubled information unnecessarily, a reasonable assumption is that an alternating system of *either* plots *or* marked-up prompter's books was in use in the early modern period, the Restoration and later. Subsequent theatrical practice certainly shows this to be the case. As late as last century, amateur players were advised that 'sometimes it is simpler to enter the calls in red in a copy of the play instead of making a call sheet. When the call boy has other backstage responsibilities, the calls can be entered in the prompt book, and the call boy sent on calls by the prompter.'[83] Probably the same distinction held between plot and marked-up playbook: which is to say that the presence of the one implies the absence of the other. Here is a reason for the absence of play-plots with theatrical books. The books that have been identified by scholars as theatrical are precisely those containing calls – and are the very books that will not, therefore, have required plots. As Baldwin enlarged, 'plays with minor actors named, as are several of Shakespeare's, were not used with a plot'; conversely, as Lawrence was first to put forward, in the plot 'we have an explanation of the striking sparsity of actors' calls in the early prompt-books'.[84]

Hence, too, the reason why such prompters' books as do exist are, in some cases, relatively 'incomplete'. Given that the prompter will hardly have wanted an incomplete performance, he must have conveyed some of the information for call-boys or other helpers by alternative means: a plot, or a series of separate call or warning documents. The fuller the playbook, the less full the plot needs to be and vice versa. This, however, raises some fundamental questions about the very definition of a prompter's book. Though it can be concluded that a book marked up for performance *is* a book for a prompter's use, it cannot be assumed that a book without performance markings *is not* a prompter's book. Definitions of what constitutes a theatrical text have all relied on their use of prompters' markings, but books not marked up with theatrical notes may still have been held by the prompter in performance: the manuscript of Philip Massinger's *Believe as You List* is an 'allowed' book without prompt markings, for instance. Both in the early modern period and later there may be many more prompters' books surviving – without prompters' marks – than have been realised.

CONCLUSION

Differing from plot-scenario and Argument, both of which anticipate being read for narrative value, the backstage-plot is a profoundly theatrical document: its creation helps formulate staging, while its use is to shape the play during performance itself. So reading it is always disappointing, as Steevens recognised when he explained, having addressed the back-stage-plots, that 'even the scenes of our author [Shakespeare] would have worn as unpromising an aspect, had their skeletons only been discovered'.[85] Moreover the backstage-plot has a vagueness about it that also sets it aside from other plots. Unlike them, it cannot work alone in its own right, requiring a document with cues to specify the actual occasions it gestures towards. A pooled selection of warnings for things to come, the backstage-plot repeatedly keeps its user alert to what is to happen and what must be readied to bring that about, but is never about 'now'. Yet as a map it has considerable advantages over other varieties of plot. It provides not the story but 'a bird's-eye view of the whole action – a grid of entrances, exits, and stage effects'.[86] And, as it is an account from the inside of the theatrical moment, it displays the most 'three-dimensional' aspects of performance. Writes Turner, 'the platt provides a structural translation of the actor's movement through space, since each box designates a discrete episode in the mimetic action'.[87]

Arising from the book, but containing information aside from it, the plot highlights and extracts the performance potential locked in the manuscript text. But the plot is not like a scroll or part: it marks a moment of to-and-fro with the entirety of the playbook, but only in performance, though its suggestions complete lacunae that the book can therefore permanently retain – or alternatively it can shape rewriting to come. What plots do indicate is why and how a 'complete' prompter's book might lack essential staging information, and why and how stage-directions might be written and contrived by people who are not the playwright, and lost before a play is ever published.

CHAPTER 8

The approved 'book' and actors' parts

INTRODUCTION

This chapter will explore the relationship between surviving full plays and performed dialogue. Were actors' parts – the scripts actors received consisting of their speeches and cues – the descendant of the playhouse book, or could they be texts originating from an earlier source? And, irrespective of source, how perfectly were actors' parts extracted from the play by copyists, and with what accuracy were they then performed?

THE APPROVED BOOK AND PERFORMANCE

A habit of claiming absolute authority for the full text as overseen and corrected by successive Masters of the Revels, Edmund Tilney (1579–1610), Sir George Buc (1603–22), Sir John Astley (1622) and Sir Henry Herbert (1623–73), has led critics to ignore how often unapproved words and passages were heard on the stage. But, as Dutton showed in 1991, 'the censorship of English Renaissance drama was neither as totalitarian nor draconian as it is often held to be'.[1] Yes, the Master of the Revels did censor most (but not all) playtexts; yes, when actors were attacked for any reason they used the Master of the Revels' approval as stated at the end of a playbook as their defence – and always, obviously, claimed to have added nothing to the dramas they performed.[2] But companies' brushes with authority illustrate the extent to which uncensored material was in fact frequently spoken onstage.

Take, for instance, what the Queen of Bohemia's or Lady Elizabeth's Company did to the censored playbook of Henry Shirley's *The Martyred Soldier* that they received back from the Master of the Revels. They blatantly reannotated it to return it to precensored form – as the outraged Henry Herbert realised when he called the text back. On it he found his own 'reformations' flanked by new annotations from the players who 'to every cross' of erasure that he had made had 'added a stet [a proofing sign for "let it stand"] of their owne'.[3] Naturally Herbert was furious, but not, it seems, so much with the performance ramifications of this, as with the liberties that had been taken with his manuscript decisions: his authority had been disregarded in its own medium, the written page. For the performed event was never expected to be controllable; it was the 'book' that sanctioned it that was.

That approved page and subsequent staging were not the same is illustrated by the story of Jonson's *The Magnetic Lady*. When the play caused offence in performance the players immediately brought out their 'book' and illustrated how it contained the licence of approval written and signed by the Master of the Revels. This was in an attempt, wrote Herbert, to blame 'me and the poet' for words that the actors had spoken; later, however, the company was forced to confess that 'the whole fault of their play' actually lay with themselves – that they had allowed unsanctioned passages to be said in performance.[4] How often this happened is hard to know: only when players are caught out will the issue be recorded, and accounts of any dealings with Tilney, Buc or Astley are scanty, their 'office books' being lost. Nevertheless, a letter survives written by George Chapman, trying to publish his play *Byron* after it had caused a furore onstage, and written probably to the then Master of the Revels, George Buc: 'I have not deserv'd what I suffer', writes Chapman from prison, 'yf the two or three lynes you crost were spoken,' for 'I see not [i.e., "do not oversee"] myne owne Plaies; Nor carrie the Actors Tongues in my Mouthe.'[5] In other words, *Byron* had received official approval – subject to alterations – for performance, but what had then been staged was the play in its precensored form, for which Chapman will take no responsibility. In both instances the difference is between a play on paper and a play onstage, a disparity regularly referred to even when issues of censorship do not come into it: Hughes' *Misfortunes of Arthur* is printed '*as it was presented, excepting certaine wordes and lines, where some of the Actors either helped their memories by brief omission: or fitted their acting by some alteration*'; Nabbes publishes *The Bride* 'with out ought taken from her that my selfe thought ornament; nor supplied with any thing which I valued but as rags'; and Dekker fronts his *Whore of Babylon* with the lament, 'Let the Poet set the note of his Nombers, even to Apolloes owne Lyre, the Player will have his owne Crochets, and sing false notes, in dispite of all the rules of Musick.'[6]

The problem is, as the examples indicate, that any text for performance can only be censored notionally, because actual speech cannot be controlled. A comment made by Francis Rous is suggestive here. Writing in 1622, the divine draws particular attention to the fact, as he perceives it, that unapproved material finds an easy outlet on the stage that it does not on paper: 'I wish Authoritie would [prevaile], and that . . . the same course may bee taken for the Scene that is for the Presse, that nothing might be acted, but that which first had beene examined.'[7] He writes in the knowledge that the Master of the Revels was technically given the task of approving all playbooks before performance, but he assumes either that this does not always happen or that it does not always happen effectively.

On occasion entire uncensored plays were played in public theatres, so Rous is right to be wary of the power of censorship. A text that was unlikely to 'pass' if the Master of the Revels saw it was sometimes simply put on without approval. Jonson and Nashe's notorious *Isle of Dogs*, 'contanynge very seditious and sclanderous matter', was 'caught' only after it had been performed at the Swan, probably by Pembroke's Men in 1597, and was, Dutton believes, not licensed by Tilney (he raises the possibility that the Surrey magistrates had looked it over).[8] And the sparse records from the time show other instances of uncensored performances put on by major London companies. Chapman, imprisoned over *Eastward Hoe* in 1605, writes to the Lord Chamberlain that his greatest regret is that 'our unhappie booke was presented without your Lordshippes allowance', explaining it was because 'our cleere opinions [were] yt nothinge it contain'd could worthely be held offensive'.[9] Yet Master of the Revels Henry Herbert was still encountering similar behaviour years later, as when he had to berate the King's Men in 1633 for not sending him their text before performing. The actors confess to him that 'not long since we acted a play called The Spanishe Viceroy, not being licensed under your worships hande, nor allowd of'; they add, 'wee . . . are very sorry for it'.[10] Other companies did not even pretend contrition. On 3 May 1640 William Beeston's Men 'Acted a new play wthout any Licence from the Mr of his Majesties revels'; asked by Herbert to stop playing at once, they simply 'Acted the sayd Play' again, flanking it with 'others to ye prjudice of his Mats service & in contempt of the office of the revels'.[11] And, though the furore surrounding these accounts shows them to be unusual, the latter only came to the Revels' attention because the play reflected on King Charles' journey to the north; other uncensored texts may have slipped through the net.

Of course, these examples have ranged over time, and there were variable habits with respect to censorship over the period depending on who was Master of the Revels, who was on the throne, and what the political situation was. Nevertheless, given that the receipt of official approval was expensive – Tilney charged Henslowe seven shillings to approve plays; by the time of Herbert the cost had risen to one (and finally two) pounds – there was always a financial incentive for a company not to submit a playbook to the Master of the Revels if it were likely to be condemned by him. The prohibition by the Master of the Revels of entire plays, which Lyly recorded in *Pappe with an Hatchet* in 1589, and Herbert exemplified years later when he burned a 'new play' of Mr Kirke's 'for the ribaldry and offense that was in it', might not necessarily have warned companies so much to steer clear of offensive material as, on specific occasions, to steer clear of the Master of the Revels.[12] That said, most plays were approved officially: official sanction protected a company from the trouble a script might subsequently bring them, and, besides, approved plays joined the collection of possible texts for royal performance, an honour also financially lucrative for a company. Yet company slackness about getting some plays censored at all should be borne in mind: if a company is not always scrupulous about obtaining approval in the first place, then when a play *is* censored, how bound will it feel to abide by the Master of the Revels' suggestions?

Two further facts need to be taken into account: that plays were regularly altered, particularly after first performances (see chapter 4), and that plays regularly received 'new additions' for revival; in neither of these instances does the Master of the Revels seem to have been asked habitually to approve the 'new' passages. So Henry Herbert, the Master of the Revels for whom a cluster of records survive, largely in copied form, repeatedly makes clear that he is only given new sections of play to assess that are substantial and self-contained – and that this is more than his predecessors did. He records a charge of ten shillings for approving a new scene in Dekker and Massinger's *The Virgin Martyr* (7 July 1624); another charge of ten shillings for allowing a 'new act in an ould play' (13 May 1629); and a £1 charge for new scenes (plural) in 'an ould play' (12 May 1636).[13] What Herbert is not, on record, asked to evaluate are single altered passages, or most of the freestanding sections discussed in this book: prologues, epilogues, songs, scrolls, arguments, internal masques or other theatrical documents that went in and out of plays at their own rates. Nor, in earlier times, were such documents independently approved by Tilney either – or, at least, the financier Henslowe, who records in his 'diary' paying playwrights for writing new prologues and epilogues in the 1590s, never records paying the Master of the Revels to see them; Ioppolo concludes from this that 'Henslowe may have assumed or been told that such products of "mending" or "altering" an old play were to be tacitly approved without the censor's actual attention or knowledge.'[14] It is worth noting that approval was likewise not sought in later time for this kind of material (though there was a sense that it should be), complaint being made in 1704 that 'Prologues, Epilogues, & Songs wch are often indecent, are brought upon ye Stage wth out his ['ye Master of ye Revels'] License.'[15]

So a few texts are not censored at all, and various types of alteration are not, as far as can be seen from surviving records, sent to the Master of the Revels. Presumably such additional passages would simply be added to a play at the company's risk, relying on the informal relationship of trust that bound Master of the Revels and acting companies together: neither wanted trouble. Thus plays in approved form were likely to be somewhat removed from the play that was performed anyway.

SCRIBES AND ACTORS' PARTS

But even if a playscript were uncontentious and received easy approval with no alterations demanded and none subsequently made, was that 'approved' copy the one that was turned into scripts for actors? Too great a reliance on the completeness of playbooks and the search to find or recover full authorial or full theatrical texts has led critics to forget that actual performances were learnt from actors' 'parts', containing speeches and cues for each character, now largely lost. Parts, of course, descended from *a* book of some kind, but is that necessarily the prompter's book, and/or the book approved by the Master of the Revels?

In the Latin 'University' part for Antoninus in *Antoninus Bassanius Caracalla*, one of the few early modern parts in existence, the text for act 2 scene 2 precedes the text for act 1: the actor's part is inscribed out of order, seemingly reflecting the copyist's piecemeal acquisition of a play in which the completed second act was 'handed over' for division into parts and learning before the first act had been completely written.[16] Nor was this unusual. Daborne the playwright writes a letter to Henslowe the financier about the 'extraordinary payns' he is taking to finish the play *Machiavelli and the Devil*: he tells Henslowe that he has not only, finally, written the end of the play, but has also altered 'one other scean in the third act which', he adds, 'they have now in parts'.[17] Here the actors have already been given their parts to learn, though the play is only semi-written; these parts are being memorised concurrently with the completion of the play, not after it. As a production consequence, the actors will technically be supposed to learn 'new' altered lines on top of old ones already distributed to them. But of course they will always be in danger of speaking onstage the pre-revision version of the play they have already committed to memory rather than the new, rewritten version of the play: this, indeed, was the very problem Chapman had encountered with his *Byron*.

Other instances too show actors learning their parts before the book has been officially approved (and changes made to it) if not before it has been fully written. With a limited time period for writing out and memorising lines, every effort was made to get texts to actors as soon as possible – and that effort, in the early modern period and later, often preceded the acquisition of official sanction for the playbook itself. On 15 January 1704, the Lord Chamberlain wrote to the company at Lincoln's Inn Fields, and then to the company at Drury Lane, about how

many of ye Old as well as New plays are still acted wth out due Care taken to leve out such Expressions as are contrary to Religion & Good Manners. And . . . this Abuse is in great Measure owing to ye Neglect of both Companys, by not sending Plays to ye Master of ye Revels, to be Licens'd but all ye Parts are got up, & ye play ready to be acted, by which Means his Censure & License cannot be so well observed.[18]

This was also true of the early modern period. Henry Herbert, Master of the Revels, asks the prompter of the King's Men, Edward Knight, to strike out several of the meatier phrases from Beaumont and Fletcher's *Womans Prize* (*Tamer Tamed*); he adds that as a consequence the actors will now have to have their parts 'purged'. 'Purge their parts, as I have the booke,' he instructs Knight, later adding as a curt note, 'the players ought not to study their parts till I have allowed of the booke'.[19]

Here the approved manuscript 'book', though it may become the prompter's book and run performances (see chapter 7 for more on the prompter and his book), need not therefore be the same text as the source for the actors' parts. T. H. Howard-Hill, discussing oddities of the manuscript play *Barnavelt*, concludes that it represents the copy from which actors' parts were made, but not the prompter's book (though Stephenson, attributing pencil markings on the book to George Buc, Master of the Revels, and to the hand of what he calls a 'book-keeper', disagrees).[20] Either way, Howard-Hill shares with Fredson Bowers the belief that the creation of a book for the prompter is likely to have been 'the final act of the play's production', following after the writing of the parts, an idea McMillin also endorses: 'the only reasonable assumption . . . is that actors' parts were copied relatively early in the process . . . and that the promptbook was prepared later'.[21] The preparation for production will actually have been less logical even than this confused hierarchy of texts might suggest, but it is useful simply to examine the taxonomy that arises from the potential distinction between controlling script and source script – that there could have been up to four full texts called, at various stages in the production, 'the book': the authorial draft texts in the form in which they were submitted to the acting company; texts marked up to be turned into parts and backstage-plots; texts used by prompters during performance; and texts approved by the Master of the Revels. Each of these texts may of course be combined in one document, but each may alternatively exist as one or more separate documents.

It is worth looking for signs that plays not necessarily for performance are marked up for the part-writing scribe. There are few clear examples, perhaps because most plays were not physically changed during the part-writing process, but in the German *Die Swen Stenndt*, or *The Two Estates* (1532), speeches are numbered to facilitate their rewriting as parts; though this does not seem to have been normal in England in the professional theatre, university plays sometimes adopted a similar habit – one of the manuscripts of Richard Legge's *Richardus Tertius* follows the end of actors' speeches with a 'pattern' made of dots and slashes, './', './.', '/./.', enabling the part-writer to see when speeches end and one part should be exchanged for another.[22] The last text does not show particular performance signs either – though, as chapter 7 has argued, that need not preclude it from being a prompter's book. The problem, however, is clear: the actors' texts learnt for performance may – but need not ever – have descended from the book held by the prompter. Which is to say that editorial 'recovery' of a theatrical text may still not recover the script(s) from which performance was made.

A related question is to what extent actors were given an accurate version of their section of the 'book' anyway, whatever the 'book' was. How closely and accurately copied were parts – and were they always rendered in the same words as full plays? Here it should be borne in mind that the creation of parts, an act of massive textual proliferation in which every play was rendered into as many documents as there were characters (plus the scrolls and papers covered in other chapters), had the potential to produce great textual difference even if the scripts were then learnt with minute accuracy.

To see what and where differences between part and play might occur, it would be necessary to compare surviving actors' parts to the full plays from which they descend. But though three of the five early modern British parts are from plays for which full playbooks also exist, the parts and the full texts are, in each instance, significantly different – they date from different periods in time, and they do not relate absolutely to one another (in no instance is there a part *and* the version of the play from which it originates).[23] This is telling in itself, showing how often different versions of a single playscript were created even over a short period of time, raising further questions about what 'the text' is. Yet it is also the case that each of the three parts and their plays have moments of close conjunction – moments where revision has not significantly altered the one from the other, and part and text are essentially dealing with the same passages. These *can* be compared for scribal accuracy. So two of the four early modern university parts that are bound together in Harvard Theater Library, the Latin Polypragmaticus (from Robert Burton's *Philosophaster*), and the English Amurath (from Thomas Goffe's *The Courageous Turk or Amurath the First*), can be looked at against surviving full texts: there are two manuscripts for Robert Burton's *Philosophaster*, and a manuscript and printed version of Goffe's *The Courageous Turk*. Likewise, Edward Alleyn's part for Orlando can be contrasted with passages from the printed quarto of the play *Orlando Furioso*.[24]

The problem is that the two first of these texts, Polypragmaticus and Amurath, are for 'university' performance at Christ Church, Oxford, and universities, obviously, did not have trained theatrical functionaries to perform menial scribal jobs: for college performances, student actors were their own copyists, so that the surviving parts may say more about amateur than professional production. William Prynne, after all, bemoaned part-*writing* as well as acting in his list of the bad occupations taken on by amateur university players – 'how many houres, evenings, halfe-dayes, dayes, and sometimes *weekes*,' are '*spent by all the Actors* (especially in solemne academicall Enterludes) *in coppying, in conning, in practising their parts*'.[25] And Polypragmaticus and Amurath are both in the hand of their player, Thomas Goffe.[26] Yet if anything this should put the parts at the accurate extreme, for Goffe is lead actor, and quite possibly organiser or prompter of both productions (he writes a note on his partbook for the provision of beer, supper and mutes for the production of *Courageous Turk*); moreover, he is also author of one of the plays, *The Courageous Turk*. As (author)-actor-prompter-scribe he could choose how accurate to be, what information he wished to give himself, and how to shape the part directly to his needs: his parts should be actors' scripts in something near ideal form.

Yet a comparison between the part for Polypragmaticus and the full play of Burton's *Philosophaster*, which survives in two revised and augmented manuscripts, reveals a surprising number of differences particularly where interchangeable words are concerned: 'quid', for instance, is rendered 'cur', which not only has the same meaning but also carries exactly the same metrical weight, as though Goffe in copying is prepared to use synonyms rather than observing word-by-word fidelity (a small change of this kind is unlikely to be a purposeful revision); some sentences even render the same ideas in different Latin, which also may be traceable to copyist rather than textual updating: so 'Vel si mavis Jesuita, ut dicam semel' in both manuscripts is, in the part, 'vel si verbo dictum vultis, sum Jesuita'.[27] Punctuation and capitalisation vary too, and here it is not that one version of the text has more and one has less of it: simply that the choices made are different. So there is a line towards the start of the part that reads 'Tu libros hos, tuque instrumenta haec cape', which in the Huntington manuscript is 'Tu libros, hos tuque instrumenta haec cape.' (line 43); a passage in 4.8 of the part, which recognises the verse form with capitals and pauses with heavy punctuation, has:

> Si quis has artes in apertum proferet
> Miserè periimus: actum de nobis erit.

But in the Huntington manuscript, where it is 4.7, it reads:

> si quis has artes in apertum proferet,
> miserè periimus, actum de nobis erit.[28]

In each instance, it seems that the player/part-writer feels bound by sense, but not punctuation and perhaps not precise word either, when the word is minor or interchangeable.

Amurath's part is even more telling, for here its copyist is author as well as scribe/prompter/player of the text. Yet it too differs from both the manuscript and the printed full book of Goffe's *The Courageous Turk* (which are also both different from one another) in ways that are not obviously traceable to revision.[29] Susan Gushee O'Malley in her edition of *The Courageous Turk* notes that the actor's part contains 122 different readings from the quarto, 19 of which she classifies as 'better', 24 of which she calls 'poorer', and 79 are 'different'; it also departs from the manuscript in 62 different readings, 6 of which are 'better', 16 'poorer', and 40 'different' (these differences, moreover, do not always concern the same quarto and manuscript passages).[30] Value-judgement aside, the differences are in fact like those for 'Polypragmaticus': synonyms are used for words so minor that they are unlikely to be specific revisions; there is differing punctuation throughout. So, for instance, the part has a section that reads:

> AM: Now Lords, who will daunce:
> A Turkish measure, Ladie, o*u*r nerves are shruncke
> And *yo*u now fix ye signe of age on us
> Y*o*u who have bloode yt leapes w*i*thin *yo*ur vaynes
> Bee nimble, as an hart, caper t'oth spheares
> O *yo*u are lyte, yt want ye weight of years

The full printed text for this passage has:

> AMUR. Now (Lords) who'le dance
> A Turkish measure? Ladies our nerves are shrunke;
> And you now fixe the signe of age on me,
> You who have bloud still flowing in your veynes,
> Be nimble as an Hart: Caper to the Sphæres!
> O you are light, that w[a]nt the weight of yeares![31]

The only substantive difference between the two passages is the word 'leapes' in the part, which is 'flowing' in the full text (but 'leaps' in the full manuscript). Punctuation, however, plus elision – 'who will' in the part is 'who'le' in the full text – joins a minor variation in singular and plural – 'ladie' in the part is 'ladies' in the full text, 'us' in the part is 'me' in the full text – to show what is often found in twice-copied full texts: that two variant playscripts for a single play will be generally unlike one another in minutiae, even when more than one of them is authorially written. Of Middleton's *Game at Chesse*, which survives in several versions, for instance, two of the manuscripts are at odds with one another at points where they are both in the playwright's hand; Ioppolo writes how both 'suggest an author rewriting slightly in the act of copying'.[32] It was this fact that led Honigmann to rethink the stability of playtexts altogether; he summarises his findings with the description:

> I was struck by the fact that authorial second thoughts can be quite indistinguishable from textual corruption. I first noticed this in later literary manuscripts, which included many variants similar to those found in corrupt texts – synonym substitution, singular–plural substitution, tense changes (spoke–spake, name–named), transposition, graphically related substitution (lipping–sipping). Some of these authorial changes seemed to be deliberate and others unconscious – for an author transcribing his own work might suffer from fatigue just like a scribe or a compositor.[33]

Any play in more than one handwritten form is changed and altered, because writing passages afresh automatically results in the making of changes in spelling, punctuation or minor synonyms, even if the author is the copyist.

What about those occasions on which the actor is not the part-writer? For in plays-within-plays actors tend to demand their scripts rather than writing them. 'Have you the Lions part written?' asks the anxious Snug to Quince in *A Midsummer Night's Dream*, 'for I am slow of studie' (TLN 329–30); 'When shall we have our parts? . . . when our parts?' clamours the scared Hobinoll when told he is to put on a play for the Prince; while the Boy in *Returne from Pernassus* blames the prompter/stage-keeper for not giving him his part earlier in the preparation process: 'Its all long of you, I could not get my part a night or two before that I might sleep on it.'[34] A part-writer of some kind or another – fellow actor or prompter – often provided the actors' scripts for professional productions. So for Jonson's *Entertainment at Britain's Burse* the actor Nathan Field is given a sum of money after he 'satt upp all night wryt[ing] the speeches, songs & inscript[ions]'; here it seems that an actor is helping out the company (for a fee) by writing the passages for the actors to learn.[35] Similarly, in 1667, Killigrew writes a note directed to a 'helper', 'Miss Hancock' (a relation of Thomas Hancock, a minor actor in his company), on a marked-up copy of *Cicilia and Clorinda*; it asks:

Miss Hancoke pray write both theis partes of Cissillia and Clorinda inteire as thay ar in this booke in to parts for they are short anufe with out cutting being in all but 92 sides in the hoell and the first part but 49 sides and the seconde but 43 sides. Tho: Killigrew/White Hall. Fe./14. 1666.[36]

Very often, and perhaps to save money, the prompter was the part-writer for professional productions. When the theatres reopened after the interregnum, John Downes the prompter recorded amongst his tedious daily jobs 'writing out all the Parts in each Play'; thereafter most stories are of parts written by or under the direction of the prompter.[37] Thus Chetwood, the Dublin prompter responsible for getting parts written in the early eighteenth century, chose to do so by hiring out the job at a profit. The poor lawyer, Whiteley, was

recommend[ed] . . . to Mr. William Rufus Chetwood, prompter of Smock-alley theatre, Dublin, as one well qualified to write out such parts as he might have occasion for; upon which an agreement was struck, and the needy lawyer was forced to the necessity of writing parts at a penny a length (42 lines each), when the unconscionable prompter charged the manager, Tom Phillips . . . no less than two-pence.[38]

But if prompter, fellow player or some other person has written the part, that puts the actor himself at a yet further distance from the 'book'.

Take the part of Orlando in Greene's *Orlando Furioso*. It is in a scribal hand, not that of its player Edward Alleyn; moreover, the scribe has himself struggled to interpret the text he is rewriting: the part contains gaps and spaces in it for moments when whatever 'book' underlay it had proved illegible. So the part is separated from the authorial text intellectually as well as physically and in terms of handwriting. That all but three of the gaps left in the manuscript have later been filled by another hand, thought to be that of its actor, Alleyn, complicates the issue further. Granted, the actor has identified with the text enough to work his way into it despite the fact that he is not its scribe, but the source for the information he supplies is unclear. Is Alleyn filling the scribe's gaps by looking at the full playscript, in which case, is he a 'better' reader of a messy text? That is possible: he has allowed three gaps to remain, perhaps because he could not read those words, but could read the others (though this raises questions: how will he handle the gaps in performance? By extemporisation?). Alternatively, Alleyn has not turned to the full play-book at all, in which case the gaps are filled either through a rehearsal held with a person who knows the missing words, or through guesswork. The part is, whatever the answer, written and annotated for performance, but still incomplete, a fact so odd that in a thoughtful chapter Michael Warren wonders whether this text can ever really have been used as the basis of a performance. Might it, rather, be a rejected part?[39] In fact, and strangely, erasures, emendations and gaps are features of theatrical parts in other countries: the cache of twenty-three Swiss parts surviving from the 1530s upwards are collectively 'carelessly written and full of error'.[40] Actors' performance documents, lacking care and textual fidelity from the start, also in their nature allowed for corrections, alterations and minor additions from the actor using them. They were somewhat different from 'the text' in use and intention.

Comparison between part and play is telling, though as ever it is skewed by the fact that both survive in non-cognate forms. The printed text of *Orlando Furioso* dates from 1594, by which time its author Greene had been accused of selling the play twice: once to the Admiral's Men; once to the Queen's Men. As the part for *Orlando Furioso* survives amongst the effects of the actor Edward Alleyn, chief player of the Admiral's Men at the time, it is probably a record of a version of the play preceding the printed one; it may also reflect a version written for

a different company.[41] Or does it? Concentration on the differences
between part and play, and a yearning, for other reasons, to see the full
Orlando play as a 'bad' quarto (in which the text is not authoritative but
corrupted by memory), have allowed scholars not to explore further the
moments of extreme similarity between full text and part.[42] So when the
part reads:

> what messenger hath Ate sent abrode,
> wth Idle look*es* to listen my lament
> sirha who wronged happy nature thus
> to spoyle thes trees wth this Angelica
> yet in hir name Orlando they are blest.[43]

the quarto, which has virtually the same words for this section, reads:

> What messenger hath Ate sent abroad,
> With idle lookes to listen my laments.
> Sirra, who wronged happy Nature so,
> To spoyle these trees with this Angelica?
> Yet in her name (Orlando) they are blest.

In some ways, the differences here – the way that the part is barely punctuated
and does not pick out its verse with capitalisation – are directly traceable to
the differences between acting a play professionally and reading it. A play
for acting needs to give certain freedoms to the actor (selecting which aspects
to emphasise and then 'pointing' them well was a skill an actor was praised
for – too much punctuation might positively get in a professional actor's
way, though an amateur might be glad of it); a play for the closet needs to
reduce those freedoms for the sake of reader-ease.[44] But other differences
are telling too: the part has 'who wronged happy nature thus' and the play
'who wronged happy Nature so', which again suggests that a part-scribe
might feel ready to exchange similar words with synonyms of his own. In
this way the part and play resemble two other copies of Middleton's *Game
at Chesse*: those written out by the scribe Ralph Crane. Crane, known to
have been a professional copyist for the King's Men, seems to have felt
comfortable 'substitut[ing] synonyms and chang[ing] words of small signifi-
cance in making two transcripts from the same copy', writes Howard-Hill;
Oxley agrees, saying of Crane's copy of *Humorous Lieutenant* that 'a major
characteristic of Crane as a copyist is his tendency to make small changes'.[45]
Non-playwright copyists were as likely to be inaccurate in a minor way as
playwright-copyists.

   The stage-directions, too, are not entirely 'shared' between part and
play; each provides information in slightly different words. It is not that

one text has stage-directions and the other does not; it is that each has the stage-directions relevant to the kind of script it is. The part is written from 'Orlando's' point of view, so its 'enters wth a mans legg' is matched by the printed book's 'Enter Orlando with a leg'; its 'he beates A' is matched by the printed book's 'He beateth him'; while the actions of other people whose motions will affect Orlando's own performance are third person in both texts 'A[rgalio]. begins to weepe' is matched by the printed book's 'Orgalio cries'.[46] But the fact that the language used for the 'shared' directions differs suggests, too, that scribes might have allowed themselves more leeway with directions than they did with dialogue. Stage-directions, already shown by other chapters to have (potential) sources in other texts as well as (potential) manifestations in other texts, are now shown to be perhaps more mutable than dialogue, altering, like punctuation, from one variety of theatrical document to another. Not only are part and playbook written at different times and by different people; they are also, and hardly surprisingly, written to convey differing material.

Thus, whether actor, prompter, scribe, or even author is the copier of parts, every individual part is mediated by someone who does not automatically have as a goal complete fidelity to a whole play, and whose use of synonyms as well as patterns of scribal punctuation and capitalisation and choice of stage-direction will have shaped the scripts he created. Perhaps the lack of accuracy was thought allowable because the parts were not going to be learnt with word-for-word fidelity anyway. At least, with the great pressures on actors to memorise and recall up to forty parts a season, it is 'a legitimate surmise', wrote Greg, 'that the actors were far from perfect in their parts'; Maguire sees the acting culture as one where 'memorisation' might be the goal, but 'remembering' might be the result.[47] There was no point stressing over copying accurately a throwaway word when actors were as likely as not to come up with a synonym in performance anyway.

EXTEMPORISATION BY CLOWNS AND OTHERS

Beyond the struggle to interpret and memorise a part with accuracy was the fact that particular actors and particular moments were designed to diverge from the text. Clowns in particular had as part of their job the ability to speak extempore: if the stage had unexpectedly emptied and there was a hiatus, it was the clown's job to improvise until the production was brought back on track. One jest records how 'hee that presented the Jester or Clowne' was in the tiring-house when he was 'called to enter, (for the Stage was emptie)'; in *The Pilgrimage to Parnassus* the clown is sent on 'when they have noe bodie to leave on the stage' with the instruction 'ether saie somwhat for thy selfe, or hang & be non plus'.[48] But even when there was no theatrical crisis, and the clown was comfortably inside the fiction of the play, he still had, if not the need, at least the liberty to comment around his text and outside it, bringing in his catchphrases and bantering with the audience: that was one of the points of clowning.

Best recorded are a series of examples involving the clown Tarlton, playing in the 1580s. His 'pleasant and extemporal invention', as an anonymous pamphlet about him had it, 'famozed all Comedies': which is to say that he improved plays in performance with his extra-textual material.[49] So in one performance Tarlton was obliged to double both as Judge (in which he had to be boxed on the ear) and as Clown (in which he had to comment on the Judge's sufferings). Having received the blow and exited as Judge, he re-entered as the Clown and was told the story of what had just happened. He responded, 'it could not be but terrible to the Judge, when the report so terrifies me, that me thinkes the blow remaines still on my cheeke, that it burnes againe'.[50] His joke was, of course, play-specific and occasion-specific: it could not be repeated in any other performance unless the same unusual doubling-emergency obtained once more. But another variety of Tarltonian jest, perhaps even more famous, was when his extempore was entirely unconnected to the play in which he was performing. The audience, if restless, were prepared to solicit Tarlton to interact with them in the middle of a production, riling him precisely in order to bring about an extemporised insult. Thus they might throw pippins and apples at him (to the first he jested '. . . Pippin you have put in, then for my grace,/Would I might put your nose in another place'; to the second '. . . as for an Apple he hath cast a Crab,/So instead of an honest woman God hath sent him a drab'); point their fingers at him (to which Tarlton responded with a two-fingered salute, and then, when challenged, quipped, 'For there is no man which in love to mee/Lends me one finger, but he shall have three'); or simply hiss at him (to which Tarlton rapped back, 'I liv'd not in that Golden Age,/When Jason wonne the Fleece./But now I am on Gotams Stage,/Where Fooles doe hisse like Geese').[51] The whole point is that Tarlton could intersperse a play with a good deal of himself, and was supposed to do so: plays containing parts for Tarlton were open and receptive to certain forms of extemporisation – and extemporisation that sailed close to the wind. Performances were 'partial' in their nature: particular parts were further from the text, as written by the author or approved by the censor, than others.

After Tarlton's death William Kempe famously became 'Jestmonger and Vice-gerent generall to the Ghost of Dicke Tarlton' and inherited some of the great clown's techniques.[52] This included extemporisation; Wiles demonstrates how plays written for Kempe are structured to let his character prepare independent material (he often has both the entrance and exit cue-lines for his sub-scene); Kempe is often also given a mono-logue of his own, presumably for embellishing, at the end of a scene.[53] And Hamlet's Folio strictures against the clowns who speak 'more then is set downe for them' (TLN 1887) are thought to be a direct reference to Kempe (they are certainly references to the ad libbing in the theatre of the time that was irritating to playwrights). The 'bad' Quarto 1 of *Hamlet* (1600) even details some of the clown's added catchphrases, suggesting a series of comic interjections that would regularly and irrelevantly find their way into numerous plays – uncensored, though at least on this occasion they are hardly libellous: 'Cannot you stay till I eate my porridge? and, you owe me/A quarters wages: and, my coate wants a cullison:/And your beere is sowre . . .'[54] When Goneril in *Lear* speaks of 'your all-lycenc'd Foole' (TLN 712), this, indicates Richard Dutton, is a real description of the early modern clown: he, but no one else, was 'licensed' as a person whatever he said.[55]

Even if later theatrical practice was to clamp down on (particular kinds of) improvisation – a player who holds 'interloqutions with the Audients' in Brome's *Antipodes* is told he is outmodedly harking back to the 'dayes of *Tarlton* and *Kempe,*/Before the stage was purg'd from barbarisme' – the habit continued to flourish on occasion, because everything that defined wit relied on it.[56] Prynne's criticism, made as late as the 1630s, was that 'sometimes such who act the Clowne or amorous person, adde many obscene lascivious jests and passages of their owne . . . to delight the auditors, which were not in their parts before', specifically singling out the difference between what was written on a part, and what was spoken on a stage.[57] His opinion too is that the clown role (or, interestingly, an amorous role) is more porous than others. In continental texts a hierarchy of codes drew attention to the fact that the clown's part had a different and more available quality from the rest of the play: Acevedo writes his clown and rustic roles in colloquial Spanish, while the rest of his plays are in formal Latin – the parts are not just linguistically different but focussed towards different audience members.[58] English texts with what are thought to be 'memorial' features often have extended fool sections: they seem to reflect parts that were consistently longer in performance than their written content; indeed, Eric Rasmussen raises the possibility that the *Book of Sir Thomas More*, in which clown additions are inserted into the margin by hand B, shows a scribe noting down some of the extemporisations that a clown had created during production.[59]

As well as deviating from known scripts, clowns were not just expected but encouraged to possess the theatrical space with their extempore talents, again showing how little the theatre cared about restricting certain players to 'allowed' passages. The end of most performances was, by design, extemporal: meaning that licensed plays usually concluded with a series of unlicensed and unwritten entertainments. At the close of a play, the clown took over with a jig, or with comic answers to 'themes' and suggestions shouted out by the audience. It was this occasion that brought the audience, sometimes by name, into the performance space, marking an unpredictable moment where the fictional just might coincide with the real – a moment that was far less structured and far more edgy than the prescribed text of an epilogue ever was. Jigs, possibly, and themes certainly, included the very kind of matter that, if written, might have been the first to be struck out by the censor's quill. When a 'gallant' came to the theatre with a rhyme designed to floor the great clown Tarlton, 'Me thinkes it is a thing unfit. /To see a Gridiron turne the Spit'; Tarlton responded not to the theme, but to the person, 'Me thinkes it is a thing unfit,/To see an Asse have any wit.'[60] His jibes might well range further to vilify particular individuals by name, though personal slights were rigorously censored in Revels' texts for the trouble they might cause. Yet Nashe relates with relish how Tarlton 'at the Theater' made pointed jests about Richard Harvey.[61] Other Tarltonian merriments included mingling personal insults with high crudity – he is hailed for bringing the term 'prepuse' (meaning 'foreskin') 'into the Theater with great applause'; a cancelled manuscript passage records in full the joke he told: he blamed his sore penis on a woman who, he opined, 'had a shimny ['chimney'] in her breeche for sewer ['sure'] she had burnt his prepuse'.[62] From later time, what appears to be a book of worked-up themes with their responses was published by Robert Armin as *Quips upon Questions*; it includes insulting personal responses (Q: 'Who comes Yonder'; A: 'yonder comes the asse that nere was wise'); monarchical slights ('The King is proud, and he would be a God'); and potential blasphemy (Q: 'Whers the Devill?' A: 'None knowes, but you may be his secretarie').[63] And, though these particular exchanges will have altered between the time of speaking and the time of printing, accounts of other theme-swapping occasions provide a similar range of insults. There was no clear expectation that all words spoken on the stage would be written, learnt, prejudged and censored: it was the off-the-cuff and uncensored that were particularly popular.

Indeed, there was even a whole variety of performance that was specifically about extemporisation where, obviously, the point was that no part or authorised text had shaped the unpredictable moment. So admired was an actor's ability to come up with (generally) risqué rhymed poetry that entire theatres might be were hired for 'wit battles': entertainments made of improvisational verse not accurate to any text at all. Robert Wilson, the clown, was singled out by Meres in 1598 as someone who 'for learning and extemporall witte . . . is without compare or compeere, as . . . he manifested in his chalenge at the Swanne on the Banke side', a 'challenge' suggesting that he took on other extemporisers and won.[64] Taylor the Waterpoet, and Fennor, self-proclaimed 'King's rhymer', both arranged to hold wit battles as popular entertainment, again in the theatrical space: public theatres were sites strongly associated with unapproved material. Taylor records how Fennor failed to turn up to their mutual and much publicised 'triall of Wit' at the Hope Playhouse (touted for 7 October 1614). Fennor replies by recalling the wit battle he had arranged some years earlier at the Fortune Playhouse with 'Kendall' (perhaps William Kendall, the actor, or possibly Timothy Kendall, a university-educated wit): Kendall, too, had not appeared, but Fennor had carried the evening on his own by extemporising to 'themes' the audience had shouted at him.[65] But successful or unsuccessful, the wit battle is predicated on material not, and never, written down. In fact, Fennor had even tried to ask Taylor for a book 'to know on what ground I might build my Invention' but that had, of course, not been provided, leading Fennor to level a totally unjustified insult at Taylor: he accused Taylor of 'studying' his would-be extempore in advance – hinting that he was sure a written text underlaid all the off-the-cuff wit – even though he had the opposite of evidence for this:

> thou knowst, thou promist in thy Bill,
> In rare extempory to shew thy skill.
> When all thou spok'st, thou studiedst had before,
> Thou know'st I know, above a month and more.[66]

Here the truth of the assertion is not the point – even if Taylor had studied his witticisms, he could hardly have given them to the Master of the Revels for approval without undercutting his entire 'extempore' claim. Rather, this illustrates and introduces the idea that entire theatres were primed for unwritten, unlearnt, unlicensed and unlicensable speech; that there were varieties of people and kinds of entertainment unlicensed in their nature; and that when plays were licensed at all it was with a potential for laxity.

This may be why the audience too might take it upon themselves to participate in the play, adding to the extempore and ensuring that unexpected material remained a feature throughout. Less often recorded than interjections from the stage, audience interruptions are regularly staged in plays-within-plays as a necessary feature of, for instance, court performances. One manuscript jest-book account relates how interruptions might be a feature of public performances too, describing how a line spoken during a Woodstock performance was responded to by 'Hoskins of Oxford' who 'standinge by as a spectator rimes openly to it'. On hearing the play's line, 'As at a banquett some meates have sweet some saure tast', Hoskins came back with 'Even soe your dublett is to short in the waste.'[67] Scripted actors' parts were entirely outside the process of extemporisation that was another element of any play whether by design or chance: so parts could only ever dictate a potential performance, not show what a real one would be like.

Moreover, it was not simply that the clown's part was fluid, as his role was. A play might be receptive to improvisation elsewhere too, indicated in a number of ways even in the 'finished' text. Instances where it was designed to happen can be seen in stage-directions like '*Enter Forrester . . . speake any thing, and Exit*'; '*Heere they two talke and rayle what they list*'; '*Jockie is led to whipping over the stage, speaking some wordes, but of no importance*'; '*Here the Queene entertaines the Ambassadors, and in their severall languages confers with them*'; and, terrifyingly, '*Tell him all the Plot.*'[68] But, such specific directions aside, other textual moments too highlight the occasions where minor extemporisation in non-clown characters – to the extent of supplying a missing word, if not more – is to take place. The gap shown by a space in the text, a dash, or more often the written sign '&c', are all used to stand in for what is to be manifested as swearing and perhaps blasphemy on the stage.

So in Thomas Middleton's *Famelie of Love* Mistress Purge asks, 'And what do they sweare by now their mony is gone [?]'; the answer is 'Why by ( ) and God refuse them'; plays in the Beaumont and Fletcher folio of 1647 include phrases such as *Bonduca*'s 'By ----' or 'a ------- consume ye': and dashes are used to a similar purpose in *Maid in the Mill, Knight of Malta, Love's Cure, Woman's Prize* and *Love's Pilgrimage*.[69] Instances of '&c' representing the same thing include Philomusus' 'I faith &c.', to which the shocked response is Stupido's 'O sweare not, sweare not,' in *Pilgrimage to Parnassus*, 'I scorne you: and you are but a &c.' in *Dr Faustus*; the Nurse's 'Out you Rogue, you arrant &c.' in *Wily Beguilde*; and 'Some Bawd of *Shoreditch*, or *Turnbul* Broker of Maidenheads, &c.' in *Hey for Honesty*.[70] The '&c' may even represent a way that a text could be approved by the Master of the Revels whilst simultaneously not hampering actors' freedoms: the text as read was 'pure', but the perform-ance might not be (though equally '&c' might represent a page doctored by the Master of the Revels when he erased a swear-word – in which case the actors would be supposed to come up with a milder expletive). Though with such instances dividing what is press censorship from what is theatrical censorship in printed plays is hard, the fact remains that a space or an '&c' will have required some stage manifestation, and that a word or words have been swallowed for the page.[71]

An '&c' on some occasions implies more fully fledged ad libbing, indicated when sentences lead up to a point and then stop (these instances too may, of course, be allowing for particularly colourful swearing): George Gascoigne produces 'I had thought to have given him these hose when I had worne them a little nearer, but he shall have a &c', 'What wil you breake? Your nose in mine &c', 'And why wouldest thou tell him? I would not for, &c'; Brome has 'Was it your mans fault Mr. *Carelesse*? if I be not reveng'd &c.'[72] Alternatively '&c' was used for a different kind of extemporal freedom: the freedom to repeat. For the term is also used for moments in which the actor is to carry on in the same vein as before; a tiny liberty that could be exploited by the player or not according to taste (it, of course, always also opens the possibility of swearing too): 'Treason! a Guard! Treason! &c.'; 'Goe from my window goe, goe from, &c. away' and 'Helpe, helpe, helpe, theeves, theeves, helpe, theeves, &c.'[73] There was, it seems, a mechanism for asking actors to extemporise: the text as written and perhaps as approved regularly expected at tiny moments to differ from the text that would be performed.

CONCLUSION

In some ways this confirms what has latterly been regularly articulated: that written plays have a different value from spoken plays and the one should not be confounded with the other. 'If the play is a book', writes Orgel matter-of-factly, 'it's not a play.'[74] The written play presented is never the script of the performed play, but a different text, neither fully a predictor nor fully a reflection of the staged performance. At the same time, however, it is nearer performance along some lines than others.

The rules of production have shown that most characters and most sections are fixed in the main, though written, learnt and spoken with mild inaccuracy; other parts, however, are only guidelines for performance, meaning that only their absolutely crucial part features – the cues that tell other actors when to speak – needed to be adhered to. Other sections still might contain moments for extempore inside what is otherwise fixed. A fully written dialogue, then, is already fragmentary, for some of its passages are the text to be acted and others are guidelines only; while any performance will conclude with (if not contain internally) a Clown's free-for-all probably featuring words and ideas that would have been censored out of the play itself.

This means that questions need to be raised about classifying surviving playbooks as showing or hiding signs of stage practices – or showing or hiding 'literary' features. The production came first and foremost out of parts; the playbook glossed and regulated rather than prescribing them. True, some playbooks are near to production, but, as has been discussed, the prompter's book and the book from which the parts descend need not be the same; and, if they are, the parts would still have been a little different in performance. Yet if playbooks are somewhat removed from performance, they contain enough performative traces to make them removed from the literary reader too. Any tiny dash, space or '&c' is a written record of words revealed only in performance – or perhaps changed from performance to performance: they are 'permissive' stage-directions.

Such books as survive in manuscript and print are, irrespective of their form – whether they are thought authorial or theatrical, prepared for the reader, or shaped to the player – neither the text performed nor the text cleared of performance features. Every 'book' retains the theatre in its gaps and lacunae; yet every book equally lacks the theatre as it differs from the scripts from which performance was made.

Conclusion: Repatching the play

Full printed and manuscript plays contain 'shadows' of their patchwork construction, and this book has shown what can be learnt about entire texts by considering what the ramifications are of writing and adapting plays by the patch. It has shown that papers likely to be taken onto the stage physically, like songs, scrolls or prologues, will not always have been written into the playbook – or at least not accurately – so that the more textual a performance moment was, the less precise the 'book' for that section might be. But it has also shown reverse moments, when a book's internal scrolls are more accurate than the rest of the text, because they have come to the printing house directly from the theatre and still in 'stage' form, integrated and 'placed' by the compositor. And, sometimes, it has shown 'exclusive' stage documents for special occasions, like the Argument that tells the story of the play, or the occasional prologue, enwrapped into a printed text, as though the book depicts a first or court performance.

In other ways, too, *Documents of Performance* has shown how elemental the 'patch' was to the construction of performance and thence to the construction of playbooks. The dialogue and all that happens within that dialogue exchange was in performance made up of separate manuscripts: learnt actors' parts; backstage-plots; and songs, scrolls, prologues and epilogues all of which might be read onstage, and all of which have their own histories. Even their story of circulation links some more closely with others – but all, often, aside from a single document. Sometimes songs, with their music, circulated in books of music containing songs by other writers and for other plays; at other times, prologues and songs, as written documents for a play, seem to have been kept with each other but away from the playscript, so that they are copied in commonplace books together, and are lost and found as twosomes. Scrolls might be kept in company with other practical documents that had a stage use, particularly phoney 'blank' scrolls which were stage props; backstage-plots seem to have been wrapped around their approved books, perhaps as folders containing some of the other play documents. So the internal texts that make up a play had an oddly metatextual and perhaps paratextual relationship to the rest of the performed play: for the play onstage was not a manifestation of one book, but an aural and visual gathering of the contents of many scattered manuscripts.

Using this information, *Documents of Performance* has interrogated two competing current schools of thought on playscripts: whether surviving playbooks are ever fully representative of plays as they were performed ('performance texts') and whether playbooks are ever fully stripped of the theatre to become plays in an ideal literary form ('literary texts'). Its material raises problems with both notions: printed texts are at a remove from performance even if they are close to the prompter's book, for the prompter's book was not necessarily the source of staged documents or, indeed, actors' parts; 'literary' texts contain lacunae, ranging from an '&c' to a missing lyric to a stranded cue, that are visibly theatrical, and bear witness – with disrupted speech-headings and (stage-)directions around internal papers – to the separate manuscript circulation of its scrolls. In all, then, this book rejects the notion of nicely divided binaries that describe playbooks – foul and fair, authorial and prompt, theatrical and literary. None of these necessarily exist, *Documents of Performance* suggests, because full texts, manuscript and print, can contain a mingled selection of the documents generated by or for performance.

For the editor who dates a play or establishes authorship for it on the basis of one of its 'removable' passages, this book provides a warning: those passages may comment on the date and author only of themselves. But this book also raises questions for the stylometricist who establishes authorship or co-authorship working from certain presumptions (that all authors wrote dialogue for the play, for instance) which this book has shown to be questionable: one of the co-authors may have plotted the play (by writing its plot-scenario) but never written any passage of it, for instance. Moreover, as many fragments can have their own life and rate of change, it has also shown that including every patch for computer analysis is problematic: the base text chosen by a stylometricist could profitably be shorn of prologues, epilogues, songs, internal masques, scrolls and (because of plot-scenarios and backstage-plots) stage-directions.

The notion of textual revision, theatrical and 'literary', also needs to be modified in the light of this book. Just as there was a variety of separate ways in which plays could be written, so there was a variety of separate ways in which they could be revised and changed. Every removable section could be taken away, added, or altered, without the necessity of taking away, adding or altering any other bit: revision might not happen over and on a whole play, but inside one of its dislocated pieces. That means that a play might always have been viewed as a selection of documents, some of which were understood to be relatively fixed, some of which were understood to be fluid, and some of which might be either: a play was made out of passages of variable permanence, for a play held in its 'patchy' structure the ability to be staged in more than one version. In particular, some play patches, though belonging to and written for their play, were designed only for single performances. Arguments, prologues and epilogues were often for first days, while playbills had long and short forms and might be rewritten for particular events. Songs might come and go depending on the singing and instrumental ability of the actors – boys' cracked voices could result in songs reduced to spoken lyrics or removed altogether – and they might equally be changed to accommodate a popular tune or alter the mood of a scene. And just as performed plays differed between first and subsequent performances, so printed and manuscript playscripts might differ too, depending on how many single-performance features they retain and how many they have sloughed off: some Arguments, some prologues and epilogues, and some internal masques were probably solely for performance at court, for instance, though they become a permanent part of the text in print. 'Long' texts that survive may, then, be books rewritten as 'literature' but may equally represent the 'long text' created for special or first performance before audience judgement modified it.

A recent interest in what Genette has called 'paratext', a term he applied to the combination of dedicatory and other material inside a work of literature ('peritext') and the other witnesses to it outside the book ('epitext'), has led to a re-examination of early modern plays in terms of their textual layout, with explorations about what title-pages and other preliminary matter do to the reading of the play. Genette saw paratext serving the function of being a 'transitional zone between text and beyond text'; he considered the impact on the reader of confronting threshold and liminal introductory material before entering a work, discussing how front matter negotiated and controlled the literature to come.[1] But he also looked at paratext inserted into the interstices between the text, like notes and chapter headings, and considered what practical bearing such structural reminders had on the text. His terminology has latterly been adopted by early modernists interested in the moment when the reader is invited inside a playbook or allowed to step back from it: for Bergeron, plays' introductory material is made up of 'discrete, introspective, set-apart rhetorical musings' which govern our responses by providing 'the last word before the playwright must release the play to readers' judgment'.[2] This is a useful way to discuss the material met with in advance of a printed play, particularly as it mirrors actual performance, where the bill and Argument are encountered before the play starts, and the prologue is heard in advance of it. Yet, as this book has shown, published plays might have disturbing paratextual matter, lacking the order and clarity that performance would have given the text: epilogues are sometimes published directly after prologues and clustered at the front or back of the book; songs might join other paratextual material before the book starts; other texts, like some Arguments and playbills, might not make it to the book at all; other texts still, like plot-scenarios and backstage-plots, shape the interstices of the book without precisely emanating from there or being directly recorded there. In questioning the paratext placed (only sometimes) before the book, and sometimes within it, *Documents of Performance* has laid the groundwork for asking where paratext starts and stops – or, rather, what in a printed playbook is *not* paratextual or epitextual in origin and, sometimes, in presentation.

In a sense, every bit of a play as it was gathered together for a production was a paratext, in that every bit of a play was 'auxiliary' to every other bit: it was performance that made a text from those paratexts, with printed plays always falling a little short because always an incomplete reflection of that. But perhaps the dislocation that has fed through from the moment of writing to the preparation for performance and thence to the play printed or written is better defined in early modern terms. It is not so much that performance, and so subsequent printed play, are made of paratexts, for that still implies that one or some documents represent 'the text' itself. Rather, a play can be, throughout, a series of patches of definable kinds, each of which might be 'liminal' and/or 'essential' depending on reader and circumstance: 'play-patchers' write some of these and playhouses come up with others. The beauty lies, *Documents of Performance* has suggested, in the constituent pieces that make up the whole. Indeed, this book takes up, to use Autolycus' phrase 'unconsidered trifles' (*Winter's Tale*, TLN 1694), recovering the fragment from within the whole, and bringing the 'grosse patchery' (*Timon*, TLN 2318) and the 'goodly patch' (*All's Well*, TLN 2578) equally to the forefront. Arising from its conclusions are a number of questions of fundamental importance to the editor (what should be used as a copytext?), to the theatre historian (how does the play performed relate to the play printed?), and to the theoretician: in a play that is at its root fragmentary, how 'authored' is each section, and what *is* the text?

Notes

INTRODUCTION: PLAYWRIGHTS AS PLAY-PATCHERS

1 Thomas Randolph, *Hey for Honesty, Down with Knavery* (1651), 15; George Wither, *Abuses Stript, and Whipt* (1613), R1b.
2 Thomas Dekker, *Newes from Hell* (1606), H1b.
3 'Constantia Munda', *The Worming of a Mad Dogge* (1617), 3; *Mercurius Rusticans* (l), Bodleian Library, MS Wood D 18 part 2.
4 George Whetstone, *Aurelia* (1593), Q1b. For more on play-patchers, see Tiffany Stern, 'Repatching the Play' in *From Script to Stage in Early Modern England*, ed. Peter Holland and Stephen Orgel (London: Palgrave, 2004), 151–77.
5 Geffrey Whitney, 'Pennæ Gloria Perennis' from *A Choice of Emblemes and other Devises* (1586), 197.
6 T. H. Howard-Hill, 'Crane's 1619 "Promptbook" of "Barnavelt" and Theatrical Processes', *Modern Philology*, 86 (1988), 146–70 (150).
7 William Rankins, *Seaven Satyres* (1598), 8.

1 PLOT-SCENARIOS

1 All from British Library MS, Add 22608, quoted in Arthur C. Kirsch, 'A Caroline Commentary on the Drama', *Modern Philology*, 66 (1969), 256–61 (258; 259; 257; 259; 257).
2 27 August 1619, S.P. PRO 14/110 fol. 57, quoted in *Calendar of State Papers, Domestic Series: 1619–23*, ed. Mary Anne Everett Green (London: Her Majesty's Stationery Office, 1856–1935), 71–3.
3 Peter Hausted, *The Rivall Friends* (1632), A4a.
4 Entry for 28 January 1633/4, quoted in N. W. Bawcutt, *The Control and Censorship of Caroline Drama* (Oxford: Clarendon Press, 1996), 187.
5 William Davenant, *The Unfortunate Lovers* (1643), A3b.
6 William Habington, 'The Prologue at the Fryers' for *The Queene of Arragon* (1640), A2b; Lodowick Carlell, *The Deserving Favorite* (1629), N3b.
7 James Shirley, *The Brothers* (1653), A4a.
8 John Tatham, *The Distracted State* (1651), A3b. See also Thomas Heywood who, in *The Foure Prentises of London* (1615), A2a, confesses that the piece

'comes short of that accuratenesse both in Plot and Stile, that these more Censorious dayes with greater curiosity acquire'. Similarly Thomas Dekker [and Thomas Middleton] in *The Roaring Girle* (1611), M3a, fear audiences who may 'floute/The plot, saying; 'tis too thinne, too weake, too meane', while Ben Jonson in *The Case is Altered* (1609), D3b, imagines one spectator who 'saies he likes not the writing, another/[who] likes not the plot, another [who likes] not the playing', and John Marston in *What You Will* (1607), A3a, has Phylomuse explain that the play is 'ill plotted, worse written'. Says Owen Felltham in *Resolves* (1623), 303–4, 'a clownish Actor in a stately Play' is in danger of disgracing 'both the plot, and the Poet'. Katharine in Richard Brome, *The Weeding of the Covent-Garden* in *Five New Playes* (1659), 51, admonishes Lucy 'as I would entreat an Auditorie, if I now were a Poet to mark the Plot, and several points of my play, that they might not say when 'tis done, they understood not this or that, or how such a part came in or went out, because they did not observe the passages'.

9   Philip Massinger, *The Emperour of the East* (1632), A4a.

10   Dryden to William Walsh, 9 or 10 May 1693 in John Dryden, *The Letters*, ed. Charles E. Ward (Durham, NC: Duke University Press, 1942), 54. Plays continued to be constructed in this way for many years. David Garrick's plot for his farce *The Newspaper* survives inside David Garrick, *Receipt Book*, Folger Shakespeare Library, MS w.b.492.

11   George Puttenham, *The Arte of English Poesie* (1589), III, ch. xxv, 256. Another writer who advises writing in prose first is Lope de Vega, who in *Arte Neuvo de Hazer Comedias en Este Tiempo* advises, 'The subject once chosen, write in prose, and divide the matter into three acts of time,' see *New Art of Making Plays in This Age*, trans. William T. Brewster (New York: Dramatic Museum of Columbia University, 1964), 31. Plutarch relates that Menander, asked whether his play was ready, replied that the plot was conceived and that 'he only had to add the words', 'Moralia 347 e' in Plutarch, *Moralia: Index*, ed. Edward N. O'Neil (Cambridge, MA: Harvard University Press, 2004), 360.

12   Jonson told Drummond in *Conversations*, Ben Jonson, *Works*, ed. C. H. Herford, Percy Simpson and Evelyn Simpson (Oxford: Clarendon Press, 1925–52), 1:143, that he wrote at least his poetry in the same way: 'he wrote all his [verses] first in prose, for so his master Camden, had learned him'.

13   Margaret Cavendish, Duchess of Newcastle, 'A General Prologue to All my Playes', in *Playes* (1662), A7a.

14   Brian Vickers, *Shakespeare Co-author* (Oxford: Oxford University Press, 2002), 21, 'The only complete example of an author-plot is in the Folger'; Neil Carson, *A Companion to Henslowe's Diary* (Cambridge: Cambridge University Press, 1988), 55, 'No complete author plot from a public theatre of the time has survived'; Grace Ioppolo, *Dramatists and Their Manuscripts in the Age of Shakespeare, Jonson, Middleton, Heywood* (New York and London: Routledge, 2006), 55, maintains, 'Greg's contention that there were 2 distinct types of plots, the author-plot (or play summary) and the theatrical plot (or list of actor entrances) may be incorrect,' and suggests that backstage-plots

were the same as author-plots. An article has, however, been written on an extant author-plot: Joseph Quincy Adams' 'The Author-Plot of an Early Seventeenth Century Play', *The Library*, 26 (1945), 17–27. Critics considering the writers of scenarios include W. J. Lawrence, 'The Elizabethan Plotter' in *Speeding Up Shakespeare* (London: Argonaut, 1937; reissued New York: Blom, 1968), 99–112, and I. A. Shapiro, 'Shakespeare and Munday', *Shakespeare Survey*, 14 (1961), 25–33.

15 Ben Jonson, *Mortimer* in *The Workes* (1641), 12Q3b.

16 Humphrey Moseley, 'To the Reader' in John Suckling, *The Last Remains* (1659), A2b.

17 Jonson, *Workes* (1640), 2Q4a–b.

18 At least two other printed plot-scenarios appear to survive but before poems rather than plays: both Arthur Brooke's *The Tragicall Historye of Romeus and Juliet* (1562), π3b, and William Shakespeare's *Lucrece* (1594), A2b, have 'arguments' different enough from the story then told to suggest that they are the printed form of summaries that preceded writing.

19 'The Trinity Manuscript', Trinity College, Cambridge, MS R.3.4, reproduced in facsimile in John Milton, *Poems: Reproduced in Facsimile from the Manuscript in Trinity College, Cambridge: With a Transcript* (Menston, UK: Scolar Press, 1970), 35. A second plot for a linked tragedy is also contained in the manuscript (40). Called ~~Adams Banishment~~ *Adam Unparadiz'd*, it takes the form of a tight paragraph beginning 'The angel Gabriel either descending or entering, shewing since this globe was created, his frequency as much in earth, as in heaven, describes Paradise'. It is not subdivided into acts or scenes, and may represent the stage before plotting: the invention of the story itself.

20 Edward Phillips, *Life of Mr John Milton* (1694), 72–3.

21 John Dryden, *The Vindication, or, the Parallel of the French Holy-League* (1683), 41.

22 [Edward Dering], *Scenario of a play set in Thrace and Macedon, c.* 1630, Folger Library, MS x.d.206; Maggs Brothers, *Shakespeare and Shakespeareana: A Catalogue*, 434 (1923), 217 (item 576; price £25).

23 *The History of King Henry IV*, Folger Library, MS v.b.34. See T. N. S. Lennam, 'Sir Edward Dering's Collection of Playbooks, 1619–1624', *Shakespeare Quarterly*, 16 (1965), 145–53; Laetitia Yeandle, 'The Dating of Sir Edward Dering's Copy of "The History of King Henry the Fourth"', *Shakespeare Quarterly*, 37 (1986), 224–6; G. Blakemore Evans, 'The Dering MS. of Shakespeare's *Henry IV* and Sir Edward Dering', *JEGP*, 54 (1955), 498–503; Hardin Craig, 'The Dering Version of Shakespeare's *Henry IV*', *Philological Quarterly*, 35 (1956), 218–19. Dering's edition of Shakespeare's *Henry IV* is reproduced in *Sir Edward Dering's Manuscript of William Shakespeare's King Henry the Fourth*, ed. George Walton Williams and Gwynne Blakemore Evans (Washington, DC: Folger Shakespeare Library, 1974).

24 [Dering], *Scenario*.

25 John Dryden, 'Preface' in Charles-Alphonse Dufresnoy, *De Arte Graphica: The Art of Painting . . . with Remarks; Translated into English, together with an*

Original Preface containing a Parallel betwixt Painting and Poetry, by Mr. Dryden (1695), xliv.

26 Abel Boyer, *The Royal Dictionary* (1699), 4F1a; Samuel Johnson, *A Dictionary of the English Language*, second edition, 2 vols. (1755–6), 23F2a.

27 Jean Guillemard, *A Combat betwixt Man and Death, translated into English by Edw. Grimeston* (1621), 378.

28 As the printer Humphrey Moseley put it in his introduction to Suckling's *Last Remains*, A2b–A3a: 'the SAD SHEPHERD . . . though it wants two entire Acts, was nevertheless judg'd a Piece of too much worth to be laid aside, by the Learned and Honorable Sir Kenelme Digby who published that [second] Volume [of Ben Jonson's plays]'.

29 Thomas Hughes, Francis Bacon, Sir Nicholas Trotte, William Fulbeck, John Lancaster, Sir Christopher Yelverton, John Penroodock and Francis Flower, *The Misfortunes of Arthur* (1587 [i.e. 1588]), c3b.

30 Ben Jonson, *Poetaster* (1602), A2a.

31 'Beaumont, & Fletcher (yt exalted pair) . . .' in *Miscellany*, Bodleian Library, MS Sancroft 53, 50.

32 Thomas Fuller, *History* (1662), oooo1b.

33 R. West, 'To the Memory of His Deare Brother Mr Thomas Randolph', in Thomas Randolph, *Poems* (1638), ***2a.

34 British Library MS, Add. 36758 in John Fletcher, *Bonduca*, ed. Walter Wilson Greg and F. P. Wilson (Oxford: Malone Society, 1951), 90.

35 Laurie E. Maguire, *Shakespearean Suspect Texts* (Cambridge: Cambridge University Press, 1996), 211.

36 Beaumont and Fletcher, *Bonduca* in Francis Beaumont and John Fletcher, *Comedies and Tragedies* (1647), 4i1b.

37 British Library MS, Add. 36758 in Fletcher, *Bonduca*, ed. Greg and Wilson, 90.

38 Paul Werstine, 'Narratives about Printed Shakespeare Texts: "Foul Papers" and "Bad Quartos"', *Shakespeare Quarterly*, 41 (1990), 65–86 (72). Werstine here also discusses Greg's attempt to fit 'foul papers' to McKerrow's idea of play 'drafts' though neither bibliographer found drafts that ideally matched the foul papers' conception.

39 Walter Wilson Greg, *The Shakespeare First Folio, Its Bibliographical and Textual History* (Oxford: Clarendon Press, 1955), 106.

40 The different ramifications of Daborne's term 'foul sheet' – and how fair sheets were usually the texts with which companies were supplied – are discussed in Paul Werstine, 'Post-Theory Problems in Shakespeare Editing', *Yearbook of English Studies*, 29 (1999), 103–17 (110). Elsewhere he notes: 'There may . . . be room for doubt about whether, in Shakespeare's time, whole plays, rather than just fragmentary versions of them, were called "foul papers",' 'Narratives about Printed Shakespeare Texts', 72. E. A. J. Honigmann, *The Stability of Shakespeare's Text* (London: Edward Arnold, 1965), 17–18, provides four other uses of cognate phrases and concludes, 'Seventeenth-century usage . . . gives no backing to the opinion that "foul papers" must be a complete draft.'

41 *Comoedia: Senilis Amor* (1635), Bodleian Library, MS Rawl. Poet 9, 80b.
42 The play itself had been entered as a Beaumont and Fletcher text – together with *A Right of Women* (also said to be by Beaumont and Fletcher), and *Madon, King of Britain* (said to be by Beaumont) – in the Stationers' Register on 29 June 1660 by Humphrey Moseley, but was never published; see W. W. Greg, *A Bibliography of the English Printed Drama to the Restoration*, 4 vols. (London: Bibliographical Society, 1959), 1:68. *Right of Women* and *Madon* are now lost, and the copy of *Faithful Friends* that survives, written probably in the 1630s, is not necessarily the same copy that Moseley entered – see Francis Beaumont and John Fletcher?, *The Faithful Friends: from the MS (Dyce 10)*, ed. G. M. Pinciss and G. R. Proudfoot (Oxford: Malone Society Reprints, 1975), v.
43 Beaumont and Fletcher?, *Faithful Friends*, ed. Pinciss and Proudfoot, 93–4.
44 Ibid., vi–vii.
45 Ioppolo, *Dramatists and Their Manuscripts*, 109.
46 Philip Henslowe, *Henslowe Papers*, ed. W. W. Greg (London: A. H. Bullen, 1907), 72.
47 Thomas Heywood, *The English Traveller* (1633), A3a.
48 Suzanne Gossett in her Arden introduction to William Shakespeare, *Pericles* (London: Thomson Learning, 2004), 60; Giorgio Melchiori in his introduction to William Shakespeare, *King Edward III* (Cambridge: Cambridge University Press, 1998), 16–17.
49 R. A. Foakes, *Henslowe's Diary* (Cambridge: Cambridge University Press, [1961] 2002), 295.
50 Ibid., 167, 168.
51 PRO STAC8 31/16 f. 30; transcribed in C. J. Sisson, *Lost Plays of Shakespeare's Age* (Cambridge: Cambridge University Press, 1936), 110.
52 W. W. Greg, *Dramatic Documents from the Elizabethan Playhouses*, 2 vols. (Oxford: Clarendon Press, 1931), 1:205.
53 Thomas Nashe, *Nashes Lenten Stuffe* (1599), B1b.
54 Letter written at the end of June 1613; transcribed in Greg, *Henslowe Papers*, 84.
55 Foakes, *Henslowe's Diary*, 73. In a later 'a cownt of All suche money I have layd owt for my lord admeralles players' between 11 October 1597 and 28 January 1598, Henslowe repeats this item; 'lent unto Bengemen Johnson the 3 of deserbz 1597 upon a boocke wch he showed the plotte unto the company wch he promised to dd unto the company at cryssmas next the some of . . . xxs' (Foakes, *Henslowe's Diary*, 85).
56 Ibid., 100.
57 Ben Jonson, 'To the Readers', *Sejanus* (1605), π2b.
58 Thomas Davies, *Wits Bedlam* (1617), K2b; Jasper Mayne, *Jonsonus Virbius* (1638), 30.
59 Foakes, *Henslowe's Diary*, 96; 123; 124.
60 Henry Parrot, *The Mastive* (1615), E1b. Attribution is made in Mark Eccles, 'Jonson and the Spies', *RES*, 13 (1937), 385–97 (389).

61 Alexander Gill, 'Uppon Ben Jonsons Magnettick Ladye: Parturient Montes Nascetur', *Miscellany*, Bodleian Library, MS Ashmole 38, 15.

62 Richard Flecknoe, *Epigrams* (1671), 51, 49. See also Edmund Gayton, *Pleasant Notes upon Don Quixote* (1654), 272, who praises Jonson for 'possibility of plot, compasse of time, and fulnesse of wit'; and Abraham Wright, *Parnassus Biceps* (1656), 130, where Jonson is heralded as one whose 'Scene was free from monsters, no hard plot/Calld down a God t'untie the unlikely knot'.

63 See title-page of *Eastward Hoe* (1605); Thomas Middleton, *The Widdow* (1652), A2a. As early as 1821 J. C. wrote in 'Notices on Old English Comedies, No. 1, *Eastward Hoe*', *Blackwood's Magazine*, 10, 127–36 (136) that *Eastward Hoe* 'bears no marks of [Jonson's] peculiar excellencies or defects . . . the style of it bears more resemblance to that of Chapman . . . Probably Jonson first sketched the plan'; in Jonson, *Works*, ed. Herford and Simpson, 11:45, the editors claim of *Eastward Hoe* that 'the proportion of features, whether of invention or of technique, which can be called distinctive, is comparatively small'; they also believe that Jonson was not responsible for the 'strong simplicity' (38) of the plot of this play; they are more clear as to *The Widow*: 'In our opinion the play shows no sign of Jonson's hand' (x:339). Suzanne Gossett and W. David Kay in their introduction to Ben Jonson, *Eastward Ho!* for *The Cambridge Edition of the Works of Ben Jonson*, ed. David Bevington, Martin Butler, Ian Donaldson and David Gants (Cambridge: Cambridge University Press, forthcoming) suggest that most of the scenes in the play were worked on by more than one author, 'assuming that the men planned the play together (or perhaps agreed to work from one of 'Benjamin's' plots)'.

64 Thomas Middleton, *The Ant, and the Nightingale: or Father Hubburds Tales* (1604), A3a. This may be a specific dig at Anthony Munday; see Adrian Weiss' edition of the text in Thomas Middleton, *The Collected Works*, ed. Gary Taylor and John Lavagnino (Oxford: Clarendon Press, 2007), 165.

65 Thomas Nashe, *Have With You to Saffron-Walden* (1596), v3a.

66 Henry More, *The Immortality of the Soul* (1659), 491; William Bosworth, 'The story of Phaon and Sappho' in 'The Historie of Arcadius and Sepha' from *The Chast and Lost Lovers* (1653), 66.

67 R. P., *Choyce Drollery* (1656), 5; Francis Meres, *Palladis Tamia* (1598), 203b.

68 A point made by Philip J. Ayres in 'Anthony Munday: "Our Best Plotter"?', *English Language Notes*, 18 (1980), 13–15.

69 Ben Jonson, *A Pleasant Comedy, called: The Case is Alterd* (1609), A3a–b.

70 Robert Tailor, *The Hogge hath Lost his Pearle* (1614), B3a; Thomas Dekker and John Ford [Middleton?], *The Spanish Gipsie* (1653), D4b.

71 George Wither, *The Great Assises Holden in Parnassus by Apollo and his Assessours* (1645), 31.

72 George Villiers, Duke of Buckingham, *Poems on Affairs of State* (1697), o8b.

73 See George McFadden, 'Political Satire in "The Rehearsal"', *Yearbook of English Studies*, 4 (1974), 120–8 (121).

74 Dryden, *The Vindication*, 42. Of the other play he co-wrote with Lee, *The Duke of Guise*, he carefully detailed the amount of the text he had himself

created (ibid., 3): 'I shall not arrogate to my self the Merits of my Friend. *Two thirds* of it belong'd to *him*; and then to me only the *First Scene* in the Play; the whole *Fourth Act*, and the *first half*, or somewhat *more* of the *Fifth.*'

75 Peter W. M. Blayney, 'The Publication of Playbooks' in *A New History of Early English Drama*, ed. John D. Cox and David Scott Kastan (New York: Columbia University Press, 1997), 383–422 (399).

76 'To the Memory of the incomparable Paire of Authors, Beaumont and Fletcher' in Francis Beaumont, *Poems* (1653), A5b.

77 *The Thespian Dictionary* (1802), 17; Francis Beaumont and John Fletcher, *The Works . . . with Some Account of the Life and Writings of the Authors*, 7 vols. (1711), 1:xxvii.

78 W. S. [Thomas Middleton], *The Puritaine* (1607), E3a–b.

79 'Upon Mr Randolph's Poems, Collected and Published After his Death', in Randolph, *Poems*, **a.

80 Letter from Thomas Wilson to Robert Cecil, 31 March 1609, quoted in Ioppolo, *Dramatists and Their Manuscripts*, 219.

81 Philip Edwards, *A Book of Masques* (Cambridge: Cambridge University Press, 1967), 127; John Chamberlain, letter of 18 February 1612, in *The Letters*, ed. Norman Egbert McClure, 2 vols. (Philadelphia: American Philosophical Society, 1939), 1:425.

82 Record for 6 February 1633 in Bawcutt, *Control and Censorship*, 187.

83 John Ford, *The Lovers Melancholy* (1629), A4b; Thomas Nabbes, *Covent Garden* (1638), A3a.

84 John Clavell, *The So[l]ddered Citizen*, ed. J. H. P. Pafford and W. W. Greg (Oxford: Malone Society, 1936), 2; Leonard Digges, 'Upon Master William Shakespeare, the Deceased Author, and his Poems', prefixed to William Shakespeare, *Poems* (1640), A3b.

85 Ioppolo, *Dramatists and Their Manuscripts*, 19.

86 See Lee Goldberg and William Rabkin, *Successful Television Writing* (Hoboken, NJ: John Wiley and Sons, 2003), 55: 'You don't want to trust someone else's note-taking skills to capture . . . your idea . . . That is where the leave-behind, the written synopsis of your idea, comes in. Not the whole story, one page tops, three paragraphs with the beginning, middle, and end, like a jacket copy on a book.'

87 William Parkes, *The Curtaine-Drawer of the World* (1612), 5.

88 A suggestion raised by Honigmann, *Stability*, 46. W. W. Greg's suggestion that this list was added with a view to publication is threatened by the misnaming in the texts, *Dramatic Documents* 1:275.

89 W[alter] M[ountfort], *The Launching of the Mary*, ed. J. H. Walter (Oxford: Malone Society, 1933), vi; William Shakespeare, *Mr. William Shakespeares Comedies, Histories, & Tragedies* (1623), 84.

90 See Gary Taylor and John Lavagnino, eds., *Thomas Middleton and Early Modern Textual Culture* (Oxford: Clarendon Press, 2007), 51–2.

91 Middleton, *Puritaine*, E1a.

92 The observation that this and *Coriolanus*' 'Enter Martius Cursing' (TLN 525) may originate in author's plots was first made by Greg in *The Shakespeare First Folio*, 164.

93 Alan C. Dessen and Leslie Thomson, *A Dictionary of Stage Directions in English Drama, 1580–1642* (Cambridge: Cambridge University Press, 1999), 90. A plot might well retain features of the source from which it is copied – which could then work their way into a play's stage-directions. For instance, Alan Dessen in a discussion on the *Shaksper* website, October 2007, reveals that the word 'pulpit' occurs in no other stage-direction in his database save *Julius Caesar*'s '*Enter Brutus and goes into the Pulpit, and Cassius, with the Plebeians*' (TLN 1528–9), and that the word comes straight from North's *Plutarch*. Possibly 'pulpit' made its way from North to the plot, and from the plot to the stage-direction.

94 Peter Alexander, *Alexander's Introductions to Shakespeare* (London and Glasgow: Collins, 1964), 99. That this might originate in shared plots is suggested in Beaurline's fascinating introduction to William Shakespeare, *King John*, ed. L. A. Beaurline (Cambridge: Cambridge University Press, 1990), 207. See also the comparison of *Taming of A Shrew* and *Taming of the Shrew* in *The Works of Mr. William Shakespear*, ed. Alexander Pope and George Sewell, 10 vols. (1728), B3b: 'There is scarce a line of this the same with the present play, yet the Plot and Scenary scarce differ at all from it.'

95 For alternative discussions of these shared moments, see E. A. J. Honigmann, '*King John, The Troublesome Reigne*, and "documentary links"', *Shakespeare Quarterly*, 38 (1987), 124–6, and the rejoinder, Paul Werstine's '"Enter a Sheriffe" and the Conjuring up of Ghosts', *Shakespeare Quarterly*, 38 (1987), 126–30. E. A. J. Honigmann had already dismissed the idea that Shakespeare wrote to plots in his *Myriad Minded Shakespeare* (New York: St. Martin's Press, 1989), 192–4, and, perhaps as a consequence, neither consider plot bleed-through as a possible source.

96 Thomas Heywood, *Pleasant Dialogues and Dramma's* (1637), 249. This point is expanded on in I. A. Shapiro, 'Stenography and Bad Quartos', *TLS* (13 May 1960), 305.

2 PLAYBILLS AND TITLE-PAGES

1 See John Orrell, 'The London Stage in the Florentine Correspondence 1604–18', *Theatre Research International*, 3 (1977–8), 157–76 (171). Moseley's prefatory verses to Francis Beaumont and John Fletcher's *Comedies and Tragedies* (1647), F6a, casually make mention of the fact that 'after th'*Epilogue* there comes some one/To tell *Spectators* what shall next be shown'. An example of the audience changing the play performed during performance itself is given by Edmund Gayton, *Pleasant Notes upon Don Quixote* (1654), 271: 'I have known . . . at *Shrove-tide*, where the Players have been appointed, notwithstanding their bils to the contrary, to act what the major part of the company

had a mind to; sometimes *Tamerlane*, sometimes *Jugurth*, sometimes the Jew of *Malta*, and sometimes parts of all these.'

2 William Rankins refers to 'Drummes and Trumpets to cal menne to Plaies' in *The Mirrour of Monsters* (1587), c1b; John Stockwood asks 'Wyll not a fylthye playe, with the blast of a Trumpette, sooner call thither a thousande, than an 24 houres tolling of a Bell, bring to the Sermon a hundred?' in *A Sermon Preached at Paules Crosse on Barthelmew Day, being the 24. of August. 1578* (1578), 23; John Fielde refers to 'Those flagges of defiance against God, & trumpets yt are blown to gather together such company [to playhouses]' in *A Godly Exhortation* (1583), 4a. But a letter from Henry Hunsdon, Lord Chamberlain, to Sir Richard Martin, Lord Mayor, on October 8th 1594, promises that his company, if given permission to play in the Cross Keys Inn, 'will nott use anie Drumes or trumpettes att all for the calling of peopell together' – see W. W. Greg, ed., *Malone Society Collections: 1 part 1* (Oxford: Malone Society, 1907), 73. It may be that, as W. J. Lawrence conjectured in 'The Ceremony of the Drum and Trumpet' in *Old Theatre Days and Ways* (1935), 11–21, the drum and trumpet ceased to be used in London around the turn of the century. When on 6 February 1599 the Admirals' Men purchased 'a drome when to go into the contry' that indicates they did not have one for London use, see Philip Henslowe, *Henslowe's Diary*, ed. R. A. Foakes (Cambridge: Cambridge University Press, 2002), 130. Drums and trumpets were, however, associated with country performance throughout the early modern period and later: Samuel Ward, *The Life of Faith in Death* (1622), 47–8 writes, 'Were it . . . but a company of Players, riding through a Market, A Drum, a Trumpet, or the least call would serve . . . to draw us out to the sight'; John Rowe, *Tragi-Comaedia. Being a Brief Relation of the Strange, and Wonderfull hand of God discovered at Witny, in the Comedy Acted there February the third, where there were some Slaine, many Hurt, with severall other Remarkable Passages* (1653), [¶ 4b] records, 'About seaven a Clock at Night they caused a Drum to beat, and a trumpet to be sounded to gather the People together. The people flocked in great multitudes, . . . and the Chamber where the Play was Acted being full, others in the Yard pressed sorely to get in.' Tate Wilkinson in *Memoirs of his Own Life*, 4 vols. (1790), III:130, records how a Lincolnshire company of players determined while at Grantham to omit the drum and trumpet ceremony, but the Marquis of Granby rebuked their manager: 'my good friend, why are you all so suddenly offended at and averse to the noble sound of a drum? – I like it, and all the inhabitants like it: Put my name on your play-bill, provided you drum, *but not otherwise.*'

3 Henry Fitzgeffrey, *Certain Elegies* (1618), D6a.

4 Reproduced in Eleanore Boswell, 'A Playbill of 1687', *The Library*, 4th series, II (1931), 499–502 (501).

5 W. J. Lawrence, *The Elizabethan Playhouse and Other Studies*, 2nd series (Stratford-upon-Avon: Shakespeare Head Press, 1913), 57–91. Lawrence's misleading title may account for E. K. Chambers' failure to assimilate the

evidence provided. Karl J. Holzknecht, 'Theatrical Billposting in the Age of Elizabeth', *Philological Quarterly*, 2 (1923), 267–81.

6 The Spanish bill is described by Hugo Albert Rennert, *The Spanish Stage* (New York: Hispanic Society of America, 1909), 133, who also records the existence of two fragments of Spanish bills probably dating from 1637. The French bill, for Théophile de Scudéry's *Ligdamon et Lidias* (1629), is now housed in the Bibliothèque de l'Arsenal in Paris. The German bill, for a strolling English performance of *Love's Sweetness turned into Deaths Bitterness* in 1628, is reproduced in Albert Cohn, *Shakespeare in Germany* (London: Asher & Co., 1865), as plate 2 (preceding p. 1). That it may be fake is raised by R. A. Foakes, 'The Image of the Swan Theatre' in *Spectacle and Image in the Renaissance*, ed. André Lascombes (Leiden: Brill, 1993), 350.

7 'How a mery man devised to cal people to a playe', jest 15 in *Mery Tales, Wittie Questions, and Quicke Answeres* (1567), J2b.

8 Marjorie Plant, *The English Book Trade* (London: George Allen & Unwin Ltd, 1965), 248. Paul J. Voss, 'Books for Sale: Advertising and Patronage in Late Elizabethan England', *Sixteenth Century Journal*, 29 (1998), 733–57 (735).

9 For the wide spread of libel bills even earlier – on posts around medieval London – see Wendy Scase, ' "Strange and Wonderful Bills": Bill-Casting and Political Discourse in Late Medieval England', *New Medieval Literatures*, 2 (1998), 225–47.

10 George Gerrard, February 1636/7, in Thomas Wentworth, Earl of Strafford, *Letters and Dispatches*, ed. William Knowler, 2 vols. (1739), II:56. See also the letter from Robert Some VC and Heads to Lord Burghley, Chancellor, of 18 September 1592, in Alan H. Nelson, ed., *Records of Early English Drama: Cambridge* (Toronto: University of Toronto Press, 1989), 1:340: 'by reason of the rifenes of the plague . . . wee sent A warrant . . . to inhibite certaine Players . . . How slightly that warrant was regarded . . . appeared by theire bills sett up upon our Colledge gates, and by theire playeinge in Chesterton.' In [John Marston's?] *Histriomastix* (1610), F2a, an actor enters 'setting uppe billes' indicating that the players are ready to perform; in Thomas Lodge, *Lady Alimony* (1659), A3a, Timon asks 'were our Bills poasted, that our House may be with a numerous Auditory stored'. Indeed, the last reference of the strolling English players who performed in the Northern Netherlands during the interregnum is that in October 1656 they posted handbills on the city gates of Dordrecht with information about their plays; see J. G. Riewald, 'New Light on the English Actors in the Netherlands, *c.* 1590–1660', *English Studies*, 41 (1960), 65–92 (91).

11 Edward Arber, *A Transcript of the Registers of the Company of Stationers of London* (1875–84), II:477. For this entire section I am grateful for the help of Peter Blayney.

12 'The Printer to the Reader' in John Lyly's *Endimion* (1591), A2a.

13 W. W. Greg and E. Boswell, *Records of the Court . . . 1576 to 1602 from Register B* (London: Bibliographical Society, 1930), 46.

14 Arber, *Transcript*, 11:652, 'plaies' corrected to 'plaiirs' by Peter Blayney, private correspondence.

15 *An Abstract of his Majesties Letters patent, granted unto Roger Wood and Thos Symcocke, for the sole printing of paper and Parchment on the one side* (1620).

16 John Chamberlain, letter of 28 October 1620 in *The Letters of John Chamberlain*, ed. Norman Egbert McClure (Philadelphia: American Philosophical Society, 1939), 11:323.

17 *To the Right Honourable the House of Commons assembled in Parliament. The Humble Petition of Thomas Man, Humfrey Lownes. . . William Jaggard . . . with Many Others* (1621).

18 Arber, *Transcript*, IV:182.

19 Taken from W. W. Greg, *The Shakespeare First Folio: Its Bibliographical and Textual History* (Oxford: Clarendon Press, 1955), 22–3. Greg here corrects some of the errors regarding playbills in Edwin E. Willoughby, *A Printer of Shakespeare* (London: Philip Allan & Co., 1934).

20 Henslowe's *Diaries* provide no clear reference to paying the playbill-printers – so it is not possible to use them to confirm this assumption.

21 An incomplete study of the ornaments owned by Charlewood, Roberts, Jaggard and Cotes has not, so far, revealed 'signs' for all the theatres – but it is, of course, possible that special fixed templates were used for playbills.

22 'Houmour of a mourning widow consider'd' in *Miscellany*, Bodleian Library, MS Rawl. Poet 152, 74a.

23 George Hakewill, *An Apologie of the Power and Providence of God* (1627), 320.

24 BL C 18 e 2/74, real size 5 13/16 by 7 ½ inches. Reproduced in William Van Lennep, 'Some English Playbills', *Harvard Library Bulletin*, 8:2 (1954), 235–41 (239). Printer identified wrongly as Jaggard by F. S. Ferguson in that same article, and as Cotes by P. W. Blayney in private correspondence.

25 This 'Wine Street' performance was presumably to take place in the theatre of that name in Bristol, thought, until now, to have ceased operating in around 1625 – see Siobhan Keenan, *Travelling Players in Shakespeare's England* (London: Palgrave Macmillan, 2002), 144–51. The Bristol Wine Street theatre must in fact have still been a performance venue after 1627, the date when Cotes started printing bills.

26 Théophile de Scudéry, *Ligdamon et Lidias* (1629); reproduced in W. J. Lawrence, 'The World's Oldest Playbills' in *The Stage Year Book*, ed. L. Carson (London: 'The Stage' Offices, 1920), 23–30.

27 Plate 2 (preceding p. 1) in Cohn, *Shakespeare in Germany*.

28 For a reference to a French bill of 1599 in which the clown was a major lure, see W. L. Wiley, *The Early Public Theatre in France* (Cambridge, MA: Harvard University Press, 1960), 219, who writes of an agreement drawn between Bonoist Petit and Valleran le Conte on 4 January 1599. Petit demanded Valleran's assurance that he would perform; otherwise, 'the said Petit will not be able in any way to name the said Valleran in the posters that will be put up'.

29 The bill is part of the collection of papers left by the great actor Edward Alleyn to Dulwich College, and is kept with the advertisement of a prize

shooting that *is* printed. W. W. Greg, ed., *Henslowe Papers* (London: A. H. Bullen, 1907), 106. It is reproduced in Jonathan Bate and Russell Jackson, eds., *The Oxford Illustrated History of Shakespeare on Stage* (Oxford: Oxford University Press, 1996), 3.

30 Lawrence, *Elizabethan Playhouse*, 61.

31 John Taylor, 'Taylors Water-Worke' in *All the Workes of John Taylor the Water-Poet* (1630), 24.

32 Greg, *Henslowe Papers*, 71.

33 John Chamberlain, letter of 19 November 1602, in *The Letters*, 1:172.

34 John Northbrooke, *A Treastise wherein Dicing, Dauncing, Vaine plaies . . . are reproved . . .* (1579), 36a.

35 Letter from a soldier to Secretary Sir Francis Walsingham, 25 January 1586/7, from Harl. MS 286 in E. K. Chambers, *The Elizabethan Stage* (Oxford: Clarendon Press, 1923), IV:303–4.

36 John Taylor, 'Wit and Mirth' in *All the Workes*, 11:183.

37 And, of course, literacy was itself determined by the ability to spell out words, not necessarily the ability to read easily or to write: the prologue-speaker in William Davenant, *The Platonick Lovers* (1636), A3a, fears that 'his Title was so hard,/'Bove halfe our Citty audience would be lost,/That knew not how to spell it on the Post', actually showing how often a title was pieced together gingerly from the advertisements; the old lady in Richard Brome's topsy-turvey *Antipodes* (1640), H1b, wants to follow bear-baitings but she is so near-sighted, argues the maid, she can 'scarce/Spell out their Bills with spectacles'.

38 Robert Chamberlain, *Jocabella* (1640), B11b–B12a.

39 George Wither, *Abuses* (1614), O4b.

40 George Silver, *Paradoxes of Defence* (1599), 66.

41 John Taylor, 'Taylors Revenge' in *All the Workes*, 11:143.

42 Ibid.

43 Ibid., 11:145: 'One swears and stormes, another laughs & smiles,/Another madly would pluck off the tiles./ . . . One valiantly stept out upon the Stage,/And would teare downe the hangings in his rage . . .'

44 Ibid., 11:147. Fennor's response – see 'Fennors Defence' in John Taylor, *All the Workes* – that he himself had once been placed in the same situation but had handled it better, provides more information about advertising challenges. Fennor had challenged Kendall the actor to a battle of wits on the Fortune stage and 'to the world did publish printed Bills,/With promise that we both would shew our skills' (11:151). Kendall had not shown up – but Fennor had simply entertained the audience with his extemporal wit. 'Kendall' is probably William Kendall, a member of the Admiral's Men in the 1590s. See Edwin Nungezer, *A Dictionary of Actors* (New Haven: Yale University Press, 1929), 223–4. Alternatively he may be Timothy Kendall, a university-educated wit. See Michelle O'Callaghan, *The English Wits: Literature and Sociability in Early Modern England* (Cambridge: Cambridge University Press, 2007), 111.

45 See Tiffany Stern, *Rehearsal from Shakespeare to Sheridan* (Oxford: Clarendon Press, 2000), 115.

46 Charles Welch, 'The City Printers', *Transactions of the Bibliographical Society*, 14 (1918), 175–241 (179).

47 Nicholas Breton, *Fantasticks: Serving for a Perpetuall Prognostication* (1626), E4b, F1a. cf. Letter from a soldier in 1586/7 in Chambers, *Elizabethan Stage*, IV:303, who draws attention to the fact that 'every day in the weake the players billes are sett upp'. Even as early as 1563–4 Edmund Grindall, Bishop of London, writes to Sir William Cecil that 'common players, . . . now daily, but specially on holy-days, set up bills, whereunto the youth resorteth excessively, and there taketh infection' – see *The Remains of Edmund Grindall D. D.*, ed. William Nicholson for the Parker Society (Cambridge: Cambridge University Press, 1843), 269.

48 John Marston, *Scourge of Villanie* (1598), B2a. See also James Shirley, *Poems* (1646), 42.

49 John Taylor, 'A Kicksey Winsey' in *All the Works*, II:40. That notices continued to be posted for perusal while pissing is confirmed by later references. Richard Leigh in *The Transproser Rehears'd* (1673), I, refers to the 'Author of most of those ingenious Labours which curious Readers admire at Pissing times in their passage between White-hall and Temple-bar'.

50 James Shirley, *The Cardinal* in *Six New Playes* (1652), B8a; John Spencer, καινα και παλαια: *Things New and Old* (1658), 105.

51 Aston Cokain, *The Obstinate Lady* (1657), 41.

52 Richard Flecknoe, *Miscellania* (1653), 141. See also John Stephens, *New Essays and Characters* (1631), 20: I shall but . . ./. . . repeate things mention'd long before/Nay things prefixt upon each Play-house doore'; [Marston?], *Histriomastix*, E4b: 'it is as dangerous to read his name at a playe-dore, As a printed bil on a plague dore'.

53 See, for instance, Edward Guilpin, *Skialetheia* (1598), A3a–b: 'every paper-clothed post in Poules,/To thee (*Deloney*) mourningly doth speake . . .'

54 Benjamin Rudyerd, *Le Prince d'Amour, or the Prince of Love* (1660), 80 (the 'Prince d'amour' was a principal personage in the Revels performed at Christmas in the Middle Temple); Silver, *Paradoxes*, 66.

55 Thomas Nashe, *Pasquill, of England, Cavaliero* (1589), D3b; Samuel Pepys, *The Diary of Samuel Pepys*, ed. Robert Latham and William Matthews (London: G. Bell and Sons Ltd, 1970–83), VII:420–1.

56 Quoted in Chambers, *Elizabethan Stage*, IV:283.

57 Robert Heath, *Clarastella* (1650), 36. The Spanish, similarly, had a habit of posting playbills for *comedias* on the corners of houses. See N. D. Shergold, *A History of the Spanish Stage* (Oxford: Clarendon Press, 1967), 514. For general bills on doors, see Thomas Hall, *The Loathsomeness of Long Hair* (1654), 108: 'Now many professe openly their inward uncleannesse by laying open to the common view, their naked Breasts, as though it were a bill affixed to the doore-posts, to signifie to the passers by, that within that place dwells an uncleane heart.'

58 Rankins, *Mirrour of Monsters*, ciia. The same is also said of Dublin in Ireland when Shirley writes his prologue to 'Another of Master Fletcher's Playes' there, see Shirley, *Poems*, 42.

59 Richard Brathwait, *Anniversaries upon his Panarete, continued* (1635), A6b. It was wise to get a servant to collect playbills rather than simply gather information from them. Sir Edmond Mundeford found this out to his cost when he sent a man to find out what was being played. 'The Virgin Martyr was upon the Post, which the Fellow rashly Apprehending, brought his Master up word, it was the Play of the Virgin Mary', Nicholas Le Strange, *Merry Passages and Jeasts: A Manuscript Jestbook of Sir Nicholas Le Strange*, ed. James Hogg (Salzburg: Institut für Englische Sprache und Literatur, 1974), 134.

60 Richard Brathwait, *The English Gentlewoman* (1631) [revised in *Times Treasury*, 1652], 53. See also Richard Brathwait, *Astraea's Teares* (1641), B6a–b: 'while their Ladies care/extended to a *Play bill*, a Caroach,/A compleat Usher, or Postillion Coach'.

61 Ben Jonson, *The Divell is an Asse* in *Bartholmew Fayre* (1631), O2b.

62 Silver, *Paradoxes*, 67.

63 Richard Brathwait, *Ar't Asleepe Husband?* (1640), 163.

64 Randle Cotgrave, *A Dictionarie of the French and English Tongues* (1611), 3Q1b.

65 John Fletcher and Philip Massinger, *The Little French Lawyer* in Beaumont and Fletcher, *Comedies and Tragedies*, H2a; John Taylor, 'The Fearefull Summer' in *All the Workes*, 1:60; Thomas Nashe, *Pierce Penilesse* (1592), D4a; Edmond Willis, *An Abreviation of Writing by Character* (1618), A3a–b.

66 Barten Holyday, *Technogamia* (1618), C2a. See also Joseph Hall, *Virgidemiarum* (1597), 39: 'Saw'st thou ever *Siquis* patch'd on *Pauls* Church dore,/ To seeke some vacant Vicarage before?' Thomas Dekker in his *Guls Horne-Booke* (1609), D3a, advises a country gentleman coming to St Paul's Cathedral not to 'cast an eye to Si-quis doore (pasted and plaistered up with serving-mens supplications)'; it is on this door – the church door in the left side aisle – that Shift in Ben Jonson's *Every Man Out* posts mock bills.

67 The picture, which comes from Joos de Damhouder's *Praxis Rerum Criminalious* (Antwerp, 1562), 398, is reproduced as plate 13 of Adam Fox's *Oral and Literate Culture in England 1500–1700* (Oxford: Clarendon Press, 2000). For other bills on doors see ibid., 38, where a Durham man in 1607 has rhymes placed above his door; 302, where a Coventry man is libelled on 'diverse and sundry doors, walls and posts to the intente that the same might be made knowne unto all mannor of persones whatsoever'; 305, where, in 1574, a group in Rye, Sussex 'affixe upon diverse men's dores certeine infamous libels and scrolls containing dishonest reproche'. See also pp. 314, 317. Other places for libels in country towns and cities include roadside posts (in 1609 one of the gamekeepers of the Earl of Pembroke set up his libels 'on the top of a post of certain rails' that adjoined the highway where they could be 'seen and redd by all passengers that way'), also whipping posts (in 1619 Lancashire tenants attached a libel to the whipping post 'standing in the most publicke place of . . . Newton'), see ibid., 315–16.

68 Ibid., 316.

69 Statutes of the Realm, 32 Henry VIII *c.*14, quoted in Holzknecht, 'Theatrical Billposting', 269.

70 Fox, *Oral,* 45; Wentworth, *Letters and Dispatches,* 1:175; Paul L. Hughes and James F. Larkin, eds., *Tudor Royal Proclamations* (New Haven and London: Yale University Press, 1969), 11:546.

71 Marjorie Plant writes, without referencing her source, that 'the title-page came to be nailed up on the whipping-posts in the streets, on the pillars in St. Paul's, and on the walls of the Inns of Courts', *English Book Trade,* 248.

72 Ben Jonson, *Epigrammes* in *The Workes* (1616), 770.

73 Henry Parrot, *The Mastive* (1615), A4b. See also John Eliot, *Poems* (1658), 10–11: 'If you . . . set to view/The Title of this Book on any Post,/I wish your expectation may be lost;/For common things . . . Are only fit for th'vulgar sort to buy.' See also Hall, *Virgidemiarum,* 63, who disdains 'Maevios' because his poetry is 'Nayl'd to an hundreth postes for noveltie,/With his big title, and Italian mott'; Thomas Campion, *Observations in the Art of English Poesie* (1602), A4b: 'Whether thus hasts my little booke so fast? . . . to stand/With one leafe like a riders cloke put up/To catch a Termer?'

74 Robert Fludd, *Answer unto M. Foster, or, The Squesing of Parson Fosters Sponge* (1631), A3b.

75 Further confirmation comes from John Davies of Hereford, *A Scourge for Paper-Persecuters* (1625), 5: 'infant-Rimers . . . pester Postes with Titles of new bookes'.

76 Nathan Field, *The Honest Man's Fortune* (1647), 90–2; John Downame, *The Account Audited* (1649), A2a.

77 A. H., *A Continued Inquisition against Paper-Persecutors* (1625), 1.

78 R. B. McKerrow, 'Booksellers, Printers, and the Stationers' Trade' in *Shakespeare's England* (Oxford: Clarendon Press, 1916), 11:212–39 (231).

79 Thomas Nashe, *Terrors of the Night* (1594), A4a. Peter W. M. Blayney, 'The Publication of Playbooks' in *A New History of Early English Drama,* ed. John D. Cox and David Scott Kastan (New York: Columbia University Press, 1997), 383–422, points out that naming a particular shop for purchase is more useful to the buyer of wholesale books than to the retail purchaser (390). Yet Nashe's confirmation that the name of the seller registered when reading title-page advertisements suggests that passers-by might also consider buying from the wholeseller's shop (it is, of course, also possible that retail sellers added to title-leaves the names of other places in which books could be bought).

80 Heath, *Clarastella,* 36.

81 Andrew Marvell, *The Rehearsall Transpros'd: the Second Part* (1673), reproduced in Andrew Marvell, *The Rehearsal Transpros'd,* ed. D. I. B. Smith (Oxford: Clarendon Press, 1971), 167.

82 T. B., *The Rebellion of Naples, or The Tragedy of Massenello* (1649), A3b.

83 Henry Peacham, *The Worth of a Peny* (1647), 3. See also Lodge, *Lady Alimony,* A3b: Trillo: 'The Title of your new Play, Sir?' Tim: 'Every Poast may sufficiently inform you'; and Richard Brathwait, *The Two Lancashire Lovers*

(1640), 196, where man's tragedy is that his 'Playbill beares no better style then A Comedy of Errors'.

84 Peter Heylin, *Observations on the Historie of the Reign of King Charles* (1656), 244.

85 *Perfect Occurrences* (3 February 1647/8), 402. This kind of advertising may have become more popular during the interregnum when plays had to be mounted in secret.

86 Letter from a soldier in 1586/7, reproduced in Chambers, *Elizabethan Stage*, IV:303–4.

87 See Alan B. Farmer and Zachary Lesser, 'Vile Arts: The Marketing of English Printed Drama, 1512–1660' in *Research Opportunities in Renaissance Drama*, 39 (2000), 77–109.

88 Wither[s], *Abuses*, o4b.

89 *A Warning for Faire Women* (1599), A3a.

90 Other printed plays of the period that do not name genre on their title-pages include Thomas Lodge, *A Looking Glasse for London and England* (1594), John Lyly, *Mother Bombie* (1594), John Lyly, *The Woman in the Moone* (1597).

91 Shirley, *Cardinal*, A4a.

92 Printed plays of around that year that do not name genre on their title-pages include John Denham's *The Sophy* (1642) and John Taylor's *A Pedlar and a Romish Priest* (1641).

93 Lodowick Carlell, *Arviragus and Philicia* (1639), A3a; Henry Peacham, *The Truth of Our Times* (1638), 90. See also Sir Samuel Tuke, *The Adventures of Five Hours* (1663), A1a, in which '*The Prologue Enters with a Playbill in his hand, and Reads,* This Day being the 15th of *December,* shall be Acted a New Play, never Plai'd before, call'd The *Adventures of Five Hours.*'

94 Thomas Campion, *The Third and Fourth Booke of Ayres* (1617), C1a.

95 For examples of readers demanding new books, see H. S. Bennett, *English Books and Readers 1558–1603* (Cambridge: Cambridge University Press, 1965), 263, 269. For continued interest in novelty as a selling-point in the early modern booktrade see his *English Books and Readers 1603–1640* (Cambridge: Cambridge University Press, 1970), 217–18.

96 John Dryden, *The Letters*, ed. Charles E. Ward (Durham, NC: Duke University Press, 1942), 113.

97 [Marston?], *Histriomastix*, E4b.

98 William Habington, *The Poems*, ed. Kenneth Allott (London: Hodder and Stoughton, 1948), 150. See also *Perfect Occurrences* (6 October 1647), for an account which seems to transcribe the playbill of a play stopped during the interregnum: 'A Stage-Play was to have been acted in Salisbury Court this day (& Bills stuck up about it) called A King and no King, formerly acted at the Black-Fryers, by his Majesties servants, about 8. yeares since, written by Francis Beaumont and John Fletcher.' A prologue written for a performance of *The Tamer Tamed* [*Woman's Prize*] on 24 June 1660, reproduced in Thomas Jordan, *A Nursery of Novelties* (1665), 20, gives Fletcher's name at least in performance, and almost certainly on the bill too. The Prologue

enters reading the bill and wondering, 'The Tamer Tam'd, what do the Players mean?'; then, still examining the bill, he explains, 'This Play, the Tamer tam'd, is Fletchers wit,/A man that pleas'd all pallats.'

99 Henry Glapthorne, *The Ladies Priviledge* (1640), A3b; Henry Moody, 'TO THE INGENIOUS AUTHOR MASTER PHILIP MASSINGER' in Philip Massinger, *A New Way to Pay Old Debts* (1633), A3a.

100 See David Scott Kastan, *Shakespeare and the Book* (Cambridge: Cambridge University Press, 2001), 31–5.

101 For the fashion in playbooks, see Farmer and Lesser, 'Vile Arts'.

102 G. E. Bentley, *The Jacobean and Caroline Stage* (Oxford: Clarendon Press, 1941–68), v:1455–6. The bill hung on the gate of the White Horse Inn, Norwich, in April 1624.

103 Thomas Overbury, *A Wife now the Widdow of Sir Tho: Overburye* (1614), A2a.

104 Henry Fitzgeffrey, *Satyres and Satyricall Epigrams* (1617), E7a–b.

105 Reproduced in William Van Lennep, 'The Earliest Known English Playbill', *Harvard Library Bulletin*, 1:3 (1947), 382–5, who also provides the bill's interregnum date. George Speaight, *The History of the Puppet Theatre* (London: George B. Harrap & Co, 1955), 152, however, redates the bill at *c.* 1700.

106 See for instance John Feeman's *A Sermon Preached Without a Text* (1643) which claims, A2b, to have a title that is 'none of mine; it had its Originall from the . . . Printers capricious conceit . . . I had no acquaintance with it, till I met it in the front of the Printed Copies'.

107 See William Shakespeare, *The Merchant of Venice*, ed. J. R. Brown (London: Methuen, 1955), xi, and William Shakespeare, *The Merchant of Venice*, ed. Jay L. Halio (Oxford: Oxford University Press, 1993), 85, in which the title-page is confined to the textual introductions; and William Shakespeare, *The Merchant of Venice*, ed. M. M. Mahood (Cambridge: Cambridge University Press, 1987), 181, in which the title-page is in the textual analysis provided after the end of the play itself. No editor provides the title-page anywhere near the title.

3 'ARGUMENTS' IN PLAYHOUSE AND BOOK

1 William Rowley, *A Tragedy called All's Lost by Lust* (1633), The Argument, A2a; Samuel Brandon, *The Tragicomoedi of the Vertuous Octavia* (1598), The Argument, A4a.

2 M. van Rossum-Steenbeek, *Greek Readers' Digests? Studies on a Selection of Subliterary Papyri* (Leiden: Brill, 1997).

3 Joseph Lowenstein, *Ben Jonson and Possessive Authorship* (Cambridge: Cambridge University Press, 2002), 201; M. J. Kidnie in her edition of Ben Jonson's *The Devil is an Ass and Other Plays* (Oxford: Oxford University Press, 2000), 332.

4 J. Rusten, 'Dicaearchus and the Tales from Euripides', *Greek, Roman and Byzantine Studies*, 23 (1982), 357–67 (358); Henry Turner, *The English Renaissance Stage* (Oxford: Oxford University Press, 2006), 225.

5 Thomas Heywood, *The Fair Maid of the West* (1631), A4a.

6 Roger Pooley, '"I Confesse it to be a Mere Toy": How to Read the Preliminary Matter to Renaissance Fiction' in *Critical Approaches to English Prose Fiction 1520–1640*, ed. Donald Beecher (Ottawa, Canada: Dovehouse Editions Inc., 1998), 110.

7 For Genette, the 'peritext' are the texts that frame the printed book and the epitext are the texts or discourses outside the book that relate to it; together peritext and epitext form 'paratext' – though latterly 'paratext' has taken over from 'peritext' as a descriptive term for front matter. See Gérard Genette, *Paratexts: Thresholds of Interpretation*, trans. Jane E. Lewin, foreword by Richard Macksey (Cambridge: Cambridge University Press, 1997), 4–5.

8 See, in particular, David M. Bergeron, 'Stuart Civic Pageants and Textual Performance', *Renaissance Quarterly*, 51 (1998), 163–83; and David M. Bergeron, *English Civic Pageantry, 1558–1642* (Tempe, AZ: Arizona Center for Medieval and Renaissance Studies, 2003); Evelyn Tribble, *Margins and Marginality* (Charlottesville: University Press of Virginia, 1993); Wendy Wall, *The Imprint of Gender* (Ithaca, NY and London: Cornell University Press, 1993).

9 For the Spanish *relación* see N. D. Shergold, *A History of the Spanish Stage* (Oxford: Clarendon Press, 1967), 254, 268. A collection of French *ballets* were gathered together and printed in 1612 as *Recueil des plus excellents ballets de ce temps*; see W. J. Lawrence, 'Early Programmes', *The Stage* (27 July 1933), 16; a later *ballet* was sent from Paris by Perwich to Sir Joseph Williamson on 25 October 1679: 'By the enclosed you see the severall entries and manner of the Balet; between every one Haines had order to dance by himselfe,' quoted in William Perwich, *The Despatches of William Perwich, English Agent in Paris, 1669–1677*, ed. M. Beryl Curran (London: Royal Historical Society, 1903), 116. Italian printed *argomenti* (often only a sheet in length) survive in some numbers; see Julie Stone Peters, *Theatre of the Book* (Oxford: Oxford University Press, 2000), 343; a *perioche* for the Play of the Dance of Death performed by Jesuits in Ingolstadt in 1606 is reproduced in George W. Brandt, ed., *German and Dutch Theatre, 1600–1848* (Cambridge: Cambridge University Press, 1993); for English *argomenti* to accompany Latin Jesuit plays performed by the exiled English Catholic community, see Suzanne Gossett, 'Drama in the English College, Rome, 1591–1660', *ELR*, 3 (1973), 60–93 (72). The idea that the audience in England might sometimes receive 'arguments' is mentioned in passing by Dieter Mehl in *The Elizabethan Dumb Show* (London and New York: Methuen, 1964), 11, and is discussed in William Martin, 'An Elizabethan Theatre Programme', *The Selborne Magazine*, 24 (1913), 16–20.

10 For the resonant and wide range of uses for the word 'plot' at the time, see Martin Brückner and Kristen Poole, 'The Plot Thickens: Surveying Manuals, Drama, and the Materiality of Narrative Form in Early Modern England', *ELH*, 69 (2002), 617–48.

11 Ben Jonson, *Loves Triumph* (1631), A2a.
12 John Ford, *The Lovers Melancholy* (1629), H1a. Misidentified as a backstage-plot in John Ford, *The Lover's Melancholy*, ed. R. F. Hill (Manchester: Manchester University Press, 1985), 108.
13 Thomas Middleton and James Shirley, *No Wit/Help like a Womans* (1657), 92.
14 James Shirley, *The Constant Maid* (1640), G4b.
15 Thomas Middleton, *Women Beware Women* in *Two New Playes* (1657), 189–90. J. R. Mulryne calls this 'a rather unusual use of plot' in his edition of Thomas Middleton's *Women Beware Women* (London: Methuen, 1977), 145, having difficulty reconciling this depiction with what he knows of backstage-plots.
16 Middleton, *Women Beware Women* (1657), 191, 193.
17 Robert White, *Cupids Banishment. A Maske Presented To Her Majesty by Younge Gentlewomen of the Ladies Hall in Deptford at Greenwich the 4th of May 1617* (contemporary copy on vellum, presented to Lucy, Countess of Bedford), Pierpont Morgan Library MS MA 1296, transcribed in S. P. Cerasano and Marion Wynne-Davies, eds., *Renaissance Drama by Women* (London and New York: Routledge, 1995), 82–9; *Vertumnus: The yeare about. as it was acted and plaide at oxeford before the Kings and Queenes Majesties, the Prince and Nobilitie, devised and written by Doctor Gwinne*, Inner Temple Library, Petyt MS 538, vol. 43 ff. 293r–v, quoted in John R. Elliott and Alan H. Nelson, eds., *Records of Early English Drama: Oxford* (Toronto: University of Toronto Press, 2004), 1:310. Edward Sherburn is quoted in Ben Jonson, *The Works of Benjamin Jonson*, ed. C. H. Herford, P. Simpson and E. Simpson (Oxford: Clarendon Press, 1925–52), x:574. As a presentation manuscript for that masque in its entirety survives, however, and as Milton at some stage read the masque (which influenced *Comus*), it is possible that an entire copy was enclosed in the letter: see ibid., vi:475.
18 Discussed in Gerard Eades Bentley, *The Jacobean and Caroline Stage* (Oxford: Clarendon Press, 1941–68), v:1231. See Erica Veevers, 'A Masque Fragment by Aurelian Townshend', *Notes and Queries*, 12 (1965), 343–5 (345).
19 Ben Jonson, *Neptunes Triumph for the Returne of Albion* (1624), A2b. In the event the masque was not performed.
20 John Day, *The Knave in Graine, New Vampt* (1640), L4a–b.
21 Ibid., L4b.
22 Thomas Kyd, *The Spanish Tragedie* (1592), K4a–b.
23 Ibid., L1a.
24 *Register of all the noble men of England*, Houghton Library, MS Eng 1285. The plot is discussed in Arthur Freeman, 'The Argument of Meleager', *English Literary Renaissance*, 1 (1971), 122–31.
25 Reproduced in W. W. Greg, *Dramatic Documents from the Elizabethan Playhouses* (Oxford: Clarendon Press, 1931), ii:viii.
26 Richard Vennar[d], *An Apology* (1614), 24.
27 John Chamberlain, *The Letters of John Chamberlain*, ed. Norman Egbert McClure (Philadelphia: American Philosophical Society, 1939), 1:172

[19 November 1602]; John Manningham, November 1602, in *The Diary of John Manningham of the Middle Temple, 1602–3*, ed. Robert Parker Sorlien (Hanover, NH: Published for the University of Rhode Island by the University Press of New England, 1976), 123; Vennar[d], *Apology*, 24.

28 Ben Jonson, *Masque of Augures* (1621), A3b–A4a.

29 *The Plot of the Play, called Englands Joy. To be Playd at the Swan this 6 of November. 1602* (1602).

30 Herbert Berry, 'Richard Vennar, "England's Joy"', *English Literary Renaissance*, 31 (2001), 240–65.

31 Fennor did actually stage *England's Joy* in 1615, as is recorded by John Taylor in *All the Workes of John Taylor the Water-Poet* (1630), 159: 'Thou [Fennor] set'st the people in a rage/In playing Englands joy, that every Man/Did judge it worse then that was done at Swan', and by Richard Brathwait, who, in *A Strappado for the Divell* (1615), 185, refers to the prohibitively expensive nature of 'that same toy . . . Fenners Englands joy'.

32 Charles Fitz-geffry, *Sir Frances Drake* (1596), B8b.

33 John Vicars, *Epigrams of that Most Wittie and Worthie Epigrammatist Mr. John Owen* (1619), D2b. The original epigrams were published in 1606 as John Owen, *Epigrammatum Libri tres autore Joanne Owen*.

34 George Villiers, Duke of Buckingham, Samuel Butler, Thomas Sprat and Martin Clifford, *The Rehearsal* (1672), 8.

35 Samuel Johnson, *Lives of the English Poets*, ed. George Birkbeck Hill (Oxford: Clarendon Press, 1905), 1:336–7: '*The Indian Emperor* . . . [was] intended for a sequel to Howard's *Indian Queen*. Of this connection notice was given to the audience by printed bills, distributed at the door; an expedient supposed to be ridiculed in *The Rehearsal*, where Bayes tells how many reams he has printed, to instil into the audience some conception of his plot.' The possibility is raised and dismissed in D. E. L. Crane's edition of George Villiers, Duke of Buckingham, *The Rehearsal* (Durham: University of Durham Press, 1976), 83.

36 John Breval, *The Play is the Plot* (1718), 55.

37 'Prince de la Grange, Lord Lieutenant of Lincoln's Inn', Εγχυχλοχορεία (1662), 3.

38 David Gowen, 'Studies in the History and Function of the British Theatre Playbill and Programme, 1564–1914' (unpublished D.Phil. thesis, University of Oxford, 1998), 42, indicates that the masque was given to members of the audience without charge, and that the publication of the document was funded by Motteaux himself.

39 *Wernerus Martyr* (1630), Folger Shakespeare Library, MS v.a.305.

40 My thanks to Alastair Blanshard for this translation from the Latin, and to Max Lieberman for confirming that the content of the German plot is the same.

41 Benjamin Griffin's description of the advantages of the Argument before the printed play of *Gorboduc*, in *Playing the Past* (Woodbridge, Suffolk: D. S. Brewer, 2001), 81.

42 *Wernerus Martyr*, A4a.

43 George Chapman, *The Memorable Maske of the two Honorable Houses or Inns of Court* (1613?), 'The aplicable argument of *the Maske*', A4a; 'The Argument' to Robert Baron, *Mirza* (1647), A8a.

44 Latin plot summaries together with a selection of 'flowers' and 'sentences' from Greek plays were published in Michael Leandro's *Aristologia Euripidea Graecolatina* (Basel, 1559): these gave diligent readers 'aids' for the Greek, and enabled the less diligent simply to pretend that they had read the Greek texts.

45 Gossett, 'Drama in the English College, Rome, 1591–1660', 72.

46 *The Argument of the Pastorall of Florimene with the Discription of the Scoenes and Intermedii Presented by the Queenes Majesties Commandment, before the Kings Majesty in the Hall at White-hall on S. Thomas day the 21 of December* (1635). N. W. Bawcutt, *The Control and Censorship of Caroline Drama* (Oxford: Clarendon Press, 1996), 196, reproduces Herbert's comment: 'The pastorall of Florimene with the description of the scenes and interludes, as it was sent mee by Mr Inigo Jones, I allowed for the press, this 14 of decemb 1635. The pastorall is in French, and tis the argument only, put into English, that I have allowed to be printed.'

47 *The Argument of the Pastorall of Florimene*, 1, 18.

48 That *Le Marriage d'Orphée et d'Eurydice* (completed by Chapoton, 1648) was performed is claimed in Samuel Pepys, *The Diary of Samuel Pepys*, ed. Robert Latham and William Matthews, 11 vols. (London: G. Bell and Sons Ltd, 1970–83), 11:165, and W. B. Van Lennep *et al.*, *The London Stage, 1660–1800* (Carbondale: Southern Illinois University Press, 1960–9), 1:32–3. Both texts trace this information to W. J. Lawrence's *The Elizabethan Playhouse, and Other Studies* (Stratford-upon-Avon: Shakespeare Head Press, 1912), 1:139–40, but in that book Lawrence correctly identifies the play and draws attention to *The Description of the Great Machines*. Presumably *The London Stage* misread Lawrence and Latham and Matthews copied the mistake.

49 A point Wendy Wall makes of the written accounts for pageants in *Imprint of Gender*, 136.

50 Quoted in Jonson, *Works*, x:449.

51 John Mason of Cambridge, *Princeps Rhetoricus or πιλομαχια the Combat of Caps* (1648), 9, performed 21 December 1647 (1), printed 19 January 1648 (20).

52 Ibid., 1, 9, 12.

53 Edmund Gayton, *Pleasant Notes upon Don Quixote* (1654), 272.

54 B. R. Pearn, 'Dumb-Show in Elizabethan Drama', *RES*, 11 (1935), 385–405 (403).

55 Chamberlain, 'Letter to Dudley Carleton', 8 March 1623 in *Letters*, 11:483.

56 Ben Jonson, *Masque of Queens*, British Library, Harley MS 6947, 143; a fair copy presented to Prince Henry also survives, British Library, Royal MS 18 A xlv.

57 William Wager, *A Comedy or Enterlude intituled, Inough is as Good as a Feast* (1570), A2b.

58 H. M. 'To the Author' in Robert Farlie, *The Kalender of Mans Life* (1638), A4a; John Suckling, *Fragmenta* (1646), 20.

4 PROLOGUES, EPILOGUES, INTERIM ENTERTAINMENTS

1 George Powell, *Alphonso* (1691), A4a. In this discussion capitals are used for the characters of Prologue and Epilogue; lower case for what they say.

2 *The Spectator* for Tuesday 1 April 1712, ed. Donald F. Bond (Oxford: Clarendon Press, 1965), III:266.

3 See, for instance, Jocelyn Powell, *Restoration Theatre Production* (London: Routledge and Kegan Paul, 1984), 16; Paulina Kewes, *Authorship and Appropriation* (Oxford: Clarendon Press, 1998), 40; Paul Salzman, *Reading Early Modern Women's Writing* (Oxford: Oxford University Press, 2006), 201.

4 Henry Glapthorne, *Poems* (1639), 28; Thomas Heywood, *Pleasant Dialogues and Dramma's* (1637), 247.

5 James Shirley, *Poems* (1646), 154; John Tatham, *The Fancies Theater* (1640), 2H2b; John Tatham, *Ostella* (1650), 101. See also epilogues referring to particular players, like Massinger's *Emperour of the East* or Heywood's prologue to the revised *Jew of Malta*, which are relevant only at very specific stages of the performers' careers. Quite often different venues altered the need, or the nature of the need, for a prologue. William Percy for *The Cuckqueans and Cuckolds Errants* (1824), 6, provides a prologue that is 'Rather to be omitted if for Powles, and another Prologue for [Tarlton's ghost] to be brought in Place'; that other prologue does not exist yet and he, or perhaps someone else, will have to write it.

6 Thomas Dekker, *The Pleasant Comedie of Old Fortunatus* (1600), A1b; Jasper Mayne, *The Citye Match* (1639), A2b; *Miscellany*, Bodleian Library, MS Add B 97, 63.

7 Thomas Heywood, *Loves Maistresse: or, The Queens Masque* (1636), A3a.

8 Ben Jonson, *The Divell is an Asse* in *Bartholmew Fayre* (1631), N2b; Lodowick Carlell, *Arviragus and Philicia* (1639), A3a. See also the prologue published both to Thomas Dekker's *The Wonder of a Kingdome* (1636), A2a, and William Rowley's *A Tragedy Called All's Lost by Lust* (1633), A3b: 'doe you but steere/His Muse, This day; and bring her toth' wished shore'; and 'Prologue to ye Mayde of honour' quoted in Peter Beal, 'Massinger at Bay: Unpublished Verses in a War of the Theatres', *Yearbook of English Studies*, 10 (1980), 190–203 (192): 'this day/looke for noe more, nor lesse, then a newe play'.

9 Ben Jonson, *Bartholmew Fayre* (1631), A2a; Margaret Cavendish, Duchess of Newcastle, *Loves Adventures* in *Playes* (1662), B1b. Other day-specific inductions include that to Thomas Lodge, *Lady Alimony* (1659), A3a, which is for the 'Poets third day'; and all the inductions concerning underprepared actors readying a first performance, including *A Pleasant Comedie, Called Wily Beguilde* (1606), A2a, where the players are 'stil poaring in their papers and never perfect'; Ben Jonson's *Staple of Newes* in *Bartholmew Fayre* (1631), 2Ab, where 'there are a set of gamesters within, in travell of a thing call'd a Play, and would faine be deliver'd of it' while the worried 'Poet . . . hath torne the booke in a *Poeticall* fury'; John Marston's *The History of Antonio and Mellida* (1602), A3a, which starts with actors who declare 'Come sirs, come: the

musique will sounde straight for entrance. Are yee readie, are yee perfect?'; his *Jacke Drums Entertainment* (1601), A2b, which is 'Wanting a Prologue, & our selves not perfect'. Similarly occasion-specific are all the inductions that state a specific amount of time that has passed since the play was written: Francis Beaumont's *The Knight of the Burning Pestle* (1613), B1b: 'You should have told us your minde a moneth since, our play is ready to begin now'; Ben Jonson's *Poetaster* (1602), A2a: 'These fifteene weekes/(So long as since the Plot was but an *Embrion*)/Have I . . . mixt vigilant thoughts,/In expectation of this hated Play.' These and other such inductions are classified as 'The Occasional Induction' in Thelma M. Greenfield, *The Induction in Elizabethan Drama* (Eugene: University of Oregon Books, 1969).

10 William Davenant, *The Platonick Lovers* (1636), A3a. John Fletcher, *The Humorous Lieutenant* in Francis Beaumont and John Fletcher, *Comedies and Tragedies* (1647), 3T2a.

11 Francis Beaumont and John Fletcher, *Loves Pilgrimage* in Beaumont and Fletcher, *Comedies and Tragedies* (1647), 8Db; Philip Massinger, 'Prologue at the Blackfriars' in *The Emperour of the East* (1632), A4a; Nathaniel Richards, *The Tragedy of Messallina* (1640), B1b; Thomas Nabbes, *The Bride* (1640), L1b; Shirley, *Poems*, 149. See also T. W., 'The Prologue to The Marriage-Broker' in *Gratiae Theatrales, or, A Choice Ternary of English Plays* (1662), *7b: '*Wellcome* to our Play./A Play span-new'.

12 Christopher Brooke, *Ghost of Richard the Third* (1614), 4πb.

13 Shirley, *Poems*, 46.

14 Nabbes, *Bride*, 13b; John Fletcher, *A Wife for a Moneth* in Beaumont and Fletcher, *Comedies and Tragedies* (1647), 612b.

15 John Fletcher and William Shakespeare, *The Two Noble Kinsmen* (1634), A1b. See a similar comment made to the reader in Thomas Middleton's *The Familie of Love* (1608), A1b: 'For Plaies in this Citie are like wenches new falne to the trade, onelie desired of your neatest gallants, whiles the'are fresh.'

16 James Shirley, [*Love Tricks or*] *The Schoole of Complement* (1631), L4b; Richards, *Tragedy of Messallina*, F8a; Philip Massinger, *Believe as You List*, from the autograph MS (Egerton 2828), licensed 6 May 1631, ed. C. J. Sisson (Oxford: Malone Society, 1927), 98; John Fletcher and Philip Massinger, *The Little French Lawyer* in Beaumont and Fletcher, *Comedies and Tragedies* (1647), L2a. See also John Fletcher's *The Chances* in Beaumont and Fletcher, *Comedies and Tragedies* (1647), 3C3a: 'Our paines were eas'd,/Could we be confident that all rise pleas'd'; Richard Brome, *The Love-sick Court* in *Five New Plays* (1659), L8a [171]: ''Tis not the Poets art. . ./Can justly make us to presume a Play/Is good till you approv't'; Thomas Heywood, *A Challenge for Beautie* (1636), K1a: 'your Smile or Frowne,/Can save, or spill; to make us swimme, or drowne'; William Habington, *The Queene of Arragon* (1640), I3b: 'may/You gently quit or else condemne the Play'; Richard Brome, *The Court Begger* in *Five New Plays* (1653), S7b: 'Ladyes, . . . Tis in you to save/Him [poet], from the rigorous censure of the rest;' Henry Glapthorne, *Wit in a Constable* (1640), A4a: 'Are you resolv'd yet Gentlemen?'

17 Edward Sharpham, *Cupid's Whirligig* (1607), L3b.
18 Stefano Guazzo, *An Italian Treat* (*c*. 1655), Folger Shakespeare Library, MS v.b.128, 99; Thomas Heywood, *A Pleasant Comedy, called A Mayden-Head Well Lost* (1634), 13a.
19 Samuel Rowley, *The Noble Souldier* (1634), H2b.
20 William B. Rye, *England as Seen by Foreigners in the Days of Elizabeth and James I* (1865), 88. For more on first-performance admission prices before the interregnum see Roslyn Lander Knutson, *The Repertory of Shakespeare's Company 1594–1613* (Fayetteville: University of Arkansas Press, 1991), 25. Samuel Pepys, 'Monday 16 December, 1661', *The Diary of Samuel Pepys*, ed. Robert Latham and William Matthews (London: G. Bell and Sons Ltd, 1970–83), 11:234. For the continuance into the eighteenth century of charging doubled or at least 'advanced' prices for first-night performances, see Alwin Thaler, *Shakspeare to Sheridan* (Cambridge, MA: Harvard University Press, 1922), 229–33.
21 Thomas Dekker, *Dekker his Dreame* (1620), D1b; Henry Peacham, *Coach and Sedan* (1636), F1a.
22 Thomas Dekker, *Newes from Hell* (1606), E1a. See also Samuel Rowlands, *Pimlico* (1609), C1a: '(As at a *New-play*) all the *Roomes*/Did swarme with *Gentiles* mix'd with *Groomes.*'
23 Abraham Wright, *Parnassus Biceps* (1656), 131.
24 Dudley North, *A Forest of Varieties* (1645), A2a.
25 W[alter] M[ountfort], *The Launching of the Mary*, ed. J. H. Walter (Oxford: Malone Society, 1933), 124.
26 'September 15, 1668' in Pepys, *The Diary*, IX:307. The editors suggest that Pepys was actually talking about Richard Flecknoe's comedy *The Damoiselles à la Mode*. Colley Cibber, *An Apology for the Life of Mr. Colley Cibber* (1740), 144.
27 Thomas Dibdin, *The Reminiscences of Thomas Dibdin* (London, 1827), 1:7.
28 William Fennor, *Fennors Descriptions* (1616), B2b; Ben Jonson, *The New Inne* (1631), (*)2a–b.
29 Peter Hausted, *The Rivall Friends* (1632), title-page; Beaumont, *Knight of the Burning Pestle* (1613), A2a; Massinger, *Emperour of the East*, A3b.
30 Richard Flecknoe, *Love's Kingdom* (1664), A2a; Henry King, *Poems, Elegies, Paradoxes, and Sonnets* (1657), 23. The poem itself dates from no later than 1636. See Henry King, *The Stoughton Manuscript*, facsim. ed. Mary Hobbs (Aldershot: Scolar, 1990), 168.
31 George Chapman [actually Glapthorne?], *Revenge for Honour* (1659), A2b; 'Mr Moores revels nere Eastgate in oxon 1636' in *Miscellany*, Bodleian Library, MS Ashmole 47, 123.
32 In William Shakespeare, *Troilus and Cressida*, 'my feare is . . . Some galled Goose of Winchester would hisse' (TLN 3589–90).
33 Thomas Middleton and James Shirley, *No Wit/Help like a Womans* (1657), H3b; R. A., *The Valiant Welshman* (1615), 14b.
34 William Shakespeare, *The Famous Historie of Troylus and Cresseid* (1609b), π2a.

35 Thomas Neale, *The Warde* (16 September 1637), Bodleian Library, MS Rawl. Poet 79, 52.

36 Ben Jonson, 'To the worthy Author M. *John Fletcher*' in John Fletcher's *The Faithfull Shepheardesse* (1629), A3a; Thomas Heywood, *The Golden Age* (1611), K2b.

37 Dekker, *The Wonder*, A2a. For the first, see Carlell, *Arviragus*, E4b: 'Our Author at the Barre of Censure stands'; for the second, see Nabbes, *Bride*, L1b: ''tis arraign'd;/And doubtful stands before your judgements barre,/Expecting what your severall censures are.' William Davenant in 'To Endimion Porter, When my comedy (call'd the Wits) was presented at Black-Fryars' in *Madagascar* (1638), 87, describes the time 'when I must come/Chain'd to the Muses Barre, to take my doome'. See also Thomas Dekker, *The Guls Horne-Booke* (1609), 29: 'by being a Justice in examining of plaies, you shall put your selfe into . . . true *Scaenicall* authority'; Francis Beaumont, John Fletcher and Philip Massinger, *The Coxcombe* in Beaumont and Fletcher, *Comedies and Tragedies* (1647), 2P3b: 'now 'tis to be tri'd/Before such Judges, 'twill not be deni'd/A . . . noble hearing'; Glapthorne, *Wit in a Constable*, A4a: 'you (who now my Judges sit)'; Henry Glapthorne, *The Ladies Privilege* (1640), A3b: 'our feare [is],/least what our Author writes should not appeare/Fit for this Judging presence'; James Shirley, *The Imposture* (1652), A4a: 'You Gentlemen, that sit/Our judges'.

38 See 'The Description of a Poet' in Fennor, *Fennor's Descriptions*, B2b–B3a: 'Sweet Poesye/Is oft convict, condem'd, and judg'd to die/Without just triall, by a multitude/Whose judgements are illiterate, and rude'; Richard Brome, *The Novella* in *Five New Playes* (1653), H4b: 'Hee'll 'bide his triall, and submits his cause/To you the Jury.' For more on the use of the word 'trial' for first performances, see Tiffany Stern, *Rehearsal from Shakespeare to Sheridan* (Oxford: Clarendon Press, 2000), 113.

39 Thomas Nabbes, *Tottenham Court* (1636), A3b; John Ford, *The Ladies Triall* (1639), K4b.

40 Thomas Middleton, *The Ant, and the Nightingale: or Father Hubburds Tales* (1604), D2b.

41 Marston, *Antonio and Mellida*, B1b.

42 Ben Jonson, *The Comicall Satyre of Every Man out of his Humor* (1600), R3a.

43 George Granville, *Heroic Love* (1678), A2a; John Dennis, *Liberty Asserted* (1704), A2b; Judith Milhous and Robert D. Hume, *Producible Interpretation* (Carbondale: Southern Illinois University Press, 1985), 44; Mary De la Rivière Manley, *Almyna* (1707), A1b. For more examples see Stern, *Rehearsal*, 187–92. Other late seventeenth-century plays that underwent alterations directly after the first night include William Killigrew's *Pandora* (1664), which was changed from a tragedy to a comedy to please the audience (A8b), and Mary De la Rivière Manley's *The Lost Lover* (1697), A4a: 'You have the Farce as 'twas Acted the first day; the latter part being left out afterwards; some few of the Audience having been offended at it, but more at the length of the act.' Eighteenth-century examples include William Popple, *Lady's Revenge* (1734),

A4a: 'The Second Night the particular Things objected to, being taken out, the Play was acted from Beginning to End, without one single Mark of Displeasure'; Theophilus Cibber, *The Lover* (1730), A4a: 'The Reader will find several Speeches printed in this Play, which were omitted in the Performance after the First Night, to avoid an improper Length'; John Vanbrugh and Colley Cibber, *The Provok'd Husband* (1728), A1a: 'the Reader will . . . find here a Scene or two of the Lower Humour that were left out after the first Day's Presentation'; Charles Macklin, *Henry VII* (1746), A1a: 'N. B. The Lines mark'd with Commas were omitted after the first Night's acting, the Play being too long in the Performance'; while Gabriel Odingsells' *Bay's Opera* (1730), A3b, notes how there were 'Interruptions of the first Night [resulting in] hasty, tho' well-meant, Amputations with which it was presented on the two following Nights'.

44 Robert Dodsley, *Sir John Cockle* (1738), A3b.

45 13 March 1703, see Emmett L. Avery, ed., *The London Stage part 2: 1700–1729* (Carbondale: Southern Illinois University Press, 1960), 33; Thomas D'Urfey, *The Banditti* (1686), A3b.

46 *Daily Post*, 17 October (1733), quoted in Arthur H. Scouten, ed., *The London Stage part 3: 1729–1747* (Carbondale: Southern Illinois University Press, 1961), clxvii.

47 John Suckling, *The Goblins* (1646), 65.

48 Samuel Harding, *Sicily and Naples* (1640), *2a.

49 Henry Killigrew, *Pallantus and Eudora* (1653), A2a.

50 Thomas Dekker [and Thomas Middleton], *The Roaring Girle* (1611), M3a; John Ford, *The Broken Heart* (1633), K4b. See also Heywood, *Mayden-Head Well Lost*, 13a: 'Our Play is new, but whether shaped well/In Act or Seane, Judge you, you best can tell'; and Ben Jonson, *A Pleasant Comedy, Called: The Case is Alterd* (1609), D3b, where, in 'Utopia', 'the sport is at a new play to observe the sway and variety of oppinion that passeth it . . . one saies he likes not the writing, another likes not the plot, another not the playing'.

51 See John Stephens, 'To his worthy Friend, H. F.' in Henry Fitzgeffrey's *Satyres and Satyricall Epigrams* (1617), F8a: 'I must . . . let *Players* know/They cannot recompence your labour: Though/They . . . take no money of you nor your Page.' Davenant confirms that this was common practice in the Restoration in *The Play-House to be Let* in *The Works* (1673), 75: '[poets] pay nothing for their entrance'.

52 Joseph Hall, Satire III of *Virgidemiarum* (1597), B5b; Henry Parrot, *Laquei Ridiculosi* (1613), c8a.

53 Gary Taylor and John Jowett, *Shakespeare Reshaped 1606–1623* (Oxford: Clarendon Press, 1993), 237.

54 George Colman, 'Preface', in Francis Beaumont and John Fletcher, *The Dramatick Works of Beaumont and Fletcher* (1778), xiv.

55 Andrew Gurr, 'Maximal and Minimal Texts: Shakespeare v. The Globe', *Shakespeare Survey*, 52 (1999), 68–87.

56 Thomas Nabbes, *Covent Garden* (1638), A3a; Richard Brome, *The Weeding of the Covent Garden* in *Five New Playes* (1659), prol., A3a.

57 John Day, *Isle of Gulls* (1606), A2a.

58 Edmund Gayton, *Pleasant Notes upon Don Quixote* (1654), 245–6.

59 Ben Jonson, *The Magnetick Lady* in *The Workes* (1640), A4a.

60 Brome, *Novella* in *Five New Playes* (1653), N2a; William Davenant, *The Unfortunate Lovers* (1643), G4b.

61 Davenant, *Play-House to Be Let*, 76; Philip Henslowe, *Henslowe Papers*, ed. Walter W. Greg (London: A. H. Bullen, 1907), 75.

62 Philip Henslowe, *Henslowe's Diary*, ed. R. A. Foakes (Cambridge: Cambridge University Press, 2002), 126, 168, 216.

63 Thomas Dekker, *If it be not Good, the Divel is in it* (1612), A4a; R. A., *Valiant Welshman*, 14b. See also 'On Christ-Church Play at Woodstock' in Richard Corbet, *Certain Elegant Poems* (1647), 71: 'If we . . . have not pleased those,/ Whose clamorous Judgments lie in urging No'es . . .'.

64 'Blasius Multibibus', *A Solemne Joviall Disputation, Theoreticke and Practicke; briefely shadowing the Law of Drinking* (1617), 159.

65 N. W. Bawcutt, *The Control and Censorship of Caroline Drama* (Oxford: Clarendon Press, 1996), 215.

66 *The Costlie Whore* (1633), H4b; James Shirley, *The Sisters* (1652), A3a; Mayne, *Citye Match*, B1a; John Denham, *The Sophy* (1642), A2a; Beaumont and Fletcher, *Comedies and Tragedies* (1647), F4b. See also Tatham, *Fancies Theater*, (*)7a: 'I shall deeme thee worthy praise, /. . . When Fancie in thy *Theater* doth play,/And wins more credit than a second day'; John Mennes, *Musarum Deliciae* (1655), 80, 'bring them into a Play,/. . ./And Ile have the second day'; Prologue to *The Scholars* in Francis Beaumont, *Poems* (1653), 79: 'Profit he knowes none/Unles that of your Approbation,/Which if your thoughts at going out will pay,/Hee'l not looke further for a *Second Day*'; Tatham, *Ostella*, III: 'Our *Author* likes the *Women* well, and says . . . on *his Day* . . . leave them not behind'; allusions from the 1650s to benefits are collected in Gerald Eades Bentley, *The Profession of Dramatist in Shakespeare's Time* (Princeton, NJ: Princeton University Press, 1986), 134.

67 William Cartwright, 'To the Memory of Ben Johnson' in *Poems* (1651), 315.

68 Bawcutt, *Control*, 166.

69 Ibid., 169, 173, 167.

70 Bentley, 'Dramatists' Pay' in *Dramatist*, 88–110.

71 Not published with *The Royall Slave*, but bound with other relevant material into a miscellany in the Bodleian Library, MS Wood D 18 part 2, 26; it is also found in a miscellany in the Folger Shakespeare Library, MS v.b.212. Heywood, *Pleasant Dialogues*, 238; 'Mr Moores revels nere Eastgate in oxon 1636' in *Miscellany*, Bodleian Library, MS Ashmole 47, 125b, 126.

72 Douglas Bruster and Robert Weimann, *Prologues to Shakespeare's Theatre: Performance and Liminality in Early Modern Drama* (London and New York: Routledge, 2004), 160.

73 Basing his argument on the fact that most positive contemporary references to 'benefits' date from the Jacobean and Caroline periods, Alwin Thaler in 'Playwrights' Benefits, and "interior gathering" in the Elizabethan Theatre',

Studies in Philology, 16 (1919), 187–96 (189), suggests that poets' benefits were not generally granted until some point after the accession of King James. With so little evidence extant on the subject, it is difficult either thoroughly to accept or thoroughly to reject his proposition.

74 William Reymes, *Self Interest, or the Belly Water*, being a verse translation . . . of Niccolo Secchi's . . . *L'Interesse c.* 1655, Folger Shakespeare Library, MS v.b.128.

75 *Miscellany*, Bodleian Library, MS Ashmole 38, 145; William Vaughan, *Golden Fleece* (1626), B2b; Gayton, *Pleasant Notes*, 220.

76 John Melton, *Astrologaster* (1620), 67.

77 *The Returne from Pernassus* (1606), A2a. In this particular text the character who is holding the book is called the 'Stagekeeper'; in the manuscript of the play the speech-prefix 'Stagekeeper' has 'prompter' written underneath: the stage-keeper here is also the prompter. Folger Shakespeare Library, MS v.a.355, 3. For more on the prompter's duties see chapter 7.

78 Thomas Goffe, *The Careles Shepherdess* (1656), 7–8.

79 T. W., *Thorny-Abbey* in *Gratiae Theatrales*, *5b. The playwright, 'T. W.', has not been identified. Baillie in *A Choice Ternary of English Plays*, ed. William M. Baillie (Binghamton, NY: Medieval and Renaissance Texts and Studies, 1984) gives a late commonwealth date for this prologue, but, given that theatres were closed during the time of Cromwell, the prologue probably continues to reflect Renaissance practice.

80 Eckehard Simon, 'Manuscript Production in Medieval Theatre: The German Carnival Plays' in *New Directions in Later Medieval Manuscript Studies*, ed. Derek Pearsall (York: York Medieval Press, 2000), 143–65 (148).

81 Reproduced in Autrey Nell Wiley, *Rare Prologues and Epilogues 1642–1700* (London: G. Allen and Unwin, 1940), 4. John Astington in 'Rereading Illustrations of the English Stage', *Shakespeare Survey*, 50 (1997), 151–70 (166) points out that the full illustration was originally designed for *The Canterburie Pilgrimage* (1641), and that it was also used as a frontispiece to *An Exact Copy of a Letter*, and *A Conspiracy of the Twelve Bishops*. Additional use of it is made for *Sir Francis Seymor, his Honourable and Worthy Speech* (1641). All are printed for H. Walker.

82 *The Prologue and Epilogue to a Comedie Presented at the Entertainment of the Prince his Highnesse by the Schollers of Trinity College in Cambridge in March last, 1641* (1642). The prologue and epilogue to the play also circulated widely in manuscripts including *Miscellany*, Bodleian Library, MS Rawl. 26; *Miscellany*, Bodleian Library, MS Douce 357; *Miscellany*, Bodleian Library, MS Malone 21; and *Miscellany*, Folger Shakespeare Library, MS v.a.322, 212b.

83 Words adopted by Bruster and Weimann, *Prologues*, 2 and *passim*.

84 Nabbes, *Covent Garden*, 3; Beal, 'Massinger at Bay', 193.

85 [John Mennes], *Wit Restor'd* in *Several Select Poems not Formerly Publish't* (1658), 162.

86 Tatham, *Ostella*, III; Richard Lovelace, *Lucasta* (1649), 75, 77; William Gager, *Ulysses Redux* (1592), F3a.

87 *Miscellany*, Bodleian Library, MS Top. Oxon e. 5, 359; 'to ye Q. by ye players 1598' in *Miscellany*, Cambridge University Library, MS Dd.5.75.

88 A. S., Gent [Richard Chamberlain], *The Booke of Bulls* (1636), c4b–c5a.

89 Lodowick Carlell, *Arviragus and Philicia*, Bodleian Library, MS Eng. Misc. d. 11, 6; Thomas Goffe, *A Critical Old Spelling Edition of Thomas Goffe's The Courageous Turke*, ed. Susan Gushee O'Malley (New York: Garland, 1979), 171; William Berkeley, *Lost Lady*, Folger Shakespeare Library, MS j.b.4; and William Berkeley, *Lost Lady* (1638) and (1639); Walter Montagu, *The Shepheards Paradise*, British Library, MS Sloane 3649 and Walter Montagu, *The Shepheards Paradise*, Folger Shakespeare Library, MS v.b.203. The other known manuscripts are British Library, MS Stowe 976, British Library, MS Add 41617 and Folger Shakespeare Library, MS v.b.204. The printed edition, without prologue or songs, is *The Shepheard's Paradise* (1659).

90 John Fletcher, *The Womans Prize* in Beaumont and Fletcher, *Comedies and Tragedies* (1647), 5Q2a. Discussed in John Fletcher, *The Woman's Prize: Or, The Tamer Tamed*, ed. George B. Ferguson (London: Mouton, 1966), 31.

91 The manuscript, Lichfield MS 68, in Lichfield Cathedral Library, is quoted here from Richard Brome, *The English Moore*, ed. Sara Jayne Steen (Columbia: University of Missouri Press, 1983), 34, 127, 93. Richard Brome, *The English Moor* (1658), A2a; G1b.

92 George Chapman, *Bussy D'Ambois* (1641), A2a–b; Thomas May, *The Heire* (1622), 13a; Thomas May, *The Heire* (1633), A4b; 13a.

93 John Marston, *The Malcontent* (1604a); John Marston, *The Malcontent* (1604b), 11b; John Marston, *The Malcontent. Augmented by Marston. With the Additions Played by the Kings Majesties Servants. Written by Jhon Webster* (1604), A3a–A4b; 14a.

94 Aston Cokain, *The Obstinate Lady* (1657), 68; Aston Cokain, *Small Poems of Divers Sorts* (1658), A3b.

95 John Mason, *The Turke* (1610), A2a–b; John Mason, *An Excellent Tragedy of Mulleasses the Turke* (1632).

96 *A Pleasant Comedie, Called Wily Beguilde* (1606), K3a; *A Pleasant Comedie, Called, Wily Beguiled* (1614). See W. W. Greg, *A Bibliography of the English Printed Drama to the Restoration* (London: Bibliographical Society, 1959), 1:234 and Stanley Wells, Gary Taylor *et al.*, *William Shakespeare: A Textual Companion* (Oxford: Clarendon Press, 1987), 375–7.

97 *The Birth of Hercules* ed. R. Warwick Bond (Oxford: Clarendon Press, 1911), 1; Edward Phillips, *The Mysteries of Love & Eloquence* (1658), A3a. See also the way Philip Massinger dismisses prologues and epilogues, perhaps for a play that never had them, or perhaps for a play in which they are lost, *The Unnaturall Combat* (1639), A2b: 'I present you with this old Tragedie, without Prologue, or Epilogue, it being composed in a time . . . when such by ornaments, were not advanced above the fabricque of the whole worke.' Bruster and Weimann, *Prologues*, 6, discuss the decline in popularity of the prologue during the later sixteenth and earlier seventeenth century, and then

its growth again; the trouble is that it is unknown how many stage-orations have been lost, so it is hard to quantify how popular the form was.

98 Agostino Lombardo, 'Fragments and Scraps: Shakespeare's *Troilus and Cressida'* in *The European Tragedy of Troilus*, ed. Piero Boitani (Oxford: Oxford University Press, 1989), 200.

99 See Peter W. M. Blayney, *The First Folio of Shakespeare* (Washington, DC: Folger Library Publications, 1991), 21.

100 Richard Brome, *The Sparagus Garden* (1640), A4a, L4b.

101 Mason, *Turke* (1610), A2b.

102 William Cavendish, Earl of Newcastle, *The Country Captaine* (1649a); William Cavendish, Earl of Newcastle, *The Country Captaine* (1649b), A1+1a–b.

103 John Fletcher, *Valentinian* in Beaumont and Fletcher, *Comedies and Tragedies* (1647), 7D2b.

104 Beaumont, *Poems*, L1b.

105 Francis Beaumont, John Fletcher and Philip Massinger, *Loves Cure* in Beaumont and Fletcher, *Comedies and Tragedies* (1647), 5s5b; Lodowick Carlell, *The Deserving Favorite* (1629), N3b.

106 John Fletcher and Philip Massinger, *The Custome of the Countrey* in Beaumont and Fletcher, *Comedies and Tragedies* (1647), 2D2a; and Beaumont, Fletcher and Massinger, *The Coxcombe* in Beaumont and Fletcher, *Comedies and Tragedies* (1647), 2P3b.

107 Beaumont and Fletcher, *Comedies and Tragedies* (1647), G2a.

108 Francis Beaumont and John Fletcher, *Fifty Comedies and Tragedies* (1679), A1a.

109 Francis Beaumont and John Fletcher, *The Captaine* in Beaumont and Fletcher, *Comedies and Tragedies* (1647), 2I5a; John Fletcher, *Beggars Bush* (1661), E2b.

110 Francis Beaumont and John Fletcher, *The Noble Gentleman* in Beaumont and Fletcher, *Comedies and Tragedies* (1647), 2F3b; John Fletcher, *The Tragedy of Thierry, King of France, and his Brother Theodoret* (1649), A1a; Francis Beaumont and John Fletcher, *The Woman Hater* (1649), A1b.

111 Thomas Heywood, *If You Know Not Me You Know No Body* (1639), A2a, G3a; Heywood, *Pleasant Dialogues*, 248–9.

112 Thomas Middleton, *The Phoenix* (1607), K3a–K3b, Huntington Library copy, STC 17892 only.

113 Shirley, *Poems*, 158, 'Prologue to his Tragedy call'd the Cardinall'.

114 Shirley, *Sisters*, A3a; James Shirley, *The Cardinal* (1652), A4a.

115 Richard Hosley in 'Was There a "Dramatic Epilogue" to *The Taming of the Shrew?' Studies in English Literature, 1500–1900*, 1 (1961), 17–34 argues against this idea, conjecturing that doubling concerns made it impossible to return to the framing story at the end of the play (31); he does not realise, however, both how seldom an induction might be used, and how easily it and papers related to it might drop away.

116 See Thomas Middleton, *Hengist, King of Kent; or the Mayor of Queenborough . . . from the Manuscript in the Folger Shakespeare Library*, ed. R. C. Bald (New York and London: Charles Scribner's Sons, 1938); Thomas Middleton,

Hengist, King of Kent [from the Portland manuscript], ed. Grace Ioppolo (Oxford: Malone Society, 2003); Thomas Middleton, *The Mayor of Quinborough a Tragedy* [*Hengist, King of Kent*] (1661).

117 Samuel Daniel, *Hymen's Triumph*, ed. John Pitcher (Oxford: Malone Society, 1994), xxxi.

118 Fulke Greville, *Mustapha* (1609), B2a; C4a; E4b; F4a; F4b.

119 The copy is now now in the Bibliothèque Nationale in Paris; see Jean Jacquot, 'Religion et Raison d'état dans l'oeuvre de Faulke Greville', *Études Anglaises*, 5 (1952), 211–22.

120 Fulke Greville, *Mustapha*, British Library, MS Add 54569. G. A. Wilkes, 'The Chorus Sacerdotum in Fulke Greville's *Mustapha*', *RES*, 49 (1998), 326–8.

121 Discussed by Ralph Alan Cohen and John Jowett in their textual notes to *Your Five Gallants* in Gary Taylor and John Lavagnino, eds., *Thomas Middleton and Early Modern Textual Culture* (Oxford: Clarendon Press, 2007), 575, and in more detail in John Jowett, 'Pre-Editorial Criticism and the Space for Editing: Examples from *Richard III* and *Your Five Gallants*', in *Problems of Editing*, ed. Christa Jansohn, special issue of *Editio*, 14 (1999), 127–49.

122 Christopher Marlowe, *Doctor Faustus A- and B- Texts*, ed. David M. Bevington and Eric Rasmussen (Manchester: Manchester University Press, 1993), 287–8.

123 Daniel, *Hymen's Triumph*, ed. Pitcher, viii.

124 See James P. Bednarz, 'When did Shakespeare Write the Choruses of *Henry V*? ', *Notes and Queries*, 53 (2006), 486–9.

125 See Andrew Gurr's introduction to his edition of Shakespeare's *Henry V* (Cambridge: Cambridge University Press, 1992), 7. For the argument that the choric apologies pertain to a specific court performance, see G. P. Jones, '*Henry V*: The Chorus and the Audience', *Shakespeare Survey*, 31 (1978), 93–104; Lawrence Danson disagrees in '*Henry V*: King, Chorus, and Critics', *Shakespeare Quarterly*, 34 (1983), 27–43.

126 Richard Farrant, *The Warres of Cyrus King of Persia* (1594), C3a.

127 Quoted in Joseph Wood Krutch, 'Governmental Attempt to Regulate the Stage after the Jeremy Collier Controversy', *PMLA*, 38 (1923), 153–74 (165); C. J. Sisson in his edition of Massinger's *Believe As You List*, xx writes: 'the Prologue and Epilogue . . . were evidently not attached to the play when it went to Herbert, or surely they would have been preserved in Massinger's hand, if by Massinger, and would have preceded the licence'.

128 Phillips, *The Mysteries of Love*, A3a; John Fletcher and Thomas Middleton, *Nice Valour* in Beaumont and Fletcher, *Comedies and Tragedies* (1647), 3x3a.

129 *Henslowe's Diary*, ed. Foakes, 207; 187.

130 Christopher Marlowe, *The Rich Jew of Malta* (1633), A3a; John Fletcher, *The Faithful Shepheardesse* (1634), A3b. These prologues and epilogues to *Game at Chesse* are not in the 1625 editions of that play; they are to be found in *Miscellany*, Bodleian Library, MS Douce 357, 40b; *Miscellany*, Bodleian

Library, MS Don. d. 58, 59a; *Miscellany*, Beinecke Library, MS Osborn
f b 106, 1a.

131 Richard Collings, *The Kingdomes Weekly Intelligencer*, Series 2, No. 198,
23 February to 2 March (1646), 438.

132 Bentley, *Dramatist*, 257.

133 Sonia Massai, 'Shakespeare, Text and Paratext', unpublished talk delivered
at the International Shakespeare Conference, Stratford-upon-Avon, 2008.
I am grateful to Sonia Massai for sending me a copy of this paper.

134 Francis Beaumont, *The Knight of the Burning Pestle* (1635), A3b–A4a; John
Lyly, *Sapho and Phao* (1584), A2a; Dekker, *The Wonder*, A2a; Rowley, *All's
Lost by Lust*, A3b.

135 John Fletcher, *Thierry, King of France*, A1a–b. Beaumont and Fletcher, *The
Noble Gentleman* in Beaumont and Fletcher, *Comedies and Tragedies* (1647),
2F3b; James Shirley, *The Changes* (1632), L1b.

136 Shirley, *Poems*, 36; 40; 35, 42; 44. Of the two named by plays, Jonson's
Alchemist and Middleton's *No Wit/Help*, both were separately published
with their own prologues.

137 Davenant, *Madagascar*, 98; 'The Prologue to the *Woman-hater*, or the
Hungry Courtier' in Beaumont and Fletcher, *The Woman Hater* (1649), A1a
(not present in the 1607 or 1648 editions of that play); Francis Beaumont and
John Fletcher, *The Woman Hater* (1607), A2a.

138 Thomas Heywood, *The Foure Prentises of London* (1615), A4a; William
Davenant, *Love and Honour* (1649), E3a; James Shirley, *The Coronation*
(1640), A2a. See also *The Second Report of Doctor John Faustus . . . Written
by an English Gentleman student in Wittenberg . . .* (1594), E2b: 'immediately
after the third sound of the Trumpets, there entreth in the Prologue attired
in a blacke vesture'.

139 Phillips, *The Mysteries of Love*, A3a; Brome, *Novella* in *Five New Plays* (1653),
H4b; Nicholas Breton, *A Poste with a Packet of Madde Letters* (1606), G1a;
Nicholas Breton, *Choice, Chance, and Change* (1606), G1a.

140 Rowlands, *Pimlico*, B2a; George Chapman, 'Vigilae Quartae & Ultimae' in
Eugenia (1614), F1b; Thomas Randolph, *Aristippus* (1630), 2. See also
Anthony Rudd, Thomas Richards and Laurence Johnson, *Misogonus* in
R. Warwick Bond, ed., *Early Plays from the Italian* (Oxford: Clarendon
Press, 1911), 174: 'ask . . . why I decke my temples thus wth bayes'; Beaumont
and Fletcher, *Woman Hater* (1607), A2a: 'A Prologue in Verse is as stale, as a
black Velvet Cloake, and a Bay Garland'; Richard Brathwait, *Barnabees
Journall* (1638), K7a: 'Prologue crown'd with a Wreath of Ivy'. It is possible
that the 'bays' were also sometimes 'awarded' to a successful play, though
references to this may be either real or metaphorical: Thomas Randolph,
Amyntas (1638), 114: 'He beggs nor Bayes, nor Ivy'; Robert Farlie, *The
Kalender of Mans Life* (1638), A4a: 'Some . . . rather doe detract than give
him Bayes,/Who merits it.'

141 Jeffrey Masten in *Textual Intercourse* (Cambridge: Cambridge University
Press, 1997), 64, explains that in the Renaissance 'author' might mean the

'person who originates or gives existence to anything' rather than 'the writer of the text'.

142 Simon Harding, *Sicily and Naples* (1640), 96; Rowley, *All's Lost by Lust*, A3b; Massinger, *Emperour of the East*, M3b.

143 Ben Jonson, *Poetaster* (1602), A3a; Glapthorne, *Wit in a Constable*, A4a. See also the prologue to Shakespeare, *Troilus and Cressida*, described as 'A prologue arm'd' (TLN 24); Marston's *Antonio and Mellida* has an armed epilogue. The vogue for the combative prologue has been traced to the theatre wars, but given its habit of cropping up over time it is more likely simply to reflect its author's preference for threatening the audience rather than begging them.

144 John Fletcher, *The Humorous Lieutenant* in Beaumont and Fletcher, *Comedies and Tragedies* (1647), 3T2a. Similarly Roger Shipman asks in *Grobiana's Nuptials*: 'can't our buisinesse bee done . . . but a Coxe-combe in a cloke must scrape his lease of leggs to begge *Sir* Tottipate's applause in dogrime verse?', quoted by G. E. Bentley in *The Jacobean and Caroline Stage* (Oxford: Clarendon Press, 1941–68), V:1055.

145 Walter F. Eggers, Jr, 'Shakespeare's Gower and the Role of the Authorial Presenter', *Philological Quarterly*, 54 (1975), 434–43 (434).

146 Jeffrey Knapp, 'What Is a Co-author?', *Representations*, 89 (2005), 1–29, argues that Renaissance writers had difficulty conceptualising multiple authorship, and points out that references to multiple authors in prologues and epilogues are extremely rare: there are no instances at all before 1600, and only one in a commercial play printed before 1642.

147 Thomas Heywood, *The Second Part of the Iron Age* in *The Iron Age* (1632), K4b. See also Chapman [Glapthorne?], *Revenge for Honour*, 63.

148 James Shirley, *The Dukes Mistris* (1638), K4b; Glapthorne, *Ladies Priviledge*, J2b; Davenant, *Madagascar*, 115. Brome, *English Moor*, 86, wants no one to claim he 'skulks behind the hangings . . . affraid/Of a hard censure'; Jonson and Brome together stood 'behind the Arras' to watch the reception of the 'new sufficient Play' of Ben Jonson's *Bartholmew Fayre*, A4a. For John Fletcher and Philip Massinger's *The Lovers Progress* in Beaumont and Fletcher, *Comedies and Tragedies* (1647), 3M2b, the revising author takes on the mantle of any other first-performance author, '*Still doubtfull, and perplex'd too, whether he/Hath done* Fletcher *right in this Historie,/The Poet sits within.*' The poet is also described as being in the tiring-house in Abraham Cowley's *Loves Riddle* (1638), G4a; and *Wily Beguilde* (1606), A2b. For more on the subject, see Tiffany Stern, 'Behind the Arras: The Prompter's Place in the Shakespearean Theatre', *Theatre Notebook*, 55 (2001), 110–18.

149 Samuel Holland, *Don Zara del Fogo* (1656), 164.

150 Beaumont and Fletcher, *Woman Hater* (1607), C3b; conversely John Stephens' *A Base Mercenary Poet* in *Satirical Essays* (1615), 292, 'when hee heares his play hissed, . . . would rather thinke bottle-Ale is opening'.

151 Prologue to Lovelace's *The Scholars* in Beaumont, *Poems*, 75; Brooke, *Ghost of Richard the Third*, 4πb. Massinger, *Emperour of the East*, D3a, gives

Philamax the role of an audience member; he chillingly reflects that, whatever 'the play may prove, . . ./I doe not like the prologue'.

152 Davenant, *Platonick Lovers,* A3a.

153 Shirley, *Cardinal,* F3b.

154 Stephens, *Satirical Essays,* 245–6.

155 For the argument that epilogues '[accommodate] the passing fiction to some sense of the actual circumstances of its production and reception' see Robert Weimann, 'Performing at the Frontiers of Representation: Epilogue and Post-Scriptural Future in Shakespeare's Plays' in *The Arts of Performance in Elizabethan and Early Stuart Drama: Essays for G. K. Hunter,* ed. Murray Biggs (Edinburgh: Edinburgh University Press, 1991), 96–112 (98). It is usual to read the epilogue to *The Tempest* as an important feature of Prospero's character. To pick just one instance, Robin Kirkpatrick in 'The Italy of *The Tempest*' in *The Tempest and Its Travels,* ed. Peter Hulme and William H. Sherman (London: Reaktion Books, 2000), 78–96 (94), discusses the epilogue as Prospero's way of locating himself on the margins of the drama he has created, putting himself in the position of the shipwreck victims he has created. Similarly Rosalind's epilogue to *As You Like It* is often seen as a telling reflection on devices in the play, particularly the playwright's comment on the reversibility of gender roles. See Michael Shapiro, *Gender in Play on the Shakespearean Stage* (Ann Arbor: University of Michigan Press, 1994), 132–3.

5 SONGS AND MASQUES

1 John Marston, *The History of Antonio and Mellida: The First Part* (1602), C3b.

2 Ibid., E2b.

3 A point made by Andrew J. Sabol, 'Two Unpublished Stage Songs for the Aery of Children', *Renaissance News,* 8 (1960), 222–32 (31); David G. O'Neill, 'The Influence of Music in the Works of John Marston', *Music & Letters,* 53 (1972), 400–10 (407).

4 Marston, *Antonio and Mellida,* A2a.

5 For statistics on numbers of lost songs per author, see William Bowden's important *The English Dramatic Lyric* (New Haven: Yale University Press, 1951), 87. Bowden calls lost songs 'blank songs'.

6 Lukas Erne, *Shakespeare as Literary Dramatist* (Cambridge: Cambridge University Press, 2003), 131–91, *passim.*

7 George Chapman, *Al Fooles* (1605), STC 4963 only. The arguments for and against this dedicatory sonnet as being definitely by Chapman are set out in Arthur Freeman and Janet Ing Freeman, *John Payne Collier* (New Haven: Yale University Press, 2004), II:1076–8.

8 George Chapman, *The Revenge of Bussy D'Ambois* (1613), A3b.

9 Bowden, *English Dramatic Lyric,* 87; Francis Beaumont and John Fletcher, *Fifty Comedies and Tragedies* (1679), A1a.

10 W. W. Greg, 'The Authorship of the Songs in Lyly's Plays', *MLR*, 1 (1905), 43–52 (46).

11 R. W. Bond, 'Addendum on Lyly's Songs', *RES*, 7 (1931), 442–7 (444).

12 Thomas Middleton, *The Witch*, ed. L. Drees and Henry de Vocht (Louvain: Librairie Universitaire, 1945), 42, 62–3.

13 Arthur Sherbo ed., *Johnson on Shakespeare*, vols. VII and VIII of *The Yale Edition of the Works of Samuel Johnson* (New Haven: Yale University Press, 1968), VII:160.

14 This description of 'Formal Song' is supplied by David Lindley, *Shakespeare and Music*, Arden Critical Companions (London: Thomson and Thomson, 2006), 168.

15 James Shirley, *The Dukes Mistris* (1638), E3b.

16 James Shirley, *Poems* (1646), 33–4. 'English Song', New York Public Library, MS Drexel 4041 (dated 1640), no number, 88b–89a; John Gamble, *Song Book*, New York Public Library, MS Drexel 4257, no. 24; discussed in Julia K. Wood, 'William Lawes's Music for Plays' in *William Lawes*, ed. Andrew Ashbee (Aldershot: Ashgate, 1998), 43. Why a song might be read is covered later in the chapter.

17 Thomas Heywood, *Rape of Lucrece* (1608), A2a.

18 Ibid., G3b.

19 Thomas Heywood, *Rape of Lucrece* (1630), H1a; Thomas Heywood, *Pleasant Dialogues and Dramma's* (1637), 262.

20 Heywood, *Rape* (1630), F4a; Thomas Heywood, *A Challenge for Beautie* (1636), I2b.

21 Robert Greene, *The Historie of Orlando Furioso, one of the Twelve Pieres of France* (1594), H4b; Robert Greene, *The Scottish Historie of James the Fourth* (1598), G4b; Thomas Heywood, *The Escapes of Jupiter*, from the autograph MS (Egerton 1994), ed. H. D. Janzen (Oxford: Malone Society, 1977), 13; John Marston [with William Barksted and Lewis Mackin], *The Insatiate Countesse* (1613), F2a.

22 A suggestion made by R. W. Bond in his edition of John Lyly, *The Complete Works* (Oxford: Clarendon Press, 1902), II:265, and disputed by Greg, 'The Authorship of the Songs in Lyly's Plays', 52.

23 *The Returne from Pernassus* (1606), H2a; William Percy, *Necromantes* in *Plays*, Huntington Library, MS HM 4, 160b.

24 John Dowland, *First Booke of Songes or Ayres* (1597), no. 6; *Everie Woman in her Humor* (1609), B2b; George Chapman, Ben Jonson and John Marston, *Eastward Hoe* (1605), D4b; Dowland, *First Booke of Songes*, no. 13; *Everie Woman in her Humor*, B1b; Chapman, Jonson and Marston, *Eastward Hoe*, A4a; Dowland, *First Booke of Songes*, no. 15; *Song Book*, British Library, MS Add 17786–91, and *'Giles Earle his Booke'*, British Library, MS Add 24665, 32; *Song Book*, Christ Church Oxford, MS Mus 439, 70; 'Songs Unto the Viol and Lute', New York Public Library, MS Drexel 4175; Francis Beaumont, *The Knight of the Burning Pestle* (1613), C4b; E3b; John Dowland, *Third and Last Booke of Songs or Aires* (1603), no. 7; George Chapman, *The Widdowes Teares* (1612), K2a.

25 John Marston, *The Dutch Courtezan* (1605), c3a; Robert Jones, *First Booke of Songes and Ayres* (1600), no. 19. *Everie Woman in her Humor*, D3b and H2a; Robert Jones, *Second Booke of Songs and Ayres* (1601), no. 5; Thomas Dekker and John Webster, *North-ward Hoe* (1607), F4a; Beaumont, *Knight of the Burning Pestle* (1613), E3b.

26 Thomas Morley, *The First Booke of Balletts* (1595), no. 4; Thomas Morley, *The First Booke of Consort Lessons* (1599), no. 12; Beaumont, *Knight of the Burning Pestle* (1613), K1b; Beaumont, *Knight of the Burning Pestle* (1613), G3b; Thomas Morley, *First Booke of Ayres* (1600), no. 6. Lindley, *Shakespeare and Music*, 198.

27 Thomas Middleton, *A Trick to Catch the Old-One* (1608), G3a; Thomas Ravenscroft, 'The Scriveners Servants Song of Holborne' in *Melismata* (1611), 12.

28 John Marston, *Jacke Drums Entertainment* (1601), 11b; Thomas Ravenscroft, *Deuteromelia* (1609), no. 17; Thomas Dekker, *Blurt Master-constable* (1602), G3a; Thomas Ravenscroft, *A Briefe Discourse* (1614), no. 15. Songs of Ravenscroft's performed after he had published them include the chorus of 'Of all the birds that ever I see' from Ravenscroft's *Deuteromelia* (1609), no. 7, in Beaumont's *Knight of the Burning Pestle* (1613), 51; 'who can sing so merry a note' from Thomas Ravenscroft's *Pammelia* (1609), no. 100, in Beaumont's *Knight of the Burning Pestle* (1613), 63; and 'Hey ho, nobody at home' from *Pammelia*, 85, in Beaumont's *Knight of the Burning Pestle* (1613), 63.

29 Thomas Campion's authorship of the poem has been a subject of mild dispute. The music and words are thought to be his by David Greer, ' "What if a day": An Examination of the Words and Music', *Music & Letters*, 43 (1962), 304–19; he is said to have reworked an old text by A. E. H. Swaen, 'The Authorship of "What if a Day," and Its Various Versions', *Modern Philology*, 4 (1907), 397–422. Richard Brome, *The Queen and Concubine* in *Five Newe Playes* (1659), A2b; *Philotus* (1603), F4b (the song is absent from the play when it is reprinted in 1612). That Brome is using Campion is a suggestion made by Felix E. Schelling in *A Book of Seventeenth Century Lyrics* (Boston, MA: Ginn and Company, 1899), 259. 'Mistris since you so much desire' is included by Philip Rosseter in his collection of Campion works in *A Booke of Ayres* (1601), xvi; Chapman, Jonson and Marston, *Eastward Hoe*, D3b. Rosseter, *Booke of Ayres*, no. 5; Beaumont, *Knight of the Burning Pestle* (1613), K2a.

30 See Linda Phyllis Austern, *Music in English Children's Drama of the Later Renaissance* (Philadelphia: Gordon and Breach Science Publishers, 1992), 205.

31 William St Clair, *The Reading Nation in the Romantic Period* (Cambridge: Cambridge University Press, 2004), 153, 697.

32 John Fletcher, *The Humorous Lieutenant* in Francis Beaumont and John Fletcher, *Comedies and Tragedies* (1647), 3S2a; John Fletcher, *Demetrius and Enanthe*, ed. Margaret McLaren Cook and F. P. Wilson (London: Malone Society, 1951), 88.

33 William Cavendish, Earl of Newcastle, *The Country Captain from British Library Harl. MS 7650*, ed. Anthony Johnson (Oxford: Malone Society, 1999),

44; William Cavendish, Earl of Newcastle, *The Country Captaine, and the Varietie* (1649), 58; Shirley, *Poems*, 51, 'A Catch'. True, Shirley was a friend of Cavendish and assisted him 'in the composure of certain Plays which the Duke afterwards published' – see Anthony Wood, *Athenae Oxonienses* (1692), 262: the song might have been freely given to Cavendish by its author. On the other hand, this play may be partly attributed to Shirley simply *because* his verse is used in it.

34 Missing from Bodleian Library MS, Rawl. Poet 214, they are to be found in British Library MS, Birch Collection, Add 4453, and Phineas Fletcher, *Sicelides a Piscatory* (1631), D2a, L3b. See Giles Fletcher and Phineas Fletcher, *Giles and Phineas Fletcher: Poetical Works*, ed. Frederick S. Boas (Cambridge: Cambridge University Press, 1908), 1:xvii.

35 Thomas Middleton, *Hengist, King of Kent, or the Mayor of Queenborough*, ed. Grace Ioppolo (Oxford: Malone Society, 2003), 4, 50 (edition of the Portland manuscript); Thomas Middleton, *Hengist, King of Kent; or the Mayor of Queenborough . . . from the Manuscript in the Folger Shakespeare Library*, ed. R. C. Bald (New York and London: Charles Scribner's Sons, 1938), 7, 62; Thomas Middleton, *The Mayor of Quinborough a Tragedy* (1661). Brome's manuscript, Lichfield MS 68 in Lichfield Cathedral Library, is quoted here from Richard Brome, *The English Moore*, ed. Sara Jayne Steen (Columbia: University of Missouri Press, 1983), 93; Richard Brome, *The English Moor* in *Five Newe Plays* (1659), 56. John Fletcher, Philip Massinger [and Francis Beaumont?], *The Beggars Bush*, Folger Shakespeare Library, MS j.b.5, 174; Fredson Bowers in Francis Beaumont and John Fletcher, *The Dramatic Works*, ed. Fredson Bowers (Cambridge: Cambridge University Press, 1966–), 111:235.

36 Thomas Heywood, *The Golden Age* (1611), 11b; Heywood, *Escapes of Jupiter*, ed. Janzen, 35.

37 Walter Montagu, *The Shepheards Paradise*, British Library, MS Sloane 3649, and Walter Montagu, *The Shepheards Paradise*, Folger Shakespeare Library, MS v.b.203, contain the songs and prologue. The latter is further annotated in pencil on the front, 'This differs very much from the other ms copy which I have. The other copy does not contain the songs between the acts,' a note thought to be by Thorn-Drury; the other known manuscripts are Walter Montagu, *The Shepheards Paradise*, British Library, MS Stowe 976; Walter Montagu, *The Shepheards Paradise*, British Library, MS Add 41617; and Walter Montagu, *The Shepheards Paradise*, Folger Shakespeare Library, MS v.b.204. The printed edition, without prologue or songs, is *The Shepheard's Paradise* (1659).

38 Alnwick Castle Library, MS Alnwick 508 lacks the songs; Alnwick Castle Library, MS Alnwick 509 contains them, largely grouped at the end of the plays as 'Songs That be vacant in the foresaid Pastoralls and Comoedyes'; they are also in *Plays*, Huntington Library, MS HM 4. See William Percy, *Mahomet and His Heaven (1601)*, ed. Matthew Dimmock (Aldershot: Ashgate, 2006), 47–8.

39 Shirley, *Poems*, 75; Thomas Goffe, *The Careles Shepherdess* (1656), 26. That John Gough may have authored *Careles Shepherdess* is argued in Norbert

F. O'Donnell, 'The Authorship of The Careless Shepherdess', *Philological Quarterly*, 33 (1954), 43–7.

40 James Shirley, *Wittie Faire One* (1633), E2a; Thomas Carew, *Poems* (1640), 184.

41 *The Wisdome of Doctor Dodypoll* (1600), A4b. George Peele, *The Hunting of Cupid* (1591), reproduced from Drummond's transcript in *The Life and Minor Works of George Peele*, ed. David H. Horne (New Haven: Yale University Press, 1952), 204–5. Music for this song survives in John Bartlet's *A Booke of Ayres* (1606), no. 14. See John P. Cutts, 'Peele's *Hunting of Cupid*', *Studies in the Renaissance*, 5 (1958), 121–32. John Suckling, *The Goblins* (1646), 25, 27; Simon Sheppard, *The Committee-man Curried* (1647), B1b, B2a.

42 John Fletcher and Thomas Middleton?, *The Nice Valour* in Beaumont and Fletcher, *Comedies and Tragedies* (1647), 3U3a. The attribution to Middleton is explored by Taylor in Gary Taylor and John Lavagnino, eds., *Thomas Middleton and Early Modern Textual Culture* (Oxford: Clarendon Press, 2007), 426–7.

43 William Percy, *The Faery Pastorall* in *The Cuckqueans and Cuckolds Errants and the Faery Pastoral* (1824), 154.

44 John Webster, *The Dutchesse of Malfy* (1623), H2a. That this was probably added by the author during proof-correction – it is only in Q1b – is pointed out in John Webster, *The Works*, ed. David Gunty, David Carnegie, Antony Hammond and Doreen DelVecchio (Cambridge: Cambridge University Press, 1995), 1:527.

45 W. J. Lawrence, 'The Date of *The Duchess of Malfi*', *Athenaeum*, 4673 (1919), 1235. John P. Cutts, 'Jacobean Masque and Stage Music', *Music & Letters*, 35 (1954), 185–201 (193).

46 Heywood, *Rape of Lucrece* (1608), K2a.

47 Thomas Killigrew, *The Second Part of Cicilia and Clorinda* in *Comedies and Tragedies* (1664), 309; the same song and note are to be found after the text and at the back of a manuscript copy of the play in the Folger Shakespeare Library, MS v.b.209, 50–1. The Folger manuscript, which contains no date, may of course be a copy of the printed text.

48 Thomas Carew, *Poems with a Maske* (1651).

49 John Lyly, *Campaspe* in *Six Court Comedies* (1632), G10b; Thomas Middleton, *A Mad World my Masters* (1640), K4a; Lyly, *Campaspe* in *Six Court Comedies*, K4a; Thomas Dekker and John Ford, *The Sun's-Darling* (1656), C1a.

50 Chapman, Jonson and Marston, *Eastward Hoe*, D4a; John Fletcher and Philip Massinger, *The Bloody Brother* (1639), H4b.

51 See John Jowett and Gary Taylor, 'With New Additions: Theatrical Interpolation in *Measure for Measure*' in *Shakespeare Reshaped*, ed. Gary Taylor and John Jowett (Oxford: Oxford University Press, 1993), 132–3.

52 Francis Quarles, *The Virgin Widow* (1649), 34; Brome, *Queen and Concubine* in *Five Newe Playes* (1659), A2b.

53 Thomas Middleton, *A Chast Mayd in Cheape-Side* (1630), 49; Thomas Middleton, *More Dissemblers Besides Women* in *Two New Playes* (1657), 19.

Beaumont, *Knight of the Burning Pestle* (1613), F1a; Francis Beaumont and John Fletcher, *The Captaine* in Beaumont and Fletcher, *Comedies and Tragedies* (1647), 2G4a. Robert Johnson's music for this song survives in '*Songs Unto the Viol and Lute*', no. 44; '*English Song*', no number, 124a; and Gamble, *Song Book*, no. 35, where it is entitled 'answer', and *Song Book*, Bodleian Library, MS CCC. 327, 11b.

54 Richard Cumberland, *Song.*, Folger Shakespeare Library, y.d.93.
55 George Jeffreys, *Musical Settings*, British Library, MS Add 10338, 46, discussed in John P. Cutts, 'Some Jacobean and Caroline Dramatic Lyrics', *Notes and Queries*, n.s. 2 (1955), 106–9.
56 Leonard Willan, *Astraea or, True Love's Myrrour* (1651), A6b, A7b.
57 Ben Jonson, *The Fountaine of Selfe-Love. Or Cynthias Revels* (1601), H2b–H3a.
58 *Song Book*, Christ Church Oxford, MS Mus 439. See Andrew J. Sabol, 'A Newly-Discovered Contemporary Song Setting for Jonson's *Cynthia's Revels*', *Notes and Queries*, 203 (1958), 384–5.
59 The music can be found in Gamble, *Song Book*, no. 109; see Catherine A. Henze, 'How Music Matters: Some Songs of Robert Johnson in the Plays of Beaumont and Fletcher', *Comparative Drama* 34:1 (2000), 1–32 (15).
60 A point made by Henze, ibid., 1.
61 Alan H. Nelson, ed., *Records of Early English Drama: Cambridge* (Toronto: University of Toronto Press, 1989), 1:535.
62 M. Hope Dodds, 'Songs in Lyly's Plays', *TLS* (28 June 1941), 311. See John Lyly, *Mydas* in *Six Court Comedies* (1632), z1b–z2a.
63 John Lyly, *Gallathea* in *Six Court Comedies* (1632), R7a–b. Lyly, *Complete Works*, ed. Bond, 11:572. The argument is also put forward by M. R. Best, 'A Note on the Songs in Lyly's Plays', *Notes and Queries*, 12 (1965), 93–4 (93).
64 A point made by G. K. Hunter, *John Lyly: The Humanist as Courtier* (London: Routledge and Kegan Paul, 1962), 367–8.
65 Thomas Ravenscroft's songbooks *Pammelia* (1609) and *Deuteromelia* (also 1609), which contain between them six Paul's Boy songs dating from between 1598 and 1604, also suggest there was a theatre library to which Ravenscroft had access – see Linda Phyllis Austern, 'Thomas Ravenscroft: Musical Chronicler of an Elizabethan Theatre Company', *Journal of the Royal Musical Association*, 38 (1985), 238–63 (240).
66 Other hints at theatrical music libraries are found in, for instance, a musical miscellany in Christ Church Oxford, which contains, muddled amongst its secular songs, a series of dramatic songs for boys that seems to reflect a choir-school manuscript, perhaps (given that it contains 'the Kisse' from Jonson's *Cynthias Revels* and 'Here's none but only I' from *Everie Woman in her Humor*) one belonging to the Children of the Chapel Royal – a suggestion made in Mary Chan, '*Cynthia's Revels* and Music for a Choir School', *Studies in the Renaissance*, 18 (1971), 134–72, but doubted by Peter Holman in 'Music for the Stage I: Before the Civil War', in *Music in Britain: The Seventeenth Century*, ed. Ian Spink (Oxford: Blackwell, 1992), 282–305 (293). '*Giles Earle his Booke*', meanwhile, a manuscript dated 1615, provides a song for Jonson's

Poetaster, 'if I freely may discover', and, next to it, a song for Marston's *Dutch Courtezan*, 'The darke is my delight'. As the first had been written for the Children of the Chapel, and the second for the Queen's Revels (the company that succeeded them and partly subsumed them), he too appears to be copying songs from a common theatre source – see David Fuller, 'Ben Jonson's Plays and Their Contemporary Music', *Music & Letters*, 58 (1977), 60–75 (64). The music that filters abroad likewise often seems to come from single collected sources: Adraen Valerius' Dutch music collection, *Nederlandtsch Gedenck-Clanck* (1626), contains among its 79 pieces at least seventeen English airs, and appears to come from a theatrical 'pool' of music gathered from a group of strolling players – see Mary Chan, *Music in the Theatre of Ben Jonson* (Oxford: Oxford University Press, 1980), 32. One Welsh manuscript details a series of tunes belonging to Tarlton, and a series belonging to Alleyn; again, a company's *cache* seems to have been circulating. See Sally Harper, *Music in Welsh Culture Before 1650* (Aldershot: Ashgate, 2007), 320–4. Every acting company, the suggestion is, had a collection of theatre songs that circulated with one another rather than (or as well as) the plays they enliven.

67 *John Sturt Lute Book*, British Library, MS Add 38539, discussed in John P. Cutts, 'The Original Music to Middleton's *The Witch*', *Shakespeare Quarterly*, 7 (1956), 203–9 (203); *Part-book in the hand of Edward Lowe*, Bodleian Library, MS Mus. d. 238, discussed in Peter Walls, 'New Light on Songs by William Lawes and John Wilson', *Music & Letters*, 57 (1976), 55–64.

68 Peter Holman, *Four and Twenty Fiddlers: The Violin at the English Court, 1540–1690* (Oxford: Clarendon Press, 1993), 188.

69 It only emerged years later in the hands of the actor and playwright Benjamin Griffin; see Thomas Middleton, *The Witch*, ed. W. W. Greg (Oxford: Malone Society, 1948 [1950]), v.

70 Ross W. Duffin, *Shakespeare's Songbook* (New York and London: W. W. Norton & Company, 2004), 32.

71 George Peele, *The Famous Chronicle of King Edward the First* (1593), C1a; Anthony Rudd, Thomas Richards and Laurence Johnson, *Misogonus* in R. W. Bond, ed., *Early Plays from the Italian* (Oxford: Clarendon Press, 1911), 197; John Pikering, *Horestes* (1567), B2b.

72 George Chapman, *The Gentleman Usher* (1606), B2a.

73 F. W. Sternfeld, *Music in Shakespearean Tragedy* (London: Routledge and Kegan Paul, 1962), 22.

74 James Shirley, *The Changes* (1632), 63.

75 Richard Brome, *The Novella* in *Five New Playes* (1653), K5a.

76 Jonson, *The Fountaine of Selfe-Love . . . Cynthias Revels*, H3a–b.

77 Thomas Dekker, *Blurt Master-constable* (1602), C3a; Nathan Field, *Amends for Ladies* (1618), F3a.

78 Ben Jonson, *The New Inne* (1631), F3a; Ben Jonson, *Sad Shepherd* in *The Workes* (1641), S3a. See also Ben Jonson, *Staple of Newes* in *Bartholmew*

Fayre (1631), G3b, where Madrigal has made a song to 'the *tune* the *Fidlers* play'd,/That we all lik'd so well': the response is 'read it, read it' – suggesting the words are written on a paper; when he has done so, Picklock suggests, 'Call in the *Fidlers. Nicke*, the boy shall sing it', and Ben Jonson, *The Divell is an Asse* in *Bartholmew Fayre* (1631), E1a–b, where Wittipol gives Manley '*a paper, wherein is the copy of a Song*' which is to be sung 'unto the ayre you love so well'; later, at the end of the scene, it is recited by Wittipol in a moment that is partly plot-point (he is overheard by the husband of the woman the song was designed to woo) and partly, it seems, another attempt to ensure that the words keep a spoken integrity aside from the tune.

79 A suggestion made by Harper, *Music in Welsh Culture*, 324–5.

80 Discussed in Philip Massinger, *Believe As You List*, from the autograph MS (Egerton 2828), licensed 6 May 1631, ed. C. J. Sisson (Oxford: Malone Society, 1927), xxv–xxvi, 67.

81 Thomas Middleton, *The Widdow* (1652), 26; *Everie Woman in her Humor*, H2a; Thomas Heywood, *The First and Second Partes of King Edward the Fourth* (1600), c8b.

82 John Fletcher, *The Wild-Goose Chase* (1652), p1b.

83 John Wilson and Edward Lowe, *Song book*, Bodleian Library, MS Mus. b. 1, 43; quoted in John P. Cutts, '"Speak–demand–we'll answer": Hecate and the Other Three Witches', *Shakespeare Jahrbuch*, 96 (1960), 173–6 (175–6).

84 See also John Fletcher and William Rowley's *Maid in the Mill* in Beaumont and Fletcher's *Comedies and Tragedies* (1647), A3b, where the song '*Come follow me (you Country-Lasses)*' ends in a chorus, '*Come follow me, come follow, &c*' – the '&c' standing in, as the surviving musical text reveals, for the single word 'mee'; 'Com follow me' in '*English Song*', no. 22. One 'etc.' song is irrecoverable because the music that survives for it is instrumental only. The Niece in James Shirley's *The Constant Maid* (1640), c3b, talks of how she could 'love an old man/Rarely, An old man with a bed full of bones, &c', and John Playford, *The Dancing Master* (1653), 6, published thirteen years later, contains a dance for a tune entitled 'An Old man is a Bed full of bones'; in this instance, the metre and the measure but not the words to the lyrics are all that posterity has been given.

85 *Ratseis Ghost* (1605), A3b.

86 See Walter Montagu, *The Shepheards Paradise*, ed. Sarah Poynting (unpublished D.Phil. thesis, University of Oxford, 1999), 71–2. There are 29 recorded copies of 'Cock-lorell', 17 copies of 'Ffrom a Gypsie in the morninge' and three other songs; see Peter Beal, *Index of English Literary Manuscripts 1450–1700*, (New York: R. R. Bowker, 1980), 11:286–9.

87 Henry Glapthorne, *The Lady Mother*, ed. Arthur Brown (Oxford: Malone Society, [1958] 1959), 26.

88 Bowden, *The English Dramatic Lyric*, 91, 93.

89 Percy, *Plays*, 191.

90 John P. Cutts, *La musique de scène de la troupe de Shakespeare* (Paris: Éditions du Centre National de la Recherche Scientifique, 1959), xv n. 10.

91 Francis Beaumont, John Fletcher and Philip Massinger, *The Coxcombe* in Beaumont and Fletcher, *Comedies and Tragedies* (1647), 2N1b, 2P3b. Suzanne Gossett, 'The Term "Masque" in Shakespeare and Fletcher and *The Coxcomb*', *Studies in English Literature*, 14 (1974), 285–95 questions that this indicates a lost masque; 'if a masque was cut, a dance certainly remained' (288).

92 Thomas May, *The Old Couple* (1658), 25. Edward Lowe, *Commonplace Book*, British Library, MS Add 29396, 21b–22; Robert Johnson's music for this song survives in '*Songs Unto the Viol and Lute*', no. 44; '*Songs Unto the Viol and Lute*', 41 (lute), 51 (viol). John P. Cutts, 'Robert Johnson: King's Musician in His Majesty's Public Entertainment', *Music & Letters*, 39 (1955), 110–26 (123); John P. Cutts, 'An Unpublished Contemporary Setting of a Shakespeare Song', *Shakespeare Survey*, 9 (1956), 86–9 (87). John Fletcher, *The Mad Lover* in Beaumont and Fletcher, *Comedies and Tragedies* (1647), C3a. In *John Bull Manuscript*, Fitzwilliam Museum, MUMS 782 [formerly MS 52. D,25], 98b–99, music for this song is situated by the original music for another song from *The Mad Lover*, 'Orpheus I am'. See also Shirley, *Dukes Mistris*, E3b, where Horatio asks Fiametta to 'Read this', and, when asked whether or not it is a song, replies, 'It may be, with a voice, and tune put too't', keeping an openness as to whether the song will be sung, perhaps because a composer could not be found, or perhaps, again, because the players did not have good enough singing voices.

93 Richmond Samuel Noble, *Shakespeare's Use of Song* (London: Oxford University Press, 1923), 77. The idea also receives acceptance from E. A. J. Honigmann, *The Texts of 'Othello' and Shakespearian Revision* (London and New York: Routledge, 1996), 40.

94 Nathaniel Richards, *The Tragedy Of Messallina* (1640), F6b.

95 Middleton, *A Chast Mayd in Cheape-Side*, 49; Middleton, *More Dissemblers* in *Two New Playes*, 19. See John Jowett, 'Middleton's Song of Cupid', *Notes and Queries*, 239 (1994), 66–70. Music for this song can be found in '*Songs Unto the Viol and Lute*', New York Public Library, nos. 24 and 56.

96 This point is regularly made by music historians, and questioned by theatre historians. It is suggested by Peter J. Seng, *The Vocal Songs in the Plays of Shakespeare: A Critical History* (Cambridge, MA: Harvard University Press, 1967), 109; Winifred Maynard, 'Ballads, Songs, and Masques in the Plays of Shakespeare' in *Elizabethan Lyric Poetry and Its Music* (Oxford: Clarendon Press, 1986), 202.

97 Middleton, *A Mad World*, K4a; Richard Flecknoe, *Love's Kingdom* (1664), G1b–G2a; Francis Beaumont and John Fletcher, *The Maids Tragedie* (1622), C2a; B4a; William Davenant, *The Unfortunate Lovers* in *The Works of Sr. William Davenant, Kt* (1673), 40.

98 Thomas Middleton, *A Faire Quarrell* (1617b), H4a.

99 Thomas Dekker, *The Shomakers Holiday* (1600), A3b–A4a. Thomas Dekker, *The Shoemaker's Holiday*, ed. Peter Smith (London: Nick Hern Books, 2004), xxx.

100 Wood, 'William Lawes's Music for Plays', 19–20.

101 Suzanne Gossett, 'Masque Influence in the Dramaturgy of Beaumont and Fletcher', *Modern Philology*, 69 (1971–2), 199–208 (199).

102 Francis Beaumont, *Masque of the Inner Temple and Gray's Inn* (1613), B2b–B3a; John Fletcher and William Shakespeare, *The Two Noble Kinsmen* (1634), 45–6; the music is probably that for 'the maypole' in *Book of Masques*, British Library, MS Add 10444; see Cutts, 'Jacobean Masque and Stage Music', 197.

103 *'Songs Unto the Viol and Lute'*, no. 43; *Song Book*, British Library, MS Add 29481, 5b–6a; *'English Song'*, no. 26. Lawrence, 'Date of *The Duchesse of Malfi'*, 1235. Cutts, 'Jacobean Masque and Stage Music', 193. The words of the song can be found freestanding in miscellanies like that in the Folger Shakespeare Library, MS v.a.124, 43b, where it is called 'Lovers deluded by their Mistresses'; they are not contained in the extant text of Campion's *Lords Maske*.

104 John Chamberlain, Letter to Dudley Carleton, 3 January 1618, in *The Letters of John Chamberlain*, ed. Norman E. McClure (Philadelphia: American Philosophical Society, 1939), 11:125–6; *Book of Masques*. Nan Cooke Carpenter, 'Shakespeare and Music: Unexplored Areas', in *Shakespeare and the Arts*, ed. Stephen Orgel and Sean Keilen (New York and London: Garland Publishing, 1999), 123–35 (133) joins Cutts and Lawrence in thinking this music relates to *Timon of Athens*; Andrew J. Sabol, *Songs and Dances for the Stuart Masque* (Providence, RI: Brown University Press, 1959), 168, disagrees, thinking this music is actually for Jonson's *Salmacida Spolia*.

105 William Shakespeare, *The Late, and much Admired Play, called Pericles, Prince of Tyre* (1609), D2a. Thomas Campion, *The Discription of a Maske, presented before the Kinges Majestie at White-Hall, on Twelfth Night Last in Honour of the Lord Hayes, and his Bride . . . their Marriage having been the same day at Court Solemnized* (1607), C4a.

106 John P. Cutts, 'Robert Johnson and the Court Masque', *Music & Letters*, 41 (1955), 110–25 (120). Ben Jonson, *Masque of Queenes* in *The Workes* (1616), 945.

107 Middleton, *The Witch*, ed. Greg, 89.

108 Irwin Smith, 'Ariel and the Masque in *The Tempest*', *Shakespeare Quarterly*, 21 (1970), 213–22. That same marriage has been put forward, by T. W. Craik in his edition of Francis Beaumont and John Fletcher, *The Maid's Tragedy* (Manchester: Manchester University Press, 1988), 34, as the reason for the additional three songs in Beaumont and Fletcher's *Maids Tragedie*.

109 John H. Long, 'Another Masque for *The Merry Wives of Windsor*', *Shakespeare Quarterly*, 3 (1952), 39–43. See also Tiffany Stern, introduction to William Shakespeare, *Merry Wives* (New York: Barnes and Noble, forthcoming).

110 See Erica Veevers, 'A Masque Fragment by Aurelian Townshend', *Notes and Queries*, 12 (1965), 343–5 (345).

111 Thomas Middleton and William Rowley, *A Courtly Masque: the Device Called, World Tost at Tennis* (1620), B1a; for the play's confusion of features for performance in the public theatre and at Denmark House, see

C. E. McGee's textual notes to *World Tossed* in Taylor and Lavagnino, eds., *Thomas Middleton*, 668 and W. L. Halstead, 'Note on Dekker's *Old Fortunatus*', *Modern Language Notes* (1939), 351–2.

112 Richard Brome, *The Weeding of the Covent-Garden* in *Five New Playes* (1659), B5b.

113 Ibid., D8b.

114 Ibid., D6b.

115 Ibid., A2a, A2b, A3a, A3b, A4a.

116 Ibid., A2b.

117 Christopher R. Wilson and Michela Calore, eds., *Music in Shakespeare: A Dictionary* (London: Continuum, 2005), 68.

118 Richard Brome, *A Joviall Crew* (1652), K3b.

119 *Miscellany*, Bodleian Library, MS Rawl. Poet 172, 60. Francis Beaumont, *Poems* (1653).

120 Brome, *Queen and Concubine* in *Five New Playes* (1659), A2b.

121 Richard Brome and Thomas Heywood, *The Late Lancashire Witches* (1634), I4a.

122 The contents of Brome's contract are extracted from a series of court cases; it is summarised in Gerard Eades Bentley, *The Jacobean and Caroline Stage* (London: Oxford University Press, 1941–68), 1:295.

123 Philip Massinger, *The Fatall Dowry* (1632), A4a–b, I1a; Dekker, *Shomakers Holiday* (1600), A3b–A4a; Thomas Dekker and John Webster, *Westward Hoe* (1607), I2b.

124 John Fletcher, *The Bloody Brother* (1639), A1b; Dabridgcourt Belchier, *Hans Beer-Pot* (1618), H2b–H3a; H3b.

125 Philip Massinger, *The Guardian* in *Three New Playes* (1655), 91–2; William Habington, *The Queene of Arragon* (1640), I2b–I3a. The copy is in The Chapin Library, Williams College, Massachusetts (library closed until 2011); it is discussed in W. W. Greg, *A Bibliography of the English Printed Drama to the Restoration* (London: Bibliographical Society, 1959), II:592.

126 *Philotus*, F4b; Heywood, *Rape of Lucrece* (1608), K2a; Middleton, *A Mad World*, K4a.

127 Beaumont and Fletcher, *Fifty Comedies and Tragedies*, A1a.

128 The statistic is from John Robert Moore, 'The Songs in Lyly's Plays', *PMLA*, 42 (1927), 623–40 (634).

129 Francis Beaumont, John Fletcher and Philip Massinger, *Loves Cure* in Beaumont and Fletcher *Comedies and Tragedies* (1647), 5R3b–5R4a.

130 Francis Beaumont and John Fletcher, *The Works*, ed. Alexander Dyce (1843–6), x:149n.

131 Robert K. Turner Jr, introduction to *Valentinian* in Beaumont and Fletcher, *Dramatic Works*, ed. Bowers, IV:269; 274.

132 Discussed in John Fletcher, *The Woman's Prize: Or, The Tamer Tamed*, ed. George B. Ferguson (London: Mouton, 1966), 31.

133 John Fletcher and William Rowley, *The Maid in the Mill* in Beaumont and Fletcher, *Comedies and Tragedies* (1647), 4C2a.

134 Ben Jonson, *Epicoene* in *Workes* (1616), 530.

135 Ibid., 530–1.

136 Ibid., 532. The song itself can be found in '*English Song*', no. 64.

137 Jonson, *The Divell is an Asse* in *Bartholmew Fayre*, E1b.

138 John Suckling, *Brennoralt* (1646), 15. William Lawes, *Songbook*, British Library, MS Add 31432, 7b–8a; discussed in Wood, 'William Lawes's Music for Plays', 41.

139 William Berkeley, *The Lost Lady* (1638), 37. William Berkeley, *The Lost Lady*, Folger Shakespeare Library, MS j.b.4.

140 William Lawes, *Songbook*, British Library, MS Add 31432 and 'Wher did you borrow' in 'English Song', New York Public Library, MS Drexel 4041, no. 5. The song is discussed in Wood, 'William Lawes's Music for Plays', 47. The additional line is retained in a neat manuscript of this play in the author's autograph made for Queen Henrietta Maria; see Folger Shakespeare Library, MS j.b.4, 151b.

141 '*SONG, by a Fairy of Oberon's Train*' in *Garrick's notes concerning a production of A Midsummer Night's Dream*, Folger Shakespeare Library, MS w.b.469.

142 '*The Musick in Mackbeth in Score*', Folger Shakespeare Library, MS w.b.537, 1–2.

143 *Music Miscellany*, Folger Shakespeare Library, MS v.a.409, 17. Discussed in Ross W. Duffin, 'Catching the Burthen: A New Round of Shakespearean Musical Hunting', *Studies in Music*, 19–20 (2000–1), 1–15 (10).

144 John Clavell, *The So[l]ddered Citizen*, ed. J. H. P. Pafford and W. W. Greg (Oxford: Malone Society, 1936), 106; *Narcissus*, ed. Margaret L. Lee (London: David Nutt, 1893), 2; Richard Brome, *The Northern Lasse* (1632), H2b.

145 William Shakespeare, *As You Like It*, ed. Juliet Dusinberre, The Arden Shakespeare (London: Thomson and Thomson, 2006), 132–3, 301. Her choice echoes a suggestion made by Peter Seng, 'The Foresters' Song in *As You Like It*', *Shakespeare Quarterly*, 10 (1959), 246–9.

146 Taylor and Lavagnino, *Thomas Middleton*, 426–7.

147 Fletcher and Middleton?, *Nice Valour* in Beaumont and Fletcher, *Comedies and Tragedies* (1647), 3U3a.

148 *Miscellany*, Bodleian Library, MS Ashmole 36–7, fol. 26.

149 Peter Beal, in *Index of English Literary Manuscripts* 1:93–5 lists 41 extant manuscripts dating from before and after the printing of *Nice Valour*, containing the words to the song. The song was first published as 'The Melancholly Lovers Song' in *A Description of the King and Queene of Fayries* (1635) without the 'O sweetest melancholy' line.

150 The music that contains the line can be found in *Song Book*, British Library, MS Egerton 2013, 3b.

151 Campion, *The Discription of a Maske, presented before the Kinges Maiestie*; Thomas Campion, *The Description of a maske: presented in the Banqueting roome at Whitehall, on Saint Stephens night last at the Mariage of the Right Honourable the Earle of Somerset: and the right noble the Lady Frances Howard*

(1614), D1b. Discussed in Frederick W. Sternfeld, 'A Song from Campion's Lord's Masque', *Journal of the Warburg and Courtauld Institutes*, 20 (1957), 373–5.

152 Massinger, *Fatall Dowry*, A4a–b, 11a. A variant of the song 'happy husband' can be found in *Miscellany*, Folger Shakespeare Library, MS v.a.308, 9.

153 *Clarke's MS Poems*, Folger Shakespeare Library, MS v.b.43, 25b.

154 Samuel Daniel, *Hymen's Triumph*, ed. John Pitcher (Oxford: Malone Society, 1994), xv.

155 *'English Song'*, no number, 127–9, first discussed in J. H. P. Pafford, 'Music and the Songs in *The Winter's Tale*', *Shakespeare Quarterly*, 10 (1959), 161–77 (165).

156 They can be found, for instance, in *Oxford Poetical Miscellanies*, Folger Shakespeare Library, MS v.a.162, 20.

157 *'Songs Unto the Viol and Lute'*, no. 41 ('To the lute'); 51 (viol); *Song Book*, British Library, MS Add 29396, 21b–22a.

158 Jonson, *Workes* (1641), E2b–E3a; see A. R. Braunmuller, 'Accounting for Absence: The Transcription of Space' in *New Ways of Looking at Old Texts*, ed. W. Speed Hill (New York: Center of Medieval and Early Renaissance Studies, 1993), 47–56 (51).

159 Fuller, 'Ben Jonson's Plays', 65.

160 *'English Song'*, no. 17; *Song Book*, Edinburgh University Library DC.1.69, 71.

161 A point made by Cutts, *La musique de scène*, 174.

162 John Fletcher, *The Pilgrim* in Beaumont and Fletcher, *Comedies and Tragedies* (1647), 4H1b–4H2a.

163 *Book of Masques*, 30b; *John Sturt Lute Book*, 19. Cutts, 'Robert Johnson: King's Musician', 122.

164 See Jowett, 'Middleton's Song of Cupid'.

165 Michael Wood, *In Search of Shakespeare*, television programme for BBC Two, first aired on 28 June 2003. The claim is not elucidated in his book of the series *In Search of Shakespeare* (London: BBC Worldwide Ltd, 2003), 315, where Wood simply states that Johnson 'composed the music for Shakespeare's collaborations with John Fletcher in *Cardenio*, *Henry VIII* and *The Two Noble Kinsmen*'.

166 Miguel de Cervantes Saavedra, *The History of the Valorous and Wittie Knight-Errant, Don-Quixote of the Mancha*, trans. Thomas Shelton (1612), 282, 299.

167 Lewis Theobald, *The Double Falshood* (1728), 48.

168 *Song Book*, Bodleian Library, MS Don. *c.* 57, 9, and *Song Book*, British Library, MS 11608, discussed in Cutts, 'Robert Johnson: King's Musician', 119–21.

169 James Shirley, *Bird in a Cage* (1633), F3a.

6 SCROLLS

1 Philip Massinger, *The Great Duke of Florence* (1636), G4a.

2 Francis Beaumont, John Fletcher and Philip Massinger, *Loves Cure* in Francis Beaumont and John Fletcher, *Comedies and Tragedies* (1647), 5S4b.

3 Francis Quarles, *The Virgin Widow* (1649), D2b.

4 Lodowick Carlell, *Arviragus and Philicia* (1639), E5b.

5 Ben Jonson, *Cynthias Revels* in *The Workes* (1616), 239.

6 Robert Tailor, *The Hogge hath Lost his Pearle* (1614), F1a–b.

7 Thomas May, *The Old Couple* (1658), 25.

8 *Tom a Lincoln*, ed. G. R. Proudfoot (Oxford: Malone Society, 1992), 75, xxvii; Francis Jaques, *The Queen of Corsica* (1642), ed. Henry D. Janzen (Oxford: Malone Society, 1989), 53–4; Walter Montagu, *The Shepherds' Paradise*, ed. Sarah Poynting (Oxford: Malone Society, 1997), 22–3.

9 Arthur Wilson, *The Swisser*, Librairie Fischbacher (Paris: Société Anonyme, 1904), 50; *Edmond Ironside*, ed. Eleanore Boswell (Oxford: Malone Society, 1927), 58.

10 Howard Marchitello, '(Dis)embodied Letters and *The Merchant of Venice*: Writing, Editing, History', *ELH*, 62 (1995), 237–65 (47); Jonathan Goldberg, 'Hamlet's Hand', *Shakespeare Quarterly*, 39 (1988), 307–27 (324–5).

11 Edward Cape Everard, *Memoirs of an Unfortunate Son of Thespis* (1818), 48–9.

12 In Robert Dodsley, *The King and the Miller of Mansfield* (1737), 13–14, the letter in question is separated from the dialogue and in italics:

> Dick alone.
>
> . . . the Letter seems to be wrote with an Air of Sincerity, I confess; and the Girl was never us'd to lie till she kept a Lord Company. Let me see, I'll read it once more.
> *Dear Richard,*
> *I am at last (tho' much too late for me) convinc'd of the Injury done to us*
> *both by that base Man, who made me think you false: . . . for your own sake I beg you to*
> *return hither, for I have some Hopes of being able to do you Justice, which is the only*
> *Comfort of your most distrest, but ever affectionate,*
> PEGGY.
> There can be no Cheat in this sure! The Letters she has sent are, I think, a Proof of her Sincerity. Well, I will go to her however . . .

13 As W. W. Greg points out in *Two Elizabethan Stage Abridgements: 'The Battle of Alcazar' and 'Orlando Furioso'* (Oxford: Malone Society, 1922), 218, 'the absence of the roundelays from A [the part of Orlando] is most instructive, since it shows that they were not learned as portions of the part but read by the actor from the actual scrolls hung up on the stage'.

14 W. W. Greg, *Dramatic Documents from the Elizabethan Playhouses* (Oxford: Clarendon Press, 1931), II: *Reproductions and Transcripts*, A, 42–8.

15 A suggestion made by Michael Warren in 'Greene's *Orlando*: W. W. Greg Furioso' in *Textual Formations and Reformations*, ed. Laurie E. Maguire and Thomas L. Berger (Newark, DE: University of Delaware Press, 1998), 67–91 (78–9).

16 Robert Greene, *The Historie of Orlando Furioso, one of the Twelve Pieres of France* (1594), D2b.

17 Lodowick Carlell, *The Passionate Lover, part i* (1655), 37; John Fletcher and Philip Massinger, *The Lovers Progress* in Beaumont and Fletcher, *Comedies and Tragedies* (1647), 3M2a; John Fletcher and Philip Massinger, *The Spanish*

Curat in Beaumont and Fletcher, *Comedies and Tragedies* (1647), E3a; Robert
Greene, *The Scottish Historie of James the Fourth* (1598), C1a.

18 Thomas Holcroft, *Try Again* (1790), Folger Shakespeare Library, Prompt
T 26, 27, 36, 53, 55; Samuel Foote, *Devil Upon Two Sticks* (1778), Folger
Shakespeare Library, Prompt D 21, 59, 58, 64.

19 Wentworth Smith, *The Hector of Germany or The Palsgrave, Prime Elector*
(1615), C4a.

20 Thomas Kyd, *Solyman and Perseda* (1592), 11b; *Charlemagne, or the Distracted
Emperor*. From the MS (Egerton 1994), ed. J. H. Walter (Oxford: Malone
Society, 1937), 62.

21 [Thomas Dekker?], *The Welsh Embassador, From the MS (Cardiff Public
Library)*, ed. H. Littledale and W. W. Greg (Oxford: Malone Society, 1920), 44.

22 Thomas Kyd, *The Spanish Tragedy* (1592), E1b. This special ink explains the
'bloodie' letters in other plays and why they are always described as looking
red (rather than brown, as actual blood would look) in appearance: 'How full
of ghastly wounds this letter shewes,' cries the Lady Honor, receiving a 'letter
written in . . . blood' before swooning in Nathan Field, *Amends for Ladies*
(1618), H1a. The same presumably goes for the 'letter written in . . . blood'
that Tamyra pens in George Chapman, *Bussy d'Amboys* (1607), 25.

23 George Whetstone, *Promos and Cassandra*, part i (1578), B1a.

24 Ben Jonson, *Bartholmew Fayre* (1631), F1b.

25 George Whetstone, *Promos and Cassandra*, part ii (1578), K1a.

26 Christopher Marlowe, *The Complete Works: Edward II*, ed. Richard Rowland
(Oxford: Oxford University Press, 1994), xxxvi; Christopher Marlowe,
Edward the Second, ed. Charles R. Forker (Manchester: Manchester University
Press, 1994), 8.

27 Christopher Marlowe, *Edward II* (1594), H1b.

28 Lewis Theobald in his edition of *The Works of Shakespeare*, 7 vols. (1733), VII:
295: 'Thus have the blundering and inadvertent Editors all along give us this
Stage-Direction.' I am grateful to Ivan Lupic for pointing out this earlier use
of the term.

29 William Shakespeare, *Hamlet* (1604), E4a.

30 Thomas Heywood, *The Fayre Mayde of the Exchange* (1607), G1a.

31 Discussed in more detail in Tiffany Stern, 'Letters, Verses and Double
Speech-Prefixes in *The Merchant of Venice*', *Notes and Queries*, 244 (1999),
231–3. Jeffrey Masten in 'Toward a Queer Address: The Taste of Letters and
Early Modern Male Friendship', *GLQ: A Journal of Lesbian and Gay Studies*,
10 (2004), 367–84 (369) disputes the implication of this reading, but not the
bibliographical evidence for it.

32 William Shakespeare, *Henry IV, Part I*, ed. David Bevington (Oxford and
New York: Oxford University Press, 1987), 206; E. K. Chambers, *William
Shakespeare: A Study of the Facts and Problems* (Oxford: Clarendon Press,
1930), 1:198.

33 William Canning, *Gesta Grayorum, or, The History of the High and Mighty
Prince, Henry Prince of Purpoole* (1688), 44.

34 *'Manuscript Speech of Henry Prince of Purpoole'*, Folger Shakespeare Library MS, v.a.190.

35 George Peele, *The Famous Chronicle of King Edward the First* (1593), G3a.

36 Philip Massinger, *Believe As You List*, from the autograph MS (Egerton 2828), licensed 6 May 1631, ed. C. J. Sisson (Oxford: Malone Society, 1927), I, II, 40, 41, 78.

37 Ibid., 99.

38 *The First Part of the Reign of King Richard the Second or Thomas of Woodstock*, ed. Wilhelmina P. Frijlinck (Oxford: Malone Society, 1929), 40, 56.

39 *Jane Shore Call-book* in 'Miscellaneous Theatrical Papers', dated 26 December 1832, Houghton Library, MS Thr 32.

40 W. Shakespeare, *Othello . . . As it is now acted at The Theatre Royal in Covent-Garden* (1761), Folger Shakespeare Library, Prompt Oth. 27, A3a; discussed in Edward Langhans, 'Othello as They Liked It', *On Stage Studies*, 7 (1983), 34–47.

41 W. Shakespeare, *Othello . . . As it is now acted at The Theatre Royal in Covent-Garden* (1761), 50.

42 Ibid., 51.

43 T. Edgar Pemberton, *A Memoir of Edward Askew Sothern* (1889), 252–4.

44 James M. Gibson, *The Philadelphia Shakespeare Story: Horace Howard Furness and the New Variorum Shakespeare* (New York: AMS Press, 1990), 188.

45 [William Shakespeare], *Passionate Pilgrim* (1599), A5a, A7a, C5a. Colin Burrow, 'Lyric in its Settings: Multiple Narratives and Lyric Voices in *Love's Labour's Lost*', unpublished paper delivered at Shakespeare Association of America, 2006; my thanks to Colin Burrow for supplying me with this text.

46 A suggestion put forward by Katherine Duncan-Jones and H. R. Woudhuysen in their excellent edition of *Shakespeare's Poems* (London: Thomson Learning, 2007), 389.

47 Burrow, 'Lyric in its Settings'.

48 [Shakespeare], *Passionate Pilgrim*, A7a; W. Shakespeare, *Love's Labour's Lost* (1598), E1b.

49 John Webster, *The Thracian Wonder* (1661), D1b, D3b.

50 Antony Hammond and Doreen Delvecchio, 'The Melbourne Manuscript and John Webster: A Reproduction and Transcripts', *Studies in Bibliography*, 41 (1988), 1–32 (27).

51 Leonard Willan, *Orgula or the Fatall Error* (1658), 78.

52 Stanley Wells, Gary Taylor, John Jowett and William Montgomery, *William Shakespeare: A Textual Companion* (Oxford: Clarendon Press, 1987), 499.

53 Robert Yarington, *Two Lamentable Tragedies* (1601), B1b.

54 *Ghismonda*, ed. Herbert G. Wright (Manchester: Manchester University Press, 1944), 141.

55 John Cooke, *Greenes Tu Quoque* (1614), C1a.

56 John Marston, *The Dutch Courtezan* (1605), D3a.

57 W. Shakespeare, *Henry VI part 3*, ed. John D. Cox and Eric Rasmussen, The Arden Shakespeare (Thomson and Thomson, 2001), 328; W. Shakespeare, *Henry VI part 3*, ed. Randall Martin (Oxford: Oxford University Press, 2001),

287; W. Shakespeare, *Henry VI part 3*, ed. Michael Hattaway (Cambridge: Cambridge University Press, 1993), 172.

58 Ben Jonson, *Every Man Out of his Humor* in *The Workes* (1616), 122–3.

59 Thomas Goffe, *The Raging Turke Or the Tragedie of Bajazet* (1631), 13a–b.

60 William Shakespeare, *Measure for Measure*, ed. Sir Arthur Quiller-Couch and John Dover Wilson (Cambridge: Cambridge University Press, 1922), 145.

61 Stephen Longstaffe in *A Critical Edition of The Life and Death of Jack Straw 1594* (Lewiston, Queenston, Lampeter: The Edwin Mellen Press, 2002), 39–40.

62 William Shakespeare, *Twelfth Night*, ed. M. M. Mahood (London: Penguin, 1966), 162. For an alternative argument – that the play employs conscious misquotations as part of its theme of identity and non-identity – see Patricia Parker, 'Altering the Letter of Twelfth Night', *Shakespeare Survey*, 59 (2006), 49–62.

63 Stephen Orgel, 'Acting Scripts, Performing Texts' in *Crisis in Editing*, ed. Randall McLeod (New York: AMS Press, 1994), 251–94 (280): the letter beginning '*Right Revererend and noble (meaning me)*' is, in one of the 1625 printed texts (1625b), E4a, headed 'The Letter.', and in italics and prose, but its continuation is in roman letters and verse; in another of the 1625 printed texts, however (1625a), E2a, it is headed '*Hee reades the Letter*', and is in italics and verse throughout; in the Huntington manuscript it is headed 'The Letter', could be said to look like verse, and is not differentiated by italics.

7 BACKSTAGE-PLOTS

1 Thomas Jordan, *Fancy's Festivals* (1657), B1a.

2 W. W. Greg, *Dramatic Documents from the Elizabethan Playhouses* (Oxford: Clarendon Press, 1931), 1:106.

3 Samuel Johnson and George Steevens, *Supplement to the Edition of Shakspeare's Plays published in 1778* (1780), 1:61.

4 David Erskine Baker, Isaac Reed and Stephen Jones, *Biographia Dramatica* (1812), 318.

5 William Shakespeare, *The Plays*, ed. George Steevens, Isaac Reed and Samuel Johnson (1803), III:414. Hereafter, for the sake of convenience, short and 'modernised' titles for the plots will be used.

6 William Shakespeare, *The Plays of William Shakspeare*, ed. Edmond Malone, Samuel Johnson, George Steevens and Isaac Reed (1793), 1:504–5.

7 Scott McMillin, 'Building Stories: Greg, Fleay and the Plot of *2 Seven Deadly Sins*', *Medieval and Renaissance Drama in England*, 4 (1989), 53–62; David Kathman, 'Reconsidering *The Seven Deadly Sins*', *Early Theatre*, 7 (2004), 13–44; Andrew Gurr, 'The Work of Elizabethan Plotters and *2 The Seven Deadly Sins*', *Early Theatre*, 10 (2007), 67–87.

8 J. Payne Collier, *The History of English Dramatic Poetry to the Time of Shakespeare* (1831), III:398–9.

9 Greg, *Dramatic Documents*, 1:21 (*et passim*).

10 Evelyn Tribble, 'Distributing Cognition in the Globe', *Shakespeare Quarterly*, 56 (2005), 135–55 (144).

11 T. J. King, *Casting Shakespeare's Plays* (Cambridge: Cambridge University Press, 1992), 7, 14; Grace Ioppolo, *Dramatists and Their Manuscripts in the Age of Shakespeare, Jonson, Middleton, Heywood* (New York and London: Routledge, 2006), 54.

12 David Bradley, *From Text to Performance in the Elizabethan Theatre* (Cambridge: Cambridge University Press, 1992), 126 (*et passim*). This led him into a major confusion about when and how the plots were written: he sometimes maintained that the plot was written near or during the 'reading' of the play to the company, and the plot then provided a framework for the subsequent making-out of actors' parts (80); he sometimes maintained it was prepared during a lengthy rehearsal period; and he sometimes held that the plot was a source of 'aides-memoire' to be channelled back into the 'book' (meaning the plot was created at some stage later in the production process still, but nevertheless before the book had been finished) (126, 80, 81). As the plot was to him a planning document, he had to maintain that it was written before the 'book' was complete, although the oddity of working out entrances and mid-scene entrances to a text not yet fully written was a problem he did not reconcile.

13 Greg, *Dramatic Documents*, 1:2.

14 For the idea that the manuscript related to the theatre but lacked evidence that it had actually been used there, see ibid., 1:191. Further books with 'playhouse notations' are discussed in W. B. Long, '"Precious Few": English Manuscript Playbooks' in *A Companion to Shakespeare*, ed. David Scott Kastan (Oxford: Blackwell, 1999), 414–33.

15 The letter is dated '8th November, 1599', see *Henslowe's Diary*, ed. R. A. Foakes (Cambridge: Cambridge University Press, 2002), 287–8. That the plot is in the handwriting of Wilson rather than, as is sometimes claimed, Shaa is pointed out by Ioppolo, *Dramatists and Their Manuscripts*, 29, 54, and can be seen by comparing the italic hand in the facsimile of the pre-plot in Greg, *Dramatic Documents*, 1, between pages 4 and 5, with the facsimile of Wilson's secretary and italic hand in Ioppolo, *Dramatists*, 18.

16 He may, however, merely be illustrating how stageable the first act of an incomplete play is; Paul Werstine reminds us that playwrights sometimes read their work to players before it was complete – see Paul Werstine, 'Post-Theory Problems in Shakespeare Editing', *Yearbook of English Studies*, 29 (1999), 103–17 (111).

17 Discussed in Andrew J. Sabol, 'New Documents on Shirley's Masque "*The Triumph of Peace*"', *Music & Letters*, 47 (1966), 10–26, and Murray Lefkowitz, 'The Longleat Papers of Bulstrode Whitelocke; New Light on Shirley's *Triumph of Peace*', *Journal of the American Musicological Society*, 18 (1965), 42–60.

18 George Steevens in *Supplement to the Edition*, ed. Johnson and Steevens, 1:61.

19 Edward Cocker, *The Pen's Triumph* (1658), B2a. The heading for *Troilus and Cressida* does not survive.

20 See Tiffany Stern, 'Watching as Reading: The Audience and Written Text in the Early Modern Playhouse' in *How to Do Things with Shakespeare*, ed. Laurie Maguire (Oxford: Blackwell, 2008), 136–59 (144–53).
21 Tribble, 'Distributing Cognition', 146.
22 Steevens in *Supplement to the Edition*, ed. Johnson and Steevens, 1:61.
23 Martin Wiggins, review of Bradley's *From Text to Performance*, *Shakespeare Survey*, 46 (1994), 229.
24 For convenience, all boxes will be referred to by the number given them by Greg on his facsimiles – confusingly, a box number in some instances, a letter in others and a scene (and act) number in others still, reflecting Greg's own confusion as to what each box represented.
25 Michela Calore, 'Elizabethan Plots: A Shared Code of Theatrical and Fictional Language', *Theatre Survey*, 44:2 (2003), 249–61 (254).
26 Greg, *Dramatic Documents*, 1:79.
27 Quotations from *Battle of Alcazar* are given from the plot as rearranged by Greg in *Dramatic Documents* rather than as preserved (with some fragments in haphazard order) by the British Library.
28 Greg, *Dramatic Documents*, 1:38. But see Kathman, who questions whether it is even always evident which players are sharers in 'Reconsidering *The Seven Deadly Sins*', 20.
29 Calore, 'Elizabethan Plots', 254.
30 Ibid., 252.
31 'Drury Lane Prompter's Callbook for *A Midsummer Night's Dream*' in David Garrick, 'Papers Connected with a Production of *A Midsummer Night's Dream c.* 1763', Folger Shakespeare Library, MS w.b.469 (6a).
32 Aaron Hill and William Popple, 12 November 1734 in *The Prompter: A Theatrical Paper (1734–1736)*, ed. William W. Appleton and Kalman A. Burnim (New York: Benjamin Blom, 1966), 2.
33 Ibid.
34 Probably he was researching his *David Garrick, Director* (Pittsburgh: University of Pittsburgh Press, 1961) at the time. For other such documents, see Charles Harlen Shattuck, *The Shakespeare Promptbooks: A Descriptive Catalogue* (Urbana and London: University of Illinois Press, 1965), where references to what Shattuck sometimes calls call-books and sometimes call-sheets are to be found on 46, 174, 218, 336, 383, 453.
35 John Brownsmith, *The Contrast; or, New Mode of Management* (1776), 16.
36 George Colman, the Younger, *Poetical Vagaries* (1812), 13.
37 George Vandenhoff, *Leaves from an Actor's Note-book* (1860), 52.
38 *Jane Shore Call-book* in 'Miscellaneous Theatrical Papers', dated 26 December 1832, Houghton Library, MS Thr 32.
39 Vandenhoff, *Leaves*, 52.
40 *Jane Shore Call-book*.
41 Thomas Goffe, *The Careles Shepherdess* (1656), 7–8; William Hawkins, *Apollo Shroving* (1627), 58; James Shirley, *Hide Parke* (1637), F2a.
42 Thomas Overbury, *Sir Thomas Overburie his Wife* (1616), M3a.

43 John Higgens, *Nomenclator* (1585), 501.

44 Fabian Philipps, *Tenenda non Tollenda* (1660), 63; John Crouch, *The Man in the Moon*, 24–31 October (1649), 221.

45 Francis Bacon, *The Historie of the Reigne of King Henry the Seventh* (1622), 21; Thomas Lodge, *Lady Alimony* (1659), A3a; Thomas Nashe, *A Pleasant Comedie, called Summers Last Will and Testament* (1600), H4b. There were, however, two other words occasionally used to describe the prompter. Thomas Vincent is called 'a Book-keeper or prompter at the Globe play-house' in John Taylor, 'Taylors Feast' in *All the Workes of John Taylor the Water-Poet* (1630), III:70; and the 'Stage keeper' in the manuscript of *Progresse to Parnassus as it was acted in St Johns Colledge in Cambridge An. 1601* (printed as *The Return from Parnassus*), Folger Shakespeare Library, MS v. a.355, 3, is also called 'prompter'. These terms, 'book-keeper' and 'stage-keeper', actually describe other aspects of the prompter's (and sometimes other people's) jobs, 'keeping' or looking after the book, and 'keeping' or looking after the management of the stage. But when the prompter additionally held these jobs, they too became wrapped up with 'prompting', for so crucial was prompting that it overtook any other aspect of the job. Thus John Florio in his *Worlde of Wordes* (1598), 51 defines 'Burriasso' as 'a prompter, or one that keepes the book for plaiers'.

46 Robert Davenport, *The City-night-cap* (1661), 40–1.

47 T. W., *Thorny-Abbey* in *Gratiae Theatrales, or, A Choice Ternary of English Plays* (1662), 5b–6a.

48 Philip Massinger, *The Roman Actor* (1629), 11a.

49 *Everie Woman in her Humor* (1609), B3a.

50 Nashe, *Summers Last Will*, B1a; Ben Jonson, *Staple of Newes* in *Bartholmew Fayre* (1631), 2A2b; George Chapman, *The Gentleman Usher* (1606), D1a.

51 Richard Brome, *The Antipodes* (1640), G4b.

52 Chapman, *Gentleman Usher*, c3b.

53 Francis Markham, *Booke of Honour* (1625), 169.

54 Robert Parsons, *The Warn-Word to Sir Francis Hastings* (1602), E2a; H1b.

55 Thomas Sheridan, *British Education* (1765), 512. Shakespeare, *The Plays of William Shakspeare*, ed. Malone *et al.* (1793), 1:7.

56 Thomas Davies, *Dramatic Micellanies* [*sic*] (1783–4), 1:112.

57 John Gee, *New Shreds of the Old Snare* (1624), 21.

58 Thomas Middleton, *The Mayor of Quinborough a Tragedy* [*Hengist, King of Kent*] (1661), 65, 'to spite thee,/A Players Boy shall bring thee *Aqua-vitæ*'; James Shirley, *The Lady of Pleasure* (1637), G4b: 'I doubt not/But in little time, I shall be impudent/As any Page or Players boy'; Ben Jonson, *Bartholmew Fayre* (1631), L1b: 'Ha' you none of your pretty impudent boyes, now; to bring stooles, fill Tabacco, fetch Ale, and beg money, as they have at other houses?'; John Day, *Isle of Gulls* (1606), A2a: 'come boy, furnish us with stooles'; Jo Healey, *Epictetus Manuall* (1616) K5a: 'At the Theater, taking the cushions from the boy, [the flatterer] setteth them up himselfe'; Thomas Dekker, *The Guls Horne-booke* (1609), 29 [c3a]: 'By sitting on the stage, you may (with

small cost) purchase the deere acquaintance of the boyes: have a good stoole for sixpence: at any time know what particular part any of the infants present'; Ben Jonson, *The Fountaine of Selfe-love. Or Cynthias Revels* (1601), A3b: 'I step foorth like one of the Children, and ask you; Would you have Stoole Sir?'; Archie Armstrong, 'A jest upon a Jester' in *A Banquet of Jests* (1633), E5a–b.

59 John Marston, *Antonios Revenge* (1602), H2a, I2b.

60 Thomas Whitfield Baldwin, *On Act and Scene Division in the Shakespeare First Folio* (Carbondale: Southern Illinois University Press, 1965), 143–4.

61 *Miscellany*, Bodleian Library, MS Rawl. Poet 117, 25.

62 Anthony Munday, *John a Kent and John a Cumber*, ed. Muriel St. Clare Byrne (Oxford: Malone Society, 1923), vii. If only Henslowe had named his scribes in his 'diary', it might have been easier to work out who wrote what – but he does not, and the important writers of books, parts and plots are unrecorded, which may possibly be (but is not necessarily) telling: it may suggest that all these tasks are completed within the playhouse by playhouse personnel.

63 Reproduced in Greg, *Dramatic Documents*, II: I.

64 An observation made by Wiggins, review, *Shakespeare Survey*, 229.

65 Arthur Ogilvy, 'Low Life on the Stage', *Once a Week*, ed. Eneas Sweetland Dallas, n.s. 4 (July–December 1867), 408–11 (409).

66 Bradley, *From Text to Performance*, 104–5.

67 Ibid., 79.

68 Ibid., 91.

69 Joseph Quincy Adams, 'The Author-Plot of an Early Seventeenth Century Play', *The Library*, 27 (1945), 17–27 (17).

70 Bernard Beckerman, 'Theatrical Plots and Elizabethan Stage Practice' in *Shakespeare and Dramatic Tradition*, ed. W. R. Elton and W. B. Long (Newark, DE: University of Delaware Press, 1989), 109–24 (109).

71 Paul N. Lazarus, *The Movie Producer: A Handbook for Producing and Picture-Making* (New York: Barnes & Noble, 1985), 109.

72 In Tiffany Stern, *Rehearsal from Shakespeare to Sheridan* (Oxford: Clarendon Press, 2000), 98, I took as a sign that plots could not be for actors' use the soubriquet 'the red fast ['faced'] fellow' (*Tamar Cam*, v.iii), which I read as an insult. I now think it may be part of a jokey theatrical terminology, a system of shared pet names, equivalent to Alleyn's apprentice John Pyk signing himself in a letter to his mistress 'yor petty pretty pratlyng parlyng pyg' – see *Henslowe's Diary*, ed. Foakes, 283.

73 Walter Raleigh, *The Poems*, ed. Michael Rudick, Renaissance English Text Society, 7th series, vol. 23 (Tempe: Arizona Center for Medieval and Renaissance Studies, 1999), 184; 'Mr Cuffe his speech at his death', *Miscellany*, Bodleian Library, MS Rawl. 26, 12b.

74 Greg, *Dramatic Documents*, I:86.

75 See Stern, *Rehearsal from Shakespeare to Sheridan*, chapters 1–2; Simon Palfrey and Tiffany Stern, *Shakespeare in Parts* (Oxford: Oxford University Press, 2007), 70–3.

76 Linda McJannet, *The Voice of Elizabethan Stage Directions* (Newark, DE: University of Delaware Press, 1999), 141.

77 Greg, *Dramatic Documents*, 1:86–7; Calore, 'Elizabethan Plots', 251, 258.

78 Scott McMillin, 'The Plots of *The Dead Man's Fortune* and *2 Seven Deadly Sins*: Inferences for Theatre Historians', *Studies in Bibliography*, 26 (1973), 235–43 (237).

79 Greg, *Dramatic Documents*, 1:218–19. 'Ready' directions are also found in the marked-up printed copy of John Cumber's *Two Merry Milkmaids* (1620), identified by Leslie Thomson in 'A Quarto "Marked for Performance": Evidence of What?', *Medieval and Renaissance Drama in England*, 8 (1996), 176–210 (182).

80 Bradley, *From Text to Performance*, 81.

81 Chapman, *Gentleman Usher*, c3b; Edward A. Langhans, *Restoration Promptbooks* (Carbondale and Edwardsville: Southern Illinois University Press, 1981), xiii.

82 Langhans, *Restoration Promptbooks*, 6, 55, 19. Langhans tabulates what constitutes a Restoration promptbook by their preference for 'call' or 'ready' and their habit of warning by character or person on 78–80.

83 William Perdue Halstead, *Stage Management for the Amateur Theatre: With an Index to the Standard* (London: George G. Harrap & Co., 1938), 117.

84 Baldwin, *On Act and Scene Division*, 39–40; W. J. Lawrence, 'Early Prompt Books' in *Pre-Restoration Stage Studies* (Cambridge, MA: Harvard University Press, 1927), 373–413 (375).

85 William Shakespeare, *The Plays and Poems*, ed. Isaac Reed, Samuel Johnson and George Steevens (1821), 1:415.

86 John Gillies, 'Introduction' in John Gillies, ed., *Playing the Globe: Genre and Geography in English Renaissance Drama* (Madison, NJ: Fairleigh Dickinson University Press, 1998), 27.

87 Henry Turner, *The English Renaissance Stage* (Oxford: Oxford University Press, 2006), 173.

8 THE APPROVED 'BOOK' AND ACTORS' PARTS

1 Richard Dutton, *Mastering the Revels* (Basingstoke: Macmillan, 1991), ix.

2 For instance, a letter from the Privy Council to Secretary Conway, 21 August 1624, relates of *A Game at Chesse*: 'We demaunding further, where there were no other parts of passages represented on the Stage, then those expressely contained in the booke, they confidentlie protested they added or varied from the same nothing at all,' quoted in N. W. Bawcutt, *The Control and Censorship of Caroline Drama* (Oxford: Clarendon Press, 1996), 154.

3 23 August, 1623, in Bawcutt, *Control and Censorship*, 143.

4 Bawcutt, *Control and Censorship*, 184.

5 Reproduced in A. R. Braunmuller, *A Seventeenth-Century Letter-Book: A Facsimile Edition of Folger MS v.a.321* (Newark, DE: University of Delaware Press, 1983), 246.

312 *Notes to pages 233–7*

6 Thomas Hughes, Francis Bacon, Sir Nicholas Trotte, William Fulbeck, John
Lancaster, Sir Christopher Yelverton, John Penroodock and Francis Flower,
The Misfortunes of Arthur (1587 [i.e. 1588]), π4b; Thomas Nabbes, *The Bride*
(1640), A3a–b; Thomas Dekker, *Whore of Babylon* (1607), A2b.
7 Francis Rous, *The Diseases of the Time* (1622), 317.
8 J. R. Dasent, ed., *Acts of the Privy Council* (London: HM Stationery Office,
1890–1907), XXVII:313. Richard Dutton, *Licensing, Censorship and Authorship*
in Early Modern England (Houndmills: Palgrave, 2000), 21. The play is
described as an 'unlicensed play, performed by an unlicensed company' in
David Thomas, David Carlton and Anne Etienne, *Theatre Censorship from*
Walpole to Wilson (Oxford: Oxford University Press, 2007), 9.
9 George Chapman reproduced in Braunmuller, *A Seventeenth-Century Letter-*
10 Bawcutt, *Control and Censorship*, 183.
12 Janet Clare, *Art Made Tongue-Tied by Authority* (Manchester and New York:
Manchester University Press, 1990), x. Bawcutt, *Control and Censorship*, 211.
13 Bawcutt, *Control and Censorship*, 153, 168, 199. Similarly, the later *Hymens*
Holliday, 'an ould play' for which Henry Herbert examined 'some alterations', was a text that he owned and had 'given unto' the theatre proprietor
Beeston. So the pound Herbert then charges Beeston for reviewing the text
appears to cover not just approving Beeston's alterations to the play but also
effectively his 'purchase' of it; Beeston was obscurely indebted to Herbert
for this entire transaction, for later that same day he bought Herbert's wife
'a payre of gloves, that cost him at least twenty shillings'. See Bawcutt, *Control*
14 Grace Ioppolo, *Dramatists and Their Manuscripts in the Age of Shakespeare,*
Jonson, Middleton and Heywood (New York and London: Routledge, 2006), 125.
15 Quoted in Joseph Wood Krutch, 'Governmental Attempt to Regulate the
Stage after the Jeremy Collier Controversy', *PMLA*, 38 (1923), 153–74 (165).
16 From *Part-book* containing Parts of Poore, Polypragmaticus, Amurath,
Antoninus, Harvard Theater Library, MS Thr 10.1.
17 Daborne to Henslowe, 25 June 1613, in Philip Henslowe, *Henslowe Papers*,
ed. W. W. Greg (London: A. H. Bullen, 1907), 73.
18 Quoted in Krutch, 'Governmental Attempt to Regulate the Stage', 165. Date
supplied in Matthew J. Kinservik, 'Theatrical Regulation during the Restoration Period' in *A Companion to Restoration Drama*, ed. Susan J. Owen
(Oxford: Blackwell, 2001), 36–52 (46).
19 Bawcutt, *Control and Censorship*, 183.
20 T. H. Howard-Hill, 'Crane's 1619 "Promptbook" of "Barnavelt" and Theatrical
Processes', *Modern Philology*, 86 (1988), 146–70; J. F. Stephenson, 'On the
Markings in the Manuscript of Sir John Van Olden Barnavelt', *Notes and*
Queries, 53 (2006), 522–4.
21 Fredson Bowers, *On Editing Shakespeare and the Elizabethan Dramatists*
(Philadelphia: University of Pennsylvania Library, 1955), 112; Scott McMillin,

The Elizabethan Theatre and the Book of Sir Thomas More (Ithaca and London: Cornell University Press, 1987), 37–8.

22 Eckehard Simon, 'Manuscript Production in Medieval Theatre: The German Carnival Plays' in *New Directions in Later Medieval Manuscript Studies*, ed. Derek Pearsall (York: York Medieval Press, 2000), 143–65 (159); Richard Legge, *Richardus Tertius*, Bodleian Library, MS Lat. Misc. e. 16.

23 The surviving parts are discussed in detail in Simon Palfrey and Tiffany Stern, *Shakespeare in Parts* (Oxford: Oxford University Press, 2007), 15–28.

24 *Part-book* containing Parts of Poore, Polypragmaticus, Amurath, Antoninus. Robert Burton, *Philosophaster*, Folger Shakespeare Library, MS v.a.315; Robert Burton, *Philosophaster*, Harvard Theater Library, MS Thr 10. Thomas Goffe, *The Tragedy of Amourath, 3rd Tyrant of the Turkes, as it was Publiquly Presented to the University of Oxon by the Students of Christchurch, Mathias day 1618*, Cheshire Record Office, MS DLT/B71; Thomas Goffe, *The Couragious Turke* (1632). *Part of Orlando*, Dulwich College, MS I Item 138; Robert Greene, *The Historie of Orlando Furioso, one of the Twelve Pieres of France* (1594).

25 William Prynne, *Histriomastix* (1633), 2R1a.

26 For the hand, see David Carnegie, 'The Identification of the Hand of Thomas Goffe, Academic Dramatist and Actor', *The Library*, 26 (1971), 161–5.

27 Burton, *Philosophaster*, Folger Shakespeare Library; Burton, *Philosophaster*, Harvard Theater Library. See Robert Burton, *Philosophaster*, ed. and trans. Connie McQuillen (New York: Medieval and Renaissance Texts and Studies, 1993), 10.

28 Reproduced in facsimile in Robert Burton, *Philosophaster*, prepared with an Introduction by Marvin Spevack (Hildesheim: Georg Olms, 1984), lines 1644–5.

29 Goffe, *The Tragedy of Amourath*; and from the printed text of Goffe's *The Couragious Turke* (1632).

30 Thomas Goffe, *A Critical Old Spelling Edition of Thomas Goffe's The Courageous Turke*, ed. Susan Gushee O'Malley (New York: Garland, 1979), 56.

31 Goffe, *Couragious Turke* (1632), F3b.

32 Ioppolo, *Dramatists and Their Manuscripts*, 100.

33 E. A. J. Honigmann, 'The New Bibliography and Its Critics' in *Textual Performances*, ed. Lucas Erne and M. J. Kidnie (Cambridge: Cambridge University Press, 2004), 84.

34 James Shirley, *The Triumph of Beautie* in *Poems* (1646), 8. *The Returne from Pernassus* (1606), A2a.

35 Quoted in Ioppolo, *Dramatists and Their Manuscripts*, 161, who believes that Field was writing as a co-author rather than a copier.

36 Quoted in William Van Lennep, 'Thomas Killigrew Prepares His Plays for Production' in *John Quincy Adams Memorial Studies*, ed. James G. McManaway et al. (Washington, DC: Folger Shakespeare Library, 1948), 803–8 (805).

37 John Downes, *Roscius Anglicanus*, ed. J. Milhous and R. D. Hume (London: Society for Theatre Research, 1987), 2.

38 Charles Lee Lewes and John Lee Lewes, *Memoirs of Charles Lee Lewes* (1805), 1:34–5.

39 Michael Warren, 'Greene's *Orlando*: W. W. Greg Furioso' in *Textual Formations and Reformations*, ed. Laurie E. Maguire and Thomas L. Berger (Newark, DE: University of Delaware Press, 1998), 67–91.

40 Graham A. Runnalls, 'Towards a Typology of Medieval French Play Manuscripts' in *The Editor and the Text*, ed. P. E. Bennett and G. A. Runnalls (Edinburgh: Edinburgh University Press, 1990), 98.

41 W. W. Greg, ed., *Two Elizabethan Stage Abridgements: 'The Battle of Alcazar' and 'Orlando Furioso'* (Oxford: Malone Society, 1922), 128.

42 Laurie E. Maguire, *Shakespearean Suspect Texts* (Cambridge: Cambridge University Press, 1996), 78–85.

43 W. W. Greg, *Dramatic Documents from the Elizabethan Playhouses* (Oxford: Clarendon Press, 1931), II: Orlando lines 62–6.

44 For more on actors and pointing see Palfrey and Stern, *Shakespeare in Parts*, 317–24.

45 T. H. Howard-Hill, quoted in Lukas Erne, *Shakespeare as Literary Dramatist* (Cambridge: Cambridge University Press, 2003), 214; Philip Oxley in his *A Critical Edition of John Fletcher's Humorous Lieutenant* (New York: Garland, 1987), 13.

46 *Part of Orlando*, Dulwich College. Greene, *The Historie of Orlando Furioso* (1594), D4b, E2b.

47 W. W. Greg in his edition of *The Merry Wives of Windsor* (Oxford: Clarendon Press, 1910), xl–xli; Maguire, *Shakespearean Suspect Texts*, 148.

48 Archie Armstrong, *A Banquet of Jests* (1633), E5a–b; Thomas Lupton, retelling the joke some years later, has it that the theatre in question was the Red Bull in *A Thousand Notable Things* (1660), 357. *The Pilgrimage to Parnassus* in *The Three Parnassus Plays*, ed. J. B. Leishman (London: Ivor Nicholson and Watson Ltd, 1949), 129–30.

49 [Richard Tarlton], *Tarltons Newes out of Purgatorie* (1590), B1a.

50 Richard Tarlton, *Tarltons Jests* (1613), C3a.

51 Ibid., B2a, B2b; ibid., B2b; William Vaughan, *Golden Fleece* (1626), B2b.

52 Thomas Nashe, *An Almond for a Parrat* (1589), A2a.

53 David Wiles, *Shakespeare's Clown* (Cambridge: Cambridge University Press, 1987), 106–7.

54 William Shakespeare, *Hamlet* (1600), F2a–b.

55 Dutton, *Licensing, Censorship and Authorship*, 36.

56 Richard Brome, *The Antipodes* (1640), D3b.

57 Prynne, *Histriomastix*, 930.

58 Malvena McKendrick, *Theatre in Spain 1490–1700* (Cambridge: Cambridge University Press, 1989), 52.

59 Eric Rasmussen, 'Setting Down What the Clown Spoke: Improvisation, Hand B, and *The Booke of Sir Thomas More*', *The Library*, 6th series, 13 (1991), 126–36.

60 Tarlton, *Tarltons Jests*, C4a–C4b.

61 Thomas Nashe, *Pierce Penilesse* (1592), 39.

62 John Harington, *A New Discourse of a Stale Subject, called the Metamorphosis of Ajax* (1596), C2b; John Harington, *A New Discourse*, British Library, MS Add 46368, 8a.

63 Robert Armin, *Quips Upon Questions, or, a Clownes Conceite on Occasion Offered* (1600), C4a, E1a, E2a.

64 Francis Meres, *Palladis Tamia* (1598), 206.

65 *Fennors Defence* in John Taylor, *All the Workes of John Taylor the Water-Poet* (1630), 142, 151.

66 *A Cast over the Water* in John Taylor, *All the Workes of John Taylor the Water-Poet* (1630), 159.

67 *Miscellany*, Folger Shakespeare Library, MS v.a.162.

68 *The History of the Tryall of Chevalry* (1605), E4a; John Cooke, *Greenes Tu Quoque* (1614), L1a; Thomas Heywood, *The Second Part of King Edward the Fourth* (1599), Y2b; Thomas Heywood, *The Second Part of, If you Know not Me, you Know No Bodie* (1606), H1a; John Marston [with William Barksted and Lewis Mackin], *The Insatiate Countesse* (1613), H2a.

69 Thomas Middleton, *The Familie of Love* (1608), B1b. For a discussion of the Beaumont and Fletcher examples see Francis Beaumont and John Fletcher, *The Dramatic Works*, ed. Fredson Bowers, IV:154, 272; VIII:355; IX:225.

70 *Pilgrimage to Parnassus* in *The Three Parnassus Plays*, ed. Leishman, 116; Christopher Marlowe, *Dr Faustus* (1604), D3b; *A Pleasant Comedie, Called Wily Beguilde* (1606), 21 [C4a]; Thomas Randolph, *Hey for Honesty, Down with Knavery* (1651), 14 [C3b].

71 All of these are probably signs of theatrical doctoring rather than printers' censorship as words could be printed that could not be spoken. See Gary Taylor and John Jowett, *Shakespeare Reshaped 1606–1623* (Oxford: Clarendon Press, 1993), 86.

72 George Gascoigne, *Supposes* in *The Pleasauntest Workes of George Gascoigne Esquire* (1587), D2b, D3a, D7a; Richard Brome, *Madd Couple Well Matcht* in *Five New Playes* (1653), D6b.

73 Richard Brome, *The Queen and Concubine* in *Five New Playes* (1659), 16; Thomas Dekker, *Blurt Master-constable* (1602), F2b, F4a.

74 Stephen Orgel, 'What Is an Editor?', *Shakespeare Studies*, 24 (1996), 23–39 (23).

CONCLUSION: REPATCHING THE PLAY

1 Gérard Genette, *Paratexts: Thresholds of Interpretation*, trans. Jane E. Lewin, foreword by Richard Macksey (Cambridge: Cambridge University Press, 1997), 2, 407.

2 David Moore Bergeron, *Textual Patronage in English Drama, 1570–1640* (Aldershot: Ashgate, 2006), 15–16.

Bibliography

PRIMARY TEXTS

MANUSCRIPTS

Book of Masques, British Library, MS Add 10444
Clarke's MS Poems, Folger Shakespeare Library, MS v.b.43
Comoedia: Senilis Amor (1635), Bodleian Library, MS Rawl. Poet 9
'*English Song*', New York Public Library, MS Drexel 4041 (dated 1640)
'*Giles Earle his Booke*', British Library, MS Add 24665
The History of King Henry IV, Folger Library, MS v.b.34
Jane Shore Call-book in 'Miscellaneous Theatrical Papers', dated 26 December
    1832, Houghton Library, MS Thr 32
John Bull Manuscript, Fitzwilliam Museum, MUMS 782 [formerly MS 52.D,25]
John Sturt Lute Book, British Library, MS Add 38539
'*Manuscript Speech of Henry Prince of Purpoole*', Folger Shakespeare Library MS,
    v.a.190
Mercurius Rusticans (l), Bodleian Library, MS Wood D 18 part 2
Miscellany, Beinecke Library, MS Osborn f b 106
Miscellany, Bodleian Library, MS Add B 97
Miscellany, Bodleian Library, MS Ashmole 36–7
Miscellany, Bodleian Library, MS Ashmole 38
Miscellany, Bodleian Library, MS Ashmole 47
Miscellany, Bodleian Library, MS Don. d. 58
Miscellany, Bodleian Library, MS Douce 357
Miscellany, Bodleian Library, MS Malone 21
Miscellany, Bodleian Library, MS Rawl. 26
Miscellany, Bodleian Library, MS Rawl. Poet 117
Miscellany, Bodleian Library, MS Rawl. Poet 152
Miscellany, Bodleian Library, MS Rawl. Poet 172
Miscellany, Bodleian Library, MS Sancroft 53
Miscellany, Bodleian Library, MS Top. Oxon e. 5, 359
Miscellany, Bodleian Library, MS Wood D 18 part 2
Miscellany, Cambridge University Library, MS Dd.5.75
Miscellany, Folger Shakespeare Library, MS v.a.124
Miscellany, Folger Shakespeare Library, MS v.a.162

Miscellany, Folger Shakespeare Library, MS v.a.308
Miscellany, Folger Shakespeare Library, MS v.a.322
Miscellany, Folger Shakespeare Library, MS v.b.212
'Mr Cuffe his speech at his death' *Miscellany,* Bodleian Library, MS Rawl. 26
'*The Musick in Mackbeth in Score*', Folger Shakespeare Library, MS w.b.537
Music Miscellany, Folger Shakespeare Library, MS v.a.409
Oxford Poetical Miscellanies, Folger Shakespeare Library, MS v.a.162
Part-book containing Parts of 'Poore', Polypragmaticus, Amurath, Antoninus, Harvard Theater Library, MS Thr 10.1
Part-book in the hand of Edward Lowe, Bodleian Library, MS Mus. d. 238
Part of Orlando, Dulwich College MS, I, Item 138
Progresse to Parnassus as it was acted in St Johns Colledge in Cambridge An. 1601, Folger Shakespeare Library, MS v.a.355
Register of all the noble men of England, Houghton Library, MS Eng 1285
Song Book, Bodleian Library, MS CCC 327
Song Book, Bodleian Library, MS Don. c. 57
Song Book, British Library, MS 11608
Song Book, British Library, MS Add 17786–91
Song Book, British Library, MS Add 29396
Song Book, British Library, MS Add 29481
Song Book, British Library, MS Egerton 2013
Song Book, Christ Church Oxford, MS Mus 439
Song Book, Edinburgh University Library Dc.1.69
'SONG, *by a Fairy of Oberon's Train*' in *Garrick's notes concerning a production of A Midsummer Night's Dream,* Folger Shakespeare Library, MS w.b.469
'*Songs Unto the Viol and Lute*', New York Public Library, MS Drexel 4175
Wernerus Martyr (1630), Folger Shakespeare Library, MS v.a.305
Berkeley, William, *The Lost Lady,* Folger Shakespeare Library, MS j.b.4
Burton, Robert, *Philosophaster,* Folger Shakespeare Library, MS v.a.315
  Philosophaster, Harvard Theater Library, MS Thr 10
Carlell, Lodowick, *Arviragus and Philicia,* Bodleian Library, MS Eng. Misc. d. 11
Cumberland, Richard, *Song.,* Folger Shakespeare Library, MS y.d.93
[Dering, Edward], *Scenario of a play set in Thrace and Macedon, c.* 1630, Folger Shakespeare Library, MS x.d.206
Fletcher, John, Philip Massinger [and Francis Beaumont?], *The Beggars Bush,* Folger Shakespeare Library, MS j.b.5
Fletcher, Phineas, *Sicelides,* Bodleian Library, MS Rawl. Poet 214
  Sicelides, British Library MS, Birch Collection, Add 4453
Foote, Samuel, *Devil Upon Two Sticks* (1778), Folger Shakespeare Library, Prompt D 21
Gamble, John, *Song Book,* New York Public Library, MS Drexel 4257
Garrick, David, 'Papers Connected with a Production of *A Midsummer Night's Dream c.* 1763', Folger Shakespeare Library, MS w.b.469
  Receipt Book, Folger Shakespeare Library, MS w.b.492

Goffe, Thomas, *The Tragedy of Amourath, 3rd Tyrant of the Turkes, as it was Publiquly Presented to the University of Oxon by the Students of Christchurch, Mathias day 1618*, Cheshire Record Office, MS DLT/B71

Greville, Fulke, *Mustapha*, British Library, MS Add 54569

Guazzo, Stefano, *An Italian Treat* (*c.* 1655), Folger Shakespeare Library, MS v.b.128

Harington, John, *A New Discourse*, British Library, MS Add 46368

Holcroft, Thomas, *Try Again* (1790), Folger Shakespeare Library, Prompt T 26

Jeffreys, George, *Musical Settings*, British Library, MS Add 10338

Jonson, Ben, *Masque of Queens*, British Library, Harley MS 6947
    Masque of Queens, British Library, Royal MS 18 A xlv

Killigrew, Thomas, *The Second Part of Cicilia and Clorinda*, Folger Shakespeare Library, MS v.b.209

Lawes, William, *Songbook*, British Library, MS Add 31432

Legge, Richard, *Richardus Tertius*, Bodleian Library, MS Lat. Misc. e. 16

Lowe, Edward, *Commonplace Book*, British Library, MS Add 29396

Montagu, Walter, *The Shepheards Paradise*, British Library, MS Add 41617
    The Shepheards Paradise, British Library, MS Sloane 3649
    The Shepheards Paradise, British Library, MS Stowe 976
    The Shepheards Paradise, Folger Shakespeare Library, MS v.b.203
    The Shepheards Paradise, Folger Shakespeare Library, MS v.b.204

Neale, Thomas, *The Warde* (16 September 1637), Bodleian Library, MS Rawl. Poet 79

Percy, William, *Plays*, Huntington Library, MS HM 4

Reymes, William, *Self Interest, or the Belly Water*, being a verse translation . . . of Niccolo Secchi's . . . *L'Interesse c.* 1655, Folger Shakespeare Library, MS v.b.128

Shakespeare, W., *Othello . . . As it is now acted at The Theatre Royal in Covent-Garden* (1761), Folger Shakespeare Library, Prompt Oth. 27

Wilson, John, and Edward Lowe, *Song book*, Bodleian Library, MS Mus. b. 1

PRINTED BOOKS

An Abstract of his Majesties Letters patent, granted unto Roger Wood and Thos Symcocke, for the sole printing of paper and Parchment on the one side (1620)

The Argument of the Pastorall of Florimene with the Discription of the Scoenes and Intermedii Presented by the Queenes Majesties Commandment, before the Kings Majesty in the Hall at White-hall on S. Thomas day the 21 of December (1635)

The Birth of Hercules, ed. R. Warwick Bond (Oxford: Clarendon Press, 1911)

Charlemagne, or the Distracted Emperor. From the MS (Egerton 1994), ed. J. H. Walter (Oxford: Malone Society, 1937)

The Costlie Whore (1633)

A Critical Edition of The Life and Death of Jack Straw 1594, ed. Stephen Longstaffe (Lewiston, Queenston, Lampeter: The Edwin Mellen Press, 2002)

A Description of the King and Queene of Fayries (1635)

Edmond Ironside, ed. Eleanore Boswell (Oxford: Malone Society, 1927)

Everie Woman in her Humor (1609)

The First Part of the Reign of King Richard the Second or Thomas of Woodstock, ed. Wilhelmina P. Frijlinck (Oxford: Malone Society, 1929)

Ghismonda, ed. Herbert G. Wright (Manchester: Manchester University Press, 1944)

The History of the Tryall of Chevalry (1605)

Mery Tales, Wittie Questions, and Quicke Answeres (1567)

Narcissus, ed. Margaret L. Lee (London: David Nutt, 1893)

Perfect Occurrences (6 October, 1647)

Perfect Occurrences (3 February, 1647/8)

Philotus (1603)

A Pleasant Comedie, Called Wily Beguilde (1606)

A Pleasant Comedie, Called, Wily Beguilde (1614)

The Plot of the Play, called Englands Joy. To be Playd at the Swan this 6 of November. 1602 (1602)

The Prologue and Epilogue to a Comedie Presented at the Entertainment of the Prince his Highnesse by the Schollers of Trinity College in Cambridge in March last, 1641 (1642)

Ratseis Ghost (1605)

The Returne from Pernassus (1606)

The Second Report of Doctor John Faustus . . . Written by an English Gentleman student in Wittenberg . . . (1594)

The Spectator, ed. Donald F. Bond, 5 vols. (Oxford: Clarendon Press, 1965)

The Thespian Dictionary (1802)

The Three Parnassus Plays, ed. J. B. Leishman (London: Ivor Nicholson and Watson Ltd, 1949)

To the Right Honourable the House of Commons assembled in Parliament. The Humble Petition of Thomas Man, Humfrey Lownes . . . William Jaggard . . . with Many Others (1621)

Tom a Lincoln, ed. G. R. Proudfoot (Oxford: Malone Society, 1992)

A Warning for Faire Women (1599)

The Wisdome of Doctor Dodypoll (1600)

A., R., *The Valiant Welshman* (1615)

Armin, Robert, *Quips Upon Questions, or, a Clownes Conceite on Occasion Offered* (1600)

Armstrong, Archie, *A Banquet of Jests* (1633)

B., T., *The Rebellion of Naples, or The Tragedy of Massenello* (1649)

Bacon, Francis, *The Historie of the Reigne of King Henry the Seventh* (1622)

Baron, Robert, *Mirza* (1647)

Bartlet, John, *A Booke of Ayres* (1606)

Beaumont, Francis, *The Knight of the Burning Pestle* (1613)

   The Knight of the Burning Pestle (1635)

   Masque of the Inner Temple and Gray's Inn (1613)

   Poems (1653)

Beaumont, Francis, and John Fletcher, *Comedies and Tragedies* (1647)
  The Dramatick Works of Beaumont and Fletcher, ed. George Colman (1778)
  The Dramatic Works, ed. Fredson Bowers, 10 vols. to date (Cambridge: Cambridge University Press, 1966–)
  Fifty Comedies and Tragedies (1679)
  The Maids Tragedie (1622)
  The Maid's Tragedy, ed. T. W. Craik (Manchester: Manchester University Press, 1988)
  The Woman Hater (1607)
  The Woman Hater (1648)
  The Woman Hater (1649)
  The Works . . . with Some Account of the Life and Writings of the Authors, 7 vols. (1711)
  The Works, ed. Alexander Dyce, 11 vols. (1843–6)
  The Faithful Friends: from the MS (Dyce 10), ed. G. M. Pinciss and G. R. Proudfoot (Oxford: Malone Society Reprints, 1975)
Belchier, Dabridgcourt, *Hans Beer-Pot* (1618)
Berkeley, William, *Lost Lady* (1638)
  Lost Lady (1639)
Bond, R. W., ed., *Early Plays from the Italian* (Oxford: Clarendon Press, 1911)
Bosworth, William, *The Chast and Lost Lovers* (1653)
Boyer, Abel, *The Royal Dictionary* (1699)
Brandon, Samuel, *The Tragicomoedi of the Vertuous Octavia* (1598)
Brathwait, Richard, *Anniversaries upon his Panarete, continued* (1635)
  Ar't Asleepe Husband? (1640)
  Astraea's Teares (1641)
  Barnabees Journall (1638)
  The English Gentlewoman (1631)
  A Strappado for the Divell (1615)
  Times Treasury (1652)
  The Two Lancashire Lovers (1640)
Breton, Nicholas, *Choice, Chance, and Change* (1606)
  Fantasticks: Serving for a Perpetuall Prognostication (1626)
  A Poste with a Packet of Madde Letters (1606)
Breval, John, *The Play is the Plot* (1718)
Brome, Richard, *The Antipodes* (1640)
  The English Moor (1658)
  The English Moore, ed. Sara Jayne Steen (Columbia: University of Missouri Press, 1983)
  Five New Playes (1653)
  Five New Playes (1659)
  A Joviall Crew (1652)
  The Northern Lasse (1632)
  The Sparagus Garden (1640)
Brome, Richard, and Thomas Heywood, *The Late Lancashire Witches* (1634)

Brooke, Arthur, *The Tragicall Historye of Romeus and Juliet* (1562)

Brooke, Christopher, *Ghost of Richard the Third* (1614)

Brownsmith, John, *The Contrast; or, New Mode of Management* (1776)

Burton, Robert, *Philosophaster*, ed. and trans. Connie McQuillen (New York: Medieval and Renaissance Texts and Studies, 1993)

 Philosophaster, prepared with an Introduction by Marvin Spevack (Hildesheim: Georg Olms, 1984)

Campion, Thomas, *The Description of a maske: presented in the Banqueting roome at Whitehall, on Saint Stephens night last at the Mariage of the Right Honourable the Earle of Somerset: and the right noble the Lady Frances Howard* (1614)

 The Discription of a Maske, presented before the Kinges Maiestie at White-Hall, on Twelfth Night last in Honour of the Lord Hayes, and his Bride . . . their Marriage having been the same day at Court Solemnized (1607)

 Observations in the Art of English Poesie (1602)

 The Third and Fourth Booke of Ayres (1617)

Canning, William, *Gesta Grayorum, or, The History of the High and Mighty Prince, Henry Prince of Purpoole* (1688)

Carew, Thomas, *Poems* (1640)

 Poems with a Maske (1651)

Carlell, Lodowick, *Arviragus and Philicia* (1639)

 The Deserving Favorite (1629)

 The Passionate Lover, part i (1655)

Cartwright, William, *Poems* (1651)

Cavendish, Margaret, Duchess of Newcastle, *Playes* (1662)

Cavendish, William, Earl of Newcastle, *The Country Captaine* (1649a)

 The Country Captaine (1649b)

 The Country Captaine, and the Varietie (1649)

 The Country Captain from British Library Harl. MS 7650, ed. Anthony Johnson (Oxford: Malone Society, 1999)

Cervantes Saavedra, Miguel de, *The History of the Valorous and Wittie Knight-Errant, Don-Quixote of the Mancha*, trans. Thomas Shelton (1612)

Chamberlain, John, *The Letters of John Chamberlain*, ed. Norman Egbert McClure, 2 vols. (Philadelphia: American Philosophical Society, 1939)

Chamberlain, Robert, *Jocabella* (1640)

Chapman, George, *Al Fooles* (1605)

 Bussy D'Ambois (1641)

 Bussy d'Amboys (1607)

 Eugenia (1614)

 The Gentleman Usher (1606)

 The Memorable Maske of the two Honorable Houses or Inns of Court (1613?)

 Pompey and Caesar (1653)

 The Revenge of Bussy D'Ambois (1613)

 The Widdowes Teares (1612)

 [actually Glapthorne?], *Revenge for Honour* (1659)

Bibliography

Chapman, George, Ben Jonson and John Marston, *Eastward Hoe* (1605)

Cibber, Colley, *An Apology for the Life of Mr. Colley Cibber* (1740)

Cibber, Theophilus, *The Lover* (1730)

Clavell, John, *The So[l]ddered Citizen*, ed. J. H. P. Pafford and W. W. Greg (Oxford: Malone Society, 1936)

Cocker, Edward, *The Pen's Triumph* (1658)

Cokain, Aston, *The Obstinate Lady* (1657)

    Small Poems of Divers Sorts (1658)

Collings, Richard, *The Kingdomes Weekly Intelligencer*, Series 2, No. 198, 23 February to 2 March (1646)

Colman, George, the Younger, *Poetical Vagaries* (1812)

Cooke, John, *Greenes Tu Quoque* (1614)

Corbet, Richard, *Certain Elegant Poems* (1647)

Cotgrave, Randle, *A Dictionarie of the French and English Tongues* (1611)

Cowley, Abraham, *Loves Riddle* (1638)

Crouch, John, *The Man in the Moon*, 24–31 October (1649)

Damhouder, Joos de, *Praxis Rerum Criminalious* (Antwerp, 1562)

Daniel, Samuel, *Hymen's Triumph*, ed. John Pitcher (Oxford: Malone Society, 1994)

Davenant, William, *Love and Honour* (1649)

    Madagascar (1638)

    The Platonick Lovers (1636)

    The Play-House to be Let in *The Works* (1673)

    The Unfortunate Lovers (1643)

    The Works of Sr. William Davenant, Kt (1673)

Davenport, Robert, *The City-night-cap* (1661)

Davies, John, of Hereford, *A Scourge for Paper-Persecuters* (1625)

Davies, Thomas, *Dramatic Micellanies [sic]*, 3 vols. (1783–4)

    Wits Bedlam (1617)

Day, John, *Isle of Gulls* (1606)

    The Knave in Graine, New Vampt (1640)

Dekker, Thomas, *Blurt Master-constable* (1602)

    Dekker his Dreame (1620)

    The Guls Horne-Booke (1609)

    If it be not Good, the Divel is in it (1612)

    Newes from Hell (1606)

    The Pleasant Comedie of Old Fortunatus (1600)

    The Shoemaker's Holiday, ed. Peter Smith (London: Nick Hern Books, 2004)

    The Shomakers Holiday (1600)

    Whore of Babylon (1607)

    The Wonder of a Kingdome (1636)

[Dekker, Thomas,?], *The Welsh Embassador, From the MS (Cardiff Public Library)*, ed. H. Littledale and W. W. Greg (Oxford: Malone Society, 1920)

Dekker, Thomas, and John Ford, *The Sun's-Darling* (1656)

    [Middleton?], *The Spanish Gipsie* (1653)

Dekker, Thomas, [and Thomas Middleton,] *The Roaring Girle* (1611)
Dekker, Thomas, and John Webster, *North-ward Hoe* (1607)
    West-ward Hoe (1607)
Denham, John, *The Sophy* (1642)
Dennis, John, *Liberty Asserted* (1704)
Dering, Edward, *Sir Edward Dering's Manuscript of William Shakespeare's King
    Henry the Fourth*, ed. George Walton Williams and Gwynne Blakemore
    Evans (Washington, DC: Folger Shakespeare Library, 1974)
Dibdin, Thomas, *The Reminiscences of Thomas Dibdin*, 2 vols. (London, 1827)
Dodsley, Robert, *The King and the Miller of Mansfield* (1737)
    Sir John Cockle (1738)
Dowland, John, *First Booke of Songes or Ayres* (1597)
    Third and Last Booke of Songs or Aires (1603)
Downame, John, *The Account Audited* (1649)
Downes, John, *Roscius Anglicanus*, ed. J. Milhous and R. D. Hume (London:
    Society for Theatre Research, 1987)
Dryden, John, *The Letters*, ed. Charles E. Ward (Durham, NC: Duke University
    Press, 1942)
    'Preface' in Charles-Alphonse Dufresnoy, *De Arte Graphica: The Art of Painting
    . . . with Remarks; Translated into English, together with an Original Preface
    containing a Parallel betwixt Painting and Poetry, by Mr. Dryden* (1695)
    The Vindication, or, the Parallel of the French Holy-League (1683)
D'Urfey, Thomas, *The Banditti* (1686)
Eliot, John, *Poems* (1658)
Everard, Edward Cape, *Memoirs of an Unfortunate Son of Thespis* (1818)
Farlie, Robert, *The Kalender of Mans Life* (1638)
Farrant, Richard, *The Warres of Cyrus King of Persia* (1594)
Feeman, John, *A Sermon Preached Without a Text* (1643)
Felltham, Owen, *Resolves* (1623)
Fennor, William, *Fennor's Descriptions* (1616)
Field, Nathan, *Amends for Ladies* (1618)
    The Honest Man's Fortune (1647)
Fielde, John, *A Godly Exhortation* (1583)
Fitzgeffrey, Henry, *Certain Elegies* (1618)
    Satyres and Satyricall Epigrams (1617)
Fitz-geffry, Charles, *Sir Frances Drake* (1596)
Flecknoe, Richard, *Epigrams* (1671)
    Love's Kingdom (1664)
    Miscellania (1653)
Fletcher, John, *Beggars Bush* (1661)
    The Bloody Brother (1639)
    Bonduca, ed. Walter Wilson Greg and F. P. Wilson (Oxford: Malone Society,
    1951)
    A Critical Edition of John Fletcher's Humorous Lieutenant, ed. Philip Oxley
    (New York: Garland, 1987)

Demetrius and Enanthe, ed. Margaret McLaren Cook and F. P. Wilson (London: Malone Society, 1951)

The Faithfull Shepheardesse (1629)

The Faithful Shepheardesse (1634)

The Tragedy of Thierry, King of France, and his Brother Theodoret (1649)

The Wild-Goose Chase (1652)

The Woman's Prize: Or, The Tamer Tamed, ed. George B. Ferguson (London: Mouton, 1966)

Fletcher, John, and Philip Massinger, *The Bloody Brother* (1639)

Fletcher, John, and William Shakespeare, *The Two Noble Kinsmen* (1634)

Fletcher, Giles, and Phineas Fletcher, *Giles and Phineas Fletcher: Poetical Works*, ed. Frederick S. Boas, 2 vols. (Cambridge: Cambridge University Press, 1908)

Fletcher, Phineas, *Sicelides a Piscatory* (1631)

Florio, John, *Worlde of Wordes* (1598)

Fludd, Robert, *Answer unto M. Foster, or, The Squesing of Parson Fosters Sponge* (1631)

Ford, John, *The Broken Heart* (1633)

    The Ladies Triall (1639)

    The Lovers Melancholy (1629)

    The Lover's Melancholy, ed. R. F. Hill (Manchester: Manchester University Press, 1985)

Fuller, Thomas, *History* (1662)

Gager, William, *Ulysses Redux* (1592)

Gascoigne, George, *Supposes* in *The Pleasauntest Workes of George Gascoigne Esquire* (1587)

Gayton, Edmund, *Pleasant Notes upon Don Quixote* (1654)

Gee, John, *New Shreds of the Old Snare* (1624)

Glapthorne, Henry, *The Ladies Priviledge* (1640)

    The Lady Mother, ed. Arthur Brown (Oxford: Malone Society, [1958] 1959)

    Poems (1639)

    Wit in a Constable (1640)

Goffe, Thomas, *The Careles Shepherdess* (1656)

    The Couragious Turke (1632)

    A Critical Old Spelling Edition of Thomas Goffe's The Courageous Turke, ed. Susan Gushee O'Malley (New York: Garland, 1979)

    The Raging Turke Or the Tragedie of Bajazet (1631)

'Grange, Prince de la, Lord Lieutenant of Lincoln's Inn', Εγχυχλοχορεία (1662)

Granville, George, *Heroic Love* (1678)

Green, Mary Anne Everett, ed., *Calendar of State Papers, Domestic Series*: 1619–23 (London: Her Majesty's Stationery Office, 1856–1935)

Greene, Robert, *The Historie of Orlando Furioso, one of the Twelve Pieres of France* (1594)

    The Scottish Historie of James the Fourth (1598)

Greville, Fulke, *Mustapha* (1609)

Grindall, Edmund, *The Remains of Edmund Grindall D. D.*, ed. William Nicholson for the Parker Society (Cambridge: Cambridge University Press, 1843)

Guillemard, Jean, *A Combat betwixt Man and Death, translated into English by Edward Grimeston* (1621)

Guilpin, Edward, *Skialetheia* (1598)

H., A., *A Continued Inquisition against Paper-Persecutors* (1625)

Habington, William, *The Poems*, ed. Kenneth Allott (London: Hodder and Stoughton, 1948)

    The Queene of Arragon (1640)

Hakewill, George, *An Apologie of the Power and Providence of God* (1627)

Hall, Joseph, *Virgidemiarum* (1597)

Hall, Thomas, *The Loathsomeness of Long Hair* (1654)

Harding, Samuel, *Sicily and Naples* (1640)

Harington, John, *A New Discourse of a Stale Subject, called the Metamorphosis of Ajax* (1596)

Hausted, Peter, *The Rivall Friends* (1632)

Hawkins, William, *Apollo Shroving* (1627)

Healey, Jo, *Epictetus Manuall* (1616)

Heath, Robert, *Clarastella* (1650)

Henslowe, Philip, *Henslowe Papers*, ed. W. W. Greg (London: A. H. Bullen, 1907)

    Henslowe's Diary, ed. R. A. Foakes (Cambridge: Cambridge University Press, 2002)

Heylin, Peter, *Observations on the Historie of the Reign of King Charles* (1656)

Heywood, Thomas, *A Challenge for Beautie* (1636)

    The English Traveller (1633)

    The Escapes of Jupiter, from the autograph MS (Egerton 1994), ed. H. D. Janzen (Oxford: Malone Society, 1977)

    The Fair Maid of the West (1631)

    The Fayre Mayde of the Exchange (1607)

    The First and Second Partes of King Edward the Fourth (1600)

    The Foure Prentises of London (1615)

    The Golden Age (1611)

    If You Know Not Me You Know No Body (1639)

    Loves Maistresse: or, The Queens Masque (1636)

    A Pleasant Comedy, called A Mayden-Head Well Lost (1634)

    Pleasant Dialogues and Dramma's (1637)

    Rape of Lucrece (1608)

    Rape of Lucrece (1630)

    The Second Part of, If you Know not Me, you Know No Bodie (1606)

    The Second Part of the Iron Age in *The Iron Age* (1632)

    The Second Part of King Edward the Fourth (1599)

Higgens, John, *Nomenclator* (1585)

Hill, Aaron, and William Popple, *The Prompter: A Theatrical Paper (1734–1736)*, ed. William W. Appleton and Kalman A. Burnim (New York: Benjamin Blom, 1966)

Holland, Samuel, *Don Zara del Fogo* (1656)

Holyday, Barten, *Technogamia* (1618)

Hughes, Paul L., and James F. Larkin, eds., *Tudor Royal Proclamations*, 3 vols. (New Haven and London: Yale University Press, 1969)

Hughes, Thomas, Francis Bacon, Sir Nicholas Trotte, William Fulbeck, John Lancaster, Sir Christopher Yelverton, John Penroodock and Francis Flower, *The Misfortunes of Arthur* (1587 [i.e. 1588])

Jaques, Francis, *The Queen of Corsica* (1642), ed. Henry D. Janzen (Oxford: Malone Society, 1989)

Johnson, Samuel, *A Dictionary of the English Language*, second edition, 2 vols. (1755–6)

    Johnson on Shakespeare, ed. Arthur Sherbo, vols. 7 and 8 of The Yale Edition of the Works of Samuel Johnson (New Haven: Yale University Press, 1968)

    Lives of the English Poets, ed. George Birkbeck Hill, 3 vols. (Oxford: Clarendon Press, 1905)

Johnson, Samuel, and George Steevens, *Supplement to the Edition of Shakspeare's Plays published in 1778*, 2 vols. (1780)

Jones, Robert, *First Booke of Songes and Ayres* (1600)

    Second Booke of Songs and Ayres (1601)

Jonson, Ben, *Bartholmew Fayre* (1631)

    The Case is Altered (1609)

    The Comicall Satyre of Every Man out of his Humor (1600)

    The Devil is an Ass and Other Plays, ed. M. J. Kidnie (Oxford: Oxford University Press, 2000)

    Eastward Ho!, ed. Suzanne Gossett and W. David Kay, *The Cambridge Edition of the Works of Ben Jonson*, ed. David Bevington, Martin Butler, Ian Donaldson and David Gants (Cambridge: Cambridge University Press, forthcoming)

    Eastward Hoe (1605)

    The Fountaine of Selfe-Love. Or Cynthias Revels (1601)

    Loves Triumph (1631)

    The Magnetick Lady (1640)

    Masque of Augures (1621)

    Neptunes Triumph for the Returne of Albion (1624)

    The New Inne (1631)

    A Pleasant Comedy, called: The Case is Alterd (1609)

    Poetaster (1602)

    Sejanus (1605)

    Staple of News (1631)

    The Workes (1616)

    The Workes (1640)

    The Workes (1641)

    The Works of Benjamin Jonson, ed. C. H. Herford, P. Simpson and E. Simpson, 11 vols. (Oxford: Clarendon Press, 1925–52)

Jordan, Thomas, *Fancy's Festivals* (1657)

    A Nursery of Novelties (1665)

Killigrew, Henry, *Pallantus and Eudora* (1653)

Killigrew, Thomas, *Comedies and Tragedies* (1664)

Killigrew, William, *Pandora* (1664)
King, Henry, *Poems, Elegies, Paradoxes, and Sonnets* (1657)
  The Stoughton Manuscript, facsim. ed. Mary Hobbs (Aldershot: Scolar, 1990)
Kyd, Thomas, *Solyman and Perseda* (1592)
  The Spanish Tragedie (1592)
Leandro, Michael, *Aristologia Euripidea Graecolatina* (Basel, 1559)
Leigh, Richard, *The Transproser Rehears'd* (1673)
Lewes, Charles Lee, and John Lee Lewes, *Memoirs of Charles Lee Lewes*, 4 vols. (1805)
Lodge, Thomas, *Lady Alimony* (1659)
  A Looking Glasse for London and England (1594)
Lovelace, Richard, *Lucasta* (1649)
Lupton, Thomas, *A Thousand Notable Things* (1660)
Lyly, John, *The Complete Works*, ed. R. W. Bond, 3 vols. (Oxford: Clarendon Press, 1902)
  Endimion (1591)
  Mother Bombie (1594)
  Sapho and Phao (1584)
  Sixe Court Comedies (1632)
  The Woman in the Moone (1597)
Macklin, Charles, *Henry VII* (1746)
Manley, Mary De la Rivière, *Almyna* (1707)
  The Lost Lover (1697)
Manningham, John, *The Diary of John Manningham of the Middle Temple, 1602–3*, ed. Robert Parker Sorlien (Hanover, NH: Published for the University of Rhode Island by the University Press of New England, 1976)
Markham, Francis, *Booke of Honour* (1625)
Marlowe, Christopher, *The Complete Works: Edward II*, ed. Richard Rowland (Oxford: Oxford University Press, 1994)
  Doctor Faustus A- and B- Texts, ed. David M. Bevington and Eric Rasmussen (Manchester: Manchester University Press, 1993)
  Dr Faustus (1604)
  Edward the Second (1594)
  Edward the Second, ed. Charles R. Forker (Manchester: Manchester University Press, 1994)
  The Rich Jew of Malta (1633)
Marston, John, *Antonios Revenge* (1602)
  The Dutch Courtezan (1605)
  The History of Antonio and Mellida (1602)
  The History of Antonio and Mellida: The First Part (1602)
  Jacke Drums Entertainment (1601)
  The Malcontent (1604a)
  The Malcontent (1604b)
  The Malcontent. Augmented by Marston. With the Additions Played by the Kings Majesties Servants. Written by Jhon Webster (1604)

Scourge of Villanie (1598)

What You Will (1607)

[Marston, John,?] *Histriomastix* (1610)

Marston, John, [with William Barksted and Lewis Mackin], *The Insatiate Countesse* (1613)

Marvell, Andrew, *The Rehearsal Transpros'd*, ed. D. I. B. Smith (Oxford: Clarendon Press, 1971)

Mason, John, *An Excellent Tragedy of Mulleasses the Turke* (1632)

The Turke (1610)

Mason, John, of Cambridge, *Princeps Rhetoricus or* πιλομαχια *the Combat of Caps* (1648)

Massinger, Philip, *Believe as You List,* from the autograph MS (Egerton 2828), licensed 6 May 1631, ed. C. J. Sisson (Oxford: Malone Society, 1927)

The Emperour of the East (1632)

The Fatall Dowry (1632)

The Great Duke of Florence (1636)

A New Way to Pay Old Debts (1633)

The Roman Actor (1629)

Three New Playes (1655)

The Unnaturall Combat (1639)

May, Thomas, *The Heire* (1622)

The Heire (1633)

The Old Couple (1658)

Mayne, Jasper, *The Citye Match* (1639)

Jonsonus Virbius (1638)

Melton, John, *Astrologaster* (1620)

Mennes, John, *Musarum Deliciae* (1655)

[Mennes, John,] *Several Select Poems not Formerly Publish't* (1658)

Meres, Francis, *Palladis Tamia* (1598)

Middleton, Thomas, *The Ant, and the Nightingale: or Father Hubburds Tales* (1604)

A Chast Mayd in Cheape-Side (1630)

The Collected Works, ed. Gary Taylor and John Lavagnino (Oxford: Clarendon Press, 2007)

A Faire Quarrell (1617a)

A Faire Quarrell (1617b)

The Familie of Love (1608)

A Game At Chesse (1625a)

A Game At Chesse (1625b)

Hengist, King of Kent, or the Mayor of Queenborough, ed. Grace Ioppolo (Oxford: Malone Society, 2003)

Hengist, King of Kent; or the Mayor of Queenborough . . . from the Manuscript in the Folger Shakespeare Library, ed. R. C. Bald (New York and London: Charles Scribner's Sons, 1938)

A Mad World my Masters (1640)

The Mayor of Quinborough a Tragedy [*Hengist, King of Kent*] (1661)

The Phoenix (1607)

A Trick to Catch the Old-One (1608)

Two New Playes (1657)

The Widdow (1652)

The Witch, ed. L. Drees and Henry de Vocht (Louvain: Librairie Universitaire, 1945)

The Witch, ed. W. W. Greg (Oxford: Malone Society, 1948 [1950])

Women Beware Women, ed. J. R. Mulryne (London: Methuen, 1977)

Middleton, Thomas, ['W. S.'], *The Puritaine* (1607)

Middleton, Thomas, and William Rowley, *A Courtly Masque: the Device Called, World Tost at Tennis* (1620)

Middleton, Thomas, and James Shirley, *No Wit/Help like a Womans* (1657)

Milton, John, *Poems: Reproduced in Facsimile from the Manuscript in Trinity College, Cambridge: With a Transcript* (Menston, UK: Scolar Press, 1970)

Montagu, Walter, *The Shepheard's Paradise* (1659)

The Shepherds' Paradise, ed. Sarah Poynting (Oxford: Malone Society, 1997)

Shepheards Paradise, ed. Sarah Poynting (unpublished D.Phil. thesis, University of Oxford, 1999)

M[ountfort], W[alter], *The Launching of the Mary*, ed. J. H. Walter (Oxford: Malone Society, 1933)

More, Henry, *The Immortality of the Soul* (1659)

Morley, Thomas, *First Booke of Ayres* (1600)

The First Booke of Balletts (1595)

The First Booke of Consort Lessons (1599)

'Multibibus, Blasius', *A Solemne Joviall Disputation, Theoreticke and Practicke; briefely shadowing the Law of Drinking* (1617)

'Munda, Constantia', *The Worming of a Mad Dogge* (1617)

Munday, Anthony, *John a Kent and John a Cumber*, ed. Muriel St. Clare Byrne (Oxford: Malone Society, 1923)

Nabbes, Thomas, *An Almond for a Parrat* (1589)

The Bride (1640)

Covent Garden (1638)

Have With You to Saffron-Walden (1596)

Nashes Lenten Stuffe (1599)

Pasquill, of England, Cavaliero (1589)

Pierce Penilesse (1592)

A Pleasant Comedie, called Summers Last Will and Testament (1600)

Terrors of the Night (1594)

Tottenham Court (1636)

North, Dudley, *A Forest of Varieties* (1645)

Northbrooke, John, *A Treastise wherein Dicing, Dauncing, Vaine plaies . . . are reproved . . .* (1579)

Odingsells, Gabriel, *Bay's Opera* (1730)

Overbury, Thomas, *Sir Thomas Overburie his Wife* (1616)

A Wife now the Widdow of Sir Tho: Overburye (1614)

P., R., *Choyce Drollery* (1656)

Parkes, William, *The Curtaine-Drawer of the World* (1612)
Parrot, Henry, *Laquei Ridiculosi* (1613)
    The Mastive (1615)
Parsons, Robert, *The Warn-Word to Sir Francis Hastinges* (1602)
Peacham, Henry, *Coach and Sedan* (1636)
    The Truth of Our Times (1638)
    The Worth of a Peny (1647)
Peele, George, *The Famous Chronicle of King Edward the First* (1593)
    The Life and Minor Works of George Peele, ed. David H. Horne (New Haven:
    Yale University Press, 1952)
Pemberton, T. Edgar, *A Memoir of Edward Askew Sothern* (1889)
Pepys, Samuel, *The Diary of Samuel Pepys*, ed. Robert Latham and William
    Matthews, 11 vols. (London: G. Bell and Sons Ltd, 1970–83)
Percy, William, *The Cuckqueans and Cuckolds Errants and the Faery Pastoral* (1824)
    Mahomet and His Heaven (1601), ed. Matthew Dimmock (Aldershot: Ashgate,
    2006)
Perwich, William, *The Despatches of William Perwich, English Agent in Paris,
    1669–1677*, ed. M. Beryl Curran (London: Royal Historical Society, 1903)
Philipps, Fabian, *Tenenda non Tollenda* (1660)
Phillips, Edward, *Life of Mr John Milton* (1694)
    The Mysteries of Love & Eloquence (1658)
Pikering, John, *Horestes* (1567)
Playford, John, *The Dancing Master* (1653)
Plutarch, *Moralia: Index*, ed. Edward N. O'Neil (Cambridge, MA: Harvard
    University Press, 2004)
Popple, William, *Lady's Revenge* (1734)
Powell, George, *Alphonso* (1691)
Prynne, William, *Histriomastix* (1633)
Puttenham, George, *The Arte of English Poesie*, 3 vols. (1589)
Quarles, Francis, *The Virgin Widow* (1649)
Raleigh, Walter, *The Poems*, ed. Michael Rudick, Renaissance English Text
    Society, 7th series, vol. 23 (Tempe: Arizona Center for Medieval and
    Renaissance Studies, 1999)
Randolph, Thomas, *Amyntas* (1638)
    Aristippus (1630)
    Hey for Honesty, Down with Knavery (1651)
    Poems (1638)
Rankins, William, *The Mirrour of Monsters* (1587)
    Seaven Satyres (1598)
Ravenscroft, Thomas, *A Briefe Discourse* (1614)
    Deuteromelia (1609)
    Melismata (1611)
    Pammelia (1609)
Richards, Nathaniel, *The Tragedy of Messallina* (1640)
Rosseter, Philip, *A Booke of Ayres* (1601)

Rous, Francis, *The Diseases of the Time* (1622)

Rowe, John, *Tragi-Comaedia. Being a Brief Relation of the Strange, and Wonderfull hand of God discovered at Witny, in the Comedy Acted there February the third, where there were some Slaine, many Hurt, with severall other Remarkable Passages* (1653)

Rowlands, Samuel, *Pimlico* (1609)

Rowley, Samuel, *The Noble Souldier* (1634)

Rowley, William, *A Tragedy called All's Lost by Lust* (1633)

Rudyerd, Benjamin, *Le Prince d'Amour, or the Prince of Love* (1660)

S., A., Gent [thought to be Richard Chamberlain], *The Booke of Bulls* (1636)

Shakespeare, William, *As You Like It*, ed. Juliet Dusinberre, The Arden Shakespeare (London: Thomson and Thomson, 2006)

The Famous Historie of Troylus and Cresseid (1609a) (1609b)

Hamlet (1600)

Hamlet (1604)

Henry IV, Part I, ed. David Bevington (Oxford and New York: Oxford University Press, 1987)

2 Henry IV (1600)

Henry V, ed. Andrew Gurr (Cambridge: Cambridge University Press, 1992)

Henry VI part 3, ed. John D. Cox and Eric Rasmussen, The Arden Shakespeare (Thomson and Thomson, 2001)

Henry VI part 3, ed. Michael Hattaway (Cambridge: Cambridge University Press, 1993)

Henry VI part 3, ed. Randall Martin (Oxford: Oxford University Press, 2001)

King Edward III, ed. Giorgio Melchiori (Cambridge: Cambridge University Press, 1998)

King John, ed. L. A. Beaurline (Cambridge: Cambridge University Press, 1990)

Love's Labour's Lost (1598)

Lucrece (1594)

Measure for Measure, ed. Sir Arthur Quiller-Couch and John Dover Wilson (Cambridge: Cambridge University Press, 1922)

The Merchant of Venice, ed. J. R. Brown (London: Methuen, 1955)

The Merchant of Venice, ed. Jay L. Halio (Oxford: Oxford University Press, 1993)

The Merchant of Venice, ed. M. M. Mahood (Cambridge: Cambridge University Press, 1987)

The Merry Wives of Windsor, ed. W. W. Greg (Oxford: Clarendon Press, 1910)

The Merry Wives of Windsor, ed. Tiffany Stern (New York: Barnes and Noble, Forthcoming)

Mr. William Shakespeares Comedies, Histories, & Tragedies (1623)

Othello . . . As it is now acted at The Theatre Royal in Covent-Garden (1761)

Pericles, Prince of Tyre (1609)

Pericles, ed. Suzanne Gossett (London: Thomson Learning, 2004)

The Plays, ed. George Steevens, Isaac Reed and Samuel Johnson, 21 vols. (1803)

The Plays and Poems, ed. Isaac Reed, Samuel Johnson and George Steevens, 21 vols. (1821)

The Plays of William Shakespeare, ed. Edmond Malone, Samuel Johnson, George Steevens and Isaac Reed, 15 vols. (1793)

Poems (1640)

Romeo and Juliet (1597)

Shakespeare's Poems, ed. Katherine Duncan-Jones and H. R. Woudhuysen (London: Thomson Learning, 2007)

Twelfth Night, ed. M. M. Mahood (London: Penguin, 1966)

The Works of Mr. William Shakespeare, ed. Alexander Pope and George Sewell, 10 vols. (1728)

The Works of Shakespeare, ed. Lewis Theobald, 7 vols. (1733)

[Shakespeare, William,] *Passionate Pilgrim* (1599)

Sharpham, Edward, *Cupid's Whirligig* (1607)

Sheppard, Simon, *The Committee-man Curried* (1647)

Sheridan, Thomas, *British Education* (1765)

Shirley, James, *Bird in a Cage* (1633)
    The Brothers (1653)
    The Cardinal (1652)
    The Changes (1632)
    The Constant Maid (1640)
    The Coronation (1640)
    The Dukes Mistris (1638)
    Hide Parke (1637)
    The Imposture (1652)
    The Lady of Pleasure (1637)
    [Love Tricks or] The Schoole of Complement (1631)
    Poems (1646)
    The Sisters (1652)
    Six New Playes (1652)
    The Triumph of Beautie in *Poems* (1646)
    Wittie Faire One (1633)

Silver, George, *Paradoxes of Defence* (1599)

Smith, Wentworth, *The Hector of Germany or The Palsgrave, Prime Elector* (1615)

Spencer, John, καινα και παλαια: *Things New and Old* (1658)

Stephens, John, *New Essays and Characters* (1631)
    Satirical Essays (1615)

Stockwood, John, *A Sermon Preached at Paules Crosse on Barthelmew Day, being the 24. of August. 1578* (1578)

Le Strange, Nicholas, *Merry Passages and Jeasts: A Manuscript Jestbook of Sir Nicholas Le Strange*, ed. James Hogg (Salzburg: Institut für Englische Sprache und Literatur, 1974)

Suckling, John, *Brennoralt* (1646)
    Fragmenta (1646)
    The Goblins (1646)
    The Last Remains of Sir John Suckling (1659)

Tailor, Robert, *The Hogge hath Lost his Pearle* (1614)
Tarlton, Richard, *Tarltons Jests* (1613)
[Tarlton, Richard], *Tarltons Newes out of Purgatorie* (1590)
Tatham, John, *The Distracted State* (1651)
    The Fancies Theater (1640)
    Ostella (1650)
Taylor, John, *All the Workes of John Taylor the Water-Poet* (1630)
    A Pedlar and a Romish Priest (1641)
Theobald, Lewis, *The Double Falshood* (1728)
Tudor Royal Proclamations
Tuke, Samuel, *The Adventures of Five Hours* (1663)
Valerius, Adraen, *Nederlandtsch Gedenck-Clanck* (1626)
Vanbrugh, John, and Colley Cibber, *The Provok'd Husband* (1728)
Vandenhoff, George, *Leaves from an Actor's Note-book* (1860)
Vaughan, William, *Golden Fleece* (1626)
Vega, Lope de, *New Art of Making Plays in This Age*, trans. William T. Brewster
    (New York: Dramatic Museum of Columbia University, 1964)
Vennar[d], Richard, *An Apology* (1614)
Vicars, John, *Epigrams of that Most Wittie and Worthie Epigrammatist Mr. John*
    Owen (1619)
Villiers, George, Duke of Buckingham, *Poems on Affairs of State* (1697)
    The Rehearsal, ed. D. E. L. Crane (Durham: University of Durham Press, 1976)
Villiers, George, Samuel Butler, Thomas Sprat and Martin Clifford, *The*
    Rehearsal (1672)
W., T., *A Choice Ternary of English Plays: Gratiae Theatrales*, ed. William M. Baillie
    (Binghamton, NY: Medieval and Renaissance Texts and Studies, 1984)
    Gratiae Theatrales, or, A Choice Ternary of English Plays (1662)
Wager, William, *A Comedy or Enterlude intituled, Inough is as Good as a Feast*
    (1570)
Ward, Samuel, *The Life of Faith in Death* (1622)
Webster, John, *The Dutchesse of Malfy* (1623)
    The Thracian Wonder (1661)
    The Works, ed. David Gunty, David Carnegie, Antony Hammond and
    Doreen DelVecchio, 3 vols. (Cambridge: Cambridge University Press, 1995)
Wentworth, Thomas, Earl of Strafford, *Letters and Dispatches*, ed. William
    Knowler, 2 vols. (1739)
Whetstone, George, *Aurelia* (1593)
    Promos and Cassandra, part i (1578)
    Promos and Cassandra, part ii (1578)
Whitney, Geffrey, 'Pennæ Gloria Perennis' from *A Choice of Emblemes and other*
    Devises (1586)
Wilkinson, Tate, *Memoirs of his Own Life*, 4 vols. (1790)
Willan, Leonard, *Astraea or, True Love's Myrrour* (1651)
    Orgula or the Fatall Error (1658)
Willis, Edmond, *An Abreviation of Writing by Character* (1618)
Wilson, Arthur, *The Swisser*, Librairie Fischbacher (Paris: Société Anonyme, 1904)

Wither, George, *Abuses* (1614)
  Abuses Stript, and Whipt (1613)
  The Great Assises Holden in Parnassus by Apollo and his Assessours (1645)
Wood, Anthony, *Athenae Oxonienses* (1692)
Wright, Abraham, *Parnassus Biceps* (1656)
Yarington, Robert, *Two Lamentable Tragedies* (1601)

SECONDARY TEXTS

Adams, Joseph Quincy, 'The Author-Plot of an Early Seventeenth Century Play',
    The Library, 27 (1945), 17–27
Alexander, Peter, *Alexander's Introductions to Shakespeare* (London and Glasgow:
    Collins, 1964)
Arber, Edward, *A Transcript of the Registers of the Company of Stationers of
    London*, 4 vols. (1875–84)
Astington, John, 'Rereading Illustrations of the English Stage', *Shakespeare
    Survey*, 50 (1997), 151–70
Austern, Linda Phyllis, *Music in English Children's Drama of the Later Renaissance*
    (Philadelphia: Gordon and Breach Science Publishers, 1992)
    'Thomas Ravenscroft: Musical Chronicler of an Elizabethan Theatre
    Company', *Journal of the Royal Musical Association*, 38 (1985), 238–63
Avery, Emmett L., ed., *The London Stage part 2: 1700–1729* (Carbondale, IL:
    Southern Illinois University Press, 1960)
Ayres, Philip J., 'Anthony Munday: "Our Best Plotter"?', *English Language Notes*,
    18 (1980), 13–15
Baker, David Erskine, Isaac Reed and Stephen Jones, *Biographia Dramatica* (1812)
Baldwin, Thomas Whitfield, *On Act and Scene Division in the Shakespeare First
    Folio* (Carbondale: Southern Illinois University Press, 1965)
Bate, Jonathan, and Russell Jackson, eds., *The Oxford Illustrated History of
    Shakespeare on Stage* (Oxford: Oxford University Press, 1996)
Bawcutt, N. W., *The Control and Censorship of Caroline Drama* (Oxford: Clarendon
    Press, 1996)
Beal, Peter, *Index of English Literary Manuscripts 1450–1700*, 2 vols. (New York:
    R. R. Bowker, 1980)
    'Massinger at Bay: Unpublished Verses in a War of the Theatres', *Yearbook of
    English Studies*, 10 (1980), 190–203
Beckerman, Bernard, 'Theatrical Plots and Elizabethan Stage Practice' in
    Shakespeare and Dramatic Tradition, ed. W. R. Elton and W. B. Long
    (Newark, DE: University of Delaware Press, 1989), 109–24
Bednarz, James P., 'When did Shakespeare Write the Choruses of *Henry V*?',
    Notes and Queries, 53 (2006), 486–9
Bennett, H. S., *English Books and Readers 1558–1603* (Cambridge: Cambridge
    University Press, 1965)
    English Books and Readers 1603–1640 (Cambridge: Cambridge University Press,
    1970)

Bentley, Gerard Eades, *The Jacobean and Caroline Stage*, 7 vols. (Oxford: Clarendon Press, 1941–68)

   The Profession of Dramatist in Shakespeare's Time (Princeton, NJ: Princeton University Press, 1986)

Bergeron, David M., *English Civic Pageantry, 1558–1642* (Tempe, AZ: Arizona Center for Medieval and Renaissance Studies, 2003)

   'Stuart Civic Pageants and Textual Performance', *Renaissance Quarterly*, 51 (1998), 163–83

   Textual Patronage in English Drama, 1570–1640 (Aldershot: Ashgate, 2006)

Berry, Herbert, 'Richard Vennar, "England's Joy"', *English Literary Renaissance*, 31 (2001), 240–65

Best, M. R., 'A Note on the Songs in Lyly's Plays', *Notes and Queries*, 12 (1965), 93–4

Blayney, Peter, W. M., *The First Folio of Shakespeare* (Washington, DC: Folger Library Publications, 1991)

   'The Publication of Playbooks' in *A New History of Early English Drama*, ed. John D. Cox and David Scott Kastan (New York: Columbia University Press, 1997), 383–422

Bond, R. W., 'Addendum on Lyly's Songs', *RES*, 7 (1931), 442–7

Boswell, Eleanore, 'A Playbill of 1687', *The Library*, 4th series, 11 (1931), 499–502

Bowden, William, *The English Dramatic Lyric* (New Haven: Yale University Press, 1951)

Bowers, Fredson, *On Editing Shakespeare and the Elizabethan Dramatists* (Philadelphia: University of Pennsylvania Library, 1955)

Bradley, David, *From Text to Performance in the Elizabethan Theatre* (Cambridge: Cambridge University Press, 1992)

Brandt, George W., ed., *German and Dutch Theatre, 1600–1848* (Cambridge: Cambridge University Press, 1993)

Braunmuller, A. R., 'Accounting for Absence: The Transcription of Space' in *New Ways of Looking at Old Texts*, ed. W. Speed Hill (New York: Center of Medieval and Early Renaissance Studies, 1993), 47–56

   A Seventeenth-Century Letter-Book: A Facsimile Edition of Folger MS v.a.321 (Newark, DE: University of Delaware Press, 1983)

Brückner, Martin, and Kristen Poole, 'The Plot Thickens: Surveying Manuals, Drama, and the Materiality of Narrative Form in Early Modern England', *ELH*, 69 (2002), 617–48

Bruster, Douglas, and Robert Weimann, *Prologues to Shakespeare's Theatre: Performance and Liminality in Early Modern Drama* (London and New York: Routledge, 2004)

Burnim, Kalman A., *David Garrick, Director* (Pittsburgh: University of Pittsburgh Press, 1961)

Burrow, Colin, 'Lyric in its Settings: Multiple Narratives and Lyric Voices in *Love's Labour's Lost*', unpublished paper delivered at Shakespeare Association of America, 2006

C., J., 'Notices on Old English Comedies, No. 1, Eastward Hoe', *Blackwood's Magazine*, 10 (1821), 127–36

Calore, Michela, 'Elizabethan Plots: A Shared Code of Theatrical and Fictional Language', *Theatre Survey*, 44:2 (2003), 249–61

Carnegie, David, 'The Identification of the Hand of Thomas Goffe, Academic Dramatist and Actor', *The Library*, 26 (1971), 161–5

Carpenter, Nan Cooke, 'Shakespeare and Music: Unexplored Areas' in *Shakespeare and the Arts*, ed. Stephen Orgel and Sean Keilen (New York and London: Garland Publishing, 1999), 123–35

Carson, Neil, *A Companion to Henslowe's Diary* (Cambridge: Cambridge University Press, 1988)

Cerasano, S. P., and Marion Wynne-Davies, eds., *Renaissance Drama by Women* (London and New York: Routledge, 1995)

Chambers, E. K., *The Elizabethan Stage*, 4 vols. (Oxford: Clarendon Press, 1923)
  William Shakespeare: A Study of the Facts and Problems, 2 vols. (Oxford: Clarendon Press, 1930)

Chan, Mary, '*Cynthia's Revels* and Music for a Choir School', *Studies in the Renaissance*, 18 (1971), 134–72
  Music in the Theatre of Ben Jonson (Oxford: Oxford University Press, 1980)

Clare, Janet, *Art Made Tongue-Tied by Authority* (Manchester and New York: Manchester University Press, 1990)

Cohn, Albert, *Shakespeare in Germany* (London: Asher & Co., 1865)

Collier, J. Payne, *The History of English Dramatic Poetry to the Time of Shakespeare*, 3 vols. (1831)

Craig, Hardin, 'The Dering Version of Shakespeare's Henry IV', *Philological Quarterly*, 35 (1956), 218–19

Cutts, John P., 'Jacobean Masque and Stage Music', *Music & Letters*, 35 (1954), 185–201
  La musique de scène de la troupe de Shakespeare (Paris: Éditions du Centre National de la Recherche Scientifique, 1959)
  'The Original Music to Middleton's *The Witch*', *Shakespeare Quarterly*, 7 (1956), 203–9
  'Peele's *Hunting of Cupid*', *Studies in the Renaissance*, 5 (1958), 121–32
  'Robert Johnson and the Court Masque', *Music & Letters*, 41 (1955), 110–25
  'Robert Johnson: King's Musician in His Majesty's Public Entertainment', *Music & Letters*, 39 (1955), 110–26
  'Some Jacobean and Caroline Dramatic Lyrics', *Notes and Queries*, n.s. 2 (1955), 106–9
  '"Speak–demand–we'll answer": Hecate and the Other Three Witches', *Shakespeare Jahrbuch*, 96 (1960), 173–6
  'An Unpublished Contemporary Setting of a Shakespeare Song', *Shakespeare Survey*, 9 (1956), 86–9

Danson, Lawrence, '*Henry V*: King, Chorus, and Critics', *Shakespeare Quarterly*, 34 (1983), 27–43

Dasent, J. R., ed., *Acts of the Privy Council*, 32 vols. (London: HM Stationery Office, 1890–1907)

Dessen, Alan C., and Leslie Thomson, *A Dictionary of Stage Directions in English Drama, 1580–1642* (Cambridge: Cambridge University Press, 1999)

Dodds, M. Hope, 'Songs in Lyly's Plays', *TLS* (28 June 1941)

Duffin, Ross W., 'Catching the Burthen: A New Round of Shakespearean Musical Hunting', *Studies in Music*, 19–20 (2000–1), 1–15

  Shakespeare's Songbook (New York and London: W. W. Norton & Company, 2004)

Dutton, Richard, *Licensing, Censorship and Authorship in Early Modern England* (Houndmills: Palgrave, 2000)

  Mastering the Revels (Basingstoke: Macmillan, 1991)

Eccles, Mark, 'Jonson and the Spies', *RES*, 13 (1937), 385–97

Edwards, Philip, *A Book of Masques* (Cambridge: Cambridge University Press, 1967)

Eggers, Walter F., Jr 'Shakespeare's Gower and the Role of the Authorial Presenter', *Philological Quarterly*, 54 (1975), 434–43

Elliott, John R., and Alan H. Nelson, eds., *Records of Early English Drama: Oxford*, 2 vols. (Toronto: University of Toronto Press, 2004)

Erne, Lukas, *Shakespeare as Literary Dramatist* (Cambridge: Cambridge University Press, 2003)

Evans, G. Blakemore, 'The Dering MS. of Shakespeare's *Henry IV* and Sir Edward Dering', *JEGP*, 54 (1955), 498–503

Farmer, Alan B., and Zachary, Lesser, 'Vile Arts: The Marketing of English Printed Drama, 1512–1660', *Research Opportunities in Renaissance Drama*, 39 (2000), 77–109

Foakes, R. A., *Henslowe's Diary* (Cambridge: Cambridge University Press, [1961] 2002)

  'The Image of the Swan Theatre' in *Spectacle and Image in the Renaissance*, ed. André Lascombes (Leiden: Brill, 1993), 337–59

Fox, Adam, *Oral and Literate Culture in England 1500–1700* (Oxford: Clarendon Press, 2000)

Freeman, Arthur, 'The Argument of Meleager', *English Literary Renaissance*, 1 (1971), 122–31

Freeman, Arthur, and Janet Ing Freeman, *John Payne Collier*, 2 vols. (New Haven: Yale University Press, 2004)

Fuller, David, 'Ben Jonson's Plays and Their Contemporary Music', *Music & Letters*, 58 (1977), 60–75

Genette, Gérard, *Paratexts: Thresholds of Interpretation*, trans. Jane E. Lewin, foreword by Richard Macksey (Cambridge: Cambridge University Press, 1997)

Gibson, James M., *The Philadelphia Shakespeare Story: Horace Howard Furness and the New Variorum Shakespeare* (New York: AMS Press, 1990)

Gillies, John, ed., *Playing the Globe: Genre and Geography in English Renaissance Drama* (Madison, NJ: Fairleigh Dickinson University Press, 1998)

Goldberg, Jonathan, 'Hamlet's Hand', *Shakespeare Quarterly*, 39 (1988), 307–27

Goldberg, Lee, and William Rabkin, *Successful Television Writing* (Hoboken, NJ: John Wiley and Sons, 2003)

Gossett, Suzanne, 'Drama in the English College, Rome, 1591–1660', *ELR*, 3 (1973), 60–93

'Masque Influence in the Dramaturgy of Beaumont and Fletcher', *Modern Philology*, 69 (1971–2), 199–208

'The Term "Masque" in Shakespeare and Fletcher and *The Coxcomb*', *Studies in English Literature*, 14 (1974), 285–95

Gowen, David, 'Studies in the History and Function of the British Theatre Playbill and Programme, 1564–1914' (unpublished D.Phil. thesis, University of Oxford, 1998)

Greenfield, Thelma M., *The Induction in Elizabethan Drama* (Eugene: University of Oregon Books, 1969)

Greer, David, '"What if a day": An Examination of the Words and Music', *Music & Letters*, 43 (1962), 304–19

Greg, W. W., 'The Authorship of the Songs in Lyly's Plays', *MLR*, 1 (1905), 43–52

A Bibliography of the English Printed Drama to the Restoration, 4 vols. (London: Bibliographical Society, 1959)

Dramatic Documents from the Elizabethan Playhouses, 2 vols. (Oxford: Clarendon Press, 1931)

The Shakespeare First Folio: Its Bibliographical and Textual History (Oxford: Clarendon Press, 1955)

Greg, W. W., ed., *Malone Society Collections: 1 part 1* (Oxford: Malone Society, 1907)

Two Elizabethan Stage Abridgements: 'The Battle of Alcazar' and 'Orlando Furioso' (Oxford: Malone Society, 1922)

Greg, W. W., and E. Boswell, *Records of the Court . . . 1576 to 1602 from Register B* (London: Bibliographical Society, 1930)

Griffin, Benjamin, *Playing the Past* (Woodbridge, Suffolk: D. S. Brewer, 2001)

Gurr, Andrew, 'Maximal and Minimal Texts: Shakespeare v. The Globe', *Shakespeare Survey*, 52 (1999), 68–87

'The Work of Elizabethan Plotters and *2 The Seven Deadly Sins*', *Early Theatre*, 10 (2007), 67–87

Halstead, W. L., 'Note on Dekker's *Old Fortunatus*', *Modern Language Notes* (1939), 351–2

Halstead, William Perdue, *Stage Management for the Amateur Theatre: With an Index to the Standard* (London: George G. Harrap & Co., 1938)

Hammond, Antony, and Doreen Delvecchio, 'The Melbourne Manuscript and John Webster: A Reproduction and Transcripts', *Studies in Bibliography*, 41 (1988), 1–32

Harper, Sally, *Music in Welsh Culture Before 1650* (Aldershot: Ashgate, 2007)

Henze, Catherine A., 'How Music Matters: Some Songs of Robert Johnson in the Plays of Beaumont and Fletcher', *Comparative Drama* 34:1 (2000), 1–32

Holman, Peter, *Four and Twenty Fiddlers: The Violin at the English Court, 1540–1690* (Oxford: Clarendon Press, 1993)

'Music for the Stage I: Before the Civil War', in *Music in Britain: The Seventeenth Century*, ed. Ian Spink (Oxford: Blackwell, 1992), 282–305

Holzknecht, Karl J., 'Theatrical Billposting in the Age of Elizabeth', *Philological Quarterly*, 2 (1923), 267–81

Honigmann, E. A. J., '*King John, The Troublesome Reigne*, and "documentary links"', *Shakespeare Quarterly*, 38 (1987), 124–6

Myriad Minded Shakespeare (New York: St. Martin's Press, 1989), 192–4

'The New Bibliography and Its Critics' in *Textual Performances*, ed. Lucas Erne and M. J. Kidnie (Cambridge: Cambridge University Press, 2004)

The Stability of Shakespeare's Text (London: Edward Arnold, 1965)

The Texts of 'Othello' and Shakespearian Revision (London and New York: Routledge, 1996)

Hosley, Richard, 'Was There a "Dramatic Epilogue" to *The Taming of the Shrew?*' *Studies in English Literature, 1500–1900*, 1 (1961), 17–34

Howard-Hill, T. H., 'Crane's 1619 "Promptbook" of "Barnavelt" and Theatrical Processes', *Modern Philology*, 86 (1988), 146–70

Hunter, G. K., *John Lyly: The Humanist as Courtier* (London: Routledge and Kegan Paul, 1962)

Ioppolo, Grace, *Dramatists and Their Manuscripts in the Age of Shakespeare, Jonson, Middleton, Heywood* (New York and London: Routledge, 2006)

Jacquot, Jean, 'Religion et Raison d'état dans l'oeuvre de Faulke Greville', *Études Anglaises*, 5 (1952), 211–22

Jones, G. P., '*Henry V*: The Chorus and the Audience', *Shakespeare Survey*, 31 (1978), 93–104

Jowett, John, 'Middleton's Song of Cupid', *Notes and Queries*, 239 (1994), 66–70

'Pre-Editorial Criticism and the Space for Editing: Examples from *Richard III* and *Your Five Gallants*', in *Problems of Editing*, ed. Christa Jansohn, special issue of *Edition*, 14 (1999), 127–49

Jowett, John, and Gary Taylor, 'With New Additions: Theatrical Interpolation in *Measure for Measure*' in *Shakespeare Reshaped*, ed. Gary Taylor and John Jowett (Oxford: Oxford University Press, 1993)

Kastan, David Scott, *Shakespeare and the Book* (Cambridge: Cambridge University Press, 2001)

Tudor Royal Proclamations, ed. Paul L. Hughes and James F. Larkin, 3 vols. (New Haven and London, Yale University Press, 1969)

Kathman, David, 'Reconsidering *The Seven Deadly Sins*', *Early Theatre*, 7 (2004), 13–44

Keenan, Siobhan, *Travelling Players in Shakespeare's England* (London: Palgrave Macmillan, 2002)

Kewes, Paulina, *Authorship and Appropriation* (Oxford: Clarendon Press, 1998)

King, T. J., *Casting Shakespeare's Plays* (Cambridge: Cambridge University Press, 1992)

Kinservik, Matthew J., 'Theatrical Regulation during the Restoration Period' in *A Companion to Restoration Drama*, ed. Susan J. Owen (Oxford: Blackwell, 2001), 36–52

Kirkpatrick, Robin, 'The Italy of *The Tempest*' in *The Tempest and Its Travels*, ed. Peter Hulme and William H. Sherman (London: Reaktion Books, 2000), 78–96

Kirsch, Arthur C., 'A Caroline Commentary on the Drama', *Modern Philology*, 66 (1969), 256–61

Knapp, Jeffrey, 'What Is a Co-author?', *Representations*, 89 (2005), 1–29

Knutson, Roslyn Lander, *The Repertory of Shakespeare's Company 1594–1613* (Fayetteville: University of Arkansas Press, 1991)

Krutch, Joseph Wood, 'Governmental Attempt to Regulate the Stage after the Jeremy Collier Controversy', *PMLA*, 38 (1923), 153–74

Langhans, Edward, '*Othello* as They Liked It', *On Stage Studies*, 7 (1983), 34–47
  Restoration Promptbooks (Carbondale and Edwardsville: Southern Illinois University Press, 1981)

Lawrence, W. J., 'The Date of *The Duchess of Malfi*', *Athenaeum*, 4673 (1919), 1235
  'Early Programmes', *The Stage* (27 July, 1933), 16
  'Early Prompt Books' in *Pre-Restoration Stage Studies* (Cambridge, MA: Harvard University Press, 1927), 373–413
  The Elizabethan Playhouse and Other Studies, 2 vols. (Stratford-upon-Avon: Shakespeare Head Press, 1913)
  'The Elizabethan Plotter' in *Speeding Up Shakespeare* (London: Argonaut, 1937; reissued New York: Blom, 1968), 99–112
  Old Theatre Days and Ways (1935)
  'The World's Oldest Playbills' in *The Stage Year Book*, ed. L. Carson (London: 'The Stage' Offices, 1920), 23–30

Lazarus, Paul N., *The Movie Producer: A Handbook for Producing and Picture-Making* (New York: Barnes & Noble, 1985)

Lefkowitz, Murray, 'The Longleat Papers of Bulstrode Whitelocke: New Light on Shirley's *Triumph of Peace*', *Journal of the American Musicological Society*, 18 (1965), 42–60

Lennam, T. N. S., 'Sir Edward Dering's Collection of Playbooks, 1619–1624', *Shakespeare Quarterly*, 16 (1965), 145–53

Lindley, David, *Shakespeare and Music*, Arden Critical Companions (London: Thomson and Thomson, 2006)

Lombardo, Agostino, 'Fragments and Scraps: Shakespeare's *Troilus and Cressida*' in *The European Tragedy of Troilus*, ed. Piero Boitani (Oxford: Oxford University Press, 1989)

Long, John H., 'Another Masque for *The Merry Wives of Windsor*', *Shakespeare Quarterly*, 3 (1952), 39–43

Long, W. B., '"Precious Few": English Manuscript Playbooks' in *A Companion to Shakespeare*, ed. David Scott Kastan (Oxford: Blackwell, 1999), 414–33

Lowenstein, Joseph, *Ben Jonson and Possessive Authorship* (Cambridge: Cambridge University Press, 2002)

Maggs, Brothers, *Shakespeare and Shakespeareana: A Catalogue*, 434 (1923)

Maguire, Laurie E., *Shakespearean Suspect Texts* (Cambridge: Cambridge University Press, 1996)

Marchitello, Howard, '(Dis)embodied Letters and *The Merchant of Venice*: Writing, Editing, History', *ELH*, 62 (1995), 237–65

Martin, William, 'An Elizabethan Theatre Programme', *The Selborne Magazine*, 24 (1913), 16–20

Massai, Sonia, 'Shakespeare, Text and Paratext', unpublished talk delivered at the International Shakespeare Conference, Stratford-upon-Avon, 2008

Masten, Jeffrey, *Textual Intercourse* (Cambridge: Cambridge University Press, 1997)
  'Toward a Queer Address: The Taste of Letters and Early Modern Male Friendship', *GLQ: A Journal of Lesbian and Gay Studies*, 10 (2004), 367–84

Maynard, Winifred, 'Ballads, Songs, and Masques in the Plays of Shakespeare' in *Elizabethan Lyric Poetry and Its Music* (Oxford: Clarendon Press, 1986)

McFadden, George, 'Political Satire in "The Rehearsal"', *Yearbook of English Studies*, 4 (1974), 120–8

McJannet, Linda, *The Voice of Elizabethan Stage Directions* (Newark, DE: University of Delaware Press, 1999)

McKendrick, Malvena, *Theatre in Spain 1490–1700* (Cambridge: Cambridge University Press, 1989)

McKerrow, R. B., *Shakespeare's England*, 2 vols. (Oxford: Clarendon Press, 1916)

McMillin, Scott, 'Building Stories: Greg, Fleay and the Plot of *2 Seven Deadly Sins*', *Medieval and Renaissance Drama in England*, 4 (1989), 53–62
  The Elizabethan Theatre and the Book of Sir Thomas More (Ithaca and London: Cornell University Press, 1987)
  'The Plots of *The Dead Man's Fortune* and *2 Seven Deadly Sins*: Inferences for Theatre Historians', *Studies in Bibliography*, 26 (1973), 235–43

Mehl, Dieter, *The Elizabethan Dumb Show* (London and New York: Methuen, 1964)

Milhous, Judith, and Robert D. Hume, *Producible Interpretation* (Carbondale: Southern Illinois University Press, 1985)

Moore, John Robert, 'The Songs in Lyly's Plays', *PMLA*, 42 (1927), 623–40

Nelson, Alan H., ed., *Records of Early English Drama: Cambridge*, 2 vols. (Toronto: University of Toronto Press, 1989)

Noble, Richmond Samuel, *Shakespeare's Use of Song* (London: Oxford University Press, 1923)

Nungezer, Edwin, *A Dictionary of Actors* (New Haven: Yale University Press, 1929)

O'Callaghan, Michelle, *The English Wits: Literature and Sociability in Early Modern England* (Cambridge: Cambridge University Press, 2007)

O'Donnell, Norbert F., 'The Authorship of *The Careless Shepherdess*', *Philological Quarterly*, 33 (1954), 43–7

Ogilvy, Arthur, 'Low Life on the Stage', *Once a Week*, ed. Eneas Sweetland Dallas, n.s. 4 (July–December 1867), 408–11

O'Neill, David G., 'The Influence of Music in the Works of John Marston', *Music & Letters*, 53 (1972), 400–10

Orgel, Stephen, 'Acting Scripts, Performing Texts' in *Crisis in Editing*, ed. Randall McLeod (New York: AMS Press, 1994), 251–94

'What Is an Editor?', *Shakespeare Studies*, 24 (1996), 23–39

Orrell, John, 'The London Stage in the Florentine Correspondence 1604–18', *Theatre Research International*, 3 (1977–8), 157–76

Pafford, H. P., 'Music and the Songs in *The Winter's Tale*', *Shakespeare Quarterly*, 10 (1959), 161–77

Palfrey, Simon, and Tiffany Stern, *Shakespeare in Parts* (Oxford: Oxford University Press, 2007)

Parker, Patricia, 'Altering the Letter of Twelfth Night', *Shakespeare Survey*, 59 (2006), 49–62

Pearn, B. R., 'Dumb-Show in Elizabethan Drama', *RES*, 11 (1935), 385–405

Pearsall, Derek, *New Directions in Later Medieval Manuscript Studies* (York: York Medieval Press, 2000), 143–65

Peters, Julie Stone, *Theatre of the Book* (Oxford: Oxford University Press, 2000)

Plant, Marjorie, *The English Book Trade* (London: George Allen & Unwin Ltd, 1965)

Pooley, Roger, ' "I Confesse it to be a Mere Toy": How to Read the Preliminary Matter to Renaissance Fiction' in *Critical Approaches to English Prose Fiction 1520–1640*, ed. Donald Beecher (Ottawa, Canada: Dovehouse Editions Inc., 1998)

Powell, Jocelyn, *Restoration Theatre Production* (London: Routledge and Kegan Paul, 1984)

Rasmussen, Eric, 'Setting Down What the Clown Spoke: Improvisation, Hand B, and *The Booke of Sir Thomas More*', *The Library*, 6th series, 13 (1991), 126–36

Rennert, Hugo Albert, *The Spanish Stage* (New York: Hispanic Society of America, 1909)

Riewald, J. G., 'New Light on the English Actors in the Netherlands, *c.* 1590–1660', *English Studies*, 41 (1960), 65–92

Runnalls, Graham A., 'Towards a Typology of Medieval French Play Manuscripts' in *The Editor and the Text*, ed. P. E. Bennett and G. A. Runnalls (Edinburgh: Edinburgh University Press, 1990)

Rusten, J., 'Dicaearchus and the Tales from Euripides', *Greek, Roman and Byzantine Studies*, 23 (1982), 357–67

Rye, William B., *England as Seen by Foreigners in the Days of Elizabeth and James I* (1865)

Sabol, Andrew J., 'New Documents on Shirley's Masque "The Triumph of Peace"', *Music & Letters*, 47 (1966), 10–26
'A Newly-Discovered Contemporary Song Setting for Jonson's *Cynthia's Revels*', *Notes and Queries*, 203 (1958), 384–5
Songs and Dances for the Stuart Masque (Providence, RI: Brown University Press, 1959)
'Two Unpublished Stage Songs for the Aery of Children', *Renaissance News*, 8 (1960), 222–32

Salzman, Paul, *Reading Early Modern Women's Writing* (Oxford: Oxford University Press, 2006)

Scase, Wendy, ' "Strange and Wonderful Bills": Bill-Casting and Political Discourse in Late Medieval England', *New Medieval Literatures*, 2 (1998), 225–47

Schelling, Felix E., *A Book of Seventeenth Century Lyrics* (Boston, MA: Ginn and Company, 1899)

Scouten, Arthur H., ed., *The London Stage part 3: 1729–1747* (Carbondale: Southern Illinois University Press, 1961)

Seng, Peter, 'The Foresters' Song in *As You Like It*', *Shakespeare Quarterly*, 10 (1959), 246–9

   The Vocal Songs in the Plays of Shakespeare: A Critical History (Cambridge, MA: Harvard University Press, 1967)

Shapiro, I. A., 'Shakespeare and Munday', *Shakespeare Survey*, 14 (1961), 25–33

   'Stenography and Bad Quartos', *TLS* (13 May, 1960), 305

Shapiro, Michael, *Gender in Play on the Shakespearean Stage* (Ann Arbor: University of Michigan Press, 1994)

Shattuck, Charles Harlen, *The Shakespeare Promptbooks: A Descriptive Catalogue* (Urbana and London: University of Illinois Press, 1965)

Shergold, N. D., *A History of the Spanish Stage* (Oxford: Clarendon Press, 1967)

Simon, Eckehard, 'Manuscript Production in Medieval Theatre: The German Carnival Plays' in *New Directions in Later Medieval Manuscript Studies*, ed. Derek Pearsall (York: York Medieval Press, 2000), 143–65

Sisson, C. J., *Lost Plays of Shakespeare's Age* (Cambridge: Cambridge University Press, 1936)

Smith, Irwin, 'Ariel and the Masque in *The Tempest*', *Shakespeare Quarterly*, 21 (1970), 213–22

Speaight, George, *The History of the Puppet Theatre* (London: George B. Harrap & Co, 1955)

St Clair, William, *The Reading Nation in the Romantic Period* (Cambridge: Cambridge University Press, 2004)

Stephenson, J. F., 'On the Markings in the Manuscript of *Sir John Van Olden Barnavelt*', *Notes and Queries*, 53 (2006), 522–4

Stern, Tiffany, 'Behind the Arras: The Prompter's Place in the Shakespearean Theatre', *Theatre Notebook*, 55 (2001), 110–18

   'Letters, Verses and Double Speech-Prefixes in *The Merchant of Venice*', *Notes and Queries*, 244 (1999), 231–3

   Rehearsal from Shakespeare to Sheridan (Oxford: Clarendon Press, 2000)

   'Repatching the Play' in *From Script to Stage in Early Modern England*, ed. Peter Holland and Stephen Orgel (London: Palgrave, 2004), 151–77

   'Watching as Reading: The Audience and Written Text in the Early Modern Playhouse' in *How to Do Things with Shakespeare*, ed. Laurie Maguire (Oxford: Blackwell, 2008), 136–59

Sternfeld, F. W., *Music in Shakespearean Tragedy* (London: Routledge and Kegan Paul, 1962)

   'A Song from Campion's Lord's Masque', *Journal of the Warburg and Courtauld Institutes*, 20 (1957), 373–5

Swaen, A. E. H., 'The Authorship of "What if a Day," and Its Various Versions', *Modern Philology*, 4 (1907), 397–422

Taylor, Gary, and John Jowett, *Shakespeare Reshaped 1606–1623* (Oxford: Clarendon Press, 1993)

Taylor, Gary, and John Lavagnino, eds., *Thomas Middleton and Early Modern Textual Culture* (Oxford: Clarendon Press, 2007)

Thaler, Alwin, 'Playwrights' Benefits, and "interior gathering" in the Elizabethan Theatre', *Studies in Philology*, 16 (1919), 187–96

   Shakspeare to Sheridan (Cambridge, MA: Harvard University Press, 1922)

Thomas, David, David Carlton and Anne Etienne, *Theatre Censorship from Walpole to Wilson* (Oxford: Oxford University Press, 2007)

Thomson, Leslie, 'A Quarto "Marked for Performance": Evidence of What?', *Medieval and Renaissance Drama in England*, 8 (1996), 176–210

Tribble, Evelyn, 'Distributing Cognition in the Globe', *Shakespeare Quarterly*, 56 (2005), 135–55

   Margins and Marginality (Charlottesville: University Press of Virginia, 1993)

Turner, Henry, *The English Renaissance Stage* (Oxford: Oxford University Press, 2006)

Van Lennep, William, 'The Earliest Known English Playbill', *Harvard Library Bulletin*, 1:3 (1947), 382–5

Van Lennep, William, Emmett L. Avery, Arthur H. Scouten, George W. Stone and Charles, B. Hogan, *The London Stage, 1660–1800*, 5 parts in 11 vols. (Carbondale: Southern Illinois University Press, 1960–9)

   'Some English Playbills', *Harvard Library Bulletin*, 8:2 (1954), 235–41

   'Thomas Killigrew Prepares His Plays for Production' in *John Quincy Adams Memorial Studies*, ed. James G. McManaway *et al.* (Washington, DC: Folger Shakespeare Library, 1948), 803–8

van Rossum-Steenbeek, M. *Greek Readers' Digests? Studies on a Selection of Subliterary Papyri* (Leiden: Brill, 1997)

Veevers, Erica, 'A Masque Fragment by Aurelian Townshend', *Notes and Queries*, 12 (1965), 343–5

Vickers, Brian, *Shakespeare Co-author* (Oxford: Oxford University Press, 2002)

Voss, Paul J., 'Books for Sale: Advertising and Patronage in Late Elizabethan England', *Sixteenth Century Journal*, 29 (1998), 733–57

Wall, Wendy, *The Imprint of Gender* (Ithaca, NY and London: Cornell University Press, 1993)

Walls, Peter, 'New Light on Songs by William Lawes and John Wilson', *Music & Letters*, 57 (1976), 55–64

Warren, Michael, 'Greene's *Orlando*: W. W. Greg Furioso' in *Textual Formations and Reformations*, ed. Laurie E. Maguire and Thomas L. Berger (Newark, DE: University of Delaware Press, 1998), 67–91

Weimann, Robert, 'Performing at the Frontiers of Representation: Epilogue and Post-Scriptural Future in Shakespeare's Plays' in *The Arts of Performance in Elizabethan and Early Stuart Drama: Essays for G. K. Hunter*, ed. Murray Biggs (Edinburgh: Edinburgh University Press, 1991), 96–112

Welch, Charles, 'The City Printers', *Transactions of the Bibliographical Society*, 14 (1918), 175–241

Wells, Stanley, Gary Taylor, John Jowett and William Montgomery, *William Shakespeare: A Textual Companion* (Oxford: Clarendon Press, 1987)

Werstine, Paul, '"Enter a Sheriffe" and the Conjuring up of Ghosts', *Shakespeare Quarterly*, 38 (1987), 126–30

'Narratives about Printed Shakespeare Texts: "Foul Papers" and "Bad Quartos"', *Shakespeare Quarterly*, 41 (1990), 65–86

'Post-Theory Problems in Shakespeare Editing', *Yearbook of English Studies*, 29 (1999), 103–17

Wiggins, Martin, review of Bradley's *From Text to Performance*, *Shakespeare Survey*, 46 (1994), 229

Wiles, David, *Shakespeare's Clown* (Cambridge: Cambridge University Press, 1987)

Wiley, Autrey Nell, *Rare Prologues and Epilogues 1642–1700* (London: G. Allen and Unwin, 1940)

Wiley, W. L., *The Early Public Theatre in France* (Cambridge, MA: Harvard University Press, 1960)

Wilkes, G. A., 'The Chorus Sacerdotum in Fulke Greville's *Mustapha*', *RES*, 49 (1998), 326–8

Willoughby, Edwin E., *A Printer of Shakespeare* (London: Philip Allan & Co., 1934)

Wilson, Christopher R., and Michela Calore, eds., *Music in Shakespeare: A Dictionary* (London: Continuum, 2005)

Wood, Julia K., 'William Lawes's Music for Plays' in *William Lawes*, ed. Andrew Ashbee (Aldershot: Ashgate, 1998)

Wood, Michael, *In Search of Shakespeare* (London: BBC Worldwide Ltd, 2003)

Yeandle, Laetitia, 'The Dating of Sir Edward Dering's Copy of "The History of King Henry the Fourth"', *Shakespeare Quarterly*, 37 (1986), 224–6

Index

Acevedo, P. Pedro Pablo 247
act division 11, 12, 14–15, 23, 24,
   see also scene division
actors' parts 3, 5, 7, 180, 195, 253
   Amurath 239, 240–1
   Antoninus 236
   contain gaps and spaces 243
   copied 3, 238–45
   disseminated before play is fully written
      236, 237–8
   lack scrolls 179
   Orlando 180, 239, 243–5
   Polypragmaticus 239–40
   relationship to 'book' 236, 254
   relationship to plots 217, 226
   scribes of 236–45
   stage-directions of 244
   Swiss 243
Adams, Joseph Quincy 226, 259 n 14
Admiral's Men 57, 243, 265 n 2
advertising 6, chapter 2 *passim*
A Larum for London 40
Alexander, Peter 264 n 93
Alexander, William, Earl of Stirling 64
Alleyn, Edward 42, 203, 239, 243–4, 267 n 29,
   296 n 66, 310 n 72
Allott, Thomas 133
allowed book 7, 20, 228
   for performance 232–6
   not for performance 238
   not precise 253
   relationship to parts 237–8
   relationship to plot 203–4
   uncensored material in 232–6
   see also printed playbook, prompter's book
An Abstract of his Majesties Letters Patent 267 n 15
Anne, Queen of England 110
antimasques 68
Antoninus Bassianus Caracalla 236
Appleton, William W. and Kalman A. Burnim
   308 n 32

'approved book' *see* allowed book
Arber, Edward 266 n 11
Arden of Feversham 40
Argument
   compared to dumb-shows 79
   compared to prologues 80
   contains character-list 6, 75
   for court performance 65, 66, 68, 69, 79, 80
   for first performance 66, 73, 74, 80, 253, 255
   for masques 65, 66–9, 71, 72, 73, 74
   for private theatre 70
   for public theatre 71–2, 74
   for puppet-shows 65, 69, 72
   for translation 75, 76–7, 78
   handed to audience 2
   in performance 4, 5, 7, 16, 66–8, 201, 253
   in printed playbook 63–5, 80, 101
   in Restoration 74
   printed and freestanding 3, 68–9, 77
   published after performance 78
   relationship to other plots 228
   revision and 89–92
   see also theatre programme
Aristophanes 63
Armin, Robert 248
   Quips Upon Questions 248
   Valiant Welshman 94, 114, 148, 280 n 33
Armstrong, Archie *Banquet of Jests* 310 n 58
Aspley, William 101, 133
Astington, John 284 n 81
Astley, John 232, 233
audience 9–10, 36–7, 65
   analyse plot 8–9
   contain faction 92
   critique play 91
   'judge' play 86
   playbill/Argument and 5
   see also damned play
Austern, Linda Phyllis 292 n 30, 295 n 65
Avery, Emmett L. 281 n 45
Ayres, Philip J. 262 n 68

B., T., *Rebellion of Naples* 56
backstage-plots 3, 5, 7, 253
  as call-sheets 214–19
  as folders for play 3, 201–2, 253
  Battle of Alcazar 202, 208, 209, 211, 212,
    213, 224, 229
  casting and 212–13
  composers of 208
  contents of 209–14
  dates of 203
  Dead Man's Fortune 202, 207, 209, 210,
    211, 212, 213, 224–5, 226, 228
  entrances on 3, 209
  exits on 210–11
  fictional characters on 211–12
  fictional place on 213
  First Part of Tamar Cam 202–3, 206, 209,
    211, 213, 224, 226, 310 n 72
  Frederick and Basilea 202–3, 207, 209, 210, 213
  headings of 208
  lack cues on 214, 216
  marginal information on 213, 216
  'personals' on 7, 211, 215
  physical characteristics of 7, 207–9
  'real' actors' names on 211–12
  relationship to playbook 3, 203–4, 227–31
  relationship to other plots 228
  relationship to stage-directions 205, 227–8, 231
  scribes of 204, 208, 213, 224–5, 228, 309
  Second Part of Fortune's Tennis 202, 209,
    210, 213, 224
  Second Part of the Seven Deadly Sins 202–3,
    207, 208, 209, 210, 211, 212, 213, 224,
    225, 228
  shorter life than playbook's 229
  Troilus and Cressida 202, 208, 209, 211, 213,
    224, 225
  see also call-sheet, pre-plot
Bacon, Sir Francis 31, 220
Baillie, William M. 284 n 79
Baker, David Erskine *et al. Biographia Dramatica*
  306 n 4
Bald, R. C. 293 n 35
Baldwin, Thomas Whitfield 223, 230
Barkstead, William 97
Baron, Robert *Mirza* 277 n 43
Barrett, Lawrence 191
Barrie, J. M. *Peter Pan* 88
Bartlet, John *Booke of Ayres* 294 n 41
Bate, Jonathan and Russell Jackson 268 n 29
Bawcutt, N. W. 257 n 4, 263 n 82, 277 n 46,
  283 nn 65, 68, 311–12 nn 2–4, 10–13, 19
Beal, Peter 278 n 8, 284 n 84, 297 n 86, 301 n 149
bear-baiting bill 37, 46–7
Beaumont, Francis 17, 29

and Fletcher 91, 104, 114, 272 n 98
Beggars' Bush 105, 129, 150
[and Fletcher] *Captaine* 105, 134, 136, 149
[and Fletcher] *Comedies and Tragedies* 105,
  121, 158, 159, 264 n 1, 283 n 66, 286 n 107
[and Fletcher and Massinger] *Coxcombe*
  281 n 37
[and Fletcher?] *Fair Maid of the Inn* 104
[and Fletcher] *Fifty Comedies* 105, 121, 146,
  158, 286 n 106
[and Fletcher] *Golden Remains* 156
[with Fletcher] *King and No King* 57
Knight of the Burning Pestle 87, 111, 126,
  127, 128, 134, 279 n 8, 292 n 28
[and Fletcher and Massinger] *Loves Cure*
  104, 150, 158, 175, 250
[and Fletcher] *Loves Pilgrimage* 250
Loyal Subject 150
Madon, King of Britain 261 n 42
[and Fletcher] *Maid's Tragedy* 17–18, 148,
  299 n 108
Masque of the Inner Temple 151
[and Bacon] *Masque of the Inner Temple
  and Gray's Inn* 31
[and Fletcher and Middleton] *Nice Valour*
  131, 163
Noble Gentleman 105, 111
Poems 156
[with Fletcher] *Right Woman* 261 n 42
Scholars 283 n 66
[and Fletcher] *Tragedy of Thierry* 111
[and Fletcher] *Woman Hater* 112, 115, 288 n 141
see also Fletcher, John
Beaurline, L. A. 264 n 94
Beckerman, Bernard 226, 227
Bednarz, James 108
Beecher, Donald 274 n 6
Beeston, Christopher 86, 312 n 13
Beeston's Boys 150, 234
Belchier, Dabridgcourt *Hans Beer-Pot* 157
Bel Savage 49
benefit performances 6, 81–2, 86, 93–6, 283
Benfield, Robert 188
Bennett, H. S. 272 n 95
Bennett, P. E. and G. A. Runnalls 314 n 40
Bentley, G. E. 273 n 102, 275 n 18, 283 n 70, 289
  n 145, 300 n 122
Bergeron, David M. 255, 274 n 8
Berkeley, William *Lost Lady* 100, 150, 161
Berry, Herbert 276
Best, M. R. 295 n 63
Bevington, David 186
  and Eric Rasmussen 108, 287 n 122
  and Martin Butler, Ian Donaldson, David
    Gants 262 n 63

Biggs, Murray 290 n 156
bill *see* bear-baiting bill, playbill,
    rope-dancing bill
Birth of Hercules 102
Blackfriars Playhouse 10, 39, 51, 54, 56, 57, 64,
    83, 90, 281 n 37
Blackfriars Playhouse in Staunton, Virginia 190
'blank' 43, 125
    type of scroll 179, 188–90, 200, 253
    see also songs: 'lost'
Blanshard, Alastair 276 n 40
Blayney, Peter W. M. 263 n 75, 266 n 11, 267
    n 24, 271 n 79, 286 n 99
Blount, Edward 122, 128, 133, 139, 158
Blunne, Thomas 45
Boas, Frederick S. 293 n 34
Boitani, Piero 286 n 98
Bond, Donald F. 278 n 2
Bond, R. Warwick 139, 285 n 97, 288 n 140,
    291 n 22, 295 n 63
'book' *see* prompter's book
Boswell, Eleanor 265 n 4, 303 n 9
Boswell, James the Younger 202
Bosworth, William 262 n 66
Bowden, William 144, 290 n 9
Bowers, Fredson 129, 237, 300 n 131, 315 n 69
Boyer, Abel *Dictionary* 15
Bracegirdle, Anne 89
Brade, William 139
Bradley, David 204, 212, 226, 227, 311 n 80
Brandon, Samuel *Vertuous Octavia* 273 n 1
Brandt, George W. 274 n 9
Brathwait, Richard
    Anniversaries 270 n 59
    Ar't Asleepe Husband? 52
    Astraea's Teares 270 n 60
    Barnabees Journall 288 n 140
    English Gentlewoman 270 n 60
    Strappado 276 n 31
    Times Treasury 270 n 60
    Two Lancashire Lovers 271 n 83
Braunmuller, A. R. 302 n 158, 311 n 5
Breton, Nicholas
    Choice, Chance and Change 288 n 140
    Fantasticks 50
    Poste 288 n 140
Breval, John *Play is the Plot* 74
Brewster, William T. 258 n 11
British Library 202
Brome, Richard 111
    Antipodes 221, 247, 268 n 37
    Court Begger 279 n 16
    English Moore 100, 129, 289 n 149
    Joviall Crew 128, 150, 156
    [and Heywood] *Late Lancashire Witches* 156

Love-sick Court 279 n 16
Mad Couple 251
Northern Lasse 150
Novella 94–5, 141, 281 n 38
Queen and Concubine 128, 134, 156, 315 n 73
Sparagus Garden 104
Weeding of the Covent-Garden 92, 154–6,
    258 n 8
Brooke, Arthur *Tragicall Historye of Romeo and
    Juliet* 259 n 18
Brooke, Christopher *Ghost of Richard III* 84, 116
Brooke, Henry, Eighth Lord Cobham 24
Brown, Arthur 297 n 87
Brown, J. R. 273 n 107
Brownsmith, John *Contrast* 216
Brückner, Martin 274 n 10
Bruster, Douglas and Robert Weimann 96, 98,
    284 n 83, 285 n 97
Buc, George 232, 233, 237
Bull Playhouse 83, 220
Bulwer-Lytton, Edward, *Lady of Lyons* 190
Burbage, Richard 224
Burghley, *see* William Cecil
Burnim, Kalman A. 216
Burre, Walter 133, 134
Burrow, Colin 191
Burton, Robert *Philosophaster* 239
Byrne, Muriel St Clare 310 n 62

Calendar of State Papers, Domestic Series: 1619–23
    257 n 2
Calore, Michela 228, 308 n 29
call-book *see* call-sheet
call-boys
    as scribes 225
    early modern 222–3
    in eighteenth century 216–17
    prompter's book and 230–1
    see also calls, call-sheet
calls 216, 222, 226, 229–31, 311 n 82
    in prompter's book 230–1, *see also* call-boys,
        call-sheet
call-sheet 189, 214–19, 226, *see also* call-boys, calls
Camden, William 258 n 12
Campion, Thomas 58, 127, 132, 157
    Lords Maske 151, 164
    Maske . . . in Honour of the Lord Hayes 151, 164
    Maske: presented . . . on Saint Stephens Night 164
    Observations 271 n 73
Carew, Thomas 98, 132–3
    Poems 131, 294 n 48
Carlell, Lodowick *Arviragus and Philicia* 58, 83,
    100, 281 n 37
    Deserving Favorite 9, 105
    Passionate Lover 181

Carleton, Dudley 8, 40, 68, 78, 277 n 55
Carnegie, David 313 n 26
Carpenter, Nan Cook 299 n 104
Carson, Neil 258 n 14
Cartwright, William 94, 203
   Royall Slave 95, 156
Cartwright, William, the Younger 203
casting 204, 212–13
casting table *see* cast-list
cast-list 3, 206, *see also* character-list
Cavendish, Margaret, Duchess of Newcastle 10
   Loves Adventures 84
Cavendish, William, Earl of Newcastle 111
   Country Captaine 104, 129, 150
   Variety 155
Cecil, Robert 30
Cecil, William, Lord Burghley 266 n 10, 269 n 47
Cerasano, S. P. and Marion Wynne-Davies
   275 n 17
challenge 37, 45, 49, 52, 53, 249
Chamberlain, John *Letters* 31, 40, 71, 268 n 33,
   277 n 55, 299 n 104
Chamberlain, Richard *Booke of Bulls* 99
Chamberlain, Robert *Jocabella* 268 n 38
Chamberlain's Men 111, 133
Chambers, E. K. 186, 265 n 5, 268 n 35, 269 n 56,
   272 n 86
Chan, Mary 295 n 66, 296 n 66
Chapman, George 23, 25, 121, 233, 234, 237
   All Fooles 121
   Bussy D'Ambois 100, 304 n 22
   Byron 233, 237
   Eugenia 113
   Gentleman Usher 141, 221, 222, 311 n 81
   Memorable Maske 65, 277 n 43
   Pompey and Caesar 64
   Revenge for Honour 280 n 31, 289 n 148
   Revenge of Bussy D'Ambois 121
   Widdowes Teares 126
Chapoton, Jean *La Descente d'Orphée* 77
   Le Marriage d'Orphée 277 n 48
character-list 6, 11, 33, *see also* cast-list
Charlemagne 182
Charles I, King of England 9, 31, 57, 77, 132,
   149, 234
Charleton, John 39–40
Charlewood, John 39–40, 267 n 21
Chettle, Henry 23
Chetwood, William Rufus 242
Children of the Chapel Royal 295 n 66
choruses and interim texts 7
   as separate documents 106–9
Cibber, Colley *Apology* 280 n 26
   Love in a Riddle 86
   Provok'd Husband 282 n 43

Cibber, Theophilus 282 n 43
Clare, Janet 312 n 12
Clavell, John 31
clowns and extemporisation 245, 252
collaboration *see* co-authorship
co-authorship
   plot-scenarios and 11, 23, 24, 32
   prologues and 105, 109–12
   scrolls and 183–4
   songs and 130
Cocker, Edward 307 n 19
Cockpit 83, 133
Codrington, Robert 16
Cohen, Ralph Alan 287 n 121
Cohn, Albert 266 n 6, 267 n 27
Cokain, Aston *Obstinate Lady* 101, 269 n 51
Cokes, John 108
Collier, John Payne 121, 204
Collings, Richard *Kingdomes Weekly Intelligencer*
   288 n 131
Colman, George, the Elder 91
Colman, George, the Younger 217
Commedia dell'Arte 204
composers 2, 3, 6, 126, 135–7
   as teachers 141
   composer-lyricists 126–8
   for court 149
   rewrite words of songs 2, 3, 127–8, 163–4
   write for theatre 168
   see also songs
Congreve, William *Double Dealer* 58
Constable, Francis 134
Cook, Margaret McLaren and F. P. Wilson
   292 n 32
Cooke, John *Greenes Tu Quoque* 194, 315 n 68
copyist *see* backstage-plots: scribes of, part-scribe,
   scribe, scroll-scribe
Corbet, Richard *Certain Elegant Poems* 283 n 63
Costlie Whore 102
Cotes, Thomas and Richard 39, 41, 43, 267 n 25
court performance 65, 66, 68, 80, 83, 95, 99,
   109, 110
   masques added for 151–3
   songs added for 147
   special version of play for 6, 118
Covent Garden 218
Cowley, Abraham 111
   Guardian 98
   Love's Riddle 289 n 149
Cox, John D. and David Scott Kastan 263 n 75,
   271 n 79
   and Eric Rasmussen 195
Craig, Hardin 259 n 23
Craik, T. W. 299 n 108
Crane, D. E. L. 276 n 35

Crane, Ralph 129, 167, 197, 244
Crook, A. and H. Brome 134
Cross Keys Inn 265 n 2
Crouch, John *Man in the Moon* 309 n 44
crying the play 36, 265–6 n 2
cues *see* actors' parts, backstage-plots, scrolls, songs
Cuffe, Henry 227
Cumber, John 311 n 79
Cumberland, Richard *Jew of Mogodore* 135
Curran, M. Beryl 274 n 9
Curtain Playhouse 36
Cutts, John P. 294 n 45, 295 n 55, 296 n 67, 297
    n 90, 299 n 104, 302 n 166

D., R, 9
Daborne, Robert 23, 25, 47, 49, 93, 236
    Machiavelli and the Devil 236
Daily Post 282 n 46
Dallas, Eneas Sweetland 310 n 65
Damhouder, Joos de 270 n 67
damned play 81, 86, 95, 97, *see* audience, first
    performance
Daniel, Samuel *Cleopatra* 64
    Hymen's Triumph 107, 108, 165
Danson, Lawrence 287 n 125
Dasent, J. R. 312 n 8
Davenant, William 112
    Love and Honour 112, 150
    Macbeth 139
    Madagascar 281 n 37, 288 n 137, 289 n 149
    Platonick Lovers 84, 268 n 37, 290 n 153
    Playhouse to be Let 93, 282 n 51
    Temple of Love 65
    Unfortunate Lovers 9, 148, 150
    Wits 9
Davenport, Robert *City-night-cap* 220
Davies, John of Herefordshire *A Scourge* 271 n 75
Davies, Thomas *Wits Bedlam* 261 n 58
Davies, Thomas *Dramatic Micellanies* [*sic*] 222
Day, John 23, 93
    Isle of Gulls 92, 309 n 58
    Knave in Graine 69
Dekker, Thomas 23, 93
    Blurt Master-constable 127, 142, 315 n 73
    Dekker his Dreame 280 n 21
    Guls Horne-Booke 270 n 66, 281 n 37, 309 n 58
    If it be not Good 58, 94
    [and Ford, Rowley, Webster] *Keep the Widow
      Waking* 24
    Newes from Hell 1, 86
    [and Webster] *North-ward Hoe* 127
    Old Fortunatus 153, 278 n 6
    Pontius Pilate 110
    [and Middleton] *Roaring Girle* 258 n 8,
      282 n 50

Shomakers Holiday 149, 157
    [and Ford] *Spanish Gipsie* 28
    [and Ford] *Sun's-Darling* 133
    [and Massinger] *Virgin Martyr* 235
    Welsh Embassador 182, 198, 229
    [and Webster] *West-ward Hoe* 40, 157
    Whore of Babylon 233
    Wonder 70, 111, 278 n 8
Denham, John *Sophy* 94, 150, 272 n 92
Dennis, John *Liberty Asserted* 89
Dering, Edward 259 n 23
    Philander King of Thrace 13–15, 16, 31
Description of the King and Queene of Fayries
    301 n 149
Dessen, Alan and Leslie Thomson 34, 264 n 92
Devereaux, Robert, Earl of Essex 109, 227
dialogue 2, 3, 11, 33, 35, 135, 141, 149, 174
    different date from prologues 118
    different date from songs 172
    made up of separate manuscripts 253
Dibdin, Thomas *Reminiscences* 87
Die Swen Stenndt 238
Digby, Kenelm 12, 19, 108, 129
Digges, Leonard 31
Dimmock, Matthew 293 n 38
Dodds, M. Hope 138
Dodsley, Robert *Miller of Mansfield* 179
    Sir John Cockle 89
Dowland, John 126
Downame, John *Account Audited* 271 n 76
Downes, John 242
Drake, Francis 73
dramatis personae *see* character-list
Drayton, Michael 23
Drees, L. and Henry de Vocht 291 n 12
Drummond, William 258 n 12
Drury-Lane Playhouse 77, 218, 237
Dryden, John 15, 58
    [with Nathaniel Lee] *Duke of Guise* 262 n 74
    Indian Emperour 74
    [with Robert Howard] *Indian Queen* 29
    Ladies à la Mode 86
    Love Triumphant 10
    [with Nathaniel Lee] *Oedipus* 29
    Sicilian Vespers 13
    Tragedy of Amboyna 13
Duffin, Ross 140, 301 n 143
Dufresnoy, Charles-Alphonse 259 n 25
Dulwich College 46, 202–3
dumb-shows 33, 79
Duncan-Jones, Katherine and H. R.
    Woudhuysen 305 n 45
D'Urfey, Thomas *Banditti* 90
    Old Mode and the New 90
Dusinberre, Juliet 163

Dutton, Richard 232, 234, 247
Dyce, Alexander 158

Earle, Giles 295 n 66
Earl of Leicester's Men 57
Earl of Oxford's Men 57
Eccles, Mark 261 n 60
Edmond Ironside 178, 182, 184
Edward III 23
Edwards, Philip 263 n 81
Eedes, Richard *Caesar Interfectus* 99
Eggers, Walter F. 114
Eliot, John *Poems* 271 n 73
Elizabeth I, Queen of England 24
Elliott, John R. and Alan H. Nelson 275 n 17
Elton, W. R. and W. B. Long 310 n 70
England's Joy see Vennar, Richard
epilogues *see* prologues
Erne, Lukas 290 n 6
'etc.' on scrolls 193
  signifying extemporisation 195
Euripides 63
Evans, G. Blakemore 259 n 23
Everard, Edward Cape 179, 189
Everie Woman in her Humor 126, 127, 143,
  295 n 66, 309 n 49
extemporisation 245–51
  indicated by 'etc.' 195, 250–1
  indicated by gap 250
  indicated with words 250–1

Farlie, Robert *Kalender of Mans Life* 277 n 58,
  288 n 141
Farmer, Alan B. and Zachary Lesser 57, 273 n 101
Farquhar, George *Beaux Stratagem* 89
Farrant, Richard *Warres of Cyrus* 109
Feeman, John 273 n 106
Felltham, Owen *Resolves* 258 n 8
Fen, Ezekiel 82–3
Fennor, William 49, 72, 249–50, 268 n 44
  Fennors Descriptions 280 n 28, 281 n 38
Ferguson, F. S. 267 n 24
Ferguson, George B. 285 n 90, 300 n 132
Field, Nathan 25, 48, 100, 313 n 35
  Amends for Ladies 142, 304 n 22
  as scribe 242
  Honest Man's Fortune 271 n 76
  Woman is a Weather-cocke 40
Fielde, John *Godly Exhortation* 265 n 2
*First Part of the Reign of King Richard the
  Second* 188
first performance 5, 6, 81, 83–93, 96, 109
  'Arguments' and 66, 73, 74, 80, 253, 255
  entrance charge for 86
  'judged' by audience 86

known as 'trial' 88–9, 92, 102
  playbills and 58
  playwrights and 115–16
  prologues and 82–93, 109, 117, 253, 255
  reunites disparate texts 3
  revision and 82–93, 119
  see also second performance, damned play
Fitzgeffrey, Henry *Certain Elegies* 265 n 3
  Satyres and Satyricall Epigrams 59, 282 n 51
Fitz-geffry, Charles *Sir Francis Drake* 276 n 32
Flecknoe, Richard 51
  Damoiselles à la Mode 280 n 26
  Epigrams 26
  Love's Dominion 148
  Love's Kingdom 87, 148
Fletcher, John 17, 21, 29, 94, 112
  and prologues 110
  [and Massinger, Jonson and Chapman]
    Bloody Brother 133–4, 150, 157
  Bonduca 18–21, 22, 23, 144, 250
  Chances 149, 279 n 16
  [and Massinger] *Cupid's Revenge* 150
  Custom of the Country 95, 286 n 106
  Faithful Friends 21–2, 23, 33, 146
  Faithful Shepheardesse 41, 88, 110, 150
  [and Massinger] *False One* 150
  [and Massinger and Field] *Honest Mans
    Fortune* 146
  Humorous Lieutenant 84, 114, 129, 244
  [and Field and Massinger] *Knight of Malta* 250
  [and Massinger] *Little French Lawyer* 270,
    279 n 16
  [and Massinger] *Lovers Progress* 149, 181,
    289 n 149
  Mad Lover 146, 149, 150
  [and Rowley] *Maid in the Mill* 159, 250,
    297 n 84
  Nice Valour 287 n 128
  Pilgrim 150, 169–70
  Queene of Corinth 150
  Sir John Van Olden Barnavelt 8–9, 237
  [and Massinger] *Spanish Curat* 150, 181, 230
  Tragedy of Thierry 106
  Valentinian 104, 136, 149, 150, 159
  Wife for a Moneth 84
  Wild-Goose Chase 143, 150
  Woman Pleas'd 150
  Womans Prize 100, 106, 159, 237, 250, 272 n 98
  see also Beaumont, Francis
Fletcher, Phineas *Sicelides* 129
Florimène 77
Florio, John *Worlde of Wordes* 309 n 45
Fludd, Robert 55
Foakes, R. A. 261 n 49, 265 n 2, 266 n 6,
  see also Henslowe 'diary'

Folger Shakespeare Library 13, 75, 135, 214
Foote, Samuel *Devil Upon Two Sticks* 181
Ford, John 23
    Broken Heart 282 n 50
    Ladies Triall 88, 150
    Lover's Melancholy 31, 66, 150
    see also Thomas Dekker
Forker, Charles R. 184
Fortune players 83
Fortune Playhouse 249
Foster, Dr William 55
'foul' papers 20–1
Fox, Adam 53
Frederick V, Elector Palatine 152
Freeman, Arthur 275 n 24 and Janet Ing
    Freeman 290 n 7
Fuller, David 296 n 66, 302 n 159
Furness, Horace Howard 191
Furness Memorial Library 191

Gager, William *Rivales* 99
    Ulysses Redux 99
Galli, Antimo 36
Gamble, John 291 n 16, 295 nn 53, 59
Garrard, George 266 n 10
Garrick, David 179, 258 n 10
    production of *Midsummer Night's Dream* 162,
    214–18
Gascoigne, George 27
    Supposes 251
Gayton, Edmund *Pleasant Notes* 79, 92,
    262 n 62, 264 n 1, 284 n 75
Gee, John *New Shreds* 223
Genette, Gérard 65, 255
Gesta Grayorum 186–7
Ghismonda 194
Gibson, James M. 305 n 44
Giles, Nathaniel 136
Gill, Alexander 262 n 61
Gillies, John 311 n 86
Glapthorne, Henry *Argalus and Parthenia* 150
    Ladies Privilege 59, 281, 289 n 149
    Lady Mother 144
    Poems 278 n 4
    Wit in a Constable 114, 157, 279 n 16, 281 n 37
Globe Playhouse 42, 83
Godbid, William 101
Goffe, Thomas 239–41
    Careles Shepherdess 64, 97, 131, 219
    Courageous Turk 100, 239, 240–1
    Raging Turke 196
Goldberg, Jonathan 179
Gossett, Suzanne 23, 76, 274 n 9, 298 n 91, 299 n 101
    and W. David Kay 262 n 63
Gowen, David 276 n 38

'Grange, Prince de la Εγχυχλοχορεία 74
Granville, George 281
Gravener, Richard 45
Gray's Inn 177, 186
Greene, Robert 27
    Friar Bacon and Friar Bungay 60, 110
    Orlando Furioso 142, 180–1, 184, 239, 243–5,
    291 n 21
    Scottish Historie 181, 291 n 21
Greenfield, Thelma M. 279 n 8
Greer, David 292 n 29
Greg, W. W. 20–1, 260 n 34, 268 n 29
    'Authorship of the Songs' 291 n 22
    Bibliography 261 n 42, 285 n 96, 300 n 125
    Dramatic Documents 204, 205, 211, 227, 228,
    263 n 87, 275 n 25, 303 n 14, 306 n 2, 307
    n 15, 308 n 27, 310 n 63, 311 n 79, 314 n 43
    edited texts by 260, 296 n 69
    Henslowe Papers 268 n 32, 312 n 17
    Malone Society Collections: I 265 n 2
    Records of the Court 266 n 15
    Shakespeare First Folio 264 n 91, 267 n 19
    Two Elizabethan Stage Abridgements 303 n 13,
    314 n 41
Greville, Fulke *Mustapha* 107
    Workes 108
Griffin, Benjamin 276 n 41
Griffin, Benjamin, actor 296 n 69
Grindall, Edmund 269 n 47
Guazzo, Stefano *Italian Treat* 280 n 18
Guillemard, Jean 15
Guilpin, Edward *Skialetheia* 269 n 391
Gunty, David *et al.* 294 n 44
Gurr, Andrew 91, 287 n 125, 306 n 7
Gwyn, Owen 137

H., A., *Continued Inquisition* 55
Habington, William *Queene of Arragon* 9, 58,
    157, 279 n 16
Hakewill, George 267 n 23
Halio, Jay L. 273 n 107
Hall, Joseph *Virgidemiarum* 270 n 66, 271 n 73,
    282 n 52
Hall, Thomas *Loathsomeness of Long Hair*
    269 n 57
Halstead, W. L. 300 n 111
Halstead, William Perdue 311 n 83
Hammond, Antony and Doreen Delvecchio
    305 n 49
Hancock, Thomas 242
Harding, Samuel *Fatal Union* 289 n 143
    Sicily and Naples 90, 113
Harington, Henry 94
Harington, John *New Discourse* 315 n 62
Harper, Sally 296 n 66, 297 n 79

Harrell, John 190
Harvey, Richard 248
Hattaway, Michael 195
Haughton, William 23
Hausted, Peter *Rivall Friends* 9, 87, 135
Hawkins, William *Apollo Shroving* 219
Haymarket Playhouse 218
Healey, Jo *Epictetus Manuall* 309 n 58
Heath, Robert 51, 56
Helmes, Henry 186
Heminges, John and Henry Condell 88
Henrietta Maria, Queen of England 178,
    301 n 140
Henry, Prince of Wales 277 n 56
Henslowe, Philip 23, 25, 47, 235, 261 n 55
    'diary' 36, 93–4, 110, 223, 232–5, 265 n 2, 267
        n 20, 283 n 62, 307 n 15, 310 n 72
    'papers' 205, 236, 283 n 61
Henze, Catherine A. 295 n 60
Herbert, Henry 9, 31, 235, 277 n 46
    approved book and 232
    book for the press and 77
    censored material and 237
    office book and 94, 110
    uncensored material and 234–6
Herbert, Mary, Countess of Pembroke
    Antonius 64
Herford, C. H., and P. and E. Simpson 262 n 63,
    275 n 17
Heylin, Peter *Observations* 272 n 84
Heywood, Thomas 23, 27, 28, 68, 93, 110
    Calisto 129–30
    Captives 229
    Challenge for Beautie 124, 279 n 16
    Edward the Fourth 143
    Escapes 291 n 21
    Fair Maid of the West 64
    Fayre Mayde of the Exchange 185
    Foure Prentises of London 112, 257 n 8
    Golden Age 87–8, 129–30
    If You Know Not Me 106
    Iron Age part II 115
    Loves Mistresse 83, 278 n 7
    Mayden-Head Well Lost 280 n 18, 282 n 50
    Pleasant Dialogues 95, 106, 124, 278 n 4,
        283 n 71
    Queen Elizabeth 34
    Rape of Lucrece 124, 132, 148, 157, 158
    Second Part of If You Know Not Me 315 n 68
    Second Part of King Edward the Fourth 315 n 68
    Silver Age 129
    Woman Killde with Kindnesse 40
Higgins, John *Nomenclator* 220
Hill, Aaron and William Popple 308 n 33
Hill, R. F. 275 n 12

Hill, W. Speed 302 n 158
Hilton, John *Catch that Catch Can* 162
History of the Tryall of Chevalry 315 n 68
Hobbs, Mary 280 n 30
Hogg, James 270 n 59
Holcroft, Thomas *Try Again* 181
Holland, Samuel *Don Zara del Fogo* 289 n 150
Holman, Peter 295 n 66, 296 n 68
Holyday, Barton *Marriage of Arts* 87
    Technogamia 53
Holzknecht, Karl J. 37, 271 n 69
Honigmann, E. A. J. 241, 260 n 40, 263 n 87,
    264 n 94
Hope Playhouse 49, 249
Horne, David H. 294 n 41
Hosley, Richard 34, 286 n 115
Houghton Library 70
Howard, Edward 28
Howard, Robert 29
    Indian Queen 276 n 35
Howard-Hill, T. H. 3, 237, 244
Hughes, Paul L. and James S. Larkin 271 n 70
Hughes, Thomas *et al. Misfortunes of Arthur* 233,
    260 n 29
Hulme, Peter 290 n 156
Hunsdon, Henry, Lord Chamberlain 265 n 2
Hunter, G. K. 295 n 64

improvisation *see* extemporisation
inductions 24, 83, 111, 278, *see also* prologues,
    choruses and interim texts
Inner Temple 186
Inns of Court 51, 88, 206
instrumentalists *see* musicians
interim entertainments 7
Ioppolo, Grace 31, 204, 235, 241, 258 n 14, 287
    n 116, 293 n 35, 307 n 15, 313 n 35

Jacquot, Jean 287 n 119
Jaggard, Isaac 39, 41
Jaggard, William 39–40, 41–2, 102, 191–2,
    267 n 21
James, King of England 96, 137, 149, 284 n 73
Jansohn, Christa 287 n 121
Janzen, Henry D. 291, 293 n 36, 303 n 8
Jaques, Francis *Queen of Corsica* 178
Jeffreys, George 135
jest-books 6
John of Bordeaux 229
Johnson, Robert 136, 137, 139, 146, 149, 150,
    151–2, 168, 170, 295 n 53
Johnson, Samuel 74
    Dictionary 15
    George Steevens and 306 n 3
    Lives 276 n 35

Johnson, Samuel (cont.)
  Plays of William Shakespeare 122
Jones, G. P. 287 n 125
Jones, Inigo 69, 277 n 46
  Britannia Triumphans 65
Jones, Robert 126–7
Jonson, Ben 28, 29, 32, 55, 64, 66, 74, 137, 261
    n 55, 262 n 62, 281 n 36, 283 n 67
  Alchemist 112
  Bartholmew Fayre 83, 183, 289 n 149, 309 n 58
  [and Sir Robert Cecil] *Britain's Burse* 30, 242
  Case is Altered 28, 258 n 8, 282 n 50
  [with Drummond] *Conversations* 258 n 12
  Cynthias Revels 136, 141, 295 n 66, 303 n 5, 310 n 58
  Divell is an Asse 52, 83, 149, 160, 168, 297 n 78
  [and Chapman and Marston] *Eastward Hoe*
    26, 47, 126, 128, 234, 262 n 63
  Epicoene 150, 160
  [and Henry Porter and Henry Chettle] *Every
    Man Out* 89, 109, 195, 270 n 66, 281 n 42
  Gypsies Metamorphosed 144, 149
  [and Porter and Chettle] *Hot Anger
    Soon Cold* 26
  Magnetick Lady 93, 233, 262 n 61
  Masque of Augurs 71
  Masque of Blackness 78
  Masque of Oberon 150
  Masque of Queens 79 n 58, 151
  Mortimer 11–12, 15, 16, 19
  Neptunes Triumph 68
  New Inne 64, 87, 142
  [and Dekker] *Page of Plymouth* 26
  Pleasure Reconciled to Virtue 68
  plots and 25–7
  Poetaster 17, 114, 279 n 8, 295 n 66
  [and Chettle, Dekker and 'other jentellman']
    Richard II 26
  Sad Shepherd 16, 142
  Salmacida Spolia 299 n 104
  Sejanus 12, 25, 64, 87
  Staple of Newes 221, 278 n 8, 296 n 78
  Volpone 86
  [and Fletcher and Middleton] *Widow* 26
  Workes 302 n 158
Jordan, Thomas *Fancy's Festivals* 201
  Nursery of Novelties 272 n 98
Jowett, John 108, 170
  and Gary Taylor 294 n 51

Kastan, David Scott 273 n 100, 307 n 14
Kathman, David 306 n 7, 308 n 28
Keegan, James 190
Keenan, Siobhan 267 n 25
Kelly, Michael 135
Kempe, William 247

Kendall, Timothy 249, 268 n 44
Kendall, William 249, 268 n 44
Ker, Robert, first Lord Roxborough 108
Kewes, Paulina 278 n 3
Kidnie, M. J. 64
Kiechel, Samuel 85
Killigrew, Henry 242
  Cicilia and Clorinda 242
  Pallantus and Eudora 90
  Pandora 281 n 43
  Second Part of Cicilia and Clorinda 132–3
King, T. J. 204
King's Men 19, 25, 66, 67, 94, 133, 134, 139–40,
    149–52, 178, 234, 244
  censorship and 237
  composers and 168
King's Revels 134
Kinservik, Matthew J. 312 n 18
Kirke, [John?] 235
Kirkpatrick, Robin 290 n 156
Kirsch, Arthur C. 257 n 1
Knapp, Jeffrey 289 n 147
Knight, Edward 19–21, 33, 142, 237
Knowler, William 266 n 10
Knutson, Roslyn Lander 280 n 20
Krutch, Joseph Wood 287 n 127, 312 n 18
Kyd, Thomas *Solyman and Perseda* 182
  Spanish Tragedy 69, 183

Lady Elizabeth's Men 11–16, 59, 134, 232
Lane, Robert 137
Langhans, Edward 305 n 40, 311 n 82
Latham, Robert and William Matthews
    269 n 55, 277
Lawes, Henry 132
Lawes, William 139, 150, 168
Lawrence, W. J., 37, 46, 230, 259 n 14, 265 n 2,
    267 n 26, 274 n 9, 294 n 45, 299 n 104
Lazarus, Paul N. 310 n 71
Leandro, Michael *Aristologia* 277 n 44
Le Conte, Valleran 267 n 28
Lee, Margaret L. 301 n 144
Lee, Nathaniel 29, *see also* Dryden, John
Lefkowitz, Murray 307 n 17
Legge, Richard *Richardus Tertius* 238
Leigh, Richard *Transproser Rehears'd* 269 n 49
Leishman, J. B. 314 n 48, 315 n 70
Lennam, T. N. S. 259 n 23
Le Strange, Nicholas *Merry Passages* 270 n 59
letters *see* scrolls
Lewes, Charles Lee and John Lee Lewes
    Memoirs 313 n 38
Lewin, Jane E. 274 n 7
libels 53, 55, 266 n 9
Lieberman, Max 276 n 40

Life and Death of Jack Straw 197
Lincoln's Inn Fields 237
Lindley, David 127, 291 n 14
Ling, Nicholas 133
Littledale, H. and W. W. Greg 304 n 21
Lively Character of the Malignant Partie 73
Locke, Matthew 139
Locke, Thomas 8
Locrine 111
Lodge, Thomas 27
   Lady Alimony 220, 266 n 10, 271 n 83, 278 n 8
   Looking Glasse 272 n 90
Lombardo, Agostino 102
London Prodigall 59
Long, John H. 299 n 109
Long, W. B. 307 n 14
Longstaffe, Stephen 197
Lord Chamberlain 234, 237
Lord Mayor 51
Lovelace, Richard *Lucasta* 99
   Scholars 99, 283, 289 n 151
Lowen, John 188
Lowenstein, Joseph 64
Lupton, Thomas *Thousand Notable Things*
   314 n 48
Lyly, John 27, 121
   Campaspe 133
   Endimion 39
   Gallathea 138
   Mother Bombie 272 n 90
   Mydas 138
   Pappe with an Hatchet 235
   Sapho and Phao 111
   Six Court Comedies 121, 128, 158
   Woman in the Moone 121, 272 n 90

Macklin, Charles *Henry VII* 282 n 43
Maggs Brothers Catalogues 13, 259 n 22
Maguire, Laurie 19, 245
   and Thomas L. Berger 303 n 15, 314 n 39
Mahood, M. M. 198, 273 n 107
Malone, Edmond 94, 222
   et al. edition of *Shakespeare's Plays* 306 n 6
Manley, Mary de la Rivière *Almyna* 89
   Lost Lover 281 n 43
Manningham, John *Diary* 71
Marchitello, Howard 303 n 10
Markham, Francis *Booke of Honour* 309 n 53
Marlowe, Christopher 93, 95
   Dr Faustus 58, 108, 251
   Edward the Second 40, 184
   Jew of Malta 110, 190, 265 n 1, 278 n 5
   Tamberlaine 265 n 1
Marston, John 120–1
   Antimasque of Mountebanks 138

Antonio and Mellida 89, 120–1, 278 n 8, 281
   n 41, 289 n 144
Antonios Revenge 223
Dutch Courtezan 126, 194, 296 n 66
Histriomastix 58, 266 n 10, 269 n 52
Insatiate Countesse 291 n 21, 315 n 68
Jacke Drums Entertainment 127, 279 n 8
Malcontent 101
Scourge of Villanie 269 n 48
What You Will 258 n 8
Martin, Randall 195
Martin, Richard 265 n 2
Martin, William 274 n 9
Marvell, Andrew 56
Mason, John *Turke* 101, 104, 106
Mason, John, of Cambridge *Princeps Rhetoricus* 78
Masque of Amazons 166
Masque of Flowers 65
masques 7, 65, 66–9, 71, 73, 74, 132, 139
   added to plays 149, 150–3
Massai, Sonia 111
Massinger, Philip 27, 28, 59
   Believe as You List 110, 142, 187, 188, 229, 230,
      279 n 16
   Emperour of the East 10, 84, 87, 99–103 n 143,
      278 n 5, 289 n 152
   [and Field] *Fatall Dowry* 149, 157, 165
   Great Duke of Florence 174
   Guardian 157
   Maid of Honour 98
   Roman Actor 221
   Spanish Viceroy 234
   Unnaturall Combat 285 n 97
   see also Fletcher, John
Masten, Jeffrey 288 n 142, 304 n 30
Master of the Revels 91, 110, 204, 232–6
   benefits for 95
   'new' passages and 235, 312 n 13
   uncensored material and 232–5, 251
May, Thomas *Heire* 101
   Old Couple 146, 149, 166
Maynard, Winifred 298 n 96
Mayne, Jasper 29
   Citye Match 94, 150, 278 n 6
   Jonsonus Virbius 261 n 58
McClure, Norman Egbert 267 n 16, 275 n 27,
   299 n 104
McFadden, George 262 n 73
McGee, C. E. 299 n 111
McJannet, Linda 311 n 76
McKendrick, Malvena 314 n 58
McKerrow, Ronald Brunlees 55, 260 n 38
McLeod, Randall 306 n 63
McManaway, James G. 313 n 36
McMillin, Scott 228, 237, 306 n 7

McQuillen, Connie 313 n 27
Mehl, Dieter 274 n 9
Melchiori, Giorgio 23
Mennes, John *Musarum Deliciae* 283 n 66
  Wit Restor'd 99
Mercurius Rusticans 257 n 3
Meres, Francis *Palladis Tamia* 27, 249
Mery Tales 38
Middleton, Thomas 110, 131, 151, 197
  Ant, and the Nightingale 89, 281 n 40
  Chast Mayd 134, 147, 170
  [and Rowley] *Faire Quarrell* 148
  Familie of Love 250, 279 n 15
  Game at Chesse 36, 111, 199, 241, 244, 311 n 2
  Hengist 99, 107, 129, 309 n 58
  Mad World my Masters 133, 148, 157
  Masque of Cupid 170
  More Dissemblers Besides Women 134, 147, 170
  [and Shirley] *No Wit/Help* 67, 112, 280 n 33
  Phoenix 106
  Puritaine 30, 34
  Trick 127
  Widdow 143, 150
  Witch 122, 139, 149, 150, 151
  Women Beware Women 67–8, 69
  [and Rowley] *World Tost at Tennis* 153
  Your Five Gallants 108
  see also Dekker, Thomas
Milhous, Judith and Robert D. Hume 281,
  313 n 37
Milton, John *Adam Unparadiz'd* 259 n 19
  Comus 275 n 17
  Paradise Lost 12–13, 15, 31
Misfortunes of Arthur 16
Misogonus 140
Montagu, Walter *Shepheards Paradise* 68, 100,
  130, 144, 152, 178
Moody, Henry 59
Moore, John Robert 300 n 128
More, Henry 262
Morley, Thomas 172
  First Booke of Ayres 127
Moseley, Humphrey 12, 134, 260 n 28, 261 n 42,
  264 n 1, *see also* Robinson, Humphrey
Motteaux, Peter *Novelty* 74
Mountfort, Walter *Launching of the Mary*
  33, 280 n 25
'Multibibus, Blasius' *Law of Drinking* 94
'Munda, Constantia' *Worming of a Mad Dogge* 1
Munday, Anthony 23, 27–8, 93, 262 n 64
  Book of Sir Thomas More 208, 224, 248
  John a Kent and John a Cumber 208, 224
Mundeford, Edmond 270 n 59
musicians 3, 6
music-list 206

Nabbes, Thomas *Bride* 84, 233, 281 n 37
  Covent Garden 31, 92, 284 n 84
  Hannibal and Scipio 16
  Tottenham Court 88
Nashe, Thomas, 27
  Almond 314 n 52
  [and Jonson] *Isle of Dogs* 24, 27, 234
  Pierce Penilesse 248, 270 n 65
  Returne of the Renowned Cavliero Pasquill 51
  Summers Last Will 220, 221
  Terrors of the Night 56
Neale, Thomas *Warde* 88
Nelson, Alan H. 266 n 10, 295 n 61
new play *see* first performance
Nicholson, William 269 n 47
North, Dudley *Forest of Varieties* 280 n 24
North, Thomas *Plutarch* 264 n 92
Northbrooke, John *Treatise* 23
Northumberland House 38
Nungezer, Edwin 268 n 44

O'Callaghan, Michelle 268 n 44
Odingsells, Gabriel 281 n 43
O'Donnell, Norbert F. 293 n 39
Ogilby's Men 67
Ogilvy, Arthur 310 n 65
O'Malley, Susan Gushee 285 n 89
O'Neill, David G. 120
Orgel, Stephen 199, 251
  and Sean Keilen 299 n 104
Orrell, John 264 n 1
Overbury, Thomas *A Wife* 273 n 103
  Sir Thomas Overburie his Wife 308 n 42
Owen, Susan J. 312 n 18
Oxford's Boys 133
Oxley, Philip 244

P., R. *Choice Drollery* 262 n 67
Pafford, J. H. P. 302 n 155
  and W. W. Greg 301 n 144
pageants 66, 78
Palfrey, Simon and Tiffany Stern 310 n 75,
  313 n 23, 314 n 44
paratext 63, 80, 255–6
Parker, Patricia 306 n 61
Parkes, William 32
Parrot, Henry *Laquei Ridiculosi* 282 n 52
  Mastive 26, 55
Parsons, Robert 222
parts *see* actors' parts
  The Warn-Word 309 n 54
part-scribe 3, 185, 206, 236–45
  is actor 239–42
  is not actor 242–5
  is prompter 242, *see also* scroll-scribe

'patches' of play 1–7, 253–6, *see also* play-patchers
Paulet, William 106
Paul's Boys 39, 70, 133, 138–9, 145, 278 n 5
Pavier quartos 40
Peacham, Henry *Coach and Sedan* 280 n 21
    Truth of Our Times 58
    Worth of a Peny 57
Pearce, Edward 127
Pearn, B. R. 277 n 54
Pearsall, Derek 284 n 80, 313 n 22
Peele, George *Edward the First* 140
    Hunting of Cupid 131
Pemberton, T. Edgar 305 n 43
Pembroke's Men 234
Penneycuicke, Andrew 133
Pepys, Samuel *Diary* 51, 86, 277 n 48, 280 n 26
Percy, William 130, 145
    Arabia Sitiens 138
    Cuckqueans 278 n 5
    Faery Pastorall 131
    Mahomet and his Heaven 293 n 38
    Necromantes 126
Perfect Occurrences 57, 272 n 98
'personals' 7, 206, 211, 215
person-list *see* character-list
Perwich, William 274 n 9
Peters, Hugh 220
Peters, Julie Stone 274 n 9
Petit, Bonoist 267 n 28
Philander King of Thrace see Dering, Edward
Philipps, Fabian *Tenenda* 309 n 44
Philips, Ambrose *Distressed Mother* 81
Phillips, Edward 13
    Livery Rake 90
    Mysteries of Love and Eloquence 102, 287 n 128,
       288 n 140
Phillips, Tom 242
Philotus 128, 157
Phoenix Playhouse 64, 83
Pickering, John *Horestes* 140
Pilgrimage to Parnassus 246, 251
Pinciss, G. M. and G. R. Proudfoot 261 n 42
Pitcher, John 287 n 123, 302 n 154
Plant, Marjory 38, 266 n 8, 271 n 71
plat(t) *see* backstage-plot
Plautus 63
playbill 4, 5, 7, 111, 255
    Bartholomew Fair bill 37, 60
    content of 43, 56–62
    flyers 6, 52, 57
    French playbill 37, 58, 266 n 6
    German playbill 37, 44, 266 n 6
    hung on posts 2, 6, 39, 50–2, 53, 55–6
    illustrations on 43
    inside houses 52–3

libels and 53–5
    number and frequency of 47–50
    other bills and 53–5
    printing and production of 3, 38–47
    puppet playbill 37
    Spanish playbill 37
    title-pages and 55–6, 62
    see also bear-baiting bill, rope-dancing bill
Playford, John *Dancing Master* 297 n 84
play-patchers 1–2, 256, *see also* patches of play
plot *see* Argument, backstage-plots,
    plot-scenarios
plot-scenarios 4, 5, 201, 204
    allow construction of play out of narrative
      order 23–4, 33
    analysed by audience 8–9
    analysed by playwrights 9
    as commodities 25
    as 'Scenary' 15, 29
    content of 11–16, 33
    messy/'foul' 18–21
    multiply distributed 23
    plotters and playwrights different 27–30, 254
    plotters of 2, 11, 14
    precedes dialogue 10, 17
    relationship to other plots 228
    reused 34
    stand in for lost dialogue 23
Pollard, Thomas 188
Pooley, Roger 274 n 6
Pope, Alexander *Works of . . . Shakespeare* 264 n 93
Popple, William *Lady's Revenge* 281 n 43
Porter, Endimion 281 n 37
Powell, George *Alphonso* 81
Powell, Jocelyn 278 n 3
Poynting, Sarah 303 n 8
pre-plot 204, 205
presenter 79, 80, 107
Prince Charles' Men 59
printed playbook 5, 7, 37
    variant states of 100–3, 104, 106–9, 129–30,
      148–9, 199, 255
    see also allowed book, prompter's book
printers 7
    and scrolls 195–9
    and songs 128–34
    of bills and Arguments 3
proclamations 54, *see also* scrolls
Progresse to Parnassus 309 n 45
prologues and epilogues 5, 7, 10, 74
    as phoney authors 113–16
    as types of scroll 6, 174, 186–7
    benefits and 81–2, 86, 93–6, 283 n 73
    choruses and 106–9
    circulating with songs 105, 107, 156–7, 171, 253

prologues and epilogues (cont.)
  clothes of 106, 112–14
  first performance and 82–93, 109, 117,
    253, 255
  for court 83, 100, 109, 110, 118, 153, 253
  for plays that are lost 99–103
  for second performance 95
  ill-learnt 97
  look and placement on page 103–4, 104–6
  lost 96, 97
  Master of the Revels and 110
  not by playwright 105, 109–12
  not in prompter's book 97
  occasion-specific 82–3
  onstage 97–8
  players of 112–17
  present/absent in variant texts 100–3, 104,
    106–9
  printed plays and 82, 117–18
  read in performance 98
  Restoration 81–2
  reuse of old 105–6, 111
  revision and 82–93, 109, 111, 118
  revivals and 94, 100, 105, 118
  separately circulating 2, 98–100, 103–6, 107,
    156, 253
  strolling players and 96–7
  see also choruses and interim texts, inductions
promptbook *see* prompter's book
prompter 19, 97
  extracts stage-directions 3
  holds book throughout performance 216–17
  is responsible for parts 242
  other words for 219–20, 309 n 45
  prompts throughout performance 219–21
  responsible for entrances 221
  supplies property-list 187
prompter's book 3, 5, 7, 181, 231
  additions in 4
  calls in 230–1
  cuts in 4
  defined 205, 229–31
  lacking arguments and scrolls in 2
  lacking masques in 153
  lacking prologues in 97
  lacking songs in 142
  not source of staged documents 254
  patches written into 3
  relationship to backstage plots 3, 203–4,
    227–31
  revisions in 4
  song in 142–3
  source for other theatrical documents 3
  see also allowed book, printed playbook
property-list 3, 187, 206

props 201
  in margins of plots 213
  scrolls as 2, 141, 179, 197, 200
Proudfoot, G. R. 303 n 8
Prynne, William 172
  Histriomastix 239, 247, 313 n 26
  Publii Ovidii Nasonis Meleager 70
Purcell, Henry 162
Purfoot, Thomas 39
Puttenham, George *Arte of English Poesie* 10
Pyk, John 310 n 72

Quarles, Francis *Virgin Widow* 134, 175
Queen Henrietta's Men 129–30, 150
Queen's Men 57, 111, 243
Queen's Revels 133, 134, 296 n 66
Quiller-Couch, Arthur 306 n 60

Raleigh, Walter *Poems* 310 n 73
Randolph, Thomas 18, 30
  Amyntas 288 n 141
  Aristippus 113
  Hey for Honesty 1, 251
Rankins, William *Mirrour of Monsters* 51, 265 n 2
  Seaven Satyres 7
Rasmussen, Eric 247
Ratseis Ghost 143
Ravenscroft, Thomas 127
  Careless Lovers 230
  Deuteromelia 292 n 28
  Pammelia 292 n 28
Recueil des Plus Excellents Ballets 274 n 9
Red Bull Players 83
Red Bull Playhouse 45, 57, 69, 82, 99
Reed, Isaac *et al. Plays and Poems of William
  Shakespeare* 311 n 85
Register of All the Noble Men 70
rehearsals 3, 140–1, 203–4, 227, 307 n 12
  of songs 6
Rennert, Hugo Albert 266 n 6
Returne from Pernassus 97, 126, 242
revision 82–93, 109, 111, 118, 145–53, 156, 157, 228,
  229, 254
revivals 84, 94–101, 105, 110, 112, 118, 122, 155, 229, 235
Reymes, William *Self Interest* 96
Richards, Nathaniel *Tragedy of Messallina* 84,
  147, 279 n 16
Riewald, J. G. 266 n 10
Roberts, James 39–40, 41–2, 71, 267 n 21
Robinson, Humphrey and Humphrey
  Moseley 134
Robinson, Richard 188
rope-dancing bill 37, 43–4, 45
Rose Playhouse 39–47
Rosseter, Philip *Booke of Ayres* 128

Rossum-Steenbeek, M. van 273 n 2
Rous, Francis *Diseases* 234
Rowe, John 265 n 2
Rowe, Nicholas *Jane Shore* 189, 218
Rowland, Richard 184
Rowlands, Samuel *Pimlico* 113, 280 n 22
Rowley, Samuel 23
    Noble Souldier 85, *see also* William Rowley
Rowley, William *All's Lost by Lust* 64, 111, 273 n 1,
    278 n 8, 289 n 143
    Hymens Holliday 312 n 13, *see also* Samuel
    Rowley
Royston, R. 134
Rudd, Anthony, Thomas Richards, Laurence
    Johnson *Misogonus* 288 n 141
Rudick, Michael 310 n 73
Rudyerd, Benjamin *Le Prince* 269 n 54
Ruggle, George *Ignoramus* 16
Runnalls, Graham A. 314 n 40
Rusten, J. 274 n 4
Rye, William B. 280 n 20

Sabol, Andrew J. 120, 295 n 58, 299 n 104, 307 n 17
Salisbury Court 59, 65, 111, 216
Salzman, Paul 278 n 3
Saviolo, Vincentio 49
Scase, Wendy 266 n 9
scenario 15, *see also* plot-scenario
scene division 14–15, 19–21, 23, *see also* act
    division
Schelling, Felix E. 292 n 29
Scouten, Arthur H. 282 n 46
scribe-directions 154, 181, 182–4,
    see also stage-directions
scribes alter texts while copying 192,
    see also backstage-plots: scribes of,
    scroll-scribe, part-scribe
scrolls 5, 6, 103, 140, 141, 144
    as props 141
    circulate as group 156
    circulate separately from text 6, 190–9,
      253, 254
    copied by scribe 2
    differ when there is variant text of same
      play 199
    distinctive in manuscript 177–8, 187
    distinctive typography 174–7, 181, 197
    'headings' for 176–7, 178, 181
    'lost' 142
    not in actors' parts 179–81
    not in playbooks 192–5
    plays not datable from 254
    property letters as 186–7, 190, 198
    with cues 182, 188–90
    with 'etc.' 193

    see also 'blank': type of scroll, scroll-scribes
scroll-scribes 159, 179–88
    copy scrolls 2, 3
    create contents of scrolls 183–4
    see also backstage-plots: scribes of, part-scribe,
      scrolls
Scudéry, Théophile 58, 266 n 6
second performance 90, 93–5, 117,
    see also first performance
Second Report of Doctor John Faustus 288 n 139
Seneca 63
Seng, Peter J. 298 n 96, 301 n 145
Senilis Amor 21, 22, 33
Shaa, Robert 201–2, 307 n 15
Shackerley, Marmion *Hollands Leaguer* 59
Shakespeare, William 18, 27, 28, 31, 34, 42,
    59, 61, 99, 111, 118, 222, 230, 231
    All's Well 34, 193, 256
    As You Like It 115, 119, 127, 142, 162, 172, 180,
      290 n 155
    [and Fletcher] *Cardenio* 149, 170
    Comedy of Errors 186
    Coriolanus 264 n 91
    Cymbeline 146, 149
    Folio text 40, 88, 102, 128, 139–40
    Hamlet 40, 79, 102, 133, 140, 147, 179, 247
    1 Henry IV 13, 74, 122, 304 n 31
    2 Henry IV 13, 114, 115, 119
    Henry V 41, 108, 119
    1 Henry VI 40
    2 Henry VI 40, 41, 102, 187, 195
    3 Henry VI 41, 194
    Henry VIII 85, 88, 103, 119
    Julius Caesar 123
    King John 29, 222
    King Lear 34, 40, 140, 199, 247
    Love's Labour's Lost 122, 191–2
    Macbeth 122, 149, 151, 162
    Measure for Measure 33, 133–4, 196
    Merchant of Venice 40, 61, 179, 185, 191
    Merry Wives 40, 102, 152
    Midsummer Night's Dream 40, 119, 122, 162,
      206, 214, 242
    Othello 8, 95, 102, 123, 128, 140, 147,
      189–90, 219
    Passionate Pilgrim 191–2
    Pericles 23, 40, 41, 114, 123, 151
    Rape of Lucrece 259 n 18
    Richard II 95
    Richard III 60, 82
    Romeo and Juliet 97, 101, 102–3, 106, 219
    Taming of the Shrew 29, 107
    Tempest 88, 102, 115, 139, 149, 152, 163
    Timon of Athens 34, 103, 168, 256
    Titus Andronicus 40, 41

Shakespeare, William (cont.)
  Troilus and Cressida 88, 102–3, 280 n 32,
    289 n 144
  Twelfth Night 87–8, 127, 139–40, 147, 166,
    175, 197–8
  [and Fletcher] *Two Noble Kinsmen* 41, 85, 151
  Winter's Tale 107, 149, 150, 166, 256
  see also Edward III
Shapiro, I. A. 259 n 14, 264 n 95
Shapiro, Michael 290 n 155
Sharpham, Edward *Cupid's Whirligig* 280 n 17
Shattock, Charles Harlen 308 n 34
Shelton, Thomas, translator *Don Quixote* 170
Sheppard, Simon *Committee-Man Curried* 131
Sherbo, Arthur 291 n 13
Sherburn, Edward 68
Shergold, N. D. 269 n 57, 274 n 9
Sheridan, Thomas *British Education* 309 n 55
Sherman, William H. 290 n 156
Shipman, Roger *Grobiana's Nuptials* 289 n 145
Shirley, Henry *Martyrd Souldier* 8, 232
Shirley, James 28, 29, 84, 112, 121, 130, 193
  Ball 230
  Bird in the Cage 172
  Brothers 9
  Cardinal 50, 57, 106, 116–17, 150
  Changes 111, 141
  Constant Maid 67, 297 n 84
  Coronation 112
  Doubtfull Heire 83
  Dukes Mistris 124, 150, 289 n 149
  [and Charles I] *Gamester* 31
  Hide Parke 308 n 41
  Imposture 281 n 37
  Lady of Pleasure 8, 309 n 58
  Poems 84, 124, 129, 156, 269 n 58, 278 n 5,
    286 n 113
  School of Complement 8, 279 n 16
  Sisters 94, 106
  Triumph of Beauty 313 n 34
  Triumph of Peace 206, 219
  Wittie Faire One 131
Sidney, Philip 131
Silver, Toby and George 49, 51, 52
Simon, Eckehard 284 n 80, 313 n 22
singers 2, 6, 134, 140
  voice-breaking 140, 146–7, 148, 255
single performances 255, *see also* first
  performances
siquis 53–4
Sir John Oldcastle 40, 41
Sisson, C. J. 261 n 51, 279 n 16, 297 n 80, 305 n 36
Smith, D. I. B. 271 n 81
Smith, Irwin 152
Smith, Peter 149

Smith, Wentworth 23
  Hector of Germany 182
Some, Robert 266 n 10
songs 3, 5, 7, 8, 22, 103, 105, 111
  added 147–53
  amongst front or back matter 157
  as types of scroll 174
  bearing theatrical traces 160–7
  circulating with prologues and epilogues
    105, 107, 156–7, 171, 253
  cut for shortening play 145–7
  'etc.' in 142–3
  'found' in music manuscripts though lost
    from play 168, 253
  in theatre library 137–40
  'lost' 120–30, 135, 144
  lyricist of 131–4
  lyrics for written by composer 2, 3, 127–8, 163–4
  not by playwright 130
  not in performance form 164–7, 195
  not in prompter's book 142
  'old' tune for 137–40
  on separate papers 135, 253
  on sheet containing music 6, 141–3
  play 'patches' and 1
  post-performance circulation of 143–4
  present/absent in variant texts 129–30,
    148–9, 255
  printed with musical notation 164
  printers of 128–34, 153–60, 160
  'random' 125
  rehearsal of 2, 6, 140–1
  revivals and 122, 155
  sent to composer 6
  with cue-list 206
  with cues 160–2, 190
  see also composers
Sorlien, Robert Parker 276 n 27
Sothern, Edward 190
Spectator 278 n 2
spectators *see* audience
speech-prefixes 174
  wayward around scrolls 184–8
Speight, George 273 n 105
Spencer, John *Things New and Old* 269 n 50
Spevack, Marvin 313 n 28
Spink, Ian 295 n 66
stage-directions 174, 204
  actors' parts and 244
  actually scribe-directions 184
  literary terms and 228
  relationship to backstage-plots 205, 227–8, 231
  relationship to plot-scenarios 11
  see also scribe-directions
Stationers' Register 39

St Clair, William 292 n 31
Steen, Sara Jayne 285 n 91, 293 n 35
Steevens, George 202–3, 206, 208, 209, 231
    et al. edition of *Shakespeare's Plays* 306 n 5,
    309 n 55
Stephens, John 282 n 51
    Satirical Essays 117, 269 n 52, 289 n 151
Stephenson, J. F. 237
Stern, Tiffany 257 n 4, 268 n 45, 281 n 37, 289 n 149,
    299 n 109, 304 n 30, 308 n 20, 310 n 75
Sternfeld, F. W. 296 n 73, 302 n 151
Stockwood, John 265 n 2
St Paul's Cathedral 51, 54
Strode, William 131, 163
strolling players 96–7, 98
stylometrics 32, 34, 172, 254
Suckling, John *Aglaura* 150, 155
    Brennoralt 150, 161
    Fragmenta 80, 277
    Goblins 90, 131, 150
    Last Remains 259 n 16, 260 n 28
    Sad One 150
Swaen, A. E. H. 292 n 29
Swan Playhouse 42, 71, 234, 249
Swanston, Eliard 187
Symcocke, Thomas 40

Tailor, Robert *Hogge Hath Lost His Pearle* 28
Taming of a Shrew 29, 107
Tarlton, Richard 97, 246–7, 248, 278 n 5,
    296 n 66
Tatham, John *Distracted State* 9
    Fancies Theater 278, 283 n 66
    Ostella 278 n 5, 283 n 66
    Whisperer 99
Taylor, Gary and John Lavagnino 262 n 64, 263
    n 90, 287 n 121, 294 n 42, 300 n 111,
    301 n 146, 315 n 71
Taylor, John, the Water-Poet
    A Kicksey Winsey 50
    All the Workes 276 n 31
    Fearefull Summer 270 n 65
    Fennors Defence 249–50
    Pedler 272 n 92
    Taylor's Feast 309 n 45
    Taylors Revenge 49
    Taylors Water-Worke 268 n 31
    Wit and Mirth 47
Taylor, Joseph 188
Tell-Tale 202
Terence 63
Thaler, Alwin 280 n 20, 283 n 73
theatre programme 6, 66, 76, *see also* Argument
Theobald, Lewis 184
    Double Falshood 170

Thomas, David and David Carlton and Anne
    Etienne 312 n 8
Thomas of Woodstock 229
Thomson, Leslie 311 n 79
Thorn-Drury, George 293 n 37
Tilney, Edmund 232, 233, 234, 235
title-pages 5, 6, 38, 43, 55–6, 57–62
Tom a Lincoln 177
*To the . . . House of Commons . . . The Humble
    Petition of Thomas Man* 267 n 17
Tourneur, Cyril 23
    Nobleman 149, 170
Townshend, Aurelian 68, 152
Tribble, Evelyn 204, 208, 274 n 8
Troublesome Reign of King John 29, 34
Tuke, Samuel *Adventures of Five Hours* 272 n 93
Turner, Henry 231, 274 n 4
Turner, Robert K. 300 n 131

university production 65, 95, 239–42
    Cambridge 16
    Oxford 95, 239
Upcott, William 135

Valerius, Adraen *Nederlandtsch Gedenck-Clanck*
    296 n 66
Vandenhoff, George *Leaves* 217, 218
Van Lennep, William 267 n 24, 273 n 105,
    277 n 48, 313 n 36
Vaughan, William *Golden Fleece* 284 n 75
Veevers, Erica 275 n 18, 299 n 110
Vega, Lope de 258 n 11
Vennar, Richard *England's Joy* 37, 47, 71–2
Vertumnus 68
Vicars, John *Epigrams* 276 n 33
Vickers, Brian 258 n 14
Villiers, George, Duke of Buckingham *Rehearsal*
    74, 262 n 72, 276 n 34
Vincent, Thomas 309 n 45
Virgil 63
Voss, Paul J. 38

W., T. *Gratiae Theatrales* 279 n 11
    Thorny-Abbey 97, 221
Wager, William *Inough is as Good* 277 n 57
Walker, H. 284 n 81
Wall, Wendy 274 n 8, 277 n 49
Walls, Peter 296 n 67
Walsh, William 10
Walsingham, Francis 268 n 35
Walter, J. H. 263 n 88, 304 n 20
Wambus, Francis 59
Ward, Charles E. 258 n 10
Ward, Samuel *Life of Faith* 265 n 2
Warning for Faire Women 57

Warren, Michael 243, 303 n 15
Waspe 229
Webster, John 23, 101, 193
  Dutchesse of Malfy 131, 149, 151
  Thracian Wonder 192
  White Devil 8
  see also Dekker, Thomas
Weimann, Robert 290 n 156
Weiss, Adrian 262 n 64
Welch, Charles 269 n 46
Wells, Stanley and Gary Taylor 193, 285 n 96
Wentworth, Thomas, Earl of Strafford 54, 266 n 10, 271 n 70
Wernerus Martyr 75–6, 77
Werstine, Paul 20, 260 n 40, 264 n 94, 307 n 16
West, Richard 18
Whetstone, George *Aurelia* 1
  Promos and Cassandra 183
  2 Promos and Cassandra 183
White Cupids Banishment 68
Whitefriars 99
Whitehall 110, 132, 151, 152, 206
Whiteley, William Rufus 242
Whitney, Geffrey 257 n 5
Wiggins, Martin 209, 225
Wiles, David 247
Wiley, Autrey Nell 284 n 81
Wiley, W. L. 267 n 28
Wilkes, G. A. 287 n 120
Wilkins, George *Miseries of Inforst Mariage* 40
  Painfull Adventure of Pericles 114
Wilkinson, Tate *Memoirs* 265 n 2
Willan, Leonard *Astraea* 136
  Orgula 193

Williams, George Walton 259 n 23
Williamson, Joseph 274 n 9
Willis, Edmond *An Abreviation of Writing* 270 n 65
Willoughby, Edwin E. 267 n 19
Wilson, Arthur *The Swisser* 178
Wilson, Christopher R. and Michela Calore 300 n 117
Wilson, John 139, 149, 168
  and Edward Lowe 297 n 83
  Cheerfull Ayres 139
Wilson, John Dover 197
Wilson, Robert, clown 249
Wilson, Robert, playwright 23, 307 n 15
  2 Henry Richmond 205–6
Wilson, Thomas 31
Wily Beguilde 101, 251, 278 n 8, 289 n 149
Windet, John 71
Wisdome of Doctor Dodypoll 131
Wither, George *Abuses* 1, 57, 268 n 39
  Great Assises 262 n 71
Wood, Anthony *Athenae Oxoniensis* 293 n 33
Wood, Julia K. 291 n 16, 299 n 100, 301 n 140
Wood, Michael 302 n 165
Wood, Roger 40
Worcester's Men 41–2
Wright, Abraham 8
  Parnassus Biceps 262 n 62, 280 n 23
  The Reformation 8
Wright, Herbert G. 305 n 54

Yarington, Robert *Two Lamentable Tragedies* 193, 305 n 53
Yeandle, Laetitia 13, 259 n 23
Yorkshire Tragedie 40, 41